Why People Go Postal

From An Inside, Personal Perspective

Lola McGee

Printed and Bound in the United States of America

Published by:
Cooper Publishing
Los Angeles, California

Distributed by:
Cooper Publishing
14005 Kornblum Avenue, Suite 215
Hawthorne, CA 90250
562-889-2662
email: LolaMcGee@LolaMcGee.com
Website: www.LolaMcGee.com

Cover layout: Richard Ike

Formatting: Professional Publishing House

First printing, February 2012

ISBN: 978-0-615-61986-6

Acknowledgments

First, I want to give all praise, glory, and honor to God for allowing me to live to tell this story in order to help myself and those who are unable to help themselves.

A special thank you to Pamela Morgan for enduring me as I went through every aspect of my illnesses and injuries, and her unwavering, unconditional love for me that she somehow continued to hold on to.

Giving all praises to God for allowing the paths of my dear friend and me to cross once again; special thanks to Sandra Ardrey.

A special thank you to my daughter for enduring the pain and suffering as she watched and cared for me during my demise. In addition, I want to thank her for monitoring my medications so they would not overtake me.

A special thank you to those who kept me living through God's Grace and Mercy: Dr. Mary J. Reed, Dr. Michael Shepard, Dr. Jimmy John Novero, Heather Harris-APN, Dr. Marian Vulpe, Dr. Mark Blizer, Dr. Marsha Simmons, Dr. Frederick Goll, III, Dr. Rick Jenkins, and Dr. Siamak Rouzroch. Thank you. Thank you. Thank you.

A special thank you to my family and friends for without your love and support, I would not have been able to hold on as tight as I did. I love you all very much.

I want to acknowledge Mr. Charles Turner, Ms. Zarita Williams, Ms. Margarite Gressman, and Mr. Michael Garrett. You all stepped up to the plate and were right there when I needed you the most. Thank you with all of my heart. I appreciate you all so much.

I would like to give a special thank you to Dr. Rosie Milligan. With great gratitude and humility, I thank God for you taking me under your wing, and with the wealth of knowledge that you have, you are truly able to understand me. I thank you for being a woman with integrity, patience, and experience, which allows me to trust you. Thank you.

Disclosure

This book consists of some statements, documents and forms I have taken the liberty to disclose, along with some of my medical documentation, so it can be truly understood the condition my body is in today, and hopefully it can help those experiencing some of my symptoms. But by all means, please don't let it get to my degree. Juggling a pain tolerance level, along with mental and other physical illnesses/injuries, is not a good place to be in.

Contents

RICK JENKINS, M.D.
A PSYCHIATRIC MEDICAL PRACTICE
420 S. BEVERLY DR., SUITE 211
BEVERLY HILLS, CA 90212

TELEPHONE (310) 552-0146
FAX (310) 552-0185

DEA NO. BJ0965876
LIC. NO. G69736

NAME Ella McGee

ADDRESS ______ DATE 11 24 10

℞ For mental health
write out in book form
events related to post
office employment

☐ LABEL

REFILL ______ TIMES

______, M.D.
DO NOT SUBSTITUTE

______, M.D.
SUBSTITUTION PERMISSIBLE

Mission Statement, In Part

The United States Postal Service will provide efficient communication to every household across America and we will secure the sanctity of the mail while it is in our possession. We will reach every place in the United States where no other company or organization even knows about.

I took this oath seriously and to heart, and I performed my duties quite well as a City Letter Carrier from June 1998 to 2000.

I was extremely proud to be a part of the United States Postal Service, wore my uniform with honor and dignity.

My country, in which I served by providing efficient communication to every household in America, WAS NO CHALLENGE TO ME; IT WAS ADMIRABLE TO BE OF SERVICE.

PREFACE

This book was inspired to help aid me back to the quality of life I once had—to be mentally, physically and emotionally sound.

Also: To help those in similar situations as mine.

To give a voice to those who passed on without having their voices heard.

To those who are "fighting their own Goliath," the way the lady on the Internet put it, who is also a federal employee.

To thank my family and true friends who assist, aid and help me to deal with the daily challenges of my new life, which I have not yet mastered.

To bring awareness to, for instance, the insurance claims representative that was on *The Oprah Winfrey Show* whose conscience finally bothered her after receiving six-figure bonuses for denying claims of people dying from lack of needed medical care and procedures.

As a woman who worked construction with men not really wanting me there, making the same salary as them, getting four hours of sleep per day while owning and operating a restaurant and catering business, or perhaps twenty-five years of recovery from alcohol and other drugs, hard work is no stranger to me.

I swear, under penalty of perjury, that the information in this book is true and factual as I have experienced it firsthand. Also, I have knowledge and will reveal it to the best of my ability.

Chapter 1
Who I Was

Acting Supervisor/204B—July 2000

I was a viable person in society that people loved to talk to, because they felt I was an old soul that possessed insight and knowledge. I was a leader in my family. I kept things together during family functions, which were going on often. I believe a family communicating around food maintains unity, closeness and togetherness. I was the backbone of my family and was respected as such, until my demise (the passing away of life as I knew it). I was a very hard worker in both my personal and professional life. In my late twenties, I owned and operated a restaurant and a catering service.

I earned an Associate of Arts Degree in Human Services and a Bachelor of Science/Business Management, along with several certificates. I went to school to give to myself and back to the community in the field of drug addiction. My first and only mental health position was as a Case Manager/Counselor at Southern California Alcohol and Drug Programs. When I told my manager, who was white, that I was leaving, she said, "As long as I'm here you will have a job." I felt appreciated as a person and a valued employee.

I was physically strong. I worked construction in my twenties and early thirties. I was mentally sound and physically healthy. I didn't start anything in my life that I couldn't finish. I was disciplined with a set of values that were to be proud of. I'm a serious, professional person with class that cannot tolerate foolishness. However, no one goes through life without making mistakes. If a mistake I made was brought to my attention, I apologized for it because it definitely was not intentional, or the behavior was worked on for the betterment of me. I believe in making people better not worse. I believe in fairness and respect along with accountability.

I raised my daughter to be a productive and achieving person, and, of course, the fruit does not fall far from the tree when it comes to her values, morals, and principals. She graduated from Howard University and Yale University, respectively, with honors and is now earning over six figures in her early thirties.

During my mid-twenties, I became the woman God continued to use and bless as He saw fit. With a giving spirit, God blessed me abundantly for giving to and helping others. I was a person who aspired to achieve and excel. I believe in growth and development, and I was more than willing to help anyone.

Chapter 2
My Tenure

Prior to my demise (the passing away of life as I knew it) at the United States Postal Service (USPS) in Nevada, hard work, multitasking, stepping outside the box, the ability to observe and see with new eyes, having innovative ideas, treating people with dignity and respect, professionalism, accountability, seriousness, leadership, success, education, entrepreneur, downsizing, minimizing, effective decision-making and communication skills were all adjectives that described my attitude, behavior, and personality. I transferred from California with this wealth of knowledge.

When I began employment with the USPS, a manager and a supervisor tried to terminate me before the end of the ninety-day probation period. However, I was efficient at my job. The reports showed that it would not be justified with the National Association of Letter Carriers Union (NALC), so I was evaluated as a career employee and the story continues.

Once I passed probation and proved myself worthy of a promotion, my goal was to obtain upward mobility. Management is the key to the success of any operation, organization, or agency. It begins and ends with effective leadership and efficient decision-making. My direct supervisor tracked my performance to justify my qualifications to be an acting supervisor (204B). After two years of carrying mail, I was finally giving the opportunity to stand up and be a 204-B.

In the interim of being a 204B, I took the USPS Supervisory Test and passed it. There was also a sixteen-week training program that you had to pass in order to complete the program and become a full fledge Associate Supervisor. I passed the course and became an Associate Supervisor in 2001.

As an Associate Supervisor, you belong to the district until you are promoted to a specific office. I worked in a few offices within the district while waiting on application processes and interviews. After eight months as a 204B (July 2000 to March 2001), four months of the Associate Supervisor Program (March 2001 to July 2001), and belonging to the district as an Associate Supervisor (August 2001 to September 2002), I applied for and was promoted to the Gardena Post Office.

I worked in California from June 1998 through May 2004. I was a supervisor for four of the six years there, which included my 204B tenure. I was still a Part-Time-Flexible (PTF) employee when I became a supervisor. As a PTF, you do not have your own route or set work hours. You are utilized on whatever route where you are needed, and at whatever time you are needed. As a PTF, I carried every route in Bell Gardens, California, and it was to my benefit when I became a 204B Supervisor.

There's a right and wrong way to do anything. My heart is right and so were my intentions when it came to managing people at the workplace. That's why, I believe, I received positive results immediately from the people I worked with after entering each new station. I did not have low self-esteem and no personal agendas while I performed my duties as a supervisor or as a manager. I expressed what I wanted, and the employees produced as I facilitated. Honesty was my best policy. The process I used was in accordance with what the senior managers required. I simply had my way of achieving the bottom line. For giving the USPS all that I had, they received a strong and positive working woman.

In 2003, I was hospitalized for Lower Bowel Obstruction and had an appendectomy. I was off work for seven weeks. In 2005, I was hospitalized for a similar problem, and I was off work for two weeks. Due to this recurring condition of Lower Bowel Obstruction, I had Family Medical Leave Act (FMLA) on file for the periodic episodes. My only episode since 2005 was in 2006 for two days. I did not have to be hospitalized. My attendance record at work spoke for itself—a loyal and dependable employee. I worked when I wasn't scheduled to work. I worked ten-to twelve-hour days. Sometimes, I worked on Saturdays. I was a salaried employee.

Me, in 2001, at my United States Postal Service
Associate Supervisor Graduation in California

Chapter 3
The Start of My Success and Demise in Nevada

After requesting a lateral transfer to the Nevada Sierra District, on May 17, 2004, I was transferred to the North Las Vegas Main Post Office (NLV). NLV has a sister station, Meadow Mesa, but my transfer was to the main office as a Supervisor, Customer Services. I requested the transfer because I loved Las Vegas so much, and I had purchased a home there. The transfer was right on-time.

When I arrived at NLV, I was assigned to the delivery unit, which wasn't performing very well. Morale was low in the office, and there was animosity between the NALC and management, from supervisors to Craig Colton, the Postmaster. I had my work cut out for me, but I'm the type of person who stays on course until it gets better. From life's experience, I recognize it is all in the approach and how you treat people. The decision-making of a good supervisor is the ability to reach the majority of workers, and hopefully the few stragglers will come around. The supervisor must not be temperamental and should have the ability to de-escalate situations. The workplace is not the place to exploit personal opinions, views or issues. Using personal issues against employees should never be a manager's way to gain control. Personal issues tend to cut deeper, causing people to retaliate. Management does not have to prove to its subordinates that it is the boss, just be the boss and do the job. The position should speak for itself.

Dr. Maya Angelou said it best: "When people show you who they are, believe them."

There was a supervisor at NLV that made it obvious he did not appreciate my skills, abilities, experiences, or acknowledge my education had anything to do with the improvement of the office's performance. He did everything he could to sabotage my performance. When I arrived, the delivery unit was 5% over budget plan hours. In four and a half months, I reduced it to 3.5% under budget plan hours. He had a bizarre and outlandish behavior that made me afraid of him. He hid my employee reports, spoke to me in a disrespectful and loud manner on the workroom floor, and told employees untruths about me, so they would turn against me. In addition, he told Craig Colton that I wasn't capturing the undertime—performing tasks without using overtime—I said I was conducting. However, the proof of the office performance reports showed my conduct to be excellent. He pulled my reports and posted them on the board and told the union steward that I was not equitable on my overtime with my employees. However, this was due to his incorrect calculations and wrong figures to reflect the report. This issue was not new and had been one of the issues he had with the union steward prior to my arrival to NLV. This issue was negated through meetings with me and the union steward weekly, regarding the overtime employee's report. Both the union steward and I would sign off on the form to ensure it was correct.

There were times when I would speak to this supervisor in the mornings, and he would walk past me as if I did not exist. Then there were times when he would approach me to talk as if nothing was wrong, and we were the best of friends. This supervisor once told me that he had to kill people in the military, and that was his job. He also told me he used to work for a security company and he and his partner had to kill someone at a casino. He had daily mood swings. He hid my employee leave slips to prevent me from knowing who was supposed to be at work, and from creating the employee schedule correctly. I called several meetings and sent emails to the Postmaster and Officer in Charge (OIC) to put a stop to this hostile work environment that he had created, but he continued to behave in this manner.

The supervisor was to turn over to me $1,000.00 in cash reserve, but he never turned it over. Postal Inspectors and Labor Relations Departments got involved regarding different issues that I had with him and other fraudulent things he did. As a result from this hostile environment, from 2004 to 2005, I sought therapy and was subsequently diagnosed with Post-Traumatic Stress Disorder, Depression, and Obsessive-Compulsive Disorder. That hostile work environment made me believe the supervisor, or someone else, would harm me at the office or at my home. I was truly afraid he would try and physically hurt me.

Eventually, the supervisor was terminated for fraudulent behavior beyond the issues he had in the office with me. I once stepped into Craig Colton's office and advised him that the supervisor's behavior did not stop there, and this behavior had a tendency to go beyond work into his personal life. Craig's reply was, "Never say that to me again."

I remember being the only black person at the 2004 Christmas party where we celebrated our success for the fiscal year. It was something that was uncommon and different for me to be a part of. It dawned on me that there were no other nationalities and I was the only African American. It would have been nice to have an array of nationalities there.

At the beginning of 2007, a hearing was held regarding the supervisor's job, and I was required to be present. I asked Dana Urbanski—Manager, Customer Services Meadow Mesa Station—if she could have the Postal Inspectors escort him in and, if possible, search him. Dana called and gave my request. Fortunately, the supervisor did not show up for the hearing, and I was allowed to leave.

Postmaster Colton allowed the supervisor's broken-down truck to stay on postal premises for over four months. It is postal policy that no personal vehicles are to be left on the premises overnight. However, Colton never enforced the policy with his terminated right-hand man. He was supposed to have it towed away on several occasions, but he never came back to the office after Colton sent the email for him to report to Meadow Mesa; after all, one of us had to go to Meadow Mesa.

Ultimately, the high-dollar pay outs for grievances stopped and the union steward became a productive employee in the workplace. He later resigned from being the National Association of Letter Carriers Union Representative for NLV.

Craig Colton's acknowledgement of performance report—Unit Feedback Report/Unit Daily 2004 shows how the delivery unit performed for the day and week!! We had the best Delivery Operating Information System (DOIS) hours!

Unit Feedback Report

RESTRICTED INFORMATION

Delivery Unit: 8903001

Service Date: 10/23/2004

Usage

Function	First Use	Last Use	Times Used
Logon	06:20	10:30	4
Capture Mail Volume - Manual	06:54	09:32	3
Capture Mail Volume - DCD	06:39	06:39	1
EOR Transfer	06:30	06:30	3
Application Version - 4.1.1	06:20	06:20	

Quality Practice

Timeliness of Reports	First Use	Last Use	Times Used
Clockring Discrepancy Report	06:57	06:57	1
Workload Status Report	07:17	09:32	2
Route/Carrier Daily Performance Report	06:20	09:33	2
MSP Overview Report	06:23	06:23	1

Miscellaneous Time	Time Added	Time Subtracted
Total Adjustment to Leave/Office Time	0:00	0:00
Total Adjustment to Return/Street Time	0:00	0:00

Daily Statistics	Quantity
Number of Operational Clockring Discrepancies	1
Number of Remaining Route Vacancies	0

Effectiveness

Overtime/Undertime Management	Start of Day	End of Day	% Reduction
Projected OT	22:42	37:10	-63.70
Projected UT	0:37	0:00	99.67

MSP Management	Value
Possible Office Scans	69
Missed Office Scans	3
Office Scan Percentage	96.00%
Possible Street Scans	238
Missed Street Scans	2
Invalid Street Scans	2
Street Scan Percentage	99.00%
On-Time Street Scan Percentage	66.00%

Metrics	Value
OT%	16.09
Office Effectiveness	2.50
Street Effectiveness	14.41
Workload Effectiveness	11.07

TIMES ON THIS REPORT ARE PRESENTED IN LOCAL TIME

10/25/2004 09:54 AM 1 GENERATED BY: COLTON, CRAIG
NLV Main, MAIN POST OFFICE, 8903001

UNIT DAILY PERFORMANCE REPORT

RESTRICTED INFORMATION

Delivery Unit:	8903001
Begin Date:	10/16/2004
End Date:	10/22/2004
Service Week:	4

Day: Thursday 10/21/2004

Mail Volumes

Cased		Delivered	
Ltr	9,462	DPS	34,507
Flt	30,712	Seq	5,630
Total	40,174	Total	80,311
		PP	308
Delayed & Curtailed			
Delayed	0		
Curtailed	889		

Work Hour Analysis

Type	Projected	Actual	Var	%Var
Office - LDC21	88:00	61:52	-26:08	-29.69
Street - LDC22	170:45	164:54	-5:51	-3.40
Other Delivery - LDC23	0:00	0:00		
Carr Cust Support - LDC26	15:33	15:33		
Collection - LDC27	2:34	2:34		
City Carr/Tert Dist - LDC28	0:00	0:00		
Rtr Ofc - LDC29	0:00	0:00		
Training - LDC92	0:00	0:00		
Total		244:53		

LDC21 & LDC22		Productivity Analysis		PD's	
Projected		**Office**		Budget	0
Act Hrs	226:46	OEI	272.26	Actual	16,845
Proj Hrs	258:45	PPH	649.33	% Var	0.00
Proj Var	-31:59	**Street**			
		MPD	0.59		
Budgeted		SEI	102.15		
Act Hrs	226:46	**Total**			
Bud Hrs	0:00	TEI	68.79		
Bud Var	226:46	WE %	12.36		
OT & Sick Leave		**OT & Sick Leave**			
OT Hrs	35:22	OT %	14.44		
Sick Leave	11:11	S/L %	4.57		

Day: Friday 10/22/2004

Mail Volumes

Cased		Delivered	
Ltr	6,492	DPS	37,133
Flt	9,775	Seq	15,482
Total	16,267	Total	68,882
		PP	256
Delayed & Curtailed			
Delayed	0		
Curtailed	0		

Work Hour Analysis

Type	Projected	Actual	Var	%Var
Office - LDC21	40:45	45:43	4:58	12.17
Street - LDC22	170:45	170:33	-0:12	-0.10
Other Delivery - LDC23	0:00	0:00		
Carr Cust Support - LDC26	6:38	6:38		
Collection - LDC27	1:59	1:59		
City Carr/Tert Dist - LDC28	0:00	0:00		
Rtr Ofc - LDC29	0:00	0:00		
Training - LDC92	0:00	0:00		
Total		224:54		

LDC21 & LDC22		Productivity Analysis		PD's	
Projected		**Office**		Budget	0
Act Hrs	216:16	OEI	368.44	Actual	16,845
Proj Hrs	211:30	PPH	355.80	% Var	0.00
Proj Var	4:46	**Street**			
		MPD	0.61		
Budgeted		SEI	98.77		
Act Hrs	216:16	**Total**			
Bud Hrs	0:00	TEI	74.90		
Bud Var	216:16	WE %	-2.25		
OT & Sick Leave		**OT & Sick Leave**			
OT Hrs	43:42	OT %	19.43		
Sick Leave	10:00	S/L %	4.45		

WEEKLY TOTALS

Mail Volumes

Cased		Delivered	
Ltr	64,664	DPS	240,923
Flt	203,689	Seq	67,544
Total	268,353	Total	576,820
		PP	1,683
Delayed & Curtailed			
Delayed	0		
Curtailed	4,756		

Work Hour Analysis

Type	Projected	Actual	Var	%Var
Office - LDC21	579:30	378:32	-200:58	-34.68
Street - LDC22	1024:30	1001:31	-22:59	-2.24
Other Delivery - LDC23	0:00	0:00		
Carr Cust Support - LDC26	69:14	69:14		
Collection - LDC27	13:31	13:31		
City Carr/Tert Dist - LDC28	0:00	0:00		
Rtr Ofc - LDC29	0:00	0:00		
Training - LDC92	0:00	0:00		
Total		1462:49		

LDC21 & LDC22		Productivity Analysis		PD's	
Projected		**Office**		Budget	0
Act Hrs	1380:03	OEI	266.97	Actual	101,056
Proj Hrs	1604:00	PPH	708.93	% Var	0.00
Proj Var	-223:57	**Street**			
		MPD	0.59		
Budgeted		SEI	100.90		
Act Hrs	1380:03	**Total**			
Bud Hrs	0:00	TEI	69.08		
Bud Var	1380:03	WE %	13.96		
OT & Sick Leave		**OT & Sick Leave**			
OT Hrs	225:09	OT %	15.39		
Sick Leave	51:03	S/L %	3.49		

BEST WEEK EVER

10/25/2004 09:53 AM 2

GENERATED BY: COLTON, CRAIG
NLV Main, MAIN POST OFFICE, 8903001

Chapter 4
Acting Manager

From April 1, 2006 to August 13, 2006, I worked at Huntridge Station in Las Vegas as Acting Manager. I did well at Huntridge, even though it was my first acting manager position. I did not have any bosses running in and out of my office or received any phone calls that weren't favorable. I kept up with upper management's pace and reply accordingly to their demands and focus. We received an External First Class Mail Audit and passed. There was no first class mail in the building that should have gone out to the street with the carriers. My staff and I put several processes in place, because it was during the time when the Nevada Sierra District became a part of the Western Area, and service, processes, and efficiency were the main focus.

From April 1, 2006 to August 25, 2008, I worked effectively as Acting Manager for the Nevada Sierra District. During that time, I applied for seventeen positions, but was never promoted. I was overlooked for two positions that remained vacant until they had someone else they wanted to fill the positions. All promoted employees were white or non-African American. I felt discriminated against based on age, sex, and race. A black, forty-six-year-old female did not stand a chance. They treated me unfairly while others were treated differently. I was lied to and disrespected, even on teleconferences. I performed well in large offices and had great performance outcomes to prove it. However, I was not good enough to be promoted. I was treated as if I was only good for repairing each post office's problems. I was never promoted to the position I was currently functioning well in. I was flown to Reno, Nevada on detail as Acting Manager and afterward returned to one of the worst offices in Las Vegas—King Station. I was acting in a manager's position that was removed from his office, and relocated by senior management due to his performance in that office.

On August 14, 2006, I was offered the detail of Acting Manager at Paradise Valley Station (PV). I called a meeting with Jennifer Vo, Robert Reynosa, and Mark Martinez. Being a serious, business-minded person, I wanted to get all parties together for a truthful discussion. However, it was not taken that way. Instead, I was disrespected and spoken to without dignity and respect. The meeting was called because I was told by Jennifer that I would be going back to North Las Vegas as a supervisor because the perception was that I had improved Huntridge Station's percent to standard by over-counting volume. My staff did not over-count mail. I was appalled at the accusation; my integrity was being questioned, which I considered a personal insult. With a condescending look, Jennifer remarked, "Lola, you can tell me that I'm full of shit if you want to." I would have never said such a thing to her. She was my boss, and I certainly would not have disrespected myself in that manner. I was shocked that she said that to me without really knowing me. That just let me know that she was being herself, and she knew that I knew she was not telling the truth. I had performed well at Huntridge, and I wanted the opportunity to continue to grow, to gain upward mobility. No one gave me any expectation at Huntridge. One thing Jennifer did say, when she gave me the opportunity was, "If I don't have to come into your station, then you are okay." Jennifer, Mark Martinez, Executive Postmaster City of Las Vegas, or Robert Reynosa, Manager, Customer Service Operations, never had to come into Huntridge and question me on any negative issues.

Mark started the meeting by asking, "Why are we here? What's going on?" I continued with, "I wanted everyone here because I want to know what I did wrong and why I'm going back to North Las Vegas (my officially promoted position—Supervisor, Customer Services) when I've worked so hard and performed well." I reminded them that Jennifer said it was being perceivedas over counted volume and that's how I reduced Percent to Standard and I didn't want to be looked at in that manner. Mark said, "No. I'll tell you why. I have a manager that is counting rubber bands and doing route inspections and I need him to be in a productive role." I respected Mark's explanation. As the meeting was ending, Mark asked Jennifer and Robert about Paradise Valley for me. He told them to work it out and told me that they would get back to me. I left the meeting with a smile on my face with the hope that all was going in a positive direction.

I worked at Paradise Valley Station as the acting manager from August 14, 2006 to March 30, 2007. When Paradise Valley Station became available, they gave the job to the white male I had replaced seven months prior. I did great work in that office with its split zone (Split Zip Code). Customers were still using the old zip code, and it made processing the mail more difficult, becausewe had to put stickers on every piece to try to get them to use the proper code. Strip Station is wherethe other routes went, and we would receive/send mail back and forth. It was challenging with getting the mail processed in time to get the carriers out on the street in a timely manner. Percent to standard isbased on a carrier processing fifteen minutes per foot, and Mail Processors cannot hold them up and have them waiting on mail.

I worked ten-to twelve-hour days and most Saturdays without any additional pay for over eight hours. I excelled in several areas. However, within a couple of weeks before I left Paradise Valley Station, my 204B (Acting Supervisor) failed to clear some mail that was left in the facility on his instructions to the carrier. I sat him down and talked with him, and I put him back on his route. Another issue was, my new supervisor failed to report to me that some mail was brought back off some business routes even though we had a plan to get it delivered.

At this same time, there were three other stations with similar mail issues. Mail was left in the building and not dispatched. There was mail in the facility that did not go out fordelivery, and nothing happened to those managers. I was given an Investigative Interview and sent back to North Las Vegas. Needless to say, I improved Paradise Valley Station with the challenges of thesplit zone and the volume that it was receiving from August 14, 2006 to March 30, 2007. Also, we were best in the city for mail processing and had a 6.9 DPH (Deliveries per Hour), which was very good at the time with the volume that we received in the station on a daily basis.

Robert said to me one day, "When you're back at North Las Vegas, think about those supervisors at Paradise Valley Station that put you there." He wanted me to change their schedules and in my attempt, they were calling in FMLA sick, and having surgeries along with transportation and childcare issues, not to mention scheduled annual leave. I asked Robert not long after if the supervisors atParadise Valley Station are in their same positions. He replied, "Yes." When the Paradise Valley position was posted, not only did I not get the job, I wasn't even given an interview. Both of our performances are a matter of record. In addition, merit time came up and Jennifer evaluated me. After all I had done to improve Huntridge Station and Paradise Valley Station, I received a low 3% rating. Even though I knew it was not right or fair for her to rate my accomplishments like that, I didn't question her. I was sent back to North Las Vegas as a supervisor.

Merit rating report equals to 3% pay increase for the year - Jennifer Vo, FY 2006

EOY Rating Report

Page 1 of 4

Rating for LOLA B. MCGEE's Contributions to Core Requirements - Fiscal Year 2006

This reflects your performance rating as of January 06, 2007.

Assignment Type	Begin Date	End Date	Finance Number	Performance Pay Program	Unit or Postmaster Level	MPOO Code	Position Type	Evaluator
Permanent	05/08/2006	09/30/2006	316200	Field EAS (District and Facility EAS)	EAS 26-21 Post Office	None	EAS Supervisor/Staff	JENNIFER T. VO

Core Requirement #1	Contributor	High Contributor	Exceptional Contributor
Achievement of target percent to standard	100% > 95%	94% > 90%	89% > 0%

Objective Approval/Disapproval Comments:	No Comments Entered.
End-of-Year Accomplishments:	I started at Huntridge the begining of qtr. 3, percent to standard was 120.83. At the end of FY 06 the percent to standard was 109.41. Now at Paradise Valley I've begun to reduce the % to standard in FY07 (wk 2)107.49. I did not meet the contributor target, but I greatly impacted the performance in the short time that I was at Huntridge. *~ Entered by LOLA B. MCGEE on 10/26/2006*
End-of-Year Evaluator Comments:	Huntridge % to standard for FY 06 was 120 based on the Western Area Variance Program compared to 135% to standard for FY05. The base is 95% compared to Earned for FY of 97 % to standard. Huntridge improved by 15% with the month of September at 111.75% to standard *~ Entered by JENNIFER T. VO on 11/20/2006*

Recommended Rating Entered by JENNIFER T. VO on 11/20/2006

Non-contributor	Contributor	High Contributor	Exceptional Contributor
0	**6**	11	14

Core Requirement #2	Contributor	High Contributor	Exceptional Contributor
Delivery Confirmation	98.0 < 98.4	98.5 < 99.0	99.1 < 100%

Objective Approval/Disapproval Comments:	No Comments Entered.
End-of-Year Accomplishments:	When I started at Huntridge the Del. Conf. score was 97.4 up to the end of qtr. 2, I improved the performance to finish the year at 98.5%. The improvement in performance was the result of my leadership for the 11/2 qtrs I was there. I am at a High Contributor level with this requirement. *~ Entered by LOLA B. MCGEE on 10/26/2006*
End-of-Year Evaluator Comments:	Huntridge started off week 39 YTD at 95.43% in Delivery Confirmation and ended the year with the highest score in the city of Las Vegas at 98.28% *~ Entered by JENNIFER T. VO on 11/20/2006*

Recommended Rating Entered by JENNIFER T. VO on 11/20/2006

Non-contributor	Contributor	High Contributor	Exceptional Contributor

0	6	11	14

Core Requirement #3	Contributor	High Contributor	Exceptional Contributor
City Carriers In by 1700	75.0 < 82.0	83.0 < 90.0	90.1 < 100%

Objective Approval/Disapproval Comments:	No Comments Entered.
End-of-Year Accomplishments:	When I arrived at Huntridge at the beginning of qtr 3 carriers returning by 1700 performance was at 72.2%. For the next two qtrs to end FY06 carriers returning by 1700 improved to 90.2 for qtr2 and 85.8 for qtr 4 even though I was asked to give help to other stations in the city. I am at a High Contributor level with this requirement. *~ Entered by LOLA B. MCGEE on 10/26/2006*
End-of-Year Evaluator Comments:	For the months that Lola was at Huntridge. It average 82.63 carriers in by 1700 based on TACS and not DOIS *~ Entered by JENNIFER T. VO on 11/20/2006*

Recommended Rating Entered by JENNIFER T. VO on 11/20/2006

Non-contributor	Contributor	High Contributor	Exceptional Contributor
0	6	11	14

Core Requirement # 4 Oral Communication

Non-Contributor	Contributor	High Contributor	Exceptional Contributor
Often has difficulty stating ideas and instructions clearly and concisely. Fails to give attention to what others are saying. Demonstrates a lack of sensitivity when communicating with others. Has difficulty in guiding staff in a positive manner. Fails to provide feedback and coaching. Does not provide a satisfactory managerial example while motivating employees to work towards goals and objectives.	Generally states ideas and instructions clearly and concisely. Gives attention to what others are saying and takes the time to understand points that are being made. Uses appropriate tone and attitude when communicating with others. Provides a satisfactory managerial example while motivating employees to work towards departmental goals and objectives. Provides practical direction to employees and communicates the department's shared vision. Available to help the team accomplish its goals. Assesses individual strengths and weaknesses and suggests methods for improvement. Supports the organizations mandate through support of its goals and values.	Consistently states ideas and instructions clearly and concisely. Gives attention to what others are saying and takes the time to understand points that are being made. Works to ensure understanding and asks for or provides clarification when needed. Uses language, examples, and concepts appropriate to the audience. Makes decisions and sets policies on controversial issues and provides innovative direction in resolving problems.	Articulates in a wide range of communication situations with all levels of the organization. Consistently states ideas and instructions clearly and concisely. Gives attention to what others are saying and takes the time to understand points that are being made. Works to ensure understanding and asks for or provides clarification when needed. Uses language, examples, and concepts appropriate to the audience. Provides exceptional leadership in planning organizing, maintaining, controlling and maximizing operations. Extends the opportunity for growth and development to all staff.

Objective Approval/Disapproval	No Comments Entered.

EOY Rating Report

Page 3 of 4

Comments:	
End-of-Year Accomplishments:	In my previous evaluations I've gotten a rating of 11-13 which is in the exceptional category. I was evaluated in the areas of ability to motivate, train, communicate, and give concise and efficient instruction to my employees. I believe that I still have the acquired skills from my previous evaluations which would put me in the Exceptional category for this requirement. *~ Entered by LOLA B. MCGEE on 10/26/2006*
End-of-Year Evaluator Comments:	Lola has improved on her communications skills as shown in the improvements in this unit. Giving the employees the vital information with the change to the Western area was a key ingredient in forming a successful transaction that efficient SERVICE is what we are about. Las Vegas for Quarter 3 made 95 in OND and 96 for Quarter 4. Huntridge ended the FY with the following: MVA 14.25 OII 8.93 Sick Leave: 3.42 Decreased OT from 18.20% FY 05 to 16.33% FY 06 *~ Entered by JENNIFER T. VO on 11/20/2006*

Recommended Rating Entered by JENNIFER T. VO on 11/20/2006

Non-contributor	Contributor	High Contributor	Exceptional Contributor
0	6	11	14

Additional End-of-Year Employee Contributions	
Additional End-of-Year Employee Contributions:	I have worked very hard on my details and I continue to improve where ever I may be placed. If the data is reviewed for the offices that I've been detailed to, it would show that improvement was acheived almost immediately upon my arrival. I have worked 11-12 hour days, and some weekends without pay. This demonstrates dedicated effort to my duties and responsibilities. *~ Entered by LOLA B. MCGEE on 10/26/2006*

Evaluator End-of-Year Overall Comment	
Evaluator End-of-Year Overall Comments:	Review completed by JENNIFER T. VO. *~ Entered by JENNIFER T. VO on 11/20/2006*

End-of-Year Discussion Date and Comments	
End-of-Year Discussion Date and Comments:	11/20/2006 - No Comments Entered.

End-of-Year Rating

End-of-year rating for the following position: Supv Customer Services - North Las Vegas Po - Field EAS (District and Facility EAS) - EAS 26-21 Post Office - EAS Supervisor/Staff

This rating accounts for 40.00000% of the Overall Performance Rating.

	Rating	Weight	Equals
Core requirement #1	6	X 0.26667	1.60000
Core requirement #2	6	X 0.26667	1.60000
Core requirement #3	6	X 0.26667	1.60000

Interim Rating

Interim rating for the following position: Supv Customer Services - North Las Vegas Po - Field EAS (District and Facility EAS) - EAS 26-21 Post Office - EAS Supervisor/Staff - Begin Date 10/01/2005 - End Date 05/07/2006

This rating accounts for 60.00000% of the Overall Performance Rating

	Rating	Weight	Equals
Core requirement #1	6	X 0.26667	1.60000
Core requirement #2	6	X 0.26667	1.60000

:OY Rating Report

Page 4 of 4

Core requirement #4	6	X 0.20000	1.20000
NPA Composite Summary	5.84	X 0.70000	4.08800
Core Requirement Rating Summary	6.00000	X 0.30000	1.80000
Overall Numeric Rating			5.88800

Core requirement #3	6	X 0.26667	1.60000
Core requirement #4	6	X 0.20000	1.20000
NPA Composite Summary	5.84	X 0.70000	4.08800
Core Requirement Rating Summary	6.00000	X 0.30000	1.80000
Overall Numeric Rating			**5.88800**

Pro-rated Overall Performance Rating :

	Numeric Rating	% of FY	
End-of-year rating	5.88800	X 0.40000	2.35520
Interim Rating	5.88800	X 0.60000	3.53280
Numeric Rating			5.88800

PES carries out to 32 decimal places when calculating and determining an employee's overall performance rating. However, for display purposes only five decimal places are displayed on the screen. It is important to note that the employee's overall performance rating is rounded to a whole number.

For example, if an employee's Numeric Rating is 8.49959, the employee's Overall Performance Rating will be rounded to a whole number of 8.

Overall Performance rating will be rounded to 6

:xport Ratings Calculation to Excel

:rint This Window

:lose Window

Some of my accomplishments can be reviewed on my eCareer profile, and my old 991s (The U.S. Postal Service Resume) I submitted for promotions on all my attempts. While on detail, I put in for several positions: Strip Station—August 2006, Winterwood Station—August 2006, Garside Station—January 2007, Huntridge—January 2007, Strip Station—January 2007 (second time) and Paradise Valley Station—January 2007. All of these stations are in the City of Las Vegas where I had been on detail for one full year. Some of the positions were filled with acting managers that had not been acting as long as I had, some had just started acting, and some, I was told, were laterals. My ability to bring my staff together and achieve the desired results, and not be considered for a position, makes one question, why me? None of the people selected for the positions were African American or women. There were only two of us acting at the time. The other African American woman stopped acting as manager because of some issues she had with a carrier.

On March 30, 2007, I called Yul Melonson at NLV (Postmaster Craig was promoted to Level 24) to introduce myself to him. After Craig left, NLV went from a Level 22 to a Level 24 post office because of growth in the city. I let Yul know that I was a supervisor at NLV, and I would be returning to my position effective tomorrow. Yul said, "No one told me that you were coming back." I told him that I was notified by Robert Reynosa and Jennifer Vo that I was returning.

I went to see Yul and told him that I was on detail for one year, and I would like to take a break for a week. When I return, I promised to have North Las Vegas running great just as I had done for Craig Colton. While sitting in the office, Yul was looking at the Flash report for Paradise Valley Station, and asked, "Why are you here?" I replied, "I don't know, but I need a week of annual to recuperate and gather myself, and I'll be ready when I come back." Yul allowed me to go on annual and when I returned he placed me at Meadow Mesa to run the largest zone there. I excelled once again and he showed his appreciation by giving me a gas card because he knew I lived on the other side of town. He gave me an excellence plaque and a monetary spot award for my part in North Las Vegas' success.

In the interim, I resumed my position at North Las Vegas Main Post Office where I excelled in my F4 duties by revamping the entire operation from distribution to the box section. I trained 204Bs, acting managers, and performed well in my operation. Also, North Las Vegas Main Post Office received "Best F4 Award for Work Hours." In addition, one day, Yul Melonson asked me to come in on a Saturday to train his supervisors on counting and transferring the vault. I did as he asked. When merit time came, he demonstrated his appreciation as well, even though he only had part of the rating and Robert Reynosa had the other part, because I was on detail in the City of Las Vegas for half of the fiscal year. Refer to my accomplishments for what I did in the City of North Las Vegas and Las Vegas on my eCareer profile and tell me if I deserved the rating that I received from Robert Reynosa in FY07. Once again, I just let it slide, and I moved on to continue to excel at whatever life brought my way.

In 2007, shortly after the New Year, Dana Urbanski was still detailed as Acting Manager, Customer Service Operations, which was the position that Jennifer Vo held. Dana and I were having a private conversation, but for the sake of this book I'm going to disclose what she asked me. Dana asked, "Why is Mark and Robert so hard on you on the telecom (telephone conference)? It just seems to me that they talk to you harder than anyone else." I said, "You can see it also? I don't know, except for the fact that I am a black, serious woman with a deep voice." I told Dana that I called a meeting with Jennifer, Robert, and Mark about how I did not want to be perceived as a person that would cheat to achieve. Dana replied, "I don't know; I don't think it is right or fair. There are other offices that are doing worse than this one, and they are not talking to them like they talk to you."

Flash = Paradise Valley Office Total Budget Performance Report, March 2007, shows total office performance for all operations

Given by Management (my Bosses

Then I was sent back as a supervisor. Doug Watson got the Job.

03/28/2007
05:01:57

Weekly Flash Report: Week 25, 2007
'ffice: LAS-PARADISE VALLEY S - 314894
Query: 890 - Las Vegas Stations

PAGE 18
unReconciled

Current Week: Act Ddays-6 Sply Ddays-6; ACT/Plan 03/17/2007 - 03/23/2007; SPLY 03/18/2006 - 03/24/2006

Month to Date: Act Ddays-20 Sply Ddays-21; ACT/Plan 03/01/2007 - 03/23/2007; SPLY 03/01/2006 - 03/24/2006

Year to Date: Act Ddays-141 Sply Ddays-143; ACT/Plan 10/01/2006 - 03/23/2007; SPLY 10/01/2005 - 03/24/2006

L\C	Description	Current Week Actual	Plan	%Plan	%SPLY	Month to Date Actual	Plan	%Plan	%SPLY	Year to Date Actual	Plan	%Plan	%SPLY
SB1	OPS MP SAL/BEN	0	0	0.0	0.0	0	0	0.0	-100.0	0	0	0.0	-100.0
20	D/S SUPERVISOR	179	167	7.2	-10.1	557	564	-1.2	-31.4	4,631	4,107	12.8	-13.4
21	OFFICE	1,002	919	9.0	-18.2	3,418	3,101	10.2	-20.7	27,380	24,079	13.7	-23.9
22	STREET	2,337	2,195	6.5	3.4	7,806	7,409	5.4	-4.0	56,490	55,053	2.6	-10.2
26	CC CUS SUPPORT	22	6	266.7	-57.7	54	19	184.2	-72.4	810	140	478.6	-33.7
27	COLLECTIONS	0	0	0.0	0.0	0	0	0.0	0.0	0	0	0.0	-100.0
92	OPNS D/S TNG HRS	0	7	-100.0	-100.0	5	24	-79.2	-83.9	150	173	-13.3	12.8
FN2C	CITY CARRIER HRS	3,339	3,114	7.2	-4.2	11,224	10,510	6.8	-9.8	83,870	79,132	6.0	-15.2
FN2B	CITY DELIVERY	3,540	3,294	7.5	-5.9	11,840	11,117	6.5	-12.2	89,461	83,552	7.1	-15.3
20OT	OT-D/S SUPERVS HRS	1	0	0.0	-98.2	6	0	0.0	-96.5	802	0	0.0	0.5
O2SR	D/S SUPERVS OT RATIO	0.56	0.00	0.0	-98.0	1.08	0.00	0.0	-94.9	17.32	0.00	0.0	16.1
OT2B	FN2B OT	428	428	0.0	-28.2	1,481	1,446	2.4	-30.9	13,354	10,507	27.1	-25.0
O2BR	FN2B OT RATIO	12.09	12.99	-6.9	-23.7	12.51	13.01	-3.8	-21.3	14.93	12.58	18.7	-11.5
PO2B	PO CITY DELIVERY	0	0	0.0	-100.0	2	0	0.0	-66.7	546	0	0.0	2.2
P2BR	FN2B PO RATIO	0.00	0.00	0.0	100.0	0.02	0.00	0.0	-62.0	0.61	0.00	0.0	20.7
SL2B	CITY DELIVERY SL	240	134	79.1	12.7	1,053	451	133.5	90.8	6,199	3,277	89.2	29.0
S2BR	CITY DEL SL RATIO	6.78	4.07	66.7	19.8	8.89	4.06	119.2	117.2	6.93	3.92	76.7	52.2
SB2B	FN2B SAL/BEN	128,029	118,939	7.6	-5.2	439,588	404,745	8.6	-8.3	3,299,548	3,092,097	6.7	-12.5
FN2	TOTAL D/S HRS	3,540	3,294	7.5	-5.9	11,840	11,117	6.5	-12.2	89,461	83,552	7.1	-15.3
38	BUILDING SERV-CUSTOD	70	78	-10.3	-2.8	234	258	-9.3	2.6	1,691	1,839	-8.0	3.4
93	OPNS V/S&P/E TNG HRS	0	0	0.0	0.0	0	0	0.0	0.0	0	7	-100.0	0.0
FN3B	TOTAL PLNT & EQUIP	70	78	-10.3	-2.8	234	258	-9.3	2.6	1,691	1,846	-8.4	3.4
38OT	OT-BLDG SERV-CUSTOD	14	0	0.0	-12.5	50	0	0.0	-3.8	440	0	0.0	4.8
P3BR	PLNT&EQUIP PO RATIO	0.00	0.00	0.0	0.0	0.00	0.00	0.0	0.0	0.00	0.00	0.0	-100.0
SB3B	PLNT & EQUIP SAL/BEN	1,877	2,626	-28.5	15.8	6,262	8,474	-26.1	21.1	45,624	61,410	-25.7	20.7
L43L	UNIT DIST HRS LETTER	30	0	0.0	0.0	95	0	0.0	0.0	746	0	0.0	0.0
L43F	UNIT DIST HRS FLATS	31	0	0.0	0.0	113	0	0.0	0.0	956	0	0.0	0.0
L43P	UNIT DIST HRS PARCEL	47	0	0.0	0.0	161	0	0.0	0.0	1,396	0	0.0	0.0
L43A	UNIT DIST HRS ALLIED	103	464	-77.8	-67.2	355	1,580	-77.5	-68.7	2,830	11,924	-76.3	-63.9
43	UNIT DIST MANUAL	211	464	-54.5	-32.8	724	1,580	-54.2	-36.1	5,928	11,924	-50.3	-24.3
44	PO BOX DIST	37	46	-19.6	-43.9	136	158	-13.9	-40.4	1,182	1,165	1.5	-21.7
45	WINDOW SERVICE	171	184	-7.1	-31.6	629	626	0.5	-31.2	4,671	4,655	0.3	-21.2
48	ADMIN MISC	184	164	12.2	-8.5	633	558	13.4	-7.9	4,384	4,145	5.8	3.3
94	OPNS C/S TNG HRS	0	2	-100.0	-100.0	0	7	-100.0	-100.0	51	63	-19.0	-66.2
FN4	TOTAL C/S HRS	603	860	-29.9	-27.8	2,122	2,929	-27.6	-28.9	16,216	21,952	-26.1	-17.6
45OT	OT-WINDOW SERVICE	4	0	0.0	-20.0	13	0	0.0	-18.8	102	0	0.0	-54.7
45PO	PO-WINDOW SERVICE	0	0	0.0	0.0	4	0	0.0	0.0	11	0	0.0	0.0
OT4	OPS RETAIL OT	61	68	-10.3	0.0	219	230	-4.8	-3.9	2,313	1,731	33.6	-2.3
OT4R	FN4 OT RATIO	10.12	7.91	27.9	38.5	10.32	7.85	31.4	35.0	14.26	7.89	80.9	18.5
PO4	OPS RETAIL POT	0	0	0.0	0.0	4	0	0.0	0.0	41	0	0.0	141.2
PO4R	FN4 PO RATIO	0.00	0.00	0.0	0.0	0.19	0.00	0.0	0.0	0.25	0.00	0.0	192.6
SL4	RETAIL SL	46	31	48.4	253.8	167	106	57.5	96.5	689	796	-13.4	-5.9
SL4R	FN4 SL RATIO	7.63	3.60	111.6	390.0	7.87	3.62	117.5	176.2	4.25	3.63	17.2	14.2
SB4	OPS RETAIL SAL/BEN	21,599	30,335	-28.8	-18.6	76,654	102,509	-25.2	-19.4	572,653	781,142	-26.7	-12.7
BOXL	BOX DIST LTRS VOL	29,737	33,435	-11.1	-26.8	105,555	114,932	-8.2	-18.8	772,708	848,407	-8.9	-5.6
BOXF	BOX DIST FLAT VOL	10,695	11,115	-3.8	5.7	30,130	38,208	-21.1	-17.4	240,420	282,045	-14.8	-15.7
BXVL	BOXF+BOXL	40,432	44,550	-9.2	-20.3	135,685	153,140	-11.4	-18.5	1,013,128	1,130,452	-10.4	-8.2
BOXP	BOX PRODUCTIVITY	1,092.76	968.48	12.8	42.1	997.68	969.24	2.9	36.6	857.13	970.35	-11.7	17.3
UDLT	UNIT DIST LTRS VOL	56,977	65,331	-12.8	-15.2	183,870	223,304	-17.7	-22.7	1,518,517	1,685,360	-9.9	4.8
UDFL	UNIT DIST FLAT VOL	50,025	60,475	-17.3	-6.9	161,920	206,706	-21.7	-20.2	1,350,445	1,560,083	-13.4	-10.2
DVP1	DIST PROD - PCS/43	507.12	271.13	87.0	31.7	477.61	272.16	75.5	22.7	483.97	272.18	77.8	28.4

Great Job!

Looks Good

Looks Good

03/28/2007
05:01:57

Weekly Flash Report: Week 25, 2007
Office: LAS-PARADISE VALLEY S - 314894
Query: 890 - Las Vegas Stations

PAGE 19
unReconciled

Act Ddays-6 Sply Ddays-6 — ACT/Plan 03/17/2007 - 03/23/2007; SPLY 03/18/2006 - 03/24/2006 — ********** Current Week ************

Act Ddays-20 Sply Ddays-21 — ACT/Plan 03/01/2007 - 03/23/2007; SPLY 03/01/2006 - 03/24/2006 — ************ Month to Date ************

Act Ddays-141 Sply Ddays-143 — ACT/Plan 10/01/2006 - 03/23/2007; SPLY 10/01/2005 - 03/24/2006 — *************** Year to Date **************

L\C	Description	Current Week Actual	Plan	%Plan	%SPLY	Month to Date Actual	Plan	%Plan	%SPLY	Year to Date Actual	Plan	%Plan	%SPLY
REHR	RETAIL REV PROD	188.63	0.00	0.0	26.0	173.13	0.00	0.0	19.3	180.03	0.00	0.0	10.6
REVP	WALKIN REV PROD	187.51	0.00	0.0	26.5	171.32	0.00	0.0	19.4	178.24	0.00	0.0	10.9
FN9	TRAINING (NON-ADD)	0	9	-100.0	-100.0	5	31	-83.9	-90.4	201	243	-17.3	-29.2
HRTT	TOTAL HOURS	4,213	4,232	-0.4	-9.8	14,196	14,304	-0.8	-14.9	107,368	107,350	0.0	-15.4
OTTA	TOTAL OVERTIME	503	499	0.8	-25.3	1,750	1,686	3.8	-27.8	16,107	12,312	30.8	-21.8
OTTR	TOTAL OT RATIO	11.94	11.79	1.3	-17.2	12.33	11.79	4.6	-15.1	15.00	11.47	30.8	-7.6
POTT	TOTAL POT	0	0	0.0	-100.0	6	0	0.0	0.0	587	0	0.0	6.1
POTR	TOTAL PO RATIO	0.00	0.00	0.0	-100.0	0.04	0.00	0.0	17.5	0.55	0.00	0.0	25.4
SLTT	TOTAL SICK LEAVE	286	168	70.2	26.5	1,220	567	115.2	91.5	6,896	4,143	66.4	24.5
SLTR	TOTAL SL RATIO	6.79	3.97	71.0	40.3	8.59	3.96	116.8	125.2	6.42	3.86	66.4	47.1
SBTT	TOTAL SAL/BEN	151,505	151,900	-0.3	-7.2	522,504	515,728	1.3	-9.9	3,917,825	3,924,622	-0.2	-12.2
39W	WALK-IN REVENUE	32,064	0	0.0	-13.4	107,761	0	0.0	-17.8	832,536	0	0.0	-12.6
39R	RETAIL REVENUE	32,255	0	0.0	-13.8	108,897	0	0.0	-17.9	840,905	0	0.0	-12.9
TREV	TOTAL REVENUE	34,464	0	0.0	-8.2	115,756	0	0.0	-14.6	869,974	0	0.0	-10.8
29A	VEH ACC TOTAL	0	0	0.0	0.0	0	0	0.0	0.0	4	0	0.0	0.0
MVAF	VECH ACC FREQ RATE	0.0	0.0	0.0	0.0	0.0	0.0	0.0	0.0	26.9	0.0	0.0	0.0
29F	TOT OSHA INJ/ILLNESS	0	0	0.0	0.0	1	0	0.0	0.0	4	0	0.0	100.0
OIIF	OSHA INJ/ILL FREQ	0.00	0.00	0.0	0.0	14.09	0.00	0.0	0.0	7.45	0.00	0.0	136.3
CSLT	CASED LETTERS	140,961	78,000	80.7	-23.3	475,663	264,000	80.2	-26.3	3,675,515	1,914,000	92.0	-29.4
CSFL	CASED FLATS	156,522	242,000	-35.3	-7.0	543,444	816,000	-33.4	-13.0	4,488,985	5,931,000	-24.3	-19.3
SEQ	SEQUENCED VOLUME	217,614	193,000	12.8	5.5	759,118	652,000	16.4	-2.4	9,127,009	4,740,000	92.6	60.7
DPS	DPS VOLUME	505,654	449,000	12.6	6.6	1,676,539	1,516,000	10.6	-4.7	12,475,588	11,025,000	13.2	-11.9
CDV	TOT CDV PIECE	1,020,751	962,000	6.1	-1.2	3,454,764	3,248,000	6.4	-9.3	29,767,097	23,610,000	26.1	-2.8
PKCC	CITY CARRIER PKGS	0	4,480	-100.0	-100.0	4,140	15,123	-72.6	-67.3	10,449	109,942	-90.5	-91.5
PK1K	PACKAGES	10,721	17,679	-39.4	-41.3	42,207	59,677	-29.3	-38.0	371,907	433,881	-14.3	-28.4
CTRT	CITY STREET ROUTES	66	67	-1.5	-2.9	66	67	-1.5	-2.9	66	67	-1.5	10.0
CUPD	CUM DELIVERIES	223,284	246,096	-9.3	0.9	744,370	819,840	-9.2	-4.0	5,254,966	5,781,233	-9.1	-11.0
SDPD	POSS DEL	37,214	41,016	-9.3	0.9	37,219	40,992	-9.2	0.8	37,269	40,713	-8.5	-9.8
CDPR	CITY DEL PER ROUTE	563.8	612.2	-7.9	3.9	563.9	611.8	-7.8	3.8	564.7	607.7	-7.1	-18.0
DPSP	DPS % - ALL OFFICES	78.2	85.2	-8.2	8.5	77.9	85.2	-8.5	6.5	77.2	85.2	-9.3	5.6
OEI	OFFICE EFF INDICATOR	222.84	267.79	-16.8	23.3	217.78	264.38	-17.6	21.1	191.93	240.09	-20.1	17.0
SEI	STREET EFF IND	95.54	112.12	-14.8	-2.5	95.36	110.65	-13.8	-0.1	93.02	105.01	-11.4	-1.0
TEI	DELIVERIES PER HOUR	66.43	78.70	-15.6	6.9	65.97	77.69	-15.1	7.7	61.95	72.77	-14.9	5.1

Flash = Huntridge Station Total Performance Report, July 2008

Last week at Huntridge
I left 7/8/08 Tuesday
Mid week 41 (08)

7/8/08
2:54:14 AM 314891

Flash Last 4 Weeks Report: Week 40 2008
Finance Office LAS-HUNTRIDGE STA - 314891
890 - Las Vegas Stations

Page 13
Unreconciled

Act Ddays 5 Sply Ddays 5 — Act/Plan 06-28-2008 - 07-04-2008; SPLY 06-30-2007 - 07-06-2007 — Current Week
Act Ddays 23 Sply Ddays 23 — Act/Plan 06-07-2008 - 07-04-2008; SPLY 06-09-2007 - 07-06-2007 — Last 4 Weeks
Act Ddays 230 Sply Ddays 229 — Act/Plan 10-01-2007 - 07-04-2008; SPLY 10-01-2006 - 07-06-2007 — Year to Date

L/C	Description	Actual	Plan	%Plan	%SPLY	Actual 4WK	Plan 4WK	%P 4WK	%S 4WK	Actual YTD	Plan YTD	%P YTD	%S YTD
SB1	OPS MP SAL/BEN	0	0	0.0	0.0	0	0	0.0	0.0	0	0	0.0	-100.0
20	D/S SUPERVISOR	104	88	18.2	-13.3	483	397	21.7	-4.2	4,472	4,175	7.1	-20.3
21	OFFICE	353	392	-9.9	-19.6	1,622	1,775	-8.6	-13.4	18,634	18,629	0.0	-13.5
22	STREET	1,160	1,145	1.3	-6.8	5,323	5,181	2.7	-5.3	54,559	54,412	0.3	-4.3
23	OTHER	0	0	0.0	0.0	0	0	0.0	0.0	27	0	0.0	0.0
26	CC CUS SUPPORT	0	3	-100.0	-100.0	3	12	-75.0	-25.0	76	120	-36.7	-13.6
92	OPNS D/S TNG HRS	0	8	-100.0	0.0	22	35	-37.1	-33.3	439	379	15.8	104.2
FN2C	CITY CARRIER HRS	1,513	1,537	-1.6	-10.1	6,945	6,956	-0.2	-7.3	73,220	73,041	0.2	-6.8
FN2B	CITY DELIVERY	1,617	1,636	-1.2	-10.4	7,453	7,400	0.7	-7.2	78,207	77,715	0.6	-7.4
20OT	OT-D/S SUPERVS HRS	0	0	0.0	-100.0	35	0	0.0	-48.5	427	0	0.0	30.2
O2SR	D/S SUPERVS OT RATIO	0.00	0.00	0.0	-100.0	7.25	0.00	0.0	-46.3	9.55	0.00	0.0	63.3
OT2C	CITY CARRIER OT	120	0	0.0	-61.7	578	0	0.0	-57.5	8,549	0	0.0	-34.6
O2CR	CITY CARR OT RATIO	7.93	0.00	0.0	-57.4	8.32	0.00	0.0	-54.1	11.68	0.00	0.0	-29.9
OT2B	FN2B OT	120	263	-54.4	-65.7	613	1,104	-44.5	-57.1	8,993	10,496	-14.3	-33.0
O2BR	FN2B OT RATIO	7.42	16.08	-53.8	-61.7	8.22	14.92	-44.9	-53.8	11.50	13.51	-14.9	-27.6
PO2C	CITY CARRIER PO	0	0	0.0	-100.0	0	0	0.0	-100.0	48	0	0.0	-74.5
P2CR	CITY CARR PO RATIO	0.00	0.00	0.0	-100.0	0.00	0.00	0.0	-100.0	0.07	0.00	0.0	-72.6
SL2B	CITY DELIVERY SL	48	71	-32.4	-63.1	261	317	-17.7	-50.0	4,366	3,369	29.6	15.3
S2CR	CITY CARR SL RATIO	3.17	0.00	0.0	-58.9	3.76	0.00	0.0	-46.1	5.92	0.00	0.0	36.3
FN2	TOTAL D/S HRS	1,617	1,636	-1.2	-10.4	7,453	7,400	0.7	-7.2	78,207	77,715	0.6	-7.4
L43L	UNIT DIST HRS LETTER	20	0	0.0	-45.9	95	0	0.0	-34.0	932	0	0.0	-30.1
L43F	UNIT DIST HRS FLATS	13	0	0.0	-31.6	56	0	0.0	-44.6	857	0	0.0	-29.1
L43P	UNIT DIST HRS PARCEL	22	0	0.0	0.0	110	0	0.0	-11.3	1,135	0	0.0	-25.2
L43A	UNIT DIST HRS ALLIED	12	107	-88.8	-78.2	31	487	-93.6	-85.6	401	5,405	-92.6	-83.6
43	UNIT DIST MANUAL	67	107	-37.4	-49.6	292	487	-40.0	-50.1	3,325	5,405	-38.5	-48.9
44	PO BOX DIST	39	24	62.5	2.6	181	107	69.2	58.8	1,584	1,177	34.6	-14.1
45	WINDOW SERVICE	133	171	-22.2	-14.7	699	775	-9.8	-14.4	7,449	8,588	-13.3	-7.5
48	ADMIN MISC	160	117	36.8	63.3	718	530	35.5	21.9	6,987	5,863	19.2	9.7
94	OPNS C/S TNG HRS	0	2	-100.0	0.0	0	8	-100.0	0.0	42	65	-35.4	-76.7
FN4	TOTAL C/S HRS	399	421	-5.2	-6.1	1,890	1,907	-0.9	-10.2	19,387	21,098	-8.1	-15.5
45OT	OT-WINDOW SERVICE	8	0	0.0	-71.4	29	0	0.0	-78.4	473	0	0.0	-58.5
45PO	PO-WINDOW SERVICE	0	0	0.0	0.0	0	0	0.0	-100.0	9	0	0.0	-25.0
OT4	OPS RETAIL OT	41	39	5.1	-53.4	132	170	-22.4	-55.7	1,739	1,809	-3.9	-45.3
OT4R	FN4 OT RATIO	10.28	9.26	10.9	-50.4	6.98	8.91	-21.7	-50.7	8.97	8.57	4.6	-35.2
PO4	OPS RETAIL POT	0	0	0.0	-100.0	1	0	0.0	-66.7	11	0	0.0	-70.3
PO4R	FN4 PO RATIO	0.00	0.00	0.0	-100.0	0.05	0.00	0.0	-62.9	0.06	0.00	0.0	-64.8
SL4	RETAIL SL	4	17	-76.5	0.0	32	78	-59.0	-39.6	257	844	-69.5	-81.0
SL4R	FN4 SL RATIO	1.00	4.04	-75.2	0.0	1.69	4.09	-58.6	-32.8	1.33	4.00	-66.9	-77.6
SB4	OPS RETAIL SAL/BEN	15,608	15,762	-1.0	1.4	69,635	71,403	-2.5	-2.8	694,561	750,835	-7.5	-13.6
BOXL	BOX DIST LTRS VOL	19,360	20,795	-6.9	-14.7	74,021	94,123	-21.4	-2.8	732,013	998,110	-26.7	-28.3
BOXF	BOX DIST FLAT VOL	2,157	4,350	-50.4	-38.0	12,019	19,687	-38.9	-11.2	137,111	208,760	-34.3	-48.1
BXVL	BOXF+BOXL	21,517	25,145	-14.4	-17.8	86,040	113,810	-24.4	-4.1	869,124	1,206,870	-28.0	-32.4
BOXP	BOX PRODUCTIVITY	551.72	1,047.71	-47.3	-19.9	475.36	1,063.64	-55.3	-39.6	548.69	1,025.38	-46.5	-21.3
UDLT	UNIT DIST LTRS VOL	21,833	50,866	-57.1	-16.1	129,205	230,235	-43.9	11.8	1,260,293	2,441,485	-48.4	-11.0
UDFL	UNIT DIST FLAT VOL	3,622	16,052	-77.4	-52.3	41,736	72,657	-42.6	14.5	441,925	770,478	-42.6	-11.6
DVP1	DIST PROD - PCS/43	379.93	625.40	-39.3	50.4	585.41	621.95	-5.9	125.3	511.95	594.26	-13.9	73.9
DVP2	DIST PROD-PCS/43+48	112.14	298.74	-62.5	-22.9	169.25	297.83	-43.2	30.7	165.07	285.05	-42.1	10.9
REHR	RETAIL REV PROD	178.08	0.00	0.0	-14.4	183.01	0.00	0.0	11.6	210.87	0.00	0.0	16.1
REVP	WALKIN REV PROD	176.42	0.00	0.0	-14.4	181.99	0.00	0.0	11.9	209.47	0.00	0.0	16.0

7/8/08
2:54:14 AM 314891

Flash Last 4 Weeks Report: Week 40 2008
Finance Office LAS-HUNTRIDGE STA - 314891
890 - Las Vegas Stations

Page 14
Unreconciled

L/C Description	Act Ddays 5 Sply Ddays 5 — Act/Plan 06-28-2008 - 07-04-2008; SPLY 06-30-2007 - 07-06-2007; Current Week: Actual	Plan	%Plan	%SPLY	Act Ddays 23 Sply Ddays 23 — Act/Plan 06-07-2008 - 07-04-2008; SPLY 06-09-2007 - 07-06-2007; Last 4 Weeks: Actual 4WK	Plan 4WK	%P 4WK	%S 4WK	Act Ddays 230 Sply Ddays 229 — Act/Plan 10-01-2007 - 07-04-2008; SPLY 10-01-2006 - 07-06-2007; Year to Date: Actual YTD	Plan YTD	%P YTD	%S YTD
FN9 TRAINING (NON-ADD)	0	10	-100.0	0.0	22	43	-48.8	-33.3	481	444	8.3	21.8
HRTT TOTAL HOURS	2,016	2,057	-2.0	-9.6	9,343	9,307	0.4	-7.9	97,594	98,813	-1.2	-9.2
OTTA TOTAL OVERTIME	161	302	-46.7	-63.2	745	1,274	-41.5	-56.9	10,732	12,305	-12.8	-35.3
OTTR TOTAL OT RATIO	7.99	14.68	-45.6	-59.4	7.97	13.69	-41.7	-53.2	11.00	12.45	-11.7	-28.8
POTT TOTAL POT	0	0	0.0	-100.0	1	0	0.0	-97.4	59	0	0.0	-73.8
POTR TOTAL PO RATIO	0.00	0.00	0.0	-100.0	0.01	0.00	0.0	-97.1	0.06	0.00	0.0	-71.1
SLTT TOTAL SICK LEAVE	52	88	-40.9	-60.0	293	395	-25.8	-49.0	4,623	4,213	9.7	-10.1
SLTR TOTAL SL RATIO	2.58	4.28	-39.7	-55.8	3.14	4.24	-26.1	-44.7	4.74	4.26	11.1	-1.0
WPTT TOTAL LWOP	50	0	0.0	-60.6	340	0	0.0	-20.9	3,527	0	0.0	-2.8
WPTR TOTAL WP RATIO	2.48	0.00	0.0	-56.5	3.64	0.00	0.0	-14.2	3.61	0.00	0.0	7.0
ALTT TOTAL AL	313	0	0.0	-11.1	1,219	0	0.0	-19.5	8,986	0	0.0	-11.1
ALTR TOTAL AL RATIO	15.53	0.00	0.0	-1.7	13.05	0.00	0.0	-12.6	9.21	0.00	0.0	-2.1
SBTT TOTAL SAL/BEN	81,600	78,250	4.3	-7.8	360,032	350,431	2.7	-6.8	3,830,632	3,755,407	2.0	-4.4
29A VEH ACC TOTAL	0	0	0.0	0.0	0	0	0.0	0.0	4	0	0.0	100.0
VACR VEH ACCIDENT RATE	0.00	0.00	0.0	0.0	0.00	0.00	0.0	0.0	36.24	0.00	0.0	104.5
29F TOT OSHA INJ/ILLNESS	0	0	0.0	0.0	0	0	0.0	0.0	4	0	0.0	100.0
OIIF OSHA INJ/ILL FREQ	0.00	0.00	0.0	0.0	0.00	0.00	0.0	0.0	8.20	0.00	0.0	120.2
CSLT CASED LETTERS	39,220	40,047	-2.1	-21.0	191,216	181,284	5.5	-15.8	1,962,573	1,922,558	2.1	-35.6
CSFL CASED FLATS	46,787	59,021	-20.7	-28.5	207,231	267,174	-22.4	-27.9	3,041,566	2,833,458	7.3	-6.7
SEQ SEQUENCED VOLUME	49,108	64,398	-23.7	-17.5	200,953	291,518	-31.1	-30.4	2,026,024	3,091,630	-34.5	-44.3
DPS CITY CARR DPS	199,166	226,931	-12.2	-22.9	939,398	1,027,272	-8.6	-9.2	10,806,820	10,894,499	-0.8	-2.5
CDV TOT CDV PIECE	334,281	390,397	-14.4	-22.8	1,538,798	1,767,248	-12.9	-16.3	17,836,983	18,742,145	-4.8	-15.1
PAK PACKAGES	3,372	8,134	-58.5	-32.6	15,305	36,817	-58.4	-25.5	249,736	390,416	-36.0	4.4
CTRT CITY STREET ROUTES	39	39	0.0	0.0	39	39	0.0	0.0	39	39	0.0	0.0
CUPD CUM DELIVERIES	90,165	90,575	-0.5	-0.4	414,777	416,645	-0.4	-0.4	4,154,234	4,166,450	-0.3	0.2
SDPD POSS DEL	18,033	18,115	-0.5	-0.4	18,034	18,115	-0.4	-0.4	18,062	18,115	-0.3	-0.3
CDPR CITY DEL PER ROUTE	462.4	464.5	-0.5	-0.4	462.4	464.5	-0.4	-0.4	463.1	464.5	-0.3	-0.3
DPSP DPS % - ALL OFFICES	83.55	85.00	-1.7	-0.4	83.09	85.00	-2.3	1.3	84.63	85.00	-0.4	7.9
OEI OFFICE EFF INDICATOR	255.42	231.06	10.5	23.9	255.72	234.73	8.9	15.0	222.94	223.65	-0.3	15.7
SEI STREET EFF IND	77.73	79.10	-1.7	6.8	77.92	80.42	-3.1	5.2	76.14	76.57	-0.6	4.7
TEI DELIVERIES PER HOUR	59.59	58.51	1.9	10.9	59.51	59.50	0.0	7.6	56.34	56.66	-0.6	7.1

Chapter 5
Continuing Demise

In September 2007, my heart was beating faster than normal. My primary doctor referred me to a Cardiologist, who diagnosed me with heart palpitations. After extensive testing, it was found to be benign. The benign heart condition ended up not being so benign. I had heart surgery on February 25, 2010. My heart was only 40% healthy, and it was beating 40,000 extra beats per day. I would have eventually died from my heart beating out completely. I believe Dr. Robert Croke was bought by the United States Postal Service at my expense. Dr. Croke told me that my condition was benign, and he would not be the person to allow me to go out on Medical Disability Retirement. I did not understand it then, but I understand it now. I also had a choking cough and sought treatment from an Ear, Nose, and Throat specialist, but he could not find the cause.

In that same month, I put in for Valle Verde Station in Henderson and received an interview (Level 22 Station), but it was given to a woman who had already been acting for about two years, but she was the type of person that spoke back to Jennifer. I did not feel that this selection was unfair. During the interview, I was given my performance report from Paradise Valley Station and Craig Colton, said he pulled the report, and it was very good. Remember, I told you we were number one in the district for Function-4 (F4 – Clerk Productivity and Mail Processing). I was told by Craig that I had a great interview, and he went back and forth while he was trying to make his decision. My skills and ability level was high, and I was very knowledgeable about the position. Craig also told me that it was a matter of when, not if, I get promoted. Then I asked Craig to give me some feedback that would help me the next time. Craig, after a sigh and hesitation, shocked me with, "You are too confident. You need to use some discretion."

Craig and I drove the same type of vehicle and lived in the same vicinity. He used to make jokes about the fact that his car had seventeen-inch rims, and mine had sixteen-inch rims. Also, the supervisor at North Las Vegas Main Post Office when I arrived was Craig's right-hand man. I worked hard for Craig, and was one of the reasons why he got his promotion from Postmaster North Las Vegas EAS-22 to Postmaster Henderson EAS-24. Craig would not promote me because he felt I forced him to do his job with his right-hand man—supervisor, and I was out of place trying to be up there with the managers. To me, Craig Colton is a wolf in sheep's clothing.

In October 2007, I put in for Sunrise Station in the City of Las Vegas EAS-21, and I received my first interview by Robert Reynosa and Mark Martinez; but I was not selected. I consoled myself by thinking, at least I got an interview, but then, there is no way at this point, with my performance, that they would be able to justify not giving me an interview, especially after receiving an interview with Craig for Valle Verde Station EAS-22. I was told by Mark and Robert that I had a great interview. Looking back in retrospect, I find it odd that Mark mentioned my daughter's Ivy League Education and Honor Achievements, and Robert had mentioned how I had purchased my home prior to moving to Las Vegas. I guess an African-American woman cannot have a child graduate from an Ivy League College, drive modern cars, and purchase a very nice home in an upscale neighborhood, but we can perform very well in a manager's position and not be promoted. The person selected for Sunrise Station EAS-21 had not been acting in any station at the time; he was going around the district doing route inspections and going station to station making sure each were properly utilizing the CSAW (Customer Service, Clerks mail volume counting program). The mail ultimately is delivered to the customer via carrier on the street or clerks putting it in the post office boxes. This was the report Craig Colton reviewed with me during my interview for Valle Verde Station. Paradise Valley Station was rated number one in Customer Service/Mail Processing. Robert, Jennifer, and Mark gave me an award for Paradise Valley Station performance, but he got the promotion.

In December 2007, I put in for Red Rock Station in the City of Las Vegas EAS-22, and I did not receive an interview. I was told that the position was given to a person whom wanted to make a lateral move, and still I was not promoted.

In January 2008, I was requested to go on detail as acting manager in Reno, Nevada, by John Morgan, Senior Manager Post Office Operations, and I accepted. Even though I'd never been in the snow, I wanted all involved in selecting me to know that I truly appreciated the offer After being in Reno for one week, I received word from Postmaster Yul Melonson that Renee Brown said I was a breath of fresh air for her in Sparks Sun Valley Station EAS-20. I trained the clerks on efficiency and productivity. I trained the supervisor on more efficient and effective scheduling forms and addressing employees. I motivated the entire office and they were happy to have me there. After being there almost a month, I received a call from Robert Reynosa asking me to come back to the City of Las Vegas, and I told him that I would call him back. I called Renee and told her that I was asked to return to Las Vegas to be the acting manager of King Station. With regret, but understanding, she said, "That's a choice you have to make, but whatever your decision is, I support you." As a token of appreciation for my performance at Sparks Sun Valley Station, I was given a Certificate of Appreciation and a copy of the Flash Report (Post Office Performance Report). I told Renee that I would probably go back. Later that day, I was scheduled to return to Las Vegas on February 23, 2008.

Merit Rating Fiscal Year 2007 (Combined from Robert (3%) and Yul 2%) = 5% total pay increase for demonstrated performance, I deserved better

EOY Rating Report   Robert/Yul Combined   Page 1 of 4

Rating for LOLA B. MCGEE, SUPV CUSTOMER SERVICES
Contributions to Core Requirements - Fiscal Year 2007

This reflects your performance rating as of January 05, 2008.

Assignment Type	Begin Date	End Date	Finance Number	Performance Pay Program	Unit or Postmaster Level	MPOO Code	Position Type	Evaluator
Permanent	04/01/2007	09/30/2007	316200	Field EAS (District and Facility EAS)	EAS 26-21 Post Office	None	EAS Supervisor/Staff	YUL J. MELONSON

Core Requirement #1	Contributor	High Contributor	Exceptional Contributor
Penalty Overtime	Reduce by .30% - .20%	Reduce by .19% - .10%	Reduce by < .10% - 0.00%

Objective Approval/Disapproval Comments: No Comments Entered

End-of-Year Accomplishments: North Las Vegas finished FY 07 at -27.3% to SPLY with the usage of 0.72% for the entire year. I arrived at the begining of quarter 3. F4 finished -42.5% with usage of 0.60% YTD. By mid year Paradise Valley was at 0.4% with penalty usage . I have met the Exceptional Contributor level for this requirement. Lola McGee 11/7/2007
~ Entered by LOLA B. MCGEE on 11/07/2007

End-of-Year Evaluator Comments: When Lola returned to North Las Vegas in April she was given the responsibility of the clerk operation at the Main Office she was able to maintain the POT at .10%
~ Entered by YUL J. MELONSON on 11/14/2007

Recommended Rating Entered by YUL J. MELONSON

Non-contributor 0	Contributor 6	**High Contributor 11**	Exceptional Contributor 14

Core Requirement #2	Contributor	High Contributor	Exceptional Contributor
Overtime % Plan	-1.0% - -2.9%	-3.0% - -3.9%	-4.0% or Better

Objective Approval/Disapproval Comments: No Comments Entered

End-of-Year Accomplishments: North Las Vegas Finished FY 07 69.7% over plan in overtime, but -6.0% under SPLY. F4 finished 150.0% over plan, but -14.4% under SPLY. There was a combination of 20% reduction in overtime eventhough I did not meet the requirement. By midyear Paradise Valley had reduced overtime by 21% for FY 07. Lola Mcgee 11/7/2007
~ Entered by LOLA B. MCGEE on 11/07/2007

End-of-Year Evaluator Comments: This is an area that Lola needs to improve on she needs to schedule the employees based on the workload utilizing the tools given her, CSAW, CSV, Advance. She needs to hold employees accountable for meeting the established benchmarks for each operation.
~ Entered by YUL J. MELONSON on 11/14/2007

Recommended Rating Entered by YUL J. MELONSON

Non-contributor	Contributor 6	High Contributor 11	Exceptional Contributor 14

https://performance.usps.gov/pls/gsaprod/GSA_EOY_2007_REPORTS_PKG.employee_... 10/20/2008

EOY Rating Report

Page 2 of 4

0			

Core Requirement #3	Contributor	High Contributor	Exceptional Contributor
Operational Productivity	DPH= 0 to 2.9% to SPLY F4 Variance= 75-85%	3.0 to 3.9% to SPLY 86-90%	4.0% or Better than SPLY 91-100%

Objective Approval/Disapproval Comments:	No Comments Entered
End-of-Year Accomplishments:	North Las Vegas finished FY 07 2.6% over SPLY in DPH, and 85.07% total F4 hour variance. This is a Contributor level. However, from my return in May 2007 to the EOY DPH had improved to 6.88%over SPLY an Exceptional Contributor, and F4 was 88.31% achieved for work hours which is a High Contributor. Paradise Valley at Midyear was at 6.9% over SPLY in DPH and 93.02% achieved for F4 workhours which in an Exceptional Contributor level. *~ Entered by LOLA B. MCGEE on 11/07/2007*
End-of-Year Evaluator Comments:	Lola was a solid contributor in improving DPH and F4 Varience. She worked with carriers to improve efficiencies. She monitored the clerk operation for clockring integrity. With continue focus on performance she will be able to maintain in FY 08. *~ Entered by YUL J. MELONSON on 11/14/2007*

Recommended Rating Entered by YUL J. MELONSON

Non-contributor 0	Contributor 6	High Contributor 11	**Exceptional Contributor 14**

Core Requirement # 4 Oral Communication

Non-Contributor	Contributor	High Contributor	Exceptional Contributor
Often has difficulty stating ideas and instructions clearly and concisely. Fails to give attention to what others are saying. Demonstrates a lack of sensitivity when communicating with others. Has difficulty in guiding staff in a positive manner. Fails to provide feedback and coaching. Does not provide a satisfactory managerial example while motivating employees to work towards goals and objectives.	Generally states ideas and instructions clearly and concisely. Gives attention to what others are saying and takes the time to understand points that are being made. Uses appropriate tone and attitude when communicating with others. Provides a satisfactory managerial example while motivating employees to work towards departmental goals and objectives. Provides practical direction to employees and communicates the department's shared vision. Available to help the team accomplish its goals. Assesses individual strengths and weaknesses and suggests methods for improvement. Supports the organizations mandate through support of its goals	Consistently states ideas and instructions clearly and concisely. Gives attention to what others are saying and takes the time to understand points that are being made. Works to ensure understanding and asks for or provides clarification when needed. Uses language, examples, and concepts appropriate to the audience. Makes decisions and sets policies on controversial issues and provides innovative direction in resolving problems.	Articulates in a wide range of communication situations with all levels of the organization. Consistently states ideas and instructions clearly and concisely. Gives attention to what others are saying and takes the time to understand points that are being made. Works to ensure understanding and asks for or provides clarification when needed. Uses language, examples, and concepts appropriate to the audience. Provides exceptional leadership in planning organizing, maintaining, controlling and maximizing operations. Extends the opportunity for growth and development to all staff.

https://performance.usps.gov/pls/gsaprod/GSA_EOY_2007_REPORTS_PKG.employee_... 10/20/2008

and values.

Objective Approval/Disapproval Comments:	No Comments Entered
End-of-Year Accomplishments:	Oral, verbal, and written communication has been demonstrated as follows: North Las Vegas finished FY 07 at 79.8% overall on VOE, and the goal is 65.9%. Discipline has been issued to hold employees accountable. North's 1700 improved from 64.% in qtr. 2 to 90.3% qtr. 3 and 91.2% for qtr. 4 FY 07. Meadow Mesa improved from 70.1% in qtr. 2 to 80.03% qtr. 3 and 87.9% qtr. 4 FY 07. Express mail for box section was scanned at 100% for qtrs 3 and 4 FY 07. Changes in distribution of processes and bids produced an improvement in F4 total operation. Training 204b's was a asset for NLV Post Office as a whole. Maintaining NLV Post Office while my PM is out attributes to the success of the whole city. Always having a team member attitude keeps the cohesiveness of management positive and ready for challenges. I do what ever is asked of me. Information is facilitated down through the channels to the employees to help keep us successful. I saved NLV thousands of dollars by acquiring the correct combo for the safe. Also, during qrts 1 and 2 at Paradise Valley there was a zone split and EXFC, 1700, % to STD, and F4 as a whole had to be maintained to great success and I managed to accomplish this in spite of momintous obsticles. I have achieved an Exceptional Contributor rating in this category. Lola McGee 11/7/2007 *~ Entered by LOLA B. MCGEE on 11/07/2007*
End-of-Year Evaluator Comments:	Lola constantly states ideas to improve the performance and workplace environment. She meets with employees to ensure employees understand what is expected from them. She notifies employees of Service, Safety, and Budget targets and achievements and the impact that North Las Vegas provides to their customers. *~ Entered by YUL J. MELONSON on 11/14/2007*

Recommended Rating Entered by YUL J. MELONSON

Non-contributor	Contributor	**High Contributor**	Exceptional Contributor
0	6	**11**	14

Additional End-of-Year Employee Contributions

Additional End-of-Year Employee Contributions:	No Comments Entered

Objective Overall Comments

Objective Overall Comments:	No Comments Entered

Evaluator End-of-Year Overall Comment

Evaluator End-of-Year Overall Comments:	With continuous improvement Lola can improve her knowledge, skills, and ability to manage at the next level. *~ Entered by YUL J. MELONSON on 11/14/2007*

End-of-Year Discussion Date and Comments

End-of-Year Discussion Date and Comments:	11/14/2007 No Comments Entered

EOY Rating Report

Page 4 of 4

End-of-Year Rating

End-of-year rating for the following position: Supv Customer Services - North Las Vegas Po - Field EAS (District and Facility EAS) - EAS 26-21 Post Office - EAS Supervisor/Staff

This rating accounts for 50.13699% of the Overall Performance Rating.

	Rating	Weight	Equals
Core requirement #1	11	X 0.26667	2.93333
Core requirement #2	0	X 0.26667	0.00000
Core requirement #3	14	X 0.26667	3.73333
Core requirement #4	11	X 0.20000	2.20000
NPA Composite Summary	7.73	X 0.70000	5.41100
Core Requirement Rating Summary	8.86667	X 0.30000	2.66000
Overall Numeric Rating			**8.07100**

Interim Rating

Interim rating for the following position: On Detail (Detailed) - LAS-PARADISE VALLEY STA (Detailed) - Field EAS (District and Facility EAS) (Detailed) - EAS 26-21 Post Office (Detailed) - EAS Manager (Detailed) - Begin Date 10/01/2006 - End Date 03/31/2007

This rating accounts for 49.86301% of the Overall Performance Rating

	Rating	Weight	Equals
Core requirement #1	0	X 0.26667	0.00000
Core requirement #2	6	X 0.26667	1.60000
Core requirement #3	14	X 0.26667	3.73333
Core requirement #4	6	X 0.20000	1.20000
NPA Composite Summary	6.83	X 0.70000	4.78100
Core Requirement Rating Summary	6.53333	X 0.30000	1.96000
Overall Numeric Rating			**6.74100**

Pro-rated Overall Performance Rating :

	Numeric Rating	% of FY	
End-of-year rating	8.07100	X 0.50137	**4.04656**
			+
Interim Rating	6.74100	X 0.49863	3.36127
Numeric Rating			**7.40782**

PES carries out to 32 decimal places when calculating and determining an employee's overall performance rating. However, for display purposes only five decimal places are displayed on the screen. It is important to note that the employee's overall performance rating is rounded to a whole number.

For example, if an employee's Numeric Rating is 8.49999, the employee's Overall Performance Rating will be rounded to a whole number of 8.

Overall Performance rating will be rounded to 7

Export Ratings Calculation to Excel

Print This Window

Close Window

https://performance.usps.gov/pls/gsaprod/GSA_EOY_2007_REPORTS_PKG.employee_... 10/20/2008

Nevada-Sierra Performance Cluster
FY 2009 NPA Goals

First-Class	Goal	Block	OSHA I & I/MVA	Goal	Block
– O/N	97.1%	15	District/Cust Serv	3.50	11
– 2-Day	95.0%	13	Plant	2.00	15
3-5 Day	94.0%	15	MVA	10.00	8
Express Mail			**VOE**		
Next-Day	97.3%	12		65.0	7
Shipping			**Efficiency**	**Workhours**	**Overtime**
Scan Rate	99.1%	13	FN 1	0% to Plan	< 5%
Pack Serv	85.0%		FN 2B	0% to Plan	< 7%
Surface	96.7%	11	FN 4	0% to Plan	< 5%
Air	94.0%	13			

UNITED STATES POSTAL SERVICE

National Performance Assessment - SEP FY2007

Restore

Report Card Detail - Updated: 11/16/2007 Post Office EAS 26-21 / North Las Vegas PO, FN 316200

Generally indicators are YTD, see More Info for details.

Corporate Indicators

	Goal	Achieved	Matrix Rank		Weight		
Priority Surface	95.0	94.5	4	x	7.5%	=	0.3000
Priority Air	90.0	91.1	8	x	7.5%	=	0.6000
Express Mail	96.0	96.5	8	x	5%	=	0.4000
First-Class ON	95.0	96.2	11	x	10%	=	1.1000
First-Class 2-Day	92.0	94.2	11	x	5%	=	0.5500
First-Class 3-Day	90.0	93.2	13	x	5%	=	0.6500
OSHA I&I Rate	5.5	4.7	10				
OSHA I&I Improvement	0.0	2.1	4				
OSHA I&I Average			7	x	10%	=	0.7000
VOE Survey Rate	63.6	64.2	6				
VOE Improvement	0.2	-2.6	0				
VOE Survey Average			3	x	10%	=	0.3000
Tot National Revenue	0.0	-0.4	4	x	20%	=	0.8000
TFP	1.00	1.70	11	x	20%	=	2.2000

Corporate Summary 7.60

Adjusted Service Commitment Period

Indicator	Achieved	Adjustment
Adj Priority Surface	83.1	0.00
Adj Priority Air	66.0	0.05
Adj Express Mail	90.5	0.05
Adj First-Class 2-Da	92.7	0.15
Adj First-Class 3-Da	87.0	0.10

Service Adjustments 0.3500

Adj Corp Summary 7.95

x 70%
5.41

No downward adjustment for service scores that result in less than zero

* Grievances Average If the Grievances Benchmark score of 1.0 was achieved then the Grievances Rate score is assigned to the Summary

Unit Indicators

	Goal	Achieved	Matrix Rank		Weight		
Retail CSM Index	584.5	530.9	4				
Retail CSM Improv.	0.0	-27.4	0				
Retail CSM Average			2	x	5%	=	0.1000
DelSig Con Scan Rate	99.1	98.5	4	x	5%	=	0.2000
Retail Effectiveness	90.5	78.4	1	x	5%	=	0.0500
Exp Mail Scan Rate	99.20	99.63	10	x	5%	=	0.5000
Carriers 1700 Rate	84.0	73.9	2				
Carriers 1700 Improv	1.0	3.5	8				
Carriers 1700 Avg			5	x	5%	=	0.2500
MVA Rate	9.9	16.6	2				
MVA Improvement	0.0	104.4	0				
MVA Average			1	x	5%	=	0.0500
Sfty Pgm Eval Guide	3.4	3.1	4	x	5%	=	0.2000
Grievances Rate	2.25	0.49	15				
Grievances Improv.	-10.0	-47.7	15				
Grievances Average			15	x	5%	=	0.7500
TOE % Plan	0.0	1.0	1	x	25%	=	0.2500
Deliv per hour	0.46	2.64	14	x	10%	=	1.4000
Retail Revenue %Plan	0.0	10.6	15	x	25%	=	3.7500

Unit Summary 7.50

Post Office EAS 26 - 21 Composite Summary

Unit Summary	7.50	x	50%	=	3.75
Adj Corp Summary	7.95	x	50%	=	3.98

Composite Summary 7.73

EAS Manager Composite Summary

Unit Summary	7.50	x	50%	=	3.75
Adj Corp Summary	7.95	x	50%	=	3.98

Composite Summary 7.73

http://npareports.usps.gov/npa/ 11/27/2007

While on detail at Sparks Sun Valley Station (Reno), I flew home and drove to California because my oldest brother (seventy-one years old) was ill and was not expected to live, and he didn't. He passed February 15, 2008, so I did not start at King Station until February 27, 2008.

The City of Las Vegas was hurting for supervisors and acting managers, and I knew it, but nevertheless, I took the opportunity and did the very best with my resources at King Station EAS-22. King was in such bad shape; it needed an overhaul. Please refer to my profile, but for the sake of this book, I'll write a few accomplishments I achieved at King Station. I cleaned up all grievances dating back a year with very little compensation paid out; I reduced the budget to -2.5% WTD; sick leave was reduced to -10%; the Managed Service Point (MSP) scanning rate increased from the low 90 to 99.4%; the Delivery Confirmation Scanning improved from 97.5 to 99.4%; the Percent to Standard, which was atrocious, improved from 157 to 124%, with my lowest day being at 107%; and the total F4 improved from 74.23 to 83.11%, and all mail was processed and the hot cases were cleared. I removed the shelves from the registry cage so the Accountable Clerk would not double-handle the mail, as an effort to get it to the carriers in a timely manner. King Station was a serious challenge, but I was determined to make it one of the best in the city.

One of my staff members told me she had been at King Station for a while, and she had never seen the distribution employees perform like they were, and it is cleaned daily. After being at King Station for the short time I was there —February 27, 2008 through May 5, 2008—and the manager returned from sick leave, I went on scheduled annual leave for two and one-half weeks.

In May 2008, I put in for Emerald Station in the City of Las Vegas EAS-22, and I did not receive an interview. I was told that no acting managers were interviewed. I felt that was okay, if it was true.

Around this time, Robert Reynosa stated to me, "If I ask Jennifer Vo what she thinks about you, she would say that you don't give enough of your time." When Robert called me while I was in Reno, he prefaced his call with "It's evident that you can communicate," and he asked me to come to King Station. I guess it was perceived that I could not communicate, which I found ludicrous and insulting.

I wrote earlier how, as a salaried employee, I worked ten- and twelve-hour days and some Saturdays, and I think that's giving an awful lot. I did not call Robert, Jennifer, or Mark to tell them I was staying in my office past eight hours nor did I call to tell them when I worked on Saturdays. Depending on which office I was working in, and that office's need, determined what I needed to do to get improved results to make it better to best performance. Vivian Green, Manager, Operations Support (2008), who supported the District Manager, Shaun Mossman, called me the clean-up woman. I worked at six different offices while the other acting managers worked at one, and they were promoted. The offices I worked were EAS-20 through EAS-22, and most of the acting managers in the City of Las Vegas were promoted from EAS-19, specifically Strip Station. I was told by Postmaster Renee Brown from Sparks, Nevada of the EAS-20, that I was over-qualified for the position, and that I was a breath of fresh air.

In May 2008, I put in for Strip Station EAS-19 (for the third time), and I did not receive an interview. I assumed I was more qualified than the other applicants, and they would not have been able to justify not given me the job, so I wasn't given the opportunity to be interviewed. The person selected for the job had not been in the city running a station, but he had been working for Robert, Mark, and Jennifer at the district office/GMF (General Mail Facility–The Mail Processing Plant). This devastated me; how can you justify not giving me an interview after I received an interview for the EAS-21 and EAS-22 positions and this was an EAS-19? Even though I accepted it and continued to be Lola, and held my head up high, I knew it was not fair or right in any stretch of the imagination.

The following three spreadsheets reference Huntridge Station.

Nevada Sierra Line of Sight Report Weeks 38-40 Fiscal Year 2008
Snap shot look at performance indicators for all offices

Nevada-Sierra Cluster Line of Sight

Supervisor's ran/I was out

Monday, July 07, 2008	Carrier after 1700 % WTD	Carriers Rpt 5 min Early % WTD	Clerks Rpt 5 min Early # WTD	DPS % WTD	Cased Letter % to SPLY WTD	% Standard WTD	OEI % SPLY WTD	SEI % SPLY WTD	TEI % SPLY WTD	Street Scan % 7/5	Late Street Scan % 7/5	Avg. PM office per Route 7/5	TEs prior to 10 AM 7/7	F2B (City Carrier Hours) % SPLY WTD	F2B OT % WTD	F2B POT % WTD	F4 Hours % SPLY WTD	F4 OT% WTD	F4 POT% WTD
Unit	< 5%	< 3%	< 5%	> 90%	< 0%	< 100%	> 5%	> 2%	> 5%	> 98%	< 15%	< .17	0	> -2.0%	< 5%	< 0.2%	> -3.0%	< 3.8%	< 0.2%
LasVegasCrossroads	29.89%	0.00%	0.00%	93.88%	-29.26%	103.50	3.0%	3.3%	3.2%	93.87	35%	0.23	0	-3.2%	10.3%	0.3%	-20.8%	10.1%	0.0%
LasVegasEastLasVegas	33.09%	3.79%	17.65%	88.13%	-17.73%	120.23	-2.2%	0.3%	0.1%	97.33	37%	0.23	0	-3.3%	10.6%	0.2%	3.5%	21.7%	0.5%
LasVegasHuntridge	9.86%	0.00%	35.71%	86.04%	28.79%	119.56	20.2%	-0.5%	4.6%	98.83	32%	0.23	0	-6.3%	8.7%	0.0%	2.6%	20.0%	0.0%
LasVegasKingStation	86.59%	2.82%	80.00%	94.29%	-59.66%	150.40	4.7%	6.8%	6.2%	90.76	65%	0.22	1	-9.3%	18.1%	5.8%	-51.4%	16.1%	0.4%
LasVegasParadiseValley	49.07%	0.00%	11.76%	84.16%	-13.15%	107.49	-1.2%	9.3%	5.6%	98.01	42%	0.23	0	-4.6%	17.1%	0.4%	1.5%	14.9%	0.0%
LasVegasSilverado	47.06%	2.27%	62.50%	92.69%	-10.13%	91.49	5.3%	5.8%	5.7%	99.14	61%	0.12	0	-0.4%	12.7%	0.3%	-19.8%	17.7%	0.0%
LasVegasStripStation	4.35%	0.00%	16.67%	93.30%	-67.10%	95.81	28.0%	5.3%	11.8%	96.08	38%	0.10	0	-18.8%	3.6%	0.0%	-36.0%	17.8%	0.0%
LasVegasSummerlin	49.51%	4.60%	29.63%	92.64%	-23.65%	103.15	12.8%	3.7%	6.6%	96.10	41%	0.25	0	-7.1%	10.2%	0.0%	-17.0%	6.8%	0.0%
LasVegasSunrise	49.62%	1.67%	37.50%	88.16%	53.42%	108.00	8.9%	5.3%	6.2%	94.24	55%	0.23	3	-5.4%	16.3%	1.2%	-12.4%	16.8%	0.0%
LasVegasWestridge	27.78%	0.00%	0.00%	95.36%	-59.95%	115.77	30.5%	5.6%	12.6%	98.13	43%	0.25	0	-11.0%	10.6%	0.1%	-18.0%	16.3%	0.0%
Reynosa	41.00%	1.63%	25.00%	91.11%	-22.38%	110.63	9.6%	4.6%	6.1%	96.36	46%	0.22	4	-6.2%	12.5%	0.8%	-17.7%	15.4%	0.1%
LasVegasEmerald	47.47%	0.00%	19.05%	87.83%	1.53%	103.77	11.7%	5.1%	7.1%	95.45	47%	0.17	0	-7.1%	13.1%	0.1%	23.7%	13.8%	0.2%
LasVegasGarside	37.07%	0.00%	0.00%	89.42%	-27.71%	114.25	12.2%	11.9%	12.0%	97.16	38%	0.21	0	-5.5%	15.2%	0.0%	-17.6%	13.0%	0.0%
LasVegasRedrockVista	34.93%	2.27%	16.00%	91.05%	57.80%	99.45	17.8%	-2.8%	3.1%	98.40	40%	0.17	4	-0.9%	13.1%	0.6%	-1.0%	7.5%	0.0%
LasVegasSpringValley	30.83%	0.85%	4.35%	89.05%	-28.06%	119.96	-0.5%	4.9%	3.0%	94.63	39%	0.28	0	-6.9%	10.5%	0.2%	-2.7%	11.5%	0.0%
LasVegasTopaz	59.74%	0.00%	18.75%	89.94%	10.42%	110.24	-2.8%	10.8%	6.9%	98.17	59%	0.17	0	1.1%	16.5%	1.0%	2.1%	10.2%	0.0%
LasVegasWinterwood	30.77%	0.00%	25.00%	92.09%	-21.34%	104.11	31.0%	7.8%	13.8%	99.31	44%	0.13	0	-10.8%	10.4%	0.2%	-23.3%	9.0%	0.0%
MCSO 2	39.17%	0.69%	18.48%	89.83%	-7.18%	108.69	10.7%	5.6%	7.1%	97.00	43%	0.20	4	-5.2%	12.6%	0.3%	-11.4%	8.8%	0.0%
LV PM	40.29%	1.27%	21.29%	90.60%	-16.42%	109.87	10.0%	5.0%	6.5%	96.61	45%	0.21	8	-5.8%	12.6%	0.6%	-14.4%	11.9%	0.1%
CarsonCity	12.50%	0.00%	16.67%	91.40%	-38.03%	92.62	12.8%	6.7%	8.8%	94.58	22%	0.22	1	-15.1%	10.7%	0.3%	-14.1%	17.4%	0.5%
CarsonCityOrmsby	35.71%	0.00%	0.00%	91.31%	-28.66%	98.17	-12.0%	-9.3%	-10.1%	91.18	27%	0.22	1	12.2%	12.3%	0.1%	5.1%	3.2%	0.0%
Depaoli	19.57%	0.00%	13.33%	91.37%	-35.31%	94.19	5.6%	1.9%	3.1%	93.50	23%	0.22	2	-8.2%	11.2%	0.2%	-9.5%	13.5%	0.3%
Henderson	17.76%	1.18%	20.83%	93.29%	-1.42%	104.27	9.7%	-3.4%	0.6%	97.51	37%	0.23	0	1.3%	10.1%	0.1%	-16.8%	8.5%	0.5%
HendersonValleVerde	18.25%	0.00%	5.41%	87.69%	42.30%	96.97	5.9%	1.5%	2.9%	94.99	43%	0.21	0	-4.6%	13.5%	0.4%	-3.2%	14.7%	0.0%
Colton	18.03%	0.51%	8.43%	90.26%	24.80%	99.78	7.4%	-0.8%	1.9%	96.11	40%	0.22	0	-1.7%	11.8%	0.3%	-9.0%	11.9%	0.1%
NorthLasVegas	20.41%	4.35%	15.38%	82.13%	145.91%	99.89	13.0%	2.2%	4.7%	97.78	32%	0.12	0	4.8%	11.3%	0.0%	-18.6%	3.5%	0.0%
NLVMeadowMesa	14.53%	13.33%	55.56%	92.96%	23.14%	89.72	38.4%	0.8%	10.1%	98.57	26%	0.17	0	-3.4%	9.0%	0.1%	-18.9%	15.4%	0.0%
NLV PM	16.27%	10.29%	38.71%	89.84%	64.83%	92.43	30.7%	1.3%	8.4%	98.32	28%	0.15	0	-1.0%	9.7%	0.1%	-18.8%	11.6%	0.0%
Reno	50.93%	1.32%	8.20%	91.52%	-56.22%	110.16	7.8%	1.1%	3.9%	94.13	31%	0.18	1	-2.0%	12.3%	0.9%	-13.4%	10.5%	0.0%
RenoDowntown	33.33%	12.90%	0.00%	85.93%	-7.54%	97.73	10.5%	5.9%	7.6%	93.14	34%	0.17	0	-8.5%	12.0%	0.3%	-15.8%	4.1%	0.0%
RenoPeavineStation	28.00%	0.00%	12.50%	92.44%	-37.31%	110.68	-5.3%	7.1%	2.7%	99.07	55%	0.25	0	1.5%	11.6%	0.0%	33.5%	6.8%	0.0%
RenoSierraStation	18.75%	0.00%	0.00%	90.54%	-22.36%	82.25	5.9%	23.9%	18.3%	96.00	13%	0.19	0	-3.5%	11.9%	0.7%	-26.5%	5.1%	0.0%
RenoSteamboatStation	26.67%	0.00%	5.56%	89.74%	-26.58%	97.41	-5.3%	20.4%	10.3%	93.75	53%	0.13	0	-3.9%	13.6%	1.0%	5.8%	14.1%	0.3%
RenoWashingtonStation	22.73%	0.00%	14.29%	90.72%	-38.38%	99.44	-5.7%	-5.6%	-5.6%	99.07	20%	0.24	0	4.0%	11.2%	0.4%	-0.5%	2.1%	0.0%
Reno PM	39.67%	2.22%	7.26%	90.51%	-44.03%	104.92	4.6%	3.0%	3.9%	95.24	31%	0.19	1	-2.0%	12.1%	0.7%	-7.9%	8.6%	0.1%
Sparks	28.33%	7.02%	12.50%	90.41%	-30.26%	93.14	-3.6%	-3.2%	-1.5%	96.58	32%	0.15	0	-0.6%	12.9%	0.0%	5.9%	1.4%	0.0%
SparksSunValleyStation	11.76%	6.67%	0.00%	93.08%	-47.95%	103.44	14.5%	-9.3%	-3.7%	98.88	15%	0.14	0	-3.3%	3.0%	0.0%	-25.7%	0.0%	0.0%
SparksVistaStation	32.89%	10.00%	30.00%	91.59%	-19.73%	89.00	12.1%	2.5%	5.6%	93.85	24%	0.17	0	-3.1%	13.0%	0.0%	-10.3%	20.9%	0.0%
Brown	28.76%	8.45%	17.24%	91.35%	-28.20%	91.50	6.4%	-1.1%	1.7%	95.49	26%	0.16	0	-2.2%	11.9%	0.0%	-4.4%	9.2%	0.0%
Fallon	0.00%	15.38%	28.57%	94.53%	-59.70%	109.95	21.1%	0.6%	6.6%	98.57	21%	0.10	1	-4.3%	14.1%	0.0%	6.2%	5.2%	0.0%
Winnemucca	0.00%	0.00%	0.00%	93.89%	-13.43%	62.80	-1.6%	38.6%	24.9%	97.56	2%	0.26	0	-17.1%	0.5%	0.0%	-1.4%	0.2%	0.0%
Yerington	0.00%	0.00%	0.00%	88.58%	-13.66%	83.46	25.7%	-7.6%	0.7%	100.00	11%	0.15	0	1.7%	4.9%	0.0%	-12.1%	0.0%	0.0%
MPOO 2	25.61%	4.14%	12.65%	90.55%	-14.29%	98.11	9.3%	1.1%	3.8%	95.93	31%	0.19	4	-2.6%	11.5%	0.3%	-8.3%	9.1%	0.1%
Alturas	33.33%	0.00%	0.00%	81.15%	40.94%	123.24	-22.6%	-13.8%	-16.9%	100.00	35%	0.18	0	-29.6%	5.2%	0.0%	16.6%	7.4%	0.0%
SusanvilleEagleStation	50.00%	0.00%	0.00%	91.61%	-37.01%	102.86	-7.4%	-2.4%	-4.2%	100.00	92%	0.10	0	7.1%	13.7%	0.6%	111.9%	19.4%	0.0%
BattleMountain	0.00%	No Data	No Data	95.09%	0.31%	87.16	8.2%	5.8%	6.5%	100.00	56%	0.24	0	-25.2%	0.0%	0.0%	-11.5%	0.0%	0.0%
BoulderCity	0.00%	0.00%	14.29%	90.54%	-7.87%	122.71	25.2%	10.4%	14.4%	97.56	31%	0.11	2	-17.6%	3.1%	0.0%	-7.2%	4.5%	0.0%
ElkoAspen	8.00%	4.17%	0.00%	95.47%	-32.79%	99.36	6.6%	7.9%	7.6%	96.36	0%	0.23	3	-2.1%	9.2%	0.0%	16.0%	15.0%	2.4%
ElkoSpringCreek	20.00%	25.00%	0.00%	96.36%	7.58%	76.17	-26.8%	-13.8%	-18.4%	92.50	0%	0.21	2	4.4%	7.8%	0.0%	-57.4%	6.2%	0.0%
Deremiah	10.00%	7.14%	0.00%	95.76%	-24.95%	92.15	-1.8%	4.2%	2.6%	95.33	0%	0.23	5	-0.9%	8.9%	0.0%	3.7%	13.6%	2.1%
Ely	0.00%	0.00%	66.67%	0.00%	0.01%	92.93	0.8%	-0.9%	-0.2%	100.00	18%	0.07	0	2.3%	1.0%	0.0%	-20.3%	50.9%	8.3%
MPOO 1	13.48%	2.82%	14.46%	87.89%	-10.08%	103.04	4.3%	4.2%	4.3%	97.54	29%	0.16	7	-6.9%	7.2%	0.1%	-9.0%	14.7%	0.8%
Cluster	34.09%	2.32%	16.88%	90.49%	-15.46%	105.08	9.6%	3.6%	5.5%	96.40	39%	0.20	19	-4.7%	12.0%	0.5%	-11.1%	11.2%	0.2%

7/8/2008 8:46 AM

Source Data WebEIS and Tacs Reports

Coray took on an

Nevada-Sierra Cluster Line of Sight

Out Sider as a Lateral that he knows,

Week 39 FY 08	Carrier after 1700 % WTD	Carriers Rpt 5 min Early % WTD	Clerks Rpt 5 min Early # WTD	DPS % WTD	Cased Letter % to SPLY WTD	% Standard WTD	OEI % SPLY WTD	SEI % SPLY WTD	TEI % SPLY WTD	Street Scan % 6/27	Late Street Scan % 6/27	Avg. PM office per Route 6/27	TEs prior to 10 AM 6/27	F2B (City Carrier Hours) % SPLY WTD	F2B OT % WTD	F2B POT % WTD	F4 Hours % SPLY WTD	F4 OT% WTD
Unit	< 5%	< 3%	< 5%	> 90%	< 0%	< 100%	> 5%	> 2%	> 5%	> 98%	< 15%	< .17	0	> -2.0%	< 5%	< 0.2%	> -3.0%	< 3.8%
LasVegasCrossroads	10.61%	0.00%	3.17%	94.65%	-35.86%	119.43	15.9%	11.0%	11.2%	98.14	9%	0.21	0	-5.7%	6.0%	0.0%	-21.1%	8.9%
LasVegasEastLasVegas	17.48%	2.44%	20.83%	89.06%	-37.12%	120.11	-0.3%	0.9%	0.6%	97.79	12%	0.23	1	-3.0%	6.9%	0.1%	-16.4%	14.3%
LasVegasHuntridge	4.76%	0.00%	14.00%	80.30%	18.51%	116.84	7.1%	6.3%	6.7%	98.56	5%	0.22	0	-9.2%	7.6%	0.0%	-12.0%	6.3%
LasVegasKingStation	33.09%	0.00%	1.96%	90.70%	-42.80%	150.01	1.9%	7.8%	6.3%	98.60	37%	0.16	0	-5.4%	9.8%	0.1%	-9.2%	6.3%
LasVegasParadiseValley	20.99%	2.07%	0.00%	84.52%	-38.70%	115.26	10.3%	7.4%	7.6%	98.39	38%	0.22	0	-7.7%	10.2%	0.4%	6.1%	6.8%
LasVegasSilverado	8.95%	0.00%	49.06%	92.69%	-26.00%	107.76	8.1%	4.6%	5.1%	99.57	32%	0.15	0	-0.1%	5.6%	0.0%	-11.3%	14.5%
LasVegasStripStation	3.80%	1.45%	3.57%	93.57%	-79.53%	117.37	56.9%	38.3%	43.3%	100.00	18%	0.17	0	-26.6%	3.0%	0.0%	-23.8%	5.6%
LasVegasSummerlin	19.23%	0.36%	8.51%	91.12%	-18.07%	106.99	21.8%	2.9%	8.4%	98.38	29%	0.24	0	-8.3%	6.9%	0.0%	-5.8%	3.1%
LasVegasSunrise	31.78%	0.53%	27.59%	89.03%	-3.95%	110.20	14.4%	5.5%	7.5%	96.28	32%	0.18	0	-7.0%	12.3%	0.5%	-20.3%	14.7%
LasVegasWestridge	10.06%	1.36%	1.23%	94.55%	-42.89%	120.89	16.4%	4.3%	7.4%	99.34	21%	0.27	0	-4.1%	9.1%	0.1%	-13.6%	8.7%
Reynosa	17.38%	0.92%	14.24%	90.69%	-30.40%	117.15	11.9%	6.0%	7.3%	98.33	24%	0.21	1	-6.1%	8.3%	0.1%	-12.9%	8.8%
LasVegasEmerald	3.82%	0.00%	8.77%	87.65%	-27.84%	108.30	18.0%	10.4%	12.2%	98.08	31%	0.18	0	-10.0%	5.6%	0.0%	-10.5%	8.5%
LasVegasGarside	12.01%	1.45%	2.60%	86.85%	-28.34%	113.28	10.3%	13.7%	13.0%	97.39	26%	0.31	0	-3.4%	7.3%	0.0%	-10.7%	9.4%
LasVegasRedrockVista	26.79%	0.74%	12.94%	92.56%	-21.91%	104.51	25.5%	7.6%	12.2%	98.27	31%	0.11	1	-7.8%	11.9%	0.4%	-1.2%	5.2%
LasVegasSpringValley	20.84%	1.87%	7.14%	89.94%	-24.32%	119.75	13.2%	3.2%	6.4%	95.97	29%	0.22	0	-7.5%	9.7%	0.4%	5.7%	9.6%
LasVegasTopaz	37.84%	0.00%	11.76%	91.24%	-13.16%	130.31	1.9%	15.0%	11.6%	98.44	29%	0.18	0	-5.2%	13.1%	0.5%	-2.9%	4.2%
LasVegasWinterwood	9.79%	2.30%	12.77%	92.84%	-26.49%	110.12	25.0%	13.2%	14.9%	97.95	29%	0.19	0	-6.0%	4.4%	0.0%	-10.3%	3.0%
MCSO 2	18.58%	1.05%	9.08%	90.33%	-24.59%	113.16	16.2%	10.5%	11.8%	97.60	29%	0.20	1	-7.5%	8.8%	0.2%	-6.3%	6.1%
LV PM	17.83%	0.97%	11.37%	90.54%	-28.12%	115.59	13.5%	7.7%	9.1%	98.05	26%	0.21	2	-6.7%	8.5%	0.2%	-9.5%	7.3%
CarsonCity	4.17%	0.56%	6.56%	91.85%	-60.94%	115.03	8.5%	4.3%	5.6%	93.55	16%	0.20	0	-10.8%	6.4%	0.0%	-11.9%	7.0%
CarsonCityOrmsby	2.20%	0.00%	0.00%	91.65%	-38.39%	107.04	5.5%	1.7%	2.8%	97.83	4%	0.23	0	7.9%	3.4%	0.1%	15.5%	1.2%
Depaoli	3.53%	0.39%	5.63%	91.79%	-55.69%	112.57	7.6%	3.5%	4.7%	94.87	13%	0.21	0	-5.3%	5.4%	0.1%	-6.3%	5.5%
Henderson	19.81%	2.75%	2.27%	88.07%	21.12%	107.90	-0.5%	3.4%	1.8%	96.06	25%	0.23	0	-2.1%	8.5%	0.1%	-3.5%	3.3%
HendersonValleVerde	10.08%	0.00%	0.00%	90.60%	7.38%	111.28	-3.5%	0.6%	-0.8%	98.38	31%	0.24	0	-1.1%	7.8%	0.1%	-8.6%	10.7%
Colton	14.43%	1.16%	0.76%	89.51%	13.70%	109.86	-2.3%	1.9%	0.4%	97.36	29%	0.24	0	-1.3%	7.9%	0.1%	-8.9%	7.1%
NorthLasVegas	15.67%	0.77%	10.91%	88.67%	0.22%	109.73	16.0%	18.5%	18.3%	95.47	29%	0.32	0	-10.4%	9.7%	0.8%	17.5%	3.7%
NLVMeadowMesa	6.96%	9.76%	4.92%	93.35%	6.77%	112.07	21.5%	3.2%	7.6%	98.00	28%	0.18	1	2.3%	7.2%	0.0%	-18.7%	8.8%
NLV PM	9.33%	6.95%	7.76%	92.24%	4.41%	111.48	19.9%	7.8%	10.7%	97.17	28%	0.22	1	-1.9%	7.9%	0.3%	-7.3%	6.7%
Reno	15.01%	1.50%	7.84%	88.13%	-35.85%	112.85	15.1%	16.1%	16.1%	97.18	17%	0.20	0	-10.8%	7.5%	0.0%	-18.0%	3.6%
RenoDowntown	9.45%	2.73%	2.08%	85.84%	-26.58%	102.69	8.3%	6.0%	6.2%	96.92	47%	0.18	0	8.3%	7.2%	0.1%	-20.4%	3.4%
RenoPeavineStation	15.94%	7.81%	14.71%	93.23%	-52.31%	117.85	28.7%	8.8%	14.4%	98.13	7%	0.17	0	5.9%	10.4%	1.2%	36.5%	4.1%
RenoSierraStation	1.92%	0.00%	0.00%	90.23%	-57.19%	86.62	24.6%	15.3%	16.6%	98.67	21%	0.22	0	0.6%	1.2%	0.0%	-9.4%	4.7%
RenoSteamboatStation	3.85%	2.38%	5.08%	85.98%	-17.60%	127.70	-3.1%	-5.5%	-4.7%	95.89	10%	0.26	0	0.3%	6.4%	0.1%	11.3%	6.9%
RenoWashingtonStation	1.74%	0.00%	10.20%	90.64%	-54.16%	104.25	19.2%	10.7%	12.8%	98.61	13%	0.27	0	-9.1%	6.9%	0.0%	-17.0%	2.7%
Reno PM	11.31%	1.91%	7.03%	88.67%	-39.21%	109.98	14.9%	12.5%	13.2%	97.44	20%	0.21	0	-5.9%	7.2%	0.1%	-9.9%	4.2%
Sparks	21.58%	7.14%	6.45%	89.51%	-29.92%	99.87	9.7%	-8.6%	-4.9%	97.12	13%	0.14	0	-0.3%	8.5%	0.0%	8.9%	5.6%
SparksSunValleyStation	8.70%	2.27%	0.00%	93.95%	-29.46%	103.70	1.0%	18.0%	13.9%	98.89	6%	0.20	0	-21.1%	1.9%	0.0%	-39.0%	0.0%
SparksVistaStation	9.39%	0.89%	27.59%	90.64%	-13.64%	101.08	7.6%	4.2%	5.2%	99.44	15%	0.20	0	-1.7%	6.8%	0.0%	-4.4%	11.0%
Brown	14.14%	3.55%	11.88%	90.73%	-21.85%	100.90	7.3%	0.0%	1.8%	98.43	13%	0.18	0	-3.4%	7.0%	0.0%	-1.9%	7.2%
Fallon	2.33%	4.88%	6.06%	87.88%	-9.45%	96.55	16.7%	2.1%	5.9%	98.55	9%	0.13	1	-9.0%	2.1%	0.0%	11.9%	4.0%
Winnemucca	0.00%	6.67%	25.00%	93.83%	-43.92%	94.49	1.4%	-7.9%	-5.4%	95.12	12%	0.14	0	-17.9%	0.2%	0.0%	-13.3%	2.0%
Yerington	0.00%	0.00%	0.00%	91.66%	-55.79%	88.36	56.2%	3.9%	15.3%	100.00	4%	0.14	0	-12.0%	1.6%	0.0%	-11.0%	0.1%
J.Morgan	11.09%	2.72%	6.38%	90.23%	-23.20%	108.42	9.4%	5.8%	6.8%	97.31	21%	0.21	2	-3.8%	7.1%	0.1%	-7.2%	5.1%
Alturas	17.65%	0.00%	No Data	84.76%	-81.89%	127.14	11.3%	-14.1%	-5.5%	95.45	32%	0.18	0	-7.9%	6.3%	0.0%	-31.5%	13.1%
SusanvilleEagleStation	0.00%	0.00%	6.67%	89.82%	-53.59%	88.44	9.5%	2.7%	4.4%	100.00	0%	0.14	0	-4.5%	5.3%	0.0%	17.6%	7.7%
BattleMountain	0.00%	No Data	0.00%	94.23%	-32.99%	79.01	22.2%	-1.8%	4.5%	100.00	6%	0.17	0	-30.7%	0.0%	0.0%	37.7%	0.0%
BoulderCity	16.05%	0.00%	0.00%	91.48%	-18.41%	117.29	15.9%	-2.0%	10.9%	100.00	13%	0.11	0	-14.7%	5.4%	0.0%	-20.1%	2.7%
ElkoAspen	12.82%	0.00%	12.50%	94.53%	-33.29%	91.08	7.4%	6.7%	28.5%	92.08	2%	0.25	3	-15.2%	4.2%	0.0%	3.8%	15.7%
ElkoSpringCreek	0.00%	0.00%	5.88%	95.53%	-24.31%	68.69	2.7%	5.7%	4.8%	95.00	0%	0.37	2	-2.1%	3.7%	0.0%	54.3%	4.2%
Deremiah	10.20%	0.00%	8.47%	94.86%	-30.93%	84.21	6.1%	6.3%	23.5%	92.91	1%	0.29	5	-12.2%	4.1%	0.0%	3.3%	12.4%
Ely	9.09%	0.00%	0.00%	0.00%	-5.74%	85.49	-4.3%	3.4%	0.7%	100.00	0%	0.20	0	5.6%	3.9%	0.0%	-26.0%	25.5%
MPOO 1	10.29%	0.00%	5.16%	87.72%	-36.85%	95.77	10.1%	1.7%	12.7%	97.26	6%	0.19	5	-8.0%	4.5%	0.0%	-9.6%	8.5%
Cluster	15.15%	1.55%	8.53%	90.36%	-26.88%	112.19	11.9%	6.9%	8.4%	97.76	24%	0.21	9	-5.7%	7.9%	0.1%	-8.6%	6.6%

Now the man is out on stress from being 1st Huntridge 2nd King = Both of the stations I applied for. (Thomas) Jack,

This was my second time at Huntridge station I did Excellent both times.

Source data WebEIS Tacs Reports

Nevada-Sierra Cluster Line of Sight

Week 40 FY 08	Carrier after 1700 % WTD	Carriers Rpt 5 min Early % WTD	Clerks Rpt 5 min Early # WTD	DPS % WTD	Cased Letter % to SPLY WTD	% Standard WTD	OEI % SPLY WTD	SEI % SPLY WTD	TEI % SPLY WTD	Street Scan % 7/3	Late Street Scan % 7/3	Avg. PM office per Route 7/3	TEs prior to 10 AM 7/3	F2B (City Carrier Hours) % SPLY WTD	F2B OT % WTD	F2B POT % WTD	F4 Hours % SPLY WTD	F4 OT% WTD
Unit	< 5%	< 3%	< 5%	> 90%	< 0%	< 100%	> 5%	> 2%	> 5%	> 98%	< 15%	< .17	0	> -2.0%	< 5%	< 0.2%	> -3.0%	< 3.8%
LasVegasCrossroads	8.02%	1.42%	20.37%	93.00%	-34.18%	118.56	-3.2%	13.9%	15.4%	99.29	14%	0.45	0	-9.7%	7.0%	0.0%	-17.9%	6.6%
LasVegasEastLasVegas	26.13%	2.81%	20.45%	87.94%	-25.56%	123.91	-5.1%	2.5%	6.6%	97.64	26%	0.28	1	-9.3%	10.3%	0.0%	-10.2%	11.0%
LasVegasHuntridge	10.59%	0.60%	45.95%	83.55%	-2.02%	114.54	1.7%	7.4%	11.4%	99.12	30%	0.21	0	-13.9%	7.0%	0.0%	1.5%	12.9%
LasVegasKingStation	39.57%	2.87%	30.23%	88.09%	-25.51%	146.75	-11.3%	7.6%	7.3%	96.99	37%	0.19	1	-7.7%	13.2%	0.2%	-13.4%	7.0%
LasVegasParadiseValley	25.55%	1.47%	0.00%	82.67%	-3.87%	119.01	-6.3%	3.4%	5.5%	98.02	30%	0.35	0	-8.0%	12.5%	0.1%	-19.3%	11.5%
LasVegasSilverado	35.57%	0.46%	60.98%	92.64%	-22.78%	105.49	4.2%	11.3%	16.6%	98.28	39%	0.17	1	-11.8%	11.4%	0.2%	-15.6%	18.6%
LasVegasStripStation	12.50%	0.00%	0.00%	91.62%	-66.45%	117.65	15.6%	18.9%	24.9%	98.21	27%	0.10	0	-22.5%	6.5%	0.0%	-35.6%	1.7%
LasVegasSummerlin	20.48%	2.73%	27.27%	93.04%	-59.31%	114.81	13.7%	8.1%	16.4%	99.39	20%	0.28	6	-15.7%	7.7%	0.1%	-21.5%	4.3%
LasVegasSunrise	60.62%	0.66%	12.50%	90.22%	-15.56%	109.43	-2.5%	4.0%	8.3%	97.37	35%	0.22	7	-6.2%	16.8%	0.5%	-21.0%	18.3%
LasVegasWestridge	10.07%	0.00%	0.00%	94.25%	-41.49%	123.98	14.7%	5.3%	14.1%	98.15	19%	0.24	0	-12.1%	8.6%	0.1%	-20.5%	9.4%
Reynosa	26.55%	1.38%	22.20%	90.40%	-28.07%	118.91	1.5%	6.8%	11.4%	98.16	28%	0.26	16	-10.7%	10.7%	0.1%	-17.5%	10.1%
LasVegasEmerald	9.96%	0.00%	8.33%	87.65%	-19.70%	113.67	-2.1%	9.7%	11.9%	95.78	33%	0.20	0	-11.4%	7.2%	0.0%	-6.8%	6.0%
LasVegasGarside	15.00%	1.10%	7.27%	86.58%	-19.27%	111.10	0.0%	15.2%	15.1%	97.88	39%	0.18	1	-7.9%	8.8%	0.0%	-31.0%	9.0%
LasVegasRedrockVista	21.47%	1.84%	26.76%	90.76%	34.71%	110.43	10.7%	5.7%	13.7%	98.99	25%	0.13	4	-10.6%	11.8%	0.3%	-1.4%	6.7%
LasVegasSpringValley	11.88%	1.31%	32.26%	88.46%	-52.76%	121.13	5.9%	10.2%	15.5%	95.45	16%	0.26	0	-15.3%	9.5%	0.1%	-4.3%	11.6%
LasVegasTopaz	26.29%	0.00%	20.51%	92.00%	-28.43%	120.60	2.1%	12.5%	16.2%	98.96	27%	0.18	1	-7.2%	13.6%	0.4%	-13.4%	7.1%
LasVegasWinterwood	24.22%	0.00%	5.26%	91.29%	-7.35%	114.51	17.2%	15.9%	22.7%	98.29	24%	0.17	0	-10.1%	8.1%	0.0%	-10.9%	6.8%
MCSO 2	17.39%	0.90%	16.14%	89.42%	-23.40%	114.89	5.0%	10.5%	14.6%	97.47	27%	0.19	6	-10.9%	9.7%	0.1%	-11.5%	6.8%
LV PM	23.06%	1.19%	18.83%	90.02%	-26.22%	117.38	2.8%	8.2%	12.6%	97.89	28%	0.23	22	-10.8%	10.3%	0.1%	-14.4%	8.4%
CarsonCity	4.38%	0.71%	17.78%	89.27%	-25.96%	99.05	-6.9%	5.8%	9.6%	90.00	12%	0.23	1	-13.6%	8.4%	0.0%	-10.3%	7.0%
CarsonCityOrmsby	7.79%	0.00%	0.00%	81.32%	74.38%	103.02	-14.5%	-10.8%	-6.9%	95.10	9%	0.16	0	15.1%	8.2%	0.0%	35.4%	1.2%
Depaoli	5.49%	0.49%	14.29%	86.58%	1.53%	100.20	-9.1%	0.6%	4.6%	91.61	11%	0.21	1	-5.9%	8.3%	0.0%	-1.3%	5.4%
Henderson	13.18%	1.94%	5.80%	86.42%	70.39%	110.97	1.4%	3.3%	8.5%	96.71	34%	0.24	0	-6.3%	9.6%	0.0%	-17.4%	2.8%
HendersonValleVerde	7.67%	0.34%	2.30%	91.62%	12.49%	117.51	-3.3%	5.4%	8.3%	98.38	34%	0.27	0	-7.9%	10.3%	0.1%	-14.4%	13.0%
Colton	10.16%	1.00%	3.60%	89.25%	39.85%	114.69	-1.4%	4.4%	8.4%	97.64	34%	0.26	0	-6.5%	9.7%	0.0%	-11.7%	7.8%
NorthLasVegas	15.79%	3.92%	9.30%	88.85%	-43.93%	95.55	7.8%	18.0%	20.2%	97.93	33%	0.16	0	-15.9%	13.0%	0.3%	3.1%	3.6%
NLVMeadowMesa	14.14%	9.24%	11.63%	92.72%	11.28%	107.25	9.2%	0.5%	7.6%	99.41	20%	0.16	0	3.4%	11.2%	0.1%	-24.8%	16.3%
NLV PM	14.60%	7.65%	10.47%	91.83%	-15.00%	104.04	8.7%	5.7%	11.4%	98.93	24%	0.16	0	-3.1%	11.7%	0.2%	-15.5%	11.1%
Reno	27.43%	1.33%	6.75%	87.72%	-10.53%	111.05	-3.9%	6.0%	9.2%	95.77	32%	0.19	5	-5.6%	9.6%	0.3%	-23.0%	2.9%
RenoDowntown	10.28%	4.30%	13.64%	80.29%	28.05%	102.00	-10.4%	9.3%	9.3%	96.91	20%	0.20	1	4.5%	8.3%	0.1%	-17.4%	3.2%
RenoPeavineStation	9.84%	0.00%	0.00%	88.94%	5.95%	126.62	0.4%	9.8%	12.9%	98.15	11%	0.19	1	6.2%	7.9%	0.2%	13.7%	1.1%
RenoSierraStation	27.78%	6.25%	0.00%	90.52%	-12.45%	75.80	12.3%	29.9%	34.4%	98.68	18%	0.21	1	-12.6%	6.0%	0.3%	-39.7%	2.0%
RenoSteamboatStation	7.32%	0.00%	4.35%	87.59%	1.41%	115.75	-19.0%	0.6%	-0.1%	98.63	48%	0.29	1	6.5%	6.1%	0.0%	6.1%	11.1%
RenoWashingtonStation	10.00%	0.00%	2.27%	90.83%	-44.96%	98.86	15.4%	11.9%	19.5%	98.60	11%	0.21	1	-12.9%	10.9%	0.0%	6.9%	1.4%
Reno PM	20.11%	1.62%	5.75%	87.34%	-8.08%	107.43	-2.5%	8.3%	11.4%	96.82	26%	0.20	10	-4.2%	9.1%	0.2%	-13.9%	3.9%
Sparks	21.52%	6.08%	2.27%	88.72%	-24.55%	96.79	2.4%	-5.8%	0.8%	98.40	14%	0.16	1	0.9%	15.3%	0.3%	-6.7%	2.1%
SparksSunValleyStation	14.63%	0.00%	0.00%	85.65%	36.68%	101.25	-6.7%	-7.5%	-3.5%	97.78	11%	0.18	0	-7.2%	7.4%	0.0%	-11.1%	1.5%
SparksVistaStation	12.87%	7.39%	20.00%	90.49%	-14.97%	94.89	-13.1%	6.5%	6.4%	98.06	11%	0.18	4	-5.3%	12.7%	0.0%	-8.8%	5.6%
Brown	16.46%	6.11%	8.14%	89.30%	-13.49%	96.04	-7.7%	-0.3%	3.1%	98.17	12%	0.17	5	-3.1%	13.2%	0.1%	-8.1%	3.4%
Fallon	0.00%	0.00%	12.50%	86.04%	-14.68%	99.39	22.4%	3.1%	16.8%	98.57	11%	0.73	1	-8.8%	7.6%	0.0%	0.6%	3.2%
Winnemucca	0.00%	0.00%	0.00%	89.69%	-17.39%	96.34	-11.5%	-9.7%	-6.1%	100.00	0%	0.30	0	-9.2%	0.1%	0.0%	-12.0%	2.8%
Yerington	0.00%	0.00%	0.00%	88.43%	-23.63%	97.01	15.4%	9.3%	11.4%	100.00	7%	0.09	0	-1.5%	0.0%	0.0%	-13.8%	0.0%
MPOO 2	14.17%	3.03%	6.75%	88.94%	-0.23%	105.74	-1.7%	4.6%	8.6%	97.15	23%	0.21	17	-4.7%	10.1%	0.1%	-11.3%	5.6%
Alturas	14.29%	0.00%	0.00%	85.59%	-59.87%	123.09	-36.6%	-2.5%	-8.5%	100.00	73%	0.28	0	-7.1%	3.2%	0.0%	-21.7%	2.8%
SusanvilleEagleStation	0.00%	0.00%	10.00%	83.50%	26.44%	91.39	-20.7%	2.1%	1.0%	96.77	0%	0.15	0	4.7%	10.8%	0.0%	42.8%	6.2%
BattleMountain	0.00%	No Data	0.00%	92.30%	-36.51%	90.61	19.9%	8.1%	16.0%	100.00	0%	0.27	0	-53.7%	0.0%	0.0%	26.0%	0.0%
BoulderCity	13.24%	0.00%	0.00%	92.21%	-27.09%	117.94	33.3%	5.5%	18.2%	99.17	12%	0.14	2	-17.0%	7.8%	0.0%	-11.7%	3.0%
ElkoAspen	4.62%	1.79%	3.45%	94.75%	-29.62%	78.91	-12.7%	5.0%	9.8%	100.00	11%	0.21	3	-7.7%	6.7%	0.0%	0.1%	12.1%
ElkoSpringCreek	0.00%	30.77%	0.00%	93.43%	6.28%	74.63	-22.7%	-4.1%	-3.8%	95.00	0%	0.14	2	-2.6%	4.3%	0.0%	-7.3%	12.7%
Deremiah	3.66%	7.25%	2.33%	94.29%	-18.63%	77.77	-15.1%	3.6%	7.3%	98.64	8%	0.19	5	-6.5%	6.1%	0.0%	-7.1%	11.6%
Ely	0.00%	0.00%	0.00%	0.00%	2.45%	87.69	-8.2%	1.1%	4.4%	97.22	0%	0.08	0	-1.1%	0.1%	0.0%	-14.3%	25.6%
MPOO 1	6.11%	2.81%	7.69%	86.03%	-10.68%	92.97	-2.0%	4.0%	9.3%	98.52	11%	0.17	7	-8.1%	6.4%	0.0%	-11.1%	7.1%
Cluster	19.27%	1.88%	12.30%	89.50%	-17.48%	111.91	1.0%	6.8%	11.1%	97.65	25%	0.22	46	-8.6%	10.1%	0.1%	-12.6%	7.0%

7/8/2008

Source data WebEIS Tacs Reports

Chapter 6
Tough Cookie

Howard University Daughter's Graduation 2002!!

As a physically-strong, mentally-stable, and emotionally-tough woman, in which I used to be, you can't imagine how emotionally hard and physically painful it is to continue to put my story in book form. It was one year prior to this when I stopped being who I knew myself to be. All I thought about was my responsibility to the postal service. I continued to perform, but it had become automatic for me. The job was never the problem; it was howI was being treated and discriminated against. Even though I was on depression medication, I now know that I was still depressed, but in denial with a choking cough and heart palpitations. I was still being treated by my doctors and having tests run because I did not know what the problems were. All I knew was that I had always been a healthy person. I even kept up with my feminine health care on an annual basis. As I stated earlier, I knew I was afraid, but I continued to persevere and not allow my fear to jeopardize my performance or a chance at a promotion.

I stopped cooking, which was something that I loved to do, and socializing. I stopped going grocery shopping and doing the laundry. If the clothes were washed, I didn't even have the strength to fold them or put them away. I stopped changing the linens on the bed. Once, I wore the same clothes to work two days in a row and did not know it until it was brought to my attention. I stopped watching movies as often. I stopped paying the mortgage because I had gotten into a habit of gambling too much. Gambling became a thing of enjoyment, even though it was going against all my disciplines, values, principals, and way of living. My bank account was questioned because of the gambling.

The more working at the post office worsened for me, the worse it got at home. My behavior changed, and I started arguments regularly. My mate and I had an agreement called No Pressure, but when things got bad, that went out the window. I was called lazy and was questioned, "How can you go to the casino, but you can't do anything around here?" My mate would ask all the time, "What is wrong? Let me help you and you have to stop bringing the office home with you." I started to forget little things and did not want to do the normal things that we did together. This was emotionally painful because my mate did not deserve who I had become. I eventually called off our relationship, and slept in another bedroom in the house. My mate knew about the continued submissions for promotion. My mate knew how it affected me when I would say that I didn't get the job. My mate also felt I was qualified for the positions, and it angered my mate, too. Sex was not on my mind anymore. All I did was sleep, work, and gamble; sometimes I wouldn't even eat dinner.

Daughter's Graduation at Yale University 5/2008!!!

Chapter 7
Back from Vacation

In June 2008, when I returned to work from being on annual, I was given another opportunity to go on detail in Las Vegas. Neither Mark Martinez nor Jennifer Vo was there. They were selected to go to other districts. Yul Melonson, Acting Executive Postmaster-City of Las Vegas, and Robert Reynosa, still the promoted manager, Customer Service Operations, (MCSO), were running the City of Las Vegas. I was called into the postmaster's office and told that I would be going to Huntridge Station as the acting manager. I said to myself, "Great, I've been there before, and I did well." I was very excited to get another shot at getting a promotion for all the hard work I had done on my details. I felt Huntridge held a special place in my heart because it was the first station where I was detailed to and performed well. When I received the notice from Robert Reynosa and Yul Melonson, I was informed that Huntridge was performing very well, and they did not want it to decline nor did they want to have to worry about the performance there. They stated in the meeting that they needed me to run the station, so they could spend their time taking care of other stations with bigger issues. I told them in the meeting that they would not have to worry about Huntridge; I will take care of it. After all, I believe that one of my jobs as a manager is to make my superiors look good, and in turn I look good.

In June 2008, I arrived at Huntridge Station and was welcomed just as I had been the first time in April 2006. I had now come full circle. I was happy and sad all at the same time, knowing I had some health issues with my heart, body, and personality, plus my hair was starting to fall out. Remember, I stated in the previous paragraph that Huntridge was supposed to be running well, and I was to maintain its performance. Well, I did not consider Huntridge to be running all that well, so I went to work with my staff and got it running better. Please refer to my eCareer personal profile, as this was a very large pill to swallow. The accomplishments achieved at this facility in just three weeks under my leadership, are too much to indicate here, but to sum it all up: we did 'excellent.' There are more details in my profile. In addition, I was called to Yul's office and was introduced to a supervisor, and he told me that I had been hand-picked to train her about the field. She worked in Human Resources for years. I said what I would always say, "No problem." I told her what time to be at the station, and I left the meeting.

On July 2, 2008, I received a call from Yul Melonson and Craig Colton asking me to go to Meadow Mesa as the acting manager and, of course, I said yes. Even though I had only been at Huntridge for three weeks, I welcomed the opportunity, once again. I asked them when did they want me, and they answered, Monday, July 7, 2008. I told them that Monday the Lord created a special day just for me, and I have scheduled leave. Craig responded, "If He created it, then I guess we'll let you have it." It was my birthday, and I had made plans for it.

I returned to Huntridge on July 8, 2008. I had empowered my supervisors with the necessary motivation, plan, and expectations they would need in my absence. I was extremely proud of my staff following through and obtaining the desired results. They performed exceptionally well for the day after the holiday (July 5, 2008) and for the Monday of July 7, 2008. Anyone in operations knows that when you can put a staff together to be the best-performing office in the city for the day after a holiday, and the Monday following, then you have arrived. To me, your leadership is measured based on how well your operations perform when you're not in the office. They made me proud, and I told them so. I could not thank them enough for their performance.

On July 10, 2008, I had my first staff meeting at Meadow Mesa Station and towards the end of it, Jerry came by to share the information that was given to him from Shaun Mossman (District Manager) and Craig Colton (Acting Manager Post Office Operations) MPOO. I tried to tell Jerry that we had talked about overtime and how we were going to capture more under time. That morning, I walked with the supervisors, demonstrating how to address the carriers. Jerry said, "Under time is hard to get," and some other words that I did not get because I was trying to get the sweat off my face that had just come over me. Jerry appeared to be paranoid about his performance at NLV because he would always say, "Shaun is going to address me for overtime, sick leave, voice of the employee (VOE)," a survey given to each employee of the postal service once a year in which ratings are calculated quarterly. It appeared that he dreaded every day's performance would not be good enough. What Jerry failed to realize was that I could help make his experience in NLV much better if he allowed me to demonstrate my skills and abilities. After all, I improved every office I worked in. However, I was never promoted.

On August 6, 2008, I was called by Corey for an interview for Huntridge Station that was scheduled for August 7, 2008 at 1:00 p.m. I was very excited, and said, "Thank you," before hanging up the phone. The next day (August 7, 2008), I prepared myself for the interview and went to work at Meadow Mesa Station. I was running a little late. According to Jerry's calculation, I was late on approximately three occasions. I will explain my lateness in a few minutes. As I was leaving for the interview for Huntridge Station, I was called back into the office to take a phone call. It was Lorraine Mims, telling me that Craig was not out of his meeting, and Corey told her to call me to let me know that they wouldn't be ready until Craig is out of his meeting. I thought to myself, Craig in a meeting, and let it go. I went to get something to eat and while I was out, I called Lorraine back. I told her to let Corey know that since I had to travel so far, I would start making my way there. I did not want Corey to call me and tell me to come on, and I had to drive that far with the anticipation of how my interview wasgoing to go. As I made it to the freeway, Lorraine called me back and said that Corey said not to come now because he did not know if the interviews were still going to be done that day or not. I then became unhappy. I returned to the office and found out that Yul Melonson and Craig Colton were trading places, and Craig and Corey were going to conduct the interviews. I was later called by Corey to inform me that my interview was rescheduled for tomorrow (August 8, 2008) at 1:30 p.m. I arrived at the interview and was told that I did very well.

On August 18, 2008, I received an eCareer email stating I was not the selected applicant. I called Corey, the selecting official, and I asked him why? Corey said that I interviewed very well, and I was right on target for what he was looking for, but he selected a guy who asked for a lateral, and he had been an EAS-22 manager before. He was from outside the district and, yet again, I could not say anything. Unlike other times, I kept my thoughts to myself, but not on this decision. When I received the news, I spoke to my staff and Jerry. I told them that I worked very hard at Huntridge, and they gave it to an outsider. I was told by Corey not to be discouraged that there would be other jobs coming up. I thought to myself, Since there are other jobs coming up then why couldn't that guy have taken one of them when they come up? Once again, I had to accept the answer that was given to me.

Non Selection letter from Corey for Huntridge Station, which was given to someone outside the district, August 18, 2008

Page 1 of 1

Attachments can contain viruses that may harm your computer. Attachments may not display correctly.

Mcgee, Lola B. - North Las Vegas, NV

From: ecareerworkflow@usps.gov [ecareerworkflow@usps.gov] **Sent:** Mon 8/18/2008 1:31 PM
To: Mcgee, Lola B. - North Las Vegas, NV
Cc:
Subject: Correspondence: Non Select
Attachments: Correspondence_Non Select.PDF(9KB)

August 18, 2008

Lola McGee
7582 CYPRESS TREE ST
LAS VEGAS NV 89123-0553
USA
Dear Lola McGee:

This letter is in reference to your application for Vacancy Announcement number 52108635 for the position of 2305-7091 MGR CUSTOMER SERVICES EAS-21 L, at the Nevada-Sierra District.

After careful review of all the applicants for this position, I have decided to select another candidate.

I want to thank you for your interest in this opportunity and encourage you to apply for other vacancies that would provide the career advancement and growth you are seeking.

Current vacancies can be searched by clicking the postal jobs link on the My Life page of Lite Blue.

Sincerely,
Corey Richards
Selecting Official

https://webmail1.usps.gov/exchange/lola.mcgee/Inbox/Correspondence:%20Non%20Selec... 8/18/2008

On Monday, August 25, 2008, I arrived at the office about 6:55 a.m. I had called my staff, as I do every morning, to find out how we're doing and what the challenges were for the day, and to give any instructions/directions that I wanted us to take.

I walked out on the floor, picked up my paperwork, and continued to sign the SPII log and observed the hot cases and continued on to the parcel area. I gave instructions to my staff and to the clerks on what needed to be done. We were inundated with parcels as usual; we had previously planned for Monday's volume by scheduling employees as best as we could with the available resources. As I continued to walk the floor, I saw Jerry Wilson approaching the supervisor's pit. I walked in his direction, and he met me. He started talking about the operation and going out on the street to let our presence be known. I told him about the hot case and the parcel area, and he asked me about the other clerk, Carrie, John Bell's wife. I told him that she had been off sick for a week now; she had surgery. He asked if I had paperwork, and I replied, "Yes. It was already planned." He went on to say, "We need to address these clerks; I don't care whose wife it is."

Consequently, I was a little perturbed because I had been at Meadow Mesa since July 9, 2008, and he had emphatically expressed his desires, and had stated his instructions with conviction. As the subordinate manager, I followed his lead, rather I liked it or not. He was not the type of person who took suggestions very well. He called the shots, and that's how he wanted it to go. I tried to inform Jerry that I was from NLV and many of the things here were done the same at both offices, and we shared the resources for the good of the city.

Later that morning, Jerry was in my office and I asked him if I could have Joe Frucione— the clerk that had a bid at Meadow Mesa. This was my third or forth time asking him for Joe. I told him that the main office had four scheme clerks with twenty-seven routes and a thirty-minute Auxiliary (Aux) route, which is a partial route and that Meadow Mesa has sixty-five city routes plus twenty or more rural routes with five scheme clerks (clerks who process/throw mail by route from their memory into a slot or hamper). Jerry's reply was, "I'll see."

Three weeks after being at Meadow Mesa, Jerry called us all together and reported that the performance of overtime the last two weeks was horrible and we have to do something about it. After the meeting, I asked Jerry if he thought the problem was me and he said, "Well, you have been here for two weeks." I said that we have a full annual leave board with long term sick leave, and the main office has Transitional Employees (TEs) that are needed over here to balance out the city during this period. I said that the main office is not splitting enough routes and not capturing enough under time.

Jerry is a disrespectful person, in my opinion. He would come to Meadow and talk to me with my staff, making decisions for us without any regard for what I'd put in place or what planning we did. One day, Jerry came to the office and called a staff meeting. He told me he was changing my start time to 8:00 a.m., because he wanted me there in the evenings and that every supervisor was going out on the streets daily to address the street expansion. I reiterated that we already had a plan in place for the street, and we would be down supervisors, so I would be running one of the zones. I also told him that I didn't have to have a change in start time to be here to five or later; I could start at 7:00 a.m. and still be here to 5:00 p.m. It's not like working long hours was new to me; I've done it my whole postal career.

There are just a few things I have to state about my experience with Jerry Wilson as my boss. It appeared to me that Jerry felt if he could make the NLV main office produce numbers, then he could pin any negative performance of Meadow Mesa on me, even though he professed he wanted the city to do good. I was assigned to NLV since May 15, 2004, and had worked at Meadow Mesa prior to coming over on detail as a manager, and we have never been a city to not do well under both leaderships with Craig Colton and Yul Melonson (both were postmasters of NLV).

One day, Jerry notified me that we needed to start doing the projections on the new Blue Share page. I took a look at the indicators and asked Jerry if they want F2 or F2B hours, and he said just the carrier hours. Craig sent out an email the next day with the variance, and I was 2% over my projection. I replied to Craig's email stating that I thought it was a 2% threshold either way. His returned email stated it was not. I called him and asked if he wanted carrier hours or total F2B because sometimes those functions were interchanged with people.

The next business, day Jerry insinuated that I had gone over his head by addressing the email and clarifying the indicator with Craig. My reply was, "No I didn't." I wanted to know what he wanted on the spreadsheet, in a jovial manner. Jerry did not say anything else to that. We went on talking about something else.

On Friday, August 22, 2008, I called NLV and asked for Jerry and was told he was at the district with Yul Melonson (Acting Postmaster Las Vegas City). I called Yul's office. I could let both know of the condition of the office for Saturday, August 23, 2008, with down and splitting routes. My supervisors made a mistake on the schedule, even though we prepared the schedule in advance. Instead of having to split five routes, we were going to split eight and case eighteen, which minimized the overtime employees. Yul was unavailable, so I left a message. Later, I called Jerry's cellphone and told him about the mistake the supervisors made, and he said we would just have to live with it, because the Scheduled Day off (SDO) employee request was already in to Shaun. I asked Jerry if we could have a TE from main office, and he said that Mel, the supervisor, already had the floor set, and he didn't think so. I told my staff we had to make the best out of it, but from this point on, I wanted them to have every 3971 (Official Employee Leave Slip) with them, and we would go route by route since those mistakes were being made.

An hour or two after talking to Jerry, while he was on his way to the airport, I received a call from Yul. I told him that I had called his office to speak with Jerry, but I'd talked with him already, and he told me that the SDO request was already in to Shaun, so it's okay. Yul asked, "Well what's wrong?" I replied, "It's okay. I don't want Jerry to think I'm going over his head." Yul persisted in a concerned manner, and I told him that my staff made mistakes with the schedule, and we were casing eighteen and splitting eight. I've already talked to Jerry, and he said no SDO employees, so I said I'll do the best that I can." Yul asked me if I had thought about bringing the TEs in early. I replied, "I can't do that because I really thought that it was a 'no-no.' He said, "Look at who could come in and manage your Percent to Standard (% to STD) and overtime." I said okay.

A few days earlier, Jerry came by the office and said to me in a by-the-way-demeanor, "You went over my head with Craig on the email," and I replied, "No. I justaddressed the email because it had my name on it along with Meadow Mesa's Variance." I just listened. I asked Jerry to go to the parcel section. "I want to show you what we have," I said, and he said, "No, I don't need to go over there. I know what it looks like." I reminded Jerry that he had told me he did not want any processes changed; so I did not change any. Jerry then responded with, "Well, if we need to change them, then do so."

Chapter 8
A Panic Attack No Investigation

On Monday, August 25, 2008, while in my office after leaving the floor, Jerry Wilson walked up to me, turned his body, in an effort to maneuver that large belly out of the way, got directly in my face and threatened me with, "You continue to go over my head with Craig and Yul, and I'm going to do something about it." To make sure I got his message and intent, Jerry was angry, abrupt, hostile, aggressive, nasty, and disrespectful in his tone. I didn't know if that meant physically or career wise. I didn't know what he was going to do, but it was the straw that broke the camel's back.

Never in my life have I ever been written up on any job. I've been loyal, respectful and a team player, and have endured rejection and disappointments. I've produced great performance records, and extended myself over and beyond. I've gone wherever asked of me, and have worked ten to twelve-hour days, and Saturdays in some offices. I did not do these positive things to be addressed with a threat of harm or receive a negative impact on my career.

As stated before, I believed Jerry to be paranoid about how he was seen in NLV. I endured the pressure he placed upon me, because I thought being a strong person, I could handle it, but that day was different.

When he left my office, I got dizzy. My head and body were experiencing shocking sensations. I advised my staff I would be leaving early, but I told them I had a reaction to some medication because I did not want them to know what happened. I was seeing double and was feeling very hot. I was hyperventilating. My head was scrabbled, and I thought I was either going to pass out or die. Either way, no one would have known the reason because I've always been the type of person to take what is dished out and make the best of it. I was in my office trying to regain my composure to drive home. I went to the restroom to see if I needed to use it. My stomach felt nauseous. I got water, and I tried to make sure it wasn't anything on my desk that I needed to address immediately. I checked my email, replied to some, and then I got my purse and left. As I was driving home, I prayed to the Lord. My brain was not acting right. I did not want to pass out or have an accident. The shocks going through my body were a great concern because I did not want to have a heart attack either. I said, "Lord, if you just let me make it home and if I don't feel any better later I will go to the hospital." At that point, I was confused, but I knew my body was not well. After two or three hours of disturbed sleep, I woke up and tried to eat a sandwich, but it made me sick to my stomach. My body was still in a traumatic state, and I could not explain it nor did I know what was going to happen next. I called my daughter around 9:00 p.m. and explained to her what was going on with me, and she said, "Mama, I'm so glad you called me because you just keep what's going on with you so private." My daughter is an Advanced Practice Nurse (Nurse Practitioner) specializing in mental health. She told me, in a nut shell, along with other things, that my body shut down after enduring all the stress and strain that the post office had put upon me. I then realized I could no longer think about the post office and my image. I had to think about my health. I could have continued being loyal to the post office and they would have eventually said, "There she lay" instead of "There she goes."

Even though I hesitated to call Jerry the night of August 25, 2008, with fear of reprisal and the fact that I would surely never get promoted now, I called Jerry Wilson that night on his cell phone. I had to make the sensible choice about my life. Still, my thoughts were racing, and I was second-guessing my decision to call. I let him know that I was claiming an on-the-job injury, and I would like for him to send me a CA-1 and a CA-2 form in the mail so that I could complete them and send them in to Injury Compensation/Office Of Workers' Compensation Programs (OWCP).

Since I had been up practically all night with my body and head condition, also my racing thoughts, I thought it best to give Jerry a call at the office at around 6:30 a.m. on Tuesday, August 26, 2008. I called NLV and Jerry answered the phone. I asked him if he got my message from last night on his cell phone, and he replied, "Yes." I asked him if he could do me a favor and look in Employee Resource Management System (eRMS) and get my address to send me a CA-1 and a CA-2 because I'm filing an on-the-job injury, and it's Stress. He said, "You know that I'm going to have to report this," and I said, "Yes." He paused for a minute and then asked, "Lola, is this about the job that you didn't get in Vegas?" I replied, "Jerry, I know that you need some information, but I will give it to you in writing." We hung up the phone.

Disclaimer:
In order to maintain authenticity,
the following correspondeces have not been altered.
* * * * *

Statements and Medical Documentation Disclosed
In Spite of the Hippa Law that protects me

August 26, 2008

My Statement of Injury on August 25, 2008
At Meadow Mesa Station – North Las Vegas

On Monday 8/25/08 I arrived at the ofice about 6:55am, after previously calling my staff as I do every morning to ind out how we are doing and what the challenges are for the day and give any instruction/direction that I want us to take, I walked out on the loor picked up my paperwork continued to sign the SPII log and observed the hot cases and continued on to the parcel area. I started giving instructions to my staff and to the clerks on what needed to be done. We were inundated with parcels as usual; we had previously planned for Monday's volume by scheduling employees as best we could with the resources we had available. As I continued to walk the loor I saw Jerry Wilson approaching the supervisor's pit I walk in his direction and he met me. He started talking about the operation and going out on the street to let our presents be known. I stated to him about the hot case and the parcel area and he asked me about the other clerk (Carrie-John Bell's wife) I told him that she has been off sick for a week now, she had surgery. He asked me if I had paperwork, and I replied yes it was already planned. He went on to say we need to address these clerks I don't care whose wife it is. I just listened. I stated to Jerry, lets go over to the parcel section I want to show you what we have and he said no I don't need to go over there I know what it looks like.

I stated to Jerry, you told me that you did not want any processes changed; so I have not changed any, Jerry then stated, well if we need to change them then do so. Consequently, I was a little perturb because I have been at Meadow Mesa since July 9, 2008 and he has emphatically expressed his desires, and has stated his instructions with conviction and as the subordinate manager to him I have just followed his lead rather I like it are not. He is not the type of person that take suggestion very well he calls the shots and that's how he wants it to go. I've tried to inform Jerry that I am from NLV and many of the things here are done the same at both ofices, but we share the resources for the good of the city.

Later that morning Jerry was in my ofice and I asked him if I could have Joe Frucione the clerk that has a bid at Meadow Mesa, this is about my third or forth time asking him for Joe. I stated that main ofice has four scheme clerks with 27 routes and a thirty minute AUX route. I stated that Meadow Mesa has 65 city routes plus twenty plus rural routes with five scheme clerks, Jerry replied I'll see.

7/10/08 I had my irst staff meeting and towards the end of it Jerry came by to share the information that was given from Shaun Mossman and Craig. In the interim I stated to Jerry that we have talked about overtime and how we are going to capture more under time. I had walked with the supervisors that morning demonstrating to them how to address the carriers, Jerry stated under time is hard to get and some other words that I did not get because I was trying to get the sweat off my face that had just come over me. Jerry appeared to me to be very paranoid about his performance at NLV because he would always state Shaun is going to address me for overtime, sick leave, VOE, and it appeared to me that he dreaded every days performance if it wasn't good enough. What Jerry failed to realize is that I could help make his experience in NLV much better if he would allow me to demonstrate to him my skills and ability. After all, I have never not improved any ofice that I've been in rather I was promoted or not. Three weeks after being at Meadow Mesa, Jerry called all of us together and stated the performance of overtime the last two weeks is horrible and we have to do something about it. Later on after the meeting I ask Jerry if he thought the problem was me and he stated well you have been here for two weeks. I stated that we have a full annual leave board with long term sick leave, and main ofice has TE's that are needed over here to balance out the city during this period. I stated that main ofice is not splitting enough routes and not capturing enough under time. Jerry is a disrespectful person in my opinion, He would come over to Meadow and talk to me with my staff and make decisions for me and them with out any regard for what I've put in place for my people are what planning we had done. Jerry came one day and called a staff meeting and told me that he was changing my start time to 8:00am because he wanted me there in the evenings and that every supervisor was going out on the streets daily to address the street expansion. I stated to Jerry that we have already had a plan for the street and we will be down supervisors so I will be running one of the zones. I stated that I don't have to have a change in start time to be here to ive or later. I said I can start at 7:00am and still be here to 5:00pm it's not like working long hours is new to me I've done it my whole postal career. This is just a few things that I have to state about my experience with Jerry Wilson as my boss. It appeared to me that Jerry thought if he made NLV main ofice have good numbers then he could pin any negative performance of Meadow Mesa's on me, even though he would state that he wants the city to do good. I have been assigned to North Las Vegas Main Post Ofice since May 15, 2004 and have worked at Meadow Mesa prior to coming over on detail as a manager, and we have never been a city to not do well under both leaderships with Craig Colton and Yul Melonson. One day recently Jerry notiied me that we needed to start doing the projections on the new Blue Share page.

I took a look at the indicators and asked Jerry if they want F2 or F2B hours he stated just the carrier hours. Craig sent out an email the next day with the variance on and I was 2% over my projection and I replied to craigs email stating that I thought it was a 2% threshold either way and he stated in an email that it was not. I called him and asked him if he wanted carrier hours or total F2B because sometimes those functions are interchanged with people. On Friday 8/22/08 I called NLV main and asked for Jerry and I was told that he was at the district with Yul, I called Yul's ofice to have both of them there to let them know of the condition of the ofice for Saturday 8/23/08 with down and splitting routes. My supervisors had made a mistake on the schedule even though we had prepared the schedule in advance. Instead of having to split 5 routes we were going to split 8 and case 18 which minimized the overtime employees. I called and left a message. Later on I called Jerry's cell phone and I got him. I told Jerry about the mistake and he said we will just have to live with it because the SDO request is already in to Shaun. I asked Jerry if we could have a TE from main ofice and he stated that Mel already has the loor set and he didn't think so. I told my staff the we have to make the best out of it but from now on I wanted them to have every 3971 with them and we will go route by route since these mistakes are being made. Within an hour or two after talking to Jerry on his way to the airport, Yul called and I told him that I was calling to speak with Jerry but I've talked with him already and he told me that the SDO request is already in to Shaun so its okay I've already talked with him. Yul stated well what's wrong and I said It's okay I don't want him to think I'm going over his head. Yul persisted in a concern manner and I told him that my staff made mistakes with the schedule and we are casing 18 and splitting 8. I've already talked to Jerry and he said know SDO's and I said I'll do the best that I can. Yul ask me if I had thought about bringing the TE's in early, I replied I can do that because I really thought that is was a NO, NO. He said look at who could come in and manage your % to STD and overtime. I said okay.

On Monday 8/25/2008 while in my ofice after leaving the loor, Jerry Wilson threatened me with an open ended statement. He stated "You continue to go over my head with Craig and Yul and I'm going to do something about it." I don't know what he was going to do but it was the straw that broke the camels back. I don't know if he means physical or paper wise, but what I do know is that I have never been written up on any job I've had in my life, I've been loyal, respectful, a team player, and have endured rejection and disappointments, I've produced great performance records, and have extended myself over and beyond, I've gone where every asked of me and have worked 10-12 hour days and Saturday's at some ofices, and I did not do these positive things to be addressed with a threat of harm are negative impact on my career. As I told you previously, I believe Jerry is paranoid about how he is seen in NLV and I have endured the pressure that he has put upon me because I'm a strong person, but this day was different. When he left my ofice I begin to get dizzy in my head and my body was having shock sensations going through it. I advised my staff that I would be leaving early but I told them that I had a reaction to some medication because I did not want them to know what had happened to me. I started to see double and my body started to get very hot. My head was scrabbled and I thought that I was either going to die or pass out either way no one would have know the reason because I've always been the type of person to just take what is dished out to me and make the best out of it. I'm in my ofice trying to get my composure to drive myself home and I go into the restroom to see if I need to use it. My stomach felt nauseous. I went and got water and I tried to make sure that it wasn't anything on my desk that I needed to address immediately. I checked my email and replied to some and I got my purse and left. As I was driving home I was praying to the lord because my brain was not acting right so I did not want to pass out or have an accident. The shocks going through my body was a great concern because I did not want to have a heart attack either. I said lord if you just let me make it home and if I don't feel any better later I will go to the hospital. At this point I was confused but I knew my body was not well.

After disturb sleep for two or three hours, I woke up and tried to eat a sandwich but it made me sick of the stomach. My body was still in this trauma state and I could not explain it nor did I know what was going to happen next. I called my daughter around 9:00pm an explained to her what was going on with me and she said mama I'm so glad you called me because you just keep what's going on with you so private. My daughter is an Advanced Practice Nurse specializing in mental health. She told me in a nut shell along with other things that my body shut down after enduring all the stress and strain that the post ofice has put upon you. I then realized that I can no longer think about the post ofice and my image I had to think about my health are I would have been loyal to the post ofice and they would have been referring to me as there she lay instead of there she go.

Even though I still hesitated to call Jerry the night of 8/25/08 with fear of reprisal and the fact that I will really not get promoted now, I had to make the sensible choice about my life. I still had the racing thoughts in my mine and I was second guessing my decision to call. I called Jerry Wilson that night on his cell phone to let him know that I am claiming an on the job injury and I would like for him to send me a CA-1, and a CA-2 form in the mail so that I can complete it. Since I had been up practically all night with my body and head condition and my racing thoughts, I thought it best to give Jerry a call at the ofice at around 6:30am on Tuesday 8/26/2008. I called North Las Vegas Post Office and Jerry answered the phone; I asked him if he got my message from last night on his cell phone and he replied yes. I asked him if he would do me a favor and look in eRMS and get my address to send me a CA-1, and a CA-2 because I'm iling an on the job injury and its Stress. He stated that "You know that I'm going to have to report this and I said yes." He paused for a minute and he stated Lola is this about the job that you didn't get in Vegas, I replied Jerry I know that you need some information but I will give it to you in writing and we hung up the phone. I later called to make an appointment for the doctor my daughter referred me to by the earliest she had was for Wednesday 8/27/08 and I took it.

Sincerely
Lola McGee

My Statement of the Occupational Disease Injury For Which I am Filing a CA-2 Form

August 27, 2008

Over the past year and a half thru two I have repeatedly endured unfair tactics and discrimination based on personal issues of my higher management, race, and gender all the while I have continued to keep my head up and excel in my work performance. In the last year are so, I have been treated for heart problems and anxiety in which I was given medication for. Even though I have never had any major health issues, I attributed my declining health to age progression. I have never been on prescribed medication for ailing health issues. I am a loyal and dedicated, to my demise, team player that strives to achieve success, growth, and development based on my own merit; however, the loyalty and dedication has not been precipitated. For the sake of my effort to explain my injury of Stress that I reported to my acting Postmaster, Jerry Wilson, on 8/25-26/08, I will start from the beginning of when I started to be treated and discriminated against which has lead to me being diagnosed with Post Traumatic Stress Disorder, and Major Depressive Disorder. I called Jerry Wilson and left a message on his cell phone stating that I was iling a claim for Stress, and I needed a CA-1 and a CA-2 form, the night of 8/25/08 sometime between the hours of 11:00pm and 12:30am, I do not remember the speciic time because I was toiling back and forth with my thoughts. I knew that with the way I had already been treated over the pass 2 years that this information was not going to be welcomed by my superiors. I take great pride in myself as a person and my work ethic, but I knew that I had to do this for my on wellbeing because if I go crazy and lose my mine not one management personnel will be there to try and bring me back. For those of you who ind it in your heart to be concern here is why my body gradually built up the Stress and it shut do because I had taken to much mistreatment. For those of you who say why did I wait so long I say it's easy for you to say that but when you are a person of respect, dignity, integrity, loyalty, and want to be respected based on your own merit it's not easy to give up and I fault to my body told me it would not endure anymore. My mine still had second thoughts of the repercussion that I would go through, but my body gave me know choice by to make sure I stopped and took care of myself, with that I believed that I am one of the most strongest women in the world, but even cast iron steel ware's out if you use it enough.

Maya Angelou said is best: "When people show you who they are believe them."

In September of 2006 I was given the opportunity for a detail as acting manager at Paradise Valley Station after calling a meeting with Jennifer Vo, Robert Reynosa, and Mark Martinez. The meeting was called by me because I had been previously told by Jennifer that I would be going back to North Las Vegas as a supervisor because the perception was that I improved

Huntridge Station's (which I had be acting manager there since from April 1, 2006 until the detail came up for Paradise Valley Station) percent to standard by over counting volume. I was appalled at the comment because my integrity was being questioned and it was a personal insult to me. All I did was looked at Jennifer and she stated with a smirk on her face "Tell me that I'm full of shit if you want to." I would not have ever said such a thing to her because she was my boss and I would not have disrespected myself in that manner. I was shocked that she would say something like that to me without really knowing me but it let me know that she was just being herself and she knew that I knew that she was not telling me the truth. I had performed well at Huntridge and all I wanted was the opportunity to continue to grow to gain upward mobility. No one gave me any expectation at Huntridge, but one thing Jennifer stated to me when she gave me the opportunity was "If I don't have to come into your station then you are okay." Jennifer, Mark, or Robert never had to come into Huntridge and question me on any negative issues. Mark started the meeting by saying why are we here, what's going on. I stated I wanted every one here because I want to know what I did wrong and why I'm going back to North Las Vegas when I've worked so hard and performed well. I stated that Jennifer said that I was being perceived as over counted volume and that how I reduced % to STD and I didn't want to be looked at in that manner. Mark stated no I'll tell you why and he said I have a manager that is counting rubber bands and during route inspections and I need him to be in a productive role. I respected Marks explanation and as the meeting was ending Mark asked Jennifer and Robert what about Paradise Valley for her. He told them to work it out and he stated to me that they would get back to me. I left the meeting with a smile on my face with the hope that all was taking in a positive manner. I worked at Paradise Valley Station as the acting manager from September 2006 thru March 2007. Shortly after the New Year (2007) Dana Urbanski was detailed into Jennifer Vo's position and we were having a private conversation but for the sake of this statement I'm going to reveal what she asked me. Dana stated to me Why is Mark and Robert so hard on you on the telecom, it just seams to me that they talk to you harder than anyone else." I stated to Dana "You can see it also; and I don't know but I am a black woman that is serious and I have a deep voice, also I called a meeting with Jennifer, Robert, and Mark to not be perceived as a person that would cheat to achieve. Dana stated "I don't know, I don't think its right or fare." I worked 10-12 hour days and was there most Saturdays without any additional pay over eight hours. I had excelled in several areas, however, within a couple of weeks before I left, my 204b failed to clear some mail that was left in the facility by his on instructions to the carrier, I sat him down. The other issue was my new supervisor failed to report to me that some mail was brought back off some business routes even though we had a plan to get it delivered. In the interim there were three other stations with similar issues, mail left in the building and not dispatched, mail in the facility that did not even go out for delivery, and nothing happened to those managers. I was given an Investigative Interview and sent back to North Las Vegas. Needless to say I improved Paradise Valley Station with the challenges of the zone split and the volume that it was receiving from 9/2006 – 3/30/2007. Robert said to me one day, when you're back at North Las Vegas think about those supervisors at PV that put you there. He wanted me to change their schedules and in my attempt they were calling in FMLA sick and having surgeries along with transportation and childcare issues. Not to mention scheduled annual leave. I asked Robert recently if the supervisors at PV are still in their same positions and he replied yes. When Paradise Valley was posted not only did I not get the job I wasn't even given an interview. The Job went to the acting manager that I had replaced 6 months prior, and both of our performances are a matter of record. In addition, merit time came up and Jennifer evaluated me, I received a low 3% rating after all I had done to improve Huntridge Station and Paradise Valley Station. Even though I knew it was not right or fare for her to rate my accomplishments like that, I didn't even question her. I was sent back to North Las Vegas as a supervisor.

Some of my accomplishments can be reviewed on my eCareer proile, and my old 991's that I submitted for promotions on all my attempts. While on detail I put in for several positions, Strip Station - 8/06, Winterwood Station - 8/06, Garside Station -1/07, Huntridge – 1/07, Strip Station - 1/07 (2nd time) and Paradise Valley Station – 1/07. All of these stations are in the City of Las Vegas where I was on detail for one (1) full year, at the time. Some of the positions were illed with acting manager that had not been acting as long as I had, some had just started acting, and some I was told were laterals. With my ability to bring my staff together and achieve the desired results, and not be considered for a position, makes one question why me, not to mention that none of the people selected for the positions were black.

When I called Yul Melonson and introduced myself to him I let him know that I am a supervisor at NLV and I will be returning back to my position effective tomorrow. He stated no one told me that you were coming back and I said that I've been notiied that I'm returning by Robert Reynosa and Jennifer Vo. I went to see Yul and I told him that I've been on detail for one year and I would like to take a break for a week but when I return I promise you that I will have North Las Vegas running great just as I had done for Craig Colton. While sitting in the ofice with Yul, he was looking at the Flash report for Paradise Valley, he stated "Why are you here" and I replied I don't know but I need a week of annual to recuperate and gather myself and I'll be ready when I come back. Yul allowed me to go on annual and when I returned he placed me at Meadow Mesa to run the largest zone there.

I excelled once again and he showed his appreciation by giving me a gas card because he knew I lived way on the other side of town. He gave me an excellence plaque and a monetary spot award for my part in North Las Vegas success. In the interim I returned back to my position at North Las Vegas Main Post Ofice where I excelled in my F4 duties. When merit time came he demonstrated he appreciation as well, even though he only had part of the rating and Robert Reynosa had the other part because I had been on detail in the City of Las Vegas for half of the Fiscal year. Refer to my accomplishments for what I did in the City of North Las Vegas and tell me if I deserved the rating that I received from Robert Reynosa, in FY07, but once again I just let it slide and I moved on to continue to excel in what ever life brought my way.

In September 2007, I put in for Valle Verde Station in Henderson and received an interview (Level 22 Station) but it was given to a lady that had already been acting for about 2 years and she was in the position at the time. I did not feel anything about this was unfair. I was told by Craig that I had a great interview and he went back and forth while he was trying to make his decision.

In October 2007 I put in for Sunrise Station in the City of Las Vegas (Level 21) and I received and interview by Robert Reynosa and Mark Martinez but I was not the one selected. I said to myself at least I've gotten to the interview, besides there is no way at this point in my performance that they would be able to justify not given me an interview, especially after receiving and interview for the level 22. I was told by Mark and Robert that I had a great interview.

In 12/2007 I put in for Red Rock Station in the City of Las Vegas (Level 22) and I did not receive an interview, I was told that they gave it to a person who wanted to lateral. In January 2008 I was requested to go on detail as acting manager in Reno Nevada, by John Morgan, and I accepted. Even though I'd never been in the snow I wanted all involved in selecting me to know that I truly appreciated the offer. After being in Reno for one week I received word from my postmaster Yul Melonson that Renee Brown said that I was a breath of fresh air for her in Sparks Sun Valley Station. After being there almost a month, I received a call from Robert Reynosa asking me to come back to the City of Las Vegas and I told him that I'll call him back. I called Renee and told her that I've been asked to come back to Las Vegas and be the acting manager of King Station. With regret but understanding she said that's a choice you have to make but what ever your decision is I support you. As a token of appreciation for my performance at Sparks Sun Valley Station, I was given a certiicate and a copy of the Flash Report. I told Renee that I will probably go back. Later on that day a date was scheduled for my return to Las Vegas on 2/23/08. While on detail at Sparks Sun Valley Station (Reno) I would ly home and drive to California because my oldest brother (71 years old) was ill and was not expected to make it and he didn't. He passed away on 2/15/08 so I did not get to start at King Station until 2/27/08.

The City of Las Vegas was hurting for supervisors let along acting managers and I knew it, but never the less I took the opportunity and I did the very best with my resources at King Station. King was in such bad shape that it needed an overhaul from front to back. Please refer to my proile, but for the sake of this statement I'll write a few accomplishments that I achieved at King Station. I cleaned up all the grievances that dated back a year with very little compensation paid out, the budget to -2.5% WTD, Sick leave was reduced to -10%, MSP scanning rate went from the low 90 to 99.4%, del cons improved from 97.5 to 99.4 % to standard, which was atrocious, improved from 157 to 124 percent, with my lowest day being at 107%, and total F4 improved from 74.23 to 83.11 percent, and all mail was being processed and the hot cases were cleared. I had the shelves taken out of the registry cage so the Accountable Clerk would not double handle the mail; this was an effort to get it to the carriers in a timely manner. King Station was a serious challenge but I was determined to make it one of the best in the city. After being at King Station for the short time that I was there 2/27/08 thru 5/05/08 the manager came back off sick leave and I went on scheduled annual for two and one half weeks.

In May 2008 I put in for Emerald Station in the City of Las Vegas (Level 22) and I did not receive an interview; I was told that no acting managers got an interview. I felt that was okay if it was true.

In May 2008 I put in for Strip Station (For the third time level 19) and I did not even receive and interview. I assumed that I was more qualiied than the other applicants and they would not have been able to justify not given me the job; so I wasn't even given the opportunity for an interview. The person that was selected for the job had not been in the city running a station but he had been working for Robert, Mark, and Jennifer. This devastated me because how can you justify not given me an interview after I have received an interview for the level 21 and 22 positions and this was a level 19. Even though I accepted it and continued to be Lola and carry my head up high, I knew it was not fare or right in any stretch of the imagination. And please believe me when I say that I don't feel any ill feelings towards the people who were selected for the positions because they are not the one's who gave themselves the positions.

When I arrived back at work I was given another opportunity to go on detail in Las Vegas, but Mark Martinez neither Jennifer Vo are here now. They have both been selected in other districts. Yul Melonson (Acting Postmaster) and Robert Reynosa (Still the promoted MCSO) were running the City of Las Vegas. I was called into the postmaster's ofice and I was told that I will be going to Huntridge Station as the acting manager. I said to myself, great I've been there before and I did well. I was very excited to get another shot at getting a promotion for all the hard work I had done on my details. I felt Huntridge had a special part in my heart because it was the irst station that I was detailed to and I had performed well. When I received the notice from Robert Reynosa and Yul Melonson, I was informed that Huntridge was performing very well and they did not want it to go down nor did they want to have to worry about the performance there. They stated in the meeting that they needed me to run the station so that they could spend their time taking care of other stations with bigger issues. I stated in the meeting that you will not have to worry about Huntridge I will take care of it. After all, I believe that one of my jobs as a manager is to make my superiors look good, in turn I look good.

I arrived at Huntridge Station in June 2008 and was welcomed just as I had been the irst time in April 2006 I had now been full circle. I was happy and sad all at the same time, because I now know that I have some health issues with my heart, body, and personality, not to mention my hair fell out. Not really knowing why but never the less I had them. Remember I stated in the previous paragraph that Huntridge was suppose to be running good and I was suppose to maintain the performance. Well when I got to Huntridge, I did not consider it running good so I went to work with my staff and we then got it to running good. Please refer to my eCareer personal proile. This is a very large pill to swallow and I can't muster up the strength to tell you my accomplishments we achieved in just three weeks under my leadership.

On 7/2/2008 I received a call from Yul Melonson and Craig Colton asking me if I would go to Meadow Mesa as the acting manager and of course I stated yes. Even though I had only been at Huntridge for three weeks, I welcomed the opportunity once again. I asked them when did they want me and they stated Monday 7/7/2008. I stated to them that Monday the Lord created a special day just for me and I have scheduled leave. Craig responded if he created it then I guess will let you have it. It was my birthday and I had plans for it. I returned back to Huntridge on 7/8/2008 (After empowering my supervisors with the necessary motivation, plan, and expectations they would need in my absence) I was very, very proud of my staff following out our desired results. They performed exceptionally well for the day after the holiday 7/5/2008 and for the Monday 7/7/2008. And anyone in operations know that when you can put a staff together to be the best performing ofice in the city for the day after a holiday and the Monday following, then you have arrived. To me your leadership is measured based on how well your operations performs when you're not in the ofice. They made me proud and I told them so, I could not thank them enough for their performance.

On July 9, 2008 I went to Meadow Mesa Station as the acting manager in North Las Vegas, my home installation. I had worked there only as a trainer and a delivery supervisor, but I was now going to be the acting manager. Refer to my statement dated 8/26/2008 for the details because I don't want to confuse anyone.

While at Meadow Mesa I put in for Huntridge Station (Level 21) in the City of Las Vegas. At this time, Yul Melonson and Corey Richards are running the city. Robert Reynosa was assigned to King Station to clean it up and I'll say refer to the reports for his performance. I was called by Corey on 8/6/2008 for an interview for Huntridge Station that was scheduled for 8/7/08 at 1:00pm. I was very excited and I said thank you before hanging up the phone. The next day 8/7/08, I prepared myself for the interview and went to work at Meadow Mesa Station. I was running a little late, which I had been late approximately three occasions according to Jerry's calculation. I will explain my lateness in a few minutes. The time arrived for me to be making it to the interview for Huntridge Station and I was called back from outside to the phone. It was Lorraine Mims and she stated to me that Craig was not out of his meeting and Corey told her to call me to let me know that they want be ready until Craig gets out of his meeting. I said to myself, Craig in a meeting and I let go. I went to get something to eat and while I was out

I called Lorraine back and told her to let Corey know that since I have to travel so far for the interview I'll just start making my way there. I did not want Corey to call me and tell me to come on and I had to drive that far with the anticipation of how my interview was going to go. As I made it to the freeway, Lorraine called me back and stated that Corey said do not come now because he did not know if the interviews were still going to be done that day or not. I then got unhappy. I went back to the ofice and I had found out that Yul Melonson and Craig Colton was trading places and Craig and Corey was going to be doing the interviews. I was later called by Corey to inform me that my interview was rescheduled for tomorrow 8/8/08 at 1:30pm. I arrived at the interview and I was told that I did very well on the interview. On 8/18/2008 I received an eCareer email which stated that I was not the selected applicant. I called Corey the selecting oficial and I asked him why. Corey stated that I interviewed very well and I was right on target for what he was looking for but he selected a guy that asked for a lateral and he had been a level 22 manager before. He was from outside the district and yet again I could not say anything. Unlike all the other times I kept my thoughts to myself I did not on this decision. I spoke to my staff and Jerry when I got the news. I told them that I worked very hard at Huntridge and they gave it to an outsider. I was told by Corey not to be discouraged that there will be other jobs coming up. I said to myself since there are other jobs coming up then why couldn't that guy have taken one of them when they come up. Once again, I had to accept the answer that was given to me.

To all the bosses that I showed up late for work in the passed year (Because it was not my behavior before now) I apologize rather you treated me fair or not. The condition that my body is in right now does not allow me to get up out of bed sometimes when I need too. It was a long time coming but as I say never the less I have to address it. If you are one that is passing judgment then just read upon Post Traumatic Stress Disorder and Major Depressive Disorder. It is by the grace of God that I have been able to perform as well as I have, but it did not get me promoted and my body has shut down and I don't have the strength, energy, or the mental stability to endure anymore. I have to heal my wounds properly. I have a family and a life but all has been affected because of the trauma the post ofice put me through. I tell you what you knocked a strong woman down to her knees and none of it was fair. I believe that I am a victim of discrimination and it is a shame especially in today's society that I have to state that claim. There is not one black manager, let alone female that is promoted in the city stations in Las Vegas. There was one, and he was forced to retire out of King Station and King Station is functioning very poorly under the leadership of Robert Reynosa and he's the Manager, Customer Services Operations. It is just not right. I don't want anyone to think that I have not made mistakes along the way and all my decisions were great and grand, because that's not true. I'm a human being who happens to be black and all I wanted was to be treated fairly and be promoted on my own merits. I did not ask anyone nor did I expect anyone to give me something for nothing, or promote me if I was a liability, all I wanted was to be treated fairly and be given my just due. I worked very hard for what I wanted but to no avail. Now I'm sick and I've been forced to ile an on the job injury and at least you can do is help me get well, I did not deserve this and my family does not deserve this. I have endured the Stress, even when I did not know it was Stress, for as long as I could now I have to take care of me and I can't worry about what somebody else may say or think.

Sincerely
Lola McGee

Statement on Notiication to My Immediate Supervisor of an Injury and Request for Medical Paperwork: CA-1 and CA-2

August 29, 2008

To Whom It May Concern:

I Lola McGee notiied Jerry Wilson, my acting postmaster, of my injury the night (8/25-26/08) I realized that I was injured from Stress. I asked Jerry to send me a CA-1 and a CA-2 in the mail to my home so that I could complete them. On 8/26/08 Jerry Wilson asked me, while I was on the phone with him, what was going on and I told him that I knew he needed information but I will put it in writing and that is what I have done with statements dating from 8/26/08 – 8/29/08.

Yesterday, 8/28/08 I went to the Las Vegas GMF to the injury compensation office and picked up a CA-1 and a CA-2 form because as of this date, Jerry Wilson has not mailed them to me.

Sincerely
Lola McGee

Statement Regarding My Call to Jerry Wilson on Completing My Reported Injury Paperwork that he Never Sent to Me CA-1 and CA-2

August 29, 2008

Today I called Jerry Wilson on his cell phone and I did not receive an answer. I then called Jerry at North Las Vegas Main Post Office and he was there. I stated to Jerry that this is Lola and I need to see you to get you the paperwork of the injury that happened on 8/25/08. I stated that I needed him to complete his portion and I wanted copies of everything.

Jerry replied by saying, it want be done today because I have a plane to catch in an hour and a half and I had all week to get it to him. I then CY, Jerry knows that I asked him to mail me the paperwork when I reported the injury. I then attempted to say something and abruptly but calmly, said okay thank you (This took place at 12:15pm today).

I then called the GMF to speak with Yul, and Lorraine told me that Yul wasn't here and neither is his secretary.

Next I called the GMF to speak with Shaun Mossman and was transferred to his office by Lorraine. I told Shaun that this is Lola McGee and I have gone through the chain of command but to know avail and I need to explain to him what Jerry told me about my paperwork on the injury claim. Shaun stated that he was not sure what I was talking about and have I talked with my POOM. I told Shaun that Yul was not at work. He said that I'll contact Yul for you what is your number and have him call you. I gave Shaun my phone number and hung up the phone.

Yul called me be within 5 to ten minutes and asked me what was going on and I explained to him what had taken place from my phone call to Jerry. I told Yul that he will find out everything that's going on with me when he gets the paperwork. I was concerned about getting the paperwork in and how I was going to be paid for the remaining four days of the week. Yul called me back and told me to take the paperwork to injury compensation at the GMF and they will give me a receipt of taking it in. I went to injury comp. and I now have signed copies of the paperwork and my 3971's were completed also.

Sincerely
Lola McGee

Jerry Wilson's September 2, 2008 statement for my claim filed on him threatening me on August 25, 2008 in my office between 9:00 a.m. and 11:00 a.m.—two pages.

Date: 09/02/2008

Subject: Statement, Lola Mcgee
CA-1, 09/02/2008

I started a detail as the OIC in North Las Vegas on 06/23/2008. On or about 07/02/2008, Craig Colton, Acting POOM2, called and stated to me that Lola Mcgee would be reporting as the Manager, Customer Services at Meadow Mesa Station in North Las Vegas on 08/08/2008. I had previously heard of Lola Mcgee but had never met her or knew of her background as a supervisor or manager. I had spoken with Lola Mcgee on 07/03/08, asking her to report to the North Las Vegas Main Office on 08/08/2008 so that I could introduce myself and go over some expectations with her. On 08/08/2008, Lola called me at around 0915 and stated that she was running late, it seemed very odd that for someone who was trying everything they could to get a promotion, that they would be late on the first day. I informed Lola that I expected her to be regular in attendance and to work on time. On 08/11/2008, Lola did not report to work until approx. 0930, she stated to me that her daughter had some issues, Lola had failed to call, I had asked how old her daughter was and she stated that she was 29 years old, I asked her if she was able to take care of herself. Lola stated that she was, I asked Lola that if she chose to report to work late and did not follow her assigned schedule, as a manager, how could she speak to her supervisors and employees with regards to addressing attendance issues, Lola stated that I was right and would correct the problem. Lola Mcgee was very difficult to speak with when it came to day to day issues with the operations, Lola made it very clear that she did not manage based on the policies and processes of the district, she made it very clear to me that she could do a better job based on her decisions. I made it clear that we would follow the policies, procedures and processes of the district and the service. Lola Mcgee had issues with when she wanted to report to work, her schedule was 0700 to 1600, I informed her that was thinking of changing her schedule to 0800 – 1700, she was adamant that she would be on time for work and asked me not too change her schedule. When Lola was informed that she did not get the Manager, Customer Services position at Huntridge Station in Las Vegas, she told me that she was considering filing a EEO because there were no black female managers in the city of Las Vegas. The following day, Lola did not report until 10:45, I asked her why she did not call me and why she was late, she stated that she went and spoke with someone about not getting Huntridge. I informed Lola that she needed to do that on her own time, I reminded Lola of the conversations that we had regarding her habits of not reporting to work on time, she stated that she did, I informed Lola that this would be her last chance that I would give her, if she reported to work late again, I would have no choice but to place her back down in her current EAS-17 position, once again, Lola assured me that she would be to work on time. With regards to Lola's allegation of a open ended threat, I very much dispute her contention of that, on 08/22/08, Lola called and asked for 3 additional SDO's for Saturday, 08/23/08, I informed Lola that the request was denied and that we would live with the mistakes that were made by herself and her supervisors regarding the schedule. I informed her that the request for SDO,s was submitted and we would follow what we had originally asked for. Lola became very agitated, I reminded Lola that the decision was mine as the OIC and we would operate based on that. Lola the contacted Yul Melonson and attempted to override my decision, Yul reminded Lola of the previous commitment made and denied her request. Yul allowed her to bring in 3 TE's at 0730AM rather than 1000AM, she the took it upon herself to bring in all 8 TE's at 0730AM, clearly not following Yul Melonson's direction. I expressed to Lola on 08/25/08 of my disappointment in her that she attempted to go over my head with Yul Melonson regarding the SDO request that I had already denied her. The six weeks that I worked with Lola Mcgee, it became very clear to me that she had issues with not getting a promotion in the city of Las Vegas and she was very displeased with a lot of people. Lola made it very clear to me that she did not agree with the decisions of others and the decision makers in the district, Lola clearly wanted to make her own decisions regardless of the policies and procedures that were in place by the Postal Service. I received a phone call at 12:32 AM on the morning of 08/26/2008 in my hotel room, I did not answer the call and listened to the message the next morning. Lola called around 0630AM on 08/26/2008, she stated to me that she would not be returning to work, that she would be filing a on the job injury for stress, I then informed Lola that I had to report this to the safety office, she then stated that when she turned in the CA1 and CA2, I would then know why, she then hung up the phone. In my opinion, I believe that Lola Mcgee has been planning this situation based on her displeasure with not being promoted in the city of Las Vegas. As the OIC in North Las Vegas, I have the administrative right to manage, set expectations, and make decisions based on the needs of the service. I set expectations with Lola Mcgee regarding her attendance issues, and her denial to follow the directions, policies and processes in place for the district and the Postal Service. Lola Mcgee made it clear to me of her displeasure of not being promoted and that she was going to do something about it, it is of my opinion that Lola Mcgee has been planning this and has finally implemented her plan, her allegations of an open door threat is just her allegation, clear expectations of her unwillingness to report to work on time and her choice not to follow the direction of the district is the root of the problem, it is clear that she is very unhappy of not being promoted and is making allegations that are not true for her benefit.

Jerry Wilson
OIC, North Las Vegas

Fax Cover Sheet For My Request to Amend
The Injury Date for My CA-2 Form From 8/25/08 to 9/2006 thru 8/18/08
Because the Injury Happened Over a Period of Time

September 4, 2008

To: Joni Payne/Injury Compensation = FAX NO. (702) 361-9404

From: Lola McGee = My home (702) 260-0876 Fax (702) 260-0876

* * * * *

September 11, 2008

My Response to Jerry Wilson's Statement
Dated 9/2/08 Regarding
CA-1 I Submitted for Stress Injury Dated 8/25/08

To: Injury Compensation/Department of Labor

I reported to my NLV-Meadow Mesa assignment on 7/9/08 and I was running late that morning but I called Jerry and he stated that it was okay but still come by the main office to see him first, so I did. As I recall, I was late approx three times I do not remember the specific time of arrival at the office but Jerry did speak to me about it on the second and third incident. Unfortunately, as I stated in my original statement dated 8/27/08 I now know why I started not being able to make it to work on time, once again I apologize.

Jerry stated in his 9/2/08 statement that I do not follow district processes and I think my decisions are better. This is not true and I would like for him to give me examples of what he means because the Nevada Sierra District operates processes and procedures that has to be followed are you will be written up for not being in compliance. I'm a professional woman who takes her job very seriously; and this has always been my character long before I ever got to the postal service. My resume states some of the accolades that I've received from following directions and being a team player. I find Jerry's statement of my work ethic untrue and I would like to know how he derived at making such a comment.

Jerry is mixing apples and oranges when he talks about changing my start time and me reporting to work on time. Jerry addressed with me about being to work on time and I agreed with him because as manager we set the example and that was my behavior until the past year I did not have an answer for it when it would periodically happen but I do now as I addressed it in my statement dated 8/27/08. Jerry came into my office one day while I was having a staff meeting and he stated that I would be starting at 8:00am because he wanted me at the office at 5:00pm when the carriers got back and I replied I can come in at 7:00am and still be here at 5:00pm when the carriers get back. My start time does not have to be changed for that reason because I worked long hours and even Saturdays during my postal career so it is not nothing new.

I want to say this as respectful as I possible can but Jerry is just out right lying in his statement when he states that I told him that I was going to file an EEO when I did not get Huntridge Station. Just think about it, does it make any logical since for me to confide in Jerry Wilson a person whom I just met and we are not the best match working together but I respect his decisions because he is the boss. Jerry Wilson needs to be put under oath and be asked if I told him that I was going to file an EEO, and I believe he got the notion of no black women in Las Vegas because he saw my statement that I wrote on 8/27/08. This is really reaching and it is no regard for the condition that I'm in. When you make a mistake be man or woman enough to admit your wrongs. I have never told a living being that I was going to file an EEO on Las Vegas because to tell you the truth I did not even know I could until the other day when I spoke with an attorney. I thought that the event had to be within a 45 day time frame and I knew that the Las Vegas issue was over a two year period. **Jerry Wilson Out Right Lied On Me and it's Not Fair; And It Should Not Be Tolerated Because Somebody Just Might Believe Him.** Also, Jerry stated that I was late the next day and I did not report until 10:45am. I'll tell you the truth about what happened on 8/19/08. I received the notice from Corey Richards on 8/18/08, which I stated in my statement, and I had a very bad evening I took my medication and I woke up late even after setting my alarm. I was depressed, refer to my statement please. Jerry stated that I go to work around 10:45 I don't believe that to be true but I cannot say anything about it because I do not know what time I actually arrived. However, I did not, I'll repeat, I did not tell Jerry Wilson that I went to speak with someone about not getting Huntridge. I told Jerry that I was distraught over not getting the job and they gave it to an outsider, but I know that I still have a responsibility and it will not happen anymore. Jerry never said to me that he was going to place me back at my supervisor position EAS-17. Jerry has never said that to me. He has said that I need you here and you need to set an example and I told him that I truly understand and I will be here on time. I can recall three occasions from 7/9/08 -8/25/08 and I'm not proud of it but at least I have answers now.

Jerry disputes my statement that he gave me an opened ended threat well all I have to say is it does not surprise me because he has said so many things that were not true and this is not different. **As I Stated In My 8/26/08 Statement Jerry Wilson Made An Open Ended Threat To Me "You Continue To Go Over My Head With Craig And Yul And I'm Going To Do Something About It."** Please refer to my statement regarding trying to contact Jerry and leaving a message at Yul's office and Yul returned my call and I explained to Yul that it was ok because I have talked with Jerry already. Yul was persistent with wanting to know what was the call regarding and what was going on in North Las Vegas, he could detect something in my voice, after all I worked for Yul from 4/1/07 – 1/12/08 at the NLV Main Post Office.

Jerry makes a lot of assumptions about who I like in Las Vegas in the district and following processes and procedures and it appears to me that all he was trying to do in his statement is discredit me rather that tell the truth, because Jerry and I only had one conversation about me being upset and that was when I disclosed to him about the district hiring an outsider. I kept my relationship with Jerry professional and tried to work with him on making North Los Vegas, as a whole, a better operating city. I respect Jerry as my boss and any thing he thinks I did intentionally to harm him I apologize because that is not my nature. I come to work to make a positive impact, not for fun or wasting my time conjuring up things to say about people. However, I take pride in having integrity.

Sincerely
Lola McGee

CA-1 form for Traumatic Injury on a specific date, time, and place, showing the filing of the injury and me being the employee meeting the criteria.

Instructions for Completing Form CA-1

Complete all items on your section of the form. If additional space is required to explain or clarify any point, attach a supplemental statement to the form. Some of the items on the form which may require further clarification are explained below.

Employee (Or person acting on the employees' behalf)

13) Cause of injury

Describe in detail how and why the injury occurred. Give appropriate details (e.g.: if you fell, how far did you fall and in what position did you land?)

14) Nature of Injury

Give a complete description of the condition(s) resulting from your injury. Specify the right or left side if applicable (e.g., fractured left leg: cut on right index finger).

15) Election of COP/Leave

If you are disabled for work as a result of this injury and filed CA-1 within thirty days of the injury, you may be entitled to receive continuation of pay (COP) from your employing agency. COP is paid for up to 45 calendar days of disability, and is not charged against sick or annual leave. If you elect sick or annual leave you may not claim compensation to repurchase leave used during the 45 days of COP entitlement.

Supervisor

At the time the form is received, complete the receipt of notice of injury and give it to the employee. In addition to completing items 17 through 39, the supervisor is responsible for obtaining the witness statement in Item 16 and for filling in the proper codes in shaded boxes a, b, and c on the front of the form. If medical expense or lost time is incurred or expected, the completed form should be sent to OWCP within 10 working days after it is received.

The supervisor should also submit any other information or evidence pertinent to the merits of this claim.

If the employing agency controverts COP, the employee should be notified and the reason for controversion explained to him or her.

17) Agency name and address of reporting office

The name and address of the office to which correspondence from OWCP should be sent (if applicable, the address of the personnel or compensation office).

18) Duty station street address and zip code

The address and zip code of the establishment where the employee actually works.

19) Employers Retirement Coverage.

Indicate which retirement system the employee is covered under.

30) Was injury caused by third party?

A third party is an individual or organization (other than the injured employee or the Federal government) who is liable for the injury. For instance, the driver of a vehicle causing an accident in which an employee is injured, the owner of a building where unsafe conditions cause an employee to fall, and a manufacturer whose defective product causes an employee's injury, could all be considered third parties to the injury.

32) Name and address of physician first providing medical care

The name and address of the physician who first provided medical care for this injury. If initial care was given by a nurse or other health professional (not a physician) in the employing agency's health unit or clinic, indicate this on a separate sheet of paper.

33) First date medical care received

The date of the first visit to the physician listed in item 31.

36) If the employing agency controverts continuation of pay, state the reason in detail.

COP may be controverted (disputed) for any reason; however, the employing agency may refuse to pay COP only if the controversion is based upon one of the nine reasons given below:

a) The disability was not caused by a traumatic injury.

b) The employee is a volunteer working without pay or for nominal pay, or a member of the office staff of a former President;

c) The employee is not a citizen or a resident of the United States or Canada;

d) The injury occurred off the employing agency's premises and the employee was not involved in official "off premise" duties;

e) The injury was proximately caused by the employee's willful misconduct, intent to bring about injury or death to self or another person, or intoxication;

f) The injury was not reported on Form CA-1 within 30 days following the injury;

g) Work stoppage first occurred 45 days or more following the injury;

h) The employee initially reported the injury after his or her employment was terminated; or

i) The employee is enrolled in the Civil Air Patrol, Peace Corps, Youth Conservation Corps, Work Study Programs, or other similar groups.

Employing Agency - Required Codes

Box a (Occupation Code), Box b (Type Code), Box c (Source Code), OSHA Site Code

The Occupational Safety and Health Administration (OSHA) requires all employing agencies to complete these items when reporting an injury. The proper codes may be found in OSHA Booklet 2014, "Recordkeeping and Reporting Guidelines.

OWCP Agency Code

This is a four-digit (or four digit plus two letter) code used by OWCP to identify the employing agency. The proper code may be obtained from your personnel or compensation office, or by contacting OWCP.

Form CA-1
Rev. Apr. 1999

05/14/2010 16:28 562--531-4400 FEDEX OFFICE 0583 PAGE 15

Traumatic Injury and Claim for Continuation of Pay/Compensation

U.S. Department of Labor
Employment Standards Administration
Office of Workers' Compensation Programs

Employee: Please complete all boxes 1 - 15 below. Do not complete shaded areas.
Witness: Complete bottom section 16.
Employing Agency (Supervisor or Compensation Specialist): Complete shaded boxes a, b, and c.

Employee Data

1. Name of employee (Last, First, Middle) McGee Lola Bonitta
2. Social Security Number
3. Date of birth Mo. Day Yr. 7 7
4. Sex ☐ Male ☒ Female
5. Home telephone
6. Grade as of date of injury CAS – 22 Level Step
7. Employee's home mailing address (include city, state, and ZIP code) 7582 Cypress Tree St. Las Vegas, NV 89123
8. Dependents ☐ Wife, Husband ☐ Children under 18 years ☐ Other N/A

Description of Injury

9. Place where injury occurred (e.g. 2nd floor, Main Post Office Bldg., 12th & Pine) North Las Vegas – Meadow Mesa Station
10. Date injury occurred Mo. Day Yr. 8 25 08 Time approx. between 9:00 – 11:00 ☒ a.m. ☐ p.m.
11. Date of this notice Mo. Day Yr. 8-25-26-08
12. Employee's occupation Permanent = Supervisor Cust. Services Acting = Manager Cust. Services
13. Cause of injury (Describe what happened and why) Jerry Wilson gave me an open ended threat "you continue to go over my head with Craig and Yul and I'm going to do something about it. I spoke to Craig once about variance projections and Yul about the condition of the office.
14. Nature of injury (identify both the injury and the part of the body, e.g., fracture of left leg) Stress = body, head shut down and I'm not functioning to my capability at this time, please refer to my statement dated 8/26/08 & 8/29/08

a. Occupation code | b. Type code | c. Source code | OWCP Use - NOI Code

Employee Signature

15. I certify, under penalty of law, that the injury described above was sustained in performance of duty as an employee of the United States Government and that it was not caused by my willful misconduct, intent to injure myself or another person, nor by my intoxication. I hereby claim medical treatment, if needed, and the following, as checked below, while disabled for work:

☒ a. Continuation of regular pay (COP) not to exceed 45 days and compensation for wage loss if disability for work continues beyond 45 days. If my claim is denied, I understand that the continuation of my regular pay shall be charged to sick or annual leave, or be deemed an overpayment within the meaning of 5 USC 5584.

☐ b. Sick and/or Annual Leave

I hereby authorize any physician or hospital (or any other person, institution, corporation, or government agency) to furnish any desired information to the U.S. Department of Labor, Office of Workers' Compensation Programs (or to its official representative). This authorization also permits any official representative of the Office to examine and to copy any records concerning me.

Signature of employee or person acting on his/her behalf Lola McGee **Date** 8/29/08

Any person who knowingly makes any false statement, misrepresentation, concealment of fact or any other act of fraud to obtain compensation as provided by the FECA or who knowingly accepts compensation to which that person is not entitled is subject to civil or administrative remedies as well as felony criminal prosecution and may, under appropriate criminal provisions, be punished by a fine or imprisonment or both.

Have your supervisor complete the receipt attached to this form and return it to you for your records.

Witness Statement

16. Statement of witness (Describe what you saw, heard, or know about this injury)

RECEIVED
SEP 04 2008
HEALTH & RESOURCES MANAGEMENT

Name of witness | Signature of witness | Date signed

Address | City | State | ZIP Code

Form CA-1
Rev. Jan. 1997

05/14/2010 16:28 562--531-4400 FEDEX OFFICE 0583 PAGE 16

Federal Employee's Notice of Traumatic Injury and Claim for Continuation of Pay/Compensation

U.S. Department of Labor
Employment Standards Administration
Office of Workers' Compensation Programs

Employee: Please complete all boxes 1 - 15 below. Do not complete shaded areas.
Witness: Complete bottom section 16.
Employing Agency (Supervisor or Compensation Specialist): Complete shaded boxes a, b, and c.

Employee Data

1. Name of employee (Last, First, Middle): McGee Lola Bonitta
2. Social Security Number:
3. Date of birth Mo. Day Yr.: 7 7
4. Sex: ☐ Male ☒ Female
5. Home telephone:
6. Grade as of date of injury Level Step: EAS - 22
7. Employee's home mailing address (include city, state, and ZIP code): 7582 Cypress Tree St. Las Vegas, NV 89123
8. Dependents: ☐ Wife, Husband ☐ Children under 18 years ☐ Other N/A

Description of Injury

9. Place where injury occurred (e.g. 2nd floor, Main Post Office Bldg., 12th & Pine): North Las Vegas - Meadow Mesa Station
10. Date injury occurred Mo. Day Yr.: 8 25 08 — Time: approx. between 9:00 - 11:00 ☒ a.m. ☐ p.m.
11. Date of this notice Mo. Day Yr.: 8-25-26-08
12. Employee's occupation: Permanent = Supervisor Cust. Services; Acting = Manager Cust. Services
13. Cause of injury (Describe what happened and why): Jerry Wilson gave me an open ended threat "You continue to go over my head with Craig and Yul and I'm going to do something about it. I spoke to Craig once about variance projections and Yul about the condition of the office.
14. Nature of injury (identify both the injury and the part of the body, e.g., fracture of left leg): stress = body, head shut down and I'm not ~~functioning to my capability at this time.~~ Please refer to my statement dated 8/26/08 & 8/29/08

a. Occupation code | b. Type code | c. Source code | OWCP Use - NOI Code

Employee Signature

15. I certify, under penalty of law, that the injury described above was sustained in performance of duty as an employee of the United States Government and that it was not caused by my willful misconduct, intent to injure myself or another person, nor by my intoxication. I hereby claim medical treatment, if needed, and the following, as checked below, while disabled for work:

☒ a. Continuation of regular pay (COP) not to exceed 45 days and compensation for wage loss if disability for work continues beyond 45 days. If my claim is denied, I understand that the continuation of my regular pay shall be charged to sick or annual leave, or be deemed an overpayment within the meaning of 5 USC 5584.

☐ b. Sick and/or Annual Leave

I hereby authorize any physician or hospital (or any other person, institution, corporation, or government agency) to furnish any desired information to the U.S. Department of Labor, Office of Workers' Compensation Programs (or to its official representative). This authorization also permits any official representative of the Office to examine and to copy any records concerning me.

Signature of employee or person acting on his/her behalf Lola McGee **Date** 8/29/08

Any person who knowingly makes any false statement, misrepresentation, concealment of fact or any other act of fraud to obtain compensation as provided by the FECA or who knowingly accepts compensation to which that person is not entitled is subject to civil or administrative remedies as well as felony criminal prosecution and may, under appropriate criminal provisions, be punished by a fine or imprisonment or both.

Have your supervisor complete the receipt attached to this form and return it to you for your records.

Witness Statement

16. Statement of witness (Describe what you saw, heard, or know about this injury)

RECEIVED
SEP 04 2008
HEALTH & RESOURCES MANAGEMENT

Name of witness | Signature of witness | Date signed

Address | City | State | ZIP Code

Form CA-1
Rev. Jan. 1997

05/14/2010 16:28 562--531-4400 FEDEX OFFICE 0583 PAGE 17

Supervisor's Report

17. Agency name and address of repor U.S. POSTAL SERVICE
INJURY COMPENSATION OFFICE
1001 E. SUNSET ROAD
LAS VEGAS, NV 89199-9998

OWCP Agency Code 566300

OSHA Site Code 89031

18. Employee's duty station (Street address and ZIP Code) Meadow Mesa Station 89031
ZIP Code

19. Employee's Retirement coverage ☐ CSRS ☒ FERS ☐ Other, (identify)

20. Regular work hours From: : ☐ a.m. ☐ p.m. To: : ☐ a.m. ☐ p.m.

21. Regular work schedule ☐ Sun. ☐ Mon. ☐ Tues. ☐ Wed. ☐ Thurs. ☐ Fri. ☐ Sat.

22. Date of injury Mo. Day Yr. 08 26 08

23. Date notice received Mo. Day Yr. 09 02 08

24. Date stopped work Mo. Day Yr. 08 26 08 Time : ☐ a.m. ☐ p.m.

25. Date pay stopped Mo. Day Yr. NA

26. Date 45 day period began Mo. Day Yr. 08 26 08

27. Date returned to work Mo. Day Yr. Time : ☐ a.m. ☐ p.m.

28. Was employee injured in performance of duty? ☐ Yes ☐ No (If "No," explain)

Unknown

29. Was injury caused by employee's willful misconduct, intoxication, or intent to injure self or another? ☐ Yes (If "Yes," explain) ☐ No

30. Was injury caused by third party? ☐ Yes ☒ No (If "No," go to item 32.)

31. Name and address of third party (include city, state, and ZIP code)

32. Name and address of physician first providing medical care (include city, state, ZIP code)
Reeds Nursing
9402 W. Lake Mead Blvd.
Las Vegas, Nv. 89134

33. First date medical care received Mo. Day Yr. 08 27 08

34. Do medical reports show employee is disabled for work? ☒ Yes ☐ No

35. Does your knowledge of the facts about this injury agree with statements of the employee and/or witness? ☐ Yes ☒ No (If "No," explain)

36. If the employing agency controverts continuation of pay, state the reason in detail.
See Attached Statements

37. Pay rate when employee stopped work $ Per

Signature of Supervisor and Filing Instructions

37. A supervisor who knowingly certifies to any false statement, misrepresentation, concealment of fact, etc., in respect of this claim may also be subject to appropriate felony criminal prosecution.

I certify that the information given above and that furnished by the employee on the reverse of this form is true to the best of my knowledge with the following exception:

Jerry A. Wilson
Name of Supervisor (Type or print)

[signature] 09-03-08
Signature of Supervisor Date

O.T.C - North Las Vegas 702-649-2368
Supervisor's Title Office phone

38. Filing instructions
☐ No lost time and no medical expense: Place this form in employee's medical folder (SF-66-D)
☐ No lost time, medical expense incurred or expected: forward this form to OWCP
☐ Lost time covered by leave, LWOP, or COP: forward this form to OWCP
☐ First Aid Injury

Form CA-1
Rev. Jan. 1997

CA-2 form for Occupational Disease, which happens over a period of time consistently, which causes injury or illness, shows the employee requirements and I met with the criteria with my correspondence.

INS, 'UCTIONS FOR COMPLETING FORM CA-2 [redacted]

Complete all items on your section of the form. If additional space is required to explain or clarify any point, attach a supplemental statement to the form. In addition to the information requested on the form, both the employee and the supervisor are required to submit additional evidence as described below. If this evidence is not submitted along with the form, the responsible party should explain the reason for the delay and state when the additional evidence will be submitted.

Employee (or person acting on the Employee's behalf)

Complete items 1 through 18 and submit the form to the employee's supervisor along with the statement and medical reports described below. Be sure to obtain the Receipt of Notice of Disease or Illness completed by the supervisor at the time the form is submitted.

1) Employee's statement

In a separate narrative statement attached to the form, the employee must submit the following information:

a) A detailed history of the disease or illness from the date it started.

b) Complete details of the conditions of employment which are believed to be responsible for the disease or illness.

c) A description of specific exposures to substances or stressful conditions causing the disease or illness, including locations where exposure or stress occurred, as well as the number of hours per day and days per week of such exposure or stress.

d) Identification of the part of the body affected. (If disability is due to a heart condition, give complete details of all activities for one week prior to the attack with particular attention to the final 24 hours of such period.)

e) A statement as to whether the employee ever suffered a similar condition. If so, provide full details of onset, history, and medical care received, along with names and addresses of physicians rendering treatment.

2) Medical report

a) Dates of examination or treatment.

b) History given to the physician by the employee.

c) Detailed description of the physician's findings.

d) Results of x-rays, laboratory tests, etc.

e) Diagnosis.

f) Clinical course of treatment.

g) Physician's opinion as to whether the disease or illness was caused or aggravated by the employment, along with an explanation of the basis for this opinion. (Medical reports that do not explain the basis for the physician's opinion are given very little weight in adjudicating the claim.)

3) Wage loss

If you have lost wages or used leave for this illness, Form CA-7 should also be submitted.

Supervisor (Or appropriate official in the employing agency)

At the time the form is received, complete the Receipt of Notice of Disease or Illness and give it to the employee. In addition to completing items 19 through 34, the supervisor is responsible for filling in the proper codes in shaded boxes a, b, and c on the front of the form. If medical expense or lost time is incurred or expected, the completed form must be sent to OWCP within ten working days after it is received. In a separate narrative statement attached to the form, the supervisor must:

a) Describe in detail the work performed by the employee. Identify fumes, chemicals, or other irritants or situations that the employee was exposed to which allegedly caused the condition. State the nature, extent, and duration of the exposure, including hours per days and days per week, requested above.

b) Attach copies of all medical reports (including x-ray reports and laboratory data) on file for the employee.

c) Attach a record of the employee's absence from work caused by any similar disease or illness. Have the employee state the reason for each absence.

d) Attach statements from each co-worker who has first-hand knowledge about the employee's condition and its cause. (The co-workers should state how such knowledge was obtained.)

e) Review and comment on the accuracy of the employee's statement requested above.

The supervisor should also submit any other information or evidence pertinent to the merits of this claim.

Item Explanation: Some of the items on the form which may require further clarification are explained below.

14. Nature of the disease or illness
Give a complete description of the disease or illness. Specify the left or right side if applicable (e.g., rash on left leg; carpal tunnel syndrome, right wrist).

19. Agency name and address of reporting office
The name and address of the off ice to which correspondence from OWCP should be sent (if applicable, the address of the personnel or compensation office).

23. Name and address of physician first providing medical care
The name and address of the physician who first provided medical care for this injury. If initial care was given by a nurse or other health professional (not a physician) in the employing agency's health unit or clinic, indicate this on a separate sheet of paper.

24. First date medical care received
The date of the first visit to the physician listed in item 23.

32. Employee's Retirement Coverage.
Indicate which retirement system the employee is covered under.

33. Was the injury caused by third party?
A third party is an individual or organization (other than the injured employee or the Federal government) who is liable for the disease. For instance, manufacturer of a chemical to which an employee was exposed might be considered a third party if improper instructions were given by the manufacturer for use of the chemical.

Employing Agency - Required Codes

Box a (Occupational Code), Box b. (Type Code), Box c (Source Code), OSHA Site Code
The Occupational Safety and Health Administration (OSHA) requires all employing agencies to complete these items when reporting an injury. The proper codes may be found in OSHA Booklet 2014, Record Keeping and Reporting Guidelines.

OWCP Agency Code
This is a four digit (or four digit two letter) code used by OWCP to identify the employing agency. The proper code may be obtained from your personnel or compensation office, or by contacting OWCP.

• U.S. GPO: 2001480-204/59062

Form CA-2
Rev.Jan.1997

05/14/2010 16:28 562--531-4400 FEDEX OFFICE 0583 PAGE 11

and Claim for Compensation

Employment Standards Administration
Office of Workers' Compensation Programs

Employee: Please complete all boxes 1 - 18 below. Do not complete shaded areas.
Employing Agency (Supervisor or Compensation Specialist): Complete shaded boxes a, b, and c.

Employee Data

1. Name of employee (Last, First, Middle): McGee Lola Bonitta
2. Social Security Number:
3. Date of birth Mo. Day Yr.: 7 7
4. Sex: Female
5. Home telephone: ( )
6. Grade as of date of last exposure Level Step: EAS-22/Acting
7. Employee's home mailing address (include city, state, and ZIP Code): 7582 Cypress Tree Street Las Vegas, NV 89123
8. Dependents
   - ☐ Wife, Husband
   - ☐ Children under 18 years
   - ☐ Other N/A

Claim Information

9. Employee's occupation: Permanent= Supervisor, Customer Services NLV-Main Acting= Manager, Customer Services NLV-Meadow Mesa

a. Occupation code

10. Location (address) where you worked when disease or illness occurred (include city, state, and ZIP Code): 4904 Camino Al Norte North Las Vegas, NV 89031 (2005) ... Swenson St. Las Vegas, NV 89119 (2006)
11. Date you first became aware of disease or illness Mo. Day Yr.: 8 25 08
12. Date you first realized the disease or illness was caused or aggravated by your employment Mo. Day Yr.: 8 25 08
13. Explain the relationship to your employment, and why you came to this realization: Please refer to my statement dated 8/27/08, 8/26/08 and 8/29/08 for specific details. For the passed 1½ thru 2 years I have endured tremendouse unfair and discrimination tactics and I allowed the Post Office to continue to use me until my body shut down and now I am disabled with health conditions.
14. Nature of disease or illness: Post Traumatic Stress Disorder Major Depressive Disorder

b. OWCP disease code c. Type code / Source code

15. If this notice and claim was not filed with the employing agency within 30 days after date shown above in item #12, explain the reason for the delay: This report would have been filed sooner than now if my Immediate Supervisor Jerry Wilson had sent me the papers.
16. If the statement requested in item 1 of the attached instructions is not submitted with this form, explain reason for delay.

RECEIVED
SEP 0 4 2008
HEALTH & RESOURCES MANAGEMENT

17. If the medical reports requested in item 2 of attached instructions are not submitted with this form, explain reason for delay.

Employee Signature

18. I certify, under penalty of law, that the disease or illness described above was the result of my employment with the United States Government, and that it was not caused by my willful misconduct, intent to injure myself or another person, nor by my intoxication. I hereby claim medical treatment, if needed, and other benefits provided by the Federal Employees' Compensation Act.

I hereby authorize any physician or hospital (or any other person, institution, corporation, or government agency) to furnish any desired information to the U.S. Department of Labor, Office of Workers' Compensation Programs (or to its official representative). This authorization also permits any official representative of the Office to examine and to copy any records concerning me.

Signature of employee or person acting on his/her behalf: Lola McGee Date 8/29/08

Have your supervisor complete the receipt attached to this form and return it to you for your records.

Any person who knowingly makes any false statement, misrepresentation, concealment of fact or any other act of fraud to obtain compensation as provided by the FECA or who knowingly accepts compensation to which that person is not entitled is subject to civil or administrative remedies as well as felony criminal prosecution and may, under appropriate criminal provisions, be punished by a fine or imprisonment or both.

For sale by the Superintendent of Documents, U.S. Government Printing Office, Washington, DC 20402

Form CA-2
Rev. Jan. 1997

05/14/2010 16:28 562--531-4400 FEDEX OFFICE 0583 PAGE 12

ial Supervisor's Report of Occupational Disease: Please complete information requested below

ervisor's Report

Agency name and address: U.S. POSTAL SERVICE / INJURY COMPENSATION OFFICE / 1001 E. SUNSET ROAD / LAS VEGAS, NV 89199-9998

ZIP Code 89431

OWCP Agency Code 5L6300

OSHA Site Code 894431

Employee's duty station (Street address and ZIP Code) Meadow Mesa Station 89431 ZIP Code

Regular work hours From: 07 00 ☒ a.m. ☐ p.m. To: 16 00 ☐ a.m. ☒ p.m.

22. Regular work schedule ☐ Sun. ☐ Mon. ☐ Tues. ☐ Wed. ☐ Thurs. ☐ Fri. ☐ Sat.

Name and address of physician first providing medical care (include city, state, ZIP code)
Leeds Nursing
9402 W. Lakemead
North Las Vegas NV. 89431

24. First date medical care received Mo. Day Yr. 08 27 08

25. Do medical reports show employee is disabled for work? ☒ Yes ☐ No

Date employee first reported condition to supervisor Mo. Day Yr. 06 26 08

27. Date and hour employee stopped work Mo. Day Yr. 06 26 08 Time 07 00 ☒ a.m. ☐ p.m.

Date and ... stopped Mo. Day Yr. N/A Time ☐ a.m. ☐ p.m.

Date employee was first ... condition ... alleged ... disease or illness Mo. Day Yr.

Date returned to work Mo. Day Yr. Time : ☐ a.m. ☐ p.m.

If employee has returned to work and work assignment has changed, describe new duties

Employee's Retirement Coverage ☐ CSRS ☒ FERS ☐ Other (Specify)

Was injury caused by third party? ☐ Yes ☒ No If "No," go to Item 35.

34. Name and address of third party (include city, state, and ZIP Code)

nature of Supervisor

A supervisor who knowingly certifies to any false statement, misrepresentation, concealment of fact, etc., in respect to this claim may also be subject to appropriate felony criminal prosecution.

I certify that the information given above and that furnished by the employee on the reverse of this form is true to the best of my knowledge with the following exception:

Jerry A. Wilson
ne of Supervisor (Type or print)

[signature] 09-03-08
nature of Supervisor Date

OIC - North Las Vegas 702-649-2658
ervisor's Title Office phone

Form CA-2
Rev. Jan. 1997

05/14/2010 16:28 562--531-4400 FEDEX OFFICE 0583 PAGE 13

Claim for Compensation

Employment Standards Administration
Office of Workers' Compensation Programs

oyee: Please complete all boxes 1 - 18 below. Do not complete shaded areas.
oying Agency (Supervisor or Compensation Specialist): Complete shaded boxes a, b, and c.

loyee Data

me of employee (Last, First, Middle): McGee Lola Bonitta

2. Social Security Number

te of birth Mo. Day Yr.: 7 7

4. Sex: Female

5. Home telephone

6. Grade as of date of last exposure: Level EAS-22 / Step Acting

ployee's home mailing address (include city, state, and ZIP Code):
582 Cypress Tree Street
as Vegas, NV 89123

8. Dependents
- ☐ Wife, Husband
- ☐ Children under 18 years
- ☐ Other N/A

Information

ployee's occupation:
rmanent = Supervisor, Customer Services NLV-Main
ting = Manager, Customer Services NLV-Meadow Mesa

Occupation code

cation (address) where you worked when disease or illness occurred (include city, state, and ZIP Code):
704 Camino Al Norte North Las Vegas NV 89031 (2008)
975 Swenson St. Las Vegas NV 89119 (2006)

11. Date you first became aware of disease or illness: Mo. Day Yr. 8 25 08

te you first realized e disease or illness as caused or aggravated your employment: Mo. Day Yr. 8 25 08

Explain the relationship to your employment, and why you came to this realization:
Please refer to my statement dated 8/27/08 8/26/08 and 8/29/08 for specific detai
the passed 1½ thru 2 years I have endured tremendouse fair and discrimination tactics and I allowed the Post Office to tinue to use me until my body shut down and now I am disabled with health conditions.

ture of disease or illness:
t Traumatic Stress Disorder
lajor Depressive Disorder

ICD-9 code / OWCP code

is notice and claim was not filed with the employing agency within 30 days after date shown above in item #12, explain the reason for the ay.
This report would have been filed sooner than now f my Immediate Supervisor Jerry Wilson had sent me the paper

e statement requested in item 1 of the attached instructions is not submitted with this form, explain reason for delay.

e medical reports requested in item 2 of attached instructions are not submitted with this form, explain reason for delay.

ee Signature

rtify, under penalty of law, that the disease or illness described above was the result of my employment with the United States ernment, and that it was not caused by my willful misconduct, intent to injure myself or another person, nor by my intoxication. reby claim medical treatment, if needed, and other benefits provided by the Federal Employees' Compensation Act.

reby authorize any physician or hospital (or any other person, institution, corporation, or government agency) to furnish any ired information to the U.S. Department of Labor, Office of Workers' Compensation Programs (or to its official representative). authorization also permits any official representative of the Office to examine and to copy any records concerning me.

re of employee or person acting on his/her behalf: [signature] Date 8/29/08

ur supervisor complete the receipt attached to this form and return it to you for your records.

son who knowingly makes any false statement, misrepresentation, concealment of fact or any other act of fraud to obtain compensation as d by the FECA or who knowingly accepts compensation to which that person is not entitled is subject to civil or administrative remedies as elony criminal prosecution and may, under appropriate criminal provisions, be punished by a fine or imprisonment or both.

For sale by the Superintendent of Documents, U.S. Government Printing Office, Washington, DC 20402 — Form CA-2 Rev. Jan. 1997

I later called to make an appointment with the doctor my daughter referred me to. The earliest she had was Wednesday, August 27, 2008. I took it.

Dr. Reed's Letter taking me off work from my August 25, 2008 injury by Jerry Wilson

Reed's Nursing Educational Services Inc.

August 27, 2008

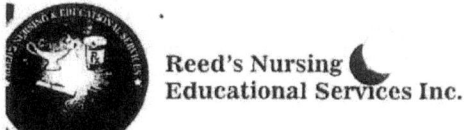

To Whom It May Concern,

Lola McGee has been under my care since 8-26-08 and is being treated for Post Traumatic Stress Disorder and Major Depressive Disorder. She is unable to return to work until her condition improves.

Sincerely,

Mary J. Reed PhD, APN

Mary J. Reed PhD, APN

Kayenta Therapy Center · 9402 W. Lake Mead Blvd. · Las Vegas, NV 89134
Tel: (702)341-0010 · Fax: (702)254-7830
drreed@nursing-edu.biz · www.nursing-edu.biz

00261

Formal Complaint
Page 107 of 244

On August 27, 2008, I was taken off work until further notice. No time period was set. I was diagnosed with Post-Traumatic Stress Disorder (PTSD), Major Depression, Anxiety, Panic Attacks, Panic Disorder, and later Agoraphobia. I still had heart palpitations, the choking cough resurfaced, and I experienced head shocks.

My family and my life were affected by the trauma the post office put me through. You knocked a strong woman down to her knees, and none of it was fair. I believe I am a victim of discrimination, and it is a shame, especially in today's society that I have to state that claim. There was not one African-American manager, let alone female, who was promoted in the city stations in Las Vegas. There was one, and he was forced to retire out of King Station, and King Station was functioning very poorly under the leadership of Robert Reynosa, the Manager, Customer Services Operations. It just was not right. I don't want anyone to think that I have not made mistakes along the way, and all my decisions were great and grand, because that's not true. I'm a human being which happens to be African-American and I only wanted to be treated fairly and promoted based on my own merits. I did not ask anyone nor did I expect anyone to give me something for nothing, or promote me if I was a liability. To be treated fairly and give my just due, was all I strived for. I worked very hard for what I wanted, but to no avail. Now, I'm sick and was forced to file an on-the-job injury, and the least you can do is help me get well. I did not deserve this, and my family does not deserve this. I have endured the stress—even when I did not know it was stress—for as long as I could. Now I have to endure the pain that the stress has brought to my life, and fight hard to recapture the life I once had. What anyone else thinks of me, at this point, is not for me to worry about.

In October 2008, I was diagnosed with Peripheral Sensory Neuropathy-Nerve Damage to both lower and upper extremities, Hearing Loss, Vision Impaired, and Lumbar Radiculopathy. Since then I have experienced blindness on two occasions in my right eye. I was told by the Orthomologist that the problem resulted from my brain. As you remember earlier I told you that something happened to my brain on 8/25/08 when I was threatened by Jerry Wilson, OIC North Las Vegas. In addition, I have tender, excruciating pain in between my buttocks.

I want it to be noted that the United States Postal Service has A Zero Tolerance Policy that is specifically detailed to include words, and jest. However there was no investigation into Jerry's threats.

UNITED STATES POSTAL SERVICE

June 1, 2006

SUBJECT: ZERO TOLERANCE POLICY STATEMENT

MEMORANDUM FOR: ALL EMPLOYEES
Nevada-Sierra District

A postal employee has a right to perform his or her assigned duties in an atmosphere free of threats, assaults, and other acts of workplace violence. We are committed in the effort to ensure a safe working environment for all employees.

Threats or assaults made directly or indirectly toward any employee or postal customer, even in the jest, will not be tolerated. This misconduct causes very real concern and apprehension on the part of people to whom this type of action is directed.

This zero tolerance policy places all employees on notice that threats, assaults, and other acts of violence committed against other employees or customers will result in severe disciplinary action up to and including removal from the Postal Service. Any employee who has been subjected to a threat or assault is by this policy instructed to immediately report the incident to a manager or supervisor and to the Inspection Service. Employees are also encouraged to report any unusual situation that has the potential to cause workplace violence. Threats of suicide are considered acts of violence. Reports to the Inspection Service, at the request of the employee who reports the incident, will be handled anonymously.

Below are definitions to help you understand and clarify when a threat, assault, or other acts of workplace violence have occurred:

Threat (broadly defined) -- a statement or act intended to inflict harm or injury on any person, or on his or her property. Threats also include words or actions intended to intimidate another person or to interfere with the performance of his or her official duties (e.g. standing in front of a corridor with a menacing posture and not permitting another person access to load a postal vehicle).

Assault (broadly defined) -- any willful attempt to inflict injury upon the person of another, when coupled with an apparent ability to do so, or any intentional display of force that would give the victim reason to fear or expect immediately bodily harm. Note: an assault may be committed without touching, striking, or doing bodily harm to another person (e.g. throwing a brick at a person that does not actually strike the person).

Violence is not limited to fatalities or physical injuries. It is recognized that any intentional words, acts, or action(s) meant to provoke another can escalate and result in injury if not immediately and appropriately addressed by management.

Johnray Egelhoff
District Manager

Lee A. Jordan
Senior Plant Manager

I want it to be noted that the claim for injury on August 25, 2008 was controverted by Grady Griffin and the United States Department of Labor denied the claim; and, their focus was on stress in the office opposed to the threat I received from Jerry Wilson. Grady Griffin stated that it was stressful but I could have refused to be on detail. Grady was not speaking logical because you would not be promoted if you refused details nor had he refused one that he wanted to get a promotion from. I was put off work on August 27, 2008.

Functioning after work 2006 - 2008!!

I was working at Meadow Mesa in April 2007 when a carrier who happened to be an official of the National Association of Letter Carriers Union took it upon himself to take his hand and cup an acting manager's mouth to shut her up. The manager sustained injury to her mouth and the carrier, after a complete and thorough investigation, was ultimately terminated. The case went through the entire grievance process. I conducted the witness statements and the Investigative Interview of the employee.

Email to Tom Martin, Manager of Labor Relations, regarding Former Union treasurer/steward Steiger 2008.

0107398289 132198863

Page 1 of 2

#132198863

[redacted]

Mcgee, Lola B. - North Las Vegas, NV

From:	Mcgee, Lola B. - North Las Vegas, NV	**Sent:**	Wed 7/23/2008 12:18 PM
To:	Martin, Tom J - Las Vegas, NV; Adams, Lewis C - Las Vegas, NV; Holmes, Lynn A - Las Vegas, NV		
Cc:	Mcgee, Lola B. - North Las Vegas, NV; Miner, Pat J - Las Vegas, NV; Melonson, Yul J - North Las Vegas, NV; Griffin, Grady E - Las Vegas, NV; Wilson, Jerry A - Reno; Colton, Craig M - Henderson, NV		
Subject:	Statement-Michael Steiger Issues today		
Attachments:			

Hello everyone,

Today I received some unwarranted and inappropriate phone calls from Mike Steiger regarding an investigative interview request that was faxed over to the NALC this morning for representation for Michelle Penko tomorrow between 8:30am and 9:00am.

Ms Penko had called in sick, linked with her SDO and annual leave, on 7/14-15/08. On 7/16/08 she was given an attendance review, which revealed that she is a 10 yr employee with 74.17 hours left of sick leave, and 10 unscheduled absences already this year. It was deemed that an investigative interview needed to be conducted. Ms Penko is a steward here at NLV-Meadow Mesa Station. My supervisor, John Bell informed me that there was no one at the union hall to represent her; and I told him to send a fax request so that it would be on record that we were trying to get her an officer representative, even if we were not obligated to. Finally, this morning the fax was sent and Mike Steiger called John back to answer the fax. John informed me that Steiger was on the phone and I went into my office to take the call.

Shortly after the fax Mike Steiger called here at Meadow Mesa and John Bell answered the phone, Mike told John that he got the fax and 9:00am tomorrow 7/24/08 would be fine. John stated to Steiger that I have to verify that you are even authorized to come on the premises. John put Steiger on hold and I (Lola McGee) took the call. I stated to Steiger "what's going on" and he told me that I was calling regarding the investigative interview for Michelle Penko. I stated to Steiger that he was no longer employed by the postal service and he was not authorized to represent my employees. He stated why don't you look in the JCAM to see that I have a right to represent her under article 17. I said Steiger I'm not going to argue with you and I'm not trying to make this a big deal and blow it out of proportion. I stated that I'll get it taking care of with the steward here and we hung up the phone. I then called and spoke with Calvin to confirm what I had told Steiger was correct, and he stated (Calvin) that Steiger has no right to come in the facility and I can used the steward that was available since there wasn't anyone at the hall to represent her. I went out to my supervisor (John Bell) to let him know that we were going to use Tim Fowler for the interview, he is an Informal-Alt and Formal A steward. At the time Michelle was at the pit and she stated to me that she wanted an officer and Steiger is an officer. She ask me to call the hall and I let her know that we have a steward here and that is who we are going to use. She mumble something under her breath and walked away. Steiger called back an stated that he was an officer of the union even though he did not work for the postal service and I am denying Michelle her rights, do you understand that, he stated to me. He stated to me "I got strung up, you know that Lola, that's why I'm not an employee of the postal service." He stated "When you look into your heart do you think what you did to me was right." I stated to Steiger that I'm not going to be talking with you because you are not even suppose to be calling here and I can't let you on the premises to represent Michelle, he then hung up in my face. A few minutes passed by and he called again; he stated that he was an officer of the union and he wanted to speak with Michelle. I stated that Michelle is performing her duties and I'm not going to let her speak with you. I stated, Steiger why are you doing this when you know that you are not to be calling here and let alone coming to represent anybody. He stated that, I'm not going to talk about personal issues anymore but as an official officer of the union I want to talk with Michelle. I stated to him that I was not going to let him talk to Michelle. He stated "You are denying me the right to speak with her" I replied, yes. He stated that she is not going in there without a branch officer, and there will not be anyone here for three weeks so you can wait three weeks are I can be there tomorrow and he hung up the phone.

Later I received a call from Jerry Wilson stating that Steiger had called him and he (Jerry Wilson) let me know that I was correct, Steiger was not to enter the building and if he came by then I was to call the police. In addition, I received a call from Tom Martin and Glen Norton, Tom let me know that we would try to accommodate Glen with the interview being held on Monday 7/28/08, by Mike Lindemon, without any timeliness issues and I agreed; however, I went in the office to stop the interview and the supervisor was writing the answer to the last question, so it was a mute point at that time. I told Tom and Glen that the interview was over and Glen stated that it is what it is.

https://webmail1.usps.gov/exchange/lola.mcgee/Inbox/Statement-Michael%20Steiger%20I... 7/23/2008

0107398289 132198863

Page 2 of 2

Thanks

Lola

#132198863

https://webmail1.usps.gov/exchange/lola.mcgee/Inbox/Statement-Michael%20Steiger%20l... 7/23/2008

Lucy James issue...NALC Union Steward, Attorney's outcome for me after NALC filed a battery charge on me with Las Vegas courts for inadvertently touching her shoulder. The below image depicts the tight walkway.

The outcome of Lucy James' battery charge against me.

CHARLES E. KELLY, ESQ.
Professional Corporation
Bar #4652
706 S. Eighth Street
Las Vegas, NV 89101
(702) 385-0777

LAS VEGAS MUNICIPAL COURT

CLARK COUNTY, NEVADA

THE STATE OF NEVADA, Plaintiff, vs. **LOLA MCGEE,** Defendant.	**Case No. C0725694A**

ACKNOWLEDGEMENT OF CASE RESOLUTION

Comes Now, Defendant Lola McGee, by and through her counsel Charles E. Kelly and hereby formally enters and acknowledges this resolution of the above case. The terms and conditions of this resolution, which the Defendant acknowledges and accepts are as follows:

1. The Parties to this resolution agree that the case will be "Submitted to the Court";
2. As part of this resolution, the Defendant specifically agrees that while the case remains under "Submission to the Court", she will remain out of trouble and incur no new, similar charges;
3. Pursuant to the terms of this agreement, the Parties request that the Court "Stay Adjudication" for a period of one year. In the event the Defendant stays out of trouble, the Court will dismiss the charges with prejudice. In the event the Defendant

-1-

fails to stay out of trouble then the Court will find her guilty of the Misdemeanor Battery charge.

As part of this resolution, I authorize my counsel to present this Acknowledgement of Case Resolution on my behalf. I am aware that I have a right to have a trial, call witnesses on my behalf, cross examine those testifying against me, and testify or not testify. I am further aware that I am waiving those rights in exchange for this resolution outlined above. Lastly, I specifically authorize my counsel to execute any documents that are necessary to fulfillment of the terms and spirit of this agreement.

LOLA McGEE, March 23, 2010

Witness

-2-

LAW DEPARTMENT – WESTERN AREA

UNITED STATES
POSTAL SERVICE

January 14, 2009

Lola McGee
7582 Cypress Tree Street
Las Vegas, NV 89123

Re: City of Las Vegas v. Lola Bonita McGee
Criminal Complaint Case No: C0725694A, Dept. 2

Dear Ms. McGee:

Enclosed is a copy of the letter I received from the Department of Justice approving your request for private legal representation in the above referenced matter. As I explained last week, you must contact an attorney of your choosing and make arrangements for that person to represent you in all legal proceedings related to this matter. Once you have chosen an attorney, please ask that person to contact me so that he/she can execute a Department of Justice approved retainer agreement.

If you have any questions, please do not hesitate to contact me.

Sincerely,

Danielle Obiorah,
Attorney

DBO/rml

Enclosure

9350 SOUTH 150 EAST, SUITE 800
SANDY, UTAH 84070-2716
TELEPHONE: (801) 984-8400
FAX: (801) 984-8401

U.S. Department of Justice

Civil Division

Deputy Assistant Attorney General

Washington, D.C. 20530

JAN - 7 2009

Danielle Obiorah
Law Department, Western Area
United States Postal Service
9350 South 150 East, Suite 800
Sandy, UT 84070-2716

RE: Representation request of United States Postal Service employee Lola Bonita McGee in the criminal matter of *City of Las Vegas v. Lola Bonita McGee*, Case No. C0725694A, Dept No. 2 (Municipal Court of the City of Las Vegas, NV)

Dear Ms. Obiorah:

Please be advised that I have considered the referenced request for private counsel representation at federal expense by United States Postal Service employee Lola Bonita McGee in the above-captioned action. From the information presently available it appears that providing Ms. McGee private counsel representation at federal expense is warranted under 28 C.F.R. §§ 50.15 and 50.16. Please advise Ms. McGee of my decision.

If you have any questions, please contact Torts Branch Trial Attorney James G. Bartolotto at (202) 616-4174.

Sincerely,

C. Frederick Beckner III

Staff and Employee Letters of Character (4)

Sep 21 09 11:18a p.1

September 20, 2009

Statement

The reason I'm writing this statement is on behalf of Lola McGee. I Charles Turner make the following statements to the best of my knowledge. Before Ms. McGee arrived at North Las Vegas Post Office (NLV), I worked for supervisor Steven Phaup from 1998–2005. Ms McGee arrived in North Las Vegas Post Office in May 2004 until she went out on higher level details in 2006.

I worked closely with Mr. Phaup on a daily basis, because at the time I was a NALC Shop Steward and a Limited Duty Carrier. Mostly on a daily basis when Mr. Phaup and I did not agree with anything dealing with union business an argument would follow rather it was in the office or on the work room floor. The arguments were always due to his lack of respect toward me as the shop steward and his dislike for African Americans with any leadership responsibility. As he and I discussed personal and workplace issues, he would more than often become very agitated and display his various behaviors of bullying, harassment, threats, and showing no mutual respect or professionalism, and leadership responsibility. These behaviors would trickle down through out the office to other employees. On several occasions I solicited help from NLV Postmaster Craig Colton and he would always take the position of Mr. Phaup.

As for as Ms. McGee I begin working for her upon her arrival. Unlike Mr. Phaup, Supervisor McGee was professional on a daily basis. Her work standards were among the best I've ever had since my tenure at the postal service. She was always fair, professional, respectful, and had concerned about all of her employees and the performance of the office. Her behavior was never a problem when dealing with Shop Steward or any other union business. There was never any disrespect, bullying, harassment, or intimidation, of any kind coming from Ms. McGee as my manager. On several occasions supervisor McGee had to take the high road when dealing with Mr. Phaup regarding supervisory issues because of his attitude and behavior towards her. On occasions there would be loud arguments on the workroom floor between Mr. Phaup and myself about several issues concerning the union contract and postal policies; however Ms. McGee, with her professional work ethics, would defuse the situation.

Sincerely

Charles R. Turner
City Letter Carrier
Meadow Mesa Station
NLV, NV 89031
(702) 644-0340

Oct 19 09 04:31p p.1

2091 Blcosoe Ln.
Las Vegas, NV 89156
September 25, 2009

To whom it may Concern:

Over the 30 years I have worked at North Las Vegas, Main Post Office 89030, there has been few supervisors that have made a great impression on me, and Lola McGee, is one of these people.

When I worked with Lola, at NLV Main, she was a supervisor that knew her job, and was fair to all the employees. She was a people person, always cheerful and understanding to the customers, when they had a problem, concerning their mail, and always willing to listen to the employees' input and suggestions, about doing their job.

Lola McGee knew what had to be done, carried her work-load, and employees were always happy to do a little more, for someone who treated them with respect.

When Lola was my supervisor, she had such special qualities, that made me want to be under her leadership. She was delightful to work with, diligent, honest, hard working, and knew her position, very well.

Sincerely,
Margaret I. Gressman
MARGARET I. GRESSMAN

Oct 19 09 04:31p p.2

Michael L. Garrett
107 Milicity Road
Henderson, NV 89012

October 8, 2009

To Whom This May Concern:

This letter is being written as a personal statement of reference and or recommendation for Lola McGee. I have known and worked with Lola McGee for over 8 years. I am a carrier that transferred to Nevada in 2001. I have been a United States letter carrier for 22 years. Lola McGee has always been a superior supervisor in my opinion. Lola has always shown a great attitude towards me and other fellow coworkers. She knows her job well and tries to get the job done fair and timely. She has always been understanding and takes the time to listen to people. It has been a pleasure working with her over the years and her presence will be truly missed. I have worked with many supervisors over the years and consider Lola McGee to be one of the most impressive considering the about of stress that came along with her position.

Sincerely,

Michael L. Garrett

AUG-31-2009 09:27P FROM: TO:2600876 P.1/1

Zarita L. Williams
3115 Olive St.
Las Vegas, NV 89104-9998

To Whom It May Concern:

I was relieved from a detail in the Human Resources department on June 30, 2008. While on detail to HR my assignment consisted of identification of the injured employees of the United States Postal. This assignment was for the Injury Compensation Department for the entire Nevada Sierra District. This program is called the National Reassessment Program (NRP) After the Area audit of the National Reassessment Program my detail ended.I was asked to assist the FMLA coordinator involving the Family Medical Leave Act in the FMLA. Department. After this detail ended; I asked Mr. Yul Melonson to assign me to a station. Mr. Yul Melonson at that time was the Acting Postmaster. Mr. Melonson detailed me to Huntridge station under the leadership of Lola McGee the Acting (A) Station manager.

Ms. Gee was very knowledgeable concerning operational procedures. Nevertheless, she was my manager for a very short period of time and reassigned to another post office as an (A) manager. However, while managing the Huntridge station she was my knowledge base concerning station procedures. Daily, Ms. Mc Gee assisted me with supervisors' task showing me the proper way to pull reports and she always explained documentation and the purpose for the documentation. I truly will always believe, the Postmaster selected Lola to train me because she was know as one who could run a post office with success. She knew what operational needs were critical and what was necessary in supervising employees.

Due to Lola honesty she has gained my trust in her as an upstanding individual believes in loyalty to our organization. I called her on numerous occasions regarding reports, systematic rules and she always explained causation of documentation to me. I consider her as one of my mentor and very stable in her judgment skills. I will always respect her as a leader in the United States Postal Service.

Yours truly,

Zarita L. Williams, Customer Service Supervisor

POSITIONS APPLIED FOR

DATE	STATION	OFFICIALS SELECT/ CONCURRING	CHAIR	COMMITTEE	SELECTION
8/2/2006	Winterwood	Reynosa/Martinez	Floyde	Bowerman, Marks	Dave Dayton
8/4/2006	Strip	Reynosa/Martinez	Floyde	Bowerman, Marks	Lynn Holmes
1/18/2007	Garside	No Selection	Colton	Cattalosse/Scrima	No Selection
1/18/2007	PV	No Selection	Colton	Cattalosse/Scrima	No Selection
	Huntridge	Reynosa/Martinez	Colton	Scrima/Cattalosse	Gerard Carraza
4/11/2007	PV	Reynosa/Martinez	Morgan	Bowerman/Floyd	Watson
4/11/2007	Garside	Reynosa/Martinez	Morgan	Bowerman/Floyd	Steve Reeves
4/11/2007	Meadow	Melonson/Morgan	Doug Hval	Renee Brown/Maryan Roach	Grady Griffin
9/12/2007	Valle Verde	Colton/Morgan	Melonson	Bowerman/Rich Wieber	Kelly McKague
10/24/2007	Sunrise	Reynosa/Martinez	N/A	No Committee	Jason McMahill
12/5/2007	Red Rock	Reynosa/Martinez	N/A	No Committee	Denise Penich
12/5/2007	Strip	Reynosa/Martinez	Roach	Morales/Roger Wagner	Tim Sampoli
5/21/2008	Emerald	Reynosa/Martinez	Richards	Roach/Cattalosse	Jason McMahill
7/16/2008	Huntridge	Richards/Colton	N/A	No Committee	Thomas Jack (L)
8/13/2008	King	Reynosa/Melonson	N/A	Tony Sequira	Thomas Jack (L)
12/9/2008	Winterwood	Reynosa/Melonson	N/A	No Committee	N/A
12/9/2008	Sunrise	Reynosa/Melonson	N/A	Unknown	Sam Pellis

United States Postal Service Resume/eCareer Profile:

United States Postal Service

Candidate Overview

Lola McGee
2121 E WARM SPRINGS RD
LAS VEGAS NV 89119-0460
7022600876
lola.mcgee@usps.gov
Position: 95589667 SUPV CUSTOMER SERVICES

Work Experience

Spring Valley Station Supervisor, Customer Services
03/09/2009 - Open

Las Vegas, NV
USA
Customer Service/Delivery
Description: Supervise a large delivery, distribution, and window operation along with collections. Manage the work of others collaborating with a team of other supervisors for the purpose of providing reliable, consistent, and quality mail service to our customers. Provide resolutions for customer complaints and inquiries. Perform route inspections and adjustments. Investigate accidents and complete safety packages.

Position Type -- Select --
Position Grade

North Las Vegas Post Office Supervisor, Customer Services
05/15/2004 - Open

North Las Vegas, NV
USA
Customer Service/Delivery
Description: Supervise a large delivery, distribution, and window operation along with collections. Manage the work of others collaborating with a team of other supervisors for the purpose of providing reliable, consistent, and quality mail service to our customers. Provide resolutions for customer complaints and inquiries. Perform route inspections and adjustments. Investigate accidents and complete safety packages.

Position Type Postal
Position Grade EAS-17

Meadow Mesa Station Manager, Customer Services/A
07/09/2008 - 03/09/2009

North Las Vegas, NV
USA
Customer Service/Delivery
Description: Manage a large delivery, distribution, collections, post office box, dispatch and retail operation thru subordinate supervisors providing efficient and quality customer service to the community in which we serve. Provide leadership, training, and development to my staff in order to achieve organizational goals. Manage a budget and provide a safe workplace. Provide clear, concise, oral and written communication to resolve customer complaints and inquiries. Maintain a positive working relationship with representatives of employee labor organizations.

Position Type Detail Assignment
Position Grade EAS-22

Work Experience

Huntridge Station Manager, Customer Services/A
06/14/2008 - 07/08/2008

Las Vegas, NV
USA
Customer Service/Delivery
Description: Manage a large delivery, distribution, collections, post office box, dispatch and retail operation thru subordinate supervisors providing efficient and quality customer service to the community in which we serve. Provide leadership, training, and development to my staff in order to achieve organizational goals. Manage a budget and provide a safe workplace. Provide clear, concise, oral and written communication to resolve customer complaints and inquiries. Maintain a positive working relationship with representatives of employee labor organizations.

Position Type Detail Assignment
Position Grade EAS-21

King Station Manager, Customer Services/A
02/23/2008 - 05/02/2008

Las Vegas, NV
USA
Customer Service/Delivery
Description: Manage a large delivery, distribution, collections, post office box, dispatch, and retail operation thru subordinate supervisors providing effecient and quality customer service to the community in which we serve. Provide leadership, training, and developement to my staff in order to achieve oganizational goals. Manage a budget and provide a safe workplace. Provide clear, concise, oral and written communication to resolve customer complaints and inquiries. Maintain a positive working relationship with representatives of employee labor organizations.

Position Type Detail Assignment
Position Grade EAS-22

Sparks-Sun Valley Station Manager, Customer Services/A
01/12/2008 - 02/22/2008

Sparks-Sun Valley, NV
USA
Customer Service/Delivery
Description: Manage a small delivery, distribution, collections, post office box, dispatch and retail operation thru subordinate supervisors providing effecient and quality customer service to the community in which we serve. Provide leadership, training, and developement to my staff in order to achieve organizational goals. Manage a budget and provide a safe workplace. Provide clear, concise, oral and written communication to resolve customer complaints and inquiries. Maintain a positive working relationship with representatives of employee labor organizations.

Position Type Detail Assignment
Position Grade EAS-20

Paradise Valley Station Manager, Customer Services/A
09/01/2006 - 03/30/2007

Las Vegas, NV
USA
Customer Service/Delivery
Description: Manage a large delivery, distribution, collections, post office box, dispatch and retail operation thru

Work Experience

subordinate supervisors providing effecient and quality customer service to the community in which we serve. Provide leadership, training, and developement to my staff in order to achieve organizational goals. Manage a budget and provide a safe workplace. Provide clear, concise, oral and written communication to resolve customer complaints and inquiries. Maintain a positive working relationship with representatives of employee labor organizations.

Position Type Detail Assignment

Position Grade EAS-22

Huntridge Station Manager, Customer Services/A

04/01/2006 - 08/31/2006

Las Vegas, NV
USA

Customer Service/Delivery

Description: Manage a large delivery, distribution, collections, post office box, dispatch and retail operation thru subordinate supervisors providing efficient and quality customer service to the community in which we serve. Provide leadership, training, and development to my staff in order to achieve organizational goals. Manage a budget and provide a safe workplace. Provide clear, concise, oral and written communication to resolve customer complaints and inquiries. Maintain a positive working relationship with representatives of employee labor organizations.

Position Type Detail Assignment

Position Grade EAS-21

Wagner Station Supervisor, Customer Services

01/13/2004 - 05/14/2004

Los Angeles, CA
USA

Customer Service/Delivery

Description: Supervise a large delivery, distribution, and window operation along with collections. Manage the work of others collaborating with a team of other supervisors for the purpose of providing reliable, consistent, and quality mail service to our customers. Provide resolutions for customer complaints and inquiries. Investigate accidents and complete safety packages. Perform route inspections and make adjustments.

Position Type Detail Assignment

Position Grade EAS-17

Gardena Post Office Supervisor, Customer Services

04/15/2002 - 01/12/2004

Gardena, CA
USA

Customer Service/Delivery

Description: Supervise a large delivery, distribution, and window operation along with collections. Manage the work of others collaborating with a team of other supervisors for the purpose of providing reliable, consistent, and quality mail service to our customers. Provide resolution for customer complaints and inquiries. Perform route inspections and make adjustments. Investigate accidents and complete safety paperwork.

Position Type Postal

Position Grade EAS-17

Seal Beach Post Office Associate Supervisor, Customer Services

11/15/2001 - 04/14/2002

Work Experience

Seal Beach, CA
USA
Customer Service/Delivery
Description: Supervise a large delivery, distribution, and window operation along with collections. Manage the work of others collaborating with a team of other supervisors for the purpose of providing reliable, consistent, and quality mail service to our customers. Provide resolution for customer complaints and inquiries. Perform route inspections and make adjustments. Investigate accidents and complete paperwork.

Position Type	Postal
Position Grade	EAS-15

La Mirada Post Office Associate Supervisor, Customer Services
07/18/2001 - 11/14/2001

La Mirada, CA
USA
Customer Service/Delivery
Description: Training in a classroom setting and hands on in the field to supervise a small to large delivery, distribution, and window operation along with collections. Manage the work of others collaborating with a team of other supervisors for the purpose of providing reliable, consistent, and quality mail service to our customers. Provide resolution for customer complaints and inquiries. Investigate accidents and complete paperwork. Perform route inspections and make adjustments.

Position Type	Postal
Position Grade	EAS-15

Bell Gardens Post Office City Letter Carrier
06/22/1998 - 07/17/2001

Bell Gardens, CA
USA

Description: Professionally trained City Letter Carrier providing mail preparation and delivery to customers on assigned routes.

Position Type	Postal
Position Grade	PS-05

Bell Gardens Post Office Supervisor, Customer Services/A
07/01/2000 - 03/16/2001

Bell Gardens, CA
USA
Customer Service/Delivery
Description: Acting supervisor for a large delivery, distribution, and window operation along with collections. Manage the work of others collaborating with a team of other supervisors for the purpose of providing reliable, consistent, and quality mail service to our customers. Provide resolutions for customer complaints and inquiries. Investigate accidents and complete safety paperwork.

Position Type	Detail Assignment
Position Grade	EAS-16

Southern California Alcohol & Drug Programs Inc. Case Manager/Counselor
06/14/1997 - 06/21/1998

Work Experience

Downey, CA
USA
Human Resources

Description: Manage clients case files to meet company's policies and regulations. Provide counseling groups, and individual sessions to motivate and encourage client participation with achieving a productive and drug free lifestyle. Create treatment plans and provide judicial representation for clients. Create the written process for achieving attitude and behavior change in clients. Assist clients with acquiring and developing coping skills to maintain a better way of living.

Position Type Non Postal
Position Grade N/A

Me & Thee (Soul Food Restaurant) Business Owner and Operator
07/01/1991 - 11/30/1994

Compton, CA
USA
Other

Description: Create an maintain a budget along with bookkeeping. Provide marketing techniques and business specials. conduct meetings with vendors and suppliers. Cook and prepare large quantities of food. Maintain public relations and health permits.

Position Type Non Postal
Position Grade N/A

Education

University of Phoenix Gardena, California	02/01/2000 - 12/31/2001 Education Level: Bachelor's Degree Subject: Business and Management
Cypress Community College Cypress, California	01/01/1995 - 06/30/1997 Education Level: Associate Degree Subject: Human Services
Cypress Community College Cypress, California	01/01/1995 - 06/30/1996 Education Level: Certificate Subject: Human Services Generalist
Cypress Community College Cypress, California	01/01/1995 - 06/30/1996 Education Level: Certificate Subject: Drug and Alcohol Studies
Trans Western Institute Long Beach, California	04/01/1988 - 04/30/1989 Education Level: Certificate Subject: Micro Computers
Los Angeles Trade Tech College Los Angeles, California	09/01/1987 - 03/31/1988 Education Level: Certificate Subject: Office Administration
Harriett Tubman High School	09/12/1977 - 06/30/1980

Education

Compton, California

Education Level: High School Graduate
Subject: High School

Special Skills / Associations

North Las Vegas Post Office - Certificate Of Appreciation - Combined Federal Campaign 2008
Sparks-Sun Valley Station - Recognition Award - Nevada Sierra District FY 2008
Going the Extra Mile Award (North Las Vegas Post Office) - 2008
Sick Leave Recognition (North Las Vegas) - 2008
North Las Vegas Post Office - Spot Award and Excellence Placque - Nevada Sierra District FY 2007
Lane C EXFC OND Recognition Award # Paradise Valley Station-Nevada Sierra District # FY 2006
Certificate Of Appreciation - Clark County School District/Nevada Reading League (2006)
Special Achievement and Monetary Award (North Las Vegas Post Office) - 2004
President#s Honor Roll # University Of Phoenix (2000-2001)
President#s Honor Roll # Cypress College (3 semesters) # 1996/1997
Certified Mental Health Counselor - Cypress College - 1996
Enterprenuer - 1991 thru 1994
#Employee Of The Quarter# Robert Kaufman Company # 1989
Compton City Council Campaign (Bernice Woods) # 1988
Parenting Award (Los Angeles Unified School District) # 1987

References

Yul Melonson	Postmaster, North Las Vegas	(702) 648-2623
Robert Reynosa	Manager, Customer Services Operations	(702) 361-9348
Renee Brown	Postmaster, Sparks	(775) 359-0720
Grady Griffin	Manager, Customer Services	(702) 657-6479
Craig Colton	Postmaster, Henderson	(702) 558-7611

Attachments

There are no attachments currently stored

Training

Start Date	End Date	Facilities	Courses
03/12/2008	04/03/2008	Online	ERMS System Change
12/07/2007	12/07/2007	Las Vegas GMF	Western Area Critical Standard Operating Instruct.
10/23/2007	10/26/2007	Las Vegas GMF	Route Inspection Training
10/18/2007	10/18/2007	Las Vegas GMF	Labor/Alternative Dispute Resolution Training
08/01/2007	08/12/2007	Las Vegas GMF	SIA/Retail/Finance Training
08/31/2006	08/31/2006	Las Vegas GMF	Labor Relations Discipline Process
06/29/2006	06/29/2006	Las Vegas GMF	EEO Rights and Remedies (No Fear Act)
06/28/2006	06/28/2006	Las Vegas GMF	Reasonable Accommodation Awareness for Postal Mgt.
04/28/2006	04/28/2006	Las Vegas GMF	EBuy Approver Training
03/17/2006	03/17/2006	Las Vegas GMF	Coach and On-Site Trainer Certification
05/20/2003	05/20/2003	Long Beach P&DC	Entry-level Interviewer Training
03/02/2002	03/02/2002	Long Beach P&DC	DOIS
01/15/2002	01/15/2002	Long Beach P&DC	Time/Attendance Collection System
03/17/2001	07/21/2001	Long Beach P&DC	Associate Supervisor Program

Summary of Accomplishments

Describe your qualifications for this vacancy by providing a brief description of your accomplishments that demonstrate that you possess the requirements stated on the job posting. These accomplishments may have occurred in various settings.

I arrived at Huntridge Station, for the second time, in June FY08. I set goals to monitor processes for efficiency and to improve service. I challenged my staff and their work ethics to improve overall performance and team accountability. Everyone maintained their assigned duties and worked as a team. In addition, it was refreshing to see that many of the processes that I had implemented during my initial tour were still being utilized. I changed supervisor schedules, clerks were utilized by processing mail according to priority and one clerk was left at the hot case to enable all mis-throws to get connected to the carriers before they left for the street. Attendance reviews were performed and discipline was given when warranted. My supervisors addressed employees with poor performance and captured under-time on a daily basis. As a result of our hard work and effort, we received 100% compliance on an EXFC service review, total F2B was -1.2 to plan and -10.4 to SPLY; F2B overtime was 7.4 and -53.8 to plan; total overtime was -45.6 to plan; carrier sick leave was 3.17 and -58.9 to SPLY; F4 was -5.2 to plan and -6.1 to SPLY; total hours were -2.0 to plan and -9.6 to SPLY; TEI was 1.9 to plan and 10.9 to SPLY; 1700 improved by 8%, and % to standard improved by 3%. I was very proud of my team our results showed that we worked hard and communicated very well together. After my arrival at King Station it became evident that much improvement was needed in several areas. I challenged my staff by given them the tasks of improving the budget, operations, staffing, safety, security, customer relations and contract violations. I began implementing my strategies for change by having a daily staff meeting. I gave techniques to utilize when addressing employees performance and behavior. DOIS and IIMS reports were addressed daily. Service standards and expectations were given to both delivery and customer service employees. I changed supervisor and employee schedules to accommodate the operations. Attendance reviews were conducted and postal policies were given to each employee. I increased requirements for safety observations and 4584 reports for the week. By week 31 FY08, I established a positive working relationship with the steward and we settled many grievances for little to no compensation. My staff and I improved the budget by -2.5% WTD, sick leave was reduced to -10.0% MTD, MSP scanning rate from 93's to 99's, delivery conf. scores from 97.5 to 99.4%, % to std. improved from 157 to 124%, and total F4 from 74.23 to 83.11%. I replaced the lobby flooring materials and the door locks to reduce any chance of an accident or security issue. Also, I accommodated a customer's request for service and received a business connect for $1600. At Sun Valley Station, I challenged my staff to improve percent to standard and overtime. With addressing performance reports and managing to the workload, we improved % to std. from 126.03 to 107.93%, and reduced overtime from 10.67 to 6.64% (-18.2). As the MIC at North Las Vegas, I gave my staff a task to meet the competition for best day after a holiday for delivery, on carriers returning by 1700. I contacted the plant, and made scheduling changes. Some employees were brought in early on heavy business routes. We curtailed 3rd class mailings and gave employees their scheduled leave time. As a result, we had the best performance in the district by having 2 out pass 1700. Also, the 204b's that I trained at NLV have been accepted into the next ASP program, and the ASP graduate that I previously trained is currently productive in many of the Las Vegas City Stations. Also, it was time for APWU negotiations. During this time it was imperative that USPS management and the APWU come together to solidify a new contract. I was asked to be apart of the local negotiation team for North Las Vegas Post Offices. Communication was accomplished through telecoms and office meetings. Our team included labor relations in the process to assure that a violation of the contract was not made. We discussed articles 8, 10, 11, 12, 13, 14, 17, 25, 37, and 38. I was very active in the decision making process through negotiations and we were very instrumental at arriving at some of the decisions. Due to its previous effectiveness, a decision was reached to keep the old contract and not change anything. Recently, the City of North Las Vegas wanted to establish delivery for some of its offices. There were 14 different entities that were in question for the North Las Vegas Post Offices. The addresses ranged from, the starting boundaries of North Las Vegas Main Post Office to the ending boundaries of the Meadow Mesa Station. I was given the task to investigate each address, identify what type of facility it was, and discover if we had delivery to it or not. As I proceeded with my investigation, I contacted other managers and supervisors, and I consulted with my postmaster. I questioned each carrier that had one of the addresses on their route to determine if they had a caller service or street delivery. As I accumulated all the information from both offices, I turned in my report and had a successful meeting with th City of North Las Vegas. At Paradise Valley Station we had a challenge to get mail delivered in a timely manner with a zone split, and to protect Lane C EXFC mail scores. I conducted staff meetings and instructed my supervisors to give employees our expectations and address deficiencies. Productivity stand - ups were given to explain our goals and feedback was given on improvements. With all of the planning and working our processes, we had mail delivered with a 6.9% TEI and F4 total work hours were at a 91.37%; of which was the best in the district for FY06 through qtr.2 FY07. We also earned the best EXFC record in the district with a 95.87% for FY06. We excelled on earned vs actual for F4 productivity rates on all mail types.

Applications

Application Date	Status	Job Posting
05/21/2008	Not Selected	MGR CUSTOMER SERVICES EAS - 22 LAS VEGAS NV NC51945217
06/04/2008	Not Selected	MGR CUSTOMER SERVICES EAS - 21 ATLANTA GA NC51966212
06/04/2008	Not Selected	POSTMASTER EAS - 22 STONE MOUNTAIN GA NC51966220
06/10/2008	Not Selected	POSTMASTER EAS - 21 DACULA GA NC51994442
07/16/2008	Not Selected	MGR CUSTOMER SERVICES EAS - 21 LAS VEGAS NV NC52108635
08/13/2008	Not Selected	MGR CUSTOMER SERVICES EAS - 22 LAS VEGAS NV NC52188820
12/09/2008	Not Selected	MGR CUSTOMER SERVICES EAS - 21 LAS VEGAS NV NC53208476
12/09/2008	In Process	MGR CUSTOMER SERVICES EAS - 21 LAS VEGAS NV NC53212633
	Draft	POSTMASTER EAS - 21 SUWANEE GA NC53761737
03/17/2009	In Process	POSTMASTER EAS - 22 COVINGTON GA NC53761725
03/17/2009	In Process	POSTMASTER EAS - 22 CUMMING GA NC53755599

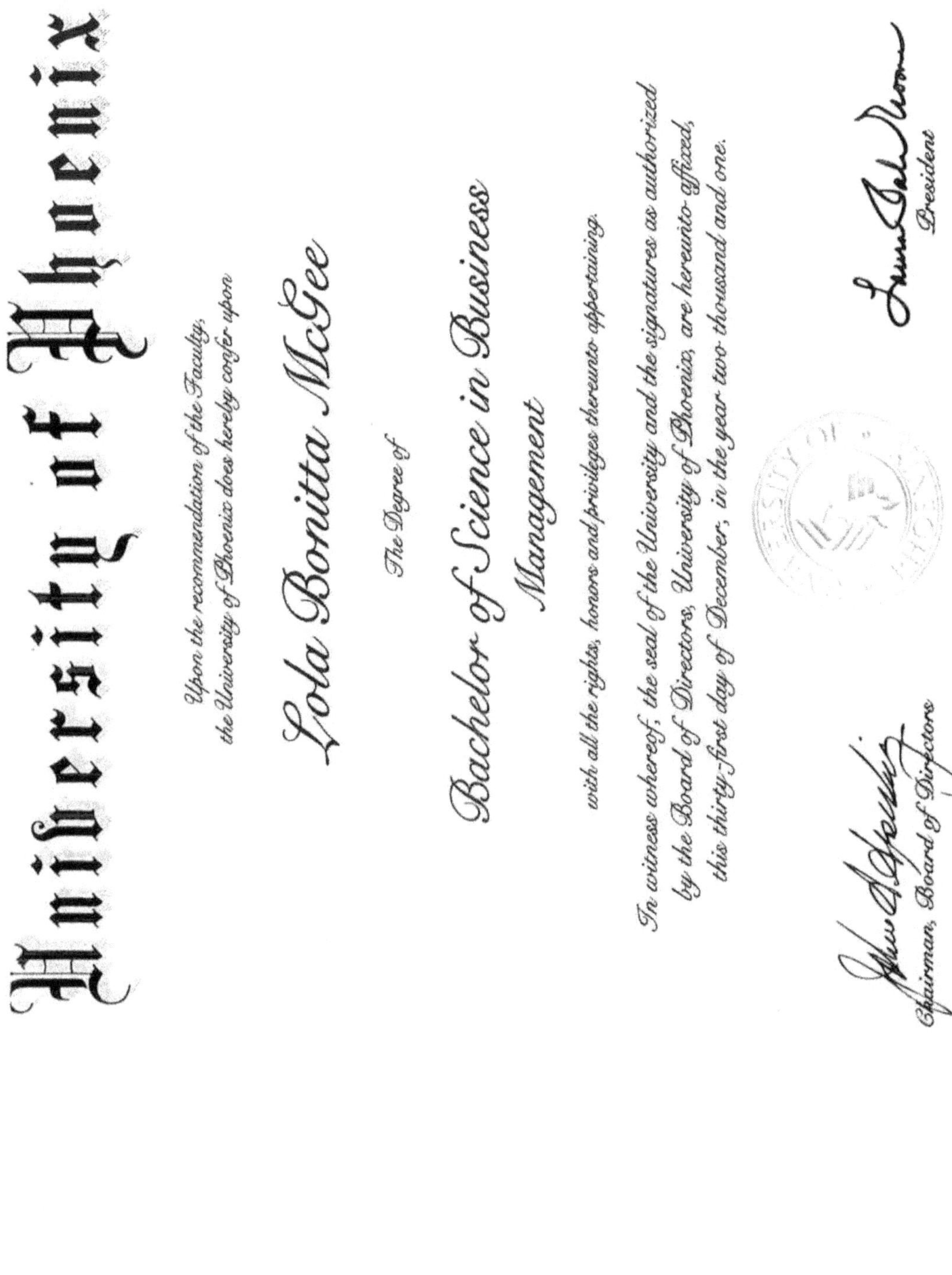

University of Phoenix

Upon the recommendation of the Faculty,
the University of Phoenix does hereby confer upon

Lola Bonitta McGee

The Degree of

Bachelor of Science in Business
Management

with all the rights, honors and privileges thereunto appertaining.

In witness whereof, the seal of the University and the signatures as authorized
by the Board of Directors, University of Phoenix, are hereunto affixed,
this thirty-first day of December, in the year two thousand and one.

Chairman, Board of Directors

President

Upon recommendation of the Faculty of the

Cypress College

and under authorization granted by the Board of Governors of the
California Community Colleges the degree of

Associate in Arts

Human Services

is hereby conferred upon

Ms. Lola Bonitta McGee

with all Rights, Benefits and Privileges appertaining thereto in token
of the satisfactory completion of a two-year curriculum

Given at Cypress, California, this month of June,
nineteen hundred ninety-seven

Chancellor

President Board of Trustees

President

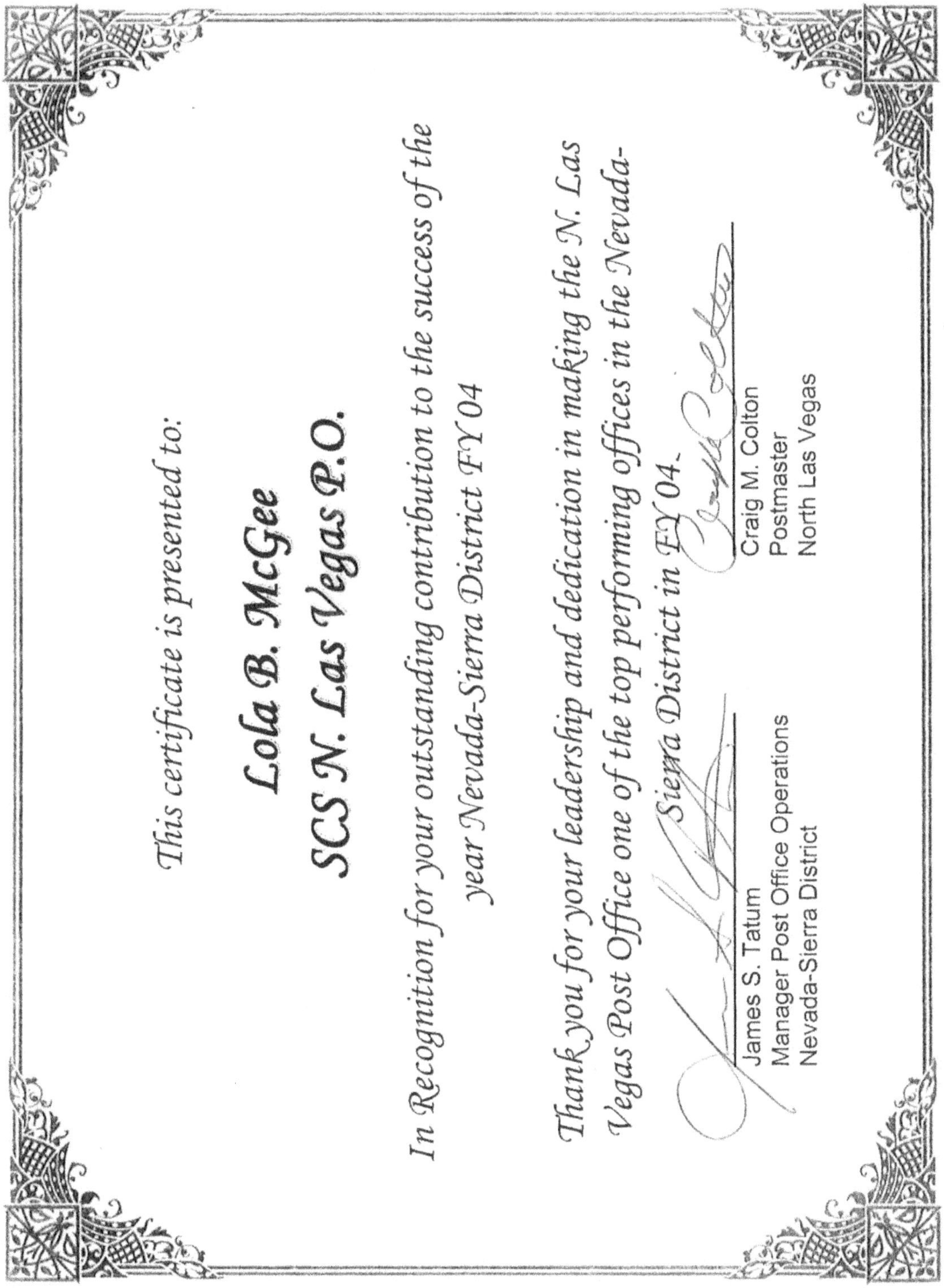

This certificate is presented to:

Lola B. McGee

SCS N. Las Vegas P.O.

In Recognition for your outstanding contribution to the success of the year Nevada-Sierra District FY 04

Thank you for your leadership and dedication in making the N. Las Vegas Post Office one of the top performing offices in the Nevada-Sierra District in FY 04.

James S. Tatum
Manager Post Office Operations
Nevada-Sierra District

Craig M. Colton
Postmaster
North Las Vegas

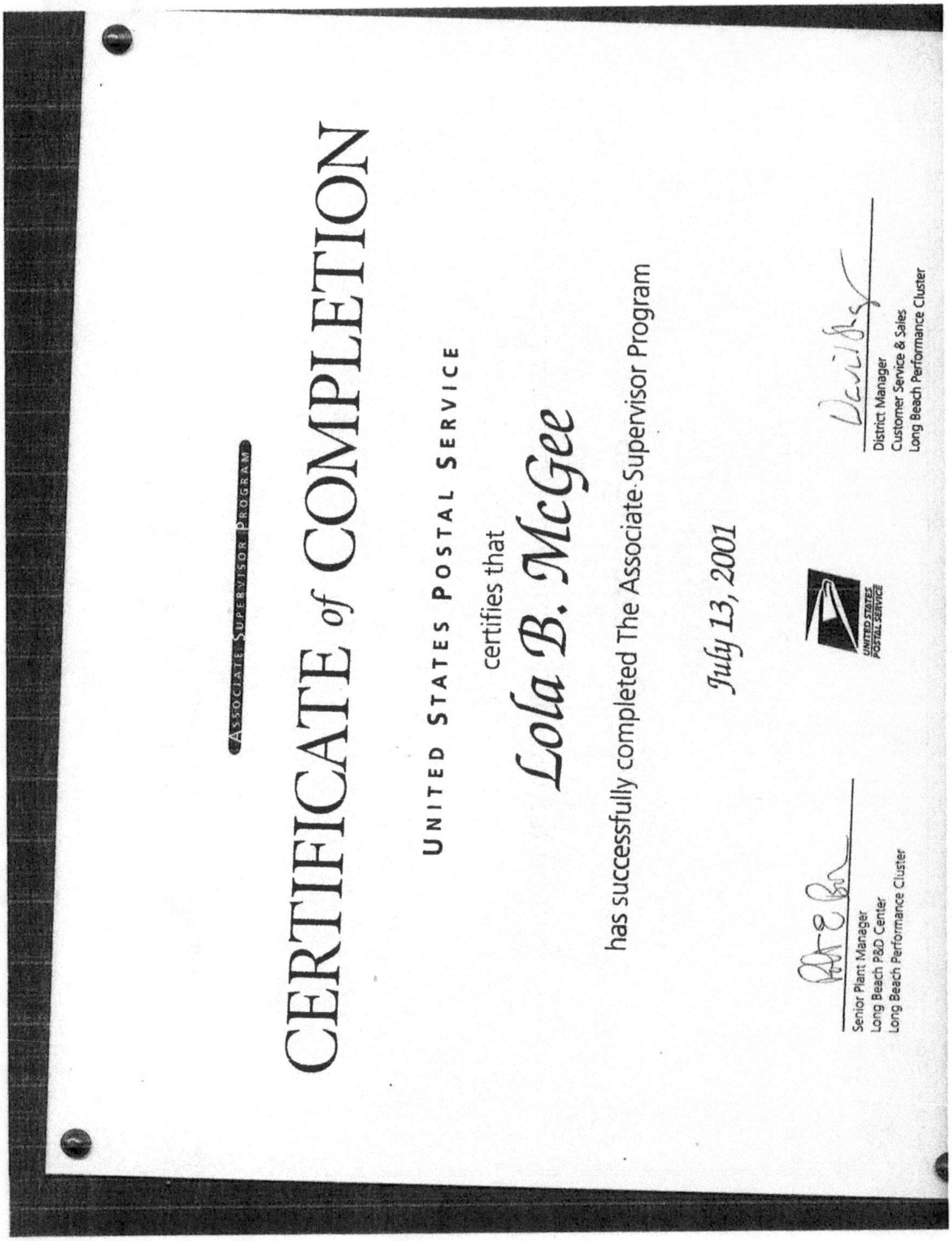
ASSOCIATE SUPERVISOR PROGRAM

CERTIFICATE *of* COMPLETION

UNITED STATES POSTAL SERVICE

certifies that

Lola B. McGee

has successfully completed The Associate Supervisor Program

July 13, 2001

Senior Plant Manager
Long Beach P&D Center
Long Beach Performance Cluster

UNITED STATES POSTAL SERVICE

District Manager
Customer Service & Sales
Long Beach Performance Cluster

CRAIG M. COLTON
POSTMASTER
NORTH LAS VEGAS POST OFFICE
UNITED STATES
POSTAL SERVICE

December, 2004

LOLA MCGEE
SUPERVISOR, CUSTOMER SERVICES
NORTH LAS VEGAS, NV

Dear Lola:

I wanted to take a few moments to thank you for your contributions to the North Las Vegas Post Office and present you with this Special Achievement Award.

In fiscal year 2004, the North Las Vegas Post Office was recognized with the highest unit score (National Performance Assessment) of all offices within the Nevada Sierra District levels 21 and above.

This success was due in large part to your willing assistance and dedication. I appreciate the 100% effort you continually gave to the Postal Service. By your example, you encouraged other employees to give their best.

Thank you for the effort that you provided to the North Las Vegas Post Office and our customers, giving excellent customer service every day.

A copy of this letter will be placed in your Official Personnel Folder.

Sincerely,

Craig M. Colton
Postmaster
North Las Vegas

cc: OPF

1414 E. LAKE MEAD BLVD.
NORTH LAS VEGAS, NV 89030-9998
702/649-4437
FAX: 702/633-5087

POST OFFICE OPERATIONS
NEVADA-SIERRA DISTRICT

UNITED STATES
POSTAL SERVICE

September 15, 2009

Lola B. McGee
P. O. Box 98272
Las Vegas, NV 89193-8272

Dear Lola:

It is with distinct pleasure that I extend my warm personal greetings on the occasion of your retirement from the United States Postal Service on September 15, 2009. A Service Award Certificate in appreciation of your more than 11 years of service is enclosed.

The Postal Service's success is due in large part to the dedication and hard work of its employees such as yourself. It is a privilege for me to recognize your years of commendable service and to personally thank you for your contributions to the Postal Service throughout your career. I wish to join with your friends and coworkers to extend my personal wishes to you for a happy and well deserved retirement.

Once again, thank you for all your contributions!

Sincerely,

Craig M. Colton
Senior Manager, Post Office Operations

cc: OPF

1001 E Sunset Rd
Las Vegas NV 89199-9992
702-361-9440
FAX (651) 675-1601

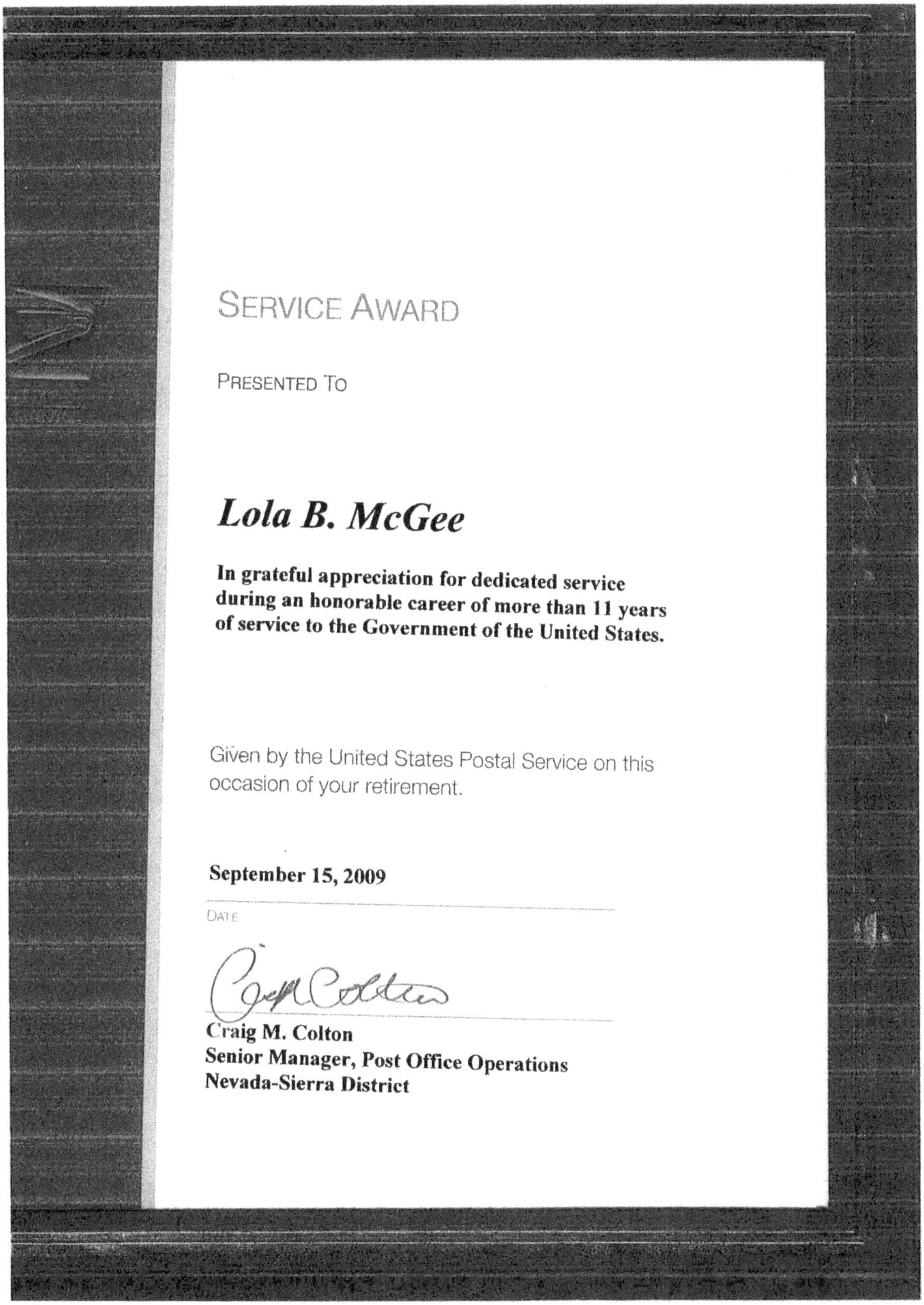

SERVICE AWARD

PRESENTED TO

Lola B. McGee

In grateful appreciation for dedicated service during an honorable career of more than 11 years of service to the Government of the United States.

Given by the United States Postal Service on this occasion of your retirement.

September 15, 2009

DATE

Craig M. Colton
Senior Manager, Post Office Operations
Nevada-Sierra District

CERTIFICATE OF APPRECIATION

This certificate of appreciation is being given to

LOLA MCGEE

For Outstanding Performance!

****

Renee M. Brown, Postmaster
Sparks, NV

02/12/2008
Date

Lola B. McGee

In recognition for your outstanding contributions to
Lane C EXFC OND Service Performance.
Best in the South, 95.53 for all of FY 2006.
Nevada-Sierra District

October 19, 2006
Date

Johnray Egelhoff, District Manager

Combined Federal Campaign

Presents

Certificate of Appreciation

To

Lola McGee

February 12, 2008

POSTMASTER

UNITED STATES
POSTAL SERVICE

September 2007

Lola McGee
North Las Vegas Post Office

Dear Lola:

Congratulations!

I am delighted to recognize you for your dedication and efforts in attaining a sick leave balance of 563 hours. The conservation of sick leave is highly valued in the Postal Service. It is important to note that it serves as insurance in the event of extended illness.

I am proud to have employees like you who appreciate the tremendous value of this benefit.

Once again, congratulations.

Sincerely,

Yul Melonson
Postmaster

1414 E. LAKE MEAD BLVD.
NORTH LAS VEGAS, NV 89030-9998
702-649-1871
FAX: 702-633-5087

UNITED STATES
POSTAL SERVICE

Going the Extra Mile Award!

Lola McGee

Congratulations on your Attendance, Safety, and Job Performance! The Postal Service relies heavily on employees as a valued resource. I appreciate your efforts and take pride in having you as one of my employees.

I would like to share with you my vision.

The North Las Vegas Post Office will become an organization where everyone, at all levels, feels the organization is theirs to improve, change, and help become what it can potentially become by sharing the "big picture" with all employees. We will become a learning organization that fosters the cross-fertilization of ideas, harnesses the synergy of group cooperation, and cultivates pride of being a valued member of one outstanding Post Office. We will take the Postal Service's core mission and make the North Las Vegas Post Office a world class organization!

A great leader doesn't necessarily do great things, but has the ability to inspire others to greatness...

Your Commitment makes the difference!

Yul Melonson
Postmaster
North Las Vegas, NV

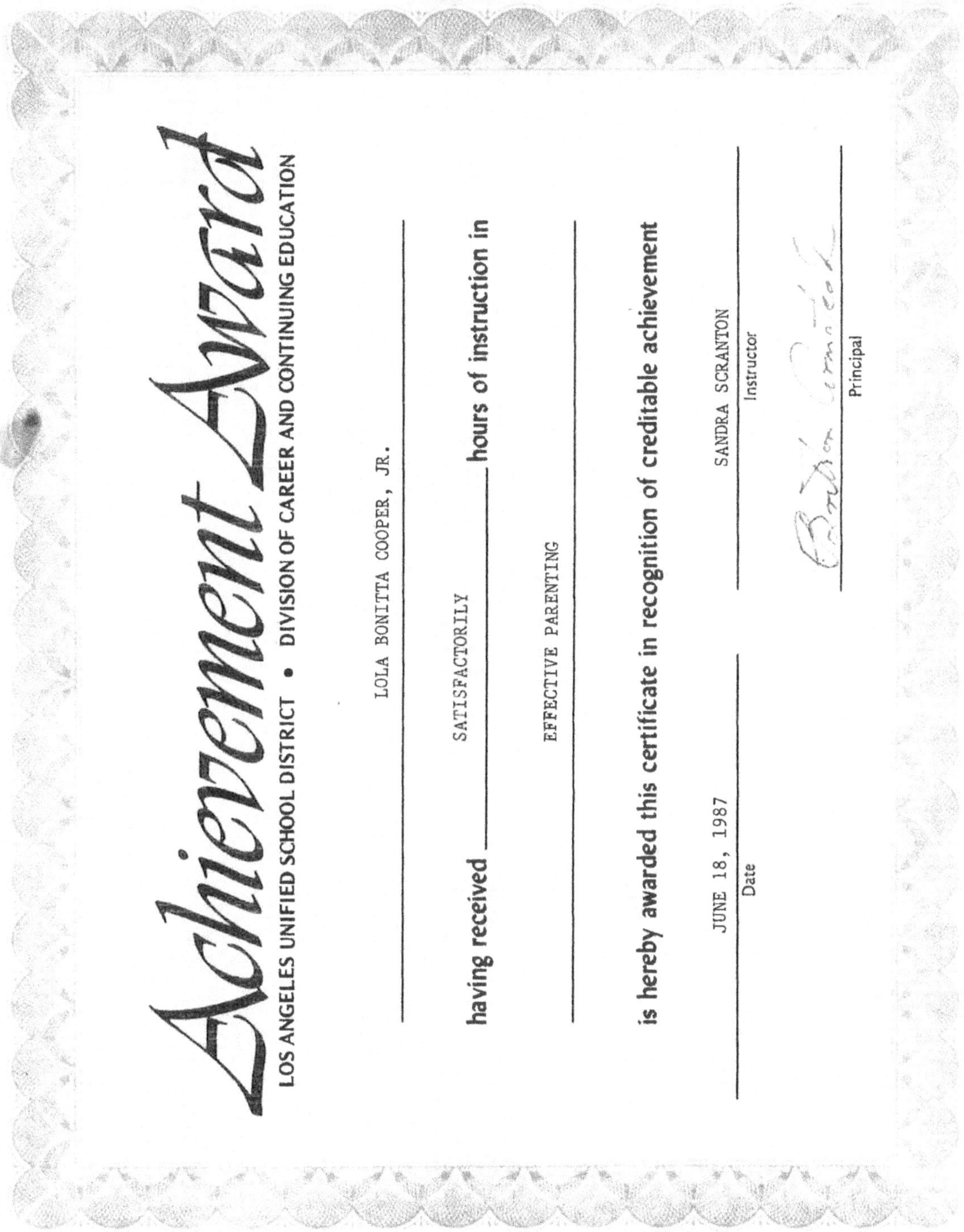

Achievement Award

LOS ANGELES UNIFIED SCHOOL DISTRICT • DIVISION OF CAREER AND CONTINUING EDUCATION

LOLA BONITTA COOPER, JR.

having received SATISFACTORILY hours of instruction in

EFFECTIVE PARENTING

is hereby awarded this certificate in recognition of creditable achievement

JUNE 18, 1987

Date

SANDRA SCRANTON

Instructor

Principal

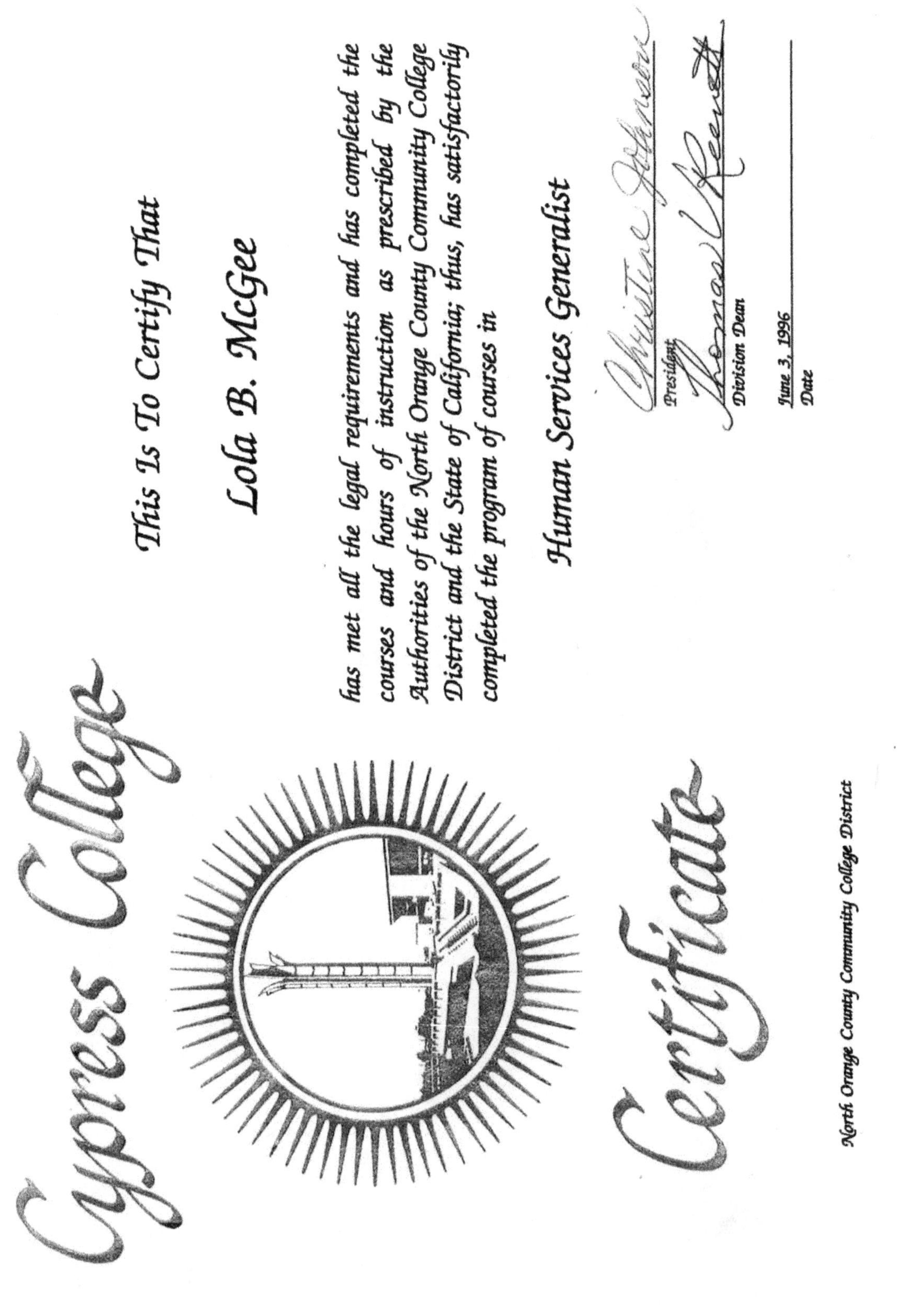

Cypress College

This Is To Certify That

Lola B. McGee

has met all the legal requirements and has completed the courses and hours of instruction as prescribed by the Authorities of the North Orange County Community College District and the State of California; thus, has satisfactorily completed the program of courses in

Human Services Generalist

Certificate

President

Division Dean

June 3, 1996
Date

North Orange County Community College District

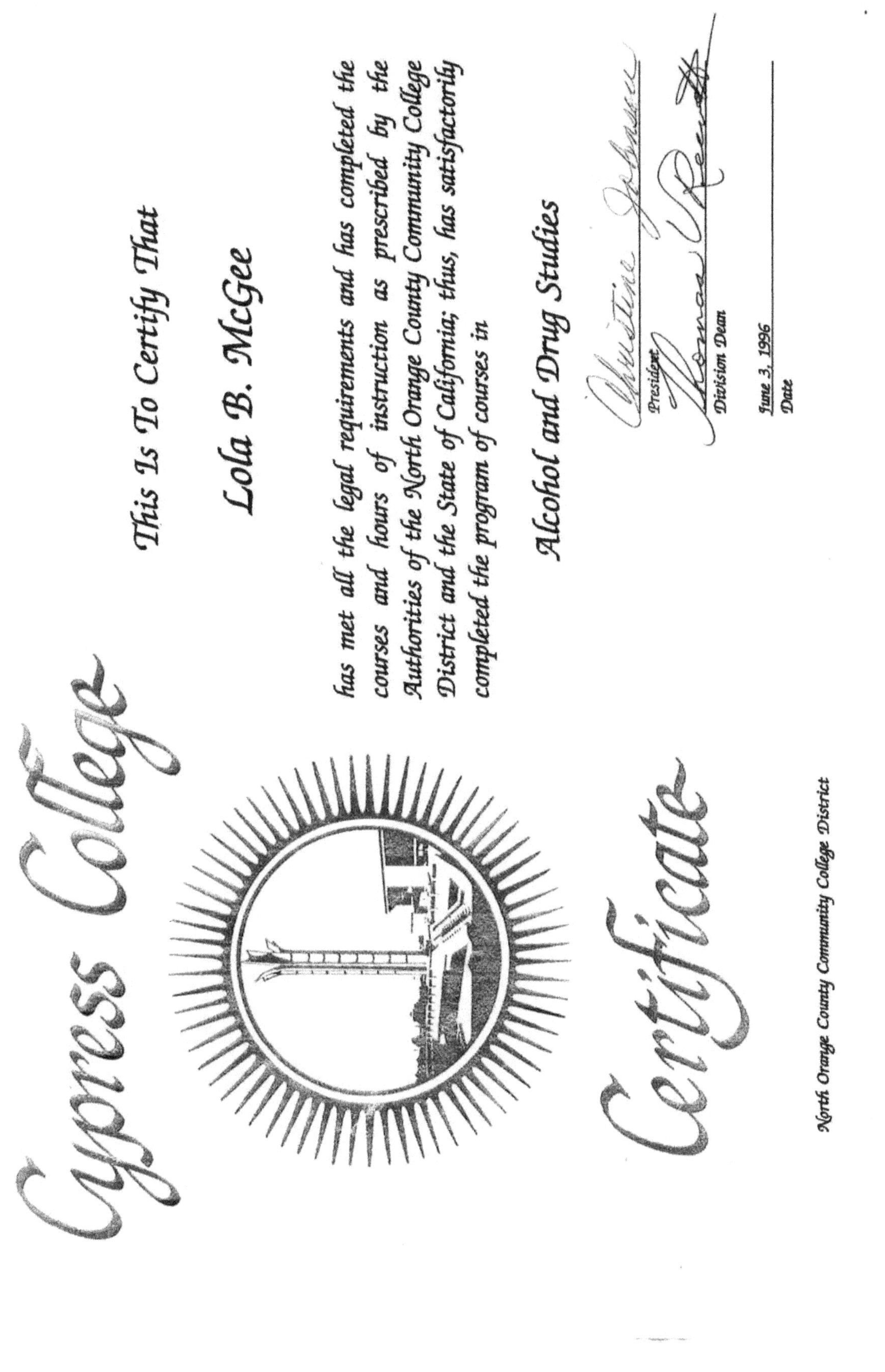

Cypress College

Certificate

This Is To Certify That

Lola B. McGee

has met all the legal requirements and has completed the courses and hours of instruction as prescribed by the Authorities of the North Orange County Community College District and the State of California; thus, has satisfactorily completed the program of courses in

Alcohol and Drug Studies

President

Division Dean

June 3, 1996

Date

North Orange County Community College District

California
Association for
Alcohol/Drug Educators

This is to certify that

Lola McGee

is a member in good standing and therefore entitled to all benefits and privileges thereof.

6-17-96
Date

President **Treasurer**

California Association for Alcohol / Drug Educators (CAADE)
San Bernardino Valley College 701 S. Mt. Vernon Ave. San Bernardino, CA 92410

June 17, 1996

Lola McGee
8739 Rose St.
Bellflower, Ca. 90706

I wish to take this opportunity to thank you for your recent membership application in the California Association for Alcohol and Drug Educators (CADDE). This letter will serve as acknowledgement that your check in the amount of $15.00 has been received and that effective June 17,1996 you are a member in good standing.

Approximately 30 days prior to expiration of your membership you will be sent a written notice for renewal. Any questions, comments or suggestions concerning membership may be directed to the undersigned.

Thank you,

Joan Harter
Chair
Membership

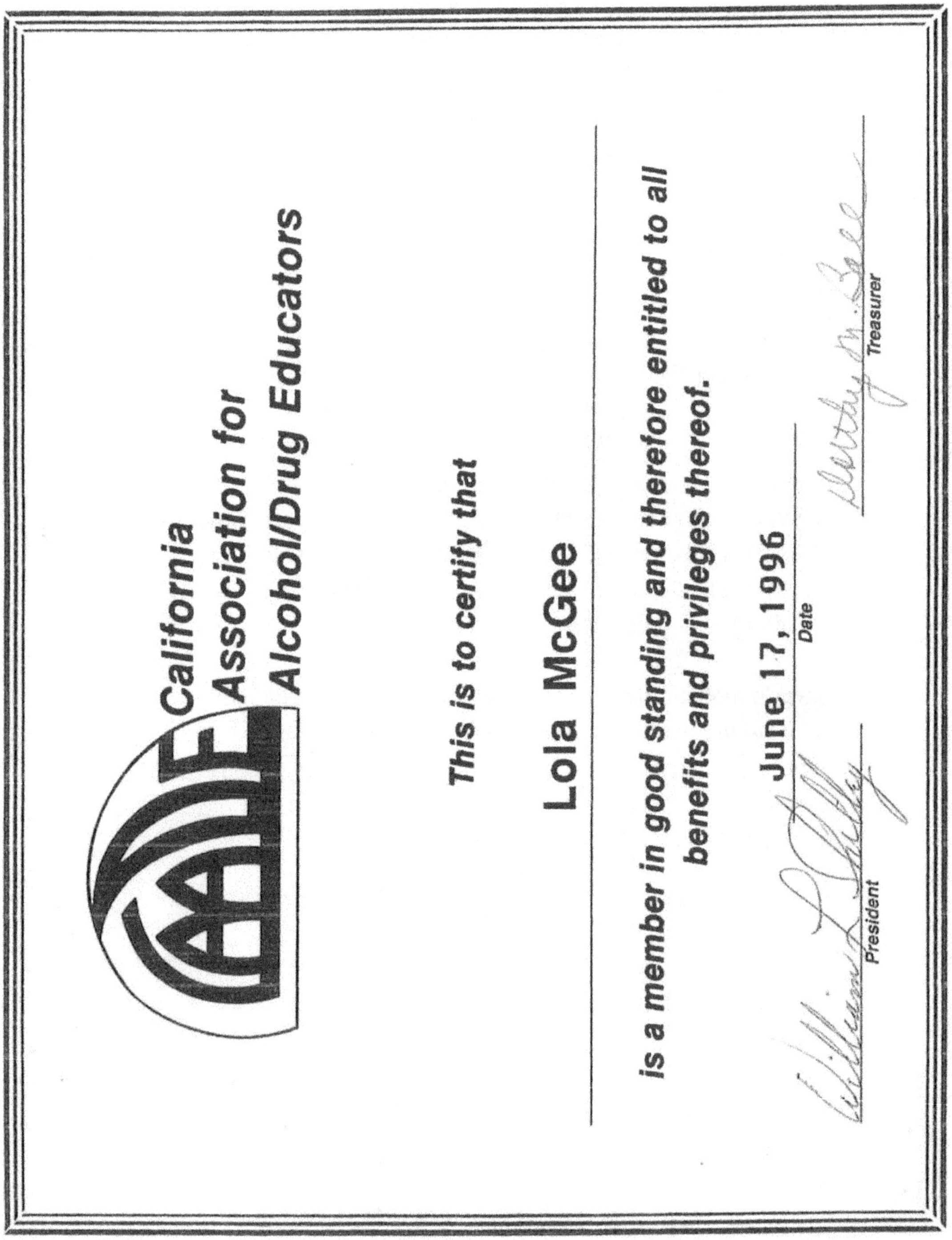

California
Association for
Alcohol/Drug Educators

This is to certify that

Lola McGee

is a member in good standing and therefore entitled to all
benefits and privileges thereof.

June 17, 1996
Date

President

Treasurer

* * * * *

Disclaimer:
In order to maintain authenticity,
the following correspondeces have not been altered.

* * * * *

Change in management (10/2/08) after the threat on (8/25/08) and 1st EEO filed (9/5/08)

Mcgee, Lola B. - North Las Vegas, NV

From:	Colton, Craig M - Las Vegas, NV	**Sent:**	Thu 10/2/2008 2:11 PM
To:	NEVADA-SIERRA JAMES C BROWN FACILITY ALL USERS; NEVADA-SIERRA AO AND STATIONS ONLY		
Cc:	Mossman, Shaun E - Las Vegas, NV; Jordan, Lee A - Las Vegas, NV; Miner, Pat J - Las Vegas, NV; Bowerman, Donna M - Las Vegas, NV; Brown, Vivian I - Las Vegas, NV; Richards, Corey D- Las Vegas, NV; Wilson, Jerry A - Reno; Gatz, Timothy R - Fernley, NV; Gray, Thomas M - Fernley, NV; DePaoli, Jerry L - Reno, NV; Melonson, Yul J - North Las Vegas, NV		
Subject:	Management Changes - Effective October 4		
Attachments:			

Effective Saturday, October 4, 2008, Corey Richards will be detailed to the position of Officer-in-Charge, North Las Vegas Post Office.

Jerry Wilson will be returning to his position of Postmaster, Fallon Post Office. Tim Gatz will be returning to his position of Postmaster, Fernley Post Office. Tom Gray will be returning to his position of Supervisor, Customer Services, Fernley Post Office.

I want to personally thank Jerry, Tim, and Tom for the excellent job they have done during the past three months. Each of them is to be commended for their dedication, as well as the results they provided to this Cluster.

Craig M. Colton
Manager, Post Office Operations
Nevada Sierra District

CONFIDENTIALITY NOTICE
This communication is intended for the sole use of the individual or entity to which it is addressed and may contain information that is privileged, confidential, and exempt from disclosure under applicable law. If the reader of this communication is not the intended recipient or the employee or agent responsible for delivering the message to the intended recipient, you are hereby notified that any dissemination, distribution, or copying of this communication may be strictly prohibited. If you have received this communication in error, please notify me immediately by telephone (702-361-9440) and return the communication to me at 1001 E. Sunset Road Las Vegas, NV 89199

Thank you.

Yul (an African-American male) was promoted to Executive Postmaster October 2008 for the first time since the inception of the Las Vegas Post Office in 1894.

UNITED STATES POSTAL SERVICE

uspsnews

It is my pleasure to announce the selection of Yul Melonson as the new PCES Postmaster, Las Vegas, NV, effective Saturday, October 11, 2008.

Yul began his Postal Service career as a letter carrier in Seattle, WA in 1978. After a promotion to Delivery Supervisor, he served in a wide array of Postal management positions in both Seattle, WA and Las Vegas NV, including Manager, Customer Services and Manager, Customer Service Operations.

Yul served as the Bulk Mail Center Manager in Los Angeles and San Francisco, CA and P&DC Manager in Reno, NV and Petaluma, CA, and International Service Center Plant Manager in Long Beach, CA. He was also a Service Team Leader for southern California and the Western Area.

Yul has been Officer-In-Charge in Henderson, NV and served as Postmaster in both Reno, NV and North Las Vegas, NV. Yul's recent assignments include A/Sr. Manager, PO Operations for the Nevada-Sierra District and Officer-In-Charge, Las Vegas, NV.

Please join with me in congratulating Yul on his appointment and extend your full support and cooperation to him in his new assignment.

Shaun E. Mossman
District Manager

PLEASE COPY AND POST ON ALL EMPLOYEE BULLETIN BOARDS.

00232

Formal Complaint
Page 78 of 244

First EEO Filed September 5, 2008 on Jerry Wilson's Threat. You will later see where the EEOC stated that I contacted them on August 18, 2008, and this will negate their plot to coincide with Jerry Wilson's statement because of the fifteen-day deadline to file the case, once contacted.

#13219886

Reference: PRE-036967-2008

Information for Pre-Complaint Counseling

Certified Mail No.	Date Mailed or Hand Delivered on
By *(Initials)*	Case No.

RECEIVED
OCT 1 0 2008
HEALTH & RESOURCES MANAGEMENT

On 8/26/2008 *(Month, Day, Year)*, you requested an appointment with a Dispute Resolution Specialist.

Important: Please read. You should complete this form and return it to the EEO office ***within10 calendar days*** of receipt. This is the only notification that you will receive regarding the necessity for you to complete this form.

A. Requester Information

Name *(Last, First, MI)*: McGee Lola B.	Social Security:	Home Telephone No.: (702) 260-0876
Your Mailing Address: 7582 Cypress Tree St, LV NV 89123		Finance Number: 316201
Name of Postal Facility Where You Work: NLV-Meadow Mesa Station 4904 Camino Al Norte NLV NV 89031		Office Telephone No.: (702) 657-647'
Address of Postal Facility: 4904 Camino Al Norte North Las Vegas NV 89031		Email Address*: lola.mcgee@usp
Employment Status *(Check One)*: ☐ Applicant ☐ Casual ☐ TE ☒ Career	Position Title: Acting/Manager Cust. Serv.	Grade Level: Level 22
Pay Location: 313 / Tour: days / Duty Hours: 7:00-1600	Off Days *(If Tour I, Show Nights Off)*: Sat./Sun.	Time in Current Position: - Years 1 Months 2 Week
Your Supervisor's Name: Jerry Wilson	Supervisor's Title: A/Postmaster-NLV	Supervisor's Telephone No.: (702) 649-2423

*Providing this information will authorize the U.S. Postal Service to send you important documents electronically.

B. Discrimination Factors

Prohibited discrimination includes actions taken based on your ***Race, Color, Religion, Sex, Age (40+), National Origin, Physical and/or Mental Disability, or in Retaliation*** *(actions based on your participation in prior EEO activity)*. These categories are referred to on this form as factors.

What factor(s) of Discrimination are you alleging? (Please be specific, i.e., Race-African American, Sex-Female).

Race = Black Sex = Female
Retaliation = Threat to do Something to me because I spoken Craig/Y

For Retaliation Allegations Only. If you are alleging retaliation discrimination, provide the date(s) and specifics of the EEO activity that you feel caused you to be retaliated against.

1. On ________ (Month, Day, Year), I engaged in EEO activity. Case No.: N/A
2. On ________ (Month, Day, Year), I engaged in EEO activity. Case No.: I have never filed an EEO before

C. Description of Incident Action

Formal Complaint Page 29 of 244

Please use the space below to briefly describe the incident or action that prompted you to seek EEO counseling at this time.

On 8/25/08 (Month, Day), 2008 (Year)

I was given an open ended Threat by Jerry Wilson. He stated "You continue to go over my head with Craig and Yul and I'm going to do Something about it." I asked Jerry what hours did Craig want on a Projection Spread sheet 72 = Carriers only 72B = Carrier and Supervisor hours. Jerry stated to me Carrier hours. That was not true because Craig sent us a nasty em

PS Form 2564-A, March 2001 (Page 1 of 3)

the next day, so I call Craig regarding the email and asked him what did he want. Craig stated F2B = Carriers and Supervisor hou

00183

doing and with persistance. I told him that my supervisor
made a mistake with the Schedule and We are Casing
18 routes and Spitting 8 routes. I told Yul that
I had already Spoke to Jerry and he told me
the SDO= overtime employees request was already
in to Shaun Mossman = District Manager.
Yul Confirmed the the SDO request Was
already in, but What about bring in your
TE's = Transitional Employees early. I replied
I Can do that he said yes, just Minimize
your overtime and 1700= Carriers out
after 5:00pm. Need-less to Say I had
My Supervisor Bring some TE's in to Case
and and some in to Carry more. However
it is my opinion that Jerry Wilson is a
paranoid, disrespectful person that does not
have the Skills to Manage. His threat to me
was the Straw that broke the Camels back. I don't
Know if he Meant doing Something Physical to me
Or paperwise, either Or none of it Was Welcomed and
it sent me into Trauma State and my body Shutdown

D. Comparisons

Explain why, based on the factors you cited in Section B, you believe that you were treated differently than other employees or applicants in similar situations

1. ______ This Was my First time Working With

(Name of Employee) Factor(s) that describe the employee, i.e., sex (male), National Origin (Hispanic)

was treated differently than I when: Jerry Wilson

2. ______

(Name of Employee) Factor(s) that describe the employee, i.e., sex (male), National Origin (Hispanic)

was treated differently than I when:

3. ______

(Name of Employee) Factor(s) that describe the employee, i.e., sex (male), National Origin (Hispanic)

was treated differently than I when:

E. Official(s) Responsible for Action(s)

List the name(s) of the official(s) who took the action that prompted you to seek counseling at this time.

1a. Name Jerry Wilson	b. Title A/Postmaster North Las Vega
c. Office North Las Vegas Post Office	d. Grade Level Level - 24
2a. Name Shaun Mossman	b. Title District Manager
c. Office District - Nevada Sierra	d. Grade Level Executive - PC.E.S

Retaliation Allegations Only: Was/were the official(s) listed in Section D above aware of your prior EEO activity?

☐ No ☐ Yes If yes, explain how the official(s) became aware: N/A

F. Resolution

What are you seeking as a resolution to your pre-complaint? Management Training for Jerry, Attitude & behavior Training for Jerry, Official and written apology, Life time medical for my Conditions, Monetary Compensation

G. Grievance MSPB Appeal

On the incident that prompted you to seek EEO counseling, have you:

1. Filed a grievance on the same issue? ☒ No ☐ Yes If yes, ______ (Date) ______ (Current Step)
2. Filed a MSPB appeal on this issue? ☒ No ☐ Yes If yes, ______ (Date Appeal Filed)

PS Form 2564-A, March 2001 (Page 2 of 3)

00185

Formal Complaint
Page 31 of 244

H. Anonymity

You have the right to remain anonymous during the pre-complaint process.

Do you desire anonymity? [X] No [ ] Yes

I. Representation

You have the right to retain representation of your choice. *(check one)* /

[ ] I waive the right to representation at this time. [ ] I authorize the person listed below to represent me.

Name of Representative	Representative's Title	
Name not available at this time but will be available by the Redress date		
Organization	Telephone Number	Email Address*
Mailing Address *(Street or P.O. Box, City, State and Zip +4)*		

* Providing this information will authorize the U.S. Postal Service to send your representative important documents electronically.

J. Documentation

Please attach any documentation you wish to submit to support your allegation(s). Include a copy of any written action(s) that caused you to seek counseling at this time.

Note: If you are alleging mental and/or physical disability, it is important for you to submit medical documentation of your disability during the pre-complaint process.

K. Privacy Act Notice

Privacy Act Notice. The collection of this information is authorized by the Equal Employment Opportunity Act of 1972, 42 U.S.C. § 2000e-16; the Age Discrimination in Employment Act of 1967, as amended, 29 U.S.C. § 633a; the Rehabilitation Act of 1973, as amended, 29 U.S.C. § 794a; and Executive Order 11478, as amended. This information will be used to adjudicate complaints of alleged discrimination and to evaluate the effectiveness of the EEO program. As a routine use, this information may be disclosed to an appropriate government agency, domestic or foreign, for law enforcement purposes; where pertinent, in a legal proceeding to which the USPS is a party or has an interest; to a government agency in order to obtain information relevant to a USPS decision concerning employment, security clearances, contracts, licenses, grants, permits or other benefits; to a government agency upon its request when relevant to its decision concerning employment, security clearances, security or suitability investigations, contracts, licenses, grants or other benefits; to a congressional office at your request, to an expert, consultant or other person under contract with the USPS to fulfill an agency function; to the Federal Records Center for storage; to the Office of Management and Budget for review of private relief legislation; to an independent certified public accountant during an official audit of USPS finances; to an investigator, administrative judge or complaints examiner appointed by the Equal Employment Opportunity Commission for investigation of a formal EEO complaint under 29 CFR 1614; to the Merit Systems Protection Board or Office of Special Counsel for proceedings or investigations involving personnel practices and other matters within their jurisdiction; and to a labor organization as required by the National Labor Relations Act. Under the Privacy Act provision, the information requested is voluntary for the complainant, and for Postal Service employees and other witnesses.

L. Authorization

I am aware that the claim(s) contained herein shall by-pass the pre-complaint process *if* like or related to a formal complaint that I have already filed, or *if* the claim(s) constitutes a spin-off complaint. (A spin-off complaint contests the manner in which a previously filed complaint is being processed.) In completing this PS Form 2564-A, *Information for Pre-complaint Counseling*, I recognize that the Manager, Dispute Resolution will review the claim(s) contained herein and determine how they shall be processed. I will be notified, in writing, if the Manager determines that my claim(s) shall be processed as amendments or appendages to a formal complaint that I have already filed.

Please print your name here	
Lola McGee	
Your Signature	Date signed
[signature]	9/5/08

Please return this form to:

National EEO Investigative Services Office
EEO Contact Center
U.S. Postal Service
PO Box 21979
Tampa FL 33622-1979

PS Form **2564-A**, March 2001 *(Page 3 of 3)*

Formal Complaint
Page 32 of 244

00186

UNITED STATES POSTAL SERVICE®

Certification of Receipt — Publication 133

Privacy Act Notice

Privacy Act Notice. The collection of this information is authorized the Equal Employment Opportunity Act of 1972, 42 U.S.C. § 2000e-16; the Age Disrimination in Employment Act of 1967, as amended, 29 U.S.C. § 633a; the Rehabilitation Act of 1973, as amended, 29 U.S.C. § 794a; and Executive Order 11478, as amended. This information will be used to adjudicate complaints of alleged discrimination and to evaluate the effectiveness of the EEO program. As a routine use, this information may be disclosed to an appropriate government agency, domestic or foreign, for law enforcement purposes; where pertinent, in a legal proceeding to which the USPS is a party or has an interest; to a government agency in order to obtain information relevant to a USPS decision concerning employment, security clearances, contracts, licenses, grants, permits or other benefits; to a government agency upon its request when relevant to its decision concerning employment, security clearances, security or suitability investigations, contracts, licenses, grants or other benefits; to a congressional office at your request; to an expert, consultant or other person under contract with the USPS to fulfill an agency function; to the Federal Records Center for storage; to the Office of Management and Budget for review of private relief legislation; to an independent certified public accountant during an official audit of USPS finances; to an investigator, administrative judge or complaints examiner appointed by the Equal Employment Opportunity Commission for investigation of a formal EEO complaint under 29 CFR 1614; to the Merit Systems Protection Board or Office of Special Counsel for proceedings or investigations involving personnel practices and other matters within their jurisdiction; and to a labor organization as required by the National Labor Relations Act. Under the Privacy Act provision, the information requested is voluntary for the complainant, and for Postal Service employees and other witnesses.

Certification of Receipt — Publication 133

I hereby certify that on this date I received a copy of Publication 133, *What You Need to Know About EEO,* to keep for my personal records.

Signature of Recipient: [signature] Date: 8/29/08

Note: Recipient, when you receive this form by mail, please sign and return it to the EEO Office at the same time you return your completed PS Form 2564-A, *Information for Pre-Complaint Counseling.*

Certification of Service — Publication 133

I hereby certify that on this date, Publication 133, *What You Need to Know About EEO,*

was mailed to 7582 Cypress Tree St. Las Vegas, NV 89123

Priority mail

via ~~Certified Mail No.~~ USPS Delivery Confimation # 0308 0730 0001 0903 1083

~~or delivered by hand to~~ Left in my Mailbox

Signature of Server | Date

PS Form **2563-A,** March 2001

00187

Formal Complaint
Page 33 of 244

Agreement to Participate in REDRESS®, an Alternative Dispute Resolution Process

Case No.
Date Initiated

I, ______________________, have been advised that, in accordance with 29 C.F.R. §1614.105(f), I have the option of participating in mediation instead of the counseling process. The EEO complaints processing office has given me information about the mediation procedure, and I voluntarily agree to participate in REDRESS® mediation during the pre-complaint processing period. I am aware that REDRESS® mediation sessions are confidential, and that resolutions reached during the procedure are handled in the same manner as are resolutions reached during the counseling process. In signing this agreement, I acknowledge that the pre-complaint processing period will be 90 calendar days. If the matter that I brought to the dispute resolution specialist's attention has not been resolved before the 90th day, I have the right to file a formal complaint at any time thereafter up to 15 calendar days after receiving my notice of right to file a discrimination complaint.

Privacy Act Notice

Privacy Act Notice. The collection of this information is authorized by the Equal Employment Opportunity Act of 1972, 42 U.S.C. § 2000e-16; the Age Discrimination in Employment Act of 1967, as amended, 29 U.S.C. § 633a; the Rehabilitation Act of 1973, as amended, 29 U.S.C. § 794a; and Executive Order 11478, as amended. This information will be used to adjudicate complaints of alleged discrimination and to evaluate the effectiveness of the EEO program. As a routine use, this information may be disclosed to an appropriate government agency, domestic or foreign, for law enforcement purposes; where pertinent, in a legal proceeding to which the USPS is a party or has an interest; to a government agency in order to obtain information relevant to a USPS decision concerning employment, security clearances, contracts, licenses, grants, permits or other benefits; to a government agency upon its request when relevant to its decision concerning employment, security clearances, security or suitability investigations, contracts, licenses, grants or other benefits; to a congressional office at your request, to an expert, consultant or other person under contract with the USPS to fulfill an agency function; to the Federal Records Center for storage; to the Office of Management and Budget for review of private relief legislation; to an independent certified public accountant during an official audit of USPS finances; to an investigator, administrative judge or complaints examiner appointed by the Equal Employment Opportunity Commission for investigation of a formal EEO complaint under 29 CFR 1614; to the Merit Systems Protection Board or Office of Special Counsel for proceedings or investigations involving personnel practices and other matters within their jurisdiction; and to a labor organization as required by the National Labor Relations Act. Under the Privacy Act provision, the information requested is voluntary for the complainant, and for Postal Service employees and other witnesses.

Signature of Counselee	Date
	9/5/08

PS Form 2567-B, March 2001

00188

Formal Complaint
Page 34 of 244

Disclaimer:
In order to maintain authenticity,
the following correspondeces have not been altered.

* * * * *

My EEO Response to their acceptance of the formal filing November 11, 2009.

December 1, 2008

United States Postal Service
Equal Employment Opportunity
In The Matter Of:

Lola McGee (Not McGhee)
7582 Cypress Tree St.
Las Vegas, Nevada 89123-0553
Complainant, Phone Number: (702) 260-0876

V.

John E. Potter
Postmaster General
United States Postal Service
Western Area
Agency.

Agency Case number: 4E-890-0120-08

Date Formal Filed: November 1, 2008

This letter is in response to the Partial Acceptance/Partial Dismissal of Formal EEO Complaint that I received on 12/1/08 Delivery Confirmation #03073330000134168378.

Unfortunately, I'm quite confused with the response. I understand that the EEO Agency has its own system and terminology in which it operates and uses, however, I would like to explain my complaints and why they were filed on the certain dates.

With the complaint filed on 9/5/08, as a result of the Threat from Jerry Wilson A/Postmaster North Las Vegas Nevada, that was a {DISCRETE ACT] that happened on 8/25/08 and the postal service has a ZERO tolerance policy on threats and violence (Even in jest or words) nevertheless something negative was going to happen because he told me so and from that day on I communicated with he via telephone, injury compensation, and fax. To this day I don't believe that the OIG or TAT team has met on the situation and management was notified via my CA-1, even though Jerry lied to the DOL and the EEO Specialist (B. J. Clay), EEO Complaint, and medical documentation. This is a separate situation from the other two EEO Complaints.

With the complaint filed on 9/18/08, I did not think that I was discriminated against until I was not selected for the position of Huntridge Station; in which, I was notified on 8/18/08. I sought out legal advice and I was told that I had been discriminated against all the time because it has been a continuing practice of the postal service with me. They continued to use me as an acting manager, but refused to promote me. Also, I was asked if all of the promoted people were white are of another race and I replied; yes. In addition, I gained more information when I sought medical attention on 8/27/08 from Dr. Mary Reed. She stated that I had a Panic Attack on 8/25/08 and I suffer from PTSD/Major Depressive Disorder because of the discrimination that I had endured for the past two (2) years. I did not know that I was discriminated against all that time, so that is why the EEO was not filed until 9/18/08. I thought that time had pasted by, not to mention, I had never filed an EEO until the Threat came from Jerry Wilson and I got so sick until I could not go to work. I had never been in this situation before in my life. I understand that each refusal to promote stands as a [DISCRETE ACT], but it's the pattern not the one job here are there. Robert Reynosa, Mark Martinez, and Jennifer Vo are pattern setting [DISCRETE ACT]. Surely, I would not have been able to possess a "Reasonable Suspicion" especially if I was not looking for one. I took every refusal as it came and tried even harder for the next one. However, when you come full circle the bell goes off as I did with Huntridge Station, it was my second time there and I did EXCELLENT. I was discriminated against based on Race: African American, Color: Black, Sex: Female, Age: 46 yrs old, Religion: Christian, Retaliation: Prior EEO Complaints, and Jerry Wilson told management that I said I was going to file an EEO when I said nothing of the sort. Please refer to my EEO dated 9/18/08 for full details. I know that it has been a long time span from 8/2006 – 8/2008, but the EEO process is suppose to be in place to help the complaint that has been discriminated against and I don't think my lack of knowledge should be a technicality that is used against me to protect those that discriminated against me. Yes, they treated me very badly but also you have to consider the retaliation that would have come up against me had I known to file earlier. Also, it wasn't mention about working Saturdays in the Formal letter but I did, and it was two 3% merit increases that I got from both Jennifer Vo (2006) and Robert Reynosa (2007). I was trying to get promoted on my own merit not fight against those who were making all of the decisions. Unfortunately, I got sick on 8/25/08 and could not return to work and the information just kept coming on how ill I really was. I would like to remind the Agency to have Dana Urbanski, and Rayshaine Hartwell as my witnesses.

With the EEO filed on 9/30/08, I reviewed the information from the EEO Specialist on 9/24/08 and it revealed Craig Colton and Cory Richards names several times with in the 15 jobs that I had applied for and I did not know that they had that much say so on as many packages as they did, they are a pattern setting [DISCRETE ACT]. I was told by the EEO Specialist that they chose the best qualified applicant that was in the package and I do not think that they are telling the truth when you have me a long time promoted supervisor, acting manager for two plus years, an BS Degree, an AA Degree along with much success in the stations along with accolades from year to year in difficult offices. Also, why would you chose a lateral person over someone whom has proven themselves right here in the district. In addition, I have why I think I was discriminated against by Craig and Cory and I painted the pictures of Steven Phaup just to explain the history that I have with Craig and Cory. I wasn't even considered for a position when they did not even have anyone else that they wanted to promote. The last position that Craig or Cory passed me by on was the Huntridge Station and they chose a lateral. Why couldn't this person have lateral to the next available position; and promote someone in the district whom has already proven to be qualified for the job. Please refer to my EEO dated 9/30/08 for details. Also, this EEO would have been filed earlier but the EEOC did not send me the paperwork until my 3rd request, B. J. Clay can attest to this information. I was discriminated based on Race: African American, Color: Black, Sex: Female, Age: 46 yrs

I believe that I was discriminated based on Race: Black, and Gender: Female. Please refer to my complaint filed 9/5/08 for more details. To date, I am still off work because of this issue old, Religion: Christian, and Retaliation: Prior EEO activity. Also, I would like to remind the Agency to have om Martin, Shelby Kruger-Duncan, Dana Urbanski, and Charles Turner to be witnesses to this particular EEO Complaint.

Sincerely

Lola McGee

January, 29 2009

To: NEEOISO
EEO Contact Center
U. S. Postal Service
P. O. Box 21979
Tampa, Florida 33622-1979

From: Lola McGee
7582 Cypress Tree St.
Las Vegas, NV 89123-0553

Dear EEO Agency,

I, Lola McGee, am writing this letter in response in reference to the Delivery Confirmation #03073330000134189526 received on 1/28/09 and the Signature Confirmation #23050270000046532674 sent on 1/15/09. The Del. Conf. was a response from your agency to the Signature Conf. that I sent regarding three (3) issues.

I find that the agency has made a mistake in my requests of the three issues that were sent in my Signature Confirmation listed above. I had two (2) items in the envelope that were to be an amendment to Case# 4E-890-0120-08 and they were my pay check stub showing that I was not paid for pay period 1-2009 and an email addressed to my Investigator Q. VanBenschoten in addition to the EEO Agency.

However, I also sent in the same package a new claim that I requested on January, 7 2009, and signed/mailed by me on 1/15/2009. This new claim was regarding new discriminating issues and some of the same from the 9/18/08 claim that was filed and the NEEOISO Dismissed the issues in the 9/18/2008 claim. Consequently, it is confusing to me that the agency would combine my two (2) amended request with the new claim. I don't know if the reason was because all three (3) issues were in the same envelope or the agency made a mistake in not realizing that it had previously dismissed the claim that was signed by me on 9/18/2008.

However, this new claim signed/mailed by me on 1/15/2009 in Signature Confirmation# 23050270000046532674 envelope has some different issues as well as some of the same issues from the 9/18/2008 claim that was sent in and dismissed. I don't see how the agency can dismiss a claim from the formal filing dated 11/1/2008 and turn right around and amend it back to my Formal Filing number 4E-890-0120-08. The initial response from the agency received by me on 12/1/2008 Delivery Confirmation number 03073330000134168378 of the Partial Acceptance/Partial Dismissal of the above case number dismissed this portion of the claim.

It is at this time that I, Lola McGee, request that the NEEOISO treat my claim signed on 1/15/09 as an individual claim based on the previously mentioned information. The claim has new/different issues along with some of the same information from the previous one; however, the timing of this claim falls within a different 45 day period with a set of different issues that should stand alone by it self. I ask that the agency do the fair and right thing in the processing of my liberty to file a claim based on being discriminated against based on a host of issues. This is one of the very reasons that I am out on job injuries and

I can't continue to get better while being treated unfairly. I'm resending this letter/claim today 1/29/2009 and remember I'm seriously ill with the postal service's treatment of me as a Black Female along with a host of other discriminating tactics and factors.

Sincerely
Lola McGee

U. S. Postal Service EEO INVESTIGATIVE AFFIDAVIT (COMPLAINANT)	Page No. 1	No. Pages 32	Case No. 4E-890-0120-08
1. Affiant's Name (First, Middle, Last) Lola B. McGEE		**2. Employing Postal Facility** NLV Main Office-Permanent/Detail EAS 22 = NLV-Meadow Mesa Station	

3. Position Title	**4. Grade Level**	**5. Postal Address and Zip + 4**	**6. Unit Assigned**
Supervisor, Customer Services/ Mgr. Cust. SVS	EAS-17/EAS- 22	1414 E. Lake Mead Blvd. NLV, NV 89030-9998/ 4904 Camino Al Norte NLV, NV 89031-9998	**Permanent: NLV – Main/ Detail: Meadow Mesa Station**

Privacy Act Notice/USPS Standards of Conduct

Privacy Act Notice. **The collection of this information is authorized by the Equal Employment Opportunity act of 1972, 42 U.S.C. § 2000e-16; the Age Discrimination in Employment Act of 1967, as amended, 29 U.S.C. § 633a; the Rehabilitation Act of 1973, as amended. This information will be used to adjudicate complaints of alleged discrimination and to evaluate the effectiveness of the EEO program. As a routine use, this information may be disclosed to an appropriate government agency, domestic or foreign, for law enforcement purposes; where pertinent, in a legal proceeding to which the USPS is a party or has an interest; to a government agency in order to obtain information relevant to a USPS decision concerning employment, security clearances, contracts, licenses, grants, permits or other benefits; to a government agency upon its request when relevant to its decision concerning employment, security clearances, security or suitability investigations, contracts, licenses, grants or other benefits; to a congressional office at your request; to an expert, consultant, or other person under contract with the USPS to fulfill an agency function; to the Federal Records Center for storage; to the Office of Management and Budget for review of private relief legislation; to an independent certified public accountant during an official audit of USPS finances; to an investigator, administrative judge or complaints examiner appointed by the Equal Employment Opportunity Commission for Investigation of a formal EEO complaint under 29 CFR 1614; to the Merit Systems Protection Board or Office of Special Counsel for proceedings or investigations involving personnel practices and other matters within their jurisdiction; and to a labor organization as required by the National Labor Relations Act. Under the Privacy Act provision, the information requested is voluntary for the complainant, and for Postal Service employees and other witnesses.**

Important Information Regarding Your Complaint

This PS Form 2568-A, EEO Investigative Affidavit (Complainant), and the other form mentioned below, are being provided for you to use to fully respond to the accompanying questions. Mail or deliver your completed statement to the EEO complaints investigator within15 calendar days of the date you received the forms. Use PS Form(s) 2569, EEO Investigative Affidavit (Continuation Sheet), as needed, to complete your written statement. Remember to number the top of each page and sign and date the bottom of each page of your statement. If you return your statement by mail, the return envelope must be postmarked on or before the 15th calendar day after the date that you received the affidavit forms.	**Failure to complete your statement and return the forms within the allotted time period could result in your complaint being dismissed based upon your failure to proceed. EEOC complaints processing regulation. 29 C.F.R. 1614.107(a)(7), states, in part, [A complaint may be dismissed] "Where the agency has provided the complainant with the written request to provide relevant information or otherwise proceed with the complaint, and the complainant has failed to respond to the request within 15 days of its receipt, or the complainant's response does not address the agency's request, provided that the request included a notice of the proposed dismissal."**
7. Statement A(Continue on Form 2569 if additional space is required)	

1. State your name and identify your home address.
ANSWER: Lola Bonitta McGee – 7582 Cypress Tree Street Las Vegas, Nevada 89123-0553

2. Identify your phone number.
ANSWER: (702) 260-0876 Home, (562) 886-2662 Cell

3. Identify your email address (if available).
ANSWER: lola.mcgee@usps.gov, and bonitta@embarqmail.com

4. Identify your RACE.
ANSWER: African American

5. Identify your COLOR.
ANSWER: Black

6. Identify your RELIGION.
ANSWER: Christian, God fearing woman believing in the Father, Son, and the Holy Ghost.

7. Identify your SEX.
ANSWER: Female

8. Identify your AGE and DATE OF BIRTH.
ANSWER: 46 years old, Born: July, 7 1962

9. Other than the current complaint, 4E-890-0120-08, do you have EEO activity? If yes, identify the complaint number, date the formal complaint was filed, and your role in the EEO activity (Complainant, Representative, or Witness).

b. Identify the USPS location to which you are assigned. Include its name and address.

ANSWER: Officially I am assigned to North Las Vegas Main Post Office located at 1414 E. Lake Mead Blvd. North Las Vegas, Nevada 89030-9998; however, on July 9, 2008, after being asked by Craig Colton the prior week while he was in Yul Melonson's office (Now the Las Vegas Postmaster, but he was acting at the time) I reported to Meadow Mesa Station as the Manager, Customer Services/A, located at 4904 Camino Al Norte North Las Vegas, Nevada 89031-9998. I had an on the job injury on 8/25/08 while I was there. Jerry Wilson (was the acting postmaster of North Las Vegas) gave me an open ended threat: "You continue to go over my head with Craig and Yul and I'm going to do something about it."

c. Identify your direct supervisor. Provide their full name, position, telephone number and email address (if known).

ANSWER: Officially my direct supervisor was Yul Melonson, North Las Vegas Postmaster and his telephone number was (702) 649-2623. I did not know his email address by hard I would just pull him up in my directory. However, he is now the promoted Postmaster of the City of Las Vegas (702) 361-9200. Since I was on detail at Meadow Mesa Station, and Jerry Wilson was on detail as the acting Postmaster of North Las Vegas then he (Jerry Wilson) was my direct supervisor (702) 649-2623. However, after they moved Jerry Wilson out, sometime after my on the job injury, Cory Richards became the acting Postmaster of North Las Vegas. And to my understanding, Cory Richards has been officially assigned to the position now (Postmaster of North Las Vegas) (702) 649-2623, and I do not know his email address.

In your complaint, you alleged that since July 12, 2008, you have been subjected to hostile work environment harassment. The following questions refer to the Issues Accepted for Investigation on this claim.

12. In your complaint, you allege that since July 12, 2008, you have not been selected for the position of Manager, Customer Service. Please identify/confirm the vacancy number(s), title(s), and location(s) for which you applied. If there is more than one, please identify them separately.

ANSWER: The heading of this section says hostile work environment/harassment, but the questions are referring to the positions I applied for. I just want to be clear and bring it to your attention. 1. 52108635, 2305-7091 Manager, Customer Services EAS-21 Las Vegas NV = Huntridge Station, 2. 51945217, 2310-0002 Manager, Customer Services EAS-22 Las Vegas NV = Emerald Station, 3. W-08082, Manager, Customer Services EAS-22 Henderson NV = Valle Verde Station, 4. W-07001, Manager, Customer Services EAS-21 Las Vegas NV = Huntridge Station, 5. W-06954, Manager, Customer Services EAS-22 Las Vegas NV = Paradise Valley Station, 6. W-06956, Manager, Customer Services EAS-22 Las Vegas NV = Garside Station.

a. When did you first become aware of the opening(s)?

ANSWER: 1. 07/01/08, 2. 5/21/08, 3. Closing date 09/12/07, 4. Closing date 01/31/07, 5. Closing date 01/18/07, 6. 01/18/07.

b. Why were you interested in or why did you want to apply for the position(s)?

ANSWER: I have excelled in the Supervisor, Customer Services position in the postal service and I wanted to broaden my horizon along with gaining upward mobility and that's why I put in for the Manager in Charge Program (MIC) in 2005. I felt I could benefit the postal service in addition to improving my skills and ability. I desire challenges and new adventures and the upward mobility would provide that benefit to me and the service. I have an AA degree in Human Services, and a BS in Business/Management which demonstrates my ability to learn at a higher level and have a minimal learning curve. I've owned my own business before along with having a small staff and employees. I was a Case Manager/Counselor before I came to the postal service and I wanted to continue my expectations of myself. I'm a high achiever and I believe in growth and development. I've trained supervisors to be an asset to the postal service in my current capacity and they have gone on to be accepted into the ASP program. I'm a wealth of knowledge and I just want to be judged on my own merit and not the color of my skin or my sex. I have demonstrated my ability to do the job and produce great results for my superiors and it baffles me to the reasoning of why I was not chosen for at least one of the 15 positions that I applied for. I'm a hard working serious professional who takes pride in what I do and my work ethic is over and beyond, and it's a shame that it has to come to this in order to be recognized. I respect any and everyone and I deserve the same in return. Respect is very, very high on my chart and no one should have to go through discrimination. The energy that is utilized to conjure up stuff and be mean or hateful to someone can be channeled in creating a better working environment. Put yourself in my shoes. If I wasn't who I am then I would have never gotten sick because I would have just treated people the way that they treated me, but I am who I am and I'm not going to disrespect me or no one else, what would that say about me. God made me who I am and I can sleep very well knowing that I have not done anyone any wrong intentionally.

c. Did you apply for the position(s)? If yes, when and how did you apply for the position(s)?

ANSWER: 1. Yes, 07/16/08, ecareer – HR Shared Services Center, 2. Yes, 05/21/08, ecareer – Shared Services Center, 3. Yes, 09/5/07, PS Form 991, 4. Yes, 01/31/07, PS Form 991, 5. Yes, 01/18/07, PS Form 991, 6. Yes, 01/18/07, PS Form 991.

d. Provide a copy of your application (e.g., PS Form 991 or other written communication regarding your interest in the position) for the position(s) and any communications you received from the USPS regarding your status in the selection process.

e. Was the selection process for this vacancy a competitive or non-competitive selection process?

ANSWER: 1. Competitive, 2. Competitive, 3.Competitive, 4. Competitive, 5. Competitive, 6. Competitive

f. Please explain your understanding of the selection process for the type you identified.

ANSWER: Competitive – there is a review committee that consist of members and the chairman is one of the members and several applicants are competing for the position based on qualifications, knowledge, skills, and ability, utilizing the STAR Format = Situation/Task Action Results, performance etc. Non-Competitive is a request for a lateral at the same level (i.e. hardship etc.)

g. Was there a review committee for this position? If yes, please identify the review committee members including name and position, if known.

ANSWER: 1. NO, I believe the person chosen was known in someway by Cory Richards (He's been promoted 3 times since I arrived in the district May 2004, we both started out as supervisors for Craig Colton – Postmaster in North Las Vegas) or his girlfriend/wife Kelly McKague, the person was a lateral from out of the district, 2. Yes, Cory Richards was the Chairman – Maryann Roach MDO tour-1, Valerie Cattalosse – Manager, Information Technology, 3. Yes, Craig Colton was the Selecting Official, - Yul Melonson was the Chairman – Donna Bowerman – Manager Retail, Richard Weber, demoted Manager Post Office Operations (MPOO) to Manager, Customer Services EAS-22, 4. Yes, Craig Colton was the Chairman (He's been promoted twice since I arrived in May 2004, Currently he's the Senior MPOO) - Valerie Cattalosse – Manager Information Technology, Paul Scrima – moved from Manager Delivery Programs to Manager Compliment Committee, 5. Yes, Craig Colton was the Chairman – Valerie Cattalosse – Manager Information Technology, Paul Scrima – Compliment Committee (No selection made), 6. Yes, Craig Colton was the Chairman – Valerie Cattalosse – Manager Information Technology, Paul Scrima – Compliment Committee (No selection made).

h. Was there a selecting official for this position? If yes, please identify the selecting official including name and position, if known.

ANSWER: 1. Yes, Cory Richards – Postmaster North Las Vegas at this time, but he was MCSO/A at that time and his permanent position was Manager, Customer Services at that time. 2. Yes, Robert Reynosa – Manager, Customer Services Operation. 3. Yes, Craig Colton – Postmaster Henderson Nevada at the time (He has since been promoted to Senior MPOO). 4. Yes, Robert Reynosa – MCSO City of

Las Vegas. 5. Yes, Robert Reynosa – MCSO (No selection made). 6. Yes, Robert Reynosa – MCSO (No selection made).

i. Was there a concurring official for this position? If yes, please identify the concurring official including name and position, if known.

ANSWER: 1. Yes, Craig Colton – Senior MPOO currently. 2. Yes, Yul Melonson – Currently Las Vegas Postmaster since October 2008 FY 2009. 3. Yes, John Morgan – Senior MPOO at the time has since left the district. 4. Yes, Mark Martinez – Las Vegas Postmaster at the time has since left the district but still in Western Area as a District Manager. 5. Yes, Mark Martinez – Las Vegas Postmaster at the time (No selection made). 6. Yes, Mark Martinez – Las Vegas Postmaster at the time (No selection made).

j. Were you recommended by the review committee for consideration by the selecting official? How were you informed of this decision?

ANSWER: 1. No Committee, I was called at Meadow Mesa Station by Cory Richards for a scheduled Interview with him and Yul Melonson on 8/7/08 and the Interview was cancelled and Cory called me back and told me to come the next day 8/8/08 to interview with him and Craig Colton. 2. No, by B. J. Clay, EEO (ADR) Specialist. 3. Yes, Craig Colton sent me a letter to my home dated 10/17/07 for an interview on 10/31/07. 4. No, B. J. Clay – EEO (ADR) Specialist, it was given to someone from out of the district. 5. No, B. J. Clay, EEO (ADR) Specialist (No selection was made). 6. No, B. J. Clay – EEO (ADR) Specialist (No selection was made).

k. Were you interviewed for the position? If yes, when were you interviewed and by whom?

ANSWER: 1. Yes, on 8/8/08 by Cory Richards and Craig Colton. 2. No. 3. Yes, on 10/31/07 by Craig Colton. For the positions 4-6 I did not receive an interview.

l. If you were not interviewed, were you provided a reason as to why you were not interviewed for the position? If yes, what was the reason and who provided this explanation.

ANSWER: For Positions 2 and 4-6 I was not interviewed and I was not provided an explanation as to why I wasn't interviewed.

m. Were you selected for the position? If not, who was selected? Please provide their full name and identify their race, color, religion, sex, age, and prior position.

ANSWER: I was not selected for any of the position 1-6 and I don't know any of their ages nor religions. 1. Thomas Jack, I believe he's Caucasian, white, male, and he was from another district and probably area, I'm not sure, I was told that he was a level 21 manager and took a lateral. 2. Jason McMahill, Caucasian, white, male, and he was originally going around the district doing route inspections and observing offices on there CSAW processes and I was in the number one CSAW operating office at Paradise Valley Station in Las Vegas. I believe I have more experience than he does, but I wasn't given the job. He was promoted twice within a year's time, Sunrise Station EAS-21 in which I interviewed on 11/28/2007. He was starting to act as manager after me. Next, he received a promotion to position (2) Emerald Station EAS-22. 3. Kelly McKague Caucasian, white, female and she was also in the MIC program. 4. Gerard Carraza, Caucasian/Hispanic (uncertain), male, another person from out of the district, and I don't know his prior position. For positions 5 and 6 there were no selections.

n. If you were not selected, were you provided a reason as to why you were not selected for the position? If yes, what was the reason and who provided this explanation.

ANSWER: 1. Yes, I was told by Cory Richards on 8/18/08 that I interviewed very, very well and I hit the points he wanted me to and it was a hard decision to make "Very hard" and Thomas Jack interviewed well also and he is already a level-21 manager. He stated "Don't give up there are more jobs coming and I'm sure you will be promoted within the next year." I did not ask Cory but I wanted to know, If there were more jobs coming, and Thomas Jack wanted a lateral, then why not tell him that there will be more jobs coming and let him put in for those. I have demonstrated to all my boss' that I can do the job and do it well, but I continued to be passed over for their on various reasons and I'm right here in the district going where ever they wanted me to go and had been at Huntridge Station twice and did an excellent job according to them, but it was not good enough to be selected for a promotion. That's when I knew something was wrong. 2. Yes, Cory Richards sent me a letter dated 6/24/08 and told me that I was not recommended by the review committee and he was the Chairman, his email address is corey.d.richards@usps.gov. 3. Yes, Craig Colton stated in a letter dated 11/5/07 in making a final selection the qualifications of each applicant were carefully evaluated but I was not selected and it doesn't reflect upon my capabilities. Instead this represents my judgment of whom in light of experience and training, was the best qualified applicant. Also, I called Craig and he stated to me that I interviewed well, my skill base is strong and it's not a matter of if I'll be promoted it's when. He also told me that I was to confident, heavy, and strong. I'm a serious person. 4, 5, and 6, No I was not provided a reason for why I was not selected for the positions.

o. Do you believe you should have been selected for the vacancy? If yes, why do you believe you should have been selected for this position?

ANSWER: Absolutely, yes I believe I should have been selected for at least one of the six not to mention I'm very qualified for all of them. I have been used to go from station to station and perform to high standards and clean up mess, but I'm not good enough to promote. If I wasn't good enough to promote then they would not have used me to manage for over two years. I was used with out any reservation and it meant nothing to them. I made a mistake by thinking I was special, and all along they had no intention on promoting me. To tell you the truth I'm over qualified for the positions I put in for considering my performance level against some stations. Craig told me to my face one time that he would take his supervisors any day and put them up against the Las Vegas Managers. I am a serious team player and I take my job seriously and I do not play games with people. I do what is asked of me and more, because it's my integrity and work ethic that is being watch. I take pride in doing anything that I do; and I'm not going to waste my time our any one else's. I did not ask anyone to give me anything I asked for the opportunity to earn it, and I have done that over and beyond. I believe in fairness and I have not been treated fairly. I want the investigator to check my performance reports: key indicators, Del. Conf., flash, 1700, % to STD, sick leave, TEI, overtime, grievance numbers, etc. from the time I arrived at a station to the time I left the station up against the reports before I got there. I would not be sitting at home ill if I did not take my job seriously. Discriminated against, yes, I was discriminated against in every way, shape, form, and fashion with a smile. Also, remember no one told me what to do at any station I just went on my own knowledge, skills, and ability to succeed, and I have had my own business so I know what ever the product or service is that's what needs to be improved. I thank God for my ability, skill/will, knowledge, perseverance, tenacity and when the processes need tweaking then adjust them. I put my heart, mind, body, and soul into the postal service and I was treated like I didn't even exist. Yes, I am a God fearing, heavy voice, black female, with confidence, and I know how to follow directions. In my book the best leader was once a good follower. Lead by example. I did not deserve this.

p. Other than the current EEO complaint, has another appeal or complaint been filed on this issue? If yes, where is it in the process? If a settlement has been reached, describe the settlement. Provide copies of any documentation and settlement (if applicable).

ANSWER: Yes, it was signed and sent on 1/15/09

q. Who do you believe was responsible for determining whether or not you would be selected for the vacancy? Please provide their name, position, email address, and office telephone number.

ANSWER: On this particular number as I understand the NEEOISO processes and procedures: It was Craig Colton the current Senior MPOO, I don't have his phone number or email address, but he can be located by calling the Las Vegas Postmaster Office secretary at (702) 361-9200 and Cory Richards North Las Vegas Postmaster, corey.d.richards@usps.gov and his telephone number is (702) 649-2623.

r. Why do you believe this individual was responsible for the decision?

ANSWER: Corey Richards – I'm black, female, and there is not one black manager in the City of Las Vegas, Henderson, or North Las Vegas Stations let alone female. They just got a black Postmaster in Las Vegas and that was in October 2008, and he's number 13 and the first installation was in the late 1800's, something is wrong with that picture. I have a serious side to me and I am misunderstood and perceived by some managers as being mean and they don't even know me. Let my work speak for me and not your perception of who I am. I would not be able to be productive in a diverse organization as a manager if I wasn't able to carry myself as a professional and provide the necessary leadership that the employees and staff needed. The decision makers of my fate as a manager are the one's who feel threatened, and its only discrimination. Craig Colton – he thinks I'm too confident and strong with my personality. It's like you are a black female and you are not to be that far up the ladder. In addition to the Steven Phaup issues that happened in North Las Vegas while he was postmaster. Steven Phaup was Craig's right hand man and he adored him. I arrived at North Las Vegas Post Office in May 2004 and delivery was 5% over SPLY in four and one half months, I reduced it to -3.5 under. Steve was jealous of my ability to communicate with the employees and produce results. Steve had a problem with the Union Steward Charles Turner and they would go back and forth hollering at each other on the workroom floor. Basically, Steve thought he ran North Las Vegas through Craig. I captured under time on a daily basis and he did not like it, so he would try devious tactics to ruin my operation (Delivery). I had Human Resources Patti Hansen and Shelby Kruger-Duncan come all the way from the GMF to Norht Las Vegas Post Office just to meet and see who Lola McGee was. Steve did not like that, he would hide my schedules, and employee leave slips, along with telling Craig I don't know what I'm doing and my carriers are not carrying the under time that I said they were carrying, but the proof was in the reports/numbers. Steve started talking unprofessional to me and I was not going to have it, so I called about three or four meetings with Craig between the forth quarter of FY 2004- the first three quarters of FY 2005. I wrote Craig emails of concern regarding Steves tactics and his disrespect towards me. We had meetings but nothing would change. Craig would take Steve to lunch, but he never took me to lunch. I also would like to know what Steven Phaup got on his merit for FY 2004 and FY 2005. To make a long story short, Dana Urbanski was the Manager at Meadow Mesa Station and she came down to work at NLV-Main Post Office in Craig's position as OIC because Craig went on a detail in the City of Las Vegas. Steve Continued to have this behavior with me and I called a meeting with Dana just as I had done with Craig. Dana tried to resolve the issues but Steve would say he would do better but he didn't. Eventually, Dana had a talk with Craig and ultimately Craig sent and email and it stated that Steve was going to be assigned to Meadow Mesa Station and he was to turn over all his stock and keys to me. Craig wanted me to run the F4 operation and he would get someone else to run delivery. I had stopped all the grievances and the union steward started working unlike when I arrived at the office. Delivery was running smoothly; and Steve was to report to Meadow Mesa within the next week after he got back from vacation leave. Steve never reported to Meadow Mesa and I was not given all the stock/cash reserve that I was suppose to have in my vault. From Aug 2005 thru Oct. 2005, Steve never showed up with the cash or reported to work so I called Maintenance to pop the lock and witness what was in the drawer. Needless to say, the money $1000.00 was not there and that led to the postal inspectors and Craig had to really get involved at that point. After going back and forth saying he was going to return and had been caught with illegal documents and other charges, Craig was forced to terminate Steven Phaup and it was very hard for him to have to do that. It is my belief that Craig would not promote me because of these issues with Steve, even though he knows that I'm capable and qualified with the necessary skills to do the job very well. He tried to get Steve promoted but he just would not act right; it is my opinion that Steve was self destructing and Craig wanted to save him because he was Craig's right hand man. So at this time, Craig will fake and shake with me but he will never willing on his own merit promote me. It is this kind of discrimination and all the rest that has me off sick because I really and truly believe in my superiors and they cared less about me. Dana Urbanski, Tom Martin, and Shelby Kruger-Duncan can be witnesses to these issues.

s. Was this individual aware of your RACE? If yes, how and when were they made aware of your RACE?

ANSWER: Yes, Craig Colton, Steven Phaup, and I all worked together at North Las Vegas Main Post Office until Steven went out on leave and never returned; but in the interim, Craig was forced to terminate him for unlawful behavior. The Postal Inspection Service/Labor Relations have a file on Steven Phaup.

i. Do you believe your RACE was a factor in the selection process? If yes, what makes you believe your RACE was a factor in the selection process?

ANSWER: It is a known universal awareness study that supports my belief and I have received the punishment first hand. Everyone that was promoted over me were White/Non Black and I was more qualified/just as qualified as they were but I never go promoted and in many cases never even go an interview in spite of my experience, skills, ability, and education and past work history before the post office. Discrimination is crystal clear if you look at the whole picture, it's a shame that I'm not judged on my on merit.

t. Was this individual aware of your COLOR? If yes, how and when were they made aware of your COLOR?

ANSWER: Yes, Craig, Corey, Steven, and I all worked in NLV together.

i. Do you believe your COLOR was a factor in the selection process? If yes, what makes you believe your COLOR was a factor in the selection process?

ANSWER: Yes, racism is a part of discrimination all day long. Every one can see that this is so not right. I'm very qualified for the positions, but I can't get promoted. I can't even get promoted for a package that they didn't even have a selection for. What do you think?

u. Was this individual aware of your RELIGION? If yes, how and when were they made aware of your RELIGION?

ANSWER: I talked with Craig about being a Christian before, and I ware a diamond cross around my neck. Also, on my cell phone voice mail, I state have a blessed day to all my callers.

i. Do you believe your RELIGION was a factor in the selection process? If yes, what makes you believe your RELIGION was a factor in the selection process?

ANSWER: Yes, some people don't like others who believe in the Father, Son, and the Holy Ghost. I have a personality that is non confrontational and I believe that with all of the mistreatment, disrespect, and discrimination they could not understand how I still kept my head up and perform my duties. It was by the Grace of God that I was allowed to do this. When people expect an adverse reaction from someone and they don't get it they feel that they don't have the power to affect you in the manner in which they want too; but it is my faith, and belief in God that he will fight my battles so I just accept the adversity and try to look at it in a different way that will be constructive for me to continue on and be productive. God is power if you have him in your life.

v. Was this individual aware of your SEX? If yes, how and when were they made aware of your SEX?

ANSWER: Yes, Craig, Corey, Steven, and I all worked together in NLV, and many men believe that women have a place in which they are suppose to stay; women are to be seen and not heard in most men's mind.

i. Do you believe your SEX was a factor in the selection process? If yes, what makes you believe your SEX was a factor in the selection process?

ANSWER: Absolutely, we have those people who think woman are not to excel like men, and I'm Black.

w. Was this individual aware of your AGE? If yes, how and when were they made aware of your AGE?

ANSWER: All they have to do is look at my OPF and everyone in NLV knows I have an adult daughter who went to Howard and Yale Universities and graduated with honors. This kind of success makes small minded people jealous.

i. Do you believe your AGE was a factor in the selection process? If yes, what makes you believe your AGE was a factor in the selection process?

ANSWER: Yes, choosing a younger person with hope that they will be faster; there are all kind of myths out there. I believe they think that people over forty are difficult to get along with and especially African American, Black, Females over 40, the odds are stacked up against me with people who are prejudice and discriminatory, along with shallow minded thinking.

x. Was this individual aware of your EEO ACTIVITY? If yes, how and when were they made aware of your EEO ACTIVITY?

ANSWER: No, I did not file my first EEO until 9/5/08 and the positions we are addressing here are from 01/18/07 closing date for position #6 (Garside Station) through 08/18/08 position #1 which is (Huntridge Station) and the date I was notified that I was not selected. These are only the positions that Craig Colton and Corey Richards had a position in the selection process. However, there has been retaliation since then because the EEO activity is now a known factor by all the district.

i. Do you believe your EEO ACTIVITY was a factor in the selection process? If yes, what makes you believe your EEO ACTIVITY was a factor in the selection process?

ANSWER: No, not for the selection that I was given to address in this case as I understand it. To my understanding this case is only to address the Corey Richards and Craig Colton positions. However, I'm not for sure because Jerry Wilson did tell a lie to other management that I said that I was going to file an EEO on Las Vegas for not getting the Huntridge Station position, and I stated nothing of the sort to him. Please refer to my Jerry Wilson EEO signed by me on 09/05/2008.

y. You identified Gerade Carraza as a comparator. Identify this individual's correct first and last name, race, color, religion, sex, and age. Was this person treated the same as you or differently from you regarding the selection for the vacancy(ies) you identified? Please specify how they were treated and why you believe they were treated this way.

ANSWER: I really don't know him and I just know his sex – male, I believe he is White/Non Black. He was from out of the district and I was qualified right here in the district and have been the acting manager at Huntridge Station before. I believe he took a lateral to Huntridge Station. I started my detail: Manager, Customer Services/A at Huntridge Station on 04/01/2006. When I state that I had come full circle after two (2) and a half years is because I was sent back to Huntridge Station on 06/14/2008 – 07/08/2008 and I was told by management that I did an Excellent job at Huntridge Station, but once again I did not get selected for the position. Aside from the discrimination, I believe that some of the laterals are friends are associated with the powers that be and that's also why I'm not considered for selections.

z. You identified Lynn Holmes as a comparator. Identify this individual's correct first and last name, race, color, religion, sex, and age. Was this person treated the same as you or differently from you regarding the selection for the vacancy(ies) you identified? Please specify how they were treated and why you believe they were treated this way.

ANSWER: Lynn Holmes is a Caucasian, White, Female and I don't know her religion or age. I know I have more experience and I graduated ASP before she did. I think we started acting around the same time, but I was in difficult offices while the others were in smaller/easier offices. In addition, they were mostly in one office while I was sent to several offices. Remember, I stated that no one briefed me on what they wanted are what they wanted me to work on are accomplish, I just went on my knowledge of experience and training, along with knowing what my postmasters would ask me for when I was in a supervisor position. I truly believe that I was never meant to succeed are do as well as I did on my details, but once they realized that I was a natural at this position then they just would send me to various offices to clean them up with never really having the idea of promoting me. If you look at all the hires and don't see any Black people being promoted but they are acting just like everyone else, it's not hard to eventually figure out discrimination especially when you come full circle like I did with Huntridge Station.

aa. You identified Thomas Jack as a comparator. Identify this individual's correct first and last name, race, color, religion, sex, and age. Was this person treated the same as you or differently from you regarding the selection for the vacancy(ies) you identified? Please specify how they were treated and why you believe they were treated this way.

ANSWER: Correct, I have never seen him before but I have talked with him over the telephone about an alleged grievance at Huntridge Station (I believe it was sometimes in September or October 2008). He was treated differently from me when he was from out of the district and he took a lateral and I was right here in the district qualified and had worked myself to my own demise. This position #1 is when the bell went off for me and I had to realize once I got sick from the Jerry Wilson threat (8/25/08) that I have to do something about this mistreatment, discrimination, racism, disrespect, and all the other negative action that was brought on by management towards me.

bb. You identified Jason MacMahill as a comparator. Identify this individual's correct first and last name, race, color, religion, sex, and age. Was this person treated the same as you or differently from you regarding the selection for the vacancy(ies) you identified? Please specify how they were treated and why you believe they were treated this way.

ANSWER: Jason McMahill is a Caucasian, White, Male and I don't know his religion or age. Jason was doing route inspections and going around the Las Vegas City making sure the stations were using the CSAW program correctly. I was at Paradise Valley Station at the time 8/2006 for two weeks and then was sent there after the Labor Day Holiday in 09/2006 – 03/30/2007 to replace Doug Watson because Jennifer Vo, Robert Reynosa, and Mark Martinez did not think that Doug Watson was doing the job in the manner that they wanted, basically Doug was not producing the numbers that they wanted. However, Doug Watson was the same person that was selected for the Paradise Valley Station position when it came up for the second time with the closing date of 04/11/07. I worked there for six (6) months with zone split challenges, late mail arriving from Strip Station which is where the split routes went, and being challenged to make all indicators along with all mail being processed and cleared from the building before the carriers left for the street. I western area compliance processes and the EXFC/EPED requirement. We succeeded with all our tasks; and were number (1) in FY2006 for EXFC/OND mail; we received an award for this. In the interim, Jason McMahill came over to Paradise Valley Station and gave a report that we were using the program very effectively to Jennifer, Robert, and Mark, and as a result we were the number one office in the Las Vegas City on CSAW performance, refer to my resume profile from ecareer. Later on Jason McMahill was sent to act as manager at Sunrise Station in Las Vegas. I have more experience in management than he did, and I sure I graduated the ASP before he did. Also, remember I have an AA Degree in Human Services, and a BS Degree in Business/Management along with having had my own business and being a manager prior to coming to the postal service, but Jason was selected for the Sunrise Station position by Robert Reynosa that closed on 10/24/07, and later promoted to the #2 position Emerald Station that I talk about in this case. Corey Richards was the Chairman and Robert Reynosa was the Selecting Official. At this time, I had been sent back to my supervisor position in North Las Vegas by Jennifer Vo, and Robert Reynosa with an explaination of mail being brought back from business routes because they had closed before the carriers got there. This is the issue when my supervisor did not inform me that mail was brought back and I was given an investigative interview and sent back to my permanent position while other managers had similar situations where mail never left the building and mail being hidden, along with green mail not even being dispatched, but nothing happened to those managers. However, I was sent back to NLV as a supervisor and that's when I met Yul Melonson for the first (1'st) time, 04/01/2007. I had been in the Las Vegas City on detail for one (1) complete year at two (2) stations, Huntridge and Paradise Valley, but when

I put in for either one of them, I was not even given an interview. I knew I had done a good job because this is when Yul looked at the Flash report for Paradise Valley Station and he asked me "Why are you here," and I replied "I don't know."

cc. You identified Tim Sampoli as a comparator. Identify this individual's correct first and last name, race, color, religion, sex, and age. Was this person treated the same as you or differently from you regarding the selection for the vacancy(ies) you identified? Please specify how they were treated and why you believe they were treated this way.

ANSWER: Correct, Tim Sampoli is a Caucasian, White, Male, and I don't know his religion or age. Tim was working in the office with Robert Reynosa, Jennifer Vo, and Mark Martinez, and he had not been out in the field acting as a Manager, Customer Services. He had been working on grievances for the Las Vegas City, and he would do individual projects and things that Robert, Jennifer, and Mark wanted him to do, miscellanies work that needed to be done. However, he did not have as much experience as I did nor do I believe he graduated the ASP class before me. I had already been in two challenging offices (Huntridge Station EAS-21, and Paradise Valley Station EAS-22) along with my private experience and my education under my belt. However, he was eventually sent to Strip Station EAS-19 for a few months and when it became open, because Lynn Holmes got a lateral into Labor Relations, he was selected for the position and I did not even get an interview. Robert Reynosa was the Selecting Official. I was very upset because how can I get an interview for an EAS-22, EAS-21, and not get an interview for an EAS-19. I figured that I was over qualified for the position and the powers that be would not have been able to justify not giving me the position. So I continued to perform my duties as a Supervisor, Customer Services in North Las Vegas. This is discrimination, racism, and any other negative thing you want to call it, but I continued to do my job and I stuffed once again, and waited for the next opportunity. I kept a positive mind set and I performed to the best of my ability and I got recognized from my postmaster with awards, gas card, and monetary gifts (Yul Melonson).

dd. You identified Doug Watson as a comparator. Identify this individual's correct first and last name, race, color, religion, sex, and age. Was this person treated the same as you or differently from you regarding the selection for the vacancy(ies) you identified? Please specify how they were treated and why you believe they were treated this way.

ANSWER: Correct, Doug Watson is a Caucasian, White, Male, and I don't know his religion or age. I addressed some of the issues with Doug in question (aa.) but he was an EAS-21 working with the route inspection team prior to coming to Paradise Valley Station in 2006. I do not know how long he was there before Jennifer, Robert, and Mark sent him back, but I was told by Jennifer when she me that I was going to Paradise Valley Station that Doug wasn't working out and let her talk to him and she would give me a report date. However, I had been sent there originally to replace him for two weeks (While he went on vacation) prior to my six month period of being the Manager, Customer Services/A. that ended on 03/30/2007. Remember, Yul Melonson asked me, after looking at the Flash Report, why are you here (Meaning North Las Vegas Main Post Office in my supervisor position), and I replied, I don't know. This is my confirmation (From an elite member of management, who is now in the PCES Postmaster position in Las Vegas) that I did a good job at a very large and difficult office (Paradise Valley Station).

Other than the comparators you previously identified, were other employees treated THE SAME as you in that they were not selected for the vacancy(ies) identified? If yes, provide their full name, position, race, color, religion, sex, and age, and a description of their situation and how it is similar to yours.

ANSWER: I do not think anyone in the district was treated, with the disrespect, misuse, discrimination, threat, cruelty, rudeness, are have managed in as many stations as I have, are have the experience I have, with the education, in the manner in which I was. I'm not aware of the packages, but I know who got promoted or a lateral over me, and I don't think, as I have stated, that it's fair are right for every one of the positions and not to have been interviewed or promoted. It just baffles me and I call it was it is: Discrimination, and unfair tactics, racism, favoritism, and a host of other adjectives that I don't care to mention. It is just wrong, unprofessional, and immaturity. I don't know who all were in the packages, but

I know who was selected, so I'm grateful for the investigation and I pray that the truth be told-revealed and justice is served in the name of the Father, Son, and the Holy Ghost, Amen.

13. In your complaint, you allege that on or around September 8, 2008, you were charged 32 hours of sick leave. For what dates were you charged 32 hours of sick leave? Were you absent on these dates? If yes, please explain how you believe the absence should have been charged and provide copies of your PS Form 3971 for those dates.

ANSWER: For the dates 09/1-5/08 with Labor Day Holiday being 91/08 I received Holiday pay and 9/2/08 Tuesday – Friday 32 hours of sick leave was taken from me. I questioned Jerry about it on 09/08/08 and he told me that he originally put me in for Leave Without Pay (LWOP) for the 32 hours, but he talked with Labor Relations and they advised him to put me in for sick leave because he did not have any paperwork for my absence. Then he replied "Do you want me to reverse the sick leave and put you back in for LWOP. I stated to Jerry that the paperwork was completed and turned in to Joni Payne in injury comp, this is the same paperwork that was signed by Grady Griffin, and he stated did you turn in a 3971 to anyone of North Las Vegas. I stated under the direction of Yul Melonson (Jerry's boss at the time) Joni Payne, and Grady Griffin, the paperwork was turned in and signed. For details of this question please refer to my EEO claim package signed by me on 09/05/2008. I have two (2) statements written on 08/29/2008 addressing my completion of my on the job injury paperwork regarding Jerry Wilson Postmaster of North Las Vegas/A at the time. Even though I called Jerry on his cell phone the night of 08/25/08 (Monday) and confirmed my notification to him around 6:30am on 08/26/08 (Tuesday), of my on the job injury, he still did not send me the paperwork for my injury. I had serious issues with dealing with Jerry concerning the paperwork and when I received the paperwork on Friday (08/29/08) from Jerry (Refer to my copies of what Jerry sent me) the letter only had two (2) CA-2 forms in the envelope. Refer to my statement where I had to go to the GMF Injury Compensation Office myself and get the necessary paperwork on (08/28/098) in order to get the claims filed and the 3971 completed for my pay. However, Yul Melonson spoke to Jerry about my paperwork on 08/29/08 and he was supposingly at the airport on his way back to Reno where he lives. Fortunately, Yul stepped in and had me go to the GMF Injury Compensation Office in Las Vegas so that I could get my paperwork turned in and my 3971 acknowledged by Grady Griffin. It was Friday (08/29/08) and the payroll had to be completed are I would not get paid. So Yul said that he would call North Las Vegas Post Office and have one of the supervisors put my time in since I had the CA-1 and the CA-2 completed. The paperwork was turned into Injury Compensation and signed and acknowledged by Grady Griffin. Joni Payne in injury comp. received the paperwork (702) 361-9330, after it was signed by Grady. She confirmed with Yul Melonson that the paperwork was in and I was to get paid for an on the job injury-Continuation of Pay (COP) for the 45 day period. However, on the following week (Pay Period 18 2008- check dated 09/05/2008) I was charged 32 hours of sick leave, and it is also the first (1'st) check that I started not getting paid higher level correctly. From that pay check to now, I'm still not being paid higher level, please refer to my letter to Jerry Wilson and Corey Richards regarding my higher level pay. In addition, I was told by Joni Payne in injury compensation that I was entitled to the pay that I was receiving at the time I was injured. It is my belief that Jerry did not want to except the CA-1 Traumatic event on 08/25/08 because he knew that it would involve him and that is why he did not send the paperwork and also why he lied to the Dept. of Labor – on the CA-1, B. J. Clay EEO (ADR) Specialist – when questioned, and all the other lies he told in his statement. All of my statements are true to the best of my knowledge, because Jerry did and said so much to me that I know I did not capture it all in my forms and statements; but what I did remember I told the truth about it. Once again please refer to my EEO signed on 9/5/08. The threat by Jerry "You continue to go over my head with Craig and Yul and I'm going to do something about it" was the straw that broke the camels back. I knew something negative was going to happen and I'm not the kind of person that desired it rather it was physically or in written form. I was afraid, nauseated, nervous, angry, upset, confused, heavy heart palpitations, my mind was disturb, and I could not think straight (I felt retarded because I could not get a logical thought processed), I vomited and had head shocks running through me, I felt like I was going to die right there in my office or the restroom where I went to put water on my face and vomit. It was horrible and I'm blessed to not have had a Stroke or Heart attack.

Instead on 8/27/08, I saw Dr. Mary J. Reed and she told me that I had a Panic Attack, and she diagnosed me with PTSD, and Major Depressive Disorder. Until this day, I am still off work and I continue to go to doctor after doctor appointments and I've been diagnosed with Neuropathy = nerve damage to both feet, but worse on my left side and it comes up to the top of my left buttocks, also, I have numbness in my feet and if I sit to long are put one foot on top of the other the numbness comes quicker, also, I have head shocks that causes sharp sensations to run down my head, neck, and lips, the left ear hearing loss, Heart Palpitations, my hair fell out and I now have very short hair so I got it cut in a kind of a style. I do not like it or the way that I look. My therapist (Dr. Mary J. Reed) said that a Panic Attack can not only cause my issues, but it can cause people to even go blind. It is my belief that I was going to have a Heart Attack or Stroke since most of the damage is on the left side of my body. I'm very grateful to God that I did not have a Heart Attack or Stroke. In addition, I was a very healthy person before all the discrimination, subtle tactics, disrespect, misuse, racism, threat, unappreciated attitude from my superiors, and being used as the clean up woman started happening to me and ultimately causing me to become very ill and I do not deserve this and all involved need to be held accountable for their attitudes and behaviors. I was a true servant of the postal service and I did it without any reservation. I just wanted to be treated fairly and on my own merit. May God bless those that played a part in my demise; and let justice be served?

a. Did you bring this to the attention of anyone in management? If yes, who did you speak with and what was their response?

ANSWER: Yes, after I left early that day because I did not know what was wrong with me, I called Jerry Wilson late that night on his cell phone (He did not answer) and I left a message that I'm not going to be coming into work tomorrow and I'm filing an on the job injury and I would like for you to send me a CA-1 and a CA-2. I confirmed with Jerry the next morning about 6:30am (Because I did not get very much sleep that night) by calling him at North Las Vegas Post Office and I asked him if he got my message last night and he replied, yes. I stated to him that I knew he needed answers and I will put them in writing with the paperwork. He stated that "You know that I'm going to have to report this and I replied, yes. Jerry asked me if this had anything to do with not getting the Las Vegas position and I stated to him that I will put it in writing and he will know everything. We then hung up the phone, and the rest of the story you have in the previous questions and please refer to my EEO package signed by me on 09/05/2008 for more details and statement information, because Jerry told lies and I responded to his statements. Also, I'm answering most of these questions by memory because the truth is the truth, but they may not be verbatim as I wrote them in the original EEO claims. However, you realize that there is a lot of information that is in other documents but mean the same thing and they will all match up. The truth is the truth I don't care how you word it.

b. Has there been a change to the leave charge since September 8, 2008? If yes, when was it changed and how was it changed?

ANSWER: Yes, originally it was changed to COP then the Dept. of Labor/OWCP combined the two (2) claims to a CA-2 (See the letter dated 11/7/08) because of the on going issues, and included the Threat as a part of the series of events that happened over time even though it was a traumatic event (Form CA-1), I had endured for the two and one half years. Since the COP had already been given to me for the 45 days and the Dept. of Labor/OWCP had combined the claims to a CA-2, I completed a 3239 PS Form to start automatic withdrawals of $100.00 from my pay check starting with pay period 6 2009. The paperwork is attached.

c. Other than the current EEO complaint, has another appeal or complaint been filed on this issue? If yes, where is it in the process? If a settlement has been reached, describe the settlement. Provide copies of any documentation and settlement (if applicable).

ANSWER: No

d. Who do you believe was responsible for charging you with sick leave on the dates identified?

ANSWER: Jerry Wilson

e. Why do you believe this individual was responsible for the decision? Please provide their name, position, email address, and office telephone number.

ANSWER: He stated to me that he did, and followed up with the sarcastic remark that I answered in question 13.

f. Was this individual aware of your RACE? If yes, how and when were they made aware of your RACE?

ANSWER: Absolutely, he was my boss and he saw me on a regular basis.

i. Do you believe your RACE was a factor in the decision to charge you with sick leave for the dates you identified? If yes, what makes you believe your RACE was a factor?

ANSWER: Yes, I believe my entire make up was a factor and his paranoid and militant attitude with his dominant, aggressive, I'm the boss and I make the decisions around here personality also played a part. Not to mention that I'm a Black female standing 5'9 with a sort of deep voice. I told him one day that we are in this together and he made no comment about what I said. When he addressed me he called me "Hey Girl."

g. Was this individual aware of your COLOR? If yes, how and when were they made aware of your COLOR?

ANSWER: Yes, I worked for him and he met me on July, 9 2008. That was my first day working at Meadow Mesa Station with him being the Officer in Charge (OIC) – North Las Vegas.

i. Do you believe your COLOR was a factor in the decision to charge you with sick leave for the dates you identified? If yes, what makes you believe your COLOR was a factor?

ANSWER: Yes, I believe he had an arrogant (who does she (Lola McGee) think she is) mentality just from my observation of his behavior while working with him for the time that I did. In my opinion he is the type of person that will throw a rock at someone and try to hide his hand, all the time he does not mean you any good. My experience working with him made me just adapt to his style and follow his instructions because he was the boss rather I agreed are not.

h. Was this individual aware of your RELIGION? If yes, how and when were they made aware of your RELIGION?

ANSWER: Yes, I have a message on my cell phone that says have a blessed day and he called me and left messages sometimes while I was working at Meadow Mesa Station. I even did projections and reports for him and I realized after the email that Craig Colton sent out to all of us (It will be in this package) he did not want to do the projection for North Las Vegas Main Post Office anymore, so he asked me to do it. I thought that he was just caught up one day and couldn't get it done until the third time I did not automatically do it and he called me and asked me why didn't I do it and I stated to him that I did not know that he wanted me to do it everyday for the entire North Las Vegas City. I believe he had Mel, a supervisor that was at the North Las Vegas Main Post Office, do it for him from that point on.

i. Do you believe your RELIGION was a factor in the decision to charge you with sick leave for the dates you identified? If yes, what makes you believe your RELIGION was a factor?

ANSWER: I'm not sure, but he was aware that I was a Christian by my message on my voice mail and the diamond cross I wear around my neck.

i. Was this individual aware of your SEX? If yes, how and when were they made aware of your SEX?

ANSWER: Yes, on 07/09/08 I met with him at the North Las Vegas Post Office.

i. Do you believe your SEX was a factor in the decision to charge you with sick leave for the dates you identified? If yes, what makes you believe your SEX was a factor?

ANSWER: Yes, because I filed an on the job injury on him and he wanted to act as if he did not know about it. It is my belief that he thought that by him sending the paperwork that he did send (the two (2) CA-2 forms that I would not get the paperwork in on time). Also, for all the other reasons that I've stated previously. I believe he is racist and he did not know that I was a Black Female until I showed up on 7/9/08, and he addressed me often as Hey Girl instead of Lola, Ms. McGee, etc. I thought it was awful but he was the boss with the dominant attitude, and I was in know position to address him because I think it would have only made things worse sooner, now that I look back on the situation.

j. Was this individual aware of your AGE? If yes, how and when were they made aware of your AGE?

ANSWER: I don't know for sure, but he knows I have an adult daughter because on one of the three occasions when I was late, I told him it was because I had to do something for my daughter and he asked me how old was she and I told him 29 years old. He told me that he had an adult daughter and she is responsible for herself. In my statements to the Dept. of Labor I addressed the lateness issues, because at the time I did not know why sometimes I just could not wake up and get to work on time. I found out on 08/27/08 when I saw Dr. Mary J. Reed and she told me that I suffered from PTSD, and Major Depressive Disorder. The Discrimination and the mistreatment had taken a told on my body. Sorry to say, but I had answers then to why I was always tired and low on energy. I stopped cleaning, cooking, doing laundry, watching my favorite shows, going out to dinner and functions, and my attitude was not the same at home anymore: I stopped having sex, going shopping for clothes and groceries, I was being called lazy and having arguments. Aside from going to work, all I had time to do was to go gamble on the weekends to a fault. Ever since I've been off the gambling has stopped and I don't need it to mask the Depression and PTSD anymore; it gave me a since of relief from the post office and I know that now, but I did not have the answers while I was in the midst of it all.

i. Do you believe your AGE was a factor in the decision to charge you with sick leave for the dates you identified? If yes, what makes you believe your AGE was a factor?

ANSWER: Yes, I believe every discriminatory factor played a part in the whole entire gamut of problems that came my way with my superiors. There is no other reason that I believe, but I was discriminated against, this came to me full force since I've been off work (08/26/08). Needless to say but I did not deserve any of it. The only thing I accept is when Jerry talked to me twice about my attendance 08/19/08 and one other time in July 2008, I don't remember the date. I'm the type of leader that leads by example, but I could not get out of bed sometimes to make it to work on time. I apologized to my boss' in the Dept. of Labor/OWCP statements. He made a comment in his statement to the Dept. of Labor and to the EEO (ADR) Specialist B. J. Clay that he talked to me about my attendance on 07/09/08 but it was not true, because this was my first day, and yes I was late, but he told me to come by the main office before I reported to Meadow Mesa so that he could meet me. As far as me being late, he stated its okay just come by here first before you go over to "Mesa," that's what he called it.

k. Was this individual aware of your EEO ACTIVITY? If yes, how and when were they made aware of your EEO ACTIVITY?

ANSWER: Yes, I filed and EEO on Jerry Wilson signed 9/5/08, and he had previously stated to management officials that I told him that I was going to file an EEO on Las Vegas for not being promoted. I did not tell Jerry anything of the sort, please refer to my Dept. of Labor statements and the statements he made to B. J. Clay during the pre-counseling period. Consequently, I did file an EEO on Robert Reynosa, Jennifer Vo, and Mark Martinez signed 9/18/08 for discrimination after I gained knowledge from a legal professional that I was within my right because it had been a continuing practice by them.

i. Do you believe your EEO ACTIVITY was a factor in the decision to charge you with sick leave for the dates you identified? If yes, what makes you believe your EEO ACTIVITY was a factor?

ANSWER: Absolutely, without a doubt, because it was on him (Jerry Wilson).

l. Were other EAS-level employees treated THE SAME as you in that they were charged sick leave under similar circumstances? If yes, provide their full name, position, race, color, religion, sex, and age, and a description of their situation (including the dates they were charged with leave) and how it is similar to yours.

ANSWER: I have no idea of any others activity as it relates to mine.

m. Were other EAS-level employees treated DIFFERENTLY than you in that they were not charged sick leave under similar circumstances? If yes, provide their full name, position, race, color, religion, sex, and age, and a description of their situation (including the dates they were absent) and how they were treated differently.

ANSWER: I have no idea of any others activity as it relates to mine.

14. In your complaint, you allege that since July 12, 2008, you have been taken off of higher level assignments. Immediately prior to or after July 12, 2008, have you held any higher level assignments? If yes, please identify the higher level assignment(s) you held including the title, grade, location, and the start and end dates of the detail(s). Identify the name, position, telephone number, and email address of your supervisor during the detail assignment. Include a copy of your PS Form 1723 for the detail(s).

ANSWER: No, I have not been back to work since the on the job injury that happened on 08/25/08.

a. Please describe the events that led up to and contributed to the end of the detail including when you were notified it would end, who informed you the detail was ending, and what reason did they provide regarding the detail ending?

ANSWER: I got my check stub for pay period 18 2008 (Check date is 9/5/08) and it was not correct for the days of 09/1-5/08, it's the same pay period that I was charged the 32 hours of sick leave instead of COP for the on the job injury dated 8/25/08 by Jerry Wilson's threat. On 09/08/08 I called North Las Vegas Post Office and spoke with Jerry. I asked him why was I taken off of higher level EAS-22 for Meadow Mesa Station, when I got sick while I was on the assignment; and he stated to me that there isn't anything in writing that says he couldn't. He stated "Do you have anything that states you're not suppose to be taken off higher level?" I stated thank you and by. I called injury compensation and spoke to Joni Payne and she stated that she is sure that I'm suppose to be paid the level that I was on when I got injured, but she would look into it and call me back and let me know. On 9/9/08, Joni called me back and told me that I was entitled to the higher level pay for sick leave and COP because I was on that level when I got injured. She stated that she talked to Jerry and he was told that he needed to make an adjustment to my pay for pay period 18-2. I made a note to myself of being in pay period 19-2 as of 9/9/08. She also said that she will send me the supervisor statements for my CA-1 and CA-2 forms. However, I was never paid correctly for higher level by Jerry Wilson to date. I continue to get my check stubs and they were not correct with higher level and by now Corey Richards is the OIC of North Las Vegas. On 11/5/08 I wrote a letter to Corey Richards and asked him to update my 1723 because when I started the detail at Meadow Mesa Station, I put an arbitrary date on it which was the end of the Fiscal Year 2008. The date I put on the 1723 is 9/30/08 and I would update it accordingly. I'm sure you have a question as to why was I doing my on 1723? It is common in the Nevada Sierra District for acting managers to put in there on 1723 to timekeeping are they won't get paid the higher level, but they will be doing the job. That is why you want see a supervisor signature on my 1723 for Meadow Mesa Station when I started on 7/9/08. Corey told me that he was not going to update my 1723 and he was not going to put me on higher level. Please refer to my letter dated 11/5/08, and my note that is written on the storage west tablet sheet of paper. Also, I was not permitted to go to the GMF and put in my FY 2009 Core Requirements for my merit at the end of the year per Corey. All of this is technicalities because of EEO Retaliation and Discrimination because on 9/30/08 I signed an EEO on Corey Richards and Craig Colton. Please refer to my EEO on Craig and Corey signed 9/30/08 and have Debbie Letts, Manager – Timekeeping (702) 361-9319 and Joni Payne – Injury Compensation Specialist (702) 361-9330 be witnesses to this information.

b. Do you believe the detail should have continued? Please explain.

ANSWER: Yes, as long as the station had an acting manager in it, then I should have been paid higher level, because if I had not gotten ill on 8/25/08 then all would have happen is I would have updated my 1723 and the rest is history. This is all retaliation and discrimination of all factors, by both Corey and Jerry.

c. Other than the current EEO complaint, has another appeal or complaint been filed on this issue? If yes, where is it in the process? If a settlement has been reached, describe the settlement. Provide copies of any documentation and settlement (if applicable).

ANSWER: No, but I sent in two (2) amendments to this complaint including this issue on Corey.

d. Who do you believe was responsible for the decision to end your detail(s)? Please provide their name, position, email address, and office telephone number.

ANSWER: Jerry Wilson – Fallen Postmaster and I don't know his email or phone number. Corey Richards, currently the North Las Vegas Postmaster corey.d.richards@usps.gov (702) 649-2623.

e. Why do you believe this individual was responsible for the decision?

ANSWER: Because both of them have been A/Postmaster at one time or another while I've been out on worker's comp.

f. Was this individual aware of your RACE? If yes, how and when were they made aware of your RACE?

ANSWER: Yes, both of them are aware of my Race because I worked for Jerry Wilson at Meadow Mesa Station and Corey Richards and I both use to be Craig Colton's supervisors in North Las Vegas when I came in 5/2004.

i. Do you believe your RACE was a factor in the decision to end your detail(s)? If yes, what makes you believe your RACE was a factor?

ANSWER: Yes, all EEO Discriminating Factors were apart of the decision to remove me from my detail by all of them, Craig Colton, Corey Richards, and Jerry Wilson. Craig Colton is the boss of both of them.

g. Was this individual aware of your COLOR? If yes, how and when were they made aware of your COLOR?

ANSWER: Yes, I'm Black and they are prejudice with a smile.

i. Do you believe your COLOR was a factor in the decision to end your detail(s)? If yes, what makes you believe your COLOR was a factor?

ANSWER: Yes, both of them behaved in the same manner and for the same reasons: EEO Retaliation, and all Factors of Discrimination, not to mention my disability at this time with my on the job injuries. My health is playing a factor also with being on worker's compensation.

h. Was this individual aware of your RELIGION? If yes, how and when were they made aware of your RELIGION?

ANSWER: Yes, all of them are as it relates to my cross and my cell phone message, and I have made verbal expressions about God, Jesus Christ, or Thank you Lord, words to that affect around Craig, Corey, and Jerry.

i. Do you believe your RELIGION was a factor in the decision to end your detail(s)? If yes, what makes you believe your RELIGION was a factor?

ANSWER: I'm not sure but I don't put it passed anyone of them.

i. Was this individual aware of your SEX? If yes, how and when were they made aware of your SEX?

ANSWER: Yes, all three of them know my sex is Female because I've worked with Craig, Corey, and Jerry.

i. Do you believe your SEX was a factor in the decision to end your detail(s)? If yes, what makes you believe your SEX was a factor?

ANSWER: Absolutely, because I'm a Black, Female that is off on worker's compensation, and I have filed EEO's on all three of them. Remember they are discriminating against me because I'm not suppose to go up the ladder that far or be in their league.

j. Was this individual aware of your AGE? If yes, how and when were they made aware of your AGE?

ANSWER: Craig is aware of my age because he had access to my OPF before they went electronic, and I'm not sure of Corey and Jerry, but all three of them know that I have an adult daughter whom is IVY League Educated and I'm very proud of her.

i. Do you believe your AGE was a factor in the decision to end your detail(s)? If yes, what makes you believe your AGE was a factor?

ANSWER: I'm not sure, I think mostly it was retaliation and discrimination on being Black and Female along with being out on workers compensation with on the job injuries.

k. Was this individual aware of your EEO ACTIVITY? If yes, how and when were they made aware of your EEO ACTIVITY?

ANSWER: Yes, all three of them, Craig, Corey, and Jerry all had EEO's filed on them. (9/5/08 and 9/30/08 were the signing dates by me. Please refer to the packages for more details.

i. Do you believe your EEO ACTIVITY was a factor in the decision to end your detail(s)? If yes, what makes you believe your EEO ACTIVITY was a factor?

ANSWER: Absolutely, Retaliation, exposing their plots, mistreatment, disrespect, using me as acting manager without the idea of promoting me, being Black and Female, African American and that's why there isn't a Black promoted in the Las Vegas, North Las Vegas, and Henderson City Stations. As I stated earlier, Yul Melonson just got promoted to PCES Postmaster of Las Vegas in October 2008 and the first installed Postmaster was in the late 1800's. To me, that says something about the culture of the Nevada Sierra Districts History. Also, my on the job injuries, and me being out on workers compensation at this time, as if I caused it upon myself. People with that type of my set do not see the hurt and harm that the cause when they discriminate against people; and what was I doing, just working harder and harder to my own demise. I'm very ill and they could care less, all they want to do is retaliate against me because they refuse to see their wrong. Jerry Wilson did not know me but his racist, domineering behavior is unacceptable; and when he threatened me, he stood right in my face to let me know that he meant business. He is very paranoid and hyper and he wanted to impress so bad that he does not care about his subordinate staff.

15. In your complaint, you allege that from July 12, 2008, you have been subjected to hostile work environment harassment including working conditions, being treated in a disrespectful, cruel, and rude manner, and receiving threats from management official(s). Identify specific events and dates since July 12, 2008 for which you believe illustrate or were part of the alleged hostile work environment harassment regarding working conditions. For each event, identify the following:

a. Who committed the alleged harassment? Identify them by name and position (if known) and their race, color, religion, sex, and age.

ANSWER: Jerry Wilson OIC of North Las Vegas is a Caucasian, White, Male and I don't know his Religion and age. Corey Richards was the OIC of North Las Vegas and now he is the Postmaster, North Las Vegas, he took a lateral to Yul Melonson's old position. Corey is a Caucasian, White, Male and I don't know his Religion and age. Craig Colton by way of Steven Phaup, Craig is a Caucasian, White, Male and I don't know his Religion and age. Steven Phaup was terminated in early 2006.

b. On what date(s) did this occur? (If you do not know the specific date, provide an approximate date or month and year).

ANSWER: Jerry Wilson = 7/10/08 – 8/25/08, Corey Richards = 10/2008 – 01/09/09, Craig Colton by was of Steven Phaup = The middle of 2004 – until and after his termination because I was fearful of his mentality and behavior.

c. Where did it occur?

ANSWER: Jerry Wilson = Meadow Mesa Station, Corey Richards = over the telephone while I'm off on workers compensation, Craig Colton by way of Steven Phaup = North Las Vegas Post Office.

d. Describe what occurred. Please be specific as to what was said or done, if it occurred once or multiple times, and if it occurred multiple times, how often it occurred.

ANSWER: Jerry Wilson came into a staff meeting of mine on 7/10/08 and abruptly started commenting on me addressing my staff regarding under time. After I stated to my staff the word under time he immediately interrupted me and stated "Under time is hard to get and he started talking telling us about something that went on in his meeting at the district or a telecom. Please refer to my CA-1, EEO package signed 9/5/08, and my letters to the Dept. of Labor and you can consult Joni Payne in Injury Compensation and Bonnie Brokofsky at Meadow Mesa Station, she was a 204B, acting supervisor while I was there. I will state some things, because so much happened on a regular basis I don't even think I got it all. He was always anxious and he would talk about the key indicators that came out daily. One day about two weeks after being there he said the last two weeks the overtime has gone up and I asked him if he was blaming me for it and he stated "You have been here for two weeks haven't you." He came into a staff meeting that I was having and he stated to me in front of my staff "Lola you are going to start coming in at 8:00am because I you here when the carriers come back. I replied, I can still come in at 7:00am and stay to 1700 when the carriers get back its no problem because I've worked long hours my whole postal career. If he wanted to talk to me and give me some instructions, I wish he would have done it privately. He stated to other management officials that I was going to file an EEO on Las Vegas and I did not even say that to anyone because at the time I did not even know that I could file an EEO on Las Vegas because it was over a long period of time and I did not know about the 45 days until I read the book and called to file an EEO on Jerry. I asked Jerry for my clerk and TE that belonged to Meadow Mesa Station and he told me that he would think about it after knowing we were struggling to get the mail out and processed. North Las Vegas-Main had 27 routes and Meadow Mesa Station had 68 city routes and 24 rural routes, and he said he would think about it. Jerry would come into my meetings and change my plans not even asking me what's going on. It was during the peak vacation period when I was at Meadow Mesa Station and my staff members also had scheduled leave, so I had made plans to help run the floor and it was all set we had a plan made. Jerry came over and told me that I was coming in late and we were going to put my 204B back on her route and I waited until the staff had left the office and I asked him if I could talk with him about what he had stated in the meeting. He did listen to me and stated it better work out. On 8/25/08 Jerry Wilson came over early in the morning and I asked him to come and look at the parcels and he stated he didn't need to look at them, "I already know what they look like." I stated to Jerry if I could have my clerk and he stated that he would think about it. Later on that morning Jerry was in my office and he walked up to me as we were talking and he gave me an open ended threat "You continue to go over my head with Craig and Yul and I'm going to do something about it." I spoke to Craig regarding a email on the projection after having asked Jerry did Craig want on the F2B indicator. Jerry was wrong and that's why I was 2% over my projection. Yul called the office after a message was left to speak to Jerry and he insisted on what was going on, so I told him that my supervisors made a mistake on the schedule and I've taken care of that issue but we are still X amount of routes to case and X amount of routes to carry. Yul suggested bringing in the Temporary employees earlier and that's what I did. Please refer to my EEO signed 9/5/08 and my statement to the Dept. of Labor. Jerry was disrespectful, rude, and hostile with me on a regular basis. Corey Richards = When he arrived in October 2008 he took me off of higher level, and told me that he was not going to use me on higher level. In an effort to convince him I wrote a letter on 11/5/08. He did not select me for a promotion 8/18/08, and told me more jobs are coming up and I'm be promoted within a year. He had my access to the GMF removed so that I could not go to injury compensation and turn in medical paperwork, Dec. 2008. Refer to Charles Turner a rehab carrier that works in the bagging office. Pay Period-1 2009, he did not pay me for week-2 (1/1-5/09). Refer to my amended email sent to NEEOISO and yourself. Craig Colton by way of Steven Phaup = I had several meetings with him and Steve regarding disrespecting behavior from Steve towards me: Steve would hide my employee reports and 3971's, move my employee schedules so that I would not know who was working on any given day, Steve would talk loud to me on the workroom floor and create a hostile working environment. He would create differences with employees to cause conflict. He would use my employees for his own benefit for what he wanted them to do. He rearranged my desk one time I was on leave. He told Craig that I was not capturing my under time like I had Craig believing but the proof was in the reports, but Craig still called me into the office with a meeting with Steve. Craig would take Steve to lunch, but he never took me to lunch. I reduced the delivery unit work hours and stopped high dollar grievance pay outs. Steve confronted Charles Turner (Steward) and asked him why didn't he file article eight grievances on me for violations. I met with Mr. Turner on a weekly basis concerning the overtime reports for the Overtime Desired List (OTDL) employees. At the end of every quarter, I OTDL employees were equitable so there wasn't any reason to file grievances on me. Steve was a very peculiar person and his mentality and behavior made me afraid of him at times, even after he was terminated because I did not trust him.

e. How did these events affect you? Did it affect your job? If yes, please describe how it affected your job.

ANSWER: They had an adverse affect on my life as I knew it. I started seeking mental health counseling (2005) and I would bring my work home. My entire life changed. I started having a different behavior as it related to my normal way of living. I was a disciplined person; in that, I operated with a system, but my life changed, and I can't tell you exactly when it happened. I believe I stopped therapy in July or August of 2005. It was difficult to attend with the hours that I had then 9:30am – 6:30pm (M-F). Also, Steve was on leave and he had not come back. Refer to Tom Martin, Dana Urbanski, Shelby Kruger-Duncan, and Charles Turner. Also, there is a Postal Inspection Service Report. I was afraid of Steve's mentality because he would tell bizarre outlandish stories everyday. I expressed my concerns to Craig and Dana. When it came time for me to go to arbitration, I requested through Dana Urbanski that a Postal Inspector be there for security purposes. I really can't explain the depth of Steven Phaup's personality are behavior, he was very dramatic as if he saw something no one else saw are believed. I was stressed to the hilt, but I tried to stay in reality and look at things in an optimistic way. I expressed my concerns to Craig but it appeared to me that he was not really worried. For the most part, it did not affect my job performance. Corey Richards = I'm off sick and the constant retaliation makes me sicker and angry. I already have good and bad days and when something else comes up I pray and ask the Lord to please help me get pass this. The stuff he's doing is just not right and it is so obvious to me that it's retaliation because of the EEO that I filed on him and Craig. Jerry Wilson = please refer to my EEO's and my statements for all of these issues. As I mentioned before, the threat made me have a Panic Attack which produced serious physical illness on my body. I have Heart Palpitations, left ear hearing loss, numbness in both feet, sharp pain at the top of my left buttocks, - Neuropathy, I have head shocks that has decreased since I've been off work and it goes down my neck and on my lips. My ears ring sometimes. I sleep all day sometimes still even though I've been off work for five (5) months. I have to adjust to walk if I'm in one position to long.

I stopped maintaining my entire household like a normal woman would. My job performance was starting to decline at Meadow Mesa Station as I now look back. I really wanted to leave after eight hours of work and some days I wanted to leave early. My energy level had gotten very low. I tried to delivery the best performance I could, considering what I was going through. I do not feel that I've been off work for five months; I just don't feel that. I feel like I went to work today, and my therapist told me that with all of the doctor appointments and the PTSD, and Major Depression I am working. She stated that it did not happen over night and it's not going to go away overnight. I have to give it some time, but sometime I feel pretty good except for the pain in my back/buttocks.

f. How did you react to these events and what response did you have when the incident(s) occurred or afterwards?

ANSWER: Craig Colton by way of Steven Phaup = I was afraid and angry, I wanted respect and to work with professionalism. I wanted us to work together because we were both very knowledgeable about our jobs. Corey Richards = I was angry and professional and I just try to deal with it the best way I can through prayer. Jerry Wilson = I was afraid and I thought I was going to die. I started shaking with sweat. I was hyperventilating and swaying back and forth. I vomited and I put water on my face. I was having head shocks going through my body. I had heart palpitations and my mind was confused. I felt like I was retarded are going crazy because I could not get and clear processing thought in my brain/mind. I really did not know what to do but I just wanted to make it home and I prayed to the Lord to let me make it home safely and if I did not feel better then I would go to the doctor. I left work at 1:00pm and I do not know how I made it home.

g. Were there any witnesses the event? If yes, please identify them by full name and position and indicate which event(s) they witnessed and, if contacted, what they will say about the event(s). If you have witness statements please include them with your affidavit.

ANSWER: Craig Colton by way of Steven Phaup = Tom Martin,- Manager of Labor Relations, Dana Urbanski, - Postmaster out of the district now, Shelby Kruger-Duncan, - Manager Organizational Behavior EAP and Threat Assessment, and Charles Turner – Rehab Carrier working down at the GMF in CFS and the Bagging Office, can all attest to the behavior, personality, attitude, and unrealistic mentality. Charles Turner can attest to the workroom floor issues with both of us. Shelby can attest to the under time and the employees point of view. Tom can attest to the unlawful issues and the termination, also of the $1000.00 dollars not being in the vault. Dana can attest to the meetings and my concerns of safety and how I wanted to work with him but he would not change his behavior. I do not have any witness statements.

h. Did you tell anyone about this interaction? If yes on what date did you FIRST notify someone of this interaction and WHO did you tell?

ANSWER: Craig Colton by way of Steven Phaup = Yes, I told Craig and Dana, (2004-2005) Corey Richards = Yes, I Corey on 11/5/2008 in a letter regarding my higher level, told Debbie Letts, and she said that she would look out for my time, Joni Payne but she could not do anything, Jerry Wilson = My CA-1 and CA-2 along with statements to management and Injury Compensation. (Joni Payne)

16. Identify specific events and dates since July 12, 2008 for which you believe illustrate or were part of the alleged hostile work environment harassment regarding being treated in a disrespectful, cruel, and rude manner. For each event, identify the following:

a. Who committed the alleged harassment? Identify them by name and position (if known) and their race, color, religion, sex, and age.

ANSWER: I have explained it all in the previous questions for all three people: Craig Colton, Corey Richards, and Jerry Wilson. Also, I'm sending the entire file so the detailed information will be all together.

b. On what date(s) did this occur? (If you do not know the specific date, provide an approximate date or month and year).

ANSWER: I have explained it all and please refer to the statements and EEO's that were signed on 9/5/08 for Jerry Wilson, 9/18/08 this was not excepted to my understanding, and 9/30/08 for Corey Richards and Craig Colton.

c. Where did it occur?

ANSWER: All of it occurred in the same places as the previous issues, I did not realize that the questions were going to be to this detail. I have put the issues all in the previous questions.

d. Describe what occurred. Please be specific as to what was said or done, if it occurred once or multiple times, and if it occurred multiple times, how often it occurred.

ANSWER: Refer to the previous answers and the EEO's signed on 9/5/08, 9/18/08 not accepted, and 9/30/08.

e. How did these events affect you? Did it affect your job? If yes, please describe how it affected your job.

ANSWER: I have answered this question previously.

f. How did you react to these events and what response did you have when the incident(s) occurred or afterwards?

ANSWER: I have answered it previously.

g. Were there any witnesses the event? If yes, please identify them by full name and position and indicate which event(s) they witnessed and, if contacted, what they will say about the event(s). If you have witness statements please include them with your affidavit.

ANSWER: I have answered it previously.

h. Did you tell anyone about this interaction? If yes on what date did you FIRST notify someone of this interaction and WHO did you tell?

ANSWER: I have answered it previously.

17. Identify specific events and dates since July 12, 2008 for which you believe illustrate or were part of the alleged hostile work environment harassment regarding receiving threats from management official(s). For each event, identify the following:

a. Who committed the alleged harassment? Identify them by name and position (if known) and their race, color, religion, sex, and age.

ANSWER: I have answered it previously.

b. On what date(s) did this occur? (If you do not know the specific date, provide an approximate date or month and year).

ANSWER: I have answered it previously.

c. Where did it occur?

ANSWER: I have answered it previously.

d. Describe what occurred. Please be specific as to what was said or done, if it occurred once or multiple times, and if it occurred multiple times, how often it occurred.

ANSWER: I have answered it previously.

e. How did these events affect you? Did it affect your job? If yes, please describe how it affected your job.

ANSWER: I have answered it previously.

f. How did you react to these events and what response did you have when the incident(s) occurred or afterwards?

ANSWER: I have answered it previously.

g. Were there any witnesses the event? If yes, please identify them by full name and position and indicate which event(s) they witnessed and, if contacted, what they will say about the event(s). If you have witness statements please include them with your affidavit.

ANSWER: I have answered it previously.

h. Did you tell anyone about this interaction? If yes on what date did you FIRST notify someone of this interaction and WHO did you tell?

ANSWER: I have answered it previously.

18. Identify any other specific events and dates since July 12, 2008 for which you believe illustrate or were part of the alleged hostile work environment harassment. For each event, identify the following:

a. Who committed the alleged harassment? Identify them by name and position (if known) and their race, color, religion, sex, and age.

ANSWER: Craig Colton by way of Steven Phaup, Corey Richards, and Jerry Wilson. They are all Caucasian, White, Males and I don't know their religion and ages. The hostile work environment harassment was explained in the previous question and I will send in more documentation. Also, please refer to the EEO's signed by me on 9/5/08, 9/18/08 not accepted, and 9/30/08 for more information. Also, please refer to my Dept. of Labor paperwork and the statements that will be apart of this package. I have explained the issues in the previous questions.

b. On what date(s) did this occur? (If you do not know the specific date, provide an approximate date or month and year).

ANSWER: I have explained in the previous questions.

c. Where did it occur?

ANSWER: I have explained in the previous questions.

d. Describe what occurred. Please be specific as to what was said or done, if it occurred once or multiple times, and if it occurred multiple times, how often it occurred.

ANSWER: I have explained in the previous questions.

e. How did these events affect you? Did it affect your job? If yes, please describe how it affected your job.

ANSWER: They made me feel worthless, and unappreciated for the work I did for the postal service along with destroying my life as I knew it.

f. How did you react to these events and what response did you have when the incident(s) occurred or afterwards?

ANSWER: I have explained it in the previous questions.

g. Were there any witnesses the event? If yes, please identify them by full name and position and indicate which event(s) they witnessed and, if contacted, what they will say about the event(s). If you have witness statements please include them with your affidavit.

ANSWER: I have listed all the witnesses that I can think of at this time in the previous questions.

h. Did you tell anyone about this interaction? If yes on what date did you FIRST notify someone of this interaction and WHO did you tell?

ANSWER: I have explained it in the previous questions.

19. Do you have any documents supporting your allegations (e.g., notes, emails, pictures, diary entries, witness statements)? If yes, provide a copy with your affidavit.

ANSWER: Yes, I will have all documents from my statements to the CA-1 and CA-2 along with the EEO's and emails and what ever notes I have from writing down things.

20. Was the individual(s) you identified as committing the alleged harassment aware of your RACE? If yes, when and how did they become aware of your RACE?

ANSWER: Yes, we have all worked together at some point.

a. Do you believe your RACE was a factor in the alleged hostile work environment and harassment? If yes, why do you believe your RACE was a factor?

ANSWER: Absolutely, all of the discriminating factors are playing a part in my harassment. I have answered the question previously.

21. Was the individual(s) you identified as committing the alleged harassment aware of your COLOR? If yes, when and how did they become aware of your COLOR?

ANSWER: Yes, we all worked together at some point.

a. Do you believe your COLOR was a factor in the alleged hostile work environment and harassment? If yes, why do you believe your COLOR was a factor?

ANSWER: Yes, They think that they are better than I am by them being White and Male and me being Black and Female. Not to mention that they are promoted managers and postmasters. I'm their subordinates.

22. Was the individual(s) you identified as committing the alleged harassment aware of your RELIGION? If yes, when and how did they become aware of your RELIGION?

ANSWER: Yes, I have answered the question previously.

a. Do you believe your RELIGION was a factor in the alleged hostile work environment and harassment? If yes, why do you believe your RELIGION was a factor?

ANSWER: I'm not sure, but they do know that I'm a Christian.

23. Was the individual(s) you identified as committing the alleged harassment aware of your SEX? If yes, when and how did they become aware of your SEX?

ANSWER: Yes, we all worked together at some time are another.

a. Do you believe your SEX was a factor in the alleged hostile work environment harassment? If yes, why do you believe your SEX was a factor?

ANSWER: Absolutely, because they think that they are superior to me by being Male and White and I'm Female and Black. Also, they are all promoted managers and postmasters.

24. Was the individual(s) you identified as committing the alleged harassment aware of your AGE? If yes, when and how did they become aware of your AGE?

ANSWER: Craig Colton is the only one that would have known my age from my OPF, and Jerry and Corey only know I have an adult daughter.

a. Do you believe your AGE was a factor in the alleged hostile work environment and harassment? If yes, why do you believe your AGE was a factor?

ANSWER: I'm not sure, but I know that I have been discriminated against and I do believe it's all the factors. When you are superior some people want the younger person because they believe they will be faster and they feel that they can teach them more and they have a perception that people over 40 years old are set in their ways.

25. Was the individual(s) you identified as committing the alleged harassment aware of your EEO ACTIVITY? If yes, when and how did they become aware of your EEO ACTIVITY?

ANSWER: Yes, I filed an EEO on all three of them Craig Colton, Jerry Wilson, and Corey Richards. The EEO (ADR) Specialist informed them and asked them questions. I don't know the dates I just got the responses.

a. Do you believe your EEO ACTIVITY was a factor in the alleged hostile work environment and harassment? If yes, why do you believe your EEO ACTIVITY was a factor?

ANSWER: Yes, Retaliation is still going on and I'm off work sick. They are finding things to try and hurt me with more are make things more complicated. Also, I'm still being passed over for promotion.

26. Is the alleged harassment continuing? If not, when did it stop?

ANSWER: Yes, It has stopped from everyone accept Corey Richards

27. Have you continued working since the period identified in your complaint (since July 12, 2008)?

ANSWER: No, I have been off work since the threat on 8/25/08 by Jerry Wilson and I'm still under the doctor's care. I'm getting better but this retaliation is only making me sicker.

a. If you have not been working, what was your last date worked and why are you not working?

ANSWER: 8/25/08, I have explained this question in length in the previous questions.

28. Please describe you understanding of the complaint procedure an employee should follow if they feel they have been subjected to hostile work environment harassment or they witness someone else being harassed?

ANSWER: They are to report it to their supervisor immediately; however, my supervisor was the one committing the harassment and I handle each situation in the manner I thought was appropriate. Craig Colton was advised of Steven Phaup issues with me and I called several meetings and sent emails to Craig with my concerns. Jerry Wilson was my boss and I tried to handle it the best way that I could, I did talk with him about it one day after a meeting. Corey Richards is just trying to continue to harass me out of retaliation and I try and communicate with him as less as possible.

29. Did you follow this procedure? If yes, on what date did you begin the complaint procedure?

ANSWER: Corey Richards I am off work and I wrote a letter to him and I also told Debbie Letts. In addition, I added the GMF issue and the pay check to the case. He will not let me come and put in my 2009 Core Requirements and that was addressed with Angie Bush and Maggie Lara, I will send the letter. Craig Colton is Corey's boss at this time, and I don't really know what to do in this situation but what I'm doing. Jerry Wilson I tried to talk to him one day after a meeting, and Craig Colton by way of Steven Phaup, I spoke to Craig immediately when it started happening. I sent emails and I called meeting with him and Steve. When Dana was there I called meetings also.

a. To whom did you make your complaint (name and position), what did you tell them, and what was their response?

ANSWER: I answered the question in #29.

b. Explain any delay between the dates you identified the alleged harassing behavior occurring (July 12, 2008) and the date you began the complaint procedure. (In other words, if there was a delay, why was there a delay?)

ANSWER: Craig Colton by way of Steven Phaup, there was no delay, Corey Richards just started after he found out about the EEO. He took me off of higher level with the 1723 technicality and I wrote a letter on that. He had my GMF access removed and he did not pay me in pp-1 wk 2, so I added it to the case. He was on leave last week, but I'll see what happens with Debbie Letts watching my time. There was not a delay to me. People do what they want too.

30. Other than this EEO complaint and investigation, has management or Human Resources conducted an investigation of your allegations of hostile work environment harassment?

ANSWER: Not to my knowledge, I only know that Jerry Wilson was sent back October, 4 2008.

a. If an investigation was conducted, were you interviewed as part of the investigation?
ANSWER: No

b. If you were interviewed, when were you interviewed and by whom?
ANSWER: Not Applicable.

c. If an investigation was conducted, is it on-going or has it been completed?
ANSWER: Unknown.

d. If the investigation is completed, were you notified of the results of the investigation? If yes, what were the results of the investigation and was any action taken regarding the individual(s) who allegedly harassed you?

ANSWER: All I know is that one day I was at injury compensation and I went on my email and I saw an email from Craig Colton regarding new assignments and Jerry Wilson was sent back to his office. I don't know anything else about any investigation and know one has told me about one.

e. Is the individual(s) who allegedly harassed you still employed with the USPS?

ANSWER: Yes, Jerry Wilson is in his office, Corey Richards just got a lateral to North Las Vegas as the Postmaster. Craig Colton by way of Steven Phaup, Craig Colton just got a promotion to Senior MPOO and Steven Phaup terminated himself by being caught doing fraudulent things.

f. If the investigation is completed, are you satisfied with the results of the investigation? If not, why not?

ANSWER: I don't know of any investigation and if it was one then I should have been made aware of it and what the outcome and findings were. In the meanwhile I'm off work sick trying to get well and Corey Richards is still harassing me with his tactics, and technicalities out of retaliation and discrimination. Something ought to be done to all the people who discriminated against me. It is just out right wrong. I'm ill and they are laughing and conjuring up more things to do to me.

31. Other than the complaint processes you have already identified, please identify any other actions or steps you took to avoid further harm by the individual(s) who committed the alleged harassment?

ANSWER: I sent several emails and asked for several meetings with Craig regarding Steven Phaup. I tried to talk with Jerry but to no avail, the threat came on 8/25/08 and I started 7/9/08. Corey just keep on doing things, I hope I get paid Friday 1/23/09. If I don't get paid Friday then I'm going to the District Manager Shaun Mossman.

32. Did the individual(s) you identified as committing the alleged harassment harass anyone else? If yes, who did they allegedly harass? Please provide their name and position and indicate if they, too, made a complaint regarding their situation/experience.

ANSWER: Yes, I believe Charles Turner was involved in some harassment by Steven Phaup and Craig Colton. I don't know if a complaint was made. Charles Turner use to be the NALC Steward at North Las Vegas Main Post Office when I arrived there in May 2004, he is now at the GMF working in CFS and bagging. I don't know if he had and issues with Jerry Wilson or Corey Richards.

33. What is your desired resolution?

ANSWER: All three men need extensive sensitivity training. I want official written apologies from all parties involved. I want Jerry Wilson to have management training if he's going to manage subordinate employees and I want Jerry to go to anger management training. I want compensation for 1 year worth of hair salon appointments on a weekly basis to grow my hair back and get it healthy. I want lifetime medical because I have major body organs that are affected as a result of the discrimination of all factors and including Retaliation from my boss.' I want to get back to being my healthy self. I want two (2) promotion levels at 10% each for pay increased at one year a piece individually calculated by the 52 weeks per year and the 26 pay period increment (EAS-19 through EAS-22). I will be placed in the higher EAS position for my permanent position. I want it to be written in the settlement that if discrimination occurs again then I will have the option to be placed in another federal position with my current rank and seniority are I will get a hardship lateral to another Postal Facility, both options will be of my choosing. The only medical problem I had before coming to the Nevada Sierra District was lower bowel obstruction and I manage that with my diet. I want my sick leave restored or compensation for it because I would not have used it had not this non- sense made me ill. I want monetary compensation for having to even endure and go through such a horrible tragedy. I would like to see more checks and balances implemented in the review committee process and vice versa with the selecting and concurring officials. The worse thing to do is give a person the power and not know if he or she can handle it because when you do you get situations like this and I do not deserve what was done to me.

34. Provide any additional statement or documentation that is relevant to the investigation being conducted. Please note, the investigation is limited to those issues accepted for investigation. Issues or events outside of the issues accepted for investigation will not be included in the investigation.

ANSWER: My health is very serious to me; I use to take much pride in my physical ability before all of this happened and I expect to get back to full capacity. I have future grandchildren that are depending on me to be there when they grow up. My life is important to me and my family as well, but I have allowed the post office to ruin my relationship, and I am selling my home because I don't know if I can trust the leaders anymore. I will come back when I'm able. I do not want to come back and be half of me. I'm a hard worker and I take pride with what has my name on it. I am somebody to me and my loved ones even though some has treated me very badly with a smile. Thank you for your integrity in this investigation. May God Bless the U. S. Postal Service and the people who operate it.

UNITED STATES POSTAL SERVICE

EEO Investigative Affidavit for Compensatory Damages

Note: Not applicable to Age Discrimination in Employment Act (ADEA) claims

Name		No.	pages
McGEE, Lola B.	4E-890-0120-08	1	3

Instructions for the Complainant

During an investigation into alleged discrimination, the Postal Service is required to gather evidence regarding appropriate remedies, which may include compensatory damages. The remedy that you are seeking to resolve this complaint includes your claim that you are entitled to receive a monetary award. Therefore, you must provide testimony and evidence concerning the nature, extent and severity of the harm you suffered due to the alleged discriminatory conduct. PS Form 2569-C contains a number of questions and/or statements regarding your claim for damages. Please read the questions or statements carefully before responding. If you need additional space, please use an additional sheet(s). Any additional sheet(s) must show the number of this form (Form 2569-C), the item number(s) to which it pertains, a page number and the total number of pages submitted for this form. *You must declare under penalty of perjury that the information you provide on this form including any attached sheets is true and correct.*

1. I experienced financial difficulties because of the discriminatory act(s) alleged in my complaint.

[X] Yes [ ] No

If yes, provide full explanation. Please include description and cause of difficulty (or difficulties) when occurred, duration of occurrence, and how severe. Ultimately Severe/Critical, Lack of Promotions (2006-2008) caused less funds to maintain my family/lifestyle. Put house up for sale at 7582 Cypress Tree St.,= down market and value is upside down in the market today/DOL,NEEOISO postage/services charges. Moved into apartment for peace of mind-double financial expenses for two places (I still have to contribute to my home even though I have an apartment 11/26/08 (Six month lease), No Higher Level Pay=less funds since I've been off sick (8/26/08), Multiple doctor visits-2-3 in one day and 3-4 days a week since 8/27/08=co-pays, medications, High gas prices, (Uhaul services, moving people, 11/2008 (TWICE), Extra household needs=food, clothes, toiletries, linens, cookware, utilities, cable, internet, telephone, domestic items-I'm forced to do for myself now daily, weekly, and monthly. My brain may not be functioning properly right now to think of everything.

2. I experienced personal medical problems because of the discriminatory act(s) alleged in my complaint.

[X] Yes [ ] No

If yes, provide full explanation. Please include description and cause of problems, when occurred, duration of occurrence, and severity. Ultimately Severe/Critical, Panic Attack=8/25/08 resulting in progressed heart palpitations, mind confusion, head shocks throughout my body, hearing loss

1

in left ear, Neuropathy-numbness in both feet and severe pain in top of left foot along with severe/cutting pain in top of left buttocks area (still exist to date and no knowledge of it going away) prolong sitting, standing, and walking aggravates it, PTSD and Major Depressive Disorder= 2005/2008 diagnosis and know knowledge of it going away (It makes me have anxiety daily along with being depressed) I'm very angry, sad, feeling used, misused, very little social time, and I sleep as long as I can, feelings of victimization, afraid in a different way – retaliation, anger from my boss', retaliation if/when I go back to work, upset with managements unfair tactics towards me, I hyperventilate sometimes depending on the situation/circumstances, anxiety when I have to go to the GMF for paperwork/injury compensation, very unhappy with the way my CA-1/CA-2 has been handled since on the job injuries were reported, I don't think like my normal self at this time; my mind is regulated by how I wake up and the events of the day, I don't have control over my personality, behavior, thinking, mood, mentality, are anything else anymore. I have head aches; I did not have them before, my life is scary to me because of the unknown of my health. The discrimination (Every factor) for two going on three years, the hostile work environment, disrespect, misuse, unfair tactics, etc. has taken a tole on my health to date. My hair has fallen out over a period of time (2005-present) and I'm now practically bald to date. I only had Lower Bowel Obstruction problems when I came to Nevada Sierra District in May/2004 and it was managed with my diet. My physical strength is very low and I was strong as the average man (If you will allow me to describe it this way). I'm very hurt. I talk loud because of my hearing loss and I ask people to tell me to quit down when I'm talking to them. I don't know what the head shocks are but it goes all through my lips/neck (It has subsided some, but it still comes maybe 3-4 times a week and it doesn't last all day anymore. Chocking cough 2007/2008 it has stopped for the most part. I know, with the left side affected so bad, that I was going to have a Stroke or Heart Attack. This is just not fair to me to be in this condition.

3. I obtained psychological or psychiatric counseling because of the discriminatory act(s) alleged in my complaint.

[X] Yes [ ] No

If yes, provide full explanation. Include description of when, the cause, its extent and severity. Critically Severe, Panic Attack, PTSD, Major Depressive Disorder: Panic Attack 8/25/08 explained in previous questions. PTSD/Depression =2005 the Steve Phaup issues that were explained in my Affidavit, along with family issues that I thought was every body else's problem but it was mine because I did not believe my behavior and how I was affecting my family and friends with these diagnosis. The job had me messed up. Also, I was just holding in all of my emotions and stuffing the work related issues. Also, I was robbed before and I had always been afraid of scary situations ever since and the Steven Phaup issue aggravated that behavior of mine so that's why I went to counseling in 2005. PTSD/Depression= 8/27/08 the threat on 8/25/08 from Jerry Wilson, the discrimination by not being promoted (2006-2008), my health and all the medical issues described above in previous questions,

2

4. I have had to take medication because of the discriminatory act(s) alleged in my complaint.

[X] Yes [ ] No

If yes, list type of medication, reason for the medication, and the cost of the medication. Motrin for pain and it cost $10.00 per bottle, Effexor for depression and it $30.00 per bottle, Clonazepam for anxiety and it cost $30.00 per bottle, Verapamil for heart palpitations and it cost $30.00 per bottle, Benzonate for choking cough $$30.00 per bottle.

Name	Case No.	Page No.	No. of pages
McGEE, Lola B.	4E-890-0120-08	2	3

5. Did any of the difficulties for which you checked "Yes" in items 1-4 exist prior to the act(s) of discrimination alleged in your complaint?

[ ] Yes [X] No

If yes, please complete question 6 below.

6. Describe for each pre-existing condition how that condition was made worse by the act(s) of discrimination alleged in your complaint. Begin each description with the item number of page 1 (items 1 through 4) to which it pertains. N/A.

7. Is there any other information or evidence regarding your claim for entitlement to compensatory damages that you want to include with this affidavit?

[X] Yes [ ] No

If yes, please provide a full explanation of the information you wish to include. Attach additional pages if necessary.
My medical/health condition may have lifetime affects and I certainly do not deserve this, not even for one second let alone a lifetime. I have lifestyle changes to adapt to with my current medical/health condition and problems. My significant other and I are having serious problems and as a result of my behavior, personality, medical condition, attitude, lack of sex drive (Libido), lack of energy, loss of love by arguing, lack of doing my part in the relationship, I have loss my love in the relationship; we have been together for eight (8) years. I believe it's irretrievable; too much damage has been done, but we are still amicable with one another. I still contribute to the household financially on a monthly basis, but this is really a hardship for me. I believe if a relationship is going to end it should be because of the two people involved not the United States Postal Service having an affect/effect on people's lives. I'm trying to gain my strength back and get well but the continued harassment, unprofessional, and unfair tactics from Corey Richards along with other issues from the postal service makes me sicker. I use to take much pride in my physical ability, but now I have to adjust to my limited physical strength. I

3

miss out on social events because I don't have the energy are mental motivation to attend. If I have free time I'd rather sleep than do something fun. I really don't have very many fun time/days in my life right now. I feel like I've been working all this time and I've been off work since 8/26/08. Half of FY 2009 has gone and I will not get evaluated for it; so I will get a lower merit increase. The fiscal year ends 9/30/2009 and it is already January, 21 2009. I'm still not promoted after continually being used as an acting manager across the district and I'm ashamed now with feelings of not even wanting to work for the postal service anymore. My dignity, respect, integrity, morals, work ethic, perseverance, drive, motivation, trust, will, performance, appears to me to have a question mark behind it now since all of this has happened. I'm very angry from being used and abused by my superiors and those that had the power to promote me and did not. I worked very hard and I was not judged on my own merit but on the color of my skin and my sex, along with the other discriminatory factors. The retaliation demonstrates their level of mentality, in the mean while I'm very ill and don't know if I will ever get back to my natural/normal self again in life. That is severe, powerful, and unfortunate for me, but the postal service will continue to go on rather I'm there are not. No harm to them. I would like for my case # 4E-890-0120-08 to be victorious for me in all that I ask for considering my mental and physical condition and all of my losses as a result of me filing this claim. I will send the co-pay, prescription, and any other small pieces of paper receipts to you shortly.

Thank you,
Lola Bonitta McGee.

PS Form 2569-C (Page 3 of 3) December 2003 **Lola Bonitta McGee**
EEO Case No. = 4E-890-0120-08

IMPORTANT!

You must attach or provide the investigator with copies of documentation, such as bills, doctor's statements, pharmacy bills, statements from other persons, or other paperwork relevant to the difficulty that you claim is related to the discriminatory act(s) alleged in your complaint. If you do not have copies of your documentation, you may provide the original to the investigator who will copy relevant records and return the original documents to you. Alternatively, for medical information and records, you may provide a signed authorization from your health care provider to the investigator permitting him/her to obtain information directly from your health care provider or pharmacy. Or, you may sign a medical information release provided by the investigator if you prefer.

Privacy Act Notice

Privacy Act Notice. The collection of this information is authorized by The Equal Employment Opportunity Act of 1972, 42 U.S.C. 2000e-16; The Age Discrimination

4

in Employment Act of 1967, as amended, 29 U.S.C.633a; The Rehabilitation Act of 1973, as amended, 29 U.S.C. 794a; and executive Order 11478, as amended. This information will be used to adjudicate complaints of alleged discrimination and to evaluate the effectiveness of the EEO program. As a routine use, this information may be disclosed to an appropriate government agency, domestic or foreign, for law enforcement purposes; where pertinent, in a legal proceeding to which the USPS is a party or has an interest; to a government agency in order to obtain information relevant to a USPS decision concerning employment, security clearances, contracts, licenses, grants, permits or other benefits; to a government agency upon its request when relevant to its decision concerning employment, security clearances, security or suitability investigations, contracts, licenses, grants or other benefits; to a congressional office at your request; to an expert, consultant, or other person under contract with the USPS to fulfill an agency function; to the Federal Records Center for storage; to the Office of Management and Budget for review of private relief legislation; to an independent certified public accountant during an official audit of USPS finances; to an investigator, administrative judge or complaints examiner appointed by the Equal Employment Opportunity Commission for Investigation of a formal EEO complaint under 29 CFR 1614; to the Merit Systems Protection Board or Office of Special Counsel for proceedings or investigations involving personnel practices and other matters within their jurisdiction; and to a labor organization as required by the National labor Relations Act. Under the Privacy Act provision, the information requested is voluntary for the complainant, and for the Postal Service employees and other witnesses.

I declare under penalty of perjury that the foregoing, including any attached sheets, is true and correct.

Affiant's Signature	**Date Signed**

<table>
<tr><td colspan="3">U. S. Postal Service
EEO INVESTIGATIVE AFFIDAVIT
(COMPLAINANT)</td><td>Page No.
1</td><td>No. Pages
23</td><td>Case No.
4E-890-0120-08</td></tr>
<tr><td colspan="4">1. Affiant's Name (First, Middle, Last)
Lola B. McGEE – SUPPLEMENTAL AFFIDAVIT
(Amended Complaint)</td><td colspan="2">2. Employing Postal Facility
North Las Vegas Post Office</td></tr>
<tr><td>3. Position Title
Supervisor, Customer Services</td><td>4. Grade Level
EAS-17</td><td colspan="2">5. Postal Address and Zip + 4
1414 E. Lake Mead Blvd.
North Las Vegas, NV
89030-9998</td><td colspan="2">6. Unit Assigned
Spring Valley Station
Las Vegas, NV 89117</td></tr>
<tr><td colspan="6">Privacy Act Notice/USPS Standards of Conduct</td></tr>
<tr><td colspan="6">Privacy Act Notice. The collection of this information is authorized by the Equal Employment Opportunity act of 1972, 42 U.S.C. § 2000e-16; the Age Discrimination in Employment Act of 1967, as amended, 29 U.S.C. § 633a; the Rehabilitation Act of 1973, as amended. This information will be used to adjudicate complaints of alleged discrimination and to evaluate the effectiveness of the EEO program. As a routine use, this information may be disclosed to an appropriate government agency, domestic or foreign, for law enforcement purposes; where pertinent, in a legal proceeding to which the USPS is a party or has an interest; to a government agency in order to obtain information relevant to a USPS decision concerning employment, security clearances, contracts, licenses, grants, permits or other benefits; to a government agency upon its request when relevant to its decision concerning employment, security clearances, security or suitability investigations, contracts, licenses, grants or other benefits; to a congressional office at your request; to an expert, consultant, or other person under contract with the USPS to fulfill an agency function; to the Federal Records Center for storage; to the Office of Management and Budget for review of private relief legislation; to an independent certified public accountant during an official audit of USPS finances; to an investigator, administrative judge or complaints examiner appointed by the Equal Employment Opportunity Commission for Investigation of a formal EEO complaint under 29 CFR 1614; to the Merit Systems Protection Board or Office of Special Counsel for proceedings or investigations involving personnel practices and other matters within their jurisdiction; and to a labor organization as required by the National Labor Relations Act. Under the Privacy Act provision, the information requested is voluntary for the complainant, and for Postal Service employees and other witnesses.</td></tr>
<tr><td colspan="6">Important Information Regarding Your Complaint</td></tr>
</table>

12

This PS Form 2568-A, EEO Investigative Affidavit (Complainant), and the other form mentioned below, are being provided for you to use to fully respond to the accompanying questions. Mail or deliver your completed statement to the EEO complaints investigator within15 calendar days of the date you received the forms. Use PS Form(s) 2569, EEO Investigative Affidavit (Continuation Sheet), as needed, to complete your written statement. Remember to number the top of each page and sign and date the bottom of each page of your statement. If you return your statement by mail, the return envelope must be postmarked on or before the 15th calendar day after the date that you received the affidavit forms.	**Failure to complete your statement and return the forms within the allotted time period could result in your complaint being dismissed based upon your failure to proceed. EEOC complaints processing regulation. 29 C.F.R. 1614.107(a)(7), states, in part, [A complaint may be dismissed] "Where the agency has provided the complainant with the written request to provide relevant information or otherwise proceed with the complaint, and the complainant has failed to respond to the request within 15 days of its receipt, or the complainant's response does not address the agency's request, provided that the request included a notice of the proposed dismissal."**
7. Statement A(Continue on Form 2569 if additional space is required)	

1. State your name.
ANSWER: Lola Bonitta McGee

2. You have the right to be accompanied by a representative of your choice when you complete this affidavit and at all times during the EEO process. Do you have a representative at this time? If yes, identify your representative by name, title (including whether or not your representative is an attorney), address, and telephone number.
ANSWER: No, but I will have one in the future.

3. In the last six months, have you had a prolonged absence from work, that is an absence of greater than 14 days? If yes, please identify your last date worked.
ANSWER: Yes, my original last date of work was 8/25/08. I started back working on 3/12/09 at Spring Valley Station as a Supervisor, Customer Services, and I don't know for how long because my on the job injury (Neuropathy) is painful while performing my duties. I didn't think that I would have to be so physical at work, it depends on the office and staffing, my legs and left top buttocks/hip pain is bothering me to the point where I have to adjust and grimmest.
a. For what period have you been absent?
ANSWER: 8/26/08 - 3/12/09

b. For what reason have you been absent?
ANSWER: I have been medically diagnosed with the following conditions: Post Traumatic Stress Disorder, Panic Attack Disorder, Hearing Loss in my left ear, Neuropathy-Nerve Damage/Numbness in my feet, up my legs, and severe pain in my left buttocks/hip, Major Depressive Disorder, Head Shocks/lips, Heart Palpitations without the presence of Heart Disease or mass blockage to my Arteries (Strictly related to Stress). These diagnoses are the results of an open ended threat from my boss. Discrimination over a two and one half year period, enduring a hostile work environment, disrespect, unfair tactic and lies by my superiors. All of these issues are a result of on the job injuries. On 8/25/08 my boss OIC, Jerry

Wilson, North Las Vegas gave me an open ended threat "You continue to go over my head with Craig and Yul and I'm going to do something about it." I knew from his (Jerry Wilson) voice, tone, gesture, words, and demeanor that something negative was going to happen, be it physical or in writing and I did not deserve any of it. I was very afraid and I lost control of myself. I started hyperventilating, my heart was beating faster, I had chest pain, I was confused in my head until I felt retarded, I had head shocks, and I thought I was going to die. I replied to an email that Craig had sent out to all his subordinate's, regarding projections, and I called him for clarity. I had originally asked Jerry Wilson what he (Craig Colton) wanted on the particular indicator F2B=Carrier and Supervisor hours, because sometimes this indicator is interchanged with managers. Jerry Wilson told me Carrier hours and that was not correct, which is the reason why Craig sent out the nasty email. On 8/22/08 I called North Las Vegas Post Office to speak with Jerry Wilson and I was told that he had gone to a meeting at the GMF. I called the postmaster's office Yul Melonson and I was told that they were in a meeting. About two hours later, I called Jerry's cell phone but I did not get an answer. Later, Jerry called me back and I told him that my supervisors had made a mistake with the schedule; and I have corrected that issue, however we are casing 18 routes and splitting 8. Jerry stated that the Scheduled Day Off projection employees report has been given to Yul Melonson and Shaun Mossman already and we will have to live with our mistakes. I asked if I could have my Transitional Employees that belong to Meadow Mesa; and he told me no, because Mel has already made his schedule, but he will call the office in the morning. I said okay and we will do the best we can. Later on after Jerry's call back, Yul Melonson calls and ask about the station and I told him that I called to speak with Jerry but I have already talked with him, its okay. Yul asked what's going on and I told him that its okay I've already spoke with Jerry. Yul persisted and I told him that my supervisors made a mistake with the schedule and Jerry has already told me that the Schedule Day Off employee's projection report has already been submitted. Yul confirmed that the Scheduled Day Off employees has been submitted but what about bringing my Transitional Employees in early, and I replied, "I can do that" and Yul said yes make sure you bring in the one's that can help you the most; and I said thank you I will. The reason I responded with such a surprise is because Shaun Mossman had mandated no Transitional Employees are to start before 10:00am. From 4/2006 – 8/2008, I had worked most of the time as an acting manager from Las Vegas to Reno; I had put in for 15 positions as Manager, Customer Services but I was never promoted, and received only four (4) interviews. I was used consistently around the Nevada Sierra District but was never selected for a position. I achieved the numbers, implemented efficient and effective processes, along with correcting deficiencies in every office I was assigned to. Jennifer Vo lied to me; and by me calling a meeting with Mark Martinez, Robert Reynosa, and her, I was never even considered for promotion. I was just used to achieve my superiors' desired results. The revelation came to me when I came full circle by being back at the first station that I had started my acting manager's position at (Huntridge Station in 6/08 – 7/08). In December 2008 I was interviewed by Robert Reynosa, while being out sick, and I was not selected because I was out sick. On 6/18/08, after being interviewed for Huntridge Station, I was informed by Corey Richards that I was not selected for the position. The position was given to a person out of the district. When I arrived at North Las Vegas in May 2004 it was performing at 5% over SPLY, under the supervising of Steven Phaup and the Postmaster was Craig Colton. By the in of the Fiscal Year 2004 I had improved it to 3.5 under plan 9/2004. Craig allowed Steve to harass me, talk loud and disrespect me in front of my employees. Also, Steve would try and sabotage my operation by hiding my employee schedule and 3971's = Leave Slips which would create problems for my operation. I called many meetings with Craig and Dana Urbanski to try and get the harassment stopped. Steve was Craig's right hand man and he did not want to do anything against his superstar. He would take him to lunch and leave me in the office and I now know that it was discrimination towards me. Steve created a very hostile work environment in North Las Vegas, even with the employees, not only would he talk bad to me but he would talk loud on the workroom floor to the employees and with the union steward (Charles Turner). Grievances were filed almost daily, along with Article 8 violations between him and Charles. Ultimately, Steven Phaup was terminated because of his fraudulent behavior and Craig had to do it. Craig will never promote me because of this. I interviewed with Craig for Valle Verde and he told me that I had a strong skill base and ability along with working knowledge, but my personality was to confident and I was to serious. Craig told me that I was to strong. When you know that you are qualified for a position and you have demonstrated your skills and ability along with being educated, it takes a toll on your health when you know that you've been discriminated against and treated unfairly because of your gender and race. I was not judged on my on merit; I was judged by the color of my skin and my gender. It's evident to me know because there is not one black let alone female promoted in the Las Vegas City Stations.

c. Have you recently returned to work or been released to return to work? If yes, on what date were you released to return to work?

ANSWER: Yes, I was released to return to work on 3/9/08. However, I had a severe flood in my home on 3/6/09 and the clean up was not completed until 3/9/09. I was notified on Saturday 3/7/09 that there had been a death in my family. There were a host of things that happened that weekend. I called Joe Acosta on Sunday 3/8/09 and told him about what had happened and I requested leave.

d. If you have returned to work, what date did you first return to work?

ANSWER: Friday 3/13/09

e. Did you provide any medical documentation regarding your ability to return to work? If yes, please provide a copy.

ANSWER: Yes, copies are attached.

4. Do you have a physical or mental medical condition or impairment? If yes, what is your medical condition or impairment? (Please do not use acronyms.)

ANSWER: I have explained it in previous questions.

a. Has or was your condition or impairment diagnosed by any healthcare provider? If yes, when was it diagnosed?

ANSWER: Yes, 2/2009, 12/2008, 11/2008, 8/27/08, 9/2007, and 2005.

b. Provide medical evidence which documents your condition or impairment. This documentation should indicate your medical diagnosis and any limitations/restrictions you may have.

c. How long is the condition expected to last? Is the medical condition you described temporary or permanent?

ANSWER: I have been released to go back to work with medication and continued doctor's visits along with Physical Therapy resuming. However, I don't know if I can work with the Neuropathy from my assessment the last two (2) days. I will be going to physical Therapy and back to my doctor to let them know how I feel. In addition, I'm going to take FMLA paperwork to my doctors and I will forward it to you once it is completed.

d. Are you currently undergoing any treatment or taking any medication(s) to help with the medical condition you described? If yes, please describe the treatment or identify the medication(s).

ANSWER: Yes, I will be scheduling Physical Therapy appointments, and I have Cardiologist and Psycho Therapy appointments. I will also schedule an appointment with my primary doctor and or my Neurologist. I take Motrin for Pain, Verapamil for my heart condition (Palpitations), Pristiq for Depression, and Clonazepam for Anxiety.

e. Is the medical condition you described from an on-the-job injury or was it a condition you had prior to or developed outside the workplace?

ANSWER: All my medical conditions are from on-the-job injuries.

f. If it is from an on-the-job injury, what was the original date of injury?

ANSWER: I did not originally know what to call the injuries when I was first seeking Psycho Therapy in 2005, all I knew is that I was scared of Steven Phaup's erratic and hyper behavior and was frustrated because of his disrespect and unprofessional behavior. I was very concern about his mentality (Craig Colton, Dana Urbanski, Shelby Kruger-Duncan, Inspector Stevens, and Tom Martin can attest to his behavior. Also, Charles Turner can attest to his behavior. Steve told bizarre stories everyday aside from his harassment towards me.

g. If it is from an on-the-job injury, has the condition been accepted by OWCP for benefits? If it has been accepted by benefits, please provide a copy of the acceptance letter from OWCP/DOL.
ANSWER: It is from on-the-job injuries, however, the DOL did not accept the claim but I will be appealing. I guess I did not explain it correctly. I don't know why but I do know that Jerry Wilson lied on several occasions in his statement and also the DOL has misquoted some information in their letter to me. I will pursue this as soon as I can, in the meanwhile I have to take care of my own health.

h. If it developed outside the workplace, provide a description of how and when it developed.
ANSWER: Absolutely, none of my conditions developed as a result of outside the workplace.

Does the medical condition you described limit any of your major life activities? If yes, describe those activities and to what degree they are limited (e.g., can not do activity at all, can only do the activity with assistive device(s) or equipment, can only do the activity for a limited period of time).
ANSWER: Anxiety causes me to be very anxious, but my medication helps. I'm not myself and I have to live with new behavior and personality. My depression causes me to be down mentally and in a slump, but my medication helps along with Psycho Therapy. Some times I don't even fill like bathing let alone any other normal life functions. I cannot hear well and I talk louder. My heart functions like a person with Heart Disease but I do not have it. Sometimes I can be setting still and my body rocks and sway on its own, which is very scary to me especially at my age (46). I'm afraid of not seeing my grandchildren grow up. It's just not fair. My Neuropathy has escalated in the last two days since I've been back at work. I am in so much more pain now down my legs, my feet, and especially my left top buttocks. I can't walk, sit, stand, bend, twist, dance, bath, shower, clean up, work, have sex, are any other movements to long and without increased pain. I grunt like an old woman and I just don't know what I'm going to do, really. Life is very different for me now know matter how hard I try to make it the same.

5. Does the medical condition you described limit your ability to perform the major job duties or functions of your position as Supervisor, Customer Service? If yes, describe those activities and to what degree they are limited (e.g., a carrier who has a limitation of no driving or use of machinery may not be able to deliver a mounted route, but may still be able to case mail or deliver mail on foot).
ANSWER: I can only say that in the past two days, I have experienced major problems that I did not expect. I thought that by me being a supervisor that I would be able to do the job, but I walk the floor, assist limited duty employees, count mail, monitor the window, go back and forth are sit at the computer to long and then move, twist to turn, make sudden moves etc. and it's a serious problem until I want to cry. I'm just not my self and I don't know what I'm going to do. I can't do the things I use to do. I was a very strong person with great physical ability and now I don't know what I can and cannot do because I'm surprised everyday. It is a chore just to complete this form because of the length. I have to stop and start. My left leg is numb right now and my back is killing me with pain. I'm rotating to the side as I set in the chair.

6. Do you require accommodations for your medical condition or limitations? If so, what are the specific accommodations? (Please be specific and provide documentation supporting your claim.)
ANSWER: I did not know that I would be like this so I'm not sure what I'm going to be requesting and what my doctors are going to say, but I have some problems and I have to look out for what's left of me. I don't know me anymore; I have to get to know what I can do and what I can't do because I've never been like this. I don't know if I'm making any since but it's real.

a. Did you request or discuss accommodations for your medical condition or limitations with management? If so, please explain to whom you made the request, when it was requested, how it was requested, and what was requested. (Please provide copies of any written requests that you may have submitted to management.)
ANSWER: I have not submitted any written request yet, I will go back to my doctor with my FMLA paperwork and I will get direction from them because I don't know at this time what to say, I can just tell you the condition that I'm in and it has only been two (2) days.

b. Were you granted any accommodations for your physical or mental impairment? If so, what? (Please provide copies of any written documentation that you may have received from management.)
ANSWER: None at this time because I was released from the doctor without any restrictions because I did not think that my job would be a problem for me.

c. Were you referred to the District Reasonable Accommodation Committee (DRAC)? If so, when and what was the outcome?
ANSWER: N/A at this time.

d. If you were not granted the accommodation you requested, did management provide alternative accommodations or options? If yes, describe the alternatives and whether you accepted the alternatives offered.
ANSWER: N/A at this time.

Claim 2: On December 9, 2008, Complainant was informed that she was not selected for Manager Position at King Station

7. Please identify the vacancy number and title, for the vacancy at King Station for which you applied.
ANSWER: Job Posting = 52188820, Job Title = 2310-0002 MGR Customer Services EAS-22 Las Vegas NV from eCareer.

8. When did you first become aware of the opening(s)?
ANSWER: 7/29/2008 and it closed on 8/13/08.
9. Why were you interested in or why did you want to apply for the position(s)?
ANSWER: I had been acting manager at King Station from 2/23/08 – 5/2/08 then I went on three (3) weeks of leave for my daughters wedding. Also, I was asked by Robert Reynosa to come and act as the manager while I was up in Reno as the acting manager. In addition, about four (4) months after I left King, Robert Reynosa's superiors sent him to King Station and my performance was better than his and he's the Manager, Customer Service Operations for Las Vegas. He is over all the managers in the Las Vegas City Stations. I was qualified for the position and I had worked hard at getting King Station up to par in the short time that I was there.

10. Did you apply for the position(s)? If yes, when and how did you apply for the position(s)?
ANSWER: Yes, I applied for the position on 8/13/08 Via the Postal eCareer website on liteblue.

11. Provide a copy of your application (e.g., PS Form 991 or other written communication regarding your interest in the position) for the position(s) and any communications you received from the USPS regarding your status in the selection process.
12. Was the selection process for this vacancy a competitive or non-competitive selection process?
ANSWER: Competitive

13. Was there a review committee for this position? If yes, please identify the review committee members including name and position, if known.
ANSWER: Yes, Robert Reynosa = Selecting Official, Yul Melonson = Concurring Official, and Tony Sequira = Retail.

14. Was there a selecting official for this position? If yes, please identify the selecting official including name and position, if known.
ANSWER: Answered already.

15. Was there a concurring official for this position? If yes, please identify the concurring official including name and position, if known.
ANSWER: Answered already.

16. Were you recommended by the review committee for consideration by the selecting official? How were you informed of this decision?
ANSWER: Yes, Robert Reynosa called me on my cell phone while I was off sick and scheduled a telephone interview.

17. Were you interviewed for the position? If yes, when were you interviewed and by whom?
ANSWER: Yes, on 12/2/08 Robert Reynosa called me and scheduled an interview for 12/4/08 at 1:15pm
If you were not interviewed, were you provided a reason as to why you were not interviewed for the position? If yes, what was the reason and who provided this explanation.
ANSWER: N/A

18. Were you selected for the position? If not, who was selected? Please provide their full name and identify their race, color, religion, sex, age, and prior position.
ANSWER: No, I was asked when will I be returning to work and I would give the answer tomorrow after I spoke with my doctor. I called back on 12/5/08 and I was told by Yul Melonson that he would let Robert know my estimated return date which I gave as the end of January according to my doctor. I was called on 12/9/08 an informed by Robert Reynosa that the person selected for King Station was Thomas Jack a White Male and I do not know his religion or age. His prior position was the manager of Huntridge Station. He's the person that was given a lateral from out of the district on the previous Huntridge Position by Corey Richards.

19. If you were not selected, were you provided a reason as to why you were not selected for the position? If yes, what was the reason and who provided this explanation.
ANSWER: No, Robert Reynosa told me that Thomas was selected and there were more positions becoming available.

20. Do you believe you should have been selected for the vacancy? If yes, why do you believe you should have been selected for this position?
ANSWER: Yes, Thomas Jack had already been given a lateral and I had worked very hard at King Station to improve it for the time that I was there. Also, my performance was better than Robert Reynosa's with less staffing.

21. Other than the current EEO complaint, has another appeal or complaint been filed on this issue? If yes, where is it in the process? If a settlement has been reached, describe the settlement. Provide copies of any documentation and settlement (if applicable).
ANSWER: No.

22. Who do you believe was responsible for determining whether or not you would be selected for the vacancy? Please provide their name, position, email address, and office telephone number.

ANSWER: Robert Reynosa = Manager, Customer Service Operations Las Vegas City. (702) 361-9348.

a. Why do you believe this individual was responsible for the decision?
ANSWER: He was the selecting official and Yul stated that he would tell Robert about my return. Also, I put in for Sunrise Station and it was filled while I was out sick and I did not get an interview. (Level-21)

23. Was this individual aware of your RACE? If yes, how and when were they made aware of your RACE?
ANSWER: Absolutely, I've worked for him more than any other manager.

a. Do you believe your RACE was a factor in the selection process? If yes, what makes you believe your RACE was a factor in the selection process?
ANSWER: Absolutely, and the fact that I have EEO activity on him along with me being out sick. This is retaliation and discrimination that has gone on ever since Mark Martinez and Jennifer Vo was here. Please refer to the entire complaints signed on 9/18/08 and 1/15/09.

24. Was this individual aware of your COLOR? If yes, how and when were they made aware of your COLOR?
ANSWER: Yes, I've worked for him.

a. Do you believe your COLOR was a factor in the selection process? If yes, what makes you believe your COLOR was a factor in the selection process?
ANSWER: Absolutely, by the way he has treated me with his unfair tactics and he has worked me the most and he has refused me the most.

25. Was this individual aware of your RELIGION? If yes, how and when were they made aware of your RELIGION?
ANSWER: He knows that I believe in God by my cell phone message, my cross around my neck and my expressions of God.

a. Do you believe your RELIGION was a factor in the selection process? If yes, what makes you believe your RELIGION was a factor in the selection process?
ANSWER: I Robert and anyone else that treat people the way that I've been treated has a problem with others who believe in God.

26. Was this individual aware of your SEX? If yes, how and when were they made aware of your SEX?
ANSWER: Yes, I've worked for him.

a. Do you believe your SEX was a factor in the selection process? If yes, what makes you believe your SEX was a factor in the selection process?
ANSWER: 100% I'm Black, Female, and educated with a child that graduated from Yale University, with Honors. He asked me one time about my home and he knows I drive two late model vehicles. He stated "You bought your home before you even moved out here" and I replied, yes.

27. Was this individual aware of your AGE? If yes, how and when were they made aware of your AGE?
ANSWER: He knows I'm over 40.

a. Do you believe your AGE was a factor in the selection process? If yes, what makes you believe your AGE was a factor in the selection process?
ANSWER: Yes, because the older you are the less productive people think you are.

28. Was this individual aware of your MEDICAL CONDITION OR LIMITATIONS? If yes, how and when were they made aware of your MEDICAL CONDITION OR LIMITATIONS?
ANSWER: Yes, he is the Manager, Customer Services Operations and he called me on 12/3/08 and made unwelcome comments. Please refer to my notes "Things that are happening."

a. Do you believe your MEDICAL CONDITION OR LIMITATIONS was a factor in the selection process? If yes, what makes you believe your MEDICAL CONDITION OR LIMITATIONS was a factor in the selection process?
ANSWER: Yes, because I had been gone over six months with two (2) claims filed with the DOL, and he acted as if he did not know what was going on with me. I worked as an acting manager for several promoted managers that were out ill for one reason are another so I know that he did not want to promote me and I'm already out sick, even though he helped to make me sick.

29. Was this individual aware of your past or current EEO ACTIVITY? If yes, how and when were they made aware of your EEO ACTIVITY?
ANSWER: Yes, one was filed on him.

a. Do you believe your past or current EEO ACTIVITY was a factor in the selection process? If yes, what makes you believe your EEO ACTIVITY was a factor in the selection process?
ANSWER: 100% yes, because he's one of the reasons why I'm sick and an EEO was filed on him.

30. Are you aware of the identity of other employees who applied for but were not selected for this position? If yes, please identify them by name, position, race, color, religion, sex, age, and limitations (if known).
ANSWER: No.

31. You identified Dave Dayton as a comparator.
a. Please identify Dayton's race, color, religion, sex, and age.
ANSWER: Caucasion, White, Male, and a promoted manager. I don't know his religion or age.
b. Identify Dayton's position.
ANSWER: Manager, Customer Services

c. Does Dayton have any limitations? If yes, please describe.
ANSWER: Not to my knowledge.

d. Did Dayton apply for the Manager position at King Station? If yes, was Dayton selected?
ANSWER: I don't know.

32. You identified Lynn Holmes as a comparator.
a. Please identify Holmes' race, color, religion, sex, and age.
ANSWER: Caucasian, White, Female who now works for Labor Relations. I don't know her religion or age.

b. Identify Holmes' position.
ANSWER: She originally was selected for Manager, Customer Services at Strip Station but she is in Labor Relations now.
c. Does Holmes have any limitations? If yes, please describe.
ANSWER: Not that I'm aware of.

d. Did Holmes apply for the Manager position at King Station? If yes, was Holmes selected?
ANSWER: I doubt it.

33. You identified Doug Watson as a comparator.
a. Please identify Watson's race, color, religion, sex, and age.
ANSWER: Caucasian, White, Male, and I don't know his religion or age.

b. Identify Watson's position.
ANSWER: Manager, Customer Services (Lateral from Paradise Valley Station).

c. Does Watson have any limitations? If yes, please describe.
ANSWER: None I'm aware of.
Did Watson apply for the Manager position at King Station? If yes, was Watson selected?
ANSWER: I doubt it.

34. You identified Gerrad Carraza as a comparator.
a. Please identify Carraza's race, color, religion, sex, and age.
ANSWER: None Black, Male and I not aware of his religion or age.

b. Identify Carraza's position.
ANSWER: Manager, Customer Services.

c. Does Carraza have any limitations? If yes, please describe.
ANSWER: None that I'm aware of.

d. Did Carraza apply for the Manager position at King Station? If yes, was Carraza selected?
ANSWER: I doubt it because King is a challenging station.

35. You identified Steve Reeves as a comparator.
a. Please identify Reeves' race, color, religion, sex, and age.
ANSWER: Caucasian, White, Male and I don't know his religion or age.

b. Identify Reeves' position.
ANSWER: Manager, Customer Services.

c. Does Reeves have any limitations? If yes, please describe.
ANSWER: None that I'm aware of.

d. Did Reeves apply for the Manager position at King Station? If yes, was Reeves selected?
ANSWER: I doubt it.
36. You identified Jason McMahill as a comparator.
a. Please identify McMahill's race, color, religion, sex, and age.
ANSWER: Caucasian, White, Male and I don't know his religion or age.
b. Identify McMahill's position.
ANSWER: Manager, Customer Services

c. Does McMahill have any limitations? If yes, please describe.
ANSWER: None that I'm aware of.

d. Did McMahill apply for the Manager position at King Station? If yes, was McMahill selected?
ANSWER: I doubt it.

37. You identified Dennis Penich as a comparator.
a. Please identify Penich's race, color, religion, sex, and age.
ANSWER: I believe he's Caucasian, White, Male and I don't know his religion or age.

b. Identify Penich's position.
ANSWER: Manager, Customer Services.

c. Does Penich have any limitations? If yes, please describe.
ANSWER: None that I know of.

d. Did Penich apply for the Manager position at King Station? If yes, was Penich selected?
ANSWER: Not that I know of.

38. You identified Tim Sampoli as a comparator.
a. Please identify Sampoli's race, color, religion, sex, and age.
ANSWER: Caucasian, White, Male and I don't know his religion or age.

b. Identify Sampoli's position.
ANSWER: Manager, Customer Services
c. Does Sampoli have any limitations? If yes, please describe.
ANSWER: Not that I know of.

d. Did Sampoli apply for the Manager position at King Station? If yes, was Sampoli selected?
ANSWER: Not that I know of.

39. You identified Thomas Jack as a comparator.
a. Please identify Jack's race, color, religion, sex, and age.
ANSWER: Caucasian, White, Male and I don't know his religion or age.

b. Identify Jack's position.
ANSWER: Manager, Customer Services.

c. Does Jack have any limitations? If yes, please describe.
ANSWER: None that I know of.

d. Did Jack apply for the Manager position at King Station? If yes, was Jack selected?
ANSWER: Yes, he was the selection according to Robert Reynosa.

Claim 3: Since August 22, 2008, Complainant has not been paid higher level pay.

40. What is your understanding of under what circumstances an employee will receive a higher level pay?
ANSWER: If an employee has been placed in a position higher than their current on then they are entitled to higher level pay. Also, if an employee was injured while on higher level then they are paid at the rate of pay that they were receiving at the time of the injury or illness. In addition, a PS Form 1723 is to be submitted by the employee's supervisor that placed them in the position. However, it is not common practice for supervisors to submit 1723 forms for their employees. Most of the time the employee completes PS Form 1723 and updates it as needed. I received that information from Injury compensation analyst Joni Payne.

41. Did you hold ana work a higher level assignment since August 22, 2008? If yes, what higher level assignment(s) were you on, what was the level of the position, for which locations did you hold the position, and for what date(s) did you work the position?
ANSWER: No.

42. Were you told that you would receive a higher level of pay for working this assignment? If yes, who told you this and what did they say?
ANSWER: N/A

43. Do you believe you should have received a higher level pay during the time frame you identified? If yes, why do you believe you should have received a higher level of pay?
ANSWER: Yes, because I was on higher level when I got injured and I submitted and arbitrary date on my PS Form 1723 and if I had not been injured when my PS Form 1723 ran out then I would have submitted another one, this is done all the time with acting managers. Most of the time the 1723 Form is submitted for one (1) year because we never know how long we will be in any given station.

44. Did you speak to anyone in management regarding your belief that you should have received a higher level of pay? If yes, who did you speak to, when did you speak with them, and what was their response?
ANSWER: Yes, I spoke with Jerry Wilson and he partially corrected my time before they sent him back to his station, after the injury to me. He did not do it totally correct. Next, I spoke with Corey Richards and I wrote him a letter after he replaced Jerry Wilson back in October 2008. Corey stated that he was not putting me on higher level and he was not going to pay me higher level. He stated that my PS Form 1723 ended on 9/30/08. All of this was retaliation from Jerry and Corey.

45. Did you ever receive a higher level of pay for the period you identified? If yes, when did you receive these additional wage(s)?
ANSWER: I received a portion that was not correct when Jerry was still there and I did not receive any since Corey has been there.

46. Other than the current EEO complaint, has another appeal or complaint been filed on this issue? If yes, where is it in the process? If a settlement has been reached, describe the settlement. Provide copies of any documentation and settlement (if applicable).
ANSWER: No.

47. Who do you believe was responsible for determining whether you would receive a higher level of pay for a higher level assignment? Please provide their name, position, email address, and office telephone number.
ANSWER: Originally Craig Colton, he has been promoted to Senior Manager Post Office Operations. You will have to contact the GMF for his email and telephone number. He was responsible for me getting paid correctly if Jerry did not. Craig is also responsible for me getting paid with Corey because Craig is over North Las Vegas Post Office as the Senior MPOO.

Why do you believe this individual was responsible for the decision?
ANSWER: He is the senior to both Jerry and Corey.

48. Was this individual aware of your RACE? If yes, how and when were they made aware of your RACE?
ANSWER: Absolutely, I worked for him as a supervisor and an acting manager.
a. Do you believe your RACE was a factor in whether or not you received a higher level of pay for a higher level assignment? If yes, what makes you believe your RACE was a factor?

ANSWER: I believe Steve Phaup, the EEO activity/retaliation, and my confident attitude along with being Black and Female had something to do with it.

49. Was this individual aware of your COLOR? If yes, how and when were they made aware of your COLOR?
ANSWER: Yes, I worked for him.

a. Do you believe your COLOR was a factor in whether or not you received a higher level of pay for a higher level assignment? If yes, what makes you believe your COLOR was a factor?
ANSWER: I answered this question earlier.

50. Was this individual aware of your RELIGION? If yes, how and when were they made aware of your RELIGION?
ANSWER: He is aware that I'm a Religious person.

a. Do you believe your RELIGION was a factor in whether or not you received a higher level of pay for a higher level assignment? If yes, what makes you believe your RELIGION was a factor?
ANSWER: No.

51. Was this individual aware of your SEX? If yes, how and when were they made aware of your SEX?
ANSWER: Yes, I worked for him.

a. Do you believe your SEX was a factor in whether or not you received a higher level of pay for a higher level assignment? If yes, what makes you believe your SEX was a factor?
ANSWER: I answered previously.

52. Was this individual aware of your AGE? If yes, how and when were they made aware of your AGE?
ANSWER: Could have been because he had access to my Official Personnel File.

a. Do you believe your AGE was a factor in whether or not you received a higher level of pay for a higher level assignment? If yes, what makes you believe your AGE was a factor?
ANSWER: No, I stated the reasons earlier.

53. Was this individual aware of your MEDICAL CONDITION OR LIMITATIONS? If yes, how and when were they made aware of your MEDICAL CONDITION OR LIMITATIONS?
ANSWER: Yes, he was Jerry's boss and it was reported to him.

a. Do you believe your MEDICAL CONDITION OR LIMITATIONS was a factor in whether or not you received a higher level of pay for a higher level assignment? If yes, what makes you believe your MEDICAL CONDITION OR LIMITATIONS was a factor?
ANSWER: Absolutely, because he would not have wanted to pay me while I was not there doing the job.

54. Was this individual aware of your current or prior EEO ACTIVITY? If yes, how and when were they made aware of your EEO ACTIVITY?
ANSWER: Yes, because one was filed on him.

a. Do you believe your current or prior EEO ACTIVITY was a factor in whether or not you received a higher level of pay for a higher level assignment? If yes, what makes you believe your EEO ACTIVITY was a factor?
ANSWER: Yes, I saw him walking down the GMF hall one day and he looked at the wall to keep from speaking are looking at me.

55. Please identify any individuals who worked the same or a similar higher level position and received higher level pay during the same time frame that you identified including their name, regular position, race, color, religion, sex, age, limitations (if known), higher level assignment, dates of the higher level assignment. Also explain how they were treated and why you believe they were treated differently than you were.
ANSWER: I don't know anyone who was injured while on a higher level assignment, however Randolph Brooks to my place as acting manager when I went out.

56. Please identify any individuals who worked the same or a similar higher level position and did not receive higher level pay during the same time frame that you identified including their name, regular position, race, color, religion, sex, age, limitations (if known), higher level assignment, dates of the higher level assignment. Also explain how they were treated and why you believe they were treated similarly to the way you were treated.
ANSWER: None that I know of.

Claim 4: Complainant was not paid for a week during pay period 1 2009 (December 20, 2008 – January 2, 2009).

57. For what time frame do you believe you were not paid correctly or at all? Please identify the date(s) and if you were paid. Include a copy of your paycheck for this time period.
ANSWER: I was not paid for week (2) of pay period (1) 12/27 – 1/2/09 No time was put in for me by Corey. This was done in retaliation to my EEO activity on him and the fact that I was out sick. Corey also displayed negative behavior towards me when he did not pay me higher level and removed my access to the GMF. It appears to me that anything that he could do to make me adversely he did. I contacted timekeeping and I was paid correctly the next pay period. (Debbie Letts – Manager of TACS (702) 361-9319.)

58. If you were not working at this time, what type of leave were you using? Please include a copy of any PS Forms 3971 which identify your request for leave.
ANSWER: The DOL had not made a decision on my on-the-job injuries so I was using my own sick leave for the hold time. I will provide 3971's to you.

59. Did you speak to anyone regarding the issues with your pay? If yes, who did you speak with, when did you speak with them, what did you tell them, and what was their response?
ANSWER: I spoke with Debbie Letts and I faxed my pay stub to Corey. Debbie stated that she would look out for my time to make sure that he is inputting it so that this does not happen again and I get paid correctly.

60. Did you receive a pay adjustment of any kind for the time period you identified? If yes, when did you receive the adjustment?
ANSWER: Yes, answered previously.

61. Other than the current EEO complaint, has another appeal or complaint been filed on this issue? If yes, where is it in the process? If a settlement has been reached, describe the settlement. Provide copies of any documentation and settlement (if applicable).
ANSWER: No.

62. Who do you believe was responsible for determining how you would be paid for the period you identified? Please provide their name, position, email address, and office telephone number.
ANSWER: Corey Richards Postmaster North Las Vegas (702) 649-2623.

a. Why do you believe this individual was responsible for the decision?
ANSWER: I was assigned to North Las Vegas and he is the Postmaster of North Las Vegas.

63. Was this individual aware of your RACE? If yes, how and when were they made aware of your RACE?
ANSWER: Yes, we were supervisors for North Las Vegas and Craig Colton was the Postmaster. (2004)

a. Do you believe your RACE was a factor in your pay for the period you identified? If yes, what makes you believe your RACE was a factor?
ANSWER: Yes, my Race, EEO activity, letter's I wrote to him along with notes, being out sick, and the fact that he retaliated against me and I addressed it.

64. Was this individual aware of your COLOR? If yes, how and when were they made aware of your COLOR?
ANSWER: Yes, I worked with him in North Las Vegas.

a. Do you believe your COLOR was a factor in your pay for the period you identified? If yes, what makes you believe your COLOR was a factor?
ANSWER: Yes, my color and every thing else. He has a very dominant aggressive attitude and personality. He throws his weight around. After all we were supervisors together and now I'm the one that has not been promoted out of all the employees that were at North Las Vegas at the time that I came. Craig once made a statement when he was detailed to the Las Vegas City, "I will put any one of my supervisors up against the managers in Las Vegas" I guess he did not include me even though I worked my tail off for him. My accolades and numbers speak for me.

65. Was this individual aware of your RELIGION? If yes, how and when were they made aware of your RELIGION?
ANSWER: Yes, he knows I believe in God.

a. Do you believe your RELIGION was a factor in your pay for the period you identified? If yes, what makes you believe your RELIGION was a factor?
ANSWER: I don't know.

66. Was this individual aware of your SEX? If yes, how and when were they made aware of your SEX?
ANSWER: Yes, I worked with him in North Las Vegas.

a. Do you believe your SEX was a factor in your pay for the period you identified? If yes, what makes you believe your SEX was a factor?
ANSWER: Absolutely, I'm Black and female and he believes he superior by being White and Male.

67. Was this individual aware of your AGE? If yes, how and when were they made aware of your AGE?
ANSWER: I don't know.

a. Do you believe your AGE was a factor in your pay for the period you identified? If yes, what makes you believe your AGE was a factor?
ANSWER: I don't know but I believe I'm older than he is.

68. Was this individual aware of your MEDICAL CONDITION OR LIMITATIONS? If yes, how and when were they made aware of your MEDICAL CONDITION OR LIMITATIONS?
ANSWER: Yes, he was the person that I faxed my 3971's to for my leave, and he asked me when was I coming back to work.

a. Do you believe your MEDICAL CONDITION OR LIMITATIONS was a factor in your pay for the period you identified? If yes, what makes you believe your MEDICAL CONDITION OR LIMITATIONS was a factor?
ANSWER: Yes, because I was making the office short staffed by being out and the fact that I filed an EEO on him. That is also why he demanded from Charles Turner that my badge access be removed from the GMF. I had to go to the GMF for Injury Compensation and Labor Relations, but anything he could do to me he did.

69. Was this individual aware of your current or prior EEO ACTIVITY? If yes, how and when were they made aware of your EEO ACTIVITY?
ANSWER: Yes, I filed one on him.

a. Do you believe your current or prior EEO ACTIVITY was a factor in your pay for the period you identified? If yes, what makes you believe your EEO ACTIVITY was a factor?
ANSWER: 100% absolutely, he did not like being exposed to the discrimination and who do I think I am.

70. Are you aware of any other individuals who have had issues with their pay under similar circumstances? If yes, please identify them including their name, position, race, color, religion, sex, age, and limitations (if known), and describe the type of pay issue they had and the dates it occurred.
ANSWER: No.

71. Are you aware of any other individuals who did not have issues with their pay under similar circumstances? If yes, please identify them including their name, position, race, color, religion, sex, age, and limitations (if known).
ANSWER: No.

Claim 5: During December 2008, management requested that Complainant's badge access to the GMF be removed.

72. Please describe the events which lead to your discovery that management requested your badge access be removed.
ANSWER: I went to use my badge in December. Also, I was told by Charles Turner that he was the one that removed it, and he explained to me the hostile behavior and attitude that Corey had when he requested that it be removed. Charles Turner is a rehab carrier that was at North Las Vegas when Corey and I were there together as supervisors. Charles is now at the GMF.

73. Was your badge actually deactivated? If yes, when was it deactivated?
ANSWER: Yes, sometime in December.

74. Did you speak to anyone in management (e.g., your supervisor) regarding your badge access? If yes, who did you speak with, when did you speak with them, what did you say, and what was their response?

ANSWER: No, I just added it to my EEO. I knew it was retaliation and there was no reason for my access to be removed when I was not a harm to anyone and I had business with Labor Relations and Injury Compensation.

75. Did you work in December 2008 at the GMF? If yes, was your badge reactivated at that time?
ANSWER: No, but I was dealing with Labor on a grievance (Lucy James) and Injury Compensation.

76. Other than the current EEO complaint, has another appeal or complaint been filed on this issue? If yes, where is it in the process? If a settlement has been reached, describe the settlement. Provide copies of any documentation and settlement (if applicable).
ANSWER: No.

77. Who do you believe was responsible for requesting your badge be deactivated or removed? Please provide their name, position, email address, and office telephone number.
ANSWER: Corey Richards according to Charles Turner.

a. Why do you believe this individual was responsible for the decision?
ANSWER: He actually went up to bagging an instructed Charles Turner to remove my access. Mr. Turner can explain it to you better in details.

78. Was this individual aware of your RACE? If yes, how and when were they made aware of your RACE?
ANSWER: Yes, I worked with Corey in North Las Vegas.

a. Do you believe your RACE was a factor in the request that your badge be deactivated or removed? If yes, what makes you believe your RACE was a factor?
ANSWER: Yes, I'm Black and female and he believes he's superior to me. Also, my EEO activity along with letter's and notes to him regarding the other issues.

79. Was this individual aware of your COLOR? If yes, how and when were they made aware of your COLOR?
ANSWER: Yes, I worked with him in North Las Vegas.

a. Do you believe your COLOR was a factor in the request that your badge be deactivated or removed? If yes, what makes you believe your COLOR was a factor?
ANSWER: Yes, answered previous.

80. Was this individual aware of your RELIGION? If yes, how and when were they made aware of your RELIGION?
ANSWER: I don't know, but he knows I believe in God.

a. Do you believe your RELIGION was a factor in the request that your badge be deactivated or removed? If yes, what makes you believe your RELIGION was a factor?
ANSWER: I don't know.

81. Was this individual aware of your SEX? If yes, how and when were they made aware of your SEX?
ANSWER: Yes, I worked with him in North Las Vegas.

a. Do you believe your SEX was a factor in the request that your badge be deactivated or removed? If yes, what makes you believe your SEX was a factor?
ANSWER: 100% absolutely, he believes he superior to me by him being a White Male.

82. Was this individual aware of your AGE? If yes, how and when were they made aware of your AGE?
ANSWER: I don't know.

a. Do you believe your AGE was a factor in the request that your badge be deactivated or removed? If yes, what makes you believe your AGE was a factor?
ANSWER: I don't know.

83. Was this individual aware of your MEDICAL CONDITION OR LIMITATION? If yes, how and when were they made aware of your MEDICAL CONDITION OR LIMITATION?
ANSWER: Yes, he was my boss when he requested that my badge access be removed.

a. Do you believe your MEDICAL CONDITION OR LIMITATION was a factor in the request that your badge be deactivated or removed? If yes, what makes you believe your MEDICAL CONDITION OR LIMITATION was a factor?
ANSWER: Yes, because I was out sick and also I had filed an EEO on him along with other issues that were previously stated.

84. Was this individual aware of your prior or current EEO ACTIVITY? If yes, how and when were they made aware of your EEO ACTIVITY?
ANSWER: Yes, I filed on him for discrimination and retaliation along with other previously stated issues.

a. Do you believe your prior or current EEO ACTIVITY was a factor in the request that your badge be deactivated or removed? If yes, what makes you believe your EEO ACTIVITY was a factor?
ANSWER: 100% absolutely. He was very angry to me when I would talk to him and Charles Turner told me the attitude that he had when he requested that my access be removed.

85. Have other employees who have had an extended absence had their badges deactivated or their access to the GMF removed? If yes, please identify them by name, position, race, color, religion, sex, age, and limitations (if known), and describe their situation and the dates their badge was deactivated.
ANSWER: I doubt it under the same situation as mine. There is no reason for access to be removed when the employee has to deal with Labor Relations and Injury Compensation offices.

86. Have other employees who have had an extended absence not had their badges deactivated or their access to the GMF removed? If yes, please identify them by name, position, race, color, religion, sex, age, and limitations (if known), and describe their situation and the dates or their absence.
ANSWER: I'm sure they have not, but I don't know of any.

UNITED STATES POSTAL SERVICE®

Agreement to Extend 180-Day EEO Investigative Process	**Case No.** 4E-890-0120-08
	Date Filed **November 1, 2008**

I, Lola B. McGEE, in accordance with 29 C.F.R. §1614.108(e), hereby agree to extend the time period for the investigation of my EEO complaint for an additional period not to exceed 90 calendar days. In signing this agreement, I understand that I retain my right to request a hearing by an EEOC Administrative Judge if my investigative file is not provided to me within 270 calendar days from the date I filed my formal complaint, and at anytime thereafter up to 30 calendar days after my receipt of the investigative file. I further understand that I retain the right to elect to request a final agency decision without a hearing within 30 calendar days of my receipt of the investigative file.

Privacy Act Notice

Privacy Act Notice. **The collection of this information is authorized by the Equal Employment Opportunity Act of 1972, 42 U.S.C. § 2000e-16; the Age Discrimination in Employment Act of 1967, as amended, 29 U.S.C. § 633a; the Rehabilitation Act of 1973, as amended, 29 U.S.C. § 794a; and Executive Order 11478, as amended. This information will be used to adjudicate complaints of alleged discrimination and to evaluate the effectiveness of the EEO program. As a routine use, this information may be disclosed to an appropriate government agency, domestic or foreign, for law enforcement purposes; where pertinent, in a legal proceeding to which the USPS is a party or has an interest; to a government agency in order to obtain information relevant to a USPS decision concerning employment, security clearances, contracts, licenses, grants, permits or other benefits; to a government agency upon its request when relevant to its decision concerning employment, security clearances, security or suitability investigations, contracts, licenses, grants or other benefits; to a congressional office at your request, to an expert, consultant or other person under contract with the USPS to fulfill an agency function; to the Federal Records Center for storage; to the Office of Management and Budget for review of private relief legislation; to an independent certified public accountant during an official audit of USPS finances; to an**

investigator, administrative judge or complaints examiner appointed by the Equal Employment Opportunity Commission for investigation of a formal EEO complaint under 29 CFR 1614; to the Merit Systems Protection Board or Office of Special Counsel for proceedings or investigations involving personnel practices and other matters within their jurisdiction; and to a labor organization as required by the National Labor Relations Act. Under the Privacy Act provision, the information requested is voluntary for the complainant, and for Postal Service employees and other witnesses.

Signature of Complainant	**Date**

PS Form 2565-C, **March 2001**

AMOUNT OF ADDITIONAL TIME REQUESTED: Ms. McGee has agreed to a two (2) week extension at the request of the investigator to provide the investigator additional time to gather relevant documentation and testimony regarding the above named complaint. This does not mean that the agency will prolong the decision for 30, 60, 90, 180, 270, or 360 days because you need additional time. I will grant you the two (2) weeks extension. Sincerely, Lola McGee 4/2/09.

Formal Filing of EEO's November 1, 2009 (The Post Office Combined all 5) Jerry's threat, and four discrimination charges for non-promotions, and this is their final decision.

UNITED STATES POSTAL SERVICE
EQUAL EMPLOYMENT OPPORTUNITY CASE
IN THE MATTER OF:

Lola B. McGee
Complainant,

v.

John E. Potter,
Postmaster General,
c/o Western Area Operations
Respondent.

Agency Case No. 4E-890-0120-08

Formal Filed: November 1, 2008

FINAL AGENCY DECISION

Introduction

Pursuant to Equal Employment Opportunity (EEOC) regulations at 29 C.F.R. §1614.110 this is the Final Agency Decision of the U.S. Postal Service regarding the complaint of discrimination identified above.

Statement of Claim

The complainant alleged discrimination based on race (African American), color (Black), religion (Baptist), sex (female), age (46, DOB; 07/07/1962), physical disability (hearing loss, heart palpitations, head shocks, neuropathy), mental disability (PTSD, anxiety disorder, panic attacks, major depressive disorder), and retaliation (prior and/or current EEO activity), in that she has been subjected to ongoing hostile work environment harassment when: 1) from July 12, 2008, the complainant has been subjected to hostile work environment harassment regarding working conditions, taken off higher level detail assignments; treated in a disrespectful, cruel, and rude manner; and received threats from management official(s); (2) on or around September 8, 2008, the complainant became aware that she had been charged 32 hours of sick leave; (3) since July 12, 2008, the complainant has not been selected for the position of Manager, Customer

However, the TACS [Time and Attendance Control System] pay adjustment indicated that the complainant was initially charged with 32 hours of LWOP [leave without pay] during Pay Period 09-01-1 (December 20, 2008 to January 2, 2009), but on January 16, 2009, that action was changed from 32 hours of LWOP to 32 hours of sick leave. It was noted, on the pay adjustment form, that the employee was "paid LWOP instead of sick leave in error." The action was authorized by Debbie Letts, TACS Manager. (IF, Exhibit 32). As the Commission held in Dionne v. United States Postal Service, EEOC Request No. 05900898 (1990), "...where a complainant fails to identify an unresolved personal harm, he or she is not aggrieved and therefore fails to state a claim within the meaning of EEOC regulations."

Accordingly, pursuant to 29 C.F.R. 1614.107 (a) (1), Allegation 3 is dismissed for failure to state a claim, as the action at issue has been resolved; and therefore, is a matter outside the gamut of Commission regulations. Despite the fact that Allegation 3 of the complainant's claim is subject to dismissal as explained above, the substance of Allegation 3 has been analyzed within the context of relevant regulations and case law. This analysis is set forth below in the section titled *Prima Facie Analysis.*

Applicable Law

Disparate Treatment

The United States Supreme Court established a burden-shifting framework for analyzing claims of discrimination in McDonnell Douglas Corporation v. Green, 411 U.S. 792 (1973), and subsequently refined that analysis in Texas Department of Community Affairs v. Burdine, 450 U.S. 248 (1981). The McDonnell Douglas and Burdine approach involves a three-step process when a complainant alleges intentional discrimination based on a disparate treatment theory. The Equal Employment Opportunity Commission has adopted this approach in its decision making. Downing v. U.S. Postal Service, EEOC Appeal No. 01822326 (September 19, 1983); Jennings v. U.S. Postal Service, EEOC Appeal No. 01932793 (April 13, 1994); and Saenz v. Department of the Navy, EEOC Request No. 05950927 (January 9, 1998). A complainant alleging discrimination must first demonstrate that there is some substance to his or her claim. To satisfy this burden, the complainant must establish a *prima facie* case of discrimination for each of the bases of discrimination alleged by a preponderance of the evidence. Furnco Construction Company v. Waters, 438 U.S. 576 (1978).

Although a complainant may establish a *prima facie* case by presenting direct evidence of discrimination, the more frequent method of establishing a *prima facie* case is through circumstantial evidence by showing that he or she: (1)

Final Agency Decision
Lola B. McGee
Agency Case No. 4E-890-0120-08
Page 4

belongs to a protected class; (2) was subjected to an adverse employment action; and (3) was treated differently in this regard than similarly situated individuals who were not members of the protected group. Mayberry v. Vought Aircraft Company, 55 F.3d 1086, at 1090 (5th Cir. 1995); Mitchell v. Toledo Hospital, 964 F.2d 577, at 582-83 (6th Cir. 1992). The failure to establish a specific element of a *prima facie* case may be overcome by presenting evidence of agency actions from which an inference of discrimination could be drawn if they remained unexplained. Day v. Postmaster General, EEOC Appeal No. 01996097 (September 18, 2000).

In a promotion claim, a complainant may establish a *prima facie* case by showing that: (1) he or she belongs to a protected class; (2) he or she applied for and was qualified for a position; (3) he or she was not selected for the position; and (4) an individual not in his or her protected class was selected under circumstances which, if left unexplained, would support an inference of discrimination. Keyes v. Secretary of the Navy, 853 F. 2d 1016 (1st Cir. 1988) and Weinstein v. U.S. Postal Service, EEOC Appeal No. 01830674 (February 8, 1984).

Once a *prima facie* case has been established, the burden of production shifts to the employer to articulate a legitimate, non-discriminatory reason for its action. Furnco, 438 U.S. at 578. See also St. Mary's Honor Center v. Hicks, 509 U.S. 502, at 506 (1993). The employer need not persuade the trier of fact that the proffered reason was its actual motivation but merely needs to raise a genuine issue of fact as to whether it discriminated against the complainant. Burdine, 450 U.S. at 254; Keval v. Commodity Futures Trading Commission, EEOC Appeal No. 01832127 (November 2, 1984); Hollis v. Department of Veterans' Affairs, EEOC Appeal No. 01934600 (May 3, 1994). If the agency offers no adequate explanation for the discrepancy in treatment between the complainant and similarly situated employees, the agency does not carry its burden of production and the complainant prevails on the basis of the inference of discrimination created by the *prima facie* case. Frady v. Postmaster General, EEOC Appeal No. 01A05317 (January 10, 2003); Houston v. Department of Veterans' Affairs, EEOC Appeal No. 01976054 (August 27, 1999); and Parker v. Postmaster General, EEOC Request No. 05900110 (April 30, 1990).

If the employer meets this burden, any presumption of discrimination created by the *prima facie* case disappears; it simply "drops from the case." Hicks, *supra*, 509 U.S. at 507; United States Postal Service Board of Governors v. Aikens, 460 U.S. 711, at 715 (1983). See also Hernandez v. Department of Transportation, EEOC Request No. 05900159 (June 28, 1990) and Peterson v. Department of Health and Human Services, EEOC Request No. 05900467 (June 8, 1990). The complainant can then prevail only if he or she proves that the employer's reasons are not only pretext but are pretext for discrimination. Hicks, 509 U.S. at 507 and 516; Nichols v. Grocer, 138 F.3d 563, at 566 (5th Cir. 1998); Swanson v. General

Final Agency Decision
Lola B. McGee
Agency Case No. 4E-890-0120-08
Page 5

Services Administration, 110 F.3d 1180, at 1185 (5th Cir. 1997). See also Papas v. Postmaster General, EEOC Appeal No. 01923753 (March 17, 1994) and Bradford v. Department of Defense, EEOC Appeal No. 01940712 (September 20, 1994). Thus, the complainant cannot create a factual issue of pretext based merely on personal speculation that there was discriminatory intent. Southard v. Texas Board of Criminal Justice, 114 F.3d 539, at 555 (5th Cir. 1997); Lyles v. U.S. Postal Service, EEOC Appeal No. 01A11110 (May 22, 2002); and Nathan v. U.S. Postal Service, EEOC Appeal No. 01995788 (August 29, 2001).

Pretext involves more than a mistake. It means that the reason offered by management is factually baseless, is not the actual motivation for the action, or is insufficient to motivate the action. Tincher v. Wal-Mart Stores, Inc., 118 F. 3d 1125, at 1130 (7th Cir. 1997) and Morgan v. Hilti, Inc., 108 F. 3d 1319, at 1323 (10th Cir. 1997). The complainant always carries the "ultimate burden of persuading the trier of fact that he has been the victim of intentional discrimination." Burdine, 450 U.S. at 254 and Hicks, 509 U.S. at 511.

At all times, the ultimate burden of persuasion remains with the complainant. Board of Trustees of Keene College v. Sweeney, 439 U.S. 24, 25 N.2 (1978). This burden was reaffirmed and clarified in St. Mary's Honor Center v. Hicks, *Id.* In Hicks, the Court held that in order to impose liability upon an employer for discriminatory employment practices, an ultimate finding of unlawful discrimination is required regardless of whether or not the employer's explanation for its action was believable. See also Brewer v. Postmaster General, EEOC Appeal No. 01941786 (June 21, 1994) and Montoya v. Department of Housing and Urban Development, EEOC Appeal No. 01940999 (August 4, 1994).

Age Discrimination

In order to establish a *prima facie* case of age discrimination, a complainant must show proof of the Title VII criteria set forth by the Supreme Court in McDonnell Douglas; *Id.* O'Connor v. Consolidated Coin Caterers Corporation, 517 U.S. 308 (1996); Loeb v. Textron, Inc., 600 F. 2d 1003 (1st Cir. 1979); and Mitchell v. Department of the Interior, EEOC Appeal No. 01990787 (January 10, 2002). The agency's burden to articulate a legitimate, nondiscriminatory reason for its action and the complainant's burden ultimately to prove pretext remain the same as in a Title VII disparate treatment case. The Court in O'Connor also held that it is not just a question of whether a comparison employee is outside the protected age category but also whether the comparator is substantially the younger than the complainant. See also Fullman v. Postmaster General, EEOC Appeal No. 01A31036 (March 18, 2004). The Supreme Court has also held that a complainant alleging age discrimination must prove not only that age was considered, but also that age *made a difference in the outcome* of the employer's decision-making process. Reeves v. Sanderson Plumbing Products, Inc., 530

Final Agency Decision
Lola B. McGee
Agency Case No. 4E-890-0120-08
Page 6

U.S. 133, at 141 (2000) and Hazen Paper Company v. Biggins, 507 U.S. 604, at 610 (1993). In other words, in age cases, the complainant must prove by a preponderance of the evidence that age was considered and that it was the *determining factor*. If the complainant's burden fails on either point, no relief is provided. Cleverly v. Western Electric Company, 594 F.2d 638, at 641 (5th Cir. 1979); Kentroti v. Frontier Airlines, 585 F.2d 967, at 974 (10th Cir. 1978); Laugeson v. Anaconda Company, 520 F.2d 307, at 317 (6th Cir. 1976). See also Sullivan v. Chairman, Tennessee Valley Authority, EEOC Appeal No. 01940217 (November 9, 1994) and Lasley v. Department of Veterans' Affairs, EEOC Appeal No. 01870615 (October 8, 1987).

Religious Discrimination

In order to establish a *prima facie* case of disparate treatment based on religion, a complainant must establish that: (1) he or she is a member of a protected class; (2) he or she was subjected to an adverse employment action; and (3) similarly situated employees outside the complainant's protected class were treated more favorably in like circumstances. Wooten v. U. S. Postal Service, EEOC Appeal No. 01980848 (February 11, 2000); Potter v. Goodwill Industries of Cleveland, 518 F. 2d 864 (6th Cir. 1975); and Furnco Construction Company v. Waters, 438 U.S. 576 (1978). A claim of religious discrimination due to disparate treatment follows the same allocation of the burdens and order of presentation of proof as in any Title VII disparate treatment claim.

In order to establish a *prima facie* case of discrimination based on a failure to accommodate religious practices or beliefs, a complainant must demonstrate by a preponderance of the evidence that he or she: (1) has a *bona fide* religious belief that conflicts with an employment requirement; (2) informed the employer of this belief and conflict; and (3) that the agency enforced the employment requirement and the complainant suffered an adverse employment action for failing to comply with the conflicting employment requirement. Green v. U. S. Postal Service, EEOC Appeal No. 01982669 (October 5, 1999) and Bishop v. Department of the Air Force, EEOC Petition No. 03970085 (September 16, 1997). See also 29 C.F.R. 1605.1 *et seq.*

Equal Employment Opportunity Commission guidelines broadly define religious practice to include moral and ethical beliefs as to what is right or wrong which are sincerely held by the individual with the strength of traditional religious views. See also United States v. Seeger, 380 U.S. 164 (1965) and Welsh v. United States, 398 U.S. 333 (1970). Title VII requires an employer to provide an accommodation unless it can show that providing the accommodation would create an undue hardship. The Supreme Court has defined undue hardship in this context as any hardship which is "...more than a *de minimis* cost." Trans World Airlines v. Hardison, 432 U.S. 63 (1977). The Court also held that an

Final Agency Decision
Lola B. McGee
Agency Case No. 4E-890-0120-08
Page 7

employer was not required to violate the seniority provisions of a collective bargaining agreement in order to achieve an accommodation of an employee's religious beliefs.

Similarly Situated Employees

One of the key elements of a *prima facie* case of disparate treatment based on an adverse employment action is proof that similarly situated comparison employees not in the complainant's protected class were treated more favorably. This is so, in part, because agencies are not monolithic entities. Turner v. Department of the Navy, EEOC Request No. 05900445 (September 25, 1990). In general, in the absence of direct evidence of discrimination, if the complainant cannot identify any similarly situated comparison employees who were treated more favorably, he or she will not prevail. Aguilar v. U.S. Postal Service, EEOC Appeal No. 01944167 (August 8, 1995).

In order for two or more employees to be considered similarly situated for the purpose of creating an inference of disparate treatment, a complainant must show that all of the relevant aspects of his or her employment situation are virtually identical to those of the other employees who he or she alleges were treated more favorably. Smith v. Monsanto Chemical Company, 770 F. 2d 719, at 723 (8th Cir. 1985); Murray v. Thistledown Racing Club, Inc., 770 F. 2d 63, at 68 (6th Cir. 1985); Nix v. WLCY Radio/Rahall Communications, 738 F. 2d 1181, at 1185 (11th Cir. 1984); Mazzella v. RCA Global Communications, Inc., 642 F. Supp. 1531, at 1547 (S.D. N.Y. 1986), *aff'd.* 814 F. 2d 653 (2nd Cir. 1987). The Equal Employment Opportunity Commission has on numerous occasions ruled in similar fashion. See, for example, Tolar v. U.S. Postal Service, EEOC Appeal No. 01965083 (December 16, 1998), citing O'Neal v. U.S. Postal Service, EEOC Request No. 05910490 (July 23, 1991); and Knapp-Huffman v. Attorney General (Bureau of Prisons), EEOC Appeal No. 01991026 (January 16, 2002).

If employees have different supervisors, perform different job functions, were subject to different job standards, engaged in different conduct, or worked during different time periods, they are not similarly situated. O'Neal, *Id.*; Allen v. Department of the Navy, EEOC Appeal No. 05900539 (June 15, 1990); Willis v. Department of the Treasury, EEOC Appeal No. 01A51459 (March 16, 2003); and Stewart v. Department of Defense, EEOC Appeal No. 01A02890 (June 27, 2001).

Person with a Disability

In order to assert a claim of disability discrimination, a complainant must satisfy the threshold requirement that he or she is a "person with a disability" as that term is defined in the Rehabilitation Act and Equal Employment Opportunity

Final Agency Decision
Lola B. McGee
Agency Case No. 4E-890-0120-08
Page 8

Commission regulations. Title 29, Code of Federal Regulations, Part 1630.2(g) defines a person with a disability as an individual who: (i) has a physical or mental impairment which substantially limits one or more of that person's major life activities; (ii) has a record of such an impairment; or (iii) is regarded as having such an impairment. See also Melahn v. Department of the Navy, EEOC Appeal No. 01832380 (October 21, 1985). Whether an individual has a disability is not based on the name or diagnosis of the impairment involved but rather the effect which that impairment has on the individual's life. Sutton *et al.* v. United Airlines, Inc., 527 U.S. 471, at 483 (1998). Also, the mere fact that an agency relied on a complainant's physical condition in taking a personnel action does not indicate that the agency perceived that the complainant had a substantially limiting condition. Kelly v. U.S. Postal Service, EEOC Appeal No. 01830028 (November 15, 1983). Similarly, the mere fact that an agency processed an employee's claim for benefits under the Federal Employees Compensation Act and/or granted the employee a modified work assignment in connection with that claim would not prove that the agency regarded the employee as disabled. Brown v. U.S. Postal Service, EEOC Appeal No. 01990686 (February 21, 2002).

According to EEOC regulations, major life activities include, but are not limited to, caring for oneself, performing manual tasks, walking, seeing, hearing, speaking, breathing, learning, and working. See 29 C.F.R. 1630.2(i). The Interpretive Appendix to the regulations also identifies sitting, standing, lifting, and reaching as other major life activities. The term "impairment" is defined broadly at 29 C.F.R. 1630.2(h) and the Commission's guidance on having a record of an impairment or being perceived as disabled appears at 29 C.F.R. 1630.2 (k) and (l).

The regulations define "substantially limited" as meaning that the individual cannot perform the major life activity at all or is significantly limited in the ability to perform the activity compared to the average person in the general population. 29 C.F.R. 1630.2(j) and Toyota Motor Manufacturing of Kentucky, Inc. v. Williams, 534 U.S. 184 (2002). See also Harrison v. Department of Justice, EEOC Appeal No. 01A03948 (July 30, 2003). Courts also look to mitigating factors such as assistive devices or medication in determining whether an individual is substantially limited. Sutton, *Id.* Temporary or intermittent conditions are not covered. Heino v. Postmaster General, EEOC Appeal No. 01994965 (January 28, 2002); Anderson v. National Gallery of Art, EEOC Appeal No. 03910108 (September 17, 1991); and Wolfe v. Postmaster General, EEOC Appeal No. 01993796 (July 8, 2002). If the major life activity of "working" is involved, the individual must be unable to perform an entire class of jobs or a broad range of jobs within the class in order to be substantially limited. 29 C.F.R. 1630.2(j)(3). See also Webber v. Department of the Air Force, EEOC Appeal No. 01989587 (March 2, 2001).

Final Agency Decision
Lola B. McGee
Agency Case No. 4E-890-0120-08
Page 9

A generalized assertion, without specific evidence to support it, that an individual is substantially limited is not sufficient to satisfy a complainant's burden of proof. Lohr v. U.S. Postal Service, EEOC Request No. 05930799 (May 19, 1994); Zeigler v. Postmaster General, EEOC Appeal No. 01930854 (May 12, 1994) and Jenkins v. Postmaster General, EEOC Appeal No. 01954572 (March 24, 1997). It is also not enough that the agency is in possession of a diagnosis; that an individual's supervisor knows that they have a particular condition; that the complainant has an approved claim with the Office of Workers Compensation Programs; or that the complainant has a percentage disability awarded by the Department of Veterans' Affairs. Black v. U.S. Postal Service, EEOC Request No. 05930748 (May 12, 1994); Pascale v. Department of the Navy, EEOC Petition No. 03850092 (March 5, 1986); Schnabele v. U.S. Postal Service, EEOC Appeal No. 01982634 (July 13, 2001); and Bono v. Postmaster General, EEOC Appeal No. 01951113 (August 11, 1997).

Disability – Disparate Treatment

Courts have adopted and applied the Title VII burdens of proof to disability discrimination claims. See, for example, Norcross v. Sneed, 755 F.2d 113 (8th Cir. 1985) and Prewitt v. United States Postal Service, 662 F.2d 292 (5th Cir. 1981). The Commission has also analyzed cases under this theory. Greathouse v. Department of the Army, EEOC Appeal No. 01984880 (May 2, 2001) and Oberg v. Secretary of the Navy, EEOC Request No. 05890451 (July 20, 1989).

In order to establish a *prima facie* case of disability discrimination, a complainant must prove, by a preponderance of the evidence, that he was treated differently than individuals not within his protected group, or that the agency failed to make a needed reasonable accommodation, resulting in adverse treatment of the complainant. See Session v. Helms, 751 F.2d 991, at 992-3 (9th Cir.), *cert.* denied, 474 U.S. 846 (1985). A complainant also must demonstrate a causal relationship between the disabling condition and the agency's reasons for the adverse employment action. Rideout v. Department of the Army, EEOC Appeal No. 01933866 (November 22, 1995); Mackey v. U.S. Postal Service, EEOC Appeal No. 01931771 (April 28, 1994); and Milder v. Department of Veterans' Affairs, EEOC Appeal No. 01971724 (January 15, 1999).

Disability – Accommodation

Assuming that a complainant has established that he or she is a person with a disability, the next element of a *prima facie* case based on a failure to accommodate is to establish that he or she is "otherwise qualified." The regulations define a "qualified individual with a disability" as a person who satisfies the requisite skill, experience, educational, and other job-related requirements of the position the individual holds or desires and who, with or

Final Agency Decision
Lola B. McGee
Agency Case No. 4E-890-0120-08
Page 10

without reasonable accommodation, can perform the essential functions of that position without endangering the health and safety of the individual or others. 29 C.F.R. 1630.2(m).

The essential functions of a position are the fundamental job duties of the position the complainant holds or desires considering whether the position exists to perform the function, whether there are a limited number of individuals available to perform the function, or whether the function is highly specialized and the incumbent was hired for his or her expertise. 29 C.F.R. 1630.2(n). The complainant has the burden of proving that he or she is a "qualified individual with a disability." Jasany v. United States Postal Service, 755 F. 2d 1244 (6th Cir. 1985). The complainant must also show that the agency was aware of the allegedly disabling condition and that an accommodation can be made. Mikovich v. Postmaster General, EEOC Appeal No. 01A11150 (June 20, 2002) and Lincovich v. U.S. Postal Service, EEOC Appeal No. 01810610 (August 9, 1982).

If it is determined that the complainant is unable to perform the essential functions of his or her position, the next inquiry is concerning whether there is any reasonable accommodation by the employer which would enable him or her to perform those functions. White v. York International Corporation, 45 F. 3d 357, at 361-362 (10th Cir. 1995). An employer is not required to provide an accommodation which does not assist the complainant in performing the essential functions of his or her position. Conley v. Postmaster General, EEOC Appeal No. 01984624 (July 6, 2001) The employer must be able to accommodate the individual without undue hardship. Brown v. Secretary of the Interior, EEOC Petition No. 03A00004 (May 22, 2002) and Hoang v. Postmaster General, EEOC Appeal No. 01923725 (March 30, 1993). The employer is not required to accommodate an individual by eliminating the essential functions of his or her job or by creating a job not already existing within the organization, including a light duty position. Turco v. Hoechst Celanese Corporation, 101 F. 3d 1090, at 1093-1094 (5th Cir. 1996); Shiring v. Runyon, Postmaster General, 90 F. 3d 827, at 831-832 (3rd Cir. 1996); and Watson v. Lithonia Lighting and National Service Industries, Inc., 304 F. 3d 749 (7th Cir. 2002), *cert.* denied 123 S. Ct. 1286 (2003).

The Rehabilitation Act does not require an employer to lower or substantially modify standards to accommodate an individual or to take an action inconsistent with the contractual rights of others under a collective bargaining agreement. Jasany, 755 F. 2d at 1250-1251; Foreman v. Babcock & Wilcox Company, 117 F. 3d 800, at 810 (5th Cir. 1997); Williams v. Widnall, 79 F. 3d 1003 (10th Cir. 1996); and Hufford-Smith v. Attorney General, EEOC Appeal No. 01995040 (February 13, 2002). In addition, a disabled worker is not entitled to the reasonable accommodation which he or she prefers and must show a connection between the disabling condition and the requested accommodation. Gile v.

United Airlines, Inc., 95 F. 3d 492, at 498 (7th Cir. 1996); Wiggins v. U.S. Postal Service, EEOC Appeal No. 01953715 (April 22, 1997); and Metzenbaum v. Office of Personnel Management, EEOC Appeal No. 01986974 (April 4, 2002).

An employer may accommodate an individual through reassignment. However, the employer does not have to accommodate him or her by promoting him to a higher level position or bumping another employee out of a job to create a vacancy. Shiring, 90 F. 3d at 832. The court held that the employee would have to establish that "...there were vacant, funded positions whose essential duties [the employee] was capable of performing, with or without reasonable accommodation, and that those positions were at an equivalent level or position [as the position the employee previously held]." Therefore, for the accommodation of reassignment to be reasonable, a position must exist within the organization and be vacant, the employee must be "otherwise qualified" to meet the criteria for this position, and the reassignment must not offend the contract rights of others under the applicable collective bargaining agreement. Foreman, 117 F. 3d at 810.

Harassment/Hostile Work Environment

Harassment of an employee that would not occur but for the employee's race, color, sex, national origin, age, disability, or religion is unlawful if it is sufficiently severe or pervasive. Wibstad v. U. S. Postal Service, EEOC Appeal No. 01972699 (August 14, 1998), citing McKinney v. Dole, 765 F. 2d 1129, at 1138-1139 (D.C. Cir. 1985), and Long v. Attorney General, EEOC Appeal No. 01984213 (July 10, 2001). See also Hubbert v. Department of the Army, EEOC Request No. 05910133 (March 19, 1991); Ortega v. Postmaster General, EEOC Appeal No. 01995243 (May 3, 2001); Humphrey v. U.S. Postal Service, EEOC Appeal No. 01965238 (October 16, 1998). Harassment due to an individual's prior EEO activity is also actionable. Roberts v. Department of Transportation, EEOC Appeal No. 01970729 (September 15, 2000).

To establish a claim of harassment, a complainant must show that: (1) she belongs to a statutorily protected class; (2) she was subjected to unwelcome verbal or physical conduct involving the protected class; (3) the harassment complained of was based on the statutorily protected class; (4) the harassment had the purpose or effect of unreasonably interfering with her work performance and/or creating an intimidating, hostile, or offensive work environment; and (5) there is a basis for imputing liability to the employer. McCleod v. Social Security Administration, EEOC Appeal No. 01963810 (August 5, 1999).

The Supreme Court has held that an employer who creates or tolerates a work environment which is permeated with "discriminatory intimidation, ridicule, and insult" that is sufficiently severe or pervasive to alter the terms and conditions of

Final Agency Decision
Lola B. McGee
Agency Case No. 4E-890-0120-08
Page 12

an individual's employment and which creates an abusive work environment is in violation of Title VII. Harris v. Forklift Systems, Inc., 510 U.S. 17 (1993), citing Meritor Savings Bank F.S.B. v. Vinson, 477 U.S. 57 (1986). The conduct in question is evaluated from the standpoint of a reasonable person, taking into account the particular context in which it occurred, including the severity and frequency of the conduct and its effect on the employee's work performance. Harris, *Id.* In order to support a finding of a hostile work environment, more than a few isolated incidents of enmity based on race, gender, national origin, religion, etc. must have occurred. Johnson v. Bunny Bread Co., 646 F. 2d 1250, at 1257 (8th Cir. 1981) and Cariddi v. Kansas City Chiefs Football Club, Inc., 568 F. 2d 87, at 88 (8th Cir. 1977. There must have been a steady barrage of opprobrious comments and not a casual comment or accidental or sporadic conversation in order to trigger an entitlement to relief. Snell v. Suffolk County, 782 F. 2d 1094 (2nd Cir. 1986).

The Equal Employment Opportunity Commission has repeatedly held that remarks unaccompanied by a concrete agency action are not a direct or personal deprivation sufficient to render an individual aggrieved. Johnson v. Department of Justice, EEOC Appeal No. 01986199 (February 18, 2000); Backo v. U. S. Postal Service, EEOC Request No. 05960227 (June 10, 1986); and Henry v. U. S. Postal Service, EEOC Request No. 05940695 (February 9, 1995). The Commission has also agreed with the courts and held that in order to establish a case of harassment that constitutes a hostile work environment, the harassment must be ongoing and continuous and that a few isolated incidents will not be sufficient to constitute discriminatory harassment. McGivern v. U. S. Postal Service, EEOC Request No. 05930481 (March 17, 1994) and Vargas v. Department of Justice, EEOC Request No. 05931047 (October 7, 1993). The conduct involved must be viewed in the context of the totality of the circumstances including, among other things, the nature and frequency of the offensive encounters and the time span over which the encounters occurred. Rabidue v. Osceola Refining Company, 805 F. 2d 611, at 620 (6th Cir. 1988) and Gilbert v. City of Little Rock, 722 F. 2d 1390, at 1394 (8th Cir. 1993).

The decisions make it clear that the anti-discrimination laws are not a "general civility code" and that the conduct complained of must be so objectively offensive as to alter the terms and conditions of one's employment. Routine work assignments, instructions, and admonishments do not rise to the level of discriminatory harassment. DiFruscio v. Social Security Administration, EEOC Appeal No. 01982006 (September 13, 2000).

Retaliation

To establish a *prima facie* case based on reprisal, a complainant must show that: (1) he or she engaged in prior protected activity; (2) the agency official was

Final Agency Decision
Lola B. McGee
Agency Case No. 4E-890-0120-08
Page 13

aware of the protected activity; (3) he or she was subsequently disadvantaged by an adverse employment action or adverse treatment; and (4) there is a causal link between the protected activity and adverse action/treatment. Hochstadt v. Worcester Foundation for Experimental Biology, Inc., 425 F. Supp. 318, 324 (D. Mass), *aff'd* 545 F.2d 222 (1st Cir. 1976); Manoharan v. Columbia University College of Physicians and Surgeons, 842 F. 2d 590, 593 (2nd Cir. 1988); Coffman v. Department of Veterans' Affairs, EEOC Request No. 05960437 (November 20, 1997); and Whitmire v. Department of the Air Force, EEOC Appeal No. 01A00340 (September 25, 2000). A complainant may establish prior EEO activity by participating at any stage of the EEO process or opposing unlawful discriminatory conduct. See, generally, Lewis v. Department of the Navy, EEOC Appeal No. 01810158 (May 22, 1981) (counseling stage); Ballard v. Postmaster General, EEOC Appeal No. 01923276 (August 17, 1992) (witness); and Burrough v. U.S. Postal Service, EEOC Appeal No. 01842417 (June 24, 1986) (representative).

A complainant may also establish a *prima facie* case by presenting evidence which, unexplained, would reasonably give rise to an inference of reprisal. Shapiro v. Social Security Administration, EEOC Request No. 05960403 (December 6, 1996). Obviously, the complainant must offer evidence that the agency officials who took the action were aware of his or her prior participation or opposition activity (Demeier v. Department of the Air Force, EEOC Appeal No. 01A11166 (May 23, 2002)) but establishing that alone will not enable a complainant to establish the causal connection element of a *prima facie* case. Garcia-Gannon v. Department of the Air Force, EEOC Appeal No. 01821195 (June 30, 1983). Adverse actions need not be ultimate employment actions, just adverse treatment based on a retaliatory motive. Burlington Northern Santa Fe Railway Company v. White, 126 S. Ct. 2405 (2006); and Lindsey v. U.S. Postal Service, EEOC Request No. 05980410 (November 4, 1999).

The causal connection may be inferred by evidence that the protected conduct was closely followed by the adverse action. Clark County School District v. Breeden, 532 U.S. 286 (2001). The Court in Breeden noted that where a complainant is relying on temporal proximity to establish a causal connection between prior protected activity and a current adverse employment action, that proximity must be "very close" and cited with approval Circuit Court of Appeals decisions holding that time gaps of three to four months between an individual's prior EEO activity and the current adverse employment action were too attenuated to suggest an inference of retaliation. The Commission has followed suit and rendered decisions establishing much shorter time frames to establish the requisite temporal proximity. See, for example, Heads v. U.S. Postal Service, EEOC Appeal No. 01A51547 (June 2, 2005); Archibald v. Department of Housing and Urban Development, EEOC Appeal No. 01A54280 (September 22, 2005);

Final Agency Decision
Lola B. McGee
Agency Case No. 4E-890-0120-08
Page 14

and Lynch v. U.S. Postal Service, EEOC Appeal No. 01A24705 (August 14, 2003).

To support a finding of unlawful retaliation, there must be proof that the agency official(s) took the action at issue because of the complainant's prior protected activity and sought to deter the complainant or others. *EEOC Compliance Manual on Retaliation*, No. 915.003 (May 20, 1998), pp. 8-16.

Background

At all times relevant to the issues raised in this complaint, the complainant was employed as a Supervisor, Customer Services, at the North Las Vegas Post Office, Nevada.[1] (IF, Affidavit A, Exhibit 1). The complainant has alleged that Corey D. Richards, Postmaster, North Las Vegas, Jerry A. Wilson, Postmaster, Fallon, Nevada, Craig M. Colton, Manager, Post Office Operations (MPOO), and Robert A. Reynosa, Manager, Customer Service Operations, intentionally discriminated against her based on race (African American), color (Black), religion (Baptist), sex (female), age (46, DOB; 07/07/1962), physical disability (hearing loss, heart palpitations, head shocks, neuropathy), mental disability (PTSD, anxiety disorder, panic attacks, major depressive disorder), and retaliation (prior and/or current EEO activity), in that she was subjected to ongoing hostile work environment harassment when: (1) from July 12, 2008, the complainant has been subjected to hostile work environment harassment regarding working conditions, taken off higher level detail assignments; treated in a disrespectful, cruel, and rude manner; and received threats from management official(s); (2) on or around September 8, 2008, the complainant became aware that she had been charged 32 hours of sick leave; (3) since July 12, 2008, the complainant has not been selected for the position of Manager, Customer Services and on December 9, 2008, the complainant was informed that she was not selected for the Manager's position at King Station; (4) since August 22, 2008, the complainant has not been paid higher level pay; (5) the complainant was not paid for a week during Pay Period 09-01-1 [Year-PP-Week] (December 20, 2008 - January 2, 2009); and (6) during December 2008, management requested that the complainant's badge access to the GMF [General Mail facility] be removed.

Allegation 1: From July 12, 2008, the complainant has been subjected to hostile work environment harassment regarding working conditions, taken off higher

[1] The complainant testified that she had been detailed to Manager, Customer Services at the Meadow Mesa Station, in North Las Vegas, for "well over two years." (IF, Affidavit A, p. 2).

level detail assignments; treated in a disrespectful, cruel, and rude manner; and received threats from management official(s).[2]

The complainant asserted that she was subjected to ongoing hostile work environment harassment at the hands of Mr. Wilson, Mr. Richards, and Mr. Colton by way of Steven Phaup, who was terminated in early 2006.[3] She alleged that Mr. Wilson harassed her from July 10, 2008, until August 25, 2008, and that Mr. Richards harassed her from October of 2008, until January 9, 2009. According to the complainant, on July 10, 2008, Mr. Wilson came into her staff meeting and abruptly started commenting about her addressing her staff regarding "under time". She contended that when she began talking to her staff about under time he interrupted her, stating that under time was hard to get and started telling them about something that went on in his meeting at the district or during a telecom. The complainant averred that Mr. Wilson was always anxious and would talk about the key indicators that would come out daily. She describe an incident that occurred about two weeks after his arrival at the facility when he stated that overtime had gone up and when she asked if he was blaming her, he responded, "You have been here for two weeks haven't you." The complainant asserted that Mr. Wilson came into a staff meeting she was having and stated in the presence of her staff that she was going to have to start coming in at 8:00 a.m. because he wanted her there when the carriers returned. She maintained that she informed him that she could still come in at 7:00 a.m. and stay until the carriers returned at 1700 because she had worked long hours all of her postal career. It was the complainant's assertion that such instructions should have been given to her privately. (IF, Affidavit A, p. 22).

The complainant averred that when she asked Mr. Wilson for a clerk and TE (Transitional Employee) that belonged to Meadow Mesa Station, he told her he would think about it even though he knew they were struggling to get the mail processed and out. She alleged that he would come into her meetings and change her plans without asking her what was going on. She related a time when she was at Meadow Mesa Station during peak vacation period when her

---

[2] The complainant's allegation relative to being taken off higher level detail assignments will be addressed in the discussion of Allegation 4.

[3] It is noted that the complainant alleged that harassment on the part of Mr. Colton was by way of Mr. Phaup, who was terminated in 2006. Since this preceded the period that was accepted for investigation, allegations relative to Mr. Colton's alleged harassment will not be addressed in this decision. Additionally, when questioned regarding specifics as to the alleged harassment the complainant referenced an incident that occurred on July 10, 2008, even though the accepted date for the beginning of the alleged harassment was July 12, 2008. The complainant alluded to other incidents for which she did not provide specific dates and elaborated repeatedly regarding Mr. Phaup, who was no longer a Postal employee during the period the accepted actions allegedly occurred. She indicated she took off work on August 25, 2008, and had not returned at the time of her affidavit on January 19, 2009. (IF, Affidavit A, pp. 22-24, 30).

Final Agency Decision
Lola B. McGee
Agency Case No. 4E-890-0120-08
Page 16

staff members had scheduled leave and she had made plans to help run the floor. She declared that Mr. Wilson came over and told her she was coming in late and that they were going to put her 204b (Acting Supervisor) back on her route. The complainant testified that she waited until the staff had left the office and asked if she could talk to him about what had happened in the meeting. She acknowledged that he did listen to her but stated that the situation had better work out. She averred that early on the morning of August 25, 2008, she asked Mr. Wilson to come and look at the parcels and he stated he did not need to look at them because he already knew what they looked like. The complainant alleged that later during that morning they were in her office and Mr. Wilson walked up to her and made an open ended threat, "You continue to go over my head with Craig and Yul and I'm going to do something about it". She explained that she had spoken to Mr. Colton regarding an email projection in which Mr. Wilson was wrong, resulting in her being 2% over projection. Also, Yul had called the office after a message had been left to speak to Mr. Wilson and when he insisted in knowing what was going on, she informed him that her supervisors had made a mistake on the schedule and although she had taken care of the issue there were still a certain amount of routes to case and carry.[4] She indicated Yul suggested bringing in the temporary employees earlier and that was what she did. The complainant declared that the threat by Mr. Wilson was the straw that broke the camel's back for her because she knew something negative was going to happen. She indicated she was afraid, nauseated, nervous, angry, upset, confused, had heavy heart palpitations, her mind was disturbed and she could not think straight. She noted that she left work early that day because she did not know what was wrong with her. She indicated that she had not been back to work since that date. The complainant maintained that Mr. Wilson was disrespectful, rude, and hostile toward her on a regular basis. (IF, Affidavit A, pp. 14-15, 19, 23).

The complainant alleged that all of the discriminatory factors played a part in her harassment. She asserted that the managers thought they were better than she was because they were White and male whereas she was Black and female; also, they were promoted managers and postmasters whereas she was their subordinate. Regarding the basis of age discrimination, the complainant testified, "When you are superior some people want the younger person because they believe they will be faster and they feel that they can teach them more and they have a perception that people over 40 years old are set in their ways." (IF, Affidavit A, pp. 28-29).

<u>Allegation 2: On or around September 8, 2008, the complainant became aware that she had been charged 32 hours of sick leave.</u>

[4] The person the complainant referred to as "Yul" was identified in the record as Yul Melonson, Postmaster. (IF, Affidavit E).

Final Agency Decision
Lola B. McGee
Agency Case No. 4E-890-0120-08
Page 17

The complainant testified that she called Mr. Wilson late on the night of August 25, 2008, on his cell phone and left a message that she would not be reporting to work on the following day and was filing an on the job injury claim and would like for him to send her a Form CA-1 and CA-2. She indicated that she called him the next morning to see if he had received her message and he responded that he had. According to the complainant, she received Holiday pay for Labor Day – Monday, September 1, 2008, and 32 hours sick leave was taken from her for Tuesday, September 2, 2008, through Friday, September 5, 2008. She asserted that when she spoke to Mr. Wilson about the matter on September 8, 2008, he informed her that he had originally put her in for 32 LWOP (Leave Without Pay) but after discussing the matter with Labor Relations they advised him to put her in for sick leave because he did not have any paperwork for her absence. She noted that he asked if she wanted him to reverse the sick leave and put her back in for LWOP. The complainant alleged that Mr. Wilson failed to provide her the requested paperwork for her COP (Continuation of Pay) claim in a timely manner, which resulted in her being charged with sick leave rather than COP for an on the job injury. She declared that every discriminatory factor played a part in the whole gamut of problems that came her way with her supervisors, noting that there was no other reason why she was discriminated against. She maintained that she did not deserve any of the treatment she received. (IF, Affidavit A, pp. 14-15, 18).

The complainant's *Employee Everything Report* for Pay Period 2008-19-1 reflects that the complainant was paid 8 hours holiday leave for September 1, 2008, and 32 hours sick leave for September 2-5, 2008. Her pay stub dated September 5, 2008, also indicates that she used 32 hours sick leave for the pay period. However, the complainant's *Employee Key Indicators Report*, which was run on March 26, 2009, reveals that the complainant was subsequently paid COP for the dates in question. (IF, Attachment to Affidavit A, p. 182; Exhibit 29, p. 17; Exhibit 30, p. 1).

Allegation 3: Since July 12, 2008, the complainant has not been selected for the position of Manager, Customer Services and on December 9, 2008, the complainant was informed that she was not selected for the Manager's position at King Station;[5]

[5] The complainant's initial EEO complaint alleged that she had been non-selected for several Manager, Customer Services positions, dating back to August 2006, however, since a non-selection is a discrete act, the non-selection allegations prior to July 12, 2008, were dismissed for untimeliness. (IF, Issues to be Investigated, p. 2). It is noted that since the complainant was non-selected for the Huntridge Station after July 12, 2008, (IF, Attachment to Affidavit A, p. 835) that claim will also be addressed in this Decision.

Final Agency Decision
Lola B. McGee
Agency Case No. 4E-890-0120-08
Page 18

The complainant alleged that she was non-selected for the Manager, Customer Service, EAS-21 Huntridge Carrier Station position and the Manager, Customer Service, EAS-22, King Carrier Station position. The complainant testified that on August 8, 2009, Mr. Richards and Mr. Colton interviewed her for the Huntridge Station position; and Mr. Richards later told her that she "interviewed very, very well and I hit the points he wanted me to, and it was a hard decision to make - Very hard." The complainant believed she should have been selected for the vacancy because she had demonstrated to all of her bosses that she "can do the job and do it well," but she was continually passed over. She averred that she was not promoted even though she had gone from station to station and performed at high standards. (IF, Affidavit A, pp. 4, 6, 7).

The evidence of record revealed a Vacancy Announcement, (Posting 52108635), with a posting period of July 1, 2008 – July 16, 2008, for the position of Manager, Customer Services, EAS-21, Las Vegas, Nevada Facility, Huntridge Station. The announcement indicated that the Functional Purpose of the position was to manage the activities of a large detached mails unit operation, on three tours, in the receipt and distribution of mails normally in an area broader than that associated with a station or branch; and to provide window services and/or mail delivery and collection. (IF, Attachment to Affidavit A, pp. 420-421).

The evidence of record revealed a letter, dated August 18, 2008, addressed to the complainant, and signed by Corey Richards, Selecting Official. The letter was in reference to her application for Vacancy Announcement number 52108635 for the position of Manager, Customer Services, EAS-21, at the Nevada-Sierra District. The complainant was advised that after careful review of all the applicants for this position, another candidate was selected. (IF, Attachment to Affidavit A, p. 835).

The complainant articulated that she applied for the position of Manager, Customer Services at King Station [EAS-22] because she was Acting Manager there from February 23, 2008 to May 2, 2008. She averred that she was qualified for the position; and had worked hard at getting King Station up to par in the short time that she was there. The complainant testified that Review Committee consisted of Mr. Reynosa, who was the Selecting Official, Postmaster Yul Melonson, the Concurring Official, and Tony Sequira, who worked in Retail. She further testified that on December 2, 2008, Mr. Reynosa called her on her cell phone, while she was off sick to schedule a telephone interview; she was interviewed for the position on December 14, 2008. However, on December 9, 2008, Mr. Reynosa called the complainant to inform her that Thomas Jack (White male, age and religion unknown), Manager of the Huntridge Station, had been selected for the position. (IF, Affidavit A, pp. 46-47).

Final Agency Decision
Lola B. McGee
Agency Case No. 4E-890-0120-08
Page 19

Record evidence revealed a Vacancy Announcement, (Posting 52188820), with a posting period of July 29, 2008 - August 13, 2008, for the position of Manager, Customer Services, EAS-22, Las Vegas, Nevada Facility, at King Station. The announcement indicated that the Functional Purpose of the position was to manage, with assistance of a large number of subordinate Supervisors, the activities of a very large carrier station with a very large number of employees providing delivery and collection services within or beyond a normal geographic area, through a very large number of carrier routes; retail services; mail distribution and dispatch; and post office box service. (IF, Attachment to Affidavit A, pp. 433-434).

The complainant testified that she believed her race was a factor in her non-selections because she had EEO activity against Mr. Reynosa; additionally she was out on sick leave; she believed her color was a factor because of the way Mr. Reynosa treated her "with his unfair tactics"; religion was a factor because Mr. Reynosa knows that she believes in God by her cell phone message, her cross around her neck and her expressions of God; sex was a factor because she is a Black female with an educated child that graduated from Yale University with Honors, and Mr. Reynosa knows that she drives two late model vehicles; her age was a factor "because the older you are the less productive people think you are"; her medical conditions/limitations were a factor in the selection process because she had been "gone over six months" with two claims filed with the DOL [Department of Labor], and Mr. Reynosa acted as if he did not know what was going on with her; and her prior/current EEO activity was a factor in the selection process because Mr. Reynosa was one of the reasons why she is sick and "an EEO was filed on him." (IF, Affidavit A, pp. 48-49).

<u>Allegations 4 & 5: The complainant has not been paid higher level pay since August 22, 2008; she was not paid for Week 1 of Pay Period 09-01.</u>

The complainant testified that it was her understanding that if an employee was injured while on higher level then he/she is paid at the rate of pay that he/she was receiving at the time of the injury or illness. Therefore, she felt she should have received a higher level pay during the time frame in question because she was on higher level when she was injured; however, Mr. Richards refused to pay her. She asserted that upon his arrival at the facility in October of 2008, he took her off higher level and told her he was not going to use her on higher level. (IF, Affidavit A, pp. 23, 53, 54).

The Time and Attendance Control System (Report of Clock Rings) for the Complainant dated July 14, 2008 indicated that the complainant's base schedule was EAS-17. For her detail assignment, she was paid at the EAS-22 level. The complainant was paid the higher level, EAS-22 from July 14, 2008 August 22,

Final Agency Decision
Lola B. McGee
Agency Case No. 4E-890-0120-08
Page 20

2008. On August 25, 2008, the complainant was returned to EAS-17 pay. (IF, Exhibit 29).

The complainant averred that her confident attitude, along with being a Black female were factors when she did not receive higher level pay. She further averred that her prior EEO activity was a factor because she saw "him"[6] walking down the GMF [General Mail Facility] hall one day and he looked at the wall to keep from speaking or looking at her. The complainant believed her medical condition was a factor because "he" would not have wanted to pay her since she was not there doing the job. (IF, Affidavit A, pp. 55, 56).

The complainant averred that she was not paid for the week of December 27, 2008 through January 2, 2009, as Mr. Richards did not input any time for her. The complainant believed that was done in retaliation for naming him in a prior EEO complaint; and because she "was out sick." However, she contacted timekeeping and was paid correctly the next pay period. (IF, Affidavit A, p. 57).

The complainant avowed that her race, color, sex, physical condition, and retaliation were all factors when she was not paid for the time frame in question. She contended that she was Black and female and Mr. Richards believed he was superior because he was a White male. Additionally, because of her, the office was short staffed, as she was out [on sick leave]; and she had filed an EEO complaint against Mr. Richards. (IF, Affidavit A, pp. 58, 59).

<u>Allegation 6: During December 2008, Management requested that the complainant's badge access to the GMF be removed</u>.

The complainant avowed that, in December (2008), when she tried to use her badge, an employee (Mail Processing Clerk Charles R. Turner), informed her that Mr. Richards had requested that her badge access be removed. The complainant noted that although she was not working at the GMF, she was "dealing with Labor on a grievance and Injury Compensation." (IF, Affidavit A, p. 60).

The complainant testified that she believed her race, color, sex, medical condition and prior EEO activity were all factors when management requested that her badge access to the GMF be removed. She alleged that she is a Black female and Mr. Richards believes "he's superior to me," and she was out on sick leave. The complainant further alleged that her prior EEO activity was a factor because she had filed an EEO on Mr. Richards, and he "was very angry to me when I would talk to him." (IF, Affidavit A, p. 61).

---

[6] Although not stated, it is assumed that the complainant was referring to Mr. Richards.

Final Agency Decision
Lola B. McGee
Agency Case No. 4E-890-0120-08
Page 21

***Prima Facie* Analysis**

Discrete Acts

The Commission has held that allegations of harassing conduct that involve discrete acts that independently state claims outside of a harassment framework are properly reviewed in the context of disparate treatment. Conlin v. Department of Veterans Affairs, EEOC Appeal No. 0120055310 (December 5, 2006). Allegations 2, 3, 4 & 5 of the accepted issues in this complaint have independently stated claims.

As is indicated above, although a complainant may establish a *prima facie* case by presenting direct evidence of discrimination, the more frequent method of establishing a *prima facie* case is through circumstantial evidence by showing that he or she (1) belongs to a protected class; (2) was subjected to an adverse employment action; and (3) was treated differently in this regard than similarly situated individuals who were not members of the protected group. Mayberry, *supra*. For promotion claims, the complainant can establish a *prima facie* case by showing that (1) she belongs to a protected class; (2) she applied for and was qualified for a position; (3) she was not selected for the position; and, (4) an individual not in her protected class was selected under circumstances which, if left unexplained, would support an inference of discrimination. Keyes v. Secretary of the Navy, 853 F. 2d 1016 (1st Cir. 1988) and Weinstein v. U.S. Postal Service, EEOC Appeal No. 01830674 (February 8, 1984).

Race, Color, Religion, Sex, and Age Discrimination

In order to establish a *prima facie* case of race, color, religion, sex, and age discrimination due to harassment, the first element the evidence must show is that the complainant is in the class of employees protected by Title VII of the Civil Rights Act of 1964, and the Age Discrimination in Employment Act (ADEA). In the instant complaint, the first element was established in that there was evidence that the complainant was African American, Black, Baptist, female, and 46 years old – her date of birth was July 7, 1962. (IF, Affidavit A, Exhibit 1).

Regarding the second element, the complainant's testimony indicates the following: 1) from July 12, 2008, the complainant has been subjected to hostile work environment harassment regarding working conditions, taken off higher level detail assignments; treated in a disrespectful, cruel, and rude manner; and received threats from management official(s); (2) on or around September 8, 2008, the complainant became aware that she had been charged 32 hours of sick leave; (3) on August 18, 2008, the complainant was advised that she was non-selected for the Manager's position at Huntridge Station; and on December 9, 2008, she was informed that she was not selected for the Manager's position

Final Agency Decision
Lola B. McGee
Agency Case No. 4E-890-0120-08
Page 22

at King Station; (4) since August 22, 2008, she has not been paid higher level pay; (5) she was not paid for a week during Pay Period 01-09; and (6) during December 2008, management requested that the complainant's badge access to the GMF [General Mail facility] be removed. (IF, Affidavit A). Accordingly, the complainant has established the second element of her *prima facie* case regarding Allegations 2, 3, 4, and 5, as she was subjected to adverse employment actions relative to those issues.

However, the complainant did not satisfy the second element relative to Allegations 1 and 6 in that she did not show that she was subjected to adverse employment actions concerning those matters. A Title VII complainant is required to demonstrate as part of her *prima facie* case a showing of "materially adverse" conditions imposed by the employer. Kocsis v. Multi-Care Management, Inc., 97 F.3d 876, 887 (6th Cir. 1996). This generally means that the complainant must show that the employer took an action adversely affecting her compensation, terms, conditions, or privileges of employment under conditions giving rise to an inference of unlawful discrimination. Galbraith v. Northern Telecom, Inc., 944 F.2d 275, 279 (6th Cir. 1991); aff'd, 503 U.S. 945 (1992). *See* Harlson v. McDonnell Douglas Corp., 37 F.3d 379, 382 (8th Cir. 1994) (plaintiff not adversely treated when reassigned because he suffered no diminution in title, salary or benefits); Flaherty v. Gas Research Institute, 31 F.3d 451, 457 (7th Cir. 1994) (personnel action that may be personally humiliating is not a materially adverse employment action); Crady v. Liberty National Bank & Trust Co., 993 F.2d 132, 136 (7th Cir. 1993) (materially adverse change in terms and conditions of employment may be indicated by termination of employment, demotion evidenced by decrease in salary, less distinguished title, material loss of benefits, significantly diminished material responsibilities, etc.); Yates v. Avco Corp., 819 F.2d 630, 638 (6th Cir. 1987) (no adverse action where plaintiff alleged that employer required her to sign an agreement stating that her transfer had been at her request and that employer had failed to properly document sick leave). There has been no showing that the issues raised in Allegations 1 and 6 adversely affected the terms, conditions, or privileges of complainant's employment under conditions giving rise to an inference of prohibited discrimination.

Although the complainant established the first and second elements of her *prima facie* case for four of the allegations, she failed to establish the third and/or fourth elements.

In reference to the complainant's non-selection for the Manager, Customer Services positions, the complainant met the burden for the first three criteria (for promotion cases), as she was a member of the protected groups indicated; she applied for and was qualified for the positions; and, she was not selected for the positions. However, the complainant did not establish that the individual not in

Final Agency Decision
Lola B. McGee
Agency Case No. 4E-890-0120-08
Page 23

her protected class was selected under circumstances which, if left unexplained, would support an inference of discrimination. For the Manager's position at the Huntridge Station, the complainant testified that she was told that the selectee, Thomas Jack (Caucasian, White, Male, DOB: 07/03/54, religion unknown) was from another District, was already a Level 21 Manager, and "took a lateral." (IF, Affidavit A, p. 6). For the King Carrier Station position, the complainant testified that she was informed that Thomas Jack was selected (again) for that vacancy (which was an EAS-22 position). (IF, Affidavit A, p. 47).

As fore stated, the complainant did not establish that Mr. Jack, the successful applicant for both positions was selected under circumstances which, if left unexplained, would support an inference of discrimination. For the Huntridge position, the complainant acknowledged that Mr. Richards had informed her that although she had interviewed well, he disclosed to her that Thomas Jack had interviewed well also, and he was already a level-21 Manager. (IF, Affidavit A, p. 7). Regarding the King position, Mr. Richards explained that Mr. Jack had been a higher level Manager/Postmaster for ten years, including EAS-levels 21 and 22. (IF, Affidavit B, p. 14). Mr. Colton averred that the selection was made based on a number of factors; and the position was given to a more experienced individual [Mr. Jack] who was a higher-level Postmaster, and who had previous experience in the position in which they were competing for. (IF, Affidavit D, p. 6). Mr. Reynosa added that Mr. Jack was selected for the Manager's position because he had a lot of experience in Route Evaluations and eliminating routes. Additionally, he had extensive experience in Function Four and Clerk operations. "We were looking for strength in these areas." (IF, Affidavit F, p. 5).

There was nothing in the evidence of record to indicate that the complainant's race, color, religion, sex and/or age were considerations or even *determining factors in* the Agency's decisions, nor did the complainant present any evidence from which one could draw an inference of discrimination. In fact, the selected applicant was 8 years older than the complainant. Therefore, for Allegation 3, the complainant failed to establish a *prima facie* case of discrimination, when she was not selected for the positions of Manager, Customer Services.

For the remaining Allegations, the third element required the complainant to show that similarly situated co-workers, not in her protected class, were treated more favorably. In order to be a valid comparator, the co-worker must be similarly situated. Michelle K. Knapp-Huffman v. John Ashcroft, Attorney General, Department of Justice, (Bureau of Prisons), No. 01991026 (January 16, 2002) ("In order to be considered similarly situated, the persons with whom the complainant is comparing herself *must be similar in substantially all aspects, so that it would be expected that they would be treated in the same manner.* Murray v. Thistledown Racing Club, Inc., 770 F.2d 63, 68 (6th Cir. 1985)" (emphasis added). *See also* Nogas v. John E. Potter, Postmaster General, United States

Final Agency Decision
Lola B. McGee
Agency Case No. 4E-890-0120-08
Page 24

Postal Service, EEOC Appeal No. 01994718 (January 30, 2002). Moreover, all relevant aspects of the employees' work situation must be identical or nearly identical, *i.e.*, that the employees report to the same supervisor, perform the same job function, and work during the same time periods. See Anderson v. Department of Treasury, EEOC Appeal No. 01A22092 (March 13, 2003); Stewart v. Department of Defense, EEOC Appeal No. 01A02890 (June 27, 2001); Jones v. United States Postal Service, EEOC Appeal No. 01983491 (April 13, 2000).

As certified in the evidence of record for Allegations 2, 4 & 5, all of which reference the complainant's pay, the complainant failed to name any similarly situated employees who were treated differently than she was under similar circumstances; and the investigation did not reveal any comparators. Likewise, in Allegations 1 & 6, the complainant failed to identify a similarly situated person who were treated more favorably than she was under the same or similar circumstances. Since the complainant failed to name any similarly situated employees who were treated more favorably than she was, or point to any evidence that supported an inference of illegal discrimination, she has failed to establish a *prima facie* case of discrimination based on race, color, religion, sex, and age.

The complainant always bears the ultimate burden of persuasion in proving that the Agency intentionally discriminated against him. United States Postal Service Board of Governors . Aikens, 460 U.S. 716 (1983). In the instant matter, you have failed to meet such a burden. In Nikki Love v. Frank, Postmaster General, U.S. Postal Service, EEOC Request No. 05890328 (May 26, 1989), the Commission held:

We agree with the court in Watson v. Megee Women's Hospital, 472 F.Supp. 325 at 330 (D.C. PA 1979):

> That an employment decision is unfortunate for the employee, unwarranted, unkind, or even unprincipled is not enough--at least, not enough to support a Title VII action. To permit such an action to succeed, without clear proof of a link between the plaintiff's protected status and the adverse employment decision, would cause Title VII to become a vehicle for providing compensation following an adverse employment decision to every person in a protected class — that is, to every citizen of either sex, any race, origin or nationality. Although ***all*** citizens are protected under Title VII, they are protected only against the specific harm of invidiously discriminatory preference by employers.

Final Agency Decision
Lola B. McGee
Agency Case No. 4E-890-0120-08
Page 25

Disability Discrimination

In order to establish a *prima facie* case of disability discrimination due to harassment, the first element that the evidence must show is that the complainant was a "person with a disability" within the meaning of the Rehabilitation Act of 1973. Thus, there must be evidence that the complainant had a physical or mental impairment which substantially impacted one or more of her major life functions, such as walking, breathing, talking, learning, seeing, hearing, thinking, eating, working, or his ability to take care of himself.

According to the complainant's testimony, on August 25, 2008, Mr. Wilson threatened her when he informed her that if she continued to go over his head to Mr. Colton and Mr. Melonson, he (Mr. Wilson) "was going to do something about it." [7] The complainant professed that Mr. Wilson's threat was the "straw that broke the camel's back". She averred that she "knew something negative was going to happen." The complainant alleged that she was afraid, nauseated, nervous, angry, upset, confused, had heavy heart palpitations, her mind was disturbed, she could not think straight, she vomited, and had head shocks running through her. She went to see Dr. Mary J. Reed (her therapist), who informed the complainant that she had had a Panic Attack. (IF, Affidavit A, pp. 14-15).

The evidence of record contained numerous medical records for the complainant; her medical history indicated that she had been diagnosed with PTSD, depression, major depressive disorder, panic disorder without agoraphobia, sensorineural hearing loss, head shocks, tinnitus, laryngopharyngeal reflux, paroxysmal ventricular tachycardia, palpitations (since childhood), heart murmur, back pain, and chest pain. (IF, Attachment to Affidavit A, pp. 68-82, 85-114, 120-123, 130-131, 166-170, 233-234, 711-722, 729-733). Her medications included motrin, pristiq, dicyclomine hydrochloride, clonazepam, and verapamil.

[7] Mr. Wilson, who was the OIC in North Las Vegas, provided the following summary of the conversations that led to the complainant's allegation of the "open ended threat": On August 22, 2008, the complainant asked for three additional SDO's (Supervisor, Distribution Operations) for Saturday, August 23, 2008. Mr. Wilson informed the complainant that the request was denied and that they would live with the mistakes that she and her Supervisors made regarding the schedule. Mr. Wilson articulated to the complainant that the request for SDO's had already been submitted and they would follow what they had originally asked for. Mr. Wilson averred that the complainant became very agitated. He reminded her that the decision was his (as the OIC) and they would operate based on that decision. The complainant contacted Postmaster Melonson and asked him to override Mr. Wilson's decision. Mr. Melonson reminded the complainant of the previous commitment made and denied her request. Mr. Wilson conveyed (to the complainant) that he was disappointed in her when she attempted to go over his head with Mr. Melonson regarding the SDO request that he had already denied her. He denied that he had threatened her. (IF, Attachment to Affidavit A, pp. 644, 645). This is an unsworn statement.

Final Agency Decision
Lola B. McGee
Agency Case No. 4E-890-0120-08
Page 26

The medical documentation from the complainant's physicians did not specifically indicate that the complainant's physical and/or mental impairments limited her major life activities in any way. On August 27, 2008, Dr. Reed indicated that the complainant had been "under my care since 8-26-08 and is being treated for Post Traumatic Stress Disorder and Major Depressive Disorder. She is unable to return to work until her condition improves." (IF, Attachment to Affidavit A, p. 164). On November 10, 2008, Shiny A. Moolakatt, MPT, from the Comprehensive [Physical] Therapy Center, wrote that the complainant "was seen here on Monday, November 10, 2008, for her Initial Evaluation for physical therapy." (IF, Attachment to Affidavit A, p. 115). In a letter dated February 17, 2009, Robert P. Croke, M.D. certified that she could "return to full-time work without any restriction;" however, she should continue the verapamil, and she required no other cardiovascular drug. (IF, Affidavit A. pp. 159-160). On February 26, 2009, Mary J. Reed, PhD, APN, notified the Postal Service that the complainant could return to work on March 9, 2009; however, she should continue her psychotherapy and medications. (IF, Attachment to Affidavit A, p. 177). [8]

At the time the instant complaint was filed, the evidence of record was devoid of any medical documentation to substantiate that the complainant had an impairment that substantially limited a major life activity, nor did the record substantiate that her condition was considered permanent in nature. Clearly excluded are temporary or transitory conditions in determining whether an individual has a disability within the meaning of the law. Alderson v. Postmaster General, 598 F. Supp. 49 (W.D. Okla. 1984). Therefore, it must be concluded that the complainant is not covered by the provisions of the Rehabilitation Act. Hence, a *prima facie* case of disability discrimination has not been established.

When all of this evidence was considered, it failed to show that the complainant was a "disabled person" within the meaning of the Rehabilitation Act. Although there was some medical evidence, there was no explanation of the impact of the medical conditions on life activities both on and off the job. The regulations defined "substantially limited" as meaning that the complainant could not perform the major life activities at all, or that she was significantly limited in her ability to perform those activities as compared to the average person in the general population. 29 C.F.R. 1630.2(j) and Toyota Motor Manufacturing of Kentucky, Inc. v. Williams, 534 U.S. 184 (2002). See also Harrison v. Department of Justice, EEOC Appeal No. 01A03948 (July 30, 2003).

[8] In her request for a Final Agency Decision, (subsequent to this Investigation) the complainant noted that her "mental and physical health has rapidly declined" to the point where she had to file for Medical Disability Retirement. She now receives "in home health care." (IF, Post Investigation, FAD Request). This is an **unsworn** statement.

Final Agency Decision
Lola B. McGee
Agency Case No. 4E-890-0120-08
Page 27

Where, as here, the major life activity of "working" was involved, the individual must be unable to perform an entire class of jobs or a broad range of jobs within the class in order to be substantially limited. 29 C.F.R. 1630.2(j)(3). See also Webber v. Department of the Air Force, EEOC Appeal No. 01989587 (March 2, 2001). There was no evidence in the record that the complainant was unable to perform an entire class of jobs, or a broad range of jobs within any class, because of her medical conditions. The evidence did not establish that the complainant was a "person with a disability" within the meaning of the Rehabilitation Act, and therefore, no *prima facie* claim for disability discrimination was established.

Harassment Claim

In order to establish a claim of harassment, the complainant must show that: (1) she belongs to a statutorily protected class; (2) she was subjected to unwelcome verbal or physical conduct involving the protected class; (3) the harassment complained of was based on the statutorily protected class; (4) the harassment had the purpose or effect of unreasonably interfering with her work performance and/or creating an intimidating, hostile, or offensive work environment; and (5) there is a basis for imputing liability to the employer. McCleod v. Social Security Administration, EEOC Appeal No. 01963810 (August 5, 1999).

As fore stated, the complainant established the first element of the harassment claim in that she was covered by Title VII of the Civil Rights Act of 1964, and the Age Discrimination in Employment Act (ADEA). (IF, Affidavit A, Exhibit 1). In a like manner, the record established that some of the incidents the complainant alleged did indeed occur; and it is safe to say that the complainant felt that these actions were "unwelcome."[9] To the extent that some of these proceedings may have occurred, we will assume that they were a direct result of the needs of the Postal Service. However, for the sake of argument only, we accept that the complainant has satisfied the second element of her *prima facie* case.

To establish the third element of this claim, the complainant must prove that the harassment complained of was based on the statutorily protected class. The complainant did not present any evidence to show that Management's actions were based on her race, color, religion, sex, age, physical disability or prior EEO activity, *i.e.,* that Management exhibited a discriminatory animus toward members of her protected groups. Her allegations were merely a hodgepodge of inconclusory accusations and conjectures unsupported by any substantive evidence that the Agency's actions were discriminatory due to the complainant's

[9] Notably, there has been no showing that the complainant was subjected to adverse working conditions, that she was treated in a disrespectful, cruel and rude manner nor is there any evidence that she was subjected to threats by her manager.

protected groups. Therefore, the complainant failed to establish the third element of her harassment claim.

To establish the fourth element of the instant harassment claim, the complainant must prove that the harassment affected a term, condition, or privilege of her employment and/or had the purpose or effect of unreasonably interfering with her work environment and/or creating a hostile, intimidating, or offensive work environment. Title VII does not serve "as a vehicle for vindicating the petty slurs suffered by the hypersensitive." Zabkowicz v. West Bend Co., 589 F.Supp. 780, 784, 35 EPD Paragraph 34, 766 (E.D. Wis. 1984); *See also* Staton v. Department of Navy, EEOC Appeal No. 01903774 (February 11, 1991). If the conduct at issue would not substantially affect the work environment of a reasonable person, no violation should be found. Staton, *supra*.

Whether the conduct is sufficiently severe or pervasive is evaluated with a two-prong test with both an objective and a subjective element: (1) The conduct must be sufficiently severe or pervasive that a reasonable person viewing the conduct from the victim's perspective would find it hostile, offensive or abusive; and (2) The conduct must have been viewed in that fashion by the complainant at the time it occurred. *See EEOC Policy Guidance on Current Issues of Sexual Harassment* (October 25, 1988), ("*Commission Policy Guidance*") p. 13.

Additionally, whether an environment is 'hostile' or 'abusive' can be determined only by looking at all the circumstances. These may include the frequency of the discriminatory conduct; its severity; whether it is physically threatening or humiliating, or a mere offensive utterance; and whether it unreasonably interferes with an employee's work performance." Harris, *supra*, at 371.

In support of her allegation of hostile work environment harassment, the complainant alleged that, in addition to not being promoted to several Manager, Customer Services positions that she applied for, Mr. Wilson was disrespectful, rude, and hostile with her on a regular basis. She cited the following examples: (1) on July 10, 2008, Mr. Wilson came into her staff meeting and interrupted it as she was talking to her staff about under time; (2) on another occasion, he came into a staff meeting and informed the complainant, in front of her staff, rather than privately, that she needed to start coming in [to work] at 8:00 AM because she needed to be there when the Carriers came back from delivering their routes. (3) Mr. Wilson would come into her staff meetings and change her decisions without asking her; (4) on August 25, 2008, Mr. Wilson threatened her; (5) in October 2008, Mr. Richards advised her that he was not going to use her on higher level; and (6) in December 2008, he (Mr. Richards) had her access to the GMF

Final Agency Decision
Lola B. McGee
Agency Case No. 4E-890-0120-08
Page 29

removed so she could not go to Injury Compensation and turn in medical paperwork.[10] (IF, Affidavit A, pp. 14-15, 22- 23, 46-47).

Assuming that the complainant established that the aforementioned incidents occurred and were based on her status as an African American, Baptist female, over 40 years of age, with a medical condition, and prior EEO activity, she failed to show that the incidents were, from the standpoint of an objective reasonable person, sufficiently severe or pervasive to rise to the level of a hostile work environment. The conduct must be "so objectively offensive as to alter the 'conditions' of the victim's employment."

Regarding Allegation 1, in which the complainant alleged that her working conditions created a hostile environment; she was treated in a disrespectful, cruel, and rude manner; and received threats from management; Mr. Wilson testified that he did not recall making any kind of threatening comment to the complainant or harassing her in any manner. He explained that there was a process whereby scheduled day off projections were made by Wednesday for the follow week. He asserted that the complainant called him on a Friday regarding a mistake that had been made and requested to call in employees who were on their scheduled day off. He indicated he informed her he was not going to request that other employees be called in on their off day and that they would have to operate with the employees they had. (IF, Affidavit C, pp. 3-5). Bonnie D. Brokofsky, Caucasian, White, Protestant, Female, age 53, Carrier Technician averred that she could not recall a staff meeting during which the complainant was harassed. She asserted that the subjects of under time and overtime were discussed at almost every staff meeting. She explained that usually the Station Manager or Postmaster would discuss the numbers and inform all supervisors of the need for improvement and they usually responded by informing them that they were trying to make improvements. (IF, Affidavit I, p. 3).

In reference to Allegation 3, *i.e.*, the complainant's non-selection for the Manager, Customer Services positions, Mr. Richards testified that he was the Selecting Official and Mr. Colton was the Concurring Official for the Huntridge Station vacancy. He avowed that the complainant was not selected for the Manager, Customer Services position for the Huntridge Station vacancy because Mr. Jack (the selectee) was more qualified and already an EAS-21. (IF, Affidavit B, pp. 11, 12). Mr. Reynosa testified that the Complainant was recommended by the Review Committee for consideration, however, focus and concern for the King Station was based on the fact that due to a reduction in mail volume, routes would have to be removed. Mr. Jack, who had been laterally moved to the Huntridge Station from the Pendleton, Oregon Post Office, was selected for the vacancy because he had lots of experience in route evaluations and elimination

[10] This is Allegation 6 of the instant complaint. (IF, Issues to be Investigated, p. 24).

of routes; and extensive experience in Function Four and clerk operations - and they were looking for strength in those areas. (IF, Affidavit F, pp. 4-5).

Concerning Allegations 2, 4 and 5, regarding the complainant's pay, Mr. Wilson declared that he put the complainant in for 32 hours sick leave during the period in question because he did not have a PS Form 3971 at the time although the complainant had notified him by phone that she would not be in. (IF, Affidavit C, 9). Mr. Richards testified that the complainant was detailed to the Acting Manager, Customer Services, at Meadow Mesa Station from July 5, 2008 through September 30, 2008. Her detail assignment ended on September 30, 2008; therefore, she was not entitled to higher level pay after that date. (IF, Affidavit B, p. 4). Ms. Letts testified that if the detail assignment ends while the employee is absent, the employee returns to their regular rate of pay. (IF, Affidavit G, p. 3). Ms. Letts explained that for Pay Period 01-09, the complainant was not paid because of a system error and a programming issue; the error affected several employees. She averred the complainant called her and asked her to take care of it if the office didn't; Ms. Letts affirmed that she submitted the adjustment for the complainant. (IF, Affidavit G, p. 5).

In reference to the complainant's allegation regarding her badge access to the GMF being removed, (Allegation 6), Mr. Richards testified that he requested "Personnel" to have the complainant's badge access deactivated because she was not in a work status at the GMF. Further, if the complainant needed to see someone at the GMF, "she would still have the ability to go to Personnel and inform the person at the desk who she was, and who she was there to visit. They would verify that the individual she was there to visit would be available and would indicate when she entered the building." (IF, Affidavit B, p. 9).

Consequently, even assuming the facts most favorably to the complainant, I find the conditions of employment were not so altered or sufficiently severe or pervasive to create a hostile work environment. Burlington Industries, Inc. v. Ellerth, 118 S.Ct. 2257 (1998); and Faragher v. City of Boca Raton, 118 S. Ct. 2275 (1998). DiFruscio v. Social Security Administration, EEOC Appeal No. 01982006 (September 13, 2000) (routine work assignments, instructions, and admonishments did not rise to a level of harassment or disparate treatment by the supervisor against the appellant).

The record evidence undoubtedly shows that the Agency officials were acting in their managerial capacity regarding the alleged allegations. The aforementioned actions were clearly within the realm of supervisory responsibility, and there was no evidence that the complainant's allegations of harassment caused a hostile work environment. Hence, a reasonable person would not perceive Management's actions as severe or pervasive. Considering the conduct was not severe or pervasive and it occurred over a relatively short period of time, the

Final Agency Decision
Lola B. McGee
Agency Case No. 4E-890-0120-08
Page 31

complainant failed to prove that, taken as a whole, the alleged harassing conduct rose to the level of a hostile work environment. Hence, the complainant failed to establish the fourth element of her hostile work environment claim, i.e., that Management's actions had the purpose or effect of unreasonably interfering with her work performance and/or creating an intimidating, hostile, or offensive work environment.

Even if all of the issues raised had been shown to be related to the complainant's race, color, religion, sex, age, medical condition, and/or prior EEO activity, which they were not, they do not reveal a work environment which was permeated with "discriminatory intimidation, ridicule, and insult" that was sufficiently severe or pervasive enough to alter the terms and conditions of her employment and create an abusive work environment in violation of Title VII. Harris v. Forklift Systems, Inc., 510 U.S. 17 (1993), citing Meritor Savings Bank F.S.B. v. Vinson, 477 U.S. 57 (1986). Evaluating the conduct in question from the standpoint of a reasonable person, taking into account the particular context in which it occurred, including its severity and frequency, the complainant has raised little more than a few isolated incidents of work centered interactions which did not render her work environment abusive or intimidating, even though some friction may have been involved. See Harris, *supra;* Johnson v. Bunny Bread Co., 646 F. 2d 1250, at 1257 (8th Cir. 1981) and Cariddi v. Kansas City Chiefs Football Club, Inc., 568 F. 2d 87, at 88 (8th Cir. 1977.

Finally, the complainant must show that there was a basis for imputing liability to the Agency. However, as noted above, an agency may generally avoid liability by showing that the acts complained of did not occur, that the conduct complained of was not unwelcome, that the alleged harassment was not "sufficiently severe or pervasive" to alter the terms or conditions of the complainant's employment or to create a hostile work environment, that immediate and appropriate corrective action was taken as soon as the employer was put on notice, or that there is no basis for imputing liability to the employer under agency principles. Crane v. Postmaster General, EEOC Appeal No. 01924585 (April 22, 1993) and Meritor Savings Bank F.S.B. v. Vinson, 477 U.S. 57 (1986).

For harassment based on comments or conduct, the Agency is only liable if a Supervisor knew or should have known of the harassment, and failed to take prompt remedial action. *See, e.g.* Tedeschi v. United States Postal Service, EEOC Appeal No. 01871031 (1988). The Postal Service has avoided liability for the complainant's alleged harassment, as Mr. Richards, Mr. Wilson, Mr. Colton, and Mr. Reynosa all testified that the complainant did not inform them at any time that she felt she was being harassed; nor did they directly witness any interactions between the complainant and any employee or Management official that they believed rose to a level that would be considered harassment or a

Final Agency Decision
Lola B. McGee
Agency Case No. 4E-890-0120-08
Page 32

hostile work environment. (IF, Affidavit B, pp. 19, 20, Affidavit C, p. 7, Affidavit D, pp. 15, 16, Affidavit F, pp. 11, 12).

Considering the foregoing, even if it is arguably assumed that the complainant established that she was subjected to hostile work environment harassment based on her protected groups, she failed to establish that there was a basis for imputing liability to the Agency.

As the complainant failed to establish elements 3, 4 and 5, she failed to establish a *prima facie* case of harassment discrimination.

Retaliation Claim

To establish a *prima facie* case based on reprisal, a complainant must show that: (1) he or she engaged in prior protected activity; (2) the agency official was aware of the protected activity; (3) he or she was subsequently disadvantaged by an adverse employment action or adverse treatment; and (4) there is a causal link between the protected activity and adverse action/treatment.

According to the complainant affidavit, when she initially sought counseling for the instant complaint (August 26, 2008), she did not have prior EEO activity. She testified that she filed an additional EEO on January 15, 2009. [11] (IF, Affidavit A, p. 2). Further, the Management Officials she named, *i.e.*, Mr. Richards, Mr. Wilson, Mr. Colton, and Mr. Reynosa, all testified that they were unaware of the complainant's prior EEO activity. (IF, Affidavit B, p. 2, Affidavit C, p. 2, Affidavit D, p. 2, Affidavit F, p. 2). Arguably, the complainant was subjected to some adverse treatment based on her claims that she was non-selected, she was not paid properly, and her badge access was removed; and because of the temporal proximity between her initial claim of hostile work environment harassment and the amended claims in the complaint, a causal connection may be inferred. However, the complainant has not satisfied the causal link of a *prima facie* case of discrimination on the basis of retaliation. The causal connection may be inferred by evidence that the cited incidents occurred in close proximity to the complainant's recent EEO involvement; it can also be argued that a causal link can be inferred between the complainant's initial EEO activity and the matters brought forth in the amendments to the complaint; however, the remainder of the evidence in the record outweighs these inferences. First, there is no evidence that management took the actions at issue because of complainant's prior protected activity and sought to deter others, as required by EEOC Compliance Manual on Retaliation, No. 915.003 (May 20, 1998), pp. 8-16. Secondly, when asked by the EEO Investigator, Mr. Richards, Mr. Wilson, Mr. Colton, and Mr.,

[11] In actuality, the complainant sought counseling January 15, 2009, and her complaint was amended accordingly. (IF, Issues to be Investigated, p. 15).

Final Agency Decision
Lola B. McGee
Agency Case No. 4E-890-0120-08
Page 33

Reynosa, all testified that complainant's prior or current EEO activity was not a factor relative to their decisions or actions regarding the complainant's claims. (IF, Affidavits B, C, D, F).

Having made that determination; however, it is important to point out that such a determination is not the equivalent of a finding of illegal discrimination. It is simply proof that, without more, the circumstances surrounding the complainant's allegations may give rise to an inference that discrimination did occur. Thus, the burden shifts to Management to produce admissible evidence that its actions were taken for legitimate, non-discriminatory reasons. As a trier of fact regarding the matters, I find that the agency has met its burden, as detailed more fully via the Managers testimonies below.

In sum, the complainant has failed to prove each element of a *prima facie* case of discrimination based on race, color, religion, sex, age, physical disability, mental disability, and/or retaliation (for prior EEO activity).

Management's Response

Assuming, for the sake of argument, that the complainant had established a *prima facie* case of discrimination based on race and retaliation, Management has articulated a legitimate, non-discriminatory explanation for their actions.

Allegation 1: From July 12, 2008, the complainant has been subjected to hostile work environment harassment regarding working conditions, taken off higher level detail assignments; treated in a disrespectful, cruel, and rude manner; and received threats from management official(s).

Mr. Wilson disavowed any knowledge of the complainant being harassed or threatened and he could not recall having commented that he was going to do something about it if she continued to go over his head. He declared that he had lots of private conversations with the complainant regarding her attendance. He explained that her work hours for her detail at Meadow Mesa were 7:00 a.m. to 4:00 p.m.; however, she did not report on her first scheduled day until 10:00 a.m. and did not notify him that she was going to be late. Mr. Wilson asserted that he ignored complainant on the first day but sat her down and had a discussion when the behavior continued during which he outlined his expectations and reiterated that her schedule was 7:00 a.m. to 4:00 p.m. He indicated that he explained that as office manager she needed to be regular in attendance and set an example for the other employees. He noted that the complainant's attendance improved after he spoke with her but subsequently regressed even though he never wrote her up or disciplined her in any way. (IF, Affidavit C, p. 5).

Final Agency Decision
Lola B. McGee
Agency Case No. 4E-890-0120-08
Page 34

Allegation 2: On or around September 8, 2008, the complainant became aware that she had been charged 32 hours of sick leave.

Mr. Wilson testified that after the complainant's attendance began deteriorating again in August of 2008 his phone rang one night around 12:00 or 12:30 a.m. He indicated that when he checked it the next morning there was a message from the complainant stating she would not be in that morning and would not be back. He contended that he returned her call that morning and asked what was going on but she would not tell him anything except to respond that if he needed to know what was going on, someone such as Safety would notify him at a later date. He asserted that he found out later the complainant had submitted a claim for stress. Mr. Wilson explained that a lot of the EAS level employees were on automatic clock rings; however, when they were on leave they needed to submit a PS Form 3971. He asserted that if the employee did not submit a Form 3971 the immediate supervisor could fill out the form for the employee and input the leave. He testified that in the instant case he input sick leave for the complainant because he did not have a Form 3971. Mr. Wilson maintained that after putting the complainant in for sick leave, Injury Compensation informed him when he returned to work on the following Monday that she would be on COP after that. He noted that the first three days for any type of on the job injury was covered by personal sick leave before being covered by COP. (IF, Affidavit C, p. 9).

Allegation 3: Since July 12, 2008, the complainant has not been selected for the position of Manager, Customer Services and on December 9, 2008, the complainant was informed that she was not selected for the Manager's position at King Station.

For the Huntridge Station position, Mr. Richards, the Selecting Official, articulated that Mr. Jack was the successful applicant for the position because he interviewed well; and he (Mr. Jack) was already in an EAS-21 Manager's position. Mr. Richards added that he had a phone conversation with the complainant and explained to her that there was someone more qualified than she was. (IF, Affidavit A, p. 11, 12, 13). Mr. Colton, who was the Concurring Official, affirmed that Mr. Jack was selected for the King Station position because he was more experienced; and had been a higher-level Postmaster. (IF, Affidavit D, p. 6)

Regarding the King position, Mr. Richards, explained that Mr. Jack was selected for the vacancy because he had been a higher level Manager/Postmaster for ten years, including EAS-levels 21 and 22. (IF, Affidavit B, p. 14). Mr. Reynosa, the Selecting Official, averred that Mr. Jack was selected for the Manager's position because he had extensive experience in Route Evaluations, eliminating routes, Function Four operations and Clerk operations. He noted that they were looking for experience in those areas." (IF, Affidavit F, p. 5). Mr. Melonson, the

Final Agency Decision
Lola B. McGee
Agency Case No. 4E-890-0120-08
Page 35

Concurring Official avowed that Mr. Jack was selected due to his experience; he had been promoted to the EAS-21 level; he had a lateral transfer from Oregon; and had years of experience at that level. (IF, Affidavit E. p. 5).

Mr. Richards, Mr. Colton, Mr. Melonson, and Mr. Reynosa all affirmed that the complainant's race, color, religion, sex, age, medical condition, nor her prior/current EEO activity were factors in their decisions/actions regarding the selection process or the individual selected for the vacancies. (IF, Affidavit B, p. 10).

Allegations 4 & 5: The complainant has not been paid higher level pay since August 22, 2008; she was not paid for a week in Pay Period 01 – 2009.

Ms. Letts noted that "generally speaking, if a person is on detail, if they have an absence of a week or two such as annual or sick leave, they continue to receive leave at higher level. If it is known that the individual may not return and another person is put on the detail, the Postmaster may have the detail ended in order to place the [second] person in the detail." Ms. Letts added that the *Employee and Labor Relations Manual (ELM), F-21*,the *Time and Attendance Handbook*, Section 421-*Higher Level*, and the *NAPS [National Association of Postal Supervisors] Agreement,* which addresses the five day waiting period for higher level details, were all utilized for guidance. (IF, Affidavit G, pp. 3, 4).

Mr. Richards disclosed that he refused to extend the complainant's detail assignment, because he had another Manager performing the duties she had. However, Mr. Richards affirmed that neither the complainant's race, color, religion, sex, age, medical condition, nor her prior/current EEO activity was a factor in his decisions/actions regarding her rate of pay or detail assignment. (IF, Affidavit B, pp. 5, 6).

Mr. Colton testified that he initiates all PS Forms 1723 for employees on details to higher level assignments. He conveyed that once the complainant was absent, another Supervisor was given the opportunity for the detail, and subsequently a permanent Manager was selected for the position. Mr. Colton also affirmed that neither the complainant's race, color, religion, sex, age, medical condition, nor her prior/current EEO activity was a factor in his decisions/actions regarding her rate of pay or detail assignment. (IF, Affidavit D, pp. 12, 13).

As mentioned earlier in this Decision, Ms. Letts explained that Pay Period 01-2009 frame in question, the complainant was not paid because of a system error and a programming issue; and the error affected several employees. A pay adjustment was made for the complainant, and she was subsequently compensated. (IF, Affidavit G, p. 5).

Final Agency Decision
Lola B. McGee
Agency Case No. 4E-890-0120-08
Page 36

Allegation 6: During December 2008, Management requested that the complainant's badge access to the GMF be removed.

Mr. Richards testified that his request to have the complainant's badge access deactivated was done in compliance with "Safety & Security" Postal Regulations, as the complainant was not in a work status at the GMF. He also testified that the complainant never contacted him with her concerns regarding her badge being deactivated for the GMF. (IF, Affidavit B, p. 9).

Mr. Richards affirmed that the complainant's race, color, religion, sex, age, medical condition, nor her prior/current EEO activity were factors in his decisions/actions regarding her badge access. (IF, Affidavit B, p. 10).

Pretext

At this point, the complainant had the burden of proving that Management's stated reason was not only pretext, but was pretext for discrimination. Tincher v. Wal-Mart Stores, Inc., 118 F.3d 1125, 1129 (7th Cir. 1997). Pretext could be demonstrated by showing "such weaknesses, impossibilities, inconsistencies, incoherencies, or contradictions in the Agency proffered reasons for its action that a reasonable fact-finder could rationally find them unworthy of credence and then infer that the employer did not act for the asserted non-discriminatory reason. Morgan v. Hiliti, Inc. 108, F.3d 1319, 1323, (10th Cir. 1997). To do this, the complainant must have shown that, in spite of the articulated non-discriminatory explanation, an overall inference of discrimination could be discerned by a preponderance of the evidence. U.S. Postal Service Board of Governors v. Aikens, 460 U.S. 711, 714-17 (1983). In other words, the complainant must have shown that the Agency was "more likely motivated by discriminatory reasons. [Citation omitted]" than not. Hill v. Social Security Administration, Appeal No. 01970512 (June 8, 2000). Or, the complainant could have shown that the proffered explanation of the Agency was unworthy of credence. Texas Dep't of Community Affairs v. Burdine, 450 U.S. 248, 256 (1981). Essentially, the record must have shown that the Agency articulated a false reason and that its real reason was discrimination. St. Mary's Honor Center v. Hicks, 509 U.S. 502, 515 (1993).

According to the Court, it was not sufficient "to disbelieve the employer; the fact finder must believe the plaintiff's explanation of intentional discrimination." Hicks, 509 U.S. at 519. The Agency was not persuaded that Management's actions were motivated by discrimination. The complainant did not offer any direct evidence, corroborating testimony from another witness, or documentation, which would have confirmed her claim that Management's actions were discriminatory. Neither did the complainant offer any evidence that showed that her race, color, religion, sex, age, medical condition, and/or prior EEO activity were

Final Agency Decision
Lola B. McGee
Agency Case No. 4E-890-0120-08
Page 37

considerations or the determining factors for the Agency's actions. Finally, the complainant did not present any evidence to indicate that the Agency officials harbored a discriminatory animus toward members of her protected group.

None of the complainant's allegations were not supported by the totality of the record; and she failed to present any plausible evidence that would have demonstrated that Management's reasons for its actions were factually baseless or not its actual motivation. Tincher v. Wal-Mart Stores, Inc. and Morgan v. Hilti, Inc., Id. It should be noted that a complainant's subjective beliefs cannot be probative evidence of pretext, and therefore, cannot be the basis of judicial relief. Elliot v. Group Medical & Surgical Service, 714 F.2d 556, 557 (5th cir. 1983), cert. denied, 467 U.S. 1215, (1984); see also, Billet v. CIGNA Corp., 940 F.2d 812, 816 (3rd Cir. 1991). The complainant cannot second-guess the wisdom of the Agency's business decisions. Thus, agencies are free to discharge, promote, demote, or transfer individuals for any reason, fair or unfair, so long as the decision is not a pretext for discrimination. Damon v. Fleming Supermarkets of Florida, Inc., 196 F.3dn 1354, 1361 (11th Cir. 1999); Nix v. WLCY Radio/Rahall Communications, 738 F.2d 1181, 1187 (11th Cir. 1984).

In other words, there was nothing that showed by a preponderance of the evidence that the legitimate explanations given by the Agency were pretexts for discrimination. Hammons v. HUD, EEOC Appeal No. 01955704 (August 20, 1997); EEOC Request No. 05971093, (May 5, 1999). Hence, the complainant did not show that the explanation of the Agency for its actions was simply a pretext for discrimination.

Based on the foregoing, it must be concluded that the complainant did not meet the burden of establishing a prima facie case of unlawful discrimination regarding the instant allegations. Hence, the complainant did not satisfy her burden of proof, and, as noted above, the complainant could not prevail.

Statement of Relief

After carefully considering the entire record, and applying the legal standards outlined in McDonnell Douglas Corporation v. Green, 411 U.S. 792 (1973); Hazen Paper Company v. Biggins, 507 U.S. 604 (1993) (applying the standard to cases brought under the ADEA); and Prewitt v. U.S. Postal Service, 662 F .2d 292 (5th Cir. 1981) (applying the standard to cases brought under the Rehabilitation Act); and Hochstadt v. Worcester Foundation for Experimental Biology, Inc., 425 F .Supp. 318 (D.Mass), aff'd 545 F .2d 222 (1st Cir. 1976) (applying the standard to reprisal cases); the evidence did not support a finding that the complainant was subjected to discrimination as alleged. Consequently, this complaint is now closed with a finding of no discrimination.

Final Agency Decision
Lola B. McGee
Agency Case No. 4E-890-0120-08
Page 38

Appeal Rights

APPEAL TO EEOC

The complainant has the right to appeal the Postal Service's final decision to the:

Director,
Office of Federal Operations
Equal Employment Opportunity Commission (EEOC)
P.O. Box 77960
Washington, DC 20013-8960

within 30 calendar days of receipt of this decision. The complainant must use EEOC Appeal Form 573, a copy of which is enclosed, in connection with the appeal. The complainant may also deliver the appeal in person or by facsimile provided that briefs filed by facsimile are ten or fewer pages in length. Any supporting statement or brief must be submitted to the EEOC within 30 calendar days of filing the appeal. Along with the appeal, the complainant must submit proof to the EEOC that a copy of the appeal and any supporting documentation and/or brief were also submitted to the:

NEEOISO – FAD
National EEO Investigative Services Office
USPS
P. O. Box 21979
Tampa, FL 33622-1979

The complainant is advised that if the complainant files an appeal beyond the 30-day period set forth in the Commission's regulations, the complainant should provide an explanation as to why the appeal should be accepted despite its untimeliness. If the complainant cannot explain why the untimeliness should be excused in accordance with EEOC Regulation 29 C.F.R. 1614.604, the Commission may dismiss the appeal as untimely.

RIGHT TO FILE A CIVIL ACTION

Alternatively, if the complainant is dissatisfied with the Postal Service's decision in this case, the complainant may file a civil action in an appropriate U.S. District Court within 90 calendar days of receipt of the Postal Service's final decision, within 90 calendar days of the EEOC's final decision on any appeal, or after 180 days from the date of filing an appeal with the EEOC if no final decision has been rendered. If the complainant chooses to file a civil action, that action should be styled **Lola B. McGee v. John E. Potter, Postmaster General**. The

Final Agency Decision
Lola B. McGee
Agency Case No. 4E-890-0120-08
Page 39

complainant may also request the court to appoint an attorney for the complainant and to authorize the commencement of that action without the payment of fees, costs, or security. Whether these requests are granted or denied is within the sole discretion of the District Judge. The application must be filed within the same 90-day time period for filing the civil action.

Doris A. Hill

Doris A. Hill Date: 8/10/09
EEO Services Analyst
National EEO Investigative Services Office
P.O. Box 21979
Tampa, FL 33622-1979

Enclosure: EEOC Appeal Form 573

cc:
Complainant
Lola B. McGee
P.O. Box 98272
Las Vegas, NV 89193-8272
Delivery Confirmation No. 0308 3390 0001 7385 5421

District Manager, Human Resources
Nevada-Sierra District
1001 East Sunset Road
Las Vegas, NV 89199-9994

Regional Manager, EEO Compliance & Appeals
USPS, Western Area Office
P. O. Box 300
Denver, Co 80201-0300

Shaun Mossman, Nevada Sierra District Manager allowed, and condoned all of this that happened to me.

Sylvester Black, Western Area Vice President allowed, and condoned all of the demise that happened to me and he is in position to correct it all.

Sunrise Station: (2009) No call for Interview

Winterwood Station: (2009) No call for Interview

Nevada's Culture and History

I did not know at the time that the Nevada Sierra District had never had a Black Postmaster since the beginning of the first installation, which was 1894 and this was 9/2008. Once I filed the EEO"s then the district promoted Yul Melonson as the first Black Executive Postmaster of the Nevada Sierra District. I made history happen by filing my EEO's in 2008. There pictures are on the wall when you walk in the lobby, it's know knowledge for all to see.

Dr. Martin Luther King Jr.

I feel and understand Dr. Martin Luther King Jr.; well he had a dream and I'm aware of the non-violent struggles and marches that he pursued, may God Rest His Soul. I thought that I was special because I did not ask anyone to give me anything, I earned it, but I was not judged on my on merit; I was judged by the color of my skin (Black) and my gender (Female) along with my age (46 yrs. old) at the time.

Dr. King I truly understand about the mountain top, because when you believe in the Lord you just out right get tired of injustice when you're trying to fight a fight that should not be yours to fight; but because you're going through it you believe as you are living the pain it's yours to fight; because faith without works is dead, and you believe that surely there is something that you have to do to help yourself as you see the demise happening to you right before your eyes. The Lord came to me and revealed that I took you through this to help my people, so I truly understand my calling just as Dr. King understood his. When he stated in his speech that "I've seen the mountain top" and he wasn't afraid; I'm not afraid anymore. Black people have endured injustice for eons and yet we still managed to respect, live, love, and work with whites and they just don't understand how we can be treated so badly as a race of people and still have integrity and love in our hearts for all mankind. I'll tell you why, because we know that God is almighty, and he is who he is regardless how others treat us. I did not say as a human being that it doesn't hurt us but deep in the core of our souls we know who sits high and looks low. All will have to account for the fruits that they bare. God knows the true heart of every man; rather you fool your boss, subordinates, employees, neighbors, children, wife, husband, or even yourself, he knows all. As Dr. King Stated: Injustice any where is a threat to justice everywhere.

In December 2008 Robert Reynosa asked me over the telephone "Why do you want to work in the field, it's so tough?" I stated to Robert that it is not the job, I don't have a problem with the position, it's the discrimination, threats, lies, use, and misuse. I told him that I can't take that. I want to be judged on my own merit.

In addition, I did not know that there had only been one black woman who had held the position as Manager, Customer Services in Las Vegas field offices since the first postmaster's installation, which was also in 1894. They were working me as the clean up woman with no intent to promote me. I was never going to be a promoted Manager, Customer Services in the Nevada Sierra District field offices because history of the town had already demonstrated that they were prejudice and racist.

I worked in a hostile work environment, and was discriminated against, lied to by management, treated without dignity and respect, used and misused, wasn't paid my wages, was not allowed to be paid higher level even though I did the work, locked out of the General Mail Facility, even though I needed to go to Injury Compensation, and Labor Relation Offices, after returning to work was not allowed to input my objectives for my FY09, required to call my own office before e coming by without any conduct issues, I was threatened by my boss without an investigation, Memory Loss, Mind Confusion, Prescribed Drugs, and Ultimately, inner Turmoil and Emotional Duress. These issues has caused me to be diagnosed with Post Traumatic Stress Disorder, Major Depressive Disorder, Obsessive Compulsive Disorder, Heart Palpitations without the presence of Heart Disease or blockages – which was considered benign, a Choking Cough, Anxiety, Panic Disorder, Panic Attacks, Agoraphobia, Hearing Loss, Vision impaired, Peripheral Sensory Neuropathy – Nerve Damage, Head Shocks,

After being off work for over six months, I thought that I could go back to work. On March 13, 2009, I was injured from lifting trays and tubs of mail into a hamper for a limited duty carrier to take to the street for other carriers. Because I had just come back to work, I tried to work off the pain but to no avail. I filed a CA-1 on 4/2/09 for injuries to my back, knees, and left thigh. I was diagnosed with Lumbar Radiculopathy–Sciatica, Cervical Facet and Thoracic Facet Syndrome, Sprain Bi-lateral Knees. I was prescribed out patient physical therapy from September 2008 to April 2009. Unfortunately, I had to be put on in home physical therapy when the 3/13/09 lifting injury happened. I had two different in home physical therapy prescriptions. The manager that witnessed the injury denied ever seeing it, but he stated that he did ask me if I was okay. My Neurologist deemed me permanent and stationary and I have just been going to doctors to keep up with my failing health.

On April 13, 2009, I went to my home office in North Las Vegas and had a meeting with my boss, who has never supervised me, and he disrespected me and was very rude, nasty, and denied me my rights. I turned in a CA-1 and a CA-2 and I asked him if he would print out a copy of my 2007 PES report and he stated, no. I then asked him if I could go on the computer and print it out for myself and he stated, no. In addition, he gave me specific instructions to call the office before I come by. I stated that I belong to this office, why do I have to call before I come by. He repeated his instructions to me and I got up and was immediately upset. I got so upset at the meeting to where I had to leave with assistance from my friend who had driven me there. Within an hour of that meeting, while at home, my right arm started hurting from my shoulder down to my finger tips and it collapsed with pain, tingling, and numbness. My heart started palpitating rapidly and I became afraid and called 911. I was taken to the emergency room and was admitted from April 13, 2009 to April 15, 2009. I do not have Hypertension, but I had an elevated blood pressure upon being initially assessed by the paramedics.

Chapter 9
Medical Disability Retirement

Due to the above physical injuries and mental illnesses, I have an attendance problem and I can't make it to work on time. I'm very forgetful and my mind sometimes does not function properly. I can no longer keep up with the fast pace of my required duties. I can not address my employees with the necessary documents of performance anymore because it calls for too much walking back and forth for me. I can not walk for consistent periods anymore. I cannot sit at the computer for any long length of time because it is to painful to sit, walk, or stand for short periods of time. I'm on a Quad cane today and that is hurtful, but I have to do whatever I can to make it easier for me to get around. I can't even brush my teeth with out dropping down to the sink for rest of my legs, knees, and back. I sit in a chair to comb my hair if I feel like combing it that day. I have assistance here now because I can't do certain things on my own. When I sit on the toilet my legs and feet exudes more numbness and pain. I wake up in the middle of the night with pain and spasms in my back, legs, and feet. I have inner turmoil which relects my inability to perform my job eficiently. Because of the pain that I endure every day, all day, I can not perform the basic functions of any job at this time. Due to my physical limitations, I am ashamed to admit that on three separate occasions I defecated on myself.

My doctors do not want me to return to work at the post ofice anymore, because it has put me through to much suffering. I was a good servant who followed instructions and was loyal to my superiors but they were not loyal to me. This entire ordeal has taken away my ability to be myself. I have lost my personality. I was once a very, very physically strong woman and now I'm reduced to barely walking, and that's with assistance. I can not walk the work room loor route to route anymore or assist customers at the window. My position calls for to much consistent different activity in order for me to perform it effectively and eficiently, not to mention the burden that it puts on my disabled body. I am no longer able to meet district policies, procedures, or processes as it relates to my duties and responsibilities of my position.

The position calls for to much activity that my body can't endure anymore. I am no longer able to meet my own standards of quality service to my position that I have achieved time and time again. Also, my mental capacity has been affected by not being able to make the best decisions for the task, and I can't concentrate on the task at hand. Also, I'm not able to set the loor, complete reports, go out on the street, and address my employees upon return like I use to be able to do. I do not have the energy, strength, or ability, and I'm ashamed to have to admit that. That is why I wanted to see if I could do my job once again when I was released to return on 3/9/09. I'm to sick; I must take care of my health. Since I'm sick now and can't do my job, I know that they will eventually terminate me for not being able to perform my required duties, and I have never been in a position like that, it hurts, mentally, physically, and emotionally. I never thought my postal career would end up like this. I worked hard and performed very well and all I wanted was to be treated with dignity, respect, and be judged on my own merit. Instead, I was used, misused, and disrespected and treated like a second class citizen when I got sick. I'm very upset and disappointed about this.

I am limited to a very different lifestyle now as it relates to the way I have to live today and perform my daily activities with my disabilities. I don't think the same way as I once did. I don't make the best decisions for the betterment of my life today because my brain does not think the same way. I do not have the confidence and conviction that I once had. I'm embarrassed by my mental and physical ability today, as it is so limited, from what it used to be. I walk with a limp from the pain. I walk slowly without the ability, to have strength, to move faster, and the pain will not allow me to move at a faster pace anyway. I'm angry, and it's unfortunate that I'm in this position. I pray to God that I get better, because the pain is too severe. It hurts me just to sit on the toilet to use the restroom. I can't even sleep or turn in the bed without pain. I'm not the type of person to take narcotic medications; however, I don't have a choice at this time in my life. I give Glory to God for my 22 years of sobriety. In spite of the medication, I'm still in pain. My pride, dignity, and self respect have been taken away from me. They used me until they could not use me anymore and now they won't even take care of me now that I'm medically disabled. I worked very hard as an acting manager for two and one half years and applied for 17 jobs, but they always found a way to tell me that I did not get the job. I was good enough to improve and clean up ofices but I was not good enough to be promoted. It hurts me to sit, walk, stand, bath, cook, clean, and any other normal duty. At one point, I was not even able to do any of these things because all I wanted to do was sleep. I use to gamble to relieve the stress, but when I went out August 26, 2008; the gambling stopped. I did not have answers to none of my adverse behaviors until August 27, 2008. While in therapy in 2005, I did not believe that I was depressed, but I knew I was in fear. I just thought that I was getting older and I did not have the energy anymore. But one thing I was able to do is go to work. I have to get assistance with daily functions. I can not even drive my vehicle properly and I'm on medication that makes me feel under the inluence and I do not like it at all, but the doctors say that it is necessary. I have gone over and beyond, demonstrated my skill, will, ability, experience, and education; however, I'm the one that is sick, needy, physically and mentally disabled, limited in daily life, libido damaged, relationship is ruined, and I have to learn on a daily basis how to live this life that I have now. It's sad to be me; but I thank God that I'm still alive.

On Februrary 11, 2009, I requested a Lateral to the City of Las Vegas. On the first day of working at the requested site I incurred a lifting injury. My request for this lateral was later denied on April 2, 2009 (the same day that I filed a CA-1 claim for the March 13, 2009 injury). I requested this lateral for several reasons. My letter states to gain continuous upward mobility; but, I intentionally left out one big reason, and that reason is that I cannot work under the current postmaster in North Las Vegas when he is one of the people who caused me to be in the condition that I'm in today. I could not put myself in a compromising position as it relates to my health. I was right; it was proven on April 13, 2009 when I went to the hospital. Due to my medical condition, it is at this time that I have no choice but to medically retire at such a young age of forty-six. It's sad to me, but my health will not allow me to continue to work. I never though that it would end this way; but, I must take care of my health.

November 5, 2008

To: U. S. Department Of Labor/OWCP – Attention: Julia Landry and Cheryl Mendoza
And Injury Compensation - Attention: Joni Payne

From: Lola McGee
File Number: 132198863

This letter is in reference to the physical and mental effects/affects of my CA-1 and CA-2 that I filed for my on the job injuries.

8/25/2008: The threat that was made by my boss Jerry Wilson "You continue to go over my head with Craig and Yul and I'm going to do something about it" made me believe that something was going to happen to me be it physical or written, all I know is that it was going to be negative upon me and I was not going to wait around to see what it was so I left early that day at 1:00pm. I did not nor have I behaved in my duties for any negative acts to be put upon me. Jerry did not know me nor did he know my history with the service, but I was a loyal high performing servant for the postal service, and I did not deserve what ever mental state he was in to be brought upon me, I protected myself while I know Jerry was in a different convicted state of mine and when he said those words to me I could fell and see it. As a result of the threat on 8/25/08 from Jerry I was informed on 8/27/2008 by my doctor (Mary Reed) that I had a Panic Attack. The affects of the Panic Attack or still being revealed as I go to the doctor (Sundance Medical – Heather Harris APN) and the results of tests come in, I will explain. I have nerve damage in both feet and I'm now going to see a Neurologist to get complete affects that the Panic Attack had on my body from head to feet, I have a problem with my equilibrium. I fell down from the floor last night trying to get up on my left leg, the strength just wasn't there. I have always been a physically strong woman, I use to work in the Oil Refineries doing Construction work in my earlier years. My left side appears to me to be the worse; I have more pain in my foot and lower sheen of my left leg. I have a discomfort pain in the top left portion of my buttocks. I have been scheduled for Physical therapy for my weight gain and for the ailing parts of my body as a result of my Panic Attack. I have partial hearing loss in my left ear as a result of my Panic Attack and I will be going to see an ear nose and throat doctor for that. My mind is confused and uncertain which is not the way it operated before the Panic Attack. I do not have clear concise decision making skills at certain times; sometimes this happens on a daily basis. I've had about 10 good days with laughter since the Panic Attack.

Things I knew about as a result of 8/25/2008, I felt threatened by my boss and something negative was going to happen. I knew I did not deserve it and I started hyperventilating, shocks were going down my neck from my head and through out my body, I was afraid, I felt nauseous and I vomited, I was dizzy, my chock coughing started to come back from treatment that I had before and it had gone away. My mind felt like I was retarded because I could not put together any logical competency through my thought process. My heart palpitations were increased and my doctor had been treating me for that for about six months to a year, I don't remember. I literally thought I was going to die because that's how I felt at that time. I was sweating and felt helpless. I felt I was a victim of a paranoid boss that did not see a solution to his success and because I talked to Craig, about the projections and Yul about the condition of the office, when he called me, he was going to hold me accountable for his boss' talking to him. I don't think this was fair nor right of Jerry, if you don't ask questions to your boss' about what they want then how can you succeed. I had already had two and a half years of success as an acting manager, but Jerry's personality and behavior could not allow him to see that. I would not have been sent there to Meadow Mesa had I not had the ability and skills to perform. The Panic Attack caused my body great dysfunction and illness beyond my imagination.

I do not think that the CA-1 should be converted all together with the CA-2 because what happened on 8/25/08 is totally different than what happen from 9/2006 – 8/2008, and I will explain. I'm now forced to use my own sick leave, pay my on co-pays, and all of this is causing me more harm while I'm off trying to get well. I feel at this time that the DOL or the Postal Service gives a dam about me as a loyal servant. I was injured on the job with a traumatic injury and I should be taking care of as if it means something to the powers that be just as well as it is devastating and troubling to me as I live with myself each and every day. I did not cause this on my self and I should not have to use my medical coverage to take care of myself because the service does not care, it's wrong. I feel that I'm still being mistreated as I will explain the CA-2 injury.

9/2006 – 8/2008 I was detailed to several offices as the acting manager and I performed very well and that is why I was continuously used as an acting manager for over two and one half years. Because of the submitting of 15 manager position over the period of time I developed depression the caused me to have the energy to perform at work only. Every refusal I kept stuffing and re-applying. I developed an automatic system that would allow me to go to work and perform but the entire rest of my life was not being performed in any way shape or form. I stopped cleaning my home. I did not have the strength to even wash the dishes. I sleep all day every day that I was off except while I went out to gamble, because it brought me a since of relief from the depression. Since I have been off work (8/25/08) I have not had one urge to gamble and I've got myself back in control of that demon. I was once an occasional gambler but with the mistreatment and Discrimination I found piece and relief to do it and I was no longer in control and I could not understand it because that is not who I am normally. I'm very responsible and I have discipline in my life, but for some reason I could not understand why I was gambling to a fault. I have that answer now, the discrimination and mistreatment needed relief in order for me to go on and endure my job under the circumstances. I felt misused and abuse, misunderstood and disrespected. I was taken for granted and I accepted it for fear of reprisal, and the opportunity of not being promoted. I stopped cooking, shopping, visiting, and even having sex. My life was out of control and I did not know how to fix it. My family and friends suffered the behavior and I could not see myself. All I thought about was the post office and my responsibility to it. I'm a very hard worker so I was able to take a lot. All I did was stuffed the disappointments and had hope for the next opportunity. The only physical affects that I had at this time were Heart Palpitations, Sleeping all day, and a Choking Cough. I love to eat but I did not even go out to dinner as I would normally do. I had no energy, and I would often as the doctor why did I not have energy to do anything (Kochy Tang) Seven Hills Medical Center. She said that I'm not eating right and stress from the job. I was lied to and it was a joke. I was never considered for promotion and I could not understand why, so I put two and two together and I realized that the only people that were being promoted were White; some of them with less experience than I did and they had not even been a promoted supervisor as long as I've been, but it was what it was. I was not represented in a concern manner by my superiors when erroneous grievances were filed against me and it was hurtful. I had no social life, and it was stressful on my significant other and my family. I was ude, critical, and disrespectful because my normal communication skills were being massed by the Major Depression. I started to forget things around late 2007, and that was really surprising because I'm normally a very thorough person. I had to have my family and friends remind me of very small things and it was embarrassing. I did not know all what was wrong with me at the time but my life was not what it once was and I could not see it nor could I help myself when I was confronted with things, I would just say what I had to say and shut them down. I was in denial and I did not believe that I had depression. I did not think like I thought a depressed person thought so I thought every one that said something to me was wrong.

The reason for this letter is to let you know the difference's between the CA-1 and the CA-2 and why it was appropriate to file both forms. The CA-1 happened at on a specific day and time that caused tremendous trauma to me and my body, and the CA-2 happened over a period of time with a host of different circumstances that I had to work under, and I was doing it until the trauma came on 8/25/08 (The threat from my boss Jerry Wilson).

I need to get well and it is not right for me to have to pay my own way for my healing when it was caused by the post office. You cannot take out the CA-1 because had it not happened then I would still be at work. Also, it has caused me a great deal of illness in which I have never had before in my life. If you take it out then you are saying that 8/25/08 happened along with 9/2006 – 8/2008 and that is not true or correct. There are different medical issues let alone different circumstances that separate the two. Also, you cannot take away the CA-2 because it has a set of continuous mistreatment, discrimination, disrespect, misuse, not being treated with dignity, and separate medical issues that goes along with it, not to mention my life style changes that has had and adverse affect on my entire life. I urge you to do the right thing and take care of me because I did not ask for this and please do not let technicalities play a part in doing me wrong, it's not fair to me. I am greatly ill and I need to be taking care of so that I can return to normalcy, I deserve that as a human being just as you would want too.

Sincerely
Lola McGee

November 5, 2008

To: Cory Richards

From: Lola McGee

Re: My updated 1723 for Meadow Mesa

Hello Cory,

This letter is in reference to the telephone conversation that I had with you today about my higher level pay for my detail at Meadow Mesa Station. I asked you to send or fax me a 1723 so that I could update it since I'm now out sick, as of 8/25/2008 and you stated to me that you were not going to send or fax me a 1723 because you were not going to put me on higher level.

It is my request that you update my 1723 higher level detail at Meadow Mesa Station because if Jerry Wilson had not threatened me on 8/25/08 then I would not have gotten sick and would currently be in my detail position. I have never been released from a detail because of my performance are lack of skill level, so I am made to believe that because my arbitrary end date that I put on my 1723, which is not unusual because we have to update 1723's all the time, was at the end of the Fiscal Year, and I just so happen to be out on an on the job injury, you are holding me responsible for being out and for filing EEO's. This is not right, fair, and it's discriminatory. This is the kind of stuff that does not allow me to get well sooner than later, it's unprofessional, immature, and lack of leadership skills rather you like that I'm out or not it is what it is and I did not do it to myself.

There are three pay periods that I need adjusted from when Jerry was there and one since you've been there.

Meadow Mesa Station still has an acting manager there an as long as I'm out I'm entitled to the EAS-22 higher level pay. I've been mistreated enough and I'm not taking it anymore, it only makes me sick. If I were not qualified for the detail then I would have never been there. I plead with you to do the right thing and pay me higher level pay, because it's the principle about the whole situation not the money.

Sincerely

Lola McGee
A/Manager, Customer Services
Meadow Mesa Station

Check stub not paid properly even though my leave slip was in a month in advance pay period—1/2009. Corey was now the post-master of North Las Vegas and he was responsible for paying me.

PAYLOC	FINANCE NO.	EMPLOYEE NAME	EMPLOYEE ID	PAY PERIOD	SERIAL NUMBER
001	31-6200	L B MCGEE	03413020	01 09	00034686

DETAIL EARNINGS

WK	RSC/LEV	RATE	CODE	TYP	HOURS	PAY
				L	4800	142963
INSURANCE INCOME					97	

GROSS TO NET

	THIS PERIOD	YEAR-TO-DATE
GROSS PAY	142963	142963
FED TAX S8	1850	1850
ST TAX NVS0	00	00
RETIRE 8	1144	1144
MEDICARE	2046	2046
UN S	800	800
ALOT	4665	4665
TSPLG	7691	7691
HP111	1957	1957
SOSEC	8748	8748

LEAVE STATUS

ANNUAL LEAVE	
FROM PREV YR	11200
EARNED THIS YR	14200
EARNED BAL	25400
USED THIS YR	12000
USED THIS PP	
BALANCE	13400
SICK LEAVE	
FROM PREV YR	59864
EARNED THIS YR	9200
USED THIS YR	46400
USED THIS PP	3200
BALANCE	22664
LEAVE WITHOUT PAY	
THIS PP	3200
CUMULATIVE	3200
BOND UNAPPL BAL #ISSUED	
EE	
I	
USPS RETIREMENT	

EARNINGS STATEMENT

PS FORM 1223-B, JUNE 1985

NET PAY 1140.62 NT BK 4116.39

!400012401071!
POSTMASTER/MANAGER
1414 E LAKE MEAD BLVD
NORTH LAS VEGAS NV 89030-9998

Cory My Check is not Correct, 32 hrs of LWOP, And my Annual is not Correct (LWOP)

DATE 01-09-2009
00034686

************AUTO** 3-DIGIT 890

LOLA B MCGEE
7582 CYPRESS TREE ST
LAS VEGAS NV 89123-0553

HUAMN RESOURCES
LAS VEGAS, NV 89199-9994
UNITED STATES
POSTAL SERVICE

DATE: November 24, 2008

SUBJECT: 2009 Core Requirements

Delivery Confirmation
#0301 0120 0008 6387 4151

TO: Lola McGee
7582 Cypress Tree Street
Las Vegas NV 89123-0553

Lola,

This correspondence is in reference to your telephone call to Maggie Lara concerning the input of your FY 2009 PES Objectives. You also shared with Ms. Lara that you are out on Workers Compensation.

The following was obtained from the Quick-Start Guide for Evaluators, Version 5, October 2008:

> **Reason for No Core Requirements:** An employee who **has not** yet submitted his/her objectives for review will be noted with an "FY XXXX Core Requirements Not Submitted" message. The employee must enter objectives and submit them to you for approval —OR— you must click the **Reason for No Core Requirements** button next to the employee's name.

The following is an excerpt from the FY 2008 Pay-for-Performance Program Administrative Rules for EAS Employees:

> What happens if an employee is on OWCP LWOP or FMLA LWOP?
>
> Employees on OWCP LWOP or FMLA LWOP for any part of the fiscal year, must be evaluated based upon his/her performance while at work.

Lola, just as Maggie and I told you over the telephone on Tuesday, November 18th, 2008, you may submit your 2009 objectives when you are cleared to come back to work.

Angela Bush
PES Coordinator
Nevada-Sierra District

cc; Corey Richards
Maggie Lara

1001 E. SUNSET RD.
LAS VEGAS, NV 89199-9994
TEL: (702) 361-9325

4/13/09 Corey Caused me to be picked up by ambulance and admitted into the Hospital after a meeting with him.

LATE NOTICE

MedicWest Ambulance, Inc.
P.O. Box 3429
Modesto, CA 95353

ACCOUNT NUMBER: 001311093

TRIP # 300-09027972-01 ACCT # 001311093
PATIENT NAME LOLA B. MCGEE
DATE OF SERVICE 04/13/2009
AMOUNT DUE 954.52 DUE DATE 07/03/2009

10Z 2465496 00 00000875 00000886
8751 AT 0.357
LOLA B. MCGEE
PO BOX 98272
LAS VEGAS NV 89193-8272

REMIT PAYMENT TO:
3000902797201

MEDICWEST AMBULANCE, INC.
PO BOX 98595
LAS VEGAS, NV 89193-8595

PLEASE CHARGE MY: ☐ VISA ☐ MASTERCARD ☐ DISCOVER ☐ AMERICAN EXPRESS
ACCOUNT ☐☐☐☐☐☐☐☐☐☐☐☐☐☐☐☐ EXPIRATION DATE ☐☐☐☐ AMOUNT PAID $ ______
CARD HOLDER NAME(PRINT): ______ SIGNATURE: ______

PLEASE DETACH AND RETURN THIS PORTION WITH YOUR PAYMENT

PATIENT NAME	ACCOUNT NO.	TRIP NO.	INVOICE DATE
LOLA B. MCGEE	001311093-0000	300-09027972-01	06/23/2009

DATE OF SERVICE	SERVICE FROM	SERVICE TO
04/13/2009	2121 E WARM SPRINGS RD 2162	ST ROSE SIENA CAMPUS

IMPORTANT MESSAGES

Your account is now PAST DUE. Your immediate response is necessary to cease further collection activity. Please remit payment today or call our customer service department at (800) 913-9106 if you have any questions. Thank you.

CODE	DESCRIPTION	UNITS	UNIT CHARGE		TOTAL CHARGE
A0427	ALS1 EMERG	1	796.74		796.74
A0425	ALS MILEAGE	7	22.54		157.78

LOLA B MCGEE
R59083999
111 06/26/2004
RX Bin # 610415
RX Group # 65006500
AdvancePCS

TOTAL CHARGES DUE 954.52

SEE REVERSE SIDE FOR INSURANCE INFORMATION

Send billing inquiries to: **MEDICWEST AMBULANCE, INC.**
P.O. BOX 3429 • MODESTO, CA 95353
Phone Number: 1-800-913-9106
Keep this portion for your records.
Fax Number: 1-209-236-8591

February 10, 2009

Change of Address Request

To: Eric Wilson/U. S. Postal Service – NEEIOSO
Investigator: Q. VanBenSchoten

From: Lola McGee
Case Number: 4E-890-0120-08 (Formal Filed November 1, 2008)

To all concerned,

Mr. Eric Wilson per our telephone conversation today, I am sending you this faxed letter to put in a request to change my address with the above mentioned people and agencies as it relates to my case number above. In our conversation today you stated it is the requirements of the NEEOISO/EEOC that the dates of my case be prolonged to 360 days because of the January 15, 2009 issues that were amended to the file. Even though I don't agree with this decision because I think it is an adverse action towards the complainant; I guess I'll have to accept it.

My old address was: 7582 Cypress Tree St. Las Vegas, Nevada 89123-0553

My new address is: P. O. Box 98272 Las Vegas, Nevada 89193-8272

My telephone numbers remain the same: Home (702) 260-0876; Cell (562) 889-2662.

Thank you
Lola McGee

* * * * *

February 11, 2009

Request for Lateral

To: Yul Melonson, Postmaster Las Vegas
Robert Reynosa, Manager, Customer Services Operations – Las Vegas
Corey Richards, Postmaster – North Las Vegas

From: Lola McGee
Supervisor, Customer Services
North Las Vegas Post Office

Hello Gentlemen,

I, Lola McGee, would like to request a lateral to the City of Las Vegas because there are more opportunities there for me. I have been assigned to North Las Vegas since I arrived in May 2004 and have excelled in my duties as a supervisor in various operations on both sides of the house. In addition, I have received several accolades for my performance and leadership; also, I have given of myself in the community of North Las Vegas by donating time to the Nevada Reading League.

It is at this time that I would like to continue to broaden my horizon and gain upward mobility; because, I have the experience, skills, ability, and desire to become a promoted Manager, Customer Services. I believe with the opportunities in the larger City of Las Vegas, I can once again utilize and demonstrate my knowledge of the positions and have a positive impact by being an asset rather than a liability.

We are in trying times now and I want to be apart of the upward spiral, to the top, for the Nevada Sierra District, once again, just as I have done in North Las Vegas under the leadership of my previous postmasters. It would be an honor for me to participate in the challenges that we face today along with rising to the occasion to help conquer the hurdles.

I want to thank you in advance for your time in acknowledging my request and I look forward to hearing from you in the near future.

Sincerely

Lola McGee
Supervisor, Customer Services
North Las Vegas Post Office
1414 E. Lake Mead Blvd.
North Las Vegas, Nevada 89030

* * * * *

Department of Labor's OWCP March 6, 2009 denial letter of August 25, 2008 claim for threat and mental illnesses.

File Number: 132198863
CA-1042-NO-0

U.S. DEPARTMENT OF LABOR

EMPLOYMENT STANDARDS ADMINISTRATION
OFFICE OF WORKERS' COMP PROGRAMS
PO BOX 8300 DISTRICT 13 SFC
LONDON, KY 40742-8300
Phone: (415) 625-7500

March 6, 2009

Date of Injury: 08/25/2008
Employee: LOLA B. MCGEE

LOLA B MCGEE
PO BOX 98272
LAS VEGAS, NV 89193-8272

Dear Ms. MCGEE:

Your claim for compensation benefits has been disallowed for the reason stated in the enclosed copy of the formal decision. This was based on all evidence of record and on the assumption that all available evidence has been submitted. If you disagree with the decision, you may follow any one of the courses of action outlined on the attached appeal rights.

Sincerely,

Cheryl Mendoza
Senior Claims Examiner

Enclosures: Formal decision with appeal rights

UNITED STATES POSTAL SERVICE
NEVADA-SIERRA PERFORMANCE CLUSTER
INJURY COMPENSATION OFFICE
1001 EAST SUNSET ROAD
LAS VEGAS, NV 89199

Case Number: 132198863
Employee: LOLA B. MCGEE
Date: March 6, 2009

FEDERAL EMPLOYEES' COMPENSATION ACT APPEAL RIGHTS

If you disagree with the attached decision, you have the right to request an appeal. If you wish to request an appeal, you should review these appeal rights carefully and decide which appeal to request. There are 3 different types of appeal: HEARING (this includes either an Oral Hearing, or a Review of the Written Record), RECONSIDERATION, and ECAB REVIEW. YOU MAY ONLY REQUEST ONE TYPE OF APPEAL AT THIS TIME.

Place an "X" on the attached form indicating which appeal you are requesting. Complete the information requested at the bottom of the form. Place the form on top of any material you are submitting. Then mail the form with attachments to the address listed for the type of appeal that you select. Always write the type of appeal you are requesting on the outside of the envelope ("HEARING REQUEST", "RECONSIDERATION REQUEST", or "ECAB REVIEW"). Your appeal rights are as follows:

1. **HEARING:** If your injury occurred on or after July 4, 1966, and you have not requested reconsideration, as described below, you may request a **Hearing**. To protect your right to a hearing, any request for a hearing must be made before any request for reconsideration by the District Office (5 U.S.C. 8124(b)(1)). **Any hearing request must also be made in writing, within 30 calendar days after the date of this decision, as determined by the postmark of your letter.** (20 C.F.R. 10.616). There are two forms of hearing. You may request either one or the other, but not both.
a. One form of Hearing is an **Oral Hearing.** An informal oral hearing is conducted by a hearing representative at a location near your home or by teleconference/videoconference. You may present oral testimony and written evidence in support of your claim. Any person authorized by you in writing may represent you at an oral hearing. At the discretion of the hearing representative, an oral hearing may be conducted by teleconference or videoconference.
b. The other form of a Hearing is a **Review of the Written Record.** This is also conducted by a hearing representative. You may submit additional written evidence, which must be sent with your request for review. You will not be asked to attend or give oral testimony.

2. **RECONSIDERATION:** If you have additional evidence or legal argument that you believe will establish your claim, you may request, in writing, that OWCP reconsider this decision. **The request must be made within one calendar year of the date of the decision**, clearly state the grounds upon which reconsideration is being requested, and be accompanied by relevant evidence not previously submitted. This evidence might include medical reports, sworn statements, or a legal argument not previously made, which apply directly to the issue addressed by this decision. In order to ensure that you receive an independent evaluation of the new evidence, persons other than those who made this determination will reconsider your case. (20 C.F.R. 10.605-610)

3. **REVIEW BY THE EMPLOYEES' COMPENSATION APPEALS BOARD (ECAB):** If you believe that all available evidence that would establish your claim has already been submitted, you have the right to request review by the ECAB (20 C.F.R. 10.625). The ECAB will review only the evidence received prior to the date of this decision (20 C.F.R. Part 501). (Effective November 19, 2008, ECAB has changed its Rules of Procedure on the time limit to appeal and has eliminated its practice of allowing one year to file an appeal. **Request for review by the ECAB must be made within 180 days from the date of this decision.** More information on the new Rules is available at www.dol.gov/ecab.

If you request reconsideration or a hearing (either oral or review of the written record), OWCP will issue a decision that includes your right to further administrative review of that decision.

File Number: 132198863
mtd-sfc-NO-0

MEMORANDUM TO THE DIRECTOR
IN THE CASE OF LOLA B. MCGEE
FILE # 132198863
March 6, 2009

The issue for determination is: whether the claimed emotional condition was sustained while in the performance of duty under the Federal Employees' Compensation Act (FECA).

The claimant, date of birth, 07/07/62, is employed a Customer Service Supervisor with the US Postal Service in Las Vegas, NV. On 08/29/08, the claimant filed a timely Notice of Occupational Disease (CA-2) and a Notice of Traumatic Injury (CA-1) claiming post-traumatic stress disorder and major depressive disorder due to unfair and discrimination tactics and verbal threats from OIC Jerry Wilson on 08/25/08.

Submitted with the CA-2 and CA-1 were two copies of a letter dated 08/18/08 from Corey Richards, Selecting Official; copy of an email from the claimant to Joni Payne, HRMS dated 09/04/08; the claimant's statements dated 08/26/08, 08/27/08, 09/02/08; the claimant's statement dated 08/29/08 regarding her request for medical paperwork; a statement dated 09/03/08 from Randy Brooks, Assistant Station Manager; a statement dated 09/03/08 from John R. Bell, Supervisor Customer Service; and a brief medical note dated 08/27/08 from Mary J. Reed, Ph.D with a diagnosis of post-traumatic stress disorder and major depressive disorder.

By letter dated 09/19/08, the Office requested additional factual evidence and a comprehensive medical report. The Office also requested the employing agency respond to the claimant's allegations by letter dated 09/19/08. On 10/10/08, the Office received an Attending Physician's Report (CA-20) dated 10/8/08 from Mary Reed, Ph.D. with a diagnosis of post-traumatic stress disorder, depression, and major depressive disorder recurrent and a CA-7 Claim for Compensation for leave without pay for the period covering 10/10/08 through 10/24/08. On 10/15/08, the Office received copies of employees' documents for Contributions to Core Requirements for Fiscal Year 2006; copy of Information for Pre-Complaint Counseling form; another copy of the claimant's 8/29/08 statement; copy of the claimant's 9/11/08 response to OIC Jerry Wilson's 9/2/08 statement ; copy of an email from the claimant to Monique Adams; another copy of the Contributions to Core Requirements documentation; copy of a Formal Step A Interview dated 9/23/08; copy of an email from Tom Martin to the claimant and other employees; copy of a letter dated 9/24/08 from the claimant to B. J. Clay; copy of an email from Phyllis Joiner to the claimant and other employees; the claimant's statement dated 10/9/08; copy of an illegible psychiatric progress note dated 6/8/07 from Eugene Rosenman, M.D.; a medical report dated 10/2/08 from Robert Croke, M.D. with a diagnosis of paroxysmal ventricular tachycardia, palpitations, heart murmur, and chest pain; copy of a 10/3/08 physical examination report; another report dated 9/19/08 with numerous medical conditions including post-traumatic stress and depression; an email dated 4/15/08 from Shelby Krueger-Duncan to the claimant and other employees; a medical report dated 10/8/08 from Mary Reed, Ph.D., with a diagnosis of depression and post-traumatic stress disorder; copy of a 8/26/08 Information for Pre-Complaint Counseling document; the claimant's statement dated 9/30/08; copy of an email dated 9/12/08 from Joe Acosta to the claimant and another employee; copy of an extensive email dated 7/23/08 from the claimant to other employees; copy of a Step A Grievance Decision dated 6/30/06 with a decision of "Not Resolved"; a medical report dated 9/9/08 with numerous diagnoses including depression and post-traumatic stress; copy of a 9/9/08 statement from the claimant regarding higher level pay, sick leave and continuation of pay; copy of a 9/25/08 Information for Pre-Complaint Counseling form; copy of the claimant's 8/29/08 statement to her immediate supervisor regarding Jerry Wilson, Acting Postmaster CA-1 and CA2 forms; another copy of the claimant's 8/29/08 statement; copy of an email dated 8/18/08 regarding the claimant's application for Vacancy Announcement for Manager Customer Service position indicating another candidate was selected; copy of the original 8/18/08 letter to the claimant from Corey Richards, Selecting Official; copy of

File Number: 132198863
mtd-sfc-NO-0

page 2 of the claimant's 9/8/08 statement; copy of an email from Joe Acosta to the claimant and another employee; another copy of the email dated 7/23/08; another copy of the 6/30/06 Step A Grievance Decision; another copy of the 4/15/08 email; copy of the claimant's statement dated 9/30/08; another copy of the Contributions to Core Requirements documents; another copy of the 9/9/08 Information for Pre-Complaint Counseling; another copy of the claimant's 8/29/08 statement; a copy of the claimant's Contributions to Core Requirements for Fiscal Year 2006 dated 1/6/07; copy of email from the claimant to Joni Payne, HRMS dated 9/4/08 regarding the claimant's CA-2; another copy of the medical report dated 10/8/08 from Mary Reed, Ph.D.; another copy of 9/9/08 medical report; another copy of the 9/19/08 medical report; another copy of the 10/3/08 medical report; another copy of the 10/2/08 medical report from Robert Croke, M.D.; another copy of the illegible 6/8/07 psychiatric progress note from Eugene Rosenman, M.D.; another copy of the 8/26/08 Information for Pre-Complain Counseling; another copy of the claimant's 9/9/08 statement regarding higher level pay, sick leave, and continuation of pay; a copy of the 9/25/08 Information for Pre-Complaint Counseling; another copy of the 8/29/08 statement from the claimant regarding Acting Postmaster Jerry Wilson; another copy of the 8/29/08 statement regarding the claimant's CA-1 and CA-2; another copy of page 2 of the claimant's 9/8/08 statement; another copy of the 8/18/08 email; another copy of the 8/18/08 letter; copy of the claimant's statement dated 10/9/08; another copy of the 9/23/08 Formal Step A Interview; copy of an email dated 6/27/08 from Tom Martin to the claimant and other employees; another copy of the 8/25/08 email; another copy of the 7/15/08 email; another copy of the 9/24/08 letter to B. J. Clay; another copy of the 10/8/08 Attending Physician's Report dated 10/8/08 from Mary Reed, Ph.D.; copy of statement dated 10/17/08 regarding why a CA-1 was filed in addition to the CA-2; another copy of the 10/17/08 letter; the claimant's statement dated 11/5/08; copy of documentation of the claimant's attendance for physical therapy dated 11/10/08; copy of physical therapy notes dated 11/10/08; copy of medical report dated 11/20/08 from Frederick Goll, III, M.D. with a diagnosis of sensorineural hearing loss, tinnitus, and laryngopharyngeal reflux; another copy of the 11/20/08 medical report; copy of physical therapy note dated 12/17/08; another copy of the claimant's 9/2/08 statement; copy of statement dated 1/9/09 from Manager Grady Griffin; copy of 10/23/08 medical report from 10/23/08 medical report from Robert Croke, M.D. with a current diagnosis of paroxysmal ventricular tachycardia, palpitations, heart murmur, chest pain; another copy of the 10/2/08 medical report from Robert Croke, M.D.; copy of 9/9/08 medical report from Robert Croke, M.D.; copy of 1/26/09 medical report from Mary Reed, Ph.D. with a diagnosis of major depressive disorder, single episode, post-traumatic stress disorder, and panic disorder without agoraphobia; another copy of the 9/9/08 Information for Pre-Complaint Counseling; copy of the claimant's resume; copy of letter to EEO dated 1/29/09 from the claimant; letter dated 2/4/09 acknowledging receipt of information; copy of 1/7/09 Information for Pre-Complaint Counseling; copy of letter dated 2/11/09 from the claimant to Yul Melonson, Postmaster; 2/10/09 Change of Address Request from the claimant to Eric Wilson and Q. VanBenSchoten; copy of an email dated 8/13/08; copy of EEO Acknowledgement of Amendment to Complaint, Revised dated 2/4/09; copy of letter dated 8/13/08 to the claimant acknowledging receipt of her application; a MRI report dated 1/26/09; another copy of the 1/26/09 medical report from Dr. Reed; a medical slip dated 2/17/09 indicating return to work once approved by psychiatry and cardiology; a medical slip dated 2/17/09 continuing physical therapy; document regarding peripheral neuropathy; copy of medical report dated 2/12/09 from Jimmy John Novero, M.D. with an impression of mild sensory peripheral neuropathy and paresthesias; copy of 1/13/09 x-ray report of the lumbar spine; copy of 1/13/09 x-ray report of the cervical spine; a medical note dated 2/26/09 from Mary Reed, Ph.D. stating the claimant can return to work on 3/9/09; a medical report dated 2/17/09 from Robert Croke, M.D. indicating the claimant is able to return to full duty.

File Number: 132198863
mtd-sfc-NO-0

THE CLAIMANT HAS ALLEGED THAT THE FOLLOWING EVENTS HAVE OCCURRED:

1) The claimant alleges she has been repeatedly subjected to unfair tactics and discrimination on the part of higher management and due to race and gender.

2) The claimant alleges she received a low rating.

3) The claimant alleges she put in for other positions but the positions were given to other employees. The only employees promoted were Caucasian

4) OIC Jerry Wilson would make decisions for the claimant and her staff.

5) OIC Jerry Wilson wanted to change the claimant's start time to 8:00 a.m.

6) On 8/25/08, the claimant alleges OIC Jerry Wilson made a threatening open-ended statement, "You continue to go over my head with Craig and Yul and I'm going to do something about it."

7) OIC Jerry Wilson did not mail the claimant Forms CA-1 and CA-2 as she requested.

8) Postmaster Craig Colton talked loud to the claimant while in front of other employees.

9) A union steward filed a Joint Statement of Violence against the claimant in retaliation for a union officer, who was a carrier at the Meadow Mesa Station.

10) The Union is trying to retaliate against the claimant for assisting in the termination of an employee.

11) Supervisor Steven Phaup used devious tactics to mess up the claimant's schedule and daily plan.

12) Postmaster Colton would take Supervisor Steven Phaup to lunch on a regular basis but never took the claimant.

OIC Jerry Wilson responded to the claimant's allegation, as follows:

1) On 8/08/08, the first day the claimant was to report to the Meadow Mesa Station, the claimant called and stated she was running late. OIC Wilson informed the claimant that he expected her to be in regular attendance and on time for work.

2) The claimant was difficult to speak with when it came to day-to-day issues with the operations. The claimant made it clear that she did not manage based on the policies and processes of the district. OIC Wilson informed the claimant that they would follow the policies, processes, and procedures of the district and service.

3) The claimant had issues with her reporting time for work. Her schedule was 7am to 4pm. OIC Wilson informed the claimant he was considering changing her schedule to 8am to 5pm. The claimant indicated she would be on time and asked for her schedule to remain 7am to 4pm.

4) The claimant informed OIC Wilson that she was considering filing an EEO complaint because she did not receive the Manager of Customer Service position at the Huntridge Station and because there were no black female managers in the city of Las Vegas.

5) The claimant did not report to work until 10:45am on 8/12/08 and when OIC Wilson asked why she did not call the claimant stated she went to speak with someone about not getting the manager position at the Huntridge Station. OIC Wilson told the claimant she needed to pursue that on her own time. He reminded the claimant of previous conversations regarding her habit of not reporting to work on time and told her this would be her last chance he would give her. If she reported to work

Department of Labor/OWCP Letter Dated September 19, 2008, questioning me again

File Number: 132198863
OD_PSY_C-O-I

U.S. DEPARTMENT OF LABOR

EMPLOYMENT STANDARDS ADMINISTRATION
OFFICE OF WORKERS' COMP PROGRAMS
PO BOX 8300 DISTRICT 13 SFC
LONDON, KY 40742-8300
Phone: (415) 625-7500

September 19, 2008

Date of Injury: 08/25/2008
Employee: LOLA B. MCGEE

LOLA B MCGEE
75282 CYPRESS TREE STREET
LAS VEGAS, NV 89123

Dear Ms. MCGEE:

I am writing in reference to the claim for benefits under the Federal Employees' Compensation Act which you filed for an emotional condition. The materials which you have submitted to date have been reviewed. We have received your CA-2, a CA-1 form, your statements dated 8/26/08, 8/27/08, and 9/2/08, and two copies of a medical note from Mary Reed, Ph.D, dated 8/27/08 diagnosing Post-Traumatic Stress Disorder and Major Depressive Disorder. This is not sufficient for this office to determine whether you are eligible for benefits under the FECA because additional factual and medical evidence is needed. Please provide the information requested below to OWCP (above address) at your earliest convenience. Please provide as much detail as possible.

Describe in detail the employment related conditions or incidents which you believe contributed to your illness. What aspects of your employment did you consider detrimental to your health? Do not respond in terms of general stress or strain. Be as specific as possible. Identify any relevant dates, locations, co-workers, supervisors, required duties, etc. For events or duties which you identify, describe how often they occurred and for how long. Provide names, addresses and phone numbers of any person who can verify your allegations. Please provide a copy of your response to this item to your employer for concurrence.

Have you filed any grievance, EEO complaint, or any other action related to the working conditions related to this claim? If so, please provide copies of all relevant documents including conclusions of fact finders and final decisions if available. If not available, when do you anticipate they will be?

Describe all sources of stress outside your Federal employment. Have you recently experienced situations in your personal or family life that include substance abuse, divorce, death or illness of a loved one? Describe your hobbies and any outside employment.

Provide details of all prior emotional conditions which you have experienced.

Have you ever been under the care of a psychiatrist, psychologist, or sought counseling? If so, for what reason? What benefit did you receive? Provide all relevant details.

Have you ever been hospitalized for an emotional condition. If so, when and where?

UNITED STATES POSTAL SERVICE
NEVADA-SIERRA PERFORMANCE CLUSTER
INJURY COMPENSATION OFFICE
1001 EAST SUNSET ROAD
LAS VEGAS, NV 89199

File Number: 132198863
OD_PSY_C-O-I

Do you, or have you ever taken medication for an emotional condition? If so, when and what medication?

Why do you feel that your job activities contributed to your condition?

Provide medical records from all prior treatment for an emotional condition.

Provide a comprehensive medical report from your treating physician (**a psychiatrist or licensed clinical psychologist**) which describes your symptoms; results of examinations and tests; diagnosis; the treatment provided; the effect of treatment; and the doctor's opinion, with medical reasons, on the cause of your condition. **Specifically, if your doctor feels that exposure or incidents in your Federal employment contributed to your condition, an explanation of which incidents and how such exposure contributed should be provided.**

OWCP may correspond directly with a physician or any other party who may be able to provide information which will help the Office make a decision on your eligibility for benefits under the FECA. Our efforts are intended to assist you in the collection of evidence. Please understand that it is ultimately your responsibility, as the claimant, to provide or ensure the provision of all evidence needed to decide your claim, including all information requested directly by the Office. Whenever a request for information is initiated by this Office, a copy will be sent to you so you may ensure that the requested information is provided as promptly as possible.

This Office is committed to rendering a timely decision on your claim. A reasonable period will be allowed for the submission of all requested evidence (approximately 30 days). If we have not received the requested information, an indication that it is forthcoming, or evidence that the information is not necessary to decide your claim, we will be required to render a decision on your claim based on the evidence in file.

If you do not understand any portion of this request, or are unable to provide all requested information for any reason, you should call or write to this Office immediately and request clarification or assistance.

Sincerely,

Julia Landry

Julia Landry
Claims Examiner 11/4/08

March 24, 2009

To: U. S. Department of Labor
Office of Workers' Comp Programs
P. O. Box 8300 District 13 SFC
London, KY 40742-8300

From: Lola McGee
P. O. Box 98272
Las Vegas, NV 89193-8272

Re: File Number: 132198863

Dear Julia Landry and Cheryl Mendoza,

I am in receipt of your denial letter of the file number listed above and I must say that it comes as a huge surprise to me because I can't believe that I was denied a CA-1 and CA-2 claim and I'm still sick from my on the job injuries. You stated that as of March 9, 2009 (Post Mark) date of your letter written on March 6, 2009 that my claim has been disallowed. I would like at this time to request the complete file that you based your decision on and all of the information that was forwarded to your office by me (Lola McGee) and the local injury compensation office. If there be any documents that I am not privy to please acknowledge them in your response. You were forwarded by the local injury compensation office the original letter from Dr. Mary Reed and a letter from Dr. Michael Shepard (The very first Certified doctor that I saw regarding the issues with Steven Phaup), and I want to know if those documents were included in the file as well when you made your decision of disallowing my claims (CA-1 and CA-2). There is a possibility that I did not explain myself correctly of the events that happened to me; however, my medical documentation is surely facts, and I live with these conditions on a daily basis.

In addition, you have misquoted me in your letter by stating that I said Postmaster Craig Colton talked loud to me while in front of other employees; I never said that.

Also, I will address the other untruths of your letter when I file my appeal. There is a lot of information that was left out and if your office has different policies and regulations than the NEEOISO, then why was the EEO activity even requested by you.

I do not understand the letter completely and I would like for the claims examiner to give me a call if it is permissible. I will send my appeal request in at a later date. Home: (702) 260-0876 and Cell: (562) 889-2662

Sincerely
Lola McGee

April 5, 2009

To: Branch of Hearings and Review
P. O. Box 37117
Washington, DC 20013-7117

From: Lola McGee
P. O. Box 89272
Las Vegas, Nevada 89193-8272

Case Number: 132198863 – Oral Hearing – By Telephone Appeal
Letter dated March 6, 2009 and Postmarked for March 9, 2009

I am asking for a Oral Hearing via telephone - Appeal of my claim number listed above based on new medical documentation that your office never received because I misplaced it in the process of trying to manage so many documents and changes that has happened in my life since your September 19, 2008 letter requesting information from me to support my claim. Also, I have up to date medical from my Neurologist (4/9/09). In addition, I will address the untruths that are in your letter that are perceived as facts.

Because of the Steven Phaup issues in 2004 and 2005, I started seeing Dr. Shepard and his letter is dated 10/20/08. I misplaced this letter as I stated above and I want to submit it with my appeal for consideration. Steven Phaup and I (Lola McGee) were supervisors at North Las Vegas Main Post Office when Craig Colton was the postmaster. Steve harassed me almost daily and I called several meetings with him and Craig in and effort to stop the hostile behavior towards me. In addition, I called meetings with OIC Dana Urbanski when Craig left and went on detail to the City of Las Vegas. The Steve Phaup issues are in my Formal EEO. I was afraid of his mentality because he had a bizarre behavior and he would do anything to try and upset me (Charles Turner, Tom Martin, and Shelby Kruger-Duncan are witnesses). Also, I'm not afraid to live alone anymore because I currently live by myself.

The Nevada Sierra District has a Zero tolerance policy to violence and threats (Even in Jest) and I will send the policy in this appeal, dated June 1, 2006.

In your letter dated March 6, 2009 you stated that I alleged that Postmaster Craig Colton talked loud to me while in front of other employees and I never said that. Steven Phaup talked loud to me in a disrespectful manner while in front of other employees on the workroom floor. This is one of the reasons mounted with others that meetings were called with Craig Colton and Dana Urbanski.

In your letter you state that OIC Jerry Wilson responded to my allegation, as follows: I will just put the truths to his responses.

1) Jerry Wilson did not address my attendance at all on 7/9/2008 (Which was my first day at Meadow Mesa) when I told him I'm running late he just stated "It's okay" come by the main before you go to Mesa so I can meet you.

2) Jerry Wilson made it very clear that no processes that we had previously put in place at NLV would be changed and they were not. It is his opinion that it was difficult to speak to me on a day to day basis, because my staff and I worked very hard together to achieve success. He states that he informed me to follow the processes, and policies of

the district, I have never-not followed the policies, and this is defamation of character. It appears to me that he is just trying to state things to make me be a non compliant employee who's hard to deal with and that is not the case. I was personally asked to come to Meadow Mesa to act as manager and I don't think that I would have been chosen if that's the kind of person that I am.

3) Jerry Wilson did not tell me that he was changing my scheduled reporting time, because I was late coming in on those three occasions, he stated that he wanted me there when the carriers got back. It was not like he was changing my time because I was late and I stated to him oh Jerry I'll be on time from now on so please don't change my time. I knew that with a station as large as Meadow Mesa I needed to start at 7:00am no later than 7:30am because decisions needed to be made according to day to day operations and issues.

4) I never had ever filed an EEO and I would not have told Jerry if at that time I had even considered filing one, because I did not even know him to talk to him that way. Jerry looked at my own statement and got the black female in his own response to make him appear knowledgeable of what I was thinking, I assume. All I know is, I never told Jerry, are any other breathing human being that I was going to file an EEO on Las Vegas because I did not know that at that time myself. Jerry just out right lied on me.

5) I told Jerry that I got my letter from Corey yesterday (8/18/2008) stating that I was not selected for the position and I was distraught and I had a bad evening. None of the rest is true, because I never went to talk to anyone and, again, why would I tell Jerry that? I just cannot believe the things that he is saying. Jerry never told me that he was going to place me back in my supervisor EAS-17 position. I stated to Jerry that he was right that I needed to set the example and be at work on time and it would not happen again.

6) Jerry was my boss and I did ask him for SDO's and my TE's that were at the main office and he told me no. All I said was ok because I knew my staff had made a mistake that I corrected for the future. Jerry stated that I became very agitated as if I were a child.

7) I did not contact Yul, he contacted me from a call I made to speak with Jerry and there was not any mention of how many Transitional Employees-TE's to bring in, he just told me to bring in the one's that could perform efficiently and that is what we did. We brought in if I remember correctly three (3) at 7:30 and two are three at 9:00, not all of them came in at 7:30am. Please pull the tacs reports to confirm what I'm saying.

8) On 8/25/2008 Jerry Wilson stood very close to me and looked at me and gave me an open ended threat "You continue to go over my head with Craig and Yul and I'm going to do something about it." Jerry is a domineering, speak with conviction, and let's you know whose the boss type of person and because he did not achieve what he wanted; and he felt intimidated by me speaking to Craig and Yul, he let it be known to me that he was going to do something about it. I was afraid and I had a Panic Attack which caused me to have increased Heart Palpitations, Hearing Loss, Neuropathy, PTSD, and Major Depression. All of Jerry's lies and I'm the one sick and on medication; does that seem fair to you? Who would you say was telling the truth me or higher management? I'm the one who suffers everyday. How would you feel if your superiors caused you all this pain and suffering?

9) First of all, I only had one (1) denial on 8/18/2008 while working with Jerry so where does he get this build up of frustration, because if I had not been doing my job in the city I would not have been continually used. Jerry found all this stuff out after the fact and he used it to make his statement to you appear strong, but I know how I respected Jerry and anyone else, because he is not the type of person that will allow you to treat him any other way, and I'm not the type of person that would disrespect anyone intentionally. I wake up to a new day everyday with God on my side. With all the things that Jerry said I did then why didn't he tell Craig that I can't work with this woman she doesn't know how to follow instructions. He did not do that because all of his made up accusations are not true.

10) Once again I followed the processes and procedures of the district, and if I did not, ask Jerry what was it that I did not do? Jerry is just stretching to try and cover up his own wrong and not be held accountable for it.
11) This is partially true, but what he forgot to put in his reply is that I asked him to send me the CA-1 and CA-2 but he did not. Jerry did not send the CA-1 because he did not want to be held accountable for the Threat and once again I'm the one who's sick.
12) Jerry is correct that he has the administrative right to manage and his statement sounds very good, but Jerry never, never, never, had to talk with me about following directions, policies, are processes. Jerry was upset that he was wrong about the projection indicator, and he had me do his projections for the next two days. On the third day he called and asked me why I did not put in his projections and I stated to him that I did not know that you wanted me to do it for you everyday. After that day, he had Mel put the projections in for him on a daily basis.

My events that were not accepted as factual:

1) My EEO activity was not filed fraudulently.
2) I sent in the PES ratings of 3% from Robert Reynosa and Jennifer Vo.
3) I've explained this over and over again and I'm the one who lives with the affects everyday. It's true, have Jerry and I take a lie detector test.
4) It's true are else I would not have had to go to Injury Comp and get my own papers. I sent in the envelope and documents that were inside. The label was from North Las Vegas Main Office 89030. This was another way he was not going to accept the (Threat) he made to me.
5) Steven Phaup did this and I addressed it in the beginning of this letter.
6) That is correct, and the Dept. of Justice is currently paying for an attorney on my behalf. Robert Reynosa did not handle the grievance properly. In addition, the steward was disciplined for an unsafe act.
7) That's true because it was mentioned at the Formal-A JSOV meeting to terminate me just like we terminated Mr. Steiger.
8) That's just some of the things that Steven Phaup did and Dana Urbanski is a witness because we had a meeting with her.
9) That's true and I worked just as hard and achieved Excellent success with delivery, Article 8 violation grievances, hostile work environment, accident free year, the union steward resigned, and countless other contributions. I even got a spot award and a plaque; however, Steve got the same thing but I wasn't taken to lunch, not even on a rotating basis.

All of my actions were acted on when I became aware of them and I have made statements, given witnesses and have told the truth, I don't know what else you want from me. I was threatened by Jerry, lied to by Jennifer, misused and abused by being used from station to station (Mark Martinez, Jennifer VO, and Robert Reynosa, Craig Colton, and Corey Richards). I have employees with less experience promoted over me and I have given names, such as Lynn Holmes, Jason McMahill, Tim Sampoli, Doug Watson, etc., and unfair tactics used to maneuver around hiring me. Having lateral transfers on competitive postings, not even being considered at all for open positions that was not even filled, disrespected, and talked to unprofessionally by my superiors on telecom's, given an investigative interview for things other promoted manager's did, but they were not given an investigative interview while guilty of the same mistake, (Dana Urbanski witness, Yul Melonson also), this is just to name a few, there are other issues that still exist to date Corey Richards not paying me (Debbie Letts), and removing my access from the GMF (Charles Turner).

Also, how can Grady Griffin answer my request when he was not even in North Las Vegas at the time; he was detailed to Henderson when I was at Meadow Mesa, and I've never worked for him in the City of Las Vegas. Yul Melonson was the Postmaster and he was on detail, so how do you derive at the truth? Bonnie Brokofsky can be a witness to the TE's coming in early.

Sincerely
Lola McGee

* * * * *

April 8, 2009

To: Yul Melonson, Postmaster Las Vegas
Robert Reynosa, Manager, Customer Service Operations Las Vegas
Corey Richards, Postmaster North Las Vegas

From: Lola McGee
Supervisor, Customer Services
North Las Vegas Main Post Office

Regarding: Response to Lateral Request Letter dated February 11, 2009

Hello Gentlemen,

I have not received a written response from my request letter dated above; however, I was assigned to Spring Valley Station in Las Vegas effective 3/9/2009. Unfortunately, I got injured on 3/13/2009 and now I'm out with an on-the-job injury. In addition, I was told to send my Continuation of Pay (COP) 3971 document to North Las Vegas Main Office rather than Spring Valley Station located at 3375 Rainbow Blvd. Las Vegas, NV 89146.

I'm confused because I have not received a written response to my February 11, 2009 Lateral Request to the City of Las Vegas. Also, I was informed by Yul that I was not to put my Core Objectives into PES because my PS Form-50 still had North Las Vegas on it; however, when I went to North Las Vegas to submit my objectives, I was told by Corey that I was not to put my requirements in there. In addition, he called Maggie Lara to get clarification and she stated that he (Corey Richards) was correct since I was in the City of Las Vegas. I explained what Yul told me to do and I stated that if I'm on a detail that I'm not required to put it into PES unless it's six (6) months or more.

To no avail, Corey refuse to let me even use the computer let alone input my Core Objectives. This will have an affect on my midyear and end of year rating for my NPA raise for fiscal year 2009. Also, I requested two (2)1 forms and a CA-2 and he refused to give me those until he called and spoke to Joni Payne in Injury Compensation. He later gave me one (1) CA-1 Form.

It is at this time that I'm requesting a written complete and absolute decision on my request for the lateral to the City of Las Vegas.

I thank you in advance for your immediate attention and concern in this matter.

Sincerely
Lola McGee

* * * * *

March 13, 2009 lifting injury (letters) and EEO filed for retaliation from Yul Melonson

Date: April 24, 2009

To: U. S. Department of Labor/OWCP
Employment Standards Administration
P. O. Box 8300 District 13 SFC
London, KY 40742-8300

From: Lola McGee
P. O. Box 98272
Las Vegas, NV 89193-8272

Subject: Date of Injury: 3/13/2009 – CA-1 Filed 4/2/2009
File Number: 132209923

Ms. Landry:

The following are the responses toward the information requested: Provide statements from any persons who witnessed your injury or had immediate knowledge of it, or other documentation that supports your claim.

1. It is up to Joe Acosta to tell the truth; and, I have already written a statement of what happened; it was given to injury compensation. State the immediate effects of the injury and what you did immediately thereafter.

2. I pushed an orange hamper over to the 89117 routes of the 89146 zone. There were some swings on the floor that were going to be taken out to the street by Karen for other carriers. K aren is a limited duty carrier and she has lifting restrictions. I turned to my left, bent my knees, and lifted the hard plastic trays of mail; also, there were 775 tubs on the floor with mail in them. I do not remember how many trays or tubs there were to be put into the hamper, but as I lifted the last tray I felt a pop/shift in my left knee and my back after which the pain followed. Both knees were in pain, but my left knee pain was more profound. My left thigh started to hurt like sharp lines of pain were running down it. As I was leaning into the hamper I sounded out in pain and I grimmest with a frown and that is when I looked and saw Joe Acosta, acting manager. He asked me if I was okay and I stated "No, but I think I'll be alright". Joe and I left the workroom floor and went into his office where I reported the injury to him that I just incurred on the workroom

floor. Through conversation I discussed with him the other on the job injuries that I had previously incurred that began to manifest on 8/25/08. I stated to Joe that I've just come back and I can't go out again and that just wouldn't look good. Joe stated that I had to take care of myself and not worry about anything else. I stated that I will do my best and we will see what happens. I do not know how heavy the trays were; but they were full of strapped out mail in an upright position. The tubs contained coverage and parcels.

Did you sustain any other injury, either on or off duty, between the date of injury, and the date it was first reported to (a) your supervisor and (b) to a doctor. If so, describe.

3. No

State the exact reason why you delayed seeking medical attention; also give the name and address of the doctor you first consulted and the date you were first examined for this injury.

4. I delayed seeking medical attention because I thought I could work off the pain, and I am still going to physical therapy for the Neuropathy; an on the job injury from 8/25/08. In addition, I had just come back from injury leave and I did not want to go back out. I wanted to try and see if the pain would go away, but to no avail. On 4/2/09 I filed the claim and I went to the emergency room at St. Rose Medical Center in Henderson. 3001 St. Rose Parkway Henderson, NV 89052. I was seen and examined for this on the job injury by R. John Balani, PAC (per FECA, a Physicians Assistants' report may be admissible if a physician cosigns the report) (http://www.dol.gov/esa/owcp/dfec/regs/compliance/DFECfolio/feca-pt3.pdf.). The attending physician that supervised and co-signed my medical record with Mr. Balani during my visit to the St. Rose ER was Dr. John Lewis, MD. The diagnosis of Sciatica pain caused by Lumbar Radiculopathy was given.

Describe (a) your condition between the date of injury and the date you first received medical attention, and (b) the nature and frequency of any home treatment.

5. From the date I was injured on 3/13/09 I have been in experienced back, both knees and left thigh pain everyday; however on 4/2/09 I just could not take this pain anymore and I sought medical treatment at St. Rose Siena ER. In spite of prescribed medications, I am in cutting pain daily. This pain is felt in my entire back. In addition to prescribed medications, I've taken Advil; I have a heating pad, and rubbing ointment. I utilize these interventions as often as my body allows. I message my body as best I can to try and take some of the pain away. I also perform stretch workouts as prescribed by my physical therapist. Some days are better than others. I have my daughter here assisting me because I'm really limited to what I can do on my own.

Did you have any similar disability or symptoms before the injury? If so, describe the prior condition. Please send records of all prior treatment.

6. My back was injured doing construction work in 1994 that resulted in disability; but, I was medically cleared in 1996. In 1998 I was deemed medically fit by a physician of the United States Postal Service without restrictions. I had no pain symptoms resulting from the 1994 injury after 1997. I was in a car accident in 2006 and received about 3 weeks of physical therapy that resulted in no disability. I had no pain symptoms from the car accident, which was minor itself. I had a Panic Attack on 8/25/08 that caused Neuropathy in my feet, legs, lower and upper left buttocks, which resulted in disability and I still suffer from this condition to date.

I will give this letter (requested information) dated 4/9/2009 to the Centennial Spine and Pain Center so that the treating doctor can address the needed information requested by your organization.

Sincerely
Lola McGee

* * * * *

Date: April 25, 2009

To: Centennial Spine and Pain Center
4640 W. Craig road N. Decatur Blvd.
Las Vegas, NV 89032

Re: Lola B. McGee (DOB: 07/07/1962)
Date of injury 3/13/09-CA – 1 filed 4/2/09
File Number: 132209923

Attn: Dr. Coppel MD or To Whom It May Concern

Dear Dr. Coppel/To Whom It May Concern:

Please answer the following information requested by U.S. Department of Labor, Employment Standards Administration, Office of Workers' Comp Programs, Attn: Ms. Julia Landry:

Have your attending physician submit a detailed, narrative medical report which includes:

history of your injury and all prior industrial and non-industrial injuries to similar parts of your body
a firm diagnosis of any condition(s) resulting from this injury (with ICD-9 diagnosis code)
findings, symptoms and/or test results which support all conditions diagnosed
treatment provided
prognosis
period and extent of disability.

Your physician (a M.D. or D.O.) must also indicate whether and explain why the condition diagnosed is believed to have been caused or aggravated by your claimed injury sustained on 3/13/2009. **A Physician's Assistant is not considered a doctor under the FECA.**

If aggravation is indicated, the physician must explain whether any such aggravation is temporary or permanent. If temporary, when will such aggravation cease? If permanent, what material change occurred to alter the course of the pre-existing condition? The physician must provide detailed medical reasoning for the conclusions drawn and explain when the diagnosed condition will return to pre-existing levels after the prescribed treatment.

This evidence is crucial in consideration of your claim. You may wish to discuss the contents of this item with your physician.

If you have not been released to full duty, please make sure you have your treating physician provide this office with appropriate work restrictions as well as a statement as to when you will be released back to full duty without restrictions.

TO THE EMPLOYING AGENCY: If the employee was treated at an agency medical facility for this injury, the employing agency must provide the treatment notes directly to OWCP.

Sincerely,
Lola McGee

May 12, 2009

To: B. J. Clay
EEO Specialist, Nevada Sierra District

From: Lola McGee
Supervisor, Customer Services
North Las Vegas Post Office

Regarding: Pre-Complaint Counseling Questions From You, Concerning Yul Melonson, City of Las Vegas Postmaster.

Hello B. J.

I would like to start by addressing the question you asked me over the telephone on May 5, 2009, before I requested you to fax the questions over to me at my home, in which you did on 5/7/09.

You asked me "Why didn't you request a Redress?" I did not request a Redress because of the information that I received from you during my first EEO complaint. I cannot afford (For health purposes) to sit in a meeting and subject myself to dishonest people where honesty and integrity is suppose to be forthcoming and it not take place. You explain to me that you could not say if they would lie or not; so I do not wish to subject myself and my health to that type of atmosphere, it affects me deeply. Higher Level Management being dishonest is one of the reasons why I'm out sick/ill to date.

B. J. in your questions you state that I'm alleging discrimination based on physical/mental disabilities, retaliation, and sex? B. J. that is correct.

Thus, you only stated for me to identify my physical/mental disabilities; I'm assuming that you do not want to know the retaliation, and sex answers to my complaint? B. J., I had an on-the-job injury on 3/13/09 which injured my entire back, both knees, and left thigh while assigned to Spring Valley Station. I have been off work under doctor's care since 4/2/09, which is the date that I filed the CA-1 claim because I could no longer endure the pain from the 3/13/09 injury. In addition, I have mental illnesses Post Traumatic Stress Disorder, Major Depression, and Panic Attacks.

I would also like for it to be noted that I suffer from Neuropathy-nerve damage in both feet and legs along with my left upper and lower buttock. I have Heart Palpitations without the presence of Heart Disease; this condition is exacerbated by stress. I have hearing loss in my left ear. All of these injuries happened while on the job.

B. J. you go on to state "I believe your issue(s) are:" (1) on 4/2/09, your detail to the Spring Valley Station was ended. (2) On 4/8/09 your request for lateral reassignment to the Las Vegas Post Office was denied, and you ask the question "Is this Correct?" I will explain what the correct information is because it appears to me, through your questioning, that you were not given all the information correctly. On 1/16/09 Yul called me and explained what was going on in the City of Las Vegas as it relates to jobs. He told me that he has several openings and he wanted to know when I would be coming back to work. I told him that it would not be probably until February or March. He stated that I need to come back because there will not be any jobs left because he had to fill his positions. Towards the end of our conversation, Yul stated that he had just interviewed for Sunrise Station. During Yul's call, I stated to him that I put in for Sunrise and I didn't get an Interview. Yul abruptly hung up the phone and I called him back several times and begged him to save me a job because I can not work for Corey because he is doing all sorts of things retaliating against me. I emphasized to Yul on his voice mail, because he would not answer my repeated calls, to "Please, Please save me a job because I can't work with Corey because of the way he is treating me." In February, I talked to Yul on the phone from his office about returning to work and I reminded him about the message that I had left on his phone. He stated to me that he could not have me come back to work and put me in an acting manager's position but he suggested that I write a letter to him and cc Robert and Corey for a lateral position in the City of Las Vegas. Yul stated that he had several supervisor positions available but I need to hurry up and get well and come back to work.

For the record, I want it to be known that Yul never told me that I would be on detail as a supervisor and my 1723 does not reflect as such. Joe Acosta put the 1723 for a year and stated your Form 50 will be cut by then. When I asked Yul about my changed PS Form 50, he stated that it takes time and he would never mislead me.

On 2/11/2009 I requested a lateral, in writing, to the City of Las Vegas and faxed it to Yul's office and confirmed receipt by Phyllis. I also asked Phyllis if she would give a copy to Robert and she acknowledged that she would. I then faxed a copy to Corey and confirmed with him that he received it.

On 2/19/09 I met with Yul in his office and we discussed what office he needed more help in because of my skills and ability to improve offices. Also, Yul stated to Joe Acosta who was the acting manager at Spring Valley Station, over a telephone conversation with me and Joe, "Lola knows what success looks like." He stated the office that is given him problems right now is Spring Valley Station. I stated then that's where I want to be. He rolled the board around and showed me the offices that had vacant supervisor positions and Spring Valley Station was one of them. I mention this because some of the offices that I talked to him about did not have vacant supervisor positions and he informed me of that. I requested a lateral and I needed to be in an office that had a vacant supervisor position.

On 3/9/09 I was released back to work and was assigned to Spring Valley Station, per Yul Melonson. Unfortunately, I had some emergencies that prevented me from actually starting on 3/9/09; and, I started on 3/13/09. This is the same day that I had the lifting injury at Spring Valley Station and it was reported and observed by Joe Acosta.

On 4/2/09 I could no longer take the pain nor let my pride get in the way of not seeking medical attention for the 3/13/09 Spring Valley Station injury. I called Joe Acosta on his cell phone to let him know that I could no longer take the pain and I would have to file a CA-1. Joe told me to take care of myself and do what I have to do.

On 4/2/09 Yul called me on my cell phone, after being notified of my CA-1 claim, and left a message that he had news for me. I was on my way to my Cardiologist appointment after calling my primary doctor's office to see if they took worker's compensation claims, they did not. Once inside the doctor's office, I called Yul back and he stated to me "Why didn't you tell me about the injury yesterday?" I replied, "I needed to put it in writing." Yul stated, "I'm sending you back to North Las Vegas and Corey has already been notified."

I want it to be noted that Yul Melonson and I had a scheduled meeting on 4/1/09 and I informed him that I was sick and I requested through him advance sick leave and he replied, "You still have annual left." This was my way of letting him know that I was sick and injured and I really could not do anything about it.

Yul was very upset and it reflected in his telephone conversation with me on 4/2/09. If he was not going to give me the lateral then I would have never been at Spring Valley Station as a supervisor. The filing of the CA-1 on 4/2/09 for the 3/13/09 injury made Yul very angry and he reacted to it by sending me back to North Las Vegas; because I did not have my official PS Form 50 processed yet.

I want it to be noted that Yul retaliated against me because I did not tell him on 4/1/09 about the injury, and the fact that I have disabilities resulting from the injury. In addition, I have prior EEO activity Case #4E-890-0120-08 and I'm a female. Females are considered weak and not able to handle the job of upper management. I called Yul the following Sunday and told him, via voicemail, that he was taking this personal and I was going to church and "Pray" for him.

B. J. your question about the detail to Spring Valley Station ended on 4/2/09 is not correct, because I was never on a detail and Yul never told me anything of that nature. I requested a lateral and he used his power to send out the letter dated 4/8/09 to justify his angry position as if it was the first time he had heard of my request for a lateral by me. This is the reason that I did not request a Redress in the beginning.

Sincerely
Lola McGee

Cover Sheet: 18 pages including Cover sheet 4E-890-0043-09

To: B. J. Clay - EEO Specialist
Nevada Sierra District

From: Lola McGee
Supervisor, Customer Services
North Las Vegas Main Post Office
1414 E. Lake Mead Blvd.
NLV, NV 89030

B. J. Here is my response to your questions/inquires that were faxed over to me on 5/7/09 (18) pages with Cover Sheet.

Lola McGee

4E-890-0043-09

Fax Cover Sheet

Date: 5/7/2009 **Time** 2:58 PM.

To: Lola McGhee **Phone:** 702-260-0876
Fax: same

From: BJ Clay **Phone:** 702-735-1056
Fax: 702-732-3235

RE: Questions

You indicated you are alleging discrimination based on physical/mental disabilities, retaliation and sex.

Please identify your physical/mental disabilities.

I believe your issue(s) are:

1. On 4/2/09, your detail to the Spring Valley Station was ended.
2. On 4/8/09, your request for lateral reassignment to the Las Vegas Post Office was denied.

Is this correct?

BJ Clay
EEO Specialist

Pages (excluding cover): 1

HP Photosmart 2610xi
Personal Printer/Fax/Copier/Scanner

Log for

4E-890-0043-09 May 07 2009 1:57PM

Last Transaction

Date	Time	Type	Identification	Duration	Pages	Result
May 7	1:56PM	Received		0:35	1	OK

Per my Request;
Sent From B. J. Clay
5/7/09 Regarding Yul Melonson's
EEO' Complaint. NO Redress
Requested By Me.

Lola McKee

PS: Called B. J. at 1:55pm
5/7/09 and told her to Fax
the information to me. She called
and left a Message 2 days ago 5/5/09.
She wanted to question me over the
phone but I wasn't trusting of that method.

May 12, 2009

To: B. J. Clay
EEO Specialist, Nevada Sierra District

From: Lola McGee
Supervisor, Customer Services
North Las Vegas Post Office

Regarding: Pre-Complaint Counseling Questions From You, Concerning Yul Melonson City of Las Vegas Postmaster.

Hello B. J.

I would like to start by addressing the question you asked me over the telephone on May 5, 2009, before I requested you to fax the questions over to me at my home, in which you did on 5/7/09.

You asked me "Why didn't you request a Redress?" I did not request a Redress because of the information that I received from you during my first EEO complaint. I cannot afford (For health purposes) to sit in a meeting and subject myself to dishonest people where honesty and integrity is suppose to be forthcoming and it not take place. You explain to me that you could not say if they would lie or not; so I do not wish to subject myself and my health to that type of atmosphere, it affects me deeply. Higher Level Management being dishonest is one of the reasons why I'm out sick/ill to date.

B. J. in your questions you state that I'm alleging discrimination based on physical/mental disabilities, retaliation, and sex? B. J. that is correct.

Thus, you only stated for me to identify my physical/mental disabilities; I'm assuming that you do not want to know the retaliation, and sex answers to my complaint? B. J., I had an on-the-job injury on 3/13/09 which injured my entire back, both knees, and left thigh while assigned to Spring Valley Station. I have been off work under doctor's care since 4/2/09, which is the date that I filed the CA-1 claim because I could no longer endure the pain from the 3/13/09 injury. In addition, I have mental illnesses Post Traumatic Stress Disorder, Major Depression, and Panic Attacks.

I would also like for it to be noted that I suffer from Neuropathy-nerve damage in both feet and legs along with my left upper and lower buttock. I have Heart Palpitations without the presence of Heart Disease; this condition is exacerbated by stress. I have hearing loss in my left ear. All of these injuries happened while on the job.

B. J. you go on to state "I believe your issue(s) are:" (1) on 4/2/09, your detail to the Spring Valley Station was ended. (2) On 4/8/09 your request for lateral reassignment to

1 of 3

the Las Vegas Post Office was denied, and you ask the question "Is this Correct?" I will explain what the correct information is because it appears to me, through your questioning, that you were not given all the information correctly. On 1/16/09 Yul called me and explained what was going on in the City of Las Vegas as it relates to jobs. He told me that he has several openings and he wanted to know when I would be coming back to work. I told him that it would not be probably until February or March. He stated that I need to come back because there will not be any jobs left because he had to fill his positions. Towards the end of our conversation, Yul stated that he had just interviewed for Sunrise Station. During Yul's call, I stated to him that I put in for Sunrise and I didn't get an Interview. Yul abruptly hung up the phone and I called him back several times and begged him to save me a job because I can not work for Corey because he is doing all sorts of things retaliating against me. I emphasized to Yul on his voice mail, because he would not answer my repeated calls, to **"Please, Please save me a job because I can't work with Corey because of the way he is treating me."** In February, I talked to Yul on the phone from his office about returning to work and I reminded him about the message that I had left on his phone. He stated to me that he could not have me come back to work and put me in an acting manager's position but he suggested that I write a letter to him and cc Robert and Corey for a lateral position in the City of Las Vegas. Yul stated that he had several supervisor positions available but I need to hurry up and get well and come back to work.

For the record, I want it to be known that Yul never told me that I would be on detail as a supervisor and my 1723 does not reflect as such. Joe Acosta put the 1723 for a year and stated your Form 50 will be cut by then. When I asked Yul about my changed PS Form 50, he stated that it takes time and he would never mislead me.

On 2/11/2009 I requested a lateral, in writing, to the City of Las Vegas and faxed it to Yul's office and confirmed receipt by Phyllis. I also asked Phyllis if she would give a copy to Robert and she acknowledged that she would. I then faxed a copy to Corey and confirmed with him that he received it.

On 2/19/09 I met with Yul in his office and we discussed what office he needed more help in because of my skills and ability to improve offices. Also, Yul stated to Joe Acosta who was the acting manager at Spring Valley Station, over a telephone conversation with me and Joe, "Lola knows what success looks like." He stated the office that is given him problems right now is Spring Valley Station. I stated then that's where I want to be. He rolled the board around and showed me the offices that had vacant supervisor positions and Spring Valley Station was one of them. I mention this because some of the offices that I talked to him about did not have vacant supervisor positions and he informed me of that. I requested a lateral and I needed to be in an office that had a vacant supervisor position.

On 3/9/09 I was released back to work and was assigned to Spring Valley Station, per Yul Melonson. Unfortunately, I had some emergencies that prevented me from actually starting on 3/9/09; and, I started on 3/13/09. This is the same day that I had

2 of 3

the lifting injury at Spring Valley Station and it was reported and observed by Joe Acosta.

On 4/2/09 I could no longer take the pain nor let my pride get in the way of not seeking medical attention for the 3/13/09 Spring Valley Station injury. I called Joe Acosta on his cell phone to let him know that I could no longer take the pain and I would have to file a CA-1. Joe told me to take care of myself and do what I have to do.

On 4/2/09 Yul called me on my cell phone, after being notified of my CA-1 claim, and left a message that he had news for me. I was on my way to my Cardiologist appointment after calling my primary doctor's office to see if they took worker's compensation claims, they did not. Once inside the doctor's office, I called Yul back and he stated to me "Why didn't you tell me about the injury yesterday?" I replied, "I needed to put it in writing." Yul stated, "I'm sending you back to North Las Vegas and Corey has already been notified."

I want it to be noted that Yul Melonson and I had a scheduled meeting on 4/1/09 and I informed him that I was sick and I requested through him advance sick leave and he replied, "You still have annual left." This was my way of letting him know that I was sick and injured and I really could not do anything about it.

Yul was very upset and it reflected in his telephone conversation with me on 4/2/09. If he was not going to give me the lateral then I would have never been at Spring Valley Station as a supervisor. The filing of the CA-1 on 4/2/09 for the 3/13/09 injury made Yul very angry and he reacted to it by sending me back to North Las Vegas; because I did not have my official PS Form 50 processed yet.

I want it to be noted that Yul retaliated against me because I did not tell him on 4/1/09 about the injury, and the fact that I have disabilities resulting from the injury. In addition, I have prior EEO activity Case #4E-890-0120-08 and I'm a female. Females are considered weak and not able to handle the job of upper management. I called Yul the following Sunday and told him, via voicemail, that he was taking this personal and I was going to church and "Pray" for him.

B. J. your question about the detail to Spring Valley Station ended on 4/2/09 is not correct, because I was never on a detail and Yul never told me anything of that nature. I requested a lateral and he used his power to send out the letter dated 4/8/09 to justify his angry position as if it was the first time he had heard of my request for a lateral by me. This is the reason that I did not request a Redress in the beginning.

Sincerely

Lola McGee

3 of 3

HP Photosmart 2610xi
Personal Printer/Fax/Copier/Scanner

Log for

May 12 2009 3:39PM

4E-890-0043-09

Last Transaction

Date	Time	Type	Identification	Duration	Pages	Result
May 12	3:30PM	Fax Sent	7323235	8:22	18	OK

Sent to B. J. Clay regarding Yul Melonson's EEO signed 4/28/09 by me. Requested on 4/21/09 from NEEOISO-EEO Agency. B.J.'s questions and my Answers.

4E-890-0043-09

Reference: PRE-021354-2009

Information for Pre-Complaint Counseling

Certified Mail No.	Date Mailed *or* Hand Delivered on
By *(Initials)*	Case No.

On 4/21/2009 *(Month, Day, Year)*, you requested an appointment with a Dispute Resolution Specialist.

Important: Please read. You should complete this form and return it to the EEO office ***within10 calendar days*** of receipt. This is the only notification that you will receive regarding the necessity for you to complete this form.

A. Requester Information

Name *(Last, First, MI)* McGee Lola B.	Social Security	Home Telephone No. (702)260-0876
Your Mailing Address P.O. Box 98272 LV, NV 89193-8272		Finance Number 316200-31489
Name of Postal Facility Where You Work Spring Valley Station		Office Telephone No. (702) 220-7237
Address of Postal Facility 3375 S. Rainbow Blvd. LV, NV 89146		Email Address* Not At Work
Employment Status *(Check One)* ☐ Applicant ☐ Casual ☐ TE ☒ Career	Position Title Supervisor, Customer SVS.	Grade Level EAS-17
Pay Location 082 · Tour days · Duty Hours 6:00-1500	Off Days *(If Tour I, Show Nights Off)* Sun/Rot.	Time in Current Position _ Years 1 Months Less Than (1)mo
Your Supervisor's Name Joe Acosta and Brad Lambertson	Supervisor's Title Acting Mgr. Cust. SVS.	Supervisor's Telephone No. (702) 220-7237

•Providing this information will authorize the U.S. Postal Service to send you important documents electronically.

B. Discrimination Factors

Prohibited discrimination includes actions taken based on your ***Race, Color, Religion, Sex, Age (40+), National Origin, Physical and/or Mental Disability, or in Retaliation*** *(actions based on your participation in prior EEO activity)*. These categories are referred to on this form as factors.

What factor(s) of Discrimination are you alleging? (Please be specific, i.e., Race-African American, Sex-Female).

Physical/Mental Disabilities, Retaliation, Female

For Retaliation Allegations Only. If you are alleging retaliation discrimination, provide the date(s) and specifics of the EEO activity that you feel caused you to be retaliated against.

1. On 11-1-08 (Month, Day, Year), I engaged in EEO activity. Case No.: 4E-890-0120-08 (4 EEO's Combined) L.M.
2. On ______ (Month, Day, Year), I engaged in EEO activity. Case No.: ______

C. Description of Incident Action

Please use the space below to briefly describe the incident or action that prompted you to seek EEO counseling at this time.

On 4/2/09 (Month, Day), 20 09 (Year)

On 2/11/09 I requested a lateral to Las Vegas City. On 2/19/09 I met with Yul Melonson to discuss which office. On 3/9/09 I was released back to work; but ~~and~~ L.M. started at Spring Valley station on 3/13/09 because of EAL and death in family. On 3/13/09 I was injured and it was reported and observed by Joe Acosta. On 4/2/09 I filed a claim because the Pain got to severe. On 4/2/09 Yul called me on my Cellphone and stated "I got news for you." He was very upset and told me that I was going back to North Las

PS Form 2564-A, March 2001 *(Page 1 of 3)*

Vegas and Corey Richards has already been notified. Yul was taken this situation personal, but I'm the one who is in pain daily. If he was not going to approve my lateral I would have never been at Spring Vall[ey] in the first Place. The injury Made him Send the 4/8/09 letter (Technicality) [illegible]

4E-890-0043-09

D. Comparisons

Explain why, based on the factors you cited in Section B, you believe that you were treated differently than other employees or applicants in similar situations

1. _______ I'm unaware of any

(Name of Employee) Factor(s) that describe the employee, i.e. sex (male), National Origin (Hispanic)

was treated differently than I when:

2. _______

(Name of Employee) Factor(s) that describe the employee, i.e., sex (male), National Origin (Hispanic)

was treated differently than I when:

3. _______

(Name of Employee) Factor(s) that describe the employee, i.e., sex (male), National Origin (Hispanic)

was treated differently than I when:

E. Official(s) Responsible for Action(s)

List the name(s) of the official(s) who took the action that prompted you to seek counseling at this time.

1a. Name Yul Melonson	b. Title Postmaster City of Los Vegas
c. Office 1001 E. SunSet Rd LV, NV 89199	d. Grade Level PCES
2a. Name	b. Title
c. Office	d. Grade Level

Retaliation Allegations Only: Was/were the official(s) listed in Section D above aware of your prior EEO activity?

☐ No ☒ Yes If yes, explain how the official(s) became aware: EEO's were filed on manages under his supervison and it's his duty to now because of his position. Also, I talked with him about the people involved

F. Resolution

What are you seeking as a resolution to your pre-complaint? Official written apology, Sensativity Training, and Monetary compensation

G. Grievance/MSPB Appeal

On the incident that prompted you to seek EEO counseling, have you:

1. Filed a grievance on the same issue? ☒ No ☐ Yes If yes, _______ (Date) _______ (Current Step)
2. Filed a MSPB appeal on this issue? ☒ No ☐ Yes If yes, _______ (Date Appeal Filed)

PS Form 2564-A, March 2001 *(Page 2 of 3)*

4E-890-0043-09

H. Anonymity

You have the right to remain anonymous during the pre-complaint process.

Do you desire anonymity? ☑ No ☐ Yes

I. Representation

You have the right to retain representation of your choice. *(check one)*

☑ I waive the right to representation at this time. → However, I will have a representative at a later da ☐ I authorize the person listed below to represent me.

Name of Representative	Representative's Title	
Organization	Telephone Number	Email Address*
Mailing Address *(Street or P.P. Box, City, State and Zip +4)*		

* Providing this information will authorize the U.S. Postal Service to send your representative important documents electronically.

J. Documentation

Please attach any documentation you wish to submit to support your allegation(s). Include a copy of any written action(s) that caused you to seek counseling at this time.

Note: If you are alleging mental and/or physical disability, it is important for you to submit medical documentation of your disability during the pre-complaint process.

K. Privacy Act Notice

Privacy Act Notice. The collection of this information is authorized by the Equal Employment Opportunity Act of 1972, 42 U.S.C. § 2000e-16; the Age Discrimination in Employment Act of 1967, as amended, 29 U.S.C. § 633a; the Rehabilitation Act of 1973, as amended, 29 U.S.C. § 794a; and Executive Order 11478, as amended. This information will be used to adjudicate complaints of alleged discrimination and to evaluate the effectiveness of the EEO program. As a routine use, this information may be disclosed to an appropriate government agency, domestic or foreign, for law enforcement purposes; where pertinent, in a legal proceeding to which the USPS is a party or has an interest; to a government agency in order to obtain information relevant to a USPS decision concerning employment, security clearances, contracts, licenses, grants, permits or other benefits; to a government agency upon its request when relevant to its decision concerning employment, security clearances, security or suitability investigations, contracts, licenses, grants or other benefits; to a congressional office at your request, to an expert, consultant or other person under contract with the USPS to fulfill an agency function; to the Federal Records Center for storage; to the Office of Management and Budget for review of private relief legislation; to an independent certified public accountant during an official audit of USPS finances; to an investigator, administrative judge or complaints examiner appointed by the Equal Employment Opportunity Commission for investigation of a formal EEO complaint under 29 CFR 1614; to the Merit Systems Protection Board or Office of Special Counsel for proceedings or investigations involving personnel practices and other matters within their jurisdiction; and to a labor organization as required by the National Labor Relations Act. Under the Privacy Act provision, the information requested is voluntary for the complainant, and for Postal Service employees and other witnesses.

L. Authorization

I am aware that the claim(s) contained herein shall by-pass the pre-complaint process *if* like or related to a formal complaint that I have already filed, or *if* the claim(s) constitutes a spin-off complaint. (A spin-off complaint contests the manner in which a previously filed complaint is being processed.) In completing this PS Form 2564-A, *Information for Pre-complaint Counseling*, I recognize that the Manager, Dispute Resolution will review the claim(s) contained herein and determine how they shall be processed. I will be notified, in writing, if the Manager determines that my claim(s) shall be processed as amendments or appendages to a formal complaint that I have already filed.

Please print your name here: Lola McGee

Your Signature	Date signed 4/28/09

Please return this form to:

☐ National EEO Investigative Services Office
EEO Contact Center
U.S. Postal Service
PO Box 21979
Tampa FL 33622-1979

PS Form **2564-A**, March 2001 *(Page 3 of 3)*

UNITED STATES POSTAL SERVICE®

4E-890-0043-09

Certification of Receipt — Publication 133

Privacy Act Notice

Privacy Act Notice. The collection of this information is authorized the Equal Employment Opportunity Act of 1972, 42 U.S.C. § 2000e-16; the Age Disrimination in Employment Act of 1967, as amended, 29 U.S.C. § 633a; the Rehabilitation Act of 1973, as amended, 29 U.S.C. § 794a; and Executive Order 11478, as amended. This information will be used to adjudicate complaints of alleged discrimination and to evaluate the effectiveness of the EEO program. As a routine use, this information may be disclosed to an appropriate government agency, domestic or foreign, for law enforcement purposes; where pertinent, in a legal proceeding to which the USPS is a party or has an interest; to a government agency in order to obtain information relevant to a USPS decision concerning employment, security clearances, contracts, licenses, grants, permits or other benefits; to a government agency upon its request when relevant to its decision concerning employment, security clearances, security or suitability investigations, contracts, licenses, grants or other benefits; to a congressional office at your request; to an expert, consultant or other person under contract with the USPS to fulfill an agency function; to the Federal Records Center for storage; to the Office of Management and Budget for review of private relief legislation; to an independent certified public accountant during an official audit of USPS finances; to an investigator, administrative judge or complaints examiner appointed by the Equal Employment Opportunity Commission for investigation of a formal EEO complaint under 29 CFR 1614; to the Merit Systems Protection Board or Office of Special Counsel for proceedings or investigations involving personnel practices and other matters within their jurisdiction; and to a labor organization as required by the National Labor Relations Act. Under the Privacy Act provision, the information requested is voluntary for the complainant, and for Postal Service employees and other witnesses.

Certification of Receipt — Publication 133

I hereby certify that on this date I received a copy of Publication 133, *What You Need to Know About EEO*, to keep for my personal records.

Signature of Recipient: Lola McGee

Date: 4/28/09

Note: Recipient, when you receive this form by mail, please sign and return it to the EEO Office at the same time you return your completed PS Form 2564-A, *Information for Pre-Complaint Counseling*.

Certification of Service — Publication 133

I hereby certify that on this date, Publication 133, *What You Need to Know About EEO*,

was mailed to Lola McGee P.O. Box 98272 LV, NV 89193-8272
Delivery Confirmation # 0309 0330 0002 1843 1630

via Certified Mail No. ______

or delivered by hand to ______

Signature of Server ______ Date ______

PS Form **2563-A,** March 2001

® EEO Investigative Affidavit for Compensatory Damages
Note: Not applicable to Age Discrimination in Employment Act (ADEA)

Name	Case No.	Page No.	No. of Pages
Lola B. McGee	4E-890-0043-09	1	2

Instructions for the Complainant:
During an investigation into alleged discrimination, The Postal Service is required to gather evidence regarding appropriate remedies, which may include compensatory damages. The remedy that you are seeking to resolve this complaint includes your claim that you are entitled to receive a monetary award. Therefore, you must provide testimony and evidence concerning the nature, extent and severity of the harm you suffered due to the alleged discriminatory conduct. PS Form 2569-C contains a number of questions and/or statements regarding your claim for damages. Please read the questions or statements carefully before responding. If you need additional space, please use an additional sheet(s). Any additional sheet(s) must show the number of this form (Form 2569-C), the item number(s) to which it pertains, a page number and the total number of pages submitted for this form. ***You must declare under penalty of perjury that the information you provide on this form including any attached sheets is true and correct.***

1. I experienced financial difficulties because of the discriminatory act(s) alleged in my complaint.

☐ **Yes** ☐ **No**

If yes, provide full explanation. Please include description and cause of difficulty(ies), when occurred, duration of occurrence, and severity.

I do not have any sick leave left and I'm not working. I've had to file Disability Retirement and Social Security Disability and there is a long waiting process. It is a very big struggle from month to month in order to pay my bills and I'm not living according to my normal lifestyle physically, mentally, are financially.

2. I experienced medical problems because of the discriminatory act(s) alleged in my complaint.

☐ **Yes** ☐ **No**

If yes, provide full explanation. Please include description and cause of problems, when occurred, duration of occurrence, and severity.

Full back, both knees, left thigh, exacerbated = Neuropathy-nerve damage, Post Traumatic Stress Disorder, Major Depression, Anxiety, and Panic Attacks.

3. I obtained psychological or psychiatric counseling and/or treatment because of the discriminatory act(s) alleged in my complaint.

☐ **Yes** ☐ **No**

If yes, provide full explanation. Please include description and cause of problems, when occurred, duration of occurrence, and severity.

From previous diagnosis of Post Traumatic Stress Disorder, Major Depression, Anxiety, and Panic Attacks, I endured severe trauma by Yul's behavior when I filed the injury on 4/2/09 and that is what lead my mental health doctor to deem me totally disabled along with Corey Richards treatment of me which lead me to be hospitalized from 4/13/09-4/15/09.

4. I have had to take medication because of the discriminatory act(s) alleged in my complaint.

☐ **Yes** ☐ **No**

If yes, list type of medication, reason for the medication, and the cost of the medication.

Lyrica for Neuropathy, Loritab for Pain, Ultram for Pain, Soma for Pain, Steroid for Pain, Verapamil for my Heart, Oitment for Pain, Motrin for Pain, Pristiq for Depression, Klonipin for Anxiety/Stress and the cost range from $6.58 - $50.00 per prescription.

5. Did any of the difficulties for which you checked "Yes" in items 1-4 exist prior to the act(s) of discrimination alleged in your complaint?

☐ **Yes** ☐ **No**

If yes, please complete question 6 below.

6. Describe for each pre-existing condition how that condition was made worse by the act(s) of discrimination alleged in your complaint. Begin each description with the item number on page 1 (items 1 through 4) to which it pertains.

Financially I was receiving a full pay check and I'm not now. I was able to walk without a cane and now I'm learning to walk without falling down. My pain is breath taking and I'm forced to take narcotic medication and I forbid against drugs. I'm proud to be a 22 year person in Sobriety, this was really an adverse life change for me. I was depressed but I was able to drive and now my condition does not allow me to do that at this time. I use to keep my hygiene up more now I very seldom even brush my teeth. The list just goes on and on.

7. **Is there any other information or evidence regarding your claim for entitlement to compensatory damages that you want to include with your affidavit?**

☐ **Yes** ☐ **No**

If yes, please provide a full explanation of the information you wish to include. Attach additional pages if necessary.

Help Me Please!!!!!!!!

IMPORTANT!

Privacy Act Notice

Privacy Act Notice. **The collection of this information is authorized by The Equal Employment Opportunity Act of 1972, 42 U.S.C. 2000e-16; The Age Discrimination in Employment Act of 1967, as amended, 29 U.S.C.633a; The Rehabilitation Act of 1973, as amended, 29 U.S.C. 794a; and Executive Order 11478, as amended. This information will be used to adjudicate complaints of alleged discrimination and to evaluate the effectiveness of the EEO program. As a routine use, this information may be disclosed to an appropriate government agency, domestic or foreign, for law enforcement purposes; where pertinent, in a legal proceeding to which the USPS is a party or has an interest; to a government agency in order to obtain information relevant to a USPS decision concerning employment, security clearances, contracts, licenses, grants, permits or other benefits; to a government agency upon its request when relevant to its decision concerning employment, security clearances, security or suitability investigations, contracts, licenses, grants or other benefits; to a congressional office at your request; to an expert, consultant, or other person under contract with the USPS to fulfill an agency function; to the Federal Records Center for storage; to the Office of Management and Budget for review of private relief legislation; to an independent certified public accountant during an official audit of USPS finances; to an investigator, administrative judge or complaints examiner appointed by the Equal Employment Opportunity Commission for Investigation of a formal EEO complaint under 29 CFR**

1614; to the Merit Systems Protection Board or Office of Special Counsel for proceedings or investigations involving personnel practices and other matters within their jurisdiction; and to a labor organization as required by the National Labor Relations Act. Under the Privacy Act provision, the information requested is voluntary for the complainant, and for Postal Service employees and other witnesses.

I declare under penalty of perjury that the foregoing, including any attached sheets, is true and correct.

Affiant's Signature	Date Signed

You must attach or provide the investigator with copies of documentation, such as bills, doctor's statements, pharmacy bills, statements from other persons, or other paperwork relevant to the difficulty that you claim is related to the discriminatory act(s) alleged in your complaint. If you do not have copies of your documentation, you may provide the original to the investigator who will copy relevant records and return the original documents to you. Alternatively, for medical information and records, you may provide a signed authorization from your health care provider to the investigator permitting him/her to obtain information directly from your health care provider or pharmacy. Or, you may sign a medical information release provided by the investigator if you prefer.

February 11, 2009 4E-890-0043-09

Request for Lateral

To: Yul Melonson, Postmaster Las Vegas
Robert Reynosa, Manager, Customer Services Operations – Las Vegas
Corey Richards, Postmaster – North Las Vegas

From: Lola McGee
Supervisor, Customer Services
North Las Vegas Post Office

Hello Gentlemen,

I, Lola McGee, would like to request a lateral to the City of Las Vegas because there are more opportunities there for me. I have been assigned to North Las Vegas since I arrived in May 2004 and have excelled in my duties as a supervisor in various operations on both sides of the house. In addition, I have received several accolades for my performance and leadership; also, I have given of myself in the community of North Las Vegas by donating time to the Nevada Reading League.

It is at this time that I would like to continue to broaden my horizon and gain upward mobility; because, I have the experience, skills, ability, and desire to become a promoted Manager, Customer Services. I believe with the opportunities in the larger City of Las Vegas, I can once again utilize and demonstrate my knowledge of the positions and have a positive impact by being an asset rather than a liability.

We are in trying times now and I want to be apart of the upward spiral, to the top, for the Nevada Sierra District, once again, just as I have done in North Las Vegas under the leadership of my previous postmasters. It would be an honor for me to participate in the challenges that we face today along with rising to the occasion to help conquer the hurdles.

I want to thank you in advance for your time in acknowledging my request and I look forward to hearing from you in the near future.

Sincerely

Lola McGee
Supervisor, Customer Services
North Las Vegas Post Office
1414 E. Lake Mead Blvd.
North Las Vegas, Nevada 89030

April 8, 2009

To: Yul Melonson, Postmaster Las Vegas
Robert Reynosa, Manager, Customer Service Operations Las Vegas
Corey Richards, Postmaster North Las Vegas

From: Lola McGee
Supervisor, Customer Services
North Las Vegas Main Post Office

Regarding: Response to Lateral Request Letter dated February 11, 2009

Hello Gentlemen,

I have not received a written response from my request letter dated above; however, I was assigned to Spring Valley Station in Las Vegas effective 3/9/2009. Unfortunately, I got injured on 3/13/2009 and now I'm out with an on-the-job injury. In addition, I was told to send my Continuation of Pay (COP) 3971 document to North Las Vegas Main Office rather than Spring Valley Station located at 3375 Rainbow Blvd. Las Vegas, NV 89146.

I'm confused because I have not received a written response to my February 11, 2009 Lateral Request to the City of Las Vegas. Also, I was informed by Yul that I was not to put my Core Objectives into PES because my PS Form-50 still had North Las Vegas on it; however, when I went to North Las Vegas to submit my objectives, I was told by Corey that I was not to put my requirements in there. In addition, he called Maggie Lara to get clarification and she stated that he (Corey Richards) was correct since I was in the City of Las Vegas. I explained what Yul told me to do and I stated that if I'm on a detail that I'm not required to put it into PES unless it's six (6) months or more.

To no avail, Corey refuse to let me even use the computer let alone input my Core Objectives. This will have an affect on my midyear and end of year rating for my NPA raise for fiscal year 2009. Also, I requested two (2)I forms and a CA-2 and he refused to give me those until he called and spoke to Joni Payne in Injury Compensation. He later gave me one (1) CA-1 Form.

It is at this time that I'm requesting a written complete and absolute decision on my request for the lateral to the City of Las Vegas.

I thank you in advance for your immediate attention and concern in this matter.

Sincerely

Lola McGee

4E-890-0043-09 **Assignment Order**

Instructions - *(Please Provide a Copy to the Employee)*

Purpose Complete this form to record management-directed assignment changes involving:

a. Temporary assignments to perform duties other than those in employee's official job description, including higher level and training assignments.

b. Scheduled hours and/or days off when schedule change is not posted.

Frequency Form is valid up to 6 months (180 days). A new form is required for assignments exceeding 180 days, or subject to local management discretion.

Approvals Assignments and changes must be approved by immediate supervisor or the manager.

Signatures If employee is unable to sign the form, the supervisor must indicate how the employee was notified in the employee signature space. Details of notification are to be provided in the form's Employee Notification Box.

Current Assignment

To: *(Name)* Lois B. McGee

Position Title: Supervisor, Customer Services

Home Installation: North Las Vegas Post Office 31-6200

Employee ID: 03413020

Employee Official Tour

Begin Tour: 09.30 | End Tour: 18.30

Lunch Out: 11.00 | Lunch Return: 12.00

Scheduled Days Off: ☑ Saturday ☐ Monday ☐ Wednesday ☐ Friday ☑ Sunday ☐ Tuesday ☐ Thursday

Des/Act Code	LDC	OPER-LU	Rate Schedule	Level	Pay Location	FLSA
09-0	20			17	001	☐ Exempt ☐ Nonexempt

New Directed Assignment

Position Title: Supervisor, Customer Services

FLSA Worksheet *(If temporary assignment includes hours outside of (paid) FLSA work week, enter FLSA work week and send copy to FLSA coordinator)* ☐ Friday ☐ Saturday

Des/Act Code	LDC	OPER-LU	Rate Schedule	Level	Pay Location	FLSA Exempt to Nonexempt Position
09-0	20 00	7050-82		17	062	☐ Yes ☐ No

Reason for Assignment ☐ *(If other, explain)* ☐ Annual Leave ☐ Vacancy ☐ Sick Leave ☐ Detail ☐ Scheduled Day Off

Employee Type: ☐ Bargaining Unit Employee - Notify by Wednesday of week preceding change *(Not required for clerk craft if detailed to a nonbargaining position)* ☑ Nonbargaining Employee - Provide 4 days notice

Location *(Give exact worksite, if route, give number)*: 3375 Rainbow Blvd.

Finance Number: 31-4897

Higher Level Authorization Method: ☐ Auto Higher Level ☐ Daily Authorization ☐ Temporary Job Assignment ☐ Timecard 1230-C

TACS ENTERED

Employee Assigned Tour

Begin Tour: 06.00 | End Tour: 15.00

Lunch Out: 11.00 | Lunch Return: 12.00

Scheduled Days Off: ☐ Saturday ☐ Monday ☐ Wednesday ☐ Friday ☑ Sunday ☐ Tuesday ☐ Thursday

Assignment Start Date: 03/09/2009 | Time: 06.00 ☑ AM ☐ PM

Assignment End Date: 09/09/2010 4-3-09 | Time: 15.00 ☐ AM ☑ PM

Start Date for RSC E or V to E or V Higher Level *(5 days after assignment start date)* | Date *(MM/DD/YYYY)*

Supervisor Name *(Print)*: Joe W. Acosta

Supervisor Signature | Date: 3/13/2009

Employee Signature | Date *(MM/DD/YYYY)*: 3/13/09

Comments on Employee Notification

Date Employee Was Notified *(MM/DD/YYYY)*

PS Form 1723, December 2000 PSN 7530-02-000-7366

1.0.0

Personal Printer/Fax/Copier/Scanner

Apr 28 2009 2:24PM

4E-890-0043-09

Last Transaction

Date	Time	Type	Identification	Duration	Pages	Result
Apr 28	2:23PM	Received	702 361 5373	0:38	1	OK

1723

Debbie Letts
Sent it to me
4/28/09

Dorman, Kristine D - Las Vegas, NV

From: Letts, Debbie M - Las Vegas, NV
Sent: Tuesday, April 07, 2009 11:24 AM
To: Dorman, Kristine D - Las Vegas, NV
Subject: FW: L. McGee

Importance: High

4E-890-0043-09

Please do...

From: Zill, Kathleen E - Las Vegas, NV
Sent: Tuesday, April 07, 2009 11:17 AM
To: Letts, Debbie M - Las Vegas, NV
Cc: Reynosa, Robert A - Las Vegas, NV
Subject: L. McGee
Importance: High

ACS ENTERED

Debbie,

Robert asked that I contact you to end L. McGee's 1723 to the City effective 4/2/2009.

Will you please?

Thanks,

Kathy Zill -
Supervisor, Customer Service Support
((702) 361-9399 FAX (651) 365-9735 Cell (702) 232-6243

CONFIDENTIALITY NOTICE
This communication is intended for the sole use of the individual or entity to which it is addressed and may contain information that is privileged, confidential, and exempt from disclosure under applicable law. If the reader of this communication is not the intended recipient or the employee or agent responsible for delivering the message to the intended recipient, you are hereby notified that any dissemination, distribution, or copying of this communication may be strictly prohibited. If you have received this communication in error, please notify me immediately by telephone (702-361-9399) and return the communication to me at 1001 E. Sunset Road Las Vegas, NV 89199

Thank you.

4E-890-0043-09

UNITED STATES POSTAL SERVICE

Request for or Notification of Absence

Employee's Name *(Last, first, M.I.)*	Employee ID	Date Submitted	No. of Hours Requested
MCGEE, LOLA B	03413020	03/08/2009	24.00

Installation *(For PM leave, show city, state and ZIP code)*	N/S Day	Pay Loc. #	D/A Code	From Date	Hour
31-6200 - NORTH LAS VEGAS NV		001	090	03/10/2009	09:00

Time of Call or Request	Scheduled Reporting Time	Employee Can Be Reached At *(If needed)*	Thru Date	Hour
08:00	09:00	☐ No Call	03/12/2009	18:00

Type of Absence
- ☐ Annual
- ☐ Holiday/AL Lv Exch
- ☐ Carrier 701 Rule
- ☐ LWOP *(See reverse)*
- ☐ Sick *(See reverse)*
- ☐ Late
- ☐ COP
- ☒ Other: AL

Documentation (For official use only)
- ☐ For FMLA Leave (Certification reviewed)
- ☐ For COP Leave (CA1 on file)
- ☐ For Advanced Sick Leave (1221 on file)
- ☐ For Military Leave (Orders reviewed)
- ☐ For Court Leave (Summons reviewed)
- ☐ For Higher Level (1723 on file)
- ☐ Scheme Training Testing, Qualifying (Memo on file)

Revised Schedule for *(Date)*

Approved in Advance ☐ Yes ☐ No

Begin Work	
Lunch-Out	
Lunch-In	
End Work	
Total Hours	

Remarks *(Do not enter medical information)*
NOT IOD; NOT FMLA

I understand that the annual leave authorized in excess of amount available to me during the leave year will be changed to LWOP.

Employee's Signature and Date	Signature of Person Recording Absence and Date	Signature of Supervisor and Date Notified
3/13/09	3/13/09	3/13/2009

Scheduled	Un-Scheduled	PP	Year
		06	2009

Scheduled	Un-Scheduled	Day	Init.	Hours
		SAT 01		
		SUN 02		
		MON 03		
		TUE 04		
		WED 05		
		THU 06		
		FRI 07		
		SAT 08		
		SUN 09		
		MON 10		
	x	TUE 11		8.00
	x	WED 12		8.00
	x	THU 13		8.00
		FRI 14		

Official Action on Application *(Return copy of signed request to employee)*

- ☐ Approved, not FMLA
- ☐ Approved FMLA/Pending Documentation Noted on Reverse.
- ☐ Approved, FMLA *(See Publication 71)*
- ☐ Disapproved (Give Reason):
- ☐ Ineligible for FMLA (Estimate eligibility date):

Signature of Supervisor and Date 3/13/2009

☐ Continued on Reverse

PS Form 3971, March 2008 (Page 1 of 2) PSN 7530-02-000-9136

Warning: The furnishing of false information on this form may result in a fine of not more than $10,000 or imprisonment of not more than 5 years, or both. *(18 U.S.C. 1001)*

Employee: Reason I Was Incapacitated for Duty During This Absence
- ☐ Sickness
- ☐ On-the-Job Injury
- ☐ Off- the-Job Injury
- ☐ Pregnancy and Confinement
- ☐ Exposed to a Contagious Disease
- ☐ Undergoing Medical, Dental, or Optical Examination or Treatment (Job related)
- ☐ Undergoing Medical, Dental, or Optical Examination or Treatment (Not job related)

Reason I Was Unavailable for Duty During This Absence
- ☐ Sick Leave for Dependent Care
- ☐ Birth of Child - Bonding
- ☐ Placement of a Child with Employee for Adoption or Foster Care

Supervisor: Additional Documentation Regarding Denial of Leave Protection Under FMLA
- ☐ Employee Not Eligible - Less than 1250 Hours Worked.
- ☐ Employee Not Eligible - Not Employed with USPS 1 Year.
- ☐ Employee Has Exhausted FMLA Entitlement in Current Leave Year.
- ☐ Absence Not for a Covered Condition.
- ☐ Absence Not for a Covered Family Member.
- ☐ Requested Documentation Not Provided.
- ☐ Documentation Provided. Does Not Meet Criteria for FMLA Protection.

Additional Documentation Required

Privacy Act Statement: Your information will be used to administer leave. Collection is authorized by 39 USC 401, 404, 1001, 1003, and 1005; and 29 USC 2601 et seq. Providing the information is voluntary, but if not provided, we may not process your request. Your information may be disclosed as follows: in relevant legal proceedings; to law enforcement when the USPS or requesting agency becomes aware of a violation of law; to a congressional office at your request; to entities under contract with USPS and/or authorized to perform audits; to labor organizations as required by law; to government agencies regarding personel matters; and to the EEOC; MSPB or Office of Special Counsel.

Leave Types *(Information Only)* — CODES

Leave Type	Time Card	FMLA Dep. Care	Time Clock
Annual- FMLA	55	01	05599
Sick- FMLA	56	02	05699
Sick - Dependent Care	56	07	05697
Absent Without Leave	24		02400
Act of God	78		07800
Blood Donor	69		06900
Civil Defense	77		07700
Civil Disorder	81		08100
COP - USPS	71		07100
COP - USPS - FMLA	71	03	07199
Convention	66		06600
Court Duty	61		06100
Donated - FMLA	46		04600
HQ Authorized Administrative	79		07900
Holiday/AL Leave Exchange	28		02800
LWOP - Part Day	59		05900
LWOP - Full Day	60		06000
LWOP - FMLA - Part Day	59	05	05999
LWOP - FMLA - Full Day	60	06	06099
LWOP - IOD/OWCP - FMLA	49	04	04999
LWOP - IOD/OWCP - not FMLA	49		04999
LWOP - Lieu of Sick Leave	59 or 60		05901 or 06001
LWOP - Maternity	59 or 6		05905 or 06005
LWOP - Military	44		04400
LWOP - Personal Reasons	59 or 60		05903 or 06003
LWOP - Proffered	59 or 6		05902 or 06002
LWOP - Suspension	59 or 6		05906 or 06006
LWOP - Suspension Pend. Term.	59 or 6		05908 or 06008
LWOP - Union Official	84		08400
Military	67		06700
Relocation	80		08000
Veteran's Funeral	86		08600
Voting Leave	85		08500
Other Paid	86		08600

Scheduled	Un-Scheduled	PP	Year

Scheduled	Un-Scheduled	Day	Init.	Hours
		SAT 01		
		SUN 02		
		MON 03		
		TUE 04		
		WED 05		
		THU 06		
		FRI 07		
		SAT 08		
		SUN 09		
		MON 10		
		TUE 11		
		WED 12		
		THU 13		
		FRI 14		

PS Form 3971, March 2008 (Page 2 of 2)

4E-890-0043-09

UNITED STATES POSTAL SERVICE

Request for or Notification of Absence

Employee's Name *(Last, first, M.I.)*: MCGEE, LOLA B
Employee ID: 03413020
Date Submitted: 03/11/2009
No. of Hours Requested: 8.00

Installation *(For PM leave, show city, state and ZIP code)*: 31-6200 - NORTH LAS VEGAS NV
N/S Day:
Pay Loc. #: 001
D/A Code: 090
From Date: 03/19/2009 Hour: 09:00

Time of Call or Request: 04:30
Scheduled Reporting Time: 09:00
Employee Can Be Reached At *(If needed)*: ☐ No Call
Thru Date: 03/19/2009 Hour: 18:00

Type of Absence
- [x] Annual
- [ ] Holiday/AL Lv Exch
- [ ] Carrier 701 Rule
- [ ] LWOP *(See reverse)*
- [ ] Sick *(See reverse)*
- [ ] Late
- [ ] COP
- [x] Other: AL

Documentation (For official use only)
- [ ] For FMLA Leave (Certification reviewed)
- [ ] For COP Leave (CA1 on file)
- [ ] For Advanced Sick Leave (1221 on file)
- [ ] For Military Leave (Orders reviewed)
- [ ] For Court Leave (Summons reviewed)
- [ ] For Higher Level (1723 on file)
- [ ] Scheme Training Testing, Qualifying (Memo on file)

Revised Schedule for *(Date)*:
Approved in Advance ☐ Yes ☐ No

Begin Work	
Lunch-Out	
Lunch-In	
End Work	
Total Hours	

Remarks *(Do not enter medical information)*
NOT IOD; NOT FMLA

Scheduled	Un-Scheduled	PP 07 / Day	Init.	Year 2009 / Hours
		SAT 01		
		SUN 02		
		MON 03		
		TUE 04		
		WED 05		
x		THU 06		8.00
		FRI 07		
		SAT 08		
		SUN 09		
		MON 10		
		TUE 11		
		WED 12		
		THU 13		
		FRI 14		

I understand that the annual leave authorized in excess of amount available to me during the leave year will be changed to LWOP.

Employee's Signature and Date: 3/13/09
Signature of Person Recording Absence and Date: 3/13/09
Signature of Supervisor and Date Notified: 3/13/09

Official Action on Application *(Return copy of signed request to employee)*

- [ ] Approved, not FMLA
- [ ] Approved FMLA Pending Documentation Noted on Reverse.
- [ ] Approved, FMLA *(See Publication 71)*
- [ ] Disapproved (Give Reason):
- [ ] Ineligible for FMLA (Estimate eligibility date):

Signature of Supervisor and Date: 3/13/09

☐ *Continued on Reverse*

PS Form 3971, March 2008 (Page 1 of 2) PSN 7530-02-000-9136

Warning: The furnishing of false information on this form may result in a fine of not more than $10,000 or imprisonment of not more than 5 years, or both. *(18 U.S.C. 1001)*

Employee: Reason I Was Incapacitated for Duty During This Absence
- [ ] Sickness
- [ ] On-the-Job Injury
- [ ] Off-the-Job Injury
- [ ] Pregnancy and Confinement
- [ ] Exposed to a Contagious Disease
- [ ] Undergoing Medical, Dental, or Optical Examination or Treatment (Job related)
- [ ] Undergoing Medical, Dental, or Optical Examination or Treatment (Not job related)

Reason I Was Unavailable for Duty During This Absence
- [ ] Sick Leave for Dependent Care
- [ ] Birth of Child - Bonding
- [ ] Placement of a Child with Employee for Adoption or Foster Care

Supervisor: Additional Documentation Regarding Denial of Leave Protection Under FMLA
- [ ] Employee Not Eligible - Less than 1250 Hours Worked.
- [ ] Employee Not Eligible - Not Employed with USPS 1 Year.
- [ ] Employee Has Exhausted FMLA Entitlement in Current Leave Year.
- [ ] Absence Not for a Covered Condition.
- [ ] Absence Not for a Covered Family Member.
- [ ] Requested Documentation Not Provided.
- [ ] Documentation Provided. Does Not Meet Criteria for FMLA Protection.

Additional Documentation Required

Privacy Act Statement: Your information will be used to administer leave. Collection is authorized by 39 USC 401, 404, 1001, 1003, and 1005; and 29 USC 2601 et seq. Providing the information is voluntary, but if not provided, we may not process your request. Your information may be disclosed as follows: in relevant legal proceedings; to law enforcement when the USPS or requesting agency becomes aware of a violation of law; to a congressional office at your request; to entities under contract with USPS and/or authorized to perform audits; to labor organizations as required by law; to government agencies regarding personel matters; and to the EEOC; MSPB or Office of Special Counsel.

Leave Types *(Information Only)* — CODES

Leave Type	Time Card	FMLA Dep. Care	Time Clock
Annual- FMLA	55	01	05599
Sick- FMLA	56	02	05699
Sick - Dependent Care	56	07	05697
Absent Without Leave	24		02400
Act of God	78		07800
Blood Donor	69		06900
Civil Defense	77		07700
Civil Disorder	81		08100
COP - USPS	71		07100
COP - USPS - FMLA	71	03	07199
Convention	66		06600
Court Duty	61		06100
Donated - FMLA	46		04600
HQ Authorized Administrative	79		07900
Holiday/AL Leave Exchange	28		02800
LWOP - Part Day	59		05900
LWOP - Full Day	60		06000
LWOP - FMLA - Part Day	59	05	05999
LWOP - FMLA - Full Day	60	06	06099
LWOP - IOD/OWCP - FMLA	49	04	04999
LWOP - IOD/OWCP - not FMLA	49		04999
LWOP - Lieu of Sick Leave	59 or 60		05901 or 06001
LWOP - Maternity	59 or 6		05905 or 06005
LWOP - Military	44		04400
LWOP - Personal Reasons	59 or 60		05903 or 06003
LWOP - Proffered	59 or 6		05902 or 06002
LWOP - Suspension	59 or 6		05906 or 06006
LWOP - Suspension Pend. Tem.	59 or 6		05908 or 06008
LWOP - Union Official	84		08400
Military	67		06700
Relocation	80		08000
Veteran's Funeral	86		08600
Voting Leave	85		08500
Other Paid	86		08600

Scheduled	Un-Scheduled	PP / Day	Init.	Year / Hours
		SAT 01		
		SUN 02		
		MON 03		
		TUE 04		
		WED 05		
		THU 06		
		FRI 07		
		SAT 08		
		SUN 09		
		MON 10		
		TUE 11		
		WED 12		
		THU 13		
		FRI 14		

PS Form 3971, March 2008 (Page 2 of 2)

4E – 890 – 0043 – 09

UNITED STATES POSTAL SERVICE

Request for or Notification of Absence

Employee's Name *(Last, first, M.I.)*	Employee ID	Date Submitted	No. of Hours Requested
MCGEE, LOLA B	03413020	03/07/2009	8.00

Installation *(For PM leave, show city, state and ZIP code)*	N/S Day	Pay Loc. #	D/A Code	From Date	Hour
31-6200 - NORTH LAS VEGAS NV		001	090	03/09/2009	09:00

Time of Call or Request	Scheduled Reporting Time	Employee Can Be Reached At *(If needed)*	Thru Date	Hour
08:00	09:00	☐ No Call	03/09/2009	18:00

Type of Absence
- ☐ Annual
- ☐ Holiday/AL Lv Exch
- ☐ Carrier 701 Rule
- ☐ LWOP *(See reverse)*
- ☐ Sick *(See reverse)*
- ☐ Late
- ☐ COP
- x Other: EAL

Documentation (For official use only)
- ☐ For FMLA Leave (Certification reviewed)
- ☐ For COP Leave (CA1 on file)
- ☐ For Advanced Sick Leave (1221 on file)
- ☐ For Military Leave (Orders reviewed)
- ☐ For Court Leave (Summons reviewed)
- ☐ For Higher Level (1723 on file)
- ☐ Scheme Training Testing, Qualifying (Memo on file)

Revised Schedule for *(Date)*

Approved in Advance ☐ Yes ☐ No

Begin Work	
Lunch-Out	
Lunch-In	
End Work	
Total Hours	

Remarks *(Do not enter medical information)*
NOT IOD; NOT FMLA - Extensive water damage requiring removal of furniture, etc.

Scheduled	Un-Scheduled	PP 06		Year 2009
		Day	Init.	Hours
		SAT 01		
		SUN 02		
		MON 03		
		TUE 04		
		WED 05		
		THU 06		
		FRI 07		
		SAT 08		
		SUN 09		
	x	MON 10		8.00
		TUE 11		
		WED 12		
		THU 13		
		FRI 14		

I understand that the annual leave authorized in excess of amount available to me during the leave year will be changed to LWOP.

Employee's Signature and Date	Signature of Person Recording Absence and Date	Signature of Supervisor and Date Notified
3/13/09	3/13/09	3/13/2009

Official Action on Application *(Return copy of signed request to employee)*

- ✓ Approved, not FMLA
- ☐ Approved FMLA, Pending Documentation Noted on Reverse.
- ☐ Approved, FMLA *(See Publication 71)*
- ☐ Disapproved (Give Reason):
- ☐ Ineligible for FMLA (Estimate eligibility date):

Signature of Supervisor and Date 3/13/2009

☐ *Continued on Reverse*

PS Form **3971**, March 2008 (Page 1 of 2) PSN 7530-02-000-9136

Warning: The furnishing of false information on this form may result in a fine of not more than $10,000 or imprisonment of not more than 5 years, or both. *(18 U.S.C. 1001)*

Employee: Reason I Was Incapacitated for Duty During This Absence
- ☐ Sickness
- ☐ On-the-Job Injury
- ☐ Off- the-Job Injury
- ☐ Pregnancy and Confinement
- ☐ Exposed to a Contagious Disease
- ☐ Undergoing Medical, Dental, or Optical Examination or Treatment (Job related)
- ☐ Undergoing Medical, Dental, or Optical Examination or Treatment (Not job related)

Reason I Was Unavailable for Duty During This Absence
- ☐ Sick Leave for Dependent Care
- ☐ Birth of Child - Bonding
- ☐ Placement of a Child with Employee for Adoption or Foster Care

Supervisor: Additional Documentation Regarding Denial of Leave Protection Under FMLA
- ☐ Employee Not Eligible - Less than 1250 Hours Worked.
- ☐ Employee Not Eligible - Not Employed with USPS 1 Year.
- ☐ Employee Has Exhausted FMLA Entitlement in Current Leave Year.
- ☐ Absence Not for a Covered Condition.
- ☐ Absence Not for a Covered Family Member.
- ☐ Requested Documentation Not Provided.
- ☐ Documentation Provided. Does Not Meet Criteria for FMLA Protection.

Additional Documentation Required

Privacy Act Statement: Your information will be used to administer leave. Collection is authorized by 39 USC 401, 404, 1001, 1003, and 1005; and 29 USC 2601 et seq. Providing the information is voluntary, but if not provided, we may not process your request. Your information may be disclosed as follows: in relevant legal proceedings; to law enforcement when the USPS or requesting agency becomes aware of a violation of law; to a congressional office at your request; to entities under contract with USPS and/or authorized to perform audits; to labor organizations as required by law; to government agencies regarding personel matters; and to the EEOC; MSPB or Office of Special Counsel.

Leave Types *(Information Only)* — CODES

Leave Type	Time Card	FMLA Dep. Care	Time Clock
Annual- FMLA	55	01	05599
Sick- FMLA	56	02	05699
Sick - Dependent Care	56	07	05697
Absent Without Leave	24		02400
Act of God	78		07800
Blood Donor	69		06900
Civil Defense	77		07700
Civil Disorder	81		08100
COP - USPS	71		07100
COP - USPS - FMLA	71	03	07199
Convention	66		06600
Court Duty	61		06100
Donated - FMLA	46		04600
HQ Authorized Administrative	79		07900
Holiday/AL Leave Exchange	28		02800
LWOP - Part Day	59		05900
LWOP - Full Day	60		06000
LWOP - FMLA - Part Day	59	05	05999
LWOP - FMLA - Full Day	60	06	06099
LWOP - IOD/OWCP - FMLA	49	04	04999
LWOP - IOD/OWCP - not FMLA	49		04999
LWOP - Lieu of Sick Leave	59 or 60		05901 or 06001
LWOP - Maternity	59 or 6		05905 or 06005
LWOP - Military	44		04400
LWOP - Personal Reasons	59 or 60		05903 or 06003
LWOP - Proffered	59 or 6		05902 or 06002
LWOP - Suspension	59 or 6		05906 or 06006
LWOP - Suspension Pend. Tem.	59 or 6		05908 or 06008
LWOP - Union Official	84		08400
Military	67		06700
Relocation	80		08000
Veteran's Funeral	86		08600
Voting Leave	85		08500
Other Paid	86		08600

Scheduled	Un-Scheduled	PP		Year
		Day	Init.	Hours
		SAT 01		
		SUN 02		
		MON 03		
		TUE 04		
		WED 05		
		THU 06		
		FRI 07		
		SAT 08		
		SUN 09		
		MON 10		
		TUE 11		
		WED 12		
		THU 13		
		FRI 14		

PS Form 3971, March 2008 (Page 2 of 2)

4E-890-0043-09

Page:	A	5 of 6
Billing Cycle Date:		03/04/09 - 04/03/09
Account Number:		534556273
Bill Reprint		

Call Detail (Continued) 562-889-

User Name: WYKEISHA COOPER — Lola McGee

Rate Code: RM90=900 Rollover Mins, UNW9=Unlimited N&W, MME0=Unlimited Expd M2M, CN3N=NTN900RUMMUNW
Rate Period (PD): DT=Daytime, NW=Nwknd
Feature: VM=VOICE MAIL, M2MC=EXPANDED M2M, CW=Call Waiting

Item	Day	Date	Time	Number Called	Call To	Min	Rate Code	Rate Pd	Feature	Airtime Charge	LD/Add'l Charge	Total Charge	
221		04/01	12:18PM	702-220-5830	LAS VE NV	2	RM90	DT				0.00	
222		04/01	12:24PM	702-301-2066	LAS VE NV	1	MME0	DT	M2MC			0.00	
223		04/01	4:32PM	702-407-0110	LAS VE NV	8	RM90	DT				0.00	
224		04/01	5:46PM	702-423-2175	LAS VE NV	21	MME0	DT	M2MC			0.00	
225		04/01	6:17PM	310-462-4271	INCOMI CL	2	RM90	DT				0.00	
226	THU	04/02	10:44AM	702-219-5432	LAS VE NV	1	RM90	DT				0.00	
227		04/02	10:45AM	702-219-5432	LAS VE NV	11	RM90	DT				0.00	
228		04/02	11:06AM	702-219-5432	LAS VE NV	2	RM90	DT				0.00	
229		04/02	11:10AM	702-806-0415	LAS VE NV	2	RM90	DT				0.00	→ JOE
230		04/02	11:29AM	702-586-4497	LAS VE NV	1	RM90	DT				0.00	
231		04/02	11:30AM	702-435-9292	LAS VE NV	1	RM90	DT				0.00	
232		04/02	12:20PM	702-806-0415	LAS VE NV	1	RM90	DT				0.00	→ JOE
233		04/02	12:32PM	702-263-4795	LAS VE NV	2	RM90	DT				0.00	
234		04/02	12:34PM	702-806-0415	INCOMI CL	6	RM90	DT				0.00	→ JOE
235		04/02	1:22PM	702-263-4795	LAS VE NV	4	RM90	DT				0.00	
236		04/02	1:26PM	702-586-4497	LAS VE NV	1	RM90	DT				0.00	
237		04/02	2:55PM	702-423-2175	INCOMI CL	1	MME0	DT	M2MC			0.00	→ YUL
238		04/02	3:22PM	801-852-8700	INCOMI CL	1	RM90	DT				0.00	
239		04/02	3:25PM	702-423-2175	LAS VE NV	5	MME0	DT	M2MC			0.00	→ YUL
240		04/02	4:23PM	702-586-4497	LAS VE NV	1	RM90	DT				0.00	
241		04/02	4:24PM	702-385-0777	LAS VE NV	2	RM90	DT				0.00	
242		04/02	4:26PM	702-434-8282	LAS VE NV	2	RM90	DT				0.00	
243		04/02	4:33PM	702-565-8911	LAS VE NV	3	RM90	DT				0.00	
244		04/02	4:35PM	702-566-5500	LAS VE NV	2	RM90	DT				0.00	
245		04/02	4:36PM	702-385-0777	CALL WAIT	6	RM90	DT	CW			0.00	
246		04/02	4:42PM	702-566-5500	LAS VE NV	6	RM90	DT				0.00	
247		04/02	4:50PM	702-361-9330	LAS VE NV	4	RM90	DT				0.00	
248		04/02	5:22PM	800-571-4501	Toll F CL	2	RM90	DT				0.00	
249		04/02	5:24PM	702-809-6858	LAS VE NV	1	RM90	DT				0.00	
250		04/02	6:42PM	702-806-0415	LAS VE NV	1	RM90	DT				0.00	
251		04/02	6:43PM	310-462-4271	INGLEW CA	1	RM90	DT				0.00	
252		04/02	6:52PM	800-727-4060	Toll F CL	3	RM90	DT				0.00	
253		04/02	6:55PM	702-586-4497	LAS VE NV	1	RM90	DT				0.00	
254		04/02	7:00PM	310-462-4271	INCOMI CL	7	RM90	DT				0.00	
255		04/02	7:06PM	310-462-4271	INGLEW CA	3	RM90	DT				0.00	
256		04/02	7:15PM	310-462-4271	INCOMI CL	1	RM90	DT				0.00	
257	FRI	04/03	7:06PM	661-703-7586	BKFD M CA	3	RM90	DT				0.00	
258		04/03	9:30PM	562-889-2662	VMAIL CL	7	UNW9	NW	VM			0.00	
259		04/03	9:38PM	661-703-7586	BKFD M CA	6	UNW9	NW				0.00	
		Subtotal Minutes				**969**						**0.00**	
Totals						**969**						**0.00**	

Interstate Calls Subtotal	0.00
Intrastate Calls Subtotal	0.00

Data Detail 562-889-

User Name: WYKEISHA COOPER

Rate Code: TMI1=Text Msg Pay Per Use
Rate Period (PD): AT=Anytime
Feature: SMH=SMS per msg $0.20 MO/MT - PPU

Item	Day	Date	Time	To/From	Type	Msg/KB/Min	Rate Code	Rate Pd	Feature	In/Out	Total Charge
1	THU	03/05	3:05PM	310-462-4271	Text Message	1 Msg	TMI1	AT	SMH	In	0.20

4E-890-0043-09

Page: A 4 of 8
Billing Cycle Date: 01/04/09 - 02/03/09
Account Number: 534556273
Bill Reprint

Call Detail (Continued) **562-889-.**

User Name: WYKEISHA COOPER – Lola McGee

Rate Code: RM60=600 Rollover Mins, UNWO=Unlimited N&W, RM13=1350 Rollover Mins, UNW9=Unlimited N&W,
ESM1=Unlimited Expd M2M, MME0=Unlimited Expd M2M
Rate Period (PD): DT=Daytime, NW=Nwknd
Feature: VM=VOICE MAIL, M2MC=EXPANDED M2M, CW=Call Waiting

Item	Day	Date	Time	Number Called	Call To	Min	Rate Code	Rate Pd	Feature	Airtime Charge	LD/Add'l Charge	Total Charge
163	FRI	01/16	8:02AM	661-703-7586	BKFD M CA	2	RM60	DT				0.00
164		01/16	11:47AM	661-703-7586	BKFD M CA	2	RM60	DT				0.00
165		01/16	12:06PM	303-856-3572	AURORA CO	1	RM60	DT				0.00
166		01/16	12:07PM	702-385-0777	LAS VE NV	2	RM60	DT				0.00
167		01/16	12:11PM	702-361-9200	LAS VE NV	2	RM60	DT				0.00
168		01/16	12:13PM	702-423-2175	LAS VE NV	2	ESM1	DT	M2MC			0.00 → yul
169		01/16	12:48PM	310-462-5811	INGLEW CA	17	RM60	DT				0.00
170		01/16	1:05PM	702-914-8987	LAS VE NV	2	RM60	DT				0.00
171		01/16	1:18PM	702-953-9733	INCOMI CL	5	RM60	DT				0.00
172		01/16	1:46PM	702-423-2175	INCOMI CL	6	ESM1	DT	M2MC			0.00
173		01/16	1:52PM	702-423-2176	LAS VE NV	1	ESM1	DT	M2MC			0.00
174		01/16	1:55PM	702-423-2175	LAS VE NV	1	ESM1	DT	M2MC			0.00
175		01/16	2:22PM	702-423-2175	LAS VE NV	3	ESM1	DT	M2MC			0.00
176		01/16	2:26PM	702-423-2175	LAS VE NV	2	ESM1	DT	M2MC			0.00
177		01/16	4:53PM	661-703-7586	BKFD M CA	2	RM60	DT				0.00
178		01/16	4:54PM	661-835-9214	BKFD S CA	3	RM60	DT				0.00
179		01/16	4:58PM	702-385-0777	LAS VE NV	1	RM60	DT				0.00
180		01/16	5:03PM	661-703-7586	INCOMI CL	50	RM60	DT				0.00
181		01/16	7:24PM	661-703-7586	INCOMI CL	16	RM60	DT				0.00
182		01/16	7:39PM	310-946-5942	CALL WAIT	27	RM60	DT	CW			0.00
183		01/16	8:06PM	661-703-7586	BKFD M CA	30	RM60	DT				0.00
184		01/16	8:35PM	661-703-7586	BKFD M CA	17	RM60	DT				0.00
185	SAT	01/17	1:37PM	702-914-8987	LAS VE NV	1	UNWO	NW				0.00
186		01/17	3:00PM	562-219-1511	INCOMI CL	1	UNWO	NW				0.00
187		01/17	5:11PM	661-703-7586	BKFD M CA	15	UNWO	NW				0.00
188		01/17	5:46PM	562-889-2662	INCOMI CL	13	UNWO	NW				0.00
189		01/17	9:14PM	661-703-7586	INCOMI CL	5	UNWO	NW				0.00
190	SUN	01/18	11:14AM	310-946-5942	INCOMI CL	3	UNWO	NW				0.00
191		01/18	11:17AM	562-889-2662	VMAIL CL	2	UNWO	NW	VM			0.00
192		01/18	12:00PM	661-703-7586	BKFD M CA	1	UNWO	NW				0.00
193		01/18	6:39PM	661-703-7586	INCOMI CL	10	UNWO	NW				0.00
194		01/18	6:49PM	661-703-7586	INCOMI CL	12	UNWO	NW				0.00
195		01/18	7:00PM	661-703-7586	BKFD M CA	1	UNWO	NW				0.00
196		01/18	7:01PM	661-835-9214	INCOMI CL	70	UNWO	NW				0.00
197		01/18	8:11PM	562-889-2662	VMAIL CL	1	UNWO	NW	VM			0.00
198		01/18	8:12PM	702-914-8987	LAS VE NV	8	UNWO	NW				0.00
199	MON	01/19	10:48AM	310-462-5811	INCOMI CL	3	RM60	DT				0.00
200		01/19	4:20PM	310-462-5811	INCOMI CL	2	RM60	DT				0.00
201	TUE	01/20	8:09AM	310-462-5811	INCOMI CL	1	RM60	DT				0.00
202		01/20	8:40AM	310-462-5811	INGLEW CA	1	RM60	DT				0.00
203		01/20	8:45AM	770-339-0214	ATLANT GA	1	RM60	DT				0.00
204		01/20	8:46AM	310-462-5811	INGLEW CA	1	RM60	DT				0.00
205		01/20	8:47AM	562-804-2613	NORWAL CA	1	RM60	DT				0.00
206		01/20	8:48AM	562-355-1604	LONG B CA	1	RM60	DT				0.00
207		01/20	8:49AM	310-462-5811	INGLEW CA	1	RM60	DT				0.00
208		01/20	8:50AM	770-339-0214	ATLANT GA	1	RM60	DT				0.00
209		01/20	9:11AM	310-462-5811	INGLEW CA	1	RM60	DT				0.00
210		01/20	9:32AM	310-462-5811	INCOMI CL	4	RM60	DT				0.00
211		01/20	9:38AM	310-462-5811	INCOMI CL	1	RM60	DT				0.00
212		01/20	9:40AM	562-355-1604	INCOMI CL	3	RM60	DT				0.00
213		01/20	11:10AM	702-914-8987	LAS VE NV	16	RM60	DT				0.00
214		01/20	11:27AM	702-914-8987	INCOMI CL	1	RM60	DT				0.00
215		01/20	12:35PM	661-703-7586	BKFD M CA	1	RM60	DT				0.00
216		01/20	12:36PM	661-703-7586	BKFD M CA	14	RM60	DT				0.00

} yuL (items 172–176)

Date: April 24, 2009

To: U. S. Department of Labor/OWCP
Employment Standards Administration
P. O. Box 8300 District 13 SFC
London, KY 40742-8300

From: Lola McGee
P. O. Box 98272
Las Vegas, NV 89193-8272

Subject: Date of Injury: 3/13/2009 – CA-1 Filed 4/2/2009
File Number: 132209923

Ms. Landry:

The following are the responses toward the information requested:

Provide statements from any persons who witnessed your injury or had immediate knowledge of it, or other documentation that supports your claim.

1. It is up to Joe Acosta to tell the truth; and, I have already written a statement of what happened; it was given to injury compensation.

State the immediate effects of the injury and what you did immediately thereafter.

2. I pushed an orange hamper over to the 89117 routes of the 89146 zone. There were some swings on the floor that were going to be taken out to the street by Karen for other carriers. Karen is a limited duty carrier and she has lifting restrictions. I turned to my left, bent my knees, and lifted the hard plastic trays of mail; also, there were 775 tubs on the floor with mail in them. I do not remember how many trays or tubs there were to be put into the hamper, but as I lifted the last tray I felt a pop/shift in my left knee and my back after which the pain followed. Both knees were in pain, but my left knee pain was more profound. My left thigh started to hurt like sharp lines of pain were running down it. As I was leaning into the hamper I sounded out in pain and I grimmest with a frown and that is when I looked and saw Joe Acosta, acting manager. He asked me if I was okay and I stated "No, but I think I'll be alright". Joe and I left the workroom floor and went into his office where I reported the injury to him that I just incurred on the workroom floor. Through conversation I discussed with him the other on the job injuries that I had previously incurred that began to manifest on 8/25/08. I stated to Joe that I've just come back and I can't go out again and that just wouldn't look good. Joe stated that I had to take care of myself and not worry about anything else. I stated that I will do my best and we will see what happens. I do not know how heavy the trays were; but they were full of strapped out mail in an upright position. The tubs contained coverage and parcels. Joe and I went to his office from the Hamper.

Did you sustain any other injury, either on or off duty, between the date of injury, and the date it was first reported to (a) your supervisor and (b) to a doctor. If so, describe.

3. No

State the exact reason why you delayed seeking medical attention; also give the name and address of the doctor you first consulted and the date you were first examined for this injury.

4. I delayed seeking medical attention because I thought I could work off the pain, and I am still going to physical therapy for the Neuropathy; an on the job injury from 8/25/08. In addition, I had just come back from injury leave and I did not want to go back out. I wanted to try and see if the pain would go away, but to no avail. On 4/2/09 I filed the claim and I went to the emergency room at St. Rose Medical Center in Henderson. 3001 St. Rose Parkway Henderson, NV 89052. I was seen and examined for this on the job injury by R. John Balani, PAC (per FECA, a Physicians Assistants' report may be admissible if a physician cosigns the report) (http://www.dol.gov/esa/owcp/dfec/regs/compliance/DFECfolio/feca-pt3.pdf.). The attending physician that supervised and co-signed my medical record with Mr. Balani during my visit to the St. Rose ER was Dr. John Lewis, MD. The diagnosis of Sciatica pain caused by Lumbar Radiculopathy was given.

Describe (a) your condition between the date of injury and the date you first received medical attention, and (b) the nature and frequency of any home treatment.

5. From the date I was injured on 3/13/09 I have been in experienced back, both knees and left thigh pain everyday; however on 4/2/09 I just could not take this pain anymore and I sought medical treatment at St. Rose Siena ER. In spite of prescribed medications, I am in cutting pain daily. This pain is felt in my entire back. In addition to prescribed medications, I've taken Advil; I have a heating pad, and rubbing ointment. I utilize these interventions as often as my body allows. I message my body as best I can to try and take some of the pain away. I also perform stretch workouts as prescribed by my physical therapist. Some days are better than others. I have my daughter here assisting me because I'm really limited to what I can do on my own.

Did you have any similar disability or symptoms before the injury? If so, describe the prior condition. Please send records of all prior treatment.

6. My back was injured doing construction work in 1994 that resulted in disability; but, I was medically cleared in 1996. In 1998 I was deemed medically fit by a physician of the United States Postal Service without restrictions. I had no pain symptoms resulting from the 1994 injury after 1997. I was in a car accident in 2006 and received about 3 weeks of physical therapy that resulted in no disability. I had no pain symptoms from the car accident, which was minor itself. I had a Panic Attack on 8/25/08 that caused Neuropathy in my feet, legs, lower and upper left buttocks, which resulted in disability and I still suffer from this condition to date.

I will give this letter (requested information) dated 4/9/2009 to the Centennial Spine and Pain Center so that the treating doctor can address the needed information requested by your organization.

Sincerely

Lola McGee

4E-890-0043-09

EMPLOYEE'S CLAIM FOR COMPENSATION/REPORT OF INITIAL TREATMENT
FORM C-4
PLEASE TYPE OR PRINT

EMPLOYEE'S CLAIM – PROVIDE ALL INFORMATION REQUESTED

First Name: Lola | M.I.: Bonitta | Last Name: McGee | Birthdate: 7-7- | Sex: ☐ M ☑ F | Claim Number (Insurer's Use Only)

Home Address: P.O. Box 98272 | Age: 46 | Height: 5'9 | Weight: 245 | Social Security Number

City: LV | State: NV | Zip: 89193-8272 | Telephone: (702) 260-0876

Physical Address: 2121 E. Warmsprings Rd | City: LV | State: NV | Zip: 89119 | Primary Language Spoken: English

INSURER: Dept. of Labor/OWCP | THIRD-PARTY ADMINISTRATOR | Employee's Occupation (Job Title) When Injury or Occupational Disease Occurred: Supervisor, Cust. Serv.

Employer's Name/Company Name: U.S. Postal Service | Telephone: (702) 361-9330

Office Mail Address (Number and Street)

Date of Injury (if applicable): 3/13/09 | Hours Injury (if applicable): 11-1:00 pm am pm | Date Employer Notified: 3/13/09 | Last Day of Work After Injury or Occupational Disease: 4/2/09 | Supervisor to Whom Injury Reported: Joe Acosta

Address or Location of Accident (if applicable): Spring Valley Station LV, NV 89146

What were you doing at the time of the accident? (if applicable): Lifting Trays and Tubs of Mail in to hamper

How did this injury or occupational disease occur? (Be specific and answer in detail. Use additional sheet if necessary): Assisting Limited duty Carriers with Lifting Trays and Tubs/Parcels of Mail in to hamper to be Carried to the street for other Carriers

If you believe that you have an occupational disease, when did you first have knowledge of the disability and its relationship to your employment? not this time

Witnesses to the Accident (if applicable): Joe Acosta

Nature of Injury or Occupational Disease: Sharp Pain in back, Knees, and left thigh | Part(s) of Body Injured or Affected: Back, Knees, Left thigh

I CERTIFY THAT THE ABOVE IS TRUE AND CORRECT TO THE BEST OF MY KNOWLEDGE AND THAT I HAVE PROVIDED THIS INFORMATION IN ORDER TO OBTAIN THE BENEFITS OF NEVADA'S INDUSTRIAL INSURANCE AND OCCUPATIONAL DISEASES ACTS (NRS 616A TO 616D, INCLUSIVE OR CHAPTER 617 OF NRS). I HEREBY AUTHORIZE ANY PHYSICIAN, CHIROPRACTOR, SURGEON, PRACTITIONER, OR OTHER PERSON, ANY HOSPITAL, INCLUDING VETERANS ADMINISTRATION OR GOVERNMENTAL HOSPITAL, ANY MEDICAL SERVICE ORGANIZATION, ANY INSURANCE COMPANY, OR OTHER INSTITUTION OR ORGANIZATION TO RELEASE TO EACH OTHER, ANY MEDICAL OR OTHER INFORMATION, INCLUDING BENEFITS PAID OR PAYABLE, PERTINENT TO THIS INJURY OR DISEASE, EXCEPT INFORMATION RELATIVE TO DIAGNOSIS, TREATMENT AND/OR COUNSELING FOR AIDS, PSYCHOLOGICAL CONDITIONS, ALCOHOL OR CONTROLLED SUBSTANCES, FOR WHICH I MUST GIVE SPECIFIC AUTHORIZATION. A PHOTOSTAT OF THIS AUTHORIZATION SHALL BE AS VALID AS THE ORIGINAL.

Date: 4/2/09 | Place: St. Rose Hospital | Employee's Signature: [signature]

THIS REPORT MUST BE COMPLETED AND MAILED WITHIN 3 WORKING DAYS OF TREATMENT

Place: St. Rose Siena ER | Name of Facility

Date: 4/2/09 | Hour: 2100 | Diagnosis and Description of Injury or Occupational Disease: lumbar radiculopathy

Is there evidence that the injured employee was under the influence of alcohol and/or another controlled substance at the time of the accident? ☑ No ☐ Yes (if yes, please explain)

Treatment: Rx meds

Have you advised the patient to remain off work five days or more?
☐ Yes Indicate dates: from __________ to __________
☑ No If no, is the injured employee capable of: ☐ full duty ☑ modified duty

X-Ray Findings:

If modified duty, specify any limitations/restrictions: No lifting more than 10 lbs.

From information given by the employee, together with medical evidence, can you directly connect this injury or occupational disease as job incurred? ☑ Yes ☐ No

Is additional medical care by a physician indicated? ☑ Yes ☐ No

Do you know of any previous injury or disease contributing to this condition or occupational disease? ☐ Yes ☑ No (Explain if yes)

Date: 4/2/09 | Print Doctor's Name: R. John Balani | I certify that the employer's copy of this form was mailed to the employer on:

Address: 3001 St. Rose Pkwy | INSURER'S USE ONLY

City: Hend | State: NV | Zip: 89052 | Provider's Tax I.D. Number | Telephone: 616 5600

Doctor's Signature: [signature] | Degree: PA-C

ORIGINAL – TREATING PHYSICIAN OR CHIROPRACTOR   PAGE 2 – INSURER/TPA   PAGE 3 – EMPLOYER   PAGE 4 – EMPLOYEE   Form C-4 (rev.01/03)

PAGE 1

4E-890-0043-09 ~~Claim # 132209923~~ LM

RECEIVED
APR 30 2009
HEALTH & RESOURCES MANAGEMENT
LM

SENT TO DOL
APR 30 2009
HEALTH & RESOURCES MANAGEMENT
LM

MP AN ARTIFICIAL WATERMARK IS ON THE BACK • HOLD AT AN ANGLE TO VIEW THIS MARK MP

St. Rose Dominican Hospitals
CHW

537550

Pt#: 56050255 MR#: 667543
MCGEE ,LOLA
07/07/1962 , F 46 04/02/09
ADR: ED, PHYSICIAN Rm: ER2
PDR: Bd: ED39P

PATIENT'S FULL NAME
ADDRESS
AGE SEX
DATE / /

℞ Please excuse from work for next 3 days

☐ *Dispense Only As Written*

☐ *Refills* 1 2 3 4
☒ *No Refills* *Void After*

Dr. R. John Bacani, PA-C
DEA # MB0767713

S734 (12/2007)

VALID FOR CONTROLLED SUBSTANCES

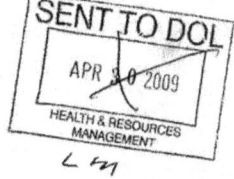

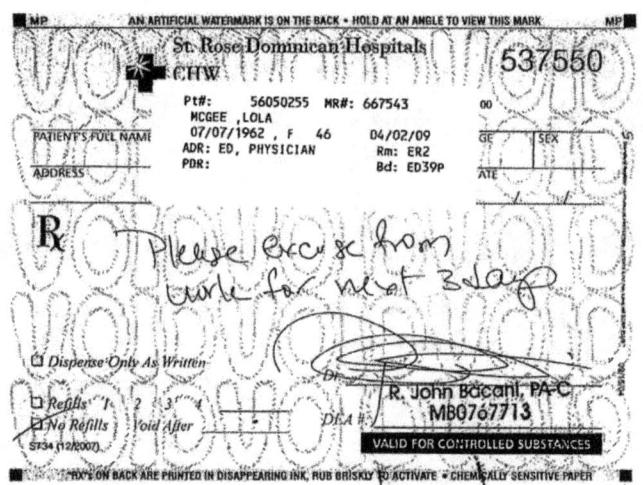

"RX"S ON BACK ARE PRINTED IN DISAPPEARING INK, RUB BRISKLY TO ACTIVATE • CHEMICALLY SENSITIVE PAPER

4E-890-0043-09 ~~132209923~~

St. ROSE DOMINICAN HOSPITAL - SIENA CAMPUS
REGISTRATION INFORMATION

NAME PFX: NAME SFX:
NAME : MCGEE ,LOLA B MR#: 667-54-3 PT#: 5605025?
ADMIT DATE: 04/02/09 TIME: 19:21 ADM PRIORITY: U ADM SOURCE: EO
COMPLAINT : PAIN BOTH KNEES PROC.:
ADM. MD : LEWIS-MD, JOHN RM/BED:
ATN. MD : LEWIS-MD, JOHN
PCP : PT. STAT: EA FC: W
ACC DATE : 03/13/09 TIME: 11:00 SER: EMR CLINIC: EMER
ORGAN DONOR: N ADV DIR: 3 DECLINED BY PATIENT
INTERPRETER: PRIMARY LANGUAGE:

PATIENT INFORMATION
DOB: 07/07/1962 AGE: 46 SEX: F M/S: S REL: BAP SS#:
ETHNICITY: 2

PATIENT ADDRESS
PO BOX 98272
LAS VEGAS NV 891938272
HOME: 702 - 260-0876

PATIENT EMPLOYER
US POSTAL SERVICE
SPRING VALLEY STATION
LAS VEGAS NV
BUSINESS: 702 - 000-0000
OCC: SUPERVISOR

EMER/PRIMARY CONTACT
COOPER HIGHSMITH ,WYKE REL: CHILD
310 - 462-4279 WK: -

LOCAL ADDRESS
GIVEN ,NONE REL: OTHER
- WK: -

GUARANTOR INFORMATION
MCGEE ,LOLA REL: SELF EMPLOYMENT: US POSTAL SERVICE
PO BOX 98272 SPRING VALLEY STATION
LAS VEGAS NV 891938272 LAS VEGAS NV
702 - 260-0876 702 - 000-0000

INSURANCE 1 COB PRIORITY: 1
INS1: US DEPT OF LABOR SUB/NAME: MCGEE ,LOLA REL: PATIENT
PLAN CODE: W22 POLICY #: GRP#: 999999
PCERT #: PENDING SUB/EMP: US POSTAL SERVICE GRP: USPS
INS PHN: 866 - 335-8319 SUB/EMP/PHN: 702 - 000-0000
INS ADDR: PO BOX 23808
INS CITY/ST/ZIP: TUCSON AZ 85734

INSURANCE 2 COB PRIORITY:
INS2: SUB/NAME: REL:
PLAN CODE: POLICY #: GRP#:
PCERT #: SUB/EMP: GRP:
INS PHN: - SUB/EMP/PHN: -
INS ADDR:
INS CITY/ST/ZIP

INSURANCE 3 COB PRIORITY:
INS3: SUB/NAME: REL:
PLAN CODE: POLICY #: GRP#:
PCERT #: SUB/EMP: GRP:
INS PHN: - SUB/EMP/PHN: -
INS ADDR:
INS CITY/ST/ZIP:

COMMENTS
040209 2033 FULL REG COMPLETED SIGNED SCANNED COAS SMOKE CESS
ACK FORM NPP UNINSURED NON PAR PROV ACK FORM PT STATED THAT
SHE WAS INJ 3/13/09 BETWEEN 11:00AM-1:00PM AT WORK PT WAS
REGISTERED BY: BMURPH PRINT DATE: 04/03/09 TIME: 00:27

RECEIVED
APR 30 2009
HEALTH & RESOURCES MANAGEMENT
LM

ADMT DX: 724.2
FINAL DX: 724.4
ICD-9 PROC:
CPT:
CODER INITIALS: CF

SENT TO DOL
APR 30 2009
HEALTH & RESOURCES MANAGEMENT
LM

4E-890-0043-09 132209923 LM

ESI ☐1 ☐2 ☐3 ☒4 ☐5 PMD 19
Upgrade ESI ____ Time ____ Initials ____ Room # ____

Patient Name	Age		Gender M / F	Triage Time 1922	Treatment Area	Chart for MD eval
McGee Lola (Last / First)						

Chief Complaint: workers comp back pain LLE pain
Assessment:

Mode of Arrival: ☐ walking ☐ crutches ☐ wheelchair ☐ Ambulance

Pre-hospital Care: ☐ C-collar ☐ backboard ☐ Blood sugar ☐ Splint ☐ IV ☐ IV Fluid ☐ Meds

RECEIVED APR 30 2009 HEALTH & RESOURCES MANAGEMENT

Past Medical History ☐ Asthma ☐ COPD ☐ Smoker ☐ MI ☐ PTCA/Stent ☐ CABG ☐ HTN ☐ A-fib ☐ CHF ☐ Dialysis ☐ Kidney Stones ☐ Renal Insuf ☐ Diabetes ☐ Hypothyroid ☐ CVA/TIA ☐ Seizures ☐ GERD ☐ PUD ☐ Gallstones ☐ Appy ☐ Choly ☐ Hyst

Medications

Pain Target ____

Vital Signs	T	P	BP	R	O2Sat	Pain Scale
1921 time	37	84	141/88	20	95%	10 /10
time						/10
time						/10

Weight ____ kg LMP ____ date Tetanus ____ yr
Allergies NKA

Physician History

☒ Dictated# 62090 ☐ Template ☐ EUS
Consultant Name / Called / Responded
Consultant Name / Called / Responded

☐ CBC with diff ☐ ER Panel (6) ☐ Chem Panel (20) ☐ Lipase ☐ CPK-MB ☐ Troponin ☐ D-Dimer ☐ PT/INR ☐ Magnesium ☐ Blood cult x ____ ☐ Lactate ☐ T&S

☐ Urinalysis (lab) ☐ Urine C/S ☐ Urine HCG (lab) ☐ Serum HCG ☐ Rh factor ☐ EKG Time ____ ☐ ABG O2 ____

☐ Port CXR ☐ PA/Lat CXR ☐ ABD (3-way) ☐ C-spine Limited — L-Spine, (B) knee
☐ CT Abd/Pelvis without contrast, R/O ☐ CT Abd/Pelvis with IV (rectal) PO contrast ☐ Full Prep R/O ☐ Rapid Prep R/O ☐ No Oral Prep R/O ☐ CT Chest with IV contrast, R/O ☐ CT Head, R/O ☐ Ultrasound ____ R/O

SENT TO DOL APR 30 2009 HEALTH & RESOURCES MANAGEMENT

INTERVENTIONS/OUTCOMES	TIME	ORDERS	ROUTE/SITE	TIME Start	Stop	RN	RB
☐ Clinical Alarms checked		All orders are one time unless otherwise indicated					
☐ Valuables checklist completed		☐ Orders Initiated Name of Order Set ☐ CP ☐ AP ☐ Other					
☐ Pre-op teaching completed		Ultram 100mg	PO	2025		M	
u-preg							

Diagnostic Impression
(1) Acute back sprain c sciatica
(B) knee sprain

TIME RESPIRATORY ORDERS TIME Start Stop RT
I have independently evaluated this patient and agree with the P.A.'s findings.
X ____

R. John Baccini, PA-C MB07513

INITIALS / NURSE SIGNATURES / RN INITIALS / NURSE SIGNATURES
Triage Nurse
Triage Nurse

PHYSICIAN SIGNATURE ____ 11839 TIME EVALUATED

PATIENT IDENTIFICATION

St. Rose Dominican Hospitals
A member of CHW
ED TREATMENT RECORD

Pt#: 56050255 MR#: 667543
MCGEE ,LOLA
07/07/1962 , F 46 04/02/09
ADR: ED, PHYSICIAN Rm: ER2
PDR: Bd: ED39P

4E-890-0043-09 #132209923 LM

U

ED Triage Form (CIS)
04/02/09 07:27 pm Performed by Gamm, Nicole RN
Entered on 04/02/09 07:39 pm

Updated on
04/02/09 07:39 pm by Gamm, Nicole RN

ED Triage

Arrival Time: 19:27
Chief Complaint ED: pt was lifting mail bins on 3/13/09, went bent over, got spasm in lt knee and lt thigh, also c/o low back pain, "now I can't don my job", c/o low back pain with radiation to lt leg
Reason for visit: LBP
Mode of Arrival: Ambulatory
Triage Acuity: 4 - Non Urgent
Accompanied By - ED: Alone
Historian: Patient
General Observation: Alert & oriented to norm, Respirations regular and unlabored, Skin warm & dry
Primary Mode of Communication: English
Temperature PO: 37.1 deg C
NIBP Systolic: 141 mm Hg
NIBP Diastolic: 88 mm Hg
Heart Rate: 84 bpm
Respiratory Rate (Monitor): 20 Breaths/Min
Pain Intensity: 10
Pain Scale Used: Numeric Rating Scale
SPO2: 99 %
Oxygen Amount: Room air
Last Tetanus: > 5 years
LMP: 4 days ago
Past Medical History: Cardiac/other, Hypertension history, Psych history, Other: "palpitations", anxiety, PTSD, major depression
Past Surgical History: appy, low bowel obstruction
Private Physician: Sundance Medical, Harris APN
Height In: 69.00 Inch
Height: 175.26 cm
Height: 175.26 cm
Weight lb: 245.00 lb
Weight - pt care: 111.364 kg
Weight Method: Stated
Weight - pt care: 111.364 kg

Ⓛ knee / LBP

+

RECEIVED APR 2009 HEALTH & RESOURCES MANAGEMENT

SENT TO DC APR 2009 HEALTH & RESOURCES MANAGEMENT

Allergies & Current Meds (CIS)

Allergy	**Reaction**
1. NKA	

Verified Prev Data - Allergies/Meds: Yes
Allergy & Medication Grid

Medication	advil	verapamil	clonazepam
Dosage	800mg at 1600	150mg daily	1mg daily
Medication	pristiq		
Dosage	50mg daily		

SRDHS (Location:SRDHS ER2 ; FT04 ; P)
Patient Name: MCGEE, LOLA   DOB / AGE / SEX: 07/07/   46 Years F
Admitting Physician: PHYSICIAN, ED
Admission Date / MRN / Financial Num: 04/02/09 667543 56050255

Page 1 of 1
Print Date: 04/02/09
Print Time: 07:42 pm
Printed by: Gamm, Nicole RN

From:7029329075 ~~#132209923~~ 04/08/2009 20:48 #607 P.004/015

4B-890-0043-09

And/Or Treatment

U.S. Department of Labor
Employment Standards Adm·:·stration
Office of Workers' Compens···n Programs

The following request for information is required under (5 USC 8101 et. seq.). Benefits and/or medical services expenses may not be paid or may be subject to suspension under this program unless this report is completed and filed as requested. Information collected will be handled and stored in compliance with the Freedom of Information Act, the Privacy Act of 1974 and OMB Cir. No. A-108.

Persons are not required to respond to this collection of information unless it displays a currently valid OMB control number.

OMB No. 1215-0103
Expires: 10-31-99

132209923

PART A - AUTHORIZATION

1. Name and Address of the Medical Facility of Physician Authorized to Provide the Medical Service:
CENTENNIAL SPINE AND PAIN CENTER
4640 W. CRAIG ROAD, LAS VEGAS, NV 89032

2. Employee's Name (last, first, middle)
McGEE, LORA

3. Date of Injury (mo., day, year)
3/13/09

4. Occupation
SCS

5. Description of Injury or Disease:
Back, knee + left thigh pain

6. You are authorized to provide medical care for the employee for a period of up to sixty days from the date shown in item 11, subject to the condition stated in item A, and to the condition indicated either 1 or 2, in item B.

A. Your signature in item 35 of Part B certifies your agreement that all fees for services shall not exceed the maximum allowable fee established by OWCP and that payment by OWCP will be accepted as payment in full for said services.

B. ☒ 1. Furnish office and/or hospital treatment as medically necessary for the effects of this injury. Any surgery other than emergency must have prior OWCP approval.

☐ 2. There is doubt whether the employee's condition is caused by an injury sustained in the performance of duty, or is otherwise related to the employment. You are authorized to examine the employee using indicated non-surgical diagnostic studies, and promptly advise the undersigned whether you believe the condition is due to the alleged injury or to any circumstances of the employment. Pending further advice you may provide necessary conservative treatment if you believe the condition may be to the injury or to the employment.

7. If a Disease or Illness is Involved, OWCP Approval for Issuing Authorization was Obtained from: (Type Name and Title of OWCP Official)

8. Signature of Authorizing Official:
[signature]

9. Name and Title of Authorizing Official: (Type or print clearly)
HRM Specialist

LM

RECEIVED
APR 10 2009
HEALTH & RESOURCES MANAGEMENT

10. Local Employing Agency Telephone Number:
702-361-9313

11. Date (mo., day, year)
4/6/09

12. Send one copy of your report: (Fill in remainder of address)

U.S. DEPARTMENT OF LABOR
Employment Standards Administration
Office of Workers' Compensation Programs

LM

SENT TO DOL
APR 10 2009
HEALTH & RESOURCES MANAGEMENT

13. Name and Address of Employee's Place of Employment:

Department of Agency

Bureau or Office

Local Address (including ZIP Code)

RECEIVED
APR 09 2009
HEALTH & RESOURCES MANAGEMENT

LM

Public Burden Statement

We estimate that it will take an average of 5 minutes to complete this collection of information, including time for reviewing instructions, searching existing data sources, gathering and maintaining the data needed, and completing and reviewing the collection of information. If you have any comments regarding these estimates or any other aspect of this collection of information, including suggestions for reducing this burden, send them to the Office of Workers' Compensation Programs, U.S. Department of Labor, Room S-3229, 200 Constitution Avenue, N.W., Washington, D.C. 20210.

DO NOT SEND THE COMPLETED FORM TO THIS OFFICE

Form CA-16
Rev. Jan. 1997

From: 7029329075 ~~[illegible]~~ 04/08/2009 20:48 #607 P.003/015

4E-890-0043-09

PART B - ATTENDING PHYSICIAN'S REPORT

14. Employee's Name (last, first, middle)
McGee, Lola

15. What History of Injury or Disease Did Employee Give You? Pain in the mid + lower back pain to the left leg and bilateral knee.

16. Is there any History or Evidence of Concurrent or Pre-existing Injury, Disease, or Physical Impairment? (If yes, please describe) Undetermined at this time further evaluation is required.
☐ Yes ☐ No

16a. IDC-9 Code

17. What are Your Findings? (Include results of X-rays, laboratory tests, etc.)
None provided. Further testing required to fully delineate the pathology of the pain generator.

18. What is Your Diagnosis?
Cervical, Thoracic & lumbar facet syndrome. lumbar radiculopathy. Knee pain

18a. IDC-9 Code
722.4 724.4 719.46

19. Do You Believe the Condition Found was Caused or Aggravated by the Employment Activity Described? (Please explain your answer if there is doubt) I was very clear with the patient that her physical examination seemed to be overly exaggerated. She was not able to perform even the most basic physical exam maneuvers. But to fully establish this further testing is recommended.
☐ Yes ☐ No

20. Did Injury Require Hospitalization? ☐ Yes ☒ No
If yes, date of admission (mo., day, year)
Date of discharge (mo., day, year)

21. Is Additional Hospitalization Required?
☐ Yes ☒ No

22. Surgery (If any, describe type)
N/A

23. Date Surgery Performed (mo., day, year)
N/A

24. What (Other) Type of Treatment Did You Provide? Just initial consultation. Recommended for patient to continue conservative therapy and obtain lumbar and bilateral knee MRI

25. What Permanent Effects, If Any, Do You Anticipate?
Undetermined

26. Date of First Examination (mo., day, year)
04-07-09

27. Date(s) of Treatment (mo., day, year)
4-7-09

28. Date of Discharge from Treatment (mo., day, year)
N/A

29. Period of Disability (mo., day, year) (If termination date unknown, so indicate)
Total Disability: From To
Partial Disability: From 4-6-09 To 4-28-09

30. Is Employee Able to Resume
Undetermined.
☐ Light Work Date:
☐ Regular Work Date:

31. If Employee is Able to Resume Work, Has He/She been Advised? ☐ Yes ☐ No If Yes, Furnish Date Advised
N/A

32. If Employee is Able to Resume Only Light Work, Indicate the Extent of Physical Limitations and the Type of Work that Could Reasonably be Performed with these Limitations.
N/A

33. General Remarks and Recommendations for Future Care, If Indicated. If you have made a Referral to Another Physician or to a Medical Facility, Provide Name and Address. Physical therapy
In the future she may benefit from diagnostic facet blocks, and epidural steroid injections.

34. Do You Specialize? ☒ Yes ☐ No (If yes, state specialty)
Pain Management

35. SIGNATURE OF PHYSICIAN. I certify that all the statements in response to the questions asked in Part B of this form are true, complete and correct to the best of my knowledge. Further, I understand that any false or misleading statement or any misrepresentation or concealment of material fact which is knowingly made may subject me to felony criminal prosecution.
[signature]

36. Address (No., Street, City, State, ZIP Code)
4454 North Decatur Blvd
Las Vegas, NV 89130

37. Tax Identification Number
20-237X045

38. National Provider System Number
1316057573

39. Date of Report
4/7/09

RECEIVED APR 30 2009 HEALTH & RESOURCE MANAGEMENT LM

RECEIVED APR 09 2009 HEALTH & RESOURCES MANAGEMENT LM

SENT TO DOL APR 30 2009 HEALTH & RESOURCES MANAGEMENT LM

MEDICAL BILL: Charges for your services should be presented to the AMA standard "Health Insurance Claim Form" (AMA OP 407/408/409; OWCP-1500a, or HCFA 1500). Service must be itemized by Current Procedural Terminology Code (CPT 4) and the form must be signed.

Dept. of Labor/OWCP decision letter May 13, 2009 for March 13, 2009 lifting injury

File Number: 132209923
nodcr-D-I

U.S. DEPARTMENT OF LABOR

EMPLOYMENT STANDARDS ADMINISTRATION
OFFICE OF WORKERS' COMP PROGRAMS
PO BOX 8300 DISTRICT 13 SFC
LONDON, KY 40742-8300
Phone: (415) 625-7500

May 13, 2009

Date of Injury: 03/13/2009
Employee: LOLA B. MCGEE

LOLA B MCGEE
PO BOX 98272
LAS VEGAS, NV 89193

Dear Ms. MCGEE:

NOTICE OF DECISION

Your claim for compensation is denied as the medical evidence does not demonstrate that the claimed medical condition is related to the established work-related event(s) as required for coverage under the Federal Employees' Compensation Act (FECA).

You are employed as a Supervisor of Customer Service with the U.S. Postal Service in Las Vegas, NV. On 04/02/2009, your filed a timely Notice of Traumatic Injury (CA-1) stating on 03/13/2009, you were assisting a limited duty employee with lifting trays and tubs of mail into a hamper to take out to carriers on the street causing back pain, knee pain, left thigh pain. You felt a pop in your knee and back. Submitted with your claim was a St. Rose Dominican Hospital Emergency Department document dated 04/02/2009 indicating sciatica and signed by John Bacani, P.A.; a C-4 Medical Form dated 04/02/2009 with a diagnosis of lumbar radiculopathy signed by a physician's assistant; a disability slip dated 04/02/2009 signed by John Bacani, P.A.

In order for a medical condition to be covered under the FECA, medical evidence must demonstrate that it is related to the accepted injury. Your physician must explain how the event(s) caused or affected your condition, based upon an accurate factual and medical history, citing objective findings in support of the physician's opinion.

You filed a timely claim establishing that you were a Federal employee who sustained an injury in the performance of duty. The medical evidence provided does not establish that the claimed medical condition resulted from the accepted event(s).

We advised you of the deficiencies of your claim in a letter dated 04/09/2009 and gave you the opportunity to provide the necessary evidence. You were advised that a physician's assistant is not considered a doctor under the FECA. You submitted the following evidence in response: two copies copy of your Request for Lateral dated 02/11/2009 to Postmaster Yul Melonson; your request dated 04/08/2009 to Postmaster Yul Melonson regarding your 02/11/2009 request; three copies of CA-16 Authorization for Treatment dated 04/07/2009 with a diagnosis of cervical, thoracic and lumbar facet syndrome and lumbar radiculopathy with no history of the injury as provided by you; copies of Emergency Department documents dated 04/02/2009 indicating sciatica; numerous copies of disability slips disabling you from work; copies of C-4 Medical forms dated 04/02/2009 with a diagnosis of lumbar radiculopathy and signed by a physician's assistant; copies of Emergency Room notes dated 04/02/2009 with clinical impression of lumbar radiculopathy; copies of St. Rose Dominican Hospital

File Number: 132209923
nodcr-D-I

Registration Documents; copy of Initial Pain Assessment by Patient dated 04/07/2009; two copies of Physical Therapy progress notes dated 04/27/2009; copy of Return Visit Progress Note dated 04/28/2009; copies of Initial Pain Assessment Report dated 04/07/2009 from Alain Coppel, M.D. with assessment of cervical facet syndrome, thoracic facet syndrome, lumbar facet syndrome, lumbar radiculopathy, and knee pain; copies of your 04/07/2009 statement of how the injury occurred; medical report dated 04/09/2009 from Jimmy Novero, M.D. with an assessment of peripheral neuropathy, pain-back, and pain-limb; copies of letters to Centennial Spine & Pain Center from you dated 04/21/09 and 04/25/2009; medical note dated 04/16/2009 from Mary Reed, Ph.D; and two copies of CA-1 Notice of Traumatic Injury. The additional evidence did not establish that the claimed condition resulted from the accepted event(s) sustained on 03/13/2009.

The Employees' Compensation Appeals Board has held that:

Appellant has the burden of establishing by the weight of the reliable, probative, and substantial evidence that his condition was causally related to factors of his employment. This burden includes the necessity of furnishing medical opinion evidence of a cause-and-effect relationship based upon a proper factual and medical background. The mere concurrence of a condition with a period of employment does not raise an inference of causal relation between the two. [Robert M. Sanford, 27 ECAB 115, 1975]

Based on these findings, the claim is denied because it is not established that the claimed medical condition is related to the established work-related event(s). Medical treatment is not authorized and prior authorization, if any, is terminated.

Your employing agency will charge any previously paid Continuation of Pay to your sick and/or annual leave balance or declare it an overpayment.

If you disagree with this decision, you should carefully review the attached appeal rights, and pursue whichever avenue is appropriate to your situation.

Sincerely,

Julia Landry
Julia Landry
Claims Examiner

Enclosure: Appeals Rights

UNITED STATES POSTAL SERVICE
NEVADA-SIERRA PERFORMANCE CLUSTER
INJURY COMPENSATION OFFICE
1001 EAST SUNSET ROAD
LAS VEGAS, NV 89199

File Number: 132209923
nodcr-D-I

Registration Documents; copy of Initial Pain Assessment by Patient dated 04/07/2009; two copies of Physical Therapy progress notes dated 04/27/2009; copy of Return Visit Progress Note dated 04/28/2009; copies of Initial Pain Assessment Report dated 04/07/2009 from Alain Coppel, M.D. with assessment of cervical facet syndrome, thoracic facet syndrome, lumbar facet syndrome, lumbar radiculopathy, and knee pain; copies of your 04/07/2009 statement of how the injury occurred; medical report dated 04/09/2009 from Jimmy Novero, M.D. with an assessment of peripheral neuropathy, pain-back, and pain-limb; copies of letters to Centennial Spine & Pain Center from you dated 04/21/09 and 04/25/2009; medical note dated 04/16/2009 from Mary Reed, Ph.D; and two copies of CA-1 Notice of Traumatic Injury. The additional evidence did not establish that the claimed condition resulted from the accepted event(s) sustained on 03/13/2009.

The Employees' Compensation Appeals Board has held that:

Appellant has the burden of establishing by the weight of the reliable, probative, and substantial evidence that his condition was causally related to factors of his employment. This burden includes the necessity of furnishing medical opinion evidence of a cause-and-effect relationship based upon a proper factual and medical background. The mere concurrence of a condition with a period of employment does not raise an inference of causal relation between the two. [Robert M. Sanford, 27 ECAB 115, 1975]

Based on these findings, the claim is denied because it is not established that the claimed medical condition is related to the established work-related event(s). Medical treatment is not authorized and prior authorization, if any, is terminated.

Your employing agency will charge any previously paid Continuation of Pay to your sick and/or annual leave balance or declare it an overpayment.

If you disagree with this decision, you should carefully review the attached appeal rights, and pursue whichever avenue is appropriate to your situation.

Sincerely,

Julia Landry

Julia Landry
Claims Examiner

Enclosure: Appeals Rights

UNITED STATES POSTAL SERVICE
NEVADA-SIERRA PERFORMANCE CLUSTER
INJURY COMPENSATION OFFICE
1001 EAST SUNSET ROAD
LAS VEGAS, NV 89199

File Number: 132198863
mtd-sfc-NO-0

In this case, the claimant is alleging treatment by OIC Jerry Wilson, lack of promotion, racism,and treatment by the employing agency has caused her psychiatric condition. The USPS provided a statement from OIC Jerry Wilson which refutes the allegations of harassment. The incidents are not accepted as factual because of the lack of probative evidence to support that these specific incidents occurred. Performance appraisals are an administrative function of the employer and not a duty of the employee. Thus an appraisal or discussion of performance, lacking evidence of error or abuse on the part of the employer does not constitute a factor of employment. {Willie Brown, Docket 89-42, 11/24/89}

No EEO findings of fact and/or settlement have been provided to substantiate any discrimination or retaliation by USPS management. Therefore, there is no finding by an adjudicatory body or administrative error. The ECAB has found that grievances and complaints, by themselves, do not establish that work place harassment or unfair treatment occurred. Neither must there be a final EEOC decision upholding harassment or discrimination before an emotional condition claim based on alleged harassment can be established. As the standards for "harassment" or "discrimination" as defined by EEOC statutory or case law is not the applicable standard for a FECA claim, the Office must make its own determination of the matter. {Parley A. Clement, 48, ECAB__(Docket No. 95-566, issued 1/17/97}

Reactions arising from the actions or inaction of the Office in consideration of a FECA claim are not in the performance of duty. {Dandy Williams, Docket 89-1787, 1/31/90}

Frustration over not being able to secure a promotion is not in the performance of duty. {Raymond Cordova, Docket 80-1734, 4/3/81}

The reaction is to being told of a shift change or a desire to work a different shift, the reaction is not in the performance of duty. {Lillian Cutler, 28 ECAB 125}

A discussion of the medical evidence is not material given that an injury occurring with the performance of duty is not demonstrated.

Conclusion: That the evidence of record fails to establish that the claimant sustained an emotional condition while in the performance of duty.

Julia Landry
Julia Landry
Claims Examiner

Response to Corey Richards Statement (not dated)

May 16, 2009

Lola McGee
Supervisor, Customer Services
North Las Vegas, NV 89030

Between 2:15-3:15pm on 4/13/09, I went to my home office North Las Vegas Post Office to speak with Postmaster Corey Richards; and, I brought a friend with me, Pamela Morgan, with the hope that Corey would not treat or talk to me in a disrespectful manner, like he has done in the past. All I wanted to do was turn in my forms and get a receipt, get my time inputted for payment for 2/18/09 and 2/19/09, and retrieve my 2007 NPA report.

Corey was very rude, abrupt, and disrespectful towards me and I did not appreciate it. We are professional people and adults. All people need to be treated with dignity and respect.

I requested my PES – NPA report for 2007 and Corey would not go on the website and print it for me nor would he allow me to go on the computer and print it for myself. Corey has treated me on several occasions in a disrespectful manner and he has retaliated against me because of EEO activity. The PES system allows access to the most current three Fiscal year information. Corey has denied me promotions, access to my home office computer, entry of my 2009 NPA objectives even though I was in work status, forms I requested, payment of higher level, input of my leave correctly, and he has deliberately not paid me even though he had my 3971 in his possession. Corey has demanded that my GMF access be removed out of retaliation for EEO activity. Corey has never supervised me and with the way that he treats me, I would not be able to work for him because of his creation of a hostile work environment with me.

I was at the office for approximately 45 minutes to an hour on 4/13/09.

On 4/15/09 I called Corey and told him that I would be filing a claim from the meeting we had on Monday 4/13/2009 for Stress, he stated what time did it happened and what did I do? I stated that I would put it in writing.

On 4/2/09 I went and tried to talk with Corey because Yul asked me to even though I told him that Corey does not treat me right and he does not talk to me respectfully. I asked Corey for some forms and he called Joni Payne and denied me all the forms except one. I also wanted to input my 2009 NPA and he denied me that also. Corey asked me why did I need the forms and I told him for injuries that happened in North Las Vegas and I had a lifting injury at Spring Valley Station. He gave me one CA-1 and that was all. I actually told him where the forms were located in the office.

I want it to be noted that I never, ever told Corey that I could not work for the postal service because people don't treat me right. Corey just lied when he stated I said that. Corey may have assumed with my injuries that I could not work anymore, but I never told him such a thing. This to me tells you about a person's character when they say things that people did not say.

Corey states that I was not in a work status as if that's the reason why I was not privy to my requests. I was allowed to input my 2008 end of year improvements, conduct business in injury compensation, be briefed and testify for Arbitration by Labor Relations, and have a telephone interview all while I was not in pay status. Thus, Corey just did not want to cooperate or oblige me because he has issues with me. It had nothing to do with work status that was just a way out for him to justify his behavior.

Corey is very aware of my EEO activity because a lot of it involves him personally.
I want it to be noted that I'm very ill because of all that I've been through in the post office. On 4/13/09 Corey Richards' behavior caused me to become ill and it put me into the hospital with Heart Palpitations, Elevated Blood Pressure, and my right arm collapsed with pain. I was hospitalized from 4/13/09-4/15/09.

Sincerely
Lola McGee

* * * * *

May 20, 2009

Statement

To: Department of Labor/OWCP and Injury Compensation

From: Lola McGee

This statement is for the injury that I suffered on 8/25/08, open ended threat committed by Jerry Wilson, Officer in Charge North Las Vegas.

On 8/25/2008 I was threatened by my boss (OIC) North Las Vegas. I was sent there to be the acting manager; however it was my permanent position as a supervisor. I did not know him and he did not know me; but he had heard of my work. During the threatening situation, he stated to me "You continue to go over my head with Craig and Yul and I'm going to do something about it." He was standing in my face, in my personal space, looking me in my eyes with a convicted, domineering tone. Once he completed this statement he turned and walked out of my office abruptly. The threat led me to believe that something negative was going to happen to me, either physical or in writing. After all that I had achieved and done during my postal career, I did not deserve any negative retaliation from him. I became afraid and I started hyperventilating, hot sweats with chills, my heart started palpitating stronger, my brain was confused and I could not think straight. I felt like I had gone retarded and I was going to die. No one was in the office with me and him so I had no witnesses. I went to the restroom to splash water over my face and I started to have a recurring chocking cough. I felt dizzy and I got me some water to drink. I tried to calm myself down to let my staff know that I would be leaving for the day. I had head shocks coming down my face and neck. Due to this incident, I was caused to leave work early that day. On 8/27/08 I went to the doctor and was diagnosed with Post Traumatic Stress Disorder, Major Depression, and Panic Attacks.

Sincerely,

Lola McGee

May 20, 2009

Statement

This CA-1 is being submitted for left ear Hearing Loss that I suffered as a result of the Panic Attack I had on 8/25/08 because my boss Jerry Wilson gave me an open ended threat "You continue to go over my head with Craig and Yul and I'm going to do something about it."

I was treated by my primary physician at Sundance Medical Center and a hearing test was conducted in her office.

Later on, I went to an Ear, Nose, and Throat Specialist and had an advanced test performed and it was confirmed that I had Hearing Loss in my left ear.

In 1998 I was physically and mentally cleared by the post office doctor test for fitness to be fit for the job and I did not have a hearing problem and I have not worked around any abnormal noise that would degenerate my hearing ability. I started not being able to hear well after the Panic Attack that I suffered on 8/25/08.

I want it to be noted that I asked my mental therapist if a Panic Attack could take away your hearing and her response was "A Panic Attack can cause you to go blind let alone affect your hearing."

Sincerely

Lola McGee

* * * * *

May 20, 2009

Statement

To: U. S Department of Labor/OWCP and Injury Compensation

From: Lola McGee

This statement is for the CA-2 submitted today for Post Traumatic Stress Disorder, Major Depression, Panic Attacks, and Obsessive Compulsive Disorder.

On 8/25/2008 I was threatened by my boss (OIC) North Las Vegas. I was sent there to be the acting manager; however it was my permanent position as a supervisor. I did not know him and he did not know me; but he had heard of my work. During the threatening situation, he stated to me "You continue to go over my head with Craig and Yul and I'm going to do something about it." He was standing in my face, in my personal space, looking me in my eyes with a convicted, domineering tone. Once he completed this statement he turned and walked out of my office abruptly. The threat led me to believe that something negative was going to happen to me, either physical or in writing. After all that I had achieved and done during my postal career, I did not deserve any negative retaliation from him. I became afraid and I started hyperventilating, hot sweats with chills, my heart started palpitating stronger, my brain was confused and I could not think straight. I felt like I had gone retarded and I was going to die. No one was in the office with me and him so I had no witnesses. I went to the restroom to splash water over my face and I started to have a recurring chocking cough. I felt dizzy and I got me some water to drink. I tried to calm myself down to let my staff know that I would be leaving for the day. I had head shocks coming down my face and neck. Due to this incident, I was caused to leave work early that day. On 8/27/08 I went to the doctor and was diagnosed with Post Traumatic Stress Disorder, Major Depression, and Panic Attacks.

From 4/2006 – 8/25/2008, I worked actively as an acting manager for the Nevada Sierra District. I applied for 17 positions and never got promoted; I wasn't even promoted in two (2) positions that they did not have selected people for. The positions were not filled until they had someone else that they wanted to put in them. All the promoted people were white/non black. I was discriminated against based on: Age-46, Sex-female, Race-African American, Color-black, Religion-Christian, Mental/Physical disability, and Retaliation, treated unfairly while others were treated differently than I was, lied to, and disrespected on telecoms. I was performing very well at large offices and had great performance outcomes to prove it; however I was not good enough to be promoted. They treated me as if I was only good for repairing the problems of each post office I was sent to; however I was never promoted to the actual position that I was already doing well in. I was even flown to Reno Nevada on detail as the acting manager and after that, they called me back to one of the worse offices in Las Vegas (King Station). In 9/2007, I felt my heart beating faster than it normally would and I was referred to a Cardiologist by my primary doctor. I was diagnosed with Heart Palpitations and with extensive testing it was determined to be benign and exacerbated by stress. Also, I had a chocking cough and I sought treatment from an Ear, Nose, and Throat Specialist and he did not find a reason.

In 2004 I requested a Lateral to North Las Vegas Post Office from California and it was granted. Consequently, there was a supervisor there that presented the appearance that he did not appreciate my skills, ability, experience, training, nor did he consider my education to improve the office performance; he did everything that he could to sabotage my performance. He had a bizarre/outlandish behavior that made me afraid of him. He would hide my employee reports, talk to me in a disrespectful, loud manner on the workroom floor, and told untruths about me to the employees so that they would turn against me. In addition, he would tell the postmaster that I wasn't capturing the under time that I said I was conducting, however the proof of the office performance reports showed my conduct to be excellent. I would speak to him in the morning and he would walk by me as if I did not speak to him. On the other hand, he would come up to me and talk to me like nothing was wrong and we were the best of friends. He would pull my reports and post them on the board and tell the union steward that I was not equitable on my overtime with my employees. However, this was due to his incorrect calculations and wrong figures to reflect the report. This issue was not new and had been one of the issues he had with the union steward prior to my arrival to the North Las Vegas Post Office. This issue was negated through the union steward and me meeting on a weekly basis regarding the overtime employees report. The union steward and I both would sign off on the form to ensure that it was correct. He told me that he had to kill people in the military and that was his job. He told me that he use to work for a security company and he and his partner had to kill someone at a casino. He had mood swings on a daily basis. He would hide my employee leave slips to prevent me from knowing who was suppose to be at work, and from creating the employee schedule correctly. I called several meetings and sent emails to the postmaster and OIC to try and stop this hostile work environment that he had created, but he continued to behave in this manner. He eventually was terminated for fraudulent behavior beyond the issues he had in the office with me. He was to turn over to me $1000.00 in cash reserve and he never turned it over to date. Postal Inspectors and Labor Relation Departments got involved regarding different issues that I had with him and the other fraudulent things that he had done. As a result from this hostile environment, in 2005 I sought therapy and was subsequently diagnosed with Post Traumatic Stress Disorder, Depression, and Obsessive Compulsive Disorder. That hostile environment made me believe that he or someone else would come and harm me at home as well as the office. I was afraid that he would one day try and physically hurt me. Later on, I was diagnosed with Heart Palpitations without Heart disease.

Sincerely

Lola McGee

* * * * *

May 27, 2009

TO: U. S. Dept. of Labor/OWCP – Attn: Brenda Buescher
Employment Standards Administration
P. O. Box 8300 District 13 SFC
London, KY 40742-8300

From: Lola McGee
P. O. Box 89272
Las Vegas, NV 89193-8272

RE: Claim #132210702

Dear Ms. Buescher,

This letter is my response to your letter dated April 29, 2009 regarding the claim number listed above. The medical evidence from Dr. Croke is attached; he is the only heart doctor that I have ever seen to date. However, I was hospitalized from 4/13/09 – 4/15/09 for chest pain, elevated blood pressure, and my right arm collapsed with pain, weakness, numbness, and tingling. I was admitted to St. Rose Hospital in Henderson, Nevada.

In addition, I have attached additional medical to be reviewed, because as a result of all the on-the-job injuries/illnesses and administrative negative issues, I have been forced to apply for Disability Retirement from the United States Postal Service at age 46.

Answers to your Questions

I will only provide the answers to your questions if it's alright with you:

1. When I begin feeling my heart beating faster than normal, I did not know what the reason was so I sought treatment (by Dr. Croke) for answers. Dr. Croke informed me that I had Heart Palpitations (My heart beats faster than it should) and he pursued vigorous testing and ultimately came up with a benign heart condition.

2. Please forgive me for indicating August 27, 2009; I made a mistake with the year. I meant 8/27/08, which is the date that I first saw Dr. Mary Reed. I explained to her my administrative issues and the condition of my heart. By the end of my appointment with her it was evident what was going on with me as it related to my health. On my next appointment with Dr. Croke, I explained to him my appointment with Dr. Reed and shared the diagnosis; he stated to me that it all makes sense now. My heart operates in that manner because of Post Traumatic Stress Disorder. I use to be afraid to stay home alone at night but that was negated when I moved by myself.

3. I have never considered my actual job duties and responsibilities harmful to me in any way. I have always been able to perform my duties well. Normal challenges have never been detrimental to me; I was able to just rise to the occasion. It is the other stuff and issues that caused me to become ill, injured, and disabled. In 2004 I requested a Lateral to North Las Vegas Post Office from California and it was granted. Consequently, there was a supervisor there that presented the appearance that he did not appreciate my skills, ability, experience, training, nor did he consider my education to improve the office performance; he did everything that he could to sabotage my performance. He had a bizarre/outlandish behavior that made me afraid of him. He would hide my employee reports, talk to me in a disrespectful, loud manner on the workroom floor, and told untruths about me to the employees so that they would turn against me. In addition, he would tell the postmaster that I wasn't capturing the under time that I said I was conducting, however the proof of the office performance reports showed my conduct to be excellent. I would speak to him in the morning and he would walk by me as if I did not speak to him. On the other hand, he would come up to me and talk to me like nothing was wrong and we were the best of friends. He would pull my reports and post them on the board and tell the union steward that I was not equitable on my overtime with my employees. However, this was due to his incorrect calculations and wrong figures to reflect the report. This issue was not new and had been one of the issues he had with the union steward prior to my arrival to the North Las Vegas Post Office. This issue was negated through the union steward and me meeting on a weekly basis regarding the overtime employees report. The union steward and I both would sign off on the form to ensure that it was correct. He told me that he had to kill people in the military and that was his job. He told me that he use to work for a security company and he and his partner had to kill someone at a casino. He had mood swings on a daily basis. He would hide my employee leave slips to prevent me from knowing who was suppose to be at work, and from creating the employee schedule correctly. I called several meetings and sent emails to the postmaster and OIC to try and stop this hostile work environment that he had created, but he continued to behave in this manner. He eventually was terminated for fraudulent behavior beyond the issues he had in the office with me. He was to turn over to me $1000.00 in cash reserve and he never turned it over to date. Postal Inspectors and Labor Relation Departments got involved regarding different issues that I had with him and the other fraudulent things that he had done. As a result from this hostile environment, in 2005 I sought therapy and was subsequently diagnosed with Post Traumatic Stress Disorder, Depression, and Obsessive Compulsive Disorder. That hostile environment made me believe that he or someone else would come and harm me at home as well as the office. I was afraid that he would one day try and physically hurt me. Later on, I was diagnosed with Heart Palpitations without Heart disease.

From 4/2006 – 8/25/2008, I worked actively as an acting manager for the Nevada Sierra District. I applied for 17 positions and never got promoted; I wasn't even promoted in two (2) positions that they did not have selected people for. The positions were not filled until they had someone else that they wanted to put in them. All the promoted people were white/non black. I was discriminated against based on: Age-46, Sex-female, Race-African American, Color-black, Religion-Christian, Mental/Physical disability, and Retaliation, treated unfairly while others were treated differently than I was, lied to, and disrespected on telecoms. I was performing very well at large offices and had great performance outcomes to prove it; however I was not good enough to be promoted. They treated me as if I was only good for repairing the problems of each post office I was sent to; however I was never promoted to the actual position that I was already doing well in. I was even flown to Reno Nevada on detail as the acting manager and after that, they called me back to one of the worse offices in Las Vegas (King Station).

In 9/2007, I felt my heart beating faster than it normally would and I was referred to a Cardiologist by my primary doctor. I was diagnosed with Heart Palpitations and with extensive testing it was determined to be benign. Also, I had a chocking cough and I sought treatment from an Ear, Nose, and Throat specialist and he could not find the cause with testing.

On 8/25/2008 I was threatened by my boss (OIC) North Las Vegas. I was sent there to be the acting manager; however it was my permanent position as a supervisor. I did not know him and he did not know me; but he had heard of my work. During the threatening situation, he stated to me "You continue to go over my head with Craig and Yul and I'm going to do something about it." He was standing in my face, in my personal space, looking me in my eyes with a convicted, domineering tone. Once he completed this statement he turned and walked out of my office abruptly. The threat led me to believe that something negative was going to happen to me, either physical or in writing. After all that I had achieved and done during my postal career, I did not deserve any negative retaliation from him. I became afraid and I started hyperventilating, hot sweats with chills, my heart started palpitating stronger, my brain was confused and I could not think straight. I felt like I had gone retarded and I was going to die. No one was in the office with me and him; so I had no witnesses. I went to the restroom to splash water over my face and I started to have a recurring chocking cough. I felt dizzy and I got me some water to drink. I tried to calm myself down to let my staff know that I would be leaving for the day. I had head shocks coming down my face and neck. Due to this incident, I was caused to leave work early that day.

On 8/27/08 I went to the doctor and was diagnosed with Post Traumatic Stress Disorder, Major Depression, Anxiety, and Panic Attacks. As a result of all I have been through, I filed on-the-job injuries and EEO's. Thus, I've been retaliated against, not paid, every claim is controverted, yet I'm so ill that I now have to seek Disability Retirement. I walk with a cane today and have assistance in my home. I take medication for all my injuries. I have a victimized mentality because of all that has happened to me. To say that I'm angry is an under statement; I have inner turmoil and I try to take it one day at a time. I'm the one that is going to be affected by my response to the district's negative behavior towards me. I will one day take the power back from them. No one could have told me that this would happen to me because I was a loyal, dedicated, team player. I did what ever was asked of me and I did it well, and I have accolades to prove it. However, I was just used as the clean up woman and now they have no use for me.

I have received medical help for everything that has happened to me, I have no choice, I'm in pain everyday and my brain does not function properly. My heart scares me to no end. Even though I have hearing loss in my left ear from the panic attack on 8/25/08, it's the only thing that I don't take medication for, I just can't hear out of my left ear.

4. Absolutely, and I met them that is why I was sent around the district from station to station to be the acting manager. I was not promoted because of discriminating factors, not my performance. Thus, they would not have used me as an acting manager if I wasn't doing the job (Rather as a supervisor or a manager). I have never had a problem performing my required duties and there is a lot of responsibility that comes with being a supervisor or a manager in the postal service.

5. Yes, for the most part. There are challenges in any position; however, you become created and rise to the occasion and do the best that you can. Yes, I was an excellent supervisor and I carried that experience with me as I managed the stations. In addition, I have higher education (AA, BS) and I'm a prior business owner. Yes, I had the tools that I needed to do my job.

6. Yes, the fear that I experienced from the supervisor at North Las Vegas Post Office, at home at night alone, low energy, going over my life to see what the problem was, I felt retarded, loss of memory, violence in the work place, discrimination, mistreatment, being used, confusion in my brain, sleeping all the time, gambling, anger, and feelings of worthlessness. I was finally convinced that I needed medication in 2007. I came to terms with Dr. Reed that I have Post Traumatic Stress Disorder, Major Depression, Anxiety, and Panic Attacks and I need medication for all of it. Life is not the same anymore since 8/25/08. My body just shut down because of the threat and it had taken to much abuse from the hands of the postal service. I did not ask anyone to give me anything; I just wanted to be judged and treated fairly according to my own merit. The benefit is still in progress. I need to get through some of my anger and self pity in order to progress. Ultimately, I have to forgive the postal service in order to move forward. I don't know what's going to happen with the physical part of my injuries. I'm a work in progress with both.

I have 22 years of sobriety from early childhood issues, and I was emotionally stable when I entered duty for the postal service. I've experienced many deaths in my family and the affect was natural of a family member. I had a solid foundation emotionally before I started with the postal service. I gained my coping skills, changed attitude, and behavior while in drug treatment. In addition, I have minimal education in mental health. I use to be afraid of staying at home alone but I now live by myself. I have been robbed years ago and I'm afraid of violence as any normal person would be.

1. Witnesses for me would be upper management and they will not write anything for fear of reprisal.
2. I brought my work home with me and it would sometimes created problems, but this was after the fact of being diagnosed with a Benign Heart Condition (Heart Palpitations). Also, I did not feel my heart beating differently until 9/2007. Most of my home problem was the result of no social life, sex, cleaning, cooking, laundry, etc.

Sincerely

Lola McGee

May 29, 2009

2:05pm

To: Doug Watson
North Las Vegas

From: Lola McGee
North Las Vegas

Hello Doug,

Per our conversation a few minutes ago, I would like to request a copy of my clock rings from 3/1/09 to present date for my personal information. I would like for the documentation to be faxed to (702) 260-0876 my home. If there be any COP time that was not approved, I will wait for the invoice to come from the ASC office so that I can address it at that time. In addition, I would like for my annual and sick leave to be used for my disability from work status until it is exhausted. I am attaching a 3971 to reflect this request. As of pay period 10, I had 130 hrs of annual leave and 12 hrs of sick leave. I started the year with 300 hrs of annual and my leave status evaporated it to 130 hrs of annual. I thank you in advance for your cooperation.

I was not paid correctly for pay period 11/2009 so I do not know what dates to put in for on my 3971 form dated 5/29/09, and I would like immediate attention to be put towards correcting my pay check. I previously submitted a 3971 through 6/1/09. If anyone took the liberty to not pay me without contacting me or applying leave that was not requested by me, I do not condone that decision.

I also want it to be noted that I was to be paid for 2/18/09 and 2/19/09 because I was working with Labor Relations on the Lucy James case for arbitration. Corey has the 1260's, I handed them to him personally on 4/13/09 and I have not been paid yet.

Sincerely
Lola McGee

June 3, 2009

To: Shaun Mossman
District Manager – Nevada Sierra

From: Lola McGee
Supervisor, Customer Services
North Las Vegas Post Office

RE: Supervisor Statement to Shared Services

Dear Mr. Mossman,

I want to start this letter by apologizing to you for having to bring something of this sort to your attention; however, I feel that it is very necessary because of the time frame that has elapsed.

I spoke with Shared Services yesterday June 2, 2009 to find out if they had received all of my documents concerning my Medical Disability Retirement and they informed me that both packages that I mailed have been received. In addition, they informed me that the Supervisor Statement was sent out via email on May 18, 2009 to Corey Richards and it has not been received yet.

It is at this time that I'm requesting your intervention in this matter because there are issues between Corey, Craig and myself. Both men have displayed negative behavior towards me and I will not subject myself to their actions because of health reasons.

Corey is my supervisor even though he has never supervised me, so that is all that needs to be reflected in the statement.

I appreciate your prompt attention in this matter because it is very important to me and my welfare.

I thank you in advance for you intervention in getting this matter taken care of.

Sincerely
Lola McGee

June 11, 2009

To: DOL DFEC Central Mailroom
P. O. Box 8300
London, KY 40742

From: Lola McGee
P. O. Box 89272
Las Vegas, Nevada 89193-8272

Case Number: 132198863 – Reconsideration Appeal (Per Louis Scolari)
Decision letter dated March 6, 2009 and Postmarked March 9, 2009
For my Oral Hearing Appeal request was untimely.

I am asking for Reconsideration Appeal of my claim number listed above based on new medical documentation that your office never received during the original consideration process. In addition, I have become medically disabled and am currently in the process of being approved for Medical Disability Retirement at age 46, and that is a shame.

I have a copy of the file that was originally considered and I will send in all medical documentation from the March 6, 2009 letter that was not given at that time. Also, I will make a copy of the old Appeal Request Form and send it in, because I do not have a new form.

In addition, I would like for the file that I sent for the Oral Hearing Appeal to the Branch of Hearings and Review to also be utilized in my Reconsideration Appeal.

Thank you
Lola McGee

June 4, 2009

To: U. S. Department Of Labor/OWCP
Employment Standards Administration
P. O. Box 8300 District 13 SFC
London, KY 40742-8300

From: Lola McGee
P. O. Box 98272
Las Vegas, NV 89193-8272

Attention: Louis Scolari, Claims Manager and Injury Compensation

RE: May 22, 2009 phone conversation/Change of Address

Dear Mr. Scolari

In our phone conversation on May 22, 2009 you stated to me that I did not file a timely Oral Appeal; in the letter it states by the postmark and to me that means envelope. Also, you stated that the claim for Neuropathy was going to be added to the original claim #132198863 because of the same events such as Panic Attack etc. The injuries stated on the CA-1 in the original claim Neuropathy = (nerve damage) numbness, weakness, tingling, burning, and pain in both feet and lower extremities going up to my left top buttocks was not in the original CA-1 or CA-2; because I did not know what the problems are terminologies were at that time. Hearing Loss was not in the original claim either. I did not know these health conditions until further testing was completed. For the two conditions Neuropathy and Hearing Loss (left ear) please refer to Sundance Medical Center reports that were completed on 10/3/08 at the center by Moises Cuevas Jr. and interpreted by Dr. Simon J. Farrow. However, I went for second opinions from Dr. Jimmy Novero - Neurologist, Neuropathy (12/16/08) and Dr. Frederick Goll, III – ENT Specialist, Hearing Loss (11/20/08).

These issues are not on the original CA-1 or CA-2 claim forms. The threat was in my opinion a CA-1 because it was a Traumatic Event that happened on 8/25/08. As a result of that Traumatic event, I had a Panic Attack which caused Neuropathy-nerve damage and Hearing Loss in my left ear. Post Traumatic Stress Disorder, Depression, Obsessive Compulsive Disorder, and Major Depression are Psychological Conditions and there are continuous events over a period of time that created those conditions ranging all the way back from 2005 to present, and some of them were in the original CA-2 form.

Thus, you stated on the phone that I did not need to file duplicate claims, please explain to me in writing which of the claims that I filed you considered duplicate.

Also, I have received correspondence from your subordinates, Julia Landry, Cheryl Mendoza, Brenda Buescher, and Nester Atienza at my Post Office Box listed above and it baffles me that the only way I knew about your letters was by calling my local injury compensation office. Your letters were addressed to my former residence and I would like to know why? I notified your department last year 2008 of my new P. O. Box address and I've received many letters from the previously named people on several occasions.

I would like for you to send me your letters directly to my P. O. Box listed above and a list of all the claim numbers, dates I signed them, and what the injury is so that I will know what to address and how in my appeal.

In addition, you stated for me to follow the appeal process in the letter that you sent to my local injury compensation office (with my wrong address on it); I would like to have the proper appeal form (s) for my response.

I want it to be noted that I was not sent the letters on May 19, 2009 and May 22, 2009 for these dates to start my clock to running. I would truly appreciate a timely response to this letter so that I can reply as soon as possible. Thank you very much. I can be reached at (702) 260-0876 home, or (562) 889-2662 cell.

Sincerely
Lola McGee

U. S. Postal Service EEO INVESTIGATIVE AFFIDAVIT (COMPLAINANT)	Page No. 1	No. Pages 14	Case No. 4E-890-0043-09

1. Affiant's Name (First, Middle, Last)	**2. Employing Postal Facility**
Lola B. McGee	North Las Vegas Post Office

3. Position Title	**4. Grade Level**	**5. Postal Address and Zip + 4**	**6. Unit Assigned**
Supervisor, Customer Service	EAS-17	1414 E. Lake Mead Blvd North Las Vegas, NV 89030	

Privacy Act Notice/USPS Standards of Conduct

Privacy Act Notice. **The collection of this information is authorized by the Equal Employment Opportunity act of 1972, 42 U.S.C. § 2000e-16; the Age Discrimination in Employment Act of 1967, as amended, 29 U.S.C. § 633a; the Rehabilitation Act of 1973, as amended. This information will be used to adjudicate complaints of alleged discrimination and to evaluate the effectiveness of the EEO program. As a routine use, this information may be disclosed to an appropriate government agency, domestic or foreign, for law enforcement purposes; where pertinent, in a legal proceeding to which the USPS is a party or has an interest; to a government agency in order to obtain information relevant to a USPS decision concerning employment, security clearances, contracts, licenses, grants, permits or other benefits; to a government agency upon its request when relevant to its decision concerning employment, security clearances, security or suitability investigations, contracts, licenses, grants or other benefits; to a congressional office at your request; to an expert, consultant, or other person under contract with the USPS to fulfill an agency function; to the Federal Records Center for storage; to the Office o Management and Budget for review of private relief legislation; to an independent certified public accountant during an official audit of USPS finances; to an investigator, administrative judge or complaints examiner appointed by the Equal Employment Opportunity Commission for Investigation of a formal EEO complaint under 29 CFR 1614; to the Merit Systems Protection Board or Office of Special Counsel for proceedings or investigations involving personnel practices and other matters within their jurisdiction; and to a labor organization as required by the National Labor Relations Act. Under the Privacy Act provision, the information requested is voluntary for the complainant, and for Postal Service employees and other witnesses.**

Important Information Regarding Your Complaint

This PS Form 2568-A, EEO Investigative Affidavit (Complainant), and the other form mentioned below, are being provided for you to use to fully respond to the accompanying questions. Mail or deliver your completed statement to the EEO complaints investigator within15 calendar days of the date you received the forms. Use PS Form(s) 2569, EEO Investigative Affidavit (Continuation Sheet), as needed, to complete your written statement. Remember to number the top of each page and sign and date the bottom of each page of your statement. If you return your statement by mail, the return envelope must be postmarked on or before the 15th calendar day after the date that you received the affidavit forms.

Failure to complete your statement and return the forms within the allotted time period could result in your complaint being dismissed based upon your failure to proceed. EEOC complaints processing regulation. 29 C.F.R. 1614.107(a)(7), states, in part, [A complaint may be dismissed] "Where the agency has provided the complainant with the written request to provide relevant information or otherwise proceed with the complaint, and the complainant has failed to respond to the request within 15 days of its receipt, or the complainant's response does not address the agency's request, provided that the request included a notice of the proposed dismissal."

Claim: You allege discrimination based on your Sex (female), Retaliation (prior EEO activity), Physical Disability (back/knees/left thigh/neuropathy-nerve damage in feet, legs and buttock/heart palpitations/hearing loss in left ear) and Mental Disability (post traumatic stress disorder/major depression/panic attacks) when: On or around April 8, 2009, you were denied a transfer to the city of Las Vegas and sent back to North Las Vegas.

1. Please state your full name, work address, title, grade, email address, and current work phone number.

Answer: Lola Bonitta McGee, 1414 E. Lake Mead Blvd., North Las Vegas, NV 89030, Supervisor, Customer Services, EAS-17, lola.mcgee@usps.gov, (702) 649-2623.

I am not at work and have been off for the second time since 4/3/09. The injury has put me in a position to file for disability retirement at age 46 and I will explain. I currently receive in home health care for my disabilities. When I returned back to work on 3/13/09, I had been off work for over six months from previous on-the-job injuries that were not healed but I thought that I would be able to maintain my job duties because I was still in mental and physical therapy with medications. Also, I was being monitored by my Cardiologist and on heart medication, and my Hearing Loss did not require a Hearing Aid at the time. I can be reached at my P. O. Box and by telephone or email information that I gave you. This Case #4E-890-0043-09 was not filed on the issues of Case #4E-890-0120-08; however, the mental anguish and exacerbated Neuropathy are apart of my body's condition and not the reasoning for the case being filed. Yul Melonson had given me a job and took it back when I got injured and I will attest to that under penalty of perjury. I was discriminated against based on gender, mental/physical disabilities, and all of it was retaliatory not just the prior EEO activity.

2. Please identify your current supervisor by name, telephone number and email address.

Answer: Corey Richards, (702)649-2623, can't remember his email. I want it to be noted that he has never supervised me; but, he was apart of the first EEO.

3. Have you selected a representative to assist you during the EEO process? If so, provide your representative's name, title, address, phone number and e-mail address.

Answer: Not at this time.

The following questions relate to your sex

4. Please identify your sex.

Answer: Female

5. Who do you believe discriminated against you? Specify their name, title and sex.

Answer: Yul Melonson, Postmaster, Las Vegas, Male.

6. Are the management officials named in your response to Question No. 5 aware of your sex? If yes, how?

Answer: Yes, I worked for him for awhile before he was promoted to Las Vegas.

The following questions relate to your prior EEO Activity

7. Please identify the prior EEO activity that you claim is a basis for discrimination by management officials in this case. If the EEO activity involved one or more prior EEO Complaints identify the complaint(s) by case number and date.

8. Answer: Yul was acting Postmaster of Las Vegas and he also responded in the investigation of case #4E-890-0120-08 filed November 1, 2008. On 3/13/09 I injured my back, left thigh, and both knees in a lifting accident at Spring Valley Station, where Yul had sent me to supervise. My back, knees, and thigh injuries exacerbated my Neuropathy-Nerve damage. Yul's retaliatory behavior affected my Post Traumatic Stress Disorder, Major Depression, and Anxiety, along with Panic Attacks. Neuropathy, Post Traumatic Stress Disorder, Major Depression, Anxiety, and Panic Attacks are disabilities from the prior case #4E-890-0120-08.

9. Please explain how the management official(s) who you allege discriminated against you were aware of your prior EEO activity. If the management official(s) were involved in the complaint, explain how and when they were involved.

10. Answer: Yul was apart of the investigation. He was the acting Postmaster of Las Vegas and the acting senior MPOO for the south. Yul's permanent position at the time was Postmaster of North Las Vegas, which is where Jerry Wilson, acting Postmaster, North Las Vegas, threatened me, and I was the acting manager of Meadow Mesa Station, which is in North Las Vegas.

The following questions relate to your alleged disability

11. Do you claim to have a physical or mental impairment? (Please provide documentation supporting your claim.)

Answer: Unfortunately yes.

12. What is your physical and/or mental impairment? (Please state the medical term for your condition or explain the nature of your condition.)

Answer: I do not know if you are asking me in totality are for the sake of this EEO #4E-890-0043-09. For the sake of this case, I have entire back pain/sprain (Sciatica), Left thigh pain, and exacerbated Lumbar Radiculopathy. Exacerbated Neuropathy = Nerve damage to both lower extremities going from my feet all the way up to my lower back causing pain, tingling, numbness, and weakness. Post Traumatic Stress Disorder, Major Depression, Anxiety, and Panic Attacks all exacerbated from prior injuries. This has caused me to need home health care and apply for Medical Disability Retirement, along with Social Security Disability at age 46, but I'm now age 47. I have three doctors that deemed me permanently disabled and can no longer work. The post office has taken a toll on my entire life.

13. Is your physical or mental impairment a permanent condition? (Please provide documentation supporting your claim.)

Answer: Yes, according to my doctor's and my self analysis of my physical and mental ability. I'm still trying to learn how to live with this drastically changed life that I live today.

12. Does your physical/mental impairment substantially limit any of the following major life activities: caring for one's self, performing manual tasks, walking, seeing, hearing, speaking, breathing, learning, or working? If so, what and how does it affect you?

(Please provide documentation on the activities affected, how they are affected, and the degree to which they are affected (i.e., can't do the activity at all, can only do the activity with assistive devices or equipment, can only do the activity for a limited period of time, etc).

Answer: Absolutely, my brain and personality does not operate in the manner it once did. I cannot perform most normal life functions in my home. Cooking, cleaning, laundry, dusting, bathing etc. I cannot stand long enough to fix a full course meal and I do have assistance now. I walk with a four Leggett cane and I have a heating pad along with a tens unit and ointment. I take narcotic medication and I'm totally against it. I also have a walker but I'm very ashamed to use it. I do very little in the kitchen and I'm a cook (My hobby/ interest). I'm getting better with dressing myself as far as socks, knee-hi's and shoes. I can only walk about 20- 40 feet, it depends on the day. Nothing I do is consistent because I don't know how I'm going to wake up in the morning are if I'm going to sleep at all that night. Most times I sleep all day everyday. I can't concentrate and my attention span is very short. I have memory loss with small things I do are need to do. I have to ask people to remind me. I recall in my mind several times to help my self remember that I took my medication. I struggle with using the toilet because of my Neuropathy and pain. My feet and legs get numb just by setting on the toilet. The longer I set at any time the more pain and numbness come. My feet and legs swell and it scares me. Then I have to deal with getting up out the chair or what ever I'm sitting on with the weakness and pain, it's a painful project. Most times, I do not keep my hygiene up because I don't feel like it physically or mentally. I got a new prescription lens in 2008 and I had to get a bifocal put in my glasses. I have never had a bifocal before. My eyes got worse in 2008. I have hearing loss in my left ear which was a part of the prior EEO, not this one. I do not speak the way I use to; I forget normal words in mid sentence. Sometimes things I know, I know I can't remember them. As far as learning, I'm just trying to re-learn how to walk and not fall down. This is embarrassing but it's true. I don't have the attention span to learn; my life and thought's at this time is to try and live and survive. I have no foundation for my future and I have no consistency in my life today. I'm out of breath when I do therapy and walk too far, or get upset at something the post office did, and they have the mitigated gall to controvert my injury claims. I was a dedicated, loyal, professional, serious, hard working, respectful, efficient, team player, and had never been disciplined are injured until I came to Las Vegas. My job duties were never a problem, it was the hostile work environment, threat, discrimination, and lifting injured that put me in this position and condition. So working is not an option for me, I have to focus on trying to learn how to live this life I have today. I already have two degrees a BS and an AA but they won't do me any good now. I know for a fact that I can not do my job that was confirmed for me when I went back to work on 3/13/09, but I though that I would see if it was because I had been out already for over six months, but that was not the case. It's also embarrassing to me that I can no longer work, my physical and mental disabilities will not allow me to and I pushed myself as long as I could (4/2/09).

13. Are you able to engage in normal life activities outside of work? If so, please describe what some of those activities might be.

Answer: No, not really. Sometimes I ride in the car to the bank or to the store. My family came to see me and they got me out of the house to go to lunch. Once a girlfriend of mine forced me to go out to dinner with her and I did, but I do not have very much activity in my life these days because I don't want to put my limitations on other people's fun. I'm limited and I don't want my pain to keep them having to look after me. I try to attend church sometimes but I desire to be regular in attendance. I'm still trying to figure out my life myself, so I know it's troublesome to others. I loved to have fun and socialize, but it is just a memory now. I use to drive to California often, which is where I'm from, but I can't even drive to get away from all this madness now.

14. Was management aware of your physical or mental impairment? If so, how were they made aware? (Please be specific and provide documentation supporting your claim.)

Answer: Absolutely, on 3/13/09 I reported my lifting injury to acting manager Joe Acosta and I even shared some of the prior injuries with him. Also, Joe Acosta who was the acting manager at Spring Valley Station was right there when I looked up from the hamper and sounded/grimmest in pain from lifting the mail. He asked me if I was ok and I stated I think all be okay. We went into his office and talked about the injury and that's when I shared with him about the previous ones. Injury Compensation has my medical documentation.

15. Have you provided management with documentation of your physical or mental impairment? If so, what did you provide, when did you provide it, and to whom did you provide it? (Provide a copy of any reports and/or records that support your claim of physical or mental impairment.)

Answer: The Injury Compensation Office has it, and I gave them the medical for the claim I filed on 4/2/09 from St. Rose Hospital Emergency Room. I also, went to Centennial Spine and Pain Center on 4/7/09 after being put off work by St. Rose Hospital. Centennial Spine and Pain Center put me off for two months and there were problems with their paperwork and my Neurologist, Jimmy John Novero took over with treatment from there. I started with in home physical therapy at that time, and the cane and Narcotics for pain.

16. What are the essential functions of your current position?

Answer: Supervising a delivery unit, distribution, and window services and any one of them calls for consistent physical and mental activity.

17. What job-related activities are affected by your physical or mental impairment, and explain how they are affected? (Please provide documentation supporting your claim.)

Answer: sitting, walking, standing, bending, attitudes, customers, employee assistance, addressing employees and getting commitments, physically monitoring every operation, counting stock and mail, reports, telecoms, computer usage, telephones, etc. My job is very active in any position and I have to look out for my health and not put it on the back burner, or else the job will still be there and I'll be dead. I have no choice in the matter and the post office saw to that.

18. Do you require accommodations for your physical or mental impairment? If so, what are the specific accommodations? (Please be specific and provide documentation supporting your claim.)

Answer: If I have to catch a plain then I need wheelchair assistance. I walk on a cane every where I go even to the toilet. I live with pain on a daily basis and it may sound sick, but I have to actually get use to a level of pain and act like it does not bother me. I have to treat it like it is normal are take heavy drugs and pass out. My heart can not take this, so I juggle the medication. The reason why I put in for the Lateral to Las Vegas in the first place is because I could not work with Corey and I thought it best to lateral and Yul was very aware of this. Corey treated me like I was a second class citizen and he did not care. Unfortunately, I had a lifting injury and Yul retaliated against me because he did not want that one his books and I did not personally tell him on 4/1/09. However, I would have never been working at Spring Valley Station it I was not going to get the lateral. My PS Form-50 states North Las Vegas as a supervisor not Las Vegas.

19. Did you request accommodations for your physical or mental impairment with management? If so, please explain to whom you made the request, when it was requested, how it was requested, and what was requested. (Please provide copies of any written requests that you may have submitted to management.)

Answer: Yes, on 2/11/09 I requested a lateral to Las Vegas per Yul's request. I faxed a letter to Yul Melonson, Robert Reynosa, and Corey Richards. On 2/19/09 I met with Yul and we decided the station that he needed more help and that had a supervisor vacancy, which was Spring Valley Station in Las Vegas. This request was for my mental disabilities and I thought that physical therapy and medication would take care of my physical disabilities; however, that was not the case.

20. Were you granted any accommodations for your physical or mental impairment? If so, what? (Please provide copies of any written documentation that you may have received from management.)

Answer: Yes, for my mental disabilities I was working at Spring Valley Station since 3/9/09. On 4/2/09, Yul called me on my cell phone and told me that he was sending me back to North Las Vegas after he learned of the lifting injury claim being filed by me that day, but the injury actually happened on 3/13/09

21. Do you have an accepted OWCP claim? If yes, state for what condition (Please provide a copy of your accepted OWCP claim).

Answer: No, I received the initial COP and it was taken back because of Centennial Spine and Pain Center's insufficient paperwork. However, it is in appeal at this time.

22. Is your position a Limited Duty position? If yes, state what duties you perform in your Limited Duty position. (Please provide a copy of your Limited Duty position description).

Answer: No.

23. Who do you believe discriminated against you because of your alleged disability? Specify their name and title.

Answer: Yul Melonson, Postmaster City of Las Vegas, he also retaliated against me based on my 3/13/09 injury, that also exacerbated prior injuries, and prior EEO activity case #4E-890-0120-08.

24. Are the management officials named in your response to Question No. 23 aware of your alleged disability? If yes, how?

Answer: 100% yes. Yul was the acting Postmaster of Las Vegas and the acting Senior MPOO of the South part of the Nevada Sierra District.

The following questions relate to your being denied a transfer to Las Vegas

25. Did you request transfer Las Vegas? If yes, when and how?

Answer: Yes, on 2/11/09 I wrote a letter to Yul, Robert, and Corey requesting a lateral to Las Vegas as a supervisor. The letter was faxed with confirmation to me from Yul's secretary Phyllis Joiner and Corey Richards himself.

26. What specific postal service locations in Las Vegas did you request a transfer to?

Answer: In my letter there was not a specific location mention; however, when I met with Yul on 2/19/09 we decided to have me be at Spring Valley Station because he needed help there and the station had a supervisor opening.

27. Who was the management official who denied your transfer to Las Vegas? Specify their name, title and sex.

Answer: Yul Melonson, Postmaster City of Las Vegas, Male, denied my lateral to Las Vegas in his letter dated 4/8/09, which is after I had been at Spring Valley Station since 3/9/09. Also, on 4/2/09 he called me on my cell phone and told me "I've got news for you I'm sending you back to North Las Vegas and Corey has already been notified."

28. When and how were you notified that you were denied a transfer to Las Vegas?

Answer: I new that my lateral was denied on 4/2/09 when Yul called me on my cell phone and told me that he had news for me and he was sending me back to North Las Vegas and Corey has already been notified. In addition, I had been out on the 3/13/09 injury and I wrote a letter on 4/8/09 to Yul and asked for an official response to my lateral request letter dated 2/11/09. Yul wrote me a letter on 4/8/09 responding to my 4/8/09 letter. However, he had already told me what he was doing over my cell phone on 4/2/09, this is discrimination and retaliation which is the reason for this EEO case #4E-890-0043-09.

29. Did management explain to you why you were denied a transfer to Las Vegas? If yes, what were you told?

Answer: In Yul's letter dated 4/8/09 he stated that he was only accepting lateral request from the restructuring employees.

30. Do you dispute the reason management gave as the basis of your being denied a transfer to Las Vegas? If yes, why? Answer: Absolutely, because I would have never been at Spring Valley Station with my lateral request if I was not going to be given the lateral. I'm a North Las Vegas supervisor and Cities do not allow promoted supervisor employees cross over and work in another city unless there has been a request for detail, lateral, higher level and that is the purpose of the request and PS Form 1723. In addition, the employees PS Form-50 states where an employee is to work and mine states North Las Vegas Post Office.

31. Please explain why you believe that your sex was a factor that was considered when you were denied a transfer to Las Vegas.

Answer: Women are considered to be weak and not able to perform at higher levels of management even though some get lucky.

32. Please explain why you believe that your prior EEO activity was a factor that was considered when you were denied a transfer to Las Vegas.

Answer: First of all it was another issue with me after the EEO. Next, Yul was an acting Postmaster of Las Vegas and the acting Senior MPOO during that time and he had to provide an affidavit in the case #4E-890-0120-08. Jerry Wilson was his subordinate and that's the person who threatened me. Also, upper management sticks together rather its right or wrong. Yul wanted to make a name for himself; and, he did not want this on his record. For him not to do something adverse towards a supervisor that filed a claim would have made him appear inefficient and not making good decision in his position. Also, I'm black and Yul is black and amongst white people he would have been looked at as favoring me because of our race. This may sound sick and crazy to you but it is reality. The bottom line is Yul was not going to back me at his expense with prior EEO activity.

33. Please explain why you believe that your alleged disability was a factor that was considered when you were denied a transfer to Las Vegas.

Answer: My injury would add to the Las Vegas OSHA Injury and illness rate indicator and I'm a supervisor with an injury and it does not look good. Nevertheless it happened and I'm the one who suffers the pain.

34. Are you aware of other employees who requested transfers to Las Vegas who were granted transfers? If yes, state the following:

a. Name and title

b. Work location

c. Management official who granted their transfer

d. Sex

e. Describe your knowledge of any medical condition affecting the employee(s).

f. Describe your knowledge of any EEO activity the employee has engaged in.

Answer: Yes, I do not know their names but I've heard that there has been some. Not only that, supervisors request laterals regularly and get them but they are not injured.

35. Are you aware of other employees who requested transfers to Las Vegas who were also denied transfers? If yes, state the following:

a. Name and title

b. Work location

c. Management official who denied their transfer

d. Sex

e. Describe your knowledge of any medical condition affecting the employee(s).

f. Describe your knowledge of any EEO activity the employee has engaged in

Answer: No.

The following questions relate to your being sent back to North Las Vegas

36. Where were you working prior to being sent back to North Las Vegas? Was this a permanent position?

Answer: I was working at Spring Valley Station in Las Vegas and I was waiting on my official PS Form-50 to be processed, which would have made me an official supervisor of Spring Valley Station in Las Vegas.

37. Who was the management official who sent you back to North Las Vegas? Specify their name, title and sex.

Answer: Yul Melonson, Postmaster of Las Vegas, Male.

38. When and how were you notified that you were being sent back to North Las Vegas?

Answer: On 4/2/09 I received a cell phone call from Yul and he told me so. Also, he sent me a letter dated 4/8/09.

39. Did management explain to you why you were being sent back to North Las Vegas? If yes, what were you told?

Answer: Yes, I was told by Yul that he was only allowing the restructuring employees to lateral.

40. Do you dispute the reason management gave as the basis of your being sent back to North Las Vegas? If yes, why?

Answer: Yes, I would have still been at Spring Valley Station had I not gotten injured on 3/13/09 and filed a claim on 4/2/09. Yul's cell phone call to me let me know that. He was very upset because I did not report the accident to him and he did not know that I had gotten injured. However, it was Joe Acosta's responsibility to report the injury to Yul. I was already trying to work it off but to no avail. In addition, Yul was not going to have me as a supervisor out sick and slotting into one of his positions. Nevertheless this is discrimination and he retaliated against me for it.

41. Please explain why you believe that your sex was a factor that was considered when you were sent back to North Las Vegas.

Answer: Simply because I am a female and injured.

42. Please explain why you believe that your prior EEO activity was a factor that was considered when you were sent back to North Las Vegas.

Answer: Previously explained.

43. Please explain why you believe that your alleged disability was a factor that was considered when you were sent back to North Las Vegas.

Answer: Previously explained.

44. Are you aware of other employees who failed to report an on-the-job injury who did not have their assignment end? If yes, state the following:

a. Name and title

b. Work location

c. Management official who did not end their assignment

d. Sex

e. Describe your knowledge of any medical condition affecting the employee(s).

f. Describe your knowledge of any EEO activity the employee has engaged in.

Answer: No, and I reported my injury to my immediate manager Joe Acosta and he also saw me when I came up from the hamper on 3/13/09. He replied are you ok and I said I think I'll be ok.

45. Are you aware of other employees who failed to report an on-the-job injury who did have their assignment end? If yes, state the following:

a. Name and title

b. Work location

c. Management official who ended their assignment

d. Sex

e. Describe your knowledge of any medical condition affecting the employee(s).

f. Describe your knowledge of any EEO activity the employee has engaged in

Answer: No, but I did report mine to Joe Acosta acting manager of Spring Valley Station at the time on 3/13/09.

<u>The following questions allow you to add information not provided in response to prior questions.</u>

21. What Postal Service rules, regulations, or policies do you feel apply to the accepted issue (s) in this complaint?

Answer: PS Form-50 gives official assignments to postal employees. Employees requesting other assignments in different cities must put in their request and be on a PS Form-1723. I requested a lateral to Las Vegas from North Las Vegas, and according to Postal Policy, I cannot be working in the city of Las Vegas without required documents and approval. I did not request a detail; I requested a lateral via letter on 2/11/09.

22. Do you feel these rules, regulations, or policies were violated or not followed? If yes, how?

Answer: They were violated, after being at Spring Valley Station for over three weeks, when Yul called me on my cell phone and told me that he was sending me back to North Las Vegas and Corey is already aware. In addition, Yul wrote a letter on 4/8/09 denying my lateral after working at Spring Valley Station over three weeks and he used a horrible excuse for the reason why, restructuring employees are being placed in the positions. Not only that, Yul knew that I could not work in North Las Vegas with Corey because of health reasons.

23. Are there witnesses you would like interviewed in regard to the accepted issue(s) in this complaint? If yes, provide their name, title, contact information and what first-hand

knowledge they will attest to.

Answer: I have not been at work since 4/2/09 so I do not know where people are in the City of Las Vegas but I will give names. Also, I just want the truth told and the people I mention may not be on my side but they know information about the situation. Joe Acosta, Yul Melonson, Phyllis Joiner, Corey Richards, Josephine, and the other supervisor lady at Spring Valley Station are a few names that comes to my mine at this time.

24. Is there anything you would like to add, in regard to the accepted issue(s) in your complaint that have not already been attested to?

Answer: I am not by any means trying to put case #4E-890-0120-08 filed November 1, 2008 with this case #4E-890-0043-09. This case is strictly discrimination and retaliation on me by Yul Melonson. The retaliation portion is not just prior EEO activity it is also not telling him personally about the injury, retaliating against me for even having the 3/13/09 injury, and filing a claim as a supervisor under his watch as the Las Vegas Postmaster.

25. What do you seek as resolution to this EEO claim of discrimination?

Answer: For case #4E-890-0043-09 based on Discrimination and Retaliation by Yul Melonson towards me (Lola McGee) I seek an official written apology, sensitivity training, full medical coverage for my physical and mental disabilities, out of pocket expenses that has already been paid, and compensation for my future salaries that I potentially would have been paid had not I had to file for Disability Retirement and Social Security Disability at age 46 with 11 years of service, and monetary compensation for punitive damages.

June 19, 2009 Delivery Confirmation #03060320000192421715

To: FADS
National EEO Investigative Services
P. O. Box 21979
Tampa, FL 33622-1979

From: Lola McGee
P. O. Box 98272
Las Vegas, NV 89193-8272

RE: Case #4E-890-0120-08

I am in receipt of the completed investigation case number listed above, received 6/18/09. It is my desire at this time to request the United States Postal Service Final Agency Decision on my Formal Complaint Dated November 1, 2008.

I want it to be noted at this time in my life, my mental and physical health has rapidly declined to the point where I had to file for Medical Disability Retirement at age 46.

In addition, I receive in home health care and I have to learn how to live a life that is extremely different from what my normal life was before all the adverse action was imposed upon me by the Nevada Sierra District.

Thus, I am requesting the Postal Service Merit Final Agency Decision.

Sincerely
Lola McGee

HARRY REID
NEVADA

MAJORITY LEADER

United States Senate

WASHINGTON, DC 20510–7012

August 11, 2009

Ms. Lola McGee
P.O. Box 98272
Las Vegas, Nevada 89193

Dear Ms. McGee:

This letter is to acknowledge receiving your request for assistance with the Department of Labor. I received your signed Privacy Release Form and have asked Charvez Foger on my Las Vegas staff to help you with this matter.

Thank you for contacting my office. If you have any questions please call Charvez Foger at (702) 388-5020 for assistance.

Sincerely,

HARRY REID
United States Senator

HR:db

United States
Office of
Personnel Management Washington, DC 20415-0001

September 10, 2009

LOLA B MCGEE
P O BOX 98272
LAS VEGAS NV 89193

CSA: 8418325

Dear Ms. McGee:

This letter is to inform you that your application for disability retirement under the Federal Employees Retirement System (FERS) has been **approved** and to provide information that will be helpful in your transition from employment to retirement. It explains the steps that must be taken before you can begin receiving annuity payments. It provides important information on other factors that may have a major impact on your disability retirement.

Interim Payments
According to the information we received from your agency, you have not been separated from Federal service. We will notify your agency that your disability retirement has been approved and ask them to separate you from Federal service. We will also ask your agency to forward your final records to us, including your last day in a pay status. Once we are advised of your last day in a pay status we will authorize interim payments, which are usually about 80 percent of the amount of your actual monthly annuity payments. You should receive your first interim payment within 10 days of your agency certifying your last day in pay to us. You will continue to receive interim payments on the first business day of each month until we complete the processing of your application for a disability retirement.

Social Security Administration Awards
We cannot start your annuity payments until we receive confirmation that you have applied for Social Security disability benefits. If you have not already done so, you must apply for them now and send us a copy of the receipt that they will send to you. If you have already sent us a copy of the receipt, you do not need to take any action.

If the Social Security Administration awards you monthly benefits, you must immediately notify us of the amount and the effective date of the monthly benefit. You can do this by sending us a photocopy of their award notice or their statement showing the monthly benefit amount and the effective date they determined your eligibility began. We conduct periodic checks against Social Security records to discover unreported awards.

You should send their application receipt and notification that you have been approved for Social Security benefits to the **U.S. Office of Personnel Management, Federal Employees Retirement System, Boyers, PA 16017.**

We will continue processing your claim after we receive the final records from your employing agency and a receipt or other confirmation that you have applied for Social Security benefits.

If you are under age 62, your FERS disability benefits for the first 12 months will be equal to 60 percent of your high-three year average salary minus 100 percent of your Social Security benefit for any month in which you are entitled to Social Security disability benefits. After the first year, your disability annuity will be equal to 40 percent of your high-three year average salary minus 60 percent of your Social Security benefit for any month in which you are entitled to Social Security disability benefits. FERS disability benefits usually begin before the claim for Social Security benefits is fully processed. **Because the FERS disability benefit must be reduced by 100 percent of any Social Security benefit payable for 12 months, Social Security checks should not be negotiated until the FERS benefit has been reduced. The Social Security checks will be needed to pay OPM for the reduction which should have been made in the FERS annuity.**

U.S. Dept. of Labor's Office of Workers' Compensation Program (OWCP) Benefits
In general, you may not receive annuity payments from both OPM and OWCP for the same period of time. However, if you are eligible to receive a civil service annuity and an OWCP Non-Scheduled Total or Partial Award for the same period of time, you may elect which benefit you want to receive. You may receive payments from both OPM and OWCP for the same period of time only if, (1) you are receiving OWCP payments for a Scheduled (loss of limb or function) Award, (2) you are receiving OWCP payments due to the death of another person and you are eligible for receiving an annuity on the basis of your own Federal service, or (3) in place of receiving an OWCP Non-Scheduled Total or Partial Award, you are receiving a Third Party Settlement from the party directly responsible for your injury. If you are receiving OWCP payments but not for one of the three reasons stated above and are also receiving payments from OPM, please contact us by calling 1(888) 767-6738, or by writing to the U.S. Office of Personnel Management, Retirement Operations Center, Boyers, PA 16017.

Recovery Situations
If you are under age 60, **we may ask you** from time to time to submit detailed medical evidence to show your condition continues to be disabling. If the medical evidence shows your condition has improved to the point where you can again perform the duties of your previous position, we will find that you are recovered from your disabling medical condition. With such a finding, annuity payments will stop on the first day of the month beginning one year after the date of the medical examination showing your recovery.

Furthermore, we will honor a written and signed statement of medical recovery that you voluntarily submit if the medical documentation on file does not demonstrate mental incompetency. Disability annuity payments will stop on the first day of the month beginning one year after the date of your voluntary statement.

If you are reemployed into a permanent position with the Federal Government at any time before age 60 at the same or higher grade/pay level and tenure as the position from which you retired, you will be found recovered. Disability annuity payments will stop on the first day of the month following the month of the recovery finding.

If you are found recovered from any of these situations, your former employing agency is not obligated to rehire you into your former position, or any other position. If your annuity payments are stopped because you are found medically recovered, you may be eligible for a deferred annuity at age 62, or at an earlier date if you meet the service criteria for a discontinued service retirement.

Restoration of Earning Capacity
If you are under age 60 and working in a non-federal position, there is a limit on the amount you can earn from wages and self-employment and still be entitled to your annuity payment. If your earnings in any calendar year equal at least 80 percent of the current salary of the position from which you retired, we will find your earning capacity to have been restored. Disability annuity payments will stop six months from the end of the calendar year in which your earning capacity is restored.

Medicare
If you believe you qualify for Medicare, you should contact the Social Security Administration promptly at 1-800-772-1213 to make arrangements for filing an application. A delay in filing could result in a delay in the date your Medicare entitlement may begin.

Reporting Responsibilities
Be sure to notify us if you are reemployed with the Federal Government, your marital status changes, or there is a change in either the address where your payments are sent or the address where you wish us to send correspondence and notices. You can report these events and ask questions concerning this letter to our **Retirement Information Office at 1(888) 767-6738, or by writing to the U.S. Office of Personnel Management, Retirement Operations Center, Boyers, PA 16017.** Be sure to include your Civil Service Annuity (CSA) claim number on any correspondence and keep this letter for future reference.

For more information about disability retirement you can visit our website at http://www.opm.gov/retire.

Sincerely,

Angela E. Lovely-Abdullah
Legal Administrative Specialist
Disability Branch
Disability, Reconsideration
And Appeals Group

3

If you are reemployed into a permanent position with the Federal Government at any time before age 60 at the same or higher grade/pay level and tenure as the position from which you retired, you will be found recovered. Disability annuity payments will stop on the

United States
Office of
Personnel Management Washington, DC 20415-0001

September 10, 2009

LOLA B MCGEE
P O BOX 98272
LAS VEGAS NV 89193

CSA: 8418325

Dear Ms. McGee:

Our records show that you claim you were disabled due to Multiple Medical Conditions and Symptoms.

In reviewing your medical records, we have found you to be disabled for your position as a Supervisor Customer Services, due to Post Traumatic Stress Disorder; Depression; Obsessive Compulsive Disorder; and Peripheral Sensory Neuropathy.

Sincerely,

Angela E. Lovely-Abdullah
Legal Administrative Specialist
Disability, Reconsideration, and
Appeals Group

September 12, 2009

To: DOL DFEC Central Mailroom
P. O. Box 8300
London, KY 40742

From: Lola McGee
P. O. Box 89272
Las Vegas, Nevada 89193-8272

RE: Case Number 132198863 – Requesting Reconsideration Appeal
Decision letter dated March 6, 2009

I am asking for a Reconsideration Appeal of my claim number listed above based on new medical documentation that your office has never received. In addition, I have research documentation that states how my medical condition derived based on the diagnosis of my doctors. Post Traumatic Stress Disorder, Major Depression, Panic Attacks, Neuropathy = Nerve damage, Hearing Loss, Heart Palpitations, Head Shocks. Also, in 2008 I had to get a much stronger prescription in my glasses because I was not able to see very well. I did not have this on any forms, but my research supports the reason why my eyes got worse. I have three prescriptions in my glasses today oppose to one before 8/25/08. I will get the eye doctor's prescription and send it in to you. I assume that all previously sent information will not need to be resent, such as statements, medical documentation, reports, forms, statements, letters, and things of that nature. If any information is not clear are other documentation is needed, please give me a call or write to me before my request receives an adverse decision.

I can be reached at (702) 260-0876 Home, (562) 889-2662 Cell.

I am using an old appeal form because I do not have a new one.

Thank you

Lola McGee

September 12, 2009 Delivery Confirmation #03060320000192421708

To: FADS
National EEO Investigative Services
P. O. Box 21979
Tampa, FL 33622-1979

From: Lola McGee
P. O. Box 98272
Las Vegas, NV 89193-8272

RE: Case #4E-890-0043-09

I am in receipt of the completed investigation case number listed above, received 9/12/09. It is my desire at this time to request the United States Postal Service Final Agency Decision on my Formal Complaint Dated May 27, 2009.

I want it to be noted at this time in my life, my mental and physical health has rapidly declined to the point where I had to file for Medical Disability Retirement and it is still being processed.

In addition, I am still receiving in home health care.

Thus, I am requesting the Postal Service Merit Final Agency Decision.

Sincerely
Lola McGee

* * * * *

September 22, 2009

Dear Shaun Mossman,

I'm giving myself a retirement party and I would like to get permission from you to have an email sent out and posted on the time clocks, for those who do not have access to the computer, notifying everyone (Employees, Managers, Supervisors, Postmasters and of course yourself) of my party.

I attempted to get the notification out from Phyllis, but she was given an answer of "No."

I'm asking you because all I want to do is to be treated fairly and with dignity and respect like anyone else that has had their retirement announced.

I can be reached at (702) 260-0876.
Thank you,
Lola McGee

I was not allowed to announce my retirement, in spite of all my correspondences to the district manager.

WELCOME ALL

U.S. POSTAL SERVICE
DISABILITY RETIREMENT PARTY
FOR

LOLA McGEE

WHEN: SATURDAY
OCTOBER 17, 2009

TIME: 6PM – UNTIL

WHERE: AVIATA APARTMENTS
CLUB HOUSE
2121 E. WARM SPRINGS RD
LAS VEGAS, NEVADA 89119

OPEN BAR
6PM – 7PM SOCIAL HOUR
7PM – 8PM PROGRAM
8PM DINNER/DANCING
LIVE DJ

Executive Postmasters, City of Las Vegas (PECS)

UNITED STATES POSTAL SERVICE
THE CITY OF LAS VEGAS POSTMASTERS

October 22, 2009

To: U. S. Department Of Labor
Employment Standards Administration
Office of Workers' Comp Programs
P. O. Box 8300 District 50
London, KY 40742-8300

From: Lola McGee
P. O. Box 98272
Las Vegas, NV 89193-8272

RE: Supplemental Factual Statement
Case Number: 132209923

Attention: Amy Towner, Hearing Representative 10/8/2009

Dear Ms. Towner,

I am sending you additional medical documentation for the above case number and there are also several pages that had misquotes but I will just send page 12, line 12. This is an attempt to provide you with the information that you said was needed. I don't know if you know but I've been through an awful lot with these claims and the whole process and it wares on my mental and physical conditions.

In reading the transcripts, I notice that there were a lot of things that I did not explain correctly and that has to do with my mental state. Sometimes I can speak and have clear understanding and sometimes I'm just really way off target. I notice that I did not follow through with some of the questions that you asked me and I did not explain them very well but it is my hope that the documentation that I'm sending will clear up some of my rambling thoughts.

Note: I have been receiving in home health care/Physical Therapy since 5/2009 and I'm on my third doctor's prescription. Dr. Jimmy Novero-Neurologist.

I can be reached at (702) 260-0876 HM, (562) 889-2662 Cell

Thank you
Lola McGee

October 22, 2009

To: DOL DFEC Central Mail Room
P. O. Box 8300
London, KY 40742

From: Lola McGee
P. O. Box 98272
Las Vegas, NV 89193-8272

RE: Reconsideration Appeal
Case Number: 132198863

Attention: Louis Scolari and Liz Villanueva

Dear Mr. Scolari and Ms. Villanueva,

I am sending you additional medical documentation for the above case number. This is an attempt to provide you with up to date information concerning the above claim number.

I also want it to be noted of the things that Corey Richards has done to me: Taking me off higher level, not paying me when he had my leave slip in his possession (PS Form 3971), not paying me for the 1260's that I personally submitted to him, not allowing me my right to my PES report for 2007, not giving me CA-1 and CA-2 Forms upon my request, removing my access to the GMF as if I was a threat, giving me specific instructions to call the office before I come, not promoting me when I was over qualified than some of the others selected. I have had to much adverse behavior from Corey and I knew it had taken a toll on me.

Note: I have been receiving in Home Health Care/Physical Therapy since 5/2009 and I'm on my third doctor's prescription. Dr. Jimmy Novero-Neurologist.

I can be reached at (702) 260-0876 HM, (562) 889-2662 Cell

Thank you
Lola McGee

October 22, 2009

To: U. S. Department Of Labor
Employment Standards Administration
Office of Workers' Comp Programs
P. O. Box 8300 District 50
London, KY 40742-8300

From: Lola McGee
P. O. Box 98272
Las Vegas, NV 89193-8272

RE: Supplemental Factual Statement
Case Number: 132210754

Attention: Amy Towner, Hearing Representative 10/8/2009

Dear Ms. Towner,

I am sending you additional medical documentation for the above case number and there are also several pages that had misquotes but I think the she words will be understood that Corey Richards is a he. This is an attempt to provide you with the information that you said was needed. I don't know if you know but I've been through an awful lot with these claims and the whole process and it wares on my mental and physical conditions.

In reading the transcripts, I notice that there were a lot of things that I did not explain correctly and that has to do with my mental state. Sometimes I can speak and have clear understanding and sometimes I'm just really way off target. I notice that I did not follow through with some of the questions that you asked me and I did not explain them very well but it is my hope that the documentation that I'm sending will clear up some of my rambling thoughts.

Some of the things that Corey Richards has done to me are: Taking me off higher level, not paying me when he had my leave slip in his possession (PS Form 3971), not paying me for the 1260's that I personally submitted to him, not allowing me my right to my PES report for 2007, not giving me CA-1 and CA-2 Forms upon my request, removing my access to the GMF as if I was a threat, giving me specific instructions to call the office before I come, not promoting me when I was over qualified than some of the others selected. I have had to much adverse behavior from Corey and I knew it had taken a toll on me.

Note: I have been receiving in home health care/Physical Therapy since 5/2009 and I'm on my third doctor's prescription. Dr. Jimmy Novero-Neurologist.

I can be reached at (702) 260-0876 HM, (562) 889-2662 Cell

Thank you
Lola McGee

November 11, 2009 Delivery Confirmation #03060320000192421814

To: United States Postal Services
National EEO Investigative Services
P. O. Box 21979
Tampa, FL 33622-1979

From: Lola McGee
P. O. Box 98272
Las Vegas, NV 89193-8272

RE: Case #4E-890-0120-08
Filed November 1, 2008

I am in receipt of the completed Final Agency Decision on my Formal Complaint received August 18, 2009.

I want it to be noted at this time in my life, my mental and physical health has rapidly declined to the point where I have been approved for Medical Disability Retirement. Thus, my physical injuries and mental illnesses were all created by the United States Postal Service.

In addition, I still receive in home health care.

I want it to be noted that this letter stands as notification that I have legal representation and I am seeking my attorney fees to be at no cost to me.

He can be reached at: David Lee Phillips & Associates, and John S. Rogers, 700 South 4th St. Las Vegas, NV 89101 Phone: (702) 386-6000

Sincerely
Lola McGee

November 20, 2009

To: U. S. Department Of Labor
Employment Standards Administration
Office of Workers' Comp Programs
P. O. Box 8300 District 50
London, KY 40742-8300

From: Lola McGee
P. O. Box 98272
Las Vegas, NV 89193-8272

RE: Supplemental Factual Statement
Case Number: 132210754

Attention: Amy Towner, Hearing Representative 10/8/2009

I am writing this letter to make sure I have a statement on file, because I really don't remember if I actually wrote a personal statement as to what happened in this situation. I know I completed the claim but I'm unsure of the statement, thus I now have Neuropathy in my right arm that collapsed on 4/13/09 when I was hospitalized. I found out later from my Therapist Dr. Mary Reed that I had a Panic Attack.

My right arm now feels like my legs and feet, with intense pain and burning all around my elbow. The other part of my arm tingles and numbs out to the point where I can't lay on it for a long time, let alone sleep on my right side. My arm goes to sleep all the way down to my finger tips and it has never done that before.4/13/09

I won't it to be noted that I am right handed and I have to use it as my strong extremity, but yet it is weak.

If you have any questions I can be reached at (702) 260-0876 HM (562) 889-2662 Cell.

Sincerely
Lola McGee

November 20, 2009 Delivery Confirmation: #03060320000192421739

To: DOL DFEC Central Mailroom
P. O. Box 8300
London, KY 40742

From: Lola McGee
P. O. Box 89272
Las Vegas, Nevada 89193-8272

RE: Case Number 132198863 – Requesting Reconsideration Appeal
Decision letter dated March 6, 2009

I am asking for a Reconsideration Appeal of my claim number listed above based on new medical documentation that your office has never received, and some that was submitted with my request dated 9/12/09, but it was not noted as being received by your office in your decision letter dated 11/12/09.

In addition, I have research documentation that was submitted and it was not noted in your decision letter as being submitted either. Also, I have a letter from the Chief, Branch of Hearings and Review that I will also submit on behalf of my Appeal request.

For the record I want to make a clear and concise statement of the work related events that caused me to file the CA-1 and CA-2 on 8/29/08. On 8/25/08 I was in my office with OIC – North Las Vegas Jerry Wilson and he gave me and open ended threat "You continue to go over my head with Craig and Yul and I'm going to do something about it." He was very upset, aggressive, and red, spoke direct and with conviction to me while he was in my face. He looked me in my eyes and abruptly turned and walked away. In addition, I endured unfair discrimination tactics will working as an acting manager for one and a half through two years. Jennifer Vo lied to me about removing me from Huntridge Station and while in the meeting with he she stated to me "Lola tell me that I'm full of shit if you want to.", I called a meeting with Robert Reynosa, Mark Martinez, and Jennifer to find out what the problem was. I was sent to Paradise Valley after the meeting. Jennifer later gave me an investigative interview for carriers bringing back closed business mail. Other offices had mail that did not even leave the building and they did not get an investigative interview. I was sent back to supervise by Jennifer and Robert. I was sent up to Reno to manage and Robert called me back and asked me to work for him in Las Vegas at King Station, then I went to Huntridge again, next Craig Colton ask me to go to Meadow Mesa, and Yul Okayed it because he was the OIC for Las Vegas. I went from station to station, applied for 17 jobs, had 4 interviews, which were all great according to them but I was never promoted. This caused me great Anxiety, Panic Disorder, Major Depression, Post Traumatic Stress Disorder, Neuropathy, Lumbar Ridiculopathy, Hearing Loss, declined Vision, Head Shocks, Heart Palpitations since 9/2007, Chest Pain, Agoraphobia, inability to make rational decisions, walking on a cane, taking medication, feeling hopeless, changed life, I can't cook my kind of meals, and I'm a cook, I have wear a pad to keep from urinating on myself or defecating and sometime I don't make it, it took my pride, dignity, and self respect, I live with pain every day, I've learned that it's apart of me now, retired from Federal Service at age 47.

I have had therapy before during the Steven Phaup tenure 2005 and I was diagnosed with Post Traumatic Stress Disorder, Obsessive Compulsive Disorder, and Depression, but I stopped going because my hours changed and Steven was gone but I was still afraid.

All of my medical documentation will explain my condition and the dates I started treatment, and other than that, I have never had any of these medical condition before.

I will explain all my medical reports that I'm submitting with this package by date and doctor. I did not have this on any forms, but my research supports the reason why my eyes got worse. I have three prescriptions in my glasses today oppose to one before 8/25/08. I assume that all previously sent information will not need to be resent, such as statements, medical documentation, reports, forms, statements, letters, and things of that nature. If any information is not clear are other documentation is needed, please give me a call or write to me.

Dr. Reed letters dated 11/19/09 and 9/11/09; Dr. Novero letters dated 8/31/09 and 5/4/09; Dr. Scheffel (eye) dated 9/14/04, Dr. Lochner III (eye) dated 9/25/08; Dr. Fredrick Goll III, 4 pages dated 11/20/08; Dr. Shepard letters dated 10/20/08 and 8/26/09; Dr. Croke letter dated 4/30/09; OPM Decision dated 9/10/09 (CSA: 8418325); Research dated 820/09 (Mayo Clinic Web Site) "Can Panic Attacks Cause Peripheral Neuropathy?" Dizziness, Causes: eyes, sensory nerves, inner ears; Panic Attacks and Panic Disorder: 2 page definition, Causes: Stress, brain function to fight or flight response; Post Traumatic Stress Disorder (PTSD): 2 page definition, Peripheral Neuropathy: Sensory Nerve Damage, 2 page definition (Traumatic Injury). NeurologyChannel.com: dated 8/18/09 3 pages explaining Neuropathy: some Neurology's develop suddenly from trauma; Helpguide.org: dated 9/12/09 5 pages of some of my feelings and symptoms.

Will you please send me another copy of the Appeal report if I'll need it, thank you?

I can be reached at (702) 260-0876 Home, (562) 889-2662 Cell.

I am using an old appeal form because I do not have a new one.

Thank you
Lola McGee

Senator Reed's office – December 7, 2009

U.S. Senator Harry Reid
Privacy Act Release Form

The Privacy Act of 1974 is a federal law designed to protect you from any unauthorized use and exchange of personal information by federal agencies. Any information that a federal agency has on file regarding your dealings with the United States government may not, with a few exceptions, be given to another agency or Member of Congress without your written permission.

To Whom It May Concern:

I hereby request the assistance of the Office of United States Senator Harry Reid to resolve the matter described on the next page(s). I authorize Senator Harry Reid and his staff to receive any information they may need to provide this assistance. The information I have provided to Senator Harry Reid is true and accurate to the best of my knowledge and belief. The assistance I have requested from Senator Reid's office is in no way an attempt to evade or violate any federal, state, or local law.

SIGNED: Lola McGee **DATE:** 12/7/09

CONTACT INFORMATION (PLEASE PRINT):

Full Name: Lola Bonitta McGee

Date of Birth: 7/7/62 Social Security Number: ____ ____ ____

Mailing Address: 360 Circular Ave, L.M. Apt/Suite: ____

City: Hamden State: CT Zip: 06514

Home Phone: [illegible] Work Phone: NA

Cell Phone: [illegible] Fax Number: NA

E-mail Address: WyKeishac@Hotmail.Com = Daughter

Case or Claim Number (if applicable): 132198863 plus ② more

Alien Number or WAC (if applicable): N/A

PAGE 1 of 2

Have you contacted another Congressional office or do you plan on contacting another Congressional office for assistance with this matter? _______YES _✓__NO

If yes, which one(s)? ______U.S. Senator John Ensign
______Congresswoman Shelly Berkley
______Congressman Dean Heller
______Congresswoman Dina Titus

BRIEF DESCRIPTION OF THE PROBLEM:

I have been dealing with the DOL on this Same Claim for over a year and a half. It has even gone to the Cheif, Hearing and Review and he wrote back that the office is/should be able to settle this matter because it is work related. I am now Medical Disability Retired and they are Still playing games with me on this Claim. The U.S. Postal Service took my life as I Know it at age 47 years old. Threat by Boss, Work for 2½ years as an acting Manager, applied for (17) Jobs and they were all given to white people/Non Black. Lifting injury on 3/13/09. 9/15/09 = Medical Disability Retirement from Federal Service. Also, is it being Reconsidered or is it being reviewed for Merit. I Just moved on 12/7/09

PLEASE RETURN THIS FORM TO:

Las Vegas
333 Las Vegas Boulevard South
Suite 8016
Las Vegas, Nevada 89101
(702) 388-5020
(702) 388-5030 Fax

Carson City
600 East William Street
Suite 302
Carson City, Nevada 89701
(775) 882-7343
(775) 883-1980

Reno
400 South Virginia Street
Suite 902
Reno, Nevada 89501
(775) 686-5750
(775) 686-5757 Fax

PAGE 2 of 2

January 9, 2010

To: United States Postal Services
National EEO Investigative Services
P. O. Box 21979
Tampa, FL 33622-1979

From: Lola McGee
43 Victor St.
East Haven, CT 06512-3759

RE: Change of Address

To all concern,

The purpose of this letter is to notify all agencies involved, regarding my Formal EEO's, of my new address, Case #4E-890-0120-08 Filed 11/1/2008; and Case #4E-890-0043-09 Filed 5/27/2009.

Sincerely
Lola McGee
(203) 903-5347-Home
(562) 889-2662-Cell

* * * * *

January 12, 2010

To: DOL DFEC Central Mailroom
P. O. Box 8300
London, KY 40742

From: Lola McGee
43 Victor St.
East Haven, CT 06512-3759

RE: New documentation from Dr. Novero; change of address; concerns about Case Number 132198863

To Whom It May Concern:

This letter is being written to notify the agency and all involved regarding the above case number, of my new address and contact phone number.

Also, I would like to know why it takes 3 to 6 months to review the case number listed above when it has been under review since its onset of 08/29/08.

I want it to be noted that the additional information that I sent in is less than 30 pages of information that the agency has never seen before. All the other documentation has been reviewed time and time again.

I am Medical Disability Retired with OPM from the issues surrounding this case. It is appalling that the Department Of Labor/Office of Workers' Compensation Programs has not yet approved this same case in spite of my medical documentation, my own statements and research that has been submitted to prove that my injuries and illnesses happened in the performance of my duties. In addition, the Chief, Branch of Hearings and Review (Chief Barnes), stated in his letter that the claim does not have to go to the appellate stage because I had already submitted documentation that proved that the injury occurred in the performance of my duties.

I want it to be noted that at this time and date I have proven over and over again that all the injuries occurred in the performance of my duties with the submitted documentation to date.

In addition, I was told by the claims examiner to get an Attorney; I want him to know that I don't believe that I need an Attorney for this matter. I just want the right thing to be done by approving my case because it continues to wear on my illnesses.

Please see attachment from my Neurologist, Dr. Novero dated January 12, 2010. This documentation diagnoses me as "permanent stationary". I can be reached at (203) 903-5347-home, (562) 889-2662-cell.

Thank you,
Lola McGee

* * * * *

February 23, 2010

To: U. S. Department Of Labor
Office of Workers' Comp Programs
P. O. Box 8300 District 1 BOS
London, KY 40742-8300

From: Lola McGee
43 Victor St.
East Haven, CT 06512

RE: Request for Reconsideration based on new factual evidence from the claimant, Case# 132198863 – Decision dated March 6, 2009

To Whom It May Concern:

I Lola McGee am writing this letter to give merit to my illnesses and injuries occurring in and out of the performance of my duties.

I would like to start by addressing the background of previous decisions rendered on my case listed above.

On 8/25/08 I Lola McGee, birth date 7/7/1962, was employed by the United States Postal Service as a Supervisor, Customer Services North Las Vegas Main Office 1414 E. Lake Mead Blvd. North Las Vegas, NV 89030.

However, on 8/25/08 I was on a detail as Manager, Customer Services at Meadow Mesa Station 4904 Camino Al Norte North Las Vegas, NV 89031 and Jerry Wilson was the Officer in Charge of North Las Vegas. On 8/25/08 at approximately 9:00am – 11:00am, I was in my office checking my emails and reviewing some performance reports that I was going to share with my staff, at our meeting, and Jerry Wilson walked into my office as I was standing near the front of the meeting table and he walked up to me, while I still had some papers left in my hand, in my face with his belly turned at an angle, to his left, and threatened me. He was in my face close enough to kiss me, and Jerry stated with anger, conviction, hostility, and in a violent tone, and breathing hard, while he looked me straight in my eyes "You continue to go over my head with Craig and Yul and I'm going to do something about it." I got very afraid and started to have heavy heart palpitations, nausea, sweating, chills, dizziness, mind confusion, and I felt retarded. I was having head shocks, and I thought that I was going to die and no one would know why. I went into the restroom to put water on my face and I vomited in the toilet. I came out and got some water from the fountain to drink. I did not know what to due, I just knew that I needed to get myself together to drive home. I gathered my reports and checked my email. I went into the senior supervisor's office and told him that I was not feeling well, and I believe it's a reaction to some medication, and I was going to be leaving. I got in my car and by the grace of God I got home. On 8/25/08 I had a Panic Attack as a result of the threat from Jerry Wilson. Please refer to my previous statements for more information.

The Postal Service has a Zero (0) tolerance policy for violence in the workplace, even in jest, or words. Jerry Wilson violated the U. S. Postal Service Policy on violence in the workplace.

I want it to be noted that the challenges of any of my duties have never been a problem; however, when you're threatened by someone that is not appropriate or safe. I knew from Jerry's expressions and demeanor that something negative or violent was going to happen, and I was not going to be there to see what it was. I was scared for my life.

In July 2008 while sitting at the conference table in my office at Meadow Mesa, during one of my staff meetings, Jerry Wilson said that he was going to change my start time to 8:00am because he wanted me there when the carriers got back. I thought it was rude and unprofessional for him to state that in front of my staff. It was one of many things that frustrated me about his inability to manage subordinates, but I still respected him as my boss. Also, on July 10, 2008, I walked with my delivery staff on their rounds and demonstrated how I wanted them to achieve under time from the carriers. Jerry came into my staff meeting that day and starting talking over me and stated to my staff that under time is hard to get. I held my head down and started to sweat. I asked Jerry, after the meeting, if he could talk to me in private when it comes to something he disagrees with regarding me and my staff.

In 2004-2005, while performing my daily delivery supervisor duties in North Las Vegas Main Post Office, Steven Phaup appeared to have jealousy problems with me regarding my skills, ability, experience, training, and he did not consider my education to improve the office performance; he did everything that he could to sabotage my performance. In four and one half months, I reduced delivery work hours from 5% over Plan to 3.5% under Plan. He had a bizarre/outlandish behavior that made me afraid of him. He would hide my employee reports, talk to me in a disrespectful, loud manner on the workroom floor, and told untruths about me to the employees so that they would turn against me. In addition, he would tell the postmaster that I wasn't capturing the under time that I said I was, however the proof of the office performance reports showed my performance to be excellent. I would speak to him in the morning and he would walk by me as if I did not speak to him. On the other hand, he would come up to me and talk to me like nothing was wrong and we were the best of friends. He would pull my reports and post them on the board and tell the union steward that I was not equitable on my overtime with my employees. However, this was due to his incorrect calculations and wrong figures to reflect the report. This issue was not new and had been one of the issues he had with the union steward prior to my arrival to the North Las Vegas Post Office. This issue was negated through the union steward and me meeting on a weekly basis regarding the overtime employees report. The union steward and I both would sign off on the form to ensure that it was correct. Steve told me that he had to kill people in the military and that was his job. He told me that he use to work for a security company and he and his partner had to kill someone at a casino.

He had mood swings on a daily basis. He would hide my employee leave slips to prevent me from knowing who was suppose to be at work, and from creating the employee schedule correctly. I called several meetings and sent emails to the Postmaster Craig Colton and Officer in Charge Dana Urbanski to try and stop this hostile work environment that he had created, but he continued to behave in this manner. He eventually was terminated for fraudulent behavior beyond the issues he had in the office with me. He was to turn over to me $1000.00 in cash reserve and he never turned it over to date. Postal Inspectors and Labor Relation Departments got involved regarding different issues that I had with him and the other fraudulent things that he had done. As a result from this hostile environment, in 2005 I sought therapy and was subsequently diagnosed with Post Traumatic Stress Disorder, Depression, and Obsessive Compulsive Disorder. That hostile environment made me believe that he or someone else would come and harm me at home as well as the office. I was afraid that he would one day try and physically hurt me. In September 2007, I was diagnosed with Heart Palpitations without Heart disease. However, I'm scheduled for a Heart Operation on February 25, 2010 from the Post Traumatic Stress Disorder daily palpitations; they have declined my Heart to 40% healthy.

From 4/2006 – 8/25/2008, I worked actively as an acting manager for the Nevada Sierra District, mainly in Las Vegas. With the two and a half years of experience, I was very qualified for a manager position that I had performed the duties of over and over again. I received an EXFC-EPED (2006) award for my performance at Paradise Valley Station in Las Vegas EAS-22 office and F4 was #1 in the district. In 2001 I graduated from the Associate Supervisor Program Class, and previously being a 204-B after carrying mail for two years, I was a manager before I got to the postal service, I've owned my own business for three (3) years, I have an AA in Human Services, and a BS in Business Management, I trained supervisors for the program, I went where ever I was asked to go, I applied for 17 positions and never got promoted; I wasn't even promoted in two (2) positions that they did not have anyone to put in it. The positions were not filled until they had someone else that they wanted to put in them. All the promoted people were white/non black. I was discriminated against based on: Age-46, Sex-female, Race-African American, Color-black, Religion-Christian, Mental/Physical disability, and Retaliation, treated unfairly while others were treated differently than I was. In August 2006 I had a meeting with my boss Jennifer VO and she stated in the meeting "Lola tell me if I'm full of shit if you want to," while she had a smirk on her face, Jennifer was sending me back to my supervisor position. I called a meeting with Jennifer VO, Mark Martinez and Robert Reynosa after the Jennifer meeting. Mark and Robert would disrespect me on telecoms by talking loud to me and talking about the performance of my office when there were other offices much worse that mine. In addition, they would say things that were rude, sarcastic, and arrogant. Dana Urbanski was sent to the City of Las Vegas as the acting Manager, Customer Service Operations, and while she was there she asked me why did Mark and Robert talk to me so bad? I told her because I'm Black and Female. She stated that your office is doing better that promoted managers and they are not talking to them that way. I was performing very well at large offices and had great performance outcomes to prove it; however I was not good enough to be promoted. They treated me as if I was only good for repairing the problems of each post office I was sent to; however I was never promoted to the actual position that I was already doing well in. I was even flown to Reno Nevada on detail as the acting manager and put processes in place there. Robert Reynosa called me and asked if I would come back to one of the worse offices in Las Vegas (King Station) and I replied, yes. As a result of all the unfair tactics, discrimination, disrespect, and blatant disregard for my work ethic, I began to have Major Depression, Post Traumatic Stress Disorder, Heart Palpitation, Anxiety, and my attendance started to be a problem as far as making it to work on time.

I want it to be noted that the City of Las Vegas had never had a Black Postmaster, from (1894 - 2008) until I filed an EEO in September 2008, then in October the first Black Postmaster was appointed to Las Vegas.

Sincerely
Lola McGee

* * * * *

March 30, 2010

To: U. S. Department Of Labor
Employment Standards Administration
Office of Workers' Comp Programs
P. O. Box 8300 District 50
London, KY 40742-8300

From: Lola McGee
P. O. Box 700
Bronx, NY 10456

RE: Change of Address: Supplemental Factual Statement Case Numbers: 132210754 and 132209923
Attention: Amy Towner, Hearing Representative 10/8/2009

Dear Ms. Towner,

This letter is to notify you and the agency of my new address for the above case numbers. I can be reached at (562) 889-2662 Cell.

Thank you
Lola McGee

* * * * *

March 30, 2010

To: State of Nevada
Department of Employment, Training, Rehabilitation
Bureau of Disability Adjudication
Phone: (775) 687-4430
Toll Free Fax: (866) 792-8244

From: Lola McGee
P. O. Box 700
Bronx, NY 10456-2019

RE: Change of Address and Phone Number
SS# ___________, Phone# (562) 889-2662 – Cell

To Whom It May Concern:

I, Lola Bonitta McGee, am writing this letter to inform the Social Security Administration of my new address and telephone number and to let the agency know that my last name is not separated (McGee).

Thank you
Lola McGee

U. S. Office of Treasure $11,266.99 pay back of Workers' Compensation per the Accounting Dept. of U. S. Postal Service because of the denied claims.

633779

UNITED STATES POSTAL SERVICE

Page 1 of 2

FINAL NOTICE

USPS DISBURSING OFFICER
ACCOUNTING SERVICE CENTER
2825 LONE OAK PKWY
EAGAN MN 55121-9640

April 14, 2010

Question or correspondence:
SEE ENCLOSED REMINDER/NOTICE.

LOLA B MCGEE
1236 W 22ST APT1
LOS ANGELES CA 90007-1770

INVOICE	REFERENCE	INVOICE DATE	DAYS LATE	ORIGINAL AMOUNT	FINANCE CHARGE	PMT/ ADJ	BALANCE DUE
701971072	F25800 PRD	24-DEC-08	446	$6,016.56	$0.00	$1,442.37	$4,574.19
702080830	F13600 PRD	25-NOV-09	110	$6,204.16	$0.00	$0.00	$6,204.16
702080831	F13610 PRD	25-NOV-09	110	$488.64	$0.00	$0.00	$488.64
					TOTAL PAST DUE:		$11,266.99

----- To ensure proper credit to your account. Please return bottom portion with your remittance -----

UNITED STATES POSTAL SERVICE

ATTN: DUNNING SECTION
ACCOUNTING SERVICE CENTER
2825 LONE OAK PKWY
EAGAN MN 55121-9616

CUSTOMER NUMBER: 03413020
LETTER DATE: April 14, 2010
TOTAL PAST DUE: $11,266.99

AMOUNT PAID: ___________.___

LOLA B MCGEE
1236 W 22ST APT1
LOS ANGELES CA 90007-1770

MAIL TO:

USPS DISBURSING OFFICER
ACCOUNTING SERVICE CENTER
2825 LONE OAK PKWY
EAGAN MN 55121-9640

☐ Check here to change address, complete new address on reverse.
Write your customer number on your check or money order. Do not send cash.

0103413020 X0000001126699X

633779

UNITED STATES
POSTAL SERVICE

Page 2 of 2

FINAL NOTICE

REF: Amount of past due debt owed to the U.S. Postal Service: $11,266.99
Account/TIN: 03413020

This is your final notice that your debt in the amount of $11,266.99 is past due. Please remit the balance in full now so we can clear your debt.

If you do not resolve your debt immediately, it will be sent to the U.S. Department of the Treasury (U.S. Treasury) for offset purposes, and a collection fee will be assessed.

If you have questions please contact us at phone number 1 (651) 681-1404, Monday through Friday (7:00 am - 3:30 pm, Central Time); fax us at 1 (651) 406-1259; or send an email to BWNKC0@USPS.GOV.

Sincerely,

Gary J. Laurant, Supervisor
Eagan Accounting Service Center

May 13, 2010

To: U. S. Department Of Labor
Employment Standards Administration
Office of Workers' Comp Programs
P. O. Box 8300 District 50
London, KY 40742-8300

From: Lola McGee
3801 E. Pacific Coast Hwy. #225
Long Beach, CA 90804

RE: Change of Address: Supplemental Factual Statement
Case Numbers: 132210754 and 132209923

Attention: Amy Towner, Hearing Representative 10/8/2009

Dear Ms. Towner,

This letter is to notify you and the agency of my new address for the above case numbers.

I can be reached at (562) 889-2662 Cell, and (562) 343-2503

Thank you
Lola McGee

* * * * *

May 13, 2010

To: DOL DFEC Central Mailroom
P. O. Box 8300
London, KY 40742

From: Lola McGee
3801 E. Pacific Coast Hwy. #225
Long Beach, CA 90804

RE: Change of Address for Case Number 132198863 and New Telephone numbers: (562) 889-2662 – Cell, (562) 343-2503 - Home

To Whom It May Concern:

This letter is being written to notify the agency and all involved regarding the above case number, of my new address and contact phone number.

Thank you,
Lola McGee

May 13, 2010

To: U. S. Department Of Labor
Employment Standards Administration
Central Mailroom
Office of Workers' Comp Programs
P. O. Box 8300
London, KY 40742-8300

From: Lola McGee
3801 E. Pacific Coast Hwy. #225
Long Beach, CA 90804

RE: My Five (5) moves in the last passed year

Attention: All concerned,

I have moved five times in the last passed year because I have not found peace of mind with myself in my current state of mind or my inner turmoil with my physical disabilities.

I am trying to find some sort of normalcy in my current condition and it has been very challenging to come to reality with my life today from what it was before my on the job injuries and illnesses. I have made very costly decisions in my moves; however, they were very necessary for my mental and physical health.

Sincerely
Lola McGee

* * * * *

May 14, 2010

To Whom It May Concern:

Claim # 132198863 (The Threat, Discrimination, and Hostile work environment were all put into this claim) In my opinion the Threat was a separate event that happen on a specific day and time it should have been treated as a Traumatic event instead of an Occupational Disease. The Dept. of Labor and the Post Office put all of it together and the Threat was not even investigated – Yul Melonson was the Manager of Jerry Wilson at the time and it was his responsibility to investigate Jerry and my claim. I filed the claims separately (Jerry Wilson, Robert Reynosa, Jennifer Vo, Mark Martinez, Steven Phaup, and Craig Colton, Corey Richards, all were responsible for my illnesses.

The threat from my boss Jerry Wilson Officer in Charge of the City of North Las Vegas Post Office, He stated "You continue to go over my head with Craig and Yul and I'm going to do something about it" I was afraid for my life and my career after all I had done for the Nevada Sierra District.

Heart Palpitations, Heart Murmur, Chest Pain, and Paroxysmal Ventricular Tachycardia, by Dr. Robert Croke in Las Vegas and he considered it a benign condition. Neuropathy: Head Shocks, Hearing Loss and Ringing, Numbness, Tingling, Swelling, Weakness and Pain in

Lower Extremities – Lumbar Ridiculopathy with severe nerve damage across my Spine and Both Buttocks (Henderson, Dr. Jimmy Novero and Las Vegas - Sundance Medical Center – Heather Harris, APN). Post Traumatic Stress Disorder, Major Depression, Obsessive Compulsive Disorder – Dr. Michael Shepard and Dr. Mary Reed - Las Vegas, Panic Attacks, Panic Disorder, Anxiety Disorder, and Agoraphobia – Dr. Mary Reed – 8/25/08.

Claim # 132209923 (I went back to work after being off for seven (7) months and requesting a lateral to Las Vegas instead of North Las Vegas – were Corey Richards was the postmaster at the time. On 3/13/09 – my first day back at work I had a lifting injury to my entire back, left thigh, and both knees while working for Yul Melonson and Joe Acosta at Spring Valley Station. This injury exacerbated my previous Neuropathy injuries and added new one's to my knees and left thigh neck and pelvic area. I was diagnosed with:
Lumbar Ridiculopathy, Cervical Facet Syndrome, Thoracic Facet Lumbar Facet Syndrome, and Knee pain because the Dept. of Labor did not authorize the MRI when it was requested by Centennial Spine and Pain Center (Las Vegas), Acute back Strain with Sciatica, and Knee Sprain – From St. Rose Hospital Emergency Room, X-Rays were taken (Las Vegas). I worked in pain while still going to physical therapy for my Neuropathy until I could not take it anymore – 4/2/09.

Claim # 132210754 was filed for an incident that happened on 4/13/09 while I went to the North Las Vegas Main Post Office, which was my official home station as a supervisor. I was still off work from the 3/13/09 injury but I needed to file some paperwork and retrieve some documents off the computer. Corey Richards was the postmaster at the time and he treated me very disrespectful, rude, and denied me my rights to file claims and access the computer. I had a witness with me Pamela Morgan and she wrote a statement to the Dept. of Labor as to how Corey treated me.
She drove me home because I was so upset, and by the time I got home within one (1) hour of leaving the office my right arm collapsed and I had chest pain, and was hyperventilating and the ambulance picked me up and I was in the St. Rose Hospital until 4/15/09.

I had to move from Las Vegas because it was a detriment to my health and life. I left my home, companion, and it destroyed my entire life as I knew it. I am a mentally and physically disabled retired person at this time and I'm still trying to learn how to exist with my life as it is today.

All of my claims started off with pay and once the post office sent in their response to the Dept. of Labor my claims were denied, yet I'm the one that is at home mentally and physically injured.

After moving to Connecticut, I went to a Cardiologist (Dr. Vulpe) and he conducted test and sent me to a specialist (Dr. Blizer) who also ran test on me and the results were deemed that I needed Heart Surgery. The Surgery was on 2/25/10 at Saint Raphael's Hospital in Connecticut.

Sincerely
Lola McGee

July 1, 2010

U. S. Dept. Of Labor/OWCP
P. O. Box 8300 District 13 SFC
London, KY 40742-8300

Lola Bonitta McGee
3801 E. Pacific Coast Hwy. #225
Long Beach, California 90804-2040

RE: Claim #132198863, 132209923, and 132210754

To all Concern:

This letter is being written to the United States Department Of Labor/OWCP, Postmaster General-John E. Potter, President- Borack Obama, and First Lady- Michelle Obama.

Claim # 132198863 8/25/08 (The Threat, Discrimination, and Hostile work environment were all put into this claim). In my opinion the Threat from my acting boss Officer In Charge, Jerry Wilson North Las Vegas was a separate event that happen on a specific day and time and it should have been treated as a Traumatic event instead of an Occupational Disease. The U. S. Postal Service has a Zero Tolerance Policy and this behavior by Mr. Wilson falls within the policy as not tolerable, yet there wasn't even an Investigation done by his boss at the time, Yul Melonson Senior, Manager Post Office Operations. I've explained in previous statements to the DOL/OWCP about Mr. Wilson's attitude and behavior, and I believe he has had prior issues regarding his conduct. Mr. Wilson stood in my face, up close and personal, with an aggressive, domineering, bullying, convicted, and harsh voice, and stated to me "You continue to go over my head with Craig and Yul and I'm going to do something about it." This threat was because of Mr. Wilson's paranoid and out of control behavior concerning an email, from Craig Colton, that was addressed to me and a phone call that I received from Yul Melonson on 8/22/08. If Mr. Wilson wanted to reprimand me are send me back to my supervisor position then he would have called me into his office with his boss and explained the situation, basically, I would have had a day in court. Mr. Wilson lied to the DOL, EEO Specialist, and EEO Investigator regarding his threat to me. Also, he lied about things he stated that I told him. Mr. Wilson actually put his lies in a statement and said I told him these things and I did not even know him. That was not the case and that was not his intent The Dept. of Labor and the Post Office put all of it together and the Threat was not even investigated – Yul Melonson was the Manager of Jerry Wilson at the time and it was his responsibility to investigate Jerry and my claim on him. As a result, Consequently, and Unfortunately, I had a Panic Attack which resulted in Peripheral Sensory Neuropathy-(nerve damage) numbness, weakness, pain, tingling, burning, spasms of my lower/upper extremities up to my spine through my buttocks, hearing loss, vision impaired, Lumbar Ridiculopathy and head shocks, recurring Major Depression, Panic Disorder, Anxiety, Post Traumatic Stress Disorder.

I want it to be known that I had no prior physical or mental health problems except Lower Bowel Obstruction in 2003 and 2005, and a construction work injury in 1994 that was healed in 1997, before my issues with the U. S. Postal Service. I filed a claim and it was denied. My attendance record speaks for my dedication of service.

This issue is regarding Discrimination and the history of the Nevada Sierra District, which was put with the CA-1 Traumatic Injury that happened on 8/25/08, the threat. For two (2) and one half years, (4/2006-8/2008) I actively worked, trained, and went over and beyond as an Acting Manager, Customer Services for the Nevada Sierra District in EAS 20-22 Level offices. I continued to demonstrate my knowledge, skill, ability, experience, education, and self motivating performance through out my career even though I was being denied positions that I knew I was qualified for. My bosses knew I was qualified also are else they would not have continued to send me around the district from office to office to improve them. I later found out that I was labeled the "Clean up Woman." During my tenure, I applied for 17 positions, but I never got promoted. All the jobs were filled by White/Non Black employees. Two (2) of the positions were not even filled until they had someone they wanted to promote in them. I worked 10-12 hour days and some Saturday's in a few offices but to no avail. I was a confident, serious, self starter, pro-active, respectful, and dignified woman who though I was going to be judged by my on merit instead of the color of my skin and my gender, but that was not the case. Of course my higher level managers found a way to cover themselves up and I meant nothing to them after I got sick. I filed six (6) EEO's and all of them were denied. I was lied to by Jennifer Vo, disrespected on telecoms by Robert Reynosa, and Mark Martinez, used, misused, abused by my upper management, and it was tolerated, all of them were White/Non- Black. I ultimately was clinically depressed and did not even know it. All I thought about was going to work and doing my job well and to the very best of my ability. I made vast improvements in the offices that I managed. Most of the promoted people in the Nevada Sierra District managed one office and it was very small, EAS-19 (Strip Station). Some were brought in from other districts, while I still was there performing and going over and beyond the call of duty. I did not ask for something for nothing nor did I ask for something that I was not qualified to do; my upper management had personal agendas that I did not know about.

I want it to be known that I could not have done any of it if it had not been for my supporting cast, my staff. I was sent to offices that they thought I would not improve because of the "Difficult Staff, Tough Union Presence, or the size of the stations." All these things were said to me, but I was able to persevere and improve each and every one of them. I must say that I did my job very well until my demise.

This issue is regarding a Hostile Work Environment. In 2004 I requested a Lateral to North Las Vegas Post Office from California and it was granted. Consequently, there was a supervisor there that presented the appearance that he did not appreciate my skills, ability, experience, training, nor did he consider my education to improve the office performance; he did everything that he could to sabotage my performance. He had a bizarre/outlandish behavior that made me afraid of him. He would hide my employee reports, talk to me in a disrespectful, loud manner on the workroom floor, and told untruths about me to the employees so that they would turn against me. In addition, he would tell the postmaster that I wasn't capturing the under time that I said I was conducting, however the proof of the office performance reports showed my conduct and performance to be excellent. I would speak to him in the morning and he would walk by me as if I did not speak to him. On the other hand, he would come up to me and talk to me like nothing was wrong and we were the best of friends. He would pull my reports and post them on the board and tell the union steward that I was not equitable on my overtime with my employees. However, this was due to his incorrect calculations and wrong figures to reflect the report. This issue was not new and had been one of the issues he had with the union steward prior to my arrival to the North Las Vegas Post Office. This issue was negated through the union steward and me meeting on a weekly basis regarding the overtime employees report. The union steward and I both would sign off on the form to ensure that it was correct. He told me that he had to kill people in the military and that was his job. He told me that he use to work for a security company and he and his partner had to kill someone at a casino. He had mood swings on a daily basis. He would hide my employee leave slips to prevent me from knowing who was suppose to be at work, and from creating the employee schedule correctly. I called several meetings and sent emails to Craig Colton Postmaster North Las Vegas, at the time. At one point Craig Colton was on detail in Las Vegas and Officer In Charge (OIC) Dana Urbanski took over while Craig was gone and I expressed my concerns to her and she tried to stop the hostile work environment that Steven Phaup had created, but he continued to behave in that manner. With Ms. Urbanski talking to Mr. Colton about the situation, Craig finally decided to send Mr. Phaup to our sister station Meadow Mesa, which is where Dana Urbanski was the Manager, Customer Services. He eventually was terminated for fraudulent behavior beyond the issues he had in the office with me. He was to turn over to me $1000.00 in cash reserve and he never turned it over to date. Postal Inspectors and Labor Relation Departments got involved regarding different issues that I had with him and the other fraudulent things that he had done. As a result of the hostile work environment, in 2005 I sought therapy and was subsequently diagnosed with Post Traumatic Stress Disorder, Depression, and Obsessive Compulsive Disorder. That hostile work environment made me believe that he or someone else would come and harm me at home as well as the office. I was afraid that he would one day try and physically hurt me. In 2007 I felt my heart beating faster than it normally did and I developed a chocking cough. Later on, I was diagnosed with Heart Palpitations without Heart disease and the Ear, Nose, and Throat Specialist could not find out why I had the cough. The Cardiologist diagnosed Heart Palpitations, Heart Murmur, Chest Pain, and Paroxysmal Ventricular Tachycardia, by Dr. Robert Croke in Las Vegas and he considered it a benign condition.

Claim # 132209923 4/2/09 (I went back to work after being off for seven (7) months and requesting a lateral to Las Vegas instead of North Las Vegas – were Corey Richards was the postmaster at the time. On 3/13/09 – my first day back at work I had a lifting injury to my entire back, left thigh, and both knees while working for Yul Melonson and Joe Acosta at Spring Valley Station. Joe Acosta, the station manager, witness the injury and he and I talked about it on 3/13/09, but when I went out on 4/2/09 with filing a claim, he stated to Yul Melonson that he did not witness the injury nor did I report the injury to him. This injury exacerbated my previous Neuropathy injuries and added new injuries to my knees, back, left thigh, neck and pelvic area. I know this information now, but at the time I submitted the claim for my back, left thigh and both knees. I was diagnosed with Lumbar Ridiculopathy, Cervical Facet Syndrome, Thoracic Facet Syndrome, and Knee pain because the Dept. of Labor did not authorize the MRI when it was requested by Centennial Spine and Pain Center (Las Vegas). My initial diagnosis was Acute back Strain with Sciatica, and Knee Sprain – From St. Rose Hospital Emergency Room, X-Rays were taken (Henderson, NV). I worked in pain while still going to physical therapy for my Neuropathy until I could not take it anymore – 4/2/09. I just did not know what to do and my pride and work ethic got in the way.

Claim # 132210754 was filed for an incident that happened on 4/13/09 while I went to the North Las Vegas Main Post Office, which was my official home station as a supervisor. I was still off work from the 3/13/09 injury but I needed to file some paperwork and retrieve some documents off the computer. Corey Richards was the postmaster at the time and he treated me very disrespectful, rude, and denied me my rights to file claims and access the computer. In addition, I was told to call the office before I came by as if I was a threat and know one else that has been out sick had to do this. Mr. Richards did not pay me higher level while I was out sick, he did not enter my time to get paid for Christmas 2008, he still, to this day, has not paid me for my Lucy James Arbitration brief and testimony days February 2009 (he was given the 1260 forms twice), he had my GMF access removed so I could not go to the Injury Compensation or Labor Relations offices. Corey Richards and I were supervisors together under Craig Colton but the both of them got promoted and I did not. Corey is one of the people who was promoted to Manager, Customer Services from Strip Station, which is the smallest station in the City of Las Vegas EAS-19. I had a witness with me, Pamela Morgan, and she wrote a statement to the Dept. of Labor as to how Corey treated me, but they did not consider it as relevant. She drove me home because I was so upset, and by the time I got home within one (1) hour of leaving the office my right arm collapsed and I had chest pain, and was hyperventilating and the ambulance picked me up and I was in the St. Rose Hospital until 4/15/09.

I had to move from Las Vegas because it was a detriment to my health and life. I left my home, companion, and it destroyed my entire life as I knew it. I am a mentally and physically disabled retired person through my work injuries with the United States Office of Personnel (OPM) at this time and I'm still trying to learn how to exist with my life as it is today at age 47.

All of my claims started off with Continuation of Pay (COP) and once the post office sent in their response to the Dept. of Labor my claims were denied, yet I'm the one that is at home mentally ill and physically injured. The Postal Service retaliated once I got sick and filed claims and EEO's against management. I was treated as if I never existed and they never had any intention on promoting me they just wanted to use me until they found a way to get me out of the way.

I went where ever they asked me to go and I performed and improved as they wanted, but the only difference is I'm Black and Female and they are White/Non-Black and Male.

Through my experience of filing claims and EEO's, I found out that the history of the Las Vegas Post Office is very prejudice. Since the late 1800's there had never been a promoted Black Postmaster until I filed my EEO on 9/18/08 and stated such. Miraculously in October 2008 Yul Melonson was appointed to the position. History was made in the City of Las Vegas at my expense.

In addition, I claimed in my EEO that there was not a promoted Black Female working in the Las Vegas field offices. Miraculously one was promoted (Donnita Mixon) and I trained her at Paradise Valley Station as a supervisor, she was one of my staff members and had just graduated from the previous supervisor class.

She had about 3-5 months of manager training before she was promoted by Yul Melonson.

After moving to Connecticut, I went to a Cardiologist (Dr. Marian Vulpe) and he conducted test and sent me to a specialist (Dr. Mark Blizer) who also ran test on me and the results were deemed that I needed Heart Surgery. The Surgery was on 2/25/10 at Saint Raphael's Hospital in Connecticut. My heart condition which is exacerbated by stress but benign to heart disease, clogs, are any blockage was beating 44,000 extra beats per day. The heart palpitations made the health of my heart decline until it was going to beat out and I was going to die, according to Dr. Vulpe and Dr. Blizer, if I had not had the operation. This is the only documentation that the Department of Labor does not have and it will be forthcoming.

I have been sent three (3) Federal Debt Case Identification numbers (2010124227A, 2010124943A, 2010124893A) from the Department Of The Treasury as it relates to all three cases. I feel that I should not have to pay back Continuation Of Pay (COP) when I was entitled to it because of my injuries and illnesses that I sustained at my workplace, the United States Postal Service-Nevada Sierra District.

In addition, I want a higher authority to look into my allegations to find that my integrity is sound. There should be a higher authority to monitor employees that have been treated this way.

I want it to be known that I have integrity, and my dignity, respect, skill, will, professionalism, serious personality, experience, knowledge, training, good decision making quality, education-BS and AA (which is not required for the position), previous business owner experience, previous manager experience, team player, leadership ability, and my own work ethic was all demonstrated and I out performed many of the promoted managers and definitely the acting managers, but I was Black, Female, and confident and they were intimidated and racist. My performance reports speak for themselves. Some were fearful of reprisal and others went along with the majority.

I was Craig Colton's supervisor before he was promoted and our office was a model. I was Yul Melonson's supervisor before he was promoted and our office was a model. I worked more for Robert Reynosa as an acting manager than anyone else and he always found a way not to promote me.

Sincerely
Lola McGee

The EEOC's response to my letter to PM General, U. S. President, July 30, 2010

MANAGER EEO COMPLIANCE & APPEALS, REGION 1
PACIFIC AREA FIELD OFFICE

UNITED STATES
POSTAL SERVICE

July 30, 2010

Lola McGee
1236 W. 22nd Street
Los Angeles, CA 90007-1770

Dear Ms McGee:

This letter is in response to your July 1 correspondence addressed to the U.S. Department of Labor, the Postmaster General and President Obama. You allege that you have been subject to threats, discrimination and a hostile work environment during your employment with the Postal Service. You also contend that you have health issues related to your Postal Employment and your claims to the Office of Worker's Compensation have been denied.

A review of records reveals that you have filed two Equal Employment Opportunity (EEO) complaints, case number 4E-890-0120-08 and case number 4E-890-0043-09 related to same issues presented in your July 1 correspondence.

Postal records indicate that you first contacted the EEO Office on August 18, 2008 (case # 4E-890-0120-08). A Final Agency Decision (Merit) was issued on August 11, 2009 and you appealed the decision to the Office of Federal Operations (OFO) on November 16, 2009. The case is currently pending an OFO decision.

You contacted the EEO Office again on April 21, 2009 (case # 4E-890-0043-09); the issue was the denial of your request for a lateral transfer to the city of Las Vegas. A formal complaint was filed on May 27, 2009 and an investigation conducted. A Final Agency Decision (Merit) was issued on October 23, 2009. No appeal was filed.

The Human Resources Management (HRM) department indicated that all of your injury compensation claims were denied. Your appeal was denied by the Office of Worker's Compensation (OWCP) and you were provided with reconsideration and appeal rights. HRM reported that you did not appeal to the Employees Compensation Appeal Board (ECAB). The Department of Labor makes determinations regarding the acceptance and amounts of Occupational Worker's Compensation. As such any issues regarding your Worker's Compensation claim must be addressed with OWCP.

For additional information related to your OWCP benefits please contact the HRM department attention: Rosie Evans, Manager HRM, 1001 E. Sunset Rd., Las Vegas, NV 89199-9446.

P.O. BOX 880546
San Francisco, CA 94188-0546
PHONE: 415.550.5152
FAX: 650.577-6155

1

MANAGER EEO COMPLIANCE & APPEALS, REGION 1
PACIFIC AREA FIELD OFFICE

Since the issued detailed in your July 1 correspondence have been addressed or are being addressed in the EEO process it would be inappropriate for me to comment on the merits of these matters.

Sincerely,

Susan Johnson

Susan Johnson
Manager, EEO Compliance & Appeals

cc: EVP ERM/CHRO
Mgr. EEO Field Operations

P.O. BOX 880546
San Francisco, CA 94188-0546
PHONE: 415.550.5152
FAX: 650.577-6155

July 7, 2010

To: US DEPARTMENT OF LABOR
OFFICE OF WORKERS' COMP PROGRAMS
PO BOX 8300 DISTRICT 13 SFC
LONDON, KY 40742- 8300

From: Lola McGee
3801 E. Pacific Coast HWY #225
Long Beach, CA 90804

RE: Request for Reconsideration Appeal case # 132209923

I am requesting and appeal on the above case number because I don't believe the agency considered the request from Centennial Spine and Pain Center. Also, I don't believe the previous Neuropathy and Lumbar Ridiculopathy injuries were considered properly.

On 4/2/09 I went to the St. Rose Emergency Room for my lifting injury that I sustained at Spring Valley Station in Las Vegas. I injured my back, left thigh, and knees, that is where I felt the pain most severely. I was given an X-Ray and examination. The diagnosis were Acute back Sprain, with Sciatica, and knee sprain. I was put off work for three (3) day until I saw a treating doctor.

On 4/7/09 I went to Centennial Spine and Pain Center and saw Dr. Coppel. I did not tell Dr. Coppel that I had previous injuries because I was only there for the 3/13/09 injury and I did not want the agency to think that I was trying to run injuries together. Dr. Coppel thought I was exaggerating during his examination because I was in such bad shape and he did not know why. Even though I was back at work, I was still in pain and going to physical therapy for my Neuropathy.

Dr. Coppel requested an MRI for my knees and your (DOL/OWCP) did not respond to the request so the only diagnosis that could be written for my knees was (Pain). The agency questioned the Pain diagnosis, but yet never responded to the request for the MRI. I do not think that this was fair are right to me. In addition to the Knee Pain diagnosis, the Centennial Spine and Pain Center diagnosed Lumbar Radiculopathy by the examination. This is the reason that the previous diagnosis was exacerbated because my Lumbar was worsened with the lifting injury. The Cervical, Lumbar, and Thoracic Facet Syndrome were diagnosis from the examination because I injured those parts of the body but all I could tell on the claim is what hurt me. I do not think the agency treated me fairly are right concerning this situation when all I was doing was trying to go by the rules of injuries on a claim.

The lifting injury took me totally out; I still walk on a claw cane to date.

Sincerely
Lola McGee

July 7, 2010

To: US DEPARTMENT OF LABOR
OFFICE OF WORKERS' COMP PROGRAMS
PO BOX 8300 DISTRICT 13 SFC
LONDON, KY 40742-8300

From: Lola McGee
3801 E. Pacific Coast HWY # 225
Long Beach, CA 90804

RE: Request for Reconsideration Appeal on case # 132210754

I am requesting reconsideration based on new medical documentation and the disparity of treatment that I received from Postmaster North Las Vegas Corey Richards.

There were several people that were out sick and Mr. Richards did not treat them in the manner that he treated me. In addition I have had a Heart Operation as a result of Post Traumatic Stress Disorder, Panic Disorder, Anxiety, Depression, and it is all related to the kind of treatment that I received from Corey Richards on 4/13/09.

Monique (Doty) Adams was out sick and she was not instructed to call the office before she came by. Ms. Adams access to the GMF was not taken away. I was told that I could input my NPA into the PES program when I returned to work, but that was not the case; I was told no when I returned on 3/13/09, but Ms. Adams was able to put he NPA into the program when she returned to work. Ms. Adams did not miss any pay periods while she had her 3971 in the office in advance. All of Ms. Adams pay was given to her while she was out and she did not miss getting paid from 1260's that she actually was suppose to get paid from, while they were in Mr. Richards possession like mine were. Until this day, I still have not gotten paid for 2/18/09 and 2/19/09. This was intentional retaliation by Mr. Richards towards me. I filed claims and EEO's on him and he reacted in an unprofessional manner towards me.

Mr. Anthony Denard was out ill but he was not treated like I was either. None of the things that happened to me happened to anyone that was out sick for an extended period of time.

Ms. Pamela Morgan's statement was not considered by the agency, but the truth of the matter is that I really thought that he would treat me differently if I had a witness with me. My health is more important to me than anything.

I will keep the original statement attached because I believe that the agency should consider it.

Between 2:15-3:15pm on 4/13/09, I went to my home office North Las Vegas Post Office to speak with Postmaster Corey Richards; and, I brought a friend with me, Pamela Morgan, with the hope that Corey would not treat or talk to me in a disrespectful manner like he has done in the past. All I wanted to do was turn in my forms and get a receipt, get my time inputted for payment for 2/18/09 and 2/19/09, and retrieve my 2007 NPA report.

Corey was very rude, abrupt, and disrespectful towards me and I did not appreciate it. We are professional people and adults. All people need to be treated with dignity and respect.

I requested my PES – NPA report for 2007 and Corey would not go on the website and print it for me nor would he allow me to go on the computer and print it for myself. Corey has treated me on several occasions in a disrespectful manner and he has retaliated against me because of EEO activity. The PES system allows access to the most current three Fiscal year information. Corey has denied me promotions, access to my home office computer, entry of my 2009 NPA objectives even though I was in work status, forms I requested, payment of higher level, input of my leave correctly, and he has deliberately not paid me even though he had my 3971 in his possession. Corey has demanded that my GMF access be removed out of retaliation for EEO activity. Corey has never supervised me and with the way that he treats me, I would not be able to work for him because of his creation of a hostile work environment with me.

I was at the office for approximately 45 minutes to an hour on 4/13/09.

On 4/15/09 I called Corey and told him that I would be filing a claim from the meeting we had on Monday 4/13/2009 for Stress, he stated what time did it happened and what did I do? I stated that I would put it in writing.

On 4/2/09 I went and tried to talk with Corey because Yul asked me to even though I told him that Corey does not treat me right and he does not talk to me respectfully. I asked Corey for some forms and he called Joni Payne and denied me all the forms except one. I also wanted to input my 2009 NPA and he denied me that also. Corey asked me why did I need the forms and I told him for injuries that happened in North Las Vegas and I had a lifting injury at Spring Valley Station. He gave me one CA-1 and that was all. I actually told him where the forms were located in the office.

I want it to be noted that I never, ever told Corey that I could not work for the postal service because people don't treat me right. Corey just lied when he stated I said that. Corey may have assumed with my injuries that I could not work anymore, but I never told him such a thing. This to me tells you about a person's character when they say things that people did not say.

Corey states that I was not in a work status as if that's the reason why I was not privy to my requests. I was allowed to input my 2008 end of year improvements, conduct business in injury compensation, be briefed and testify for Arbitration by Labor Relations, and have a telephone interview all while I was not in pay status. Thus, Corey just did not want to cooperate or oblige me because he has issues with me. It had nothing to do with work status that was just a way out for him to justify his behavior.

Corey is very aware of my EEO activity because a lot of it involves him personally.

I want it to be noted that I'm very ill because of all that I've been through in the post office. On 4/13/09 Corey Richards' behavior caused me to become ill and it put me into the hospital with Heart Palpitations, Elevated Blood Pressure, and my right arm collapsed with pain. I was hospitalized from 4/13/09-4/15/09.

Sincerely
Lola McGee

July 7, 2010

To: U. S. Treasury – Dispute Department

Attn: Cherry

From: Lola McGee
3801 E. Pacific Coast HWY #225
Long Beach, CA 90804

RE: Fed Debt Case Identification: 2010124227A, 2010124893A, and 2010124943A

I am writing this letter to notify the United States Treasury Department that I have filed appeals on the above case I.D. numbers. I apologize for not having them prepared when I stated I would, but I have mental illnesses that prevent me from taking care of my business in a timely manner, sometimes.

I will fax over the documentation that I mailed to the Department of Labor concerning the three dollar amounts that your office shows as debts. They are not debts, they are injury and illnesses claims that I sustained while working for the U. S. Postal Service.

Thank you
Lola McGee

Author's Note:

I'm still paying the postal service for this debt in which I really do not owe, because I got injured on the job and was entitled to be compensated for workers compensation Continuation of Pay (COP) August 17, 2011. The U. S. Department of Treasure actually takes approximately $500.00 out of my pension monthly for a debt the postal service maliciously controverted and lied about, so they say I have to pay $12,000.00 because of denied claims. This is just ruthless, maggot; mentality on both parts the postal service and the Dept. of Labor. They took my health, life, family, significant other, friends, and my ability to be who I was, now they want even pay for me to try and get well.

Author's Note:
Second attempt to Postmaster General for intervention with DOL, Postal Services and NEEOISO.

September 30, 2010

To: United States Postmaster General
John E. Potter
Washington, D. C. 20210

From: Lola Bonitta McGee
1236 W. 22nd St. #1
Los Angeles, California 90007-1770

RE: Your intervention with the Nevada Sierra District, Department Of Labor/OWCP, NEEOISO/EEOC, Claim #132198863, #132209923, #132210754, and Formal EEO Case #4E-890-0120-08, and #4E-890-0043-09

Dear Mr. Potter,

First I would like to apologize for having to bring these issues to your attention, especially in today's time with your schedule in trying to keep the postal service viable; however, it is very necessary that I address you with this matter because it is a matter of life are death to my mental illnesses, and physical injuries, in which I sustained while working for the postal service.

I want you to know that my illnesses and injuries that I sustained while working for the United States Postal Service are the reason why I received a from the Office Of Personnel Management/OPM.

I wrote a letter dated July 1, 2010 to the DOL/OWCP, concerning my claims, and Formal cases with the NEEOISO/EEOC and I received a reply dated July 30, 2010, and it was not correct; neither did Susan Johnson, Manager, EEO Compliance & Appeals give the integrity of the cases and claims.

Sir, this is the reason why I am writing you to intervene and investigate the issues yourself. My life, health, sanity, and welfare depend on the truth of the claims and cases to be approved. I want you to know that if I had not gotten mentally ill and physically injured from the postal service then I would still be employed.

I have always been a woman of integrity and I'll be that until the day the Lord calls me home. I believed in my superiors and I was a model employee that went over and beyond. My knowledge, skills/will, ability, integrity, experience, professionalism, seriousness, education, and presence allowed me to perform. I worked 10/12 hour days, and some Saturday's at some stations, and was a team player, but I did not know that the team was not on my side, they were prejudice, insecure, and afraid of my unknown because I am not the type of person who goes to work to gossip and play. I was not treated fairly, and unbeknownst to me, I was not to do anything but perform. I had great leadership qualities as I performed my duties as a supervisor, trainer, and acting manager, that's why I was used all around the district for 2 ½ years (4/2006–8/2008) and applied for 17 positions, received four (4) interviews which were all great, but the positions were given to employees younger than I was, Non Black, and the majority were White Males. Those that were promoted worked in smaller offices with 15 routes EAS-19 and I worked in EAS-20 – EAS-22 offices. I was called the clean up woman by the Manager, Operations Support (Vivian Green). There are several things that happened over the 2 ½ years with senior managers, such as Mark Martinez, Robert Reynosa, Jennifer Vo, Shaun Mossman, Craig Colton, Yul Melonson, Corey Richards, Pat Miner, Sylvester Black, and Jerry Wilson, as it relates to the things they said and the decisions they made or delegated, all I can say is they are ruthless people and I don't understand how they sleep at night. I was diagnosed with Post Traumatic Stress Disorder, and Major Depression, and Anxiety.

In 2004 I worked in a hostile work environment and the office was performing very poorly along with high volume NALC payouts. Postmaster (Craig Colton) did nothing about the harassment even though it was brought to his attention by me. Nevertheless, I cleaned it up in four and a half months (4 ½). I started Psycho Therapy and was diagnosed with Post Traumatic Stress Disorder, Depression, Obsessive Compulsive Disorder, later on my heart started beating faster (Heart Palpitations), and I developed a Choking Cough. I was treated for both conditions but at the time I only knew that I was afraid of the Supervisor's, Steven Phaup, Mentality, he was very bizarre and tried to sabotage my operation on a daily basis.

On 8/25/08 I was threatened by paranoid, aggressive, and heartless, OIC-Jerry Wilson who did not treat me with dignity and respect, as a matter of fact, Jerry addressed me as "Hey Girl", he did not know how to manage subordinates, and especially one with skill, ability, and experience. I was diagnosed with Post Traumatic Stress Disorder, Major Depression, Anxiety, Panic Attacks, Panic Disorder, Neuropathy, Hearing Loss, Vision Impaired, and Lumbar Radiculopathy, Choking Cough, and Heart Palpitations go worse. Yul Melonson was the senior manager to investigate the threat, but there was no investigation done.

I also want it to be noted that history was made in Nevada, because there had never been a Black Postmaster in the City of Las Vegas, since the first Postmaster Installation in 1894, until I filed my Exeo's in September 2008. Also, there had only been one (1) Black Female that had served during this period.

On 3/9/09 I was released to return to work by all of my doctors except Dr. Jimmy Novero-Neurologist. My primary physician (Heather Harris-APN), some how, left him out of the loop. I actually returned to work on 3/13/09 and that same day I had a lifting injury. I reported the injury to my Acting Manager, Joe Acosta and he actually was there when the injury happened. He asked me if I was ok and I replied, I think I'll be ok and I'll just do the best that I can to work it off. My pride, work ethic, and responsibility to my career, at the postal service, made me try and work it off since I was still going to Physical Therapy, Psycho Therapy, and my Cardiologist. Unfortunately, I was not able to work it off and on 4/1/09 I had a meeting with Promoted Executive Postmaster (Yul Melonson) and I told him that I was sick and I asked him for advance sick leave, because I had used a lot of saved leave up from the previous seven (7) months of being out. He stated to me that I have annual still left so he can't give me the advance sick leave. It still did not register with me that I was too ill to perform my duties and that is the reason why I asked for the advance sick leave. On 4/2/09, which happened to be my last day of working for the United States Postal Service, I had to file a claim on the lifting injury. I was diagnosed with Lumbar Radiculopathy-Sciatica, Back Strain, Bi-Lateral Knee Strain, Cervical and Thoracic Facet Syndrome.

Once Yul found out he called my cell phone and left me a message that stated "I got news for you, you are going back to North Las Vegas and Corey has already been notified". I called Yul Melonson back and he repeated the same thing to me that I just previously put in quotes; and Yul asked me "Why didn't I tell him on yesterday" (4/1/09), and I stated to Yul that I reported it to Joe, and he was suppose to tell you. Physical Therapy was reduced to in home health care because my health declined to not being able to walk and I was put on a four (4) leg cane, walker, in home tens unit, heating pad, prescribe ointment with medication in it, along with .

On 4/13/09 I went to the North Las Vegas Main Post Office, and I had a friend with me with the hope that Corey Richards would treat me with dignity and respect; unfortunately that was not the case. Corey disrespected me and denied me my rights as an employee of the office. I was hospitalized from 4/13/09 – 4/15/09 and I filed a claim for stress. I had elevated blood pressure, my right arm collapsed, and my heart palpitations were excessive. I want it to be noted that I have not been paid for 2/18/09 and 2/19/09 for my briefing and testimony in the Lucy James case which was very beneficial to the postal service, because the arbitrator's decision denied a lot of JSOV grievances.

I want it to be noted that I am in need of a powered scooter and The Scooter Store states that Federal Blue Cross Blue Shield will not pay for it because the injuries happened as a result of work, so this is another reason why I'm bringing this matter to your attention. All of my claims have been denied erroneously and it just causes me more stress and pain to have to keep addressing the appeals. I really thought that the postal service would have integrity at least in the investigations, but to no avail.

In addition, the Nevada Sierra District is taking money out of my pension for injuries that I sustained on the job. If it were not true then I would not have filed any claims are cases. I would like a complete copy of my claim files, because I need this information for my personal use. If I have a portion of the file, then send me the remaining portion that I do not have.

Ms. Johnson states in her letter that my claims to OWCP and the DOL were denied and that I should speak with Rosie Evans regarding any benefits. On 9/17/10 I spoke with Ms. Evans and she stated that she did not know of any approved claims. This is my life we are talking about here not a game.

Regarding Ms. Johnson's reply concerning my EEO cases, any correspondence or filing that was done for one case was done for the other case.

I want you to know that all of the issues are not the same as it was stated in Ms. Johnson's letter dated 7/30/10.

Since the NEEOISO put EEO complaints together, I want you to know the truth why they were filed and I'm going to go by the date that I signed them.

On 9/5/08 I filed an EEO on Acting Manager, Jerry Wilson for the aggressive, convicted, up close, in my face and personal threat he made to me on 8/25/08. Mr. Wilson Stated "You continue to go over my head with Craig and Yul and I'm going to do something about it."

On 9/18/08 I filed an EEO on Jennifer Vo, Mark Martinez, and Robert Reynosa for discrimination and retaliation after not being promoted to station manager after working as an acting manager for over 2 ½ years. Jennifer lied to me and I called a meeting with her Mark and Robert. I was talked to disrespectfully on telecoms and it was noticed by Dana Urbanski, I was asked by Yul why am I back at the office after he reviewed the flash report for Paradise Valley Station, Robert wanted me to removed the supervisors at Paradise Valley Station, but the were still there after they promoted the person that I had replaced seven (7) months prior, I received an award for best EXFC/EPED with having a zone split station with 66 routes still in it. Paradise Valley was the number one station in the district for F4 productivity with the volume that it received (8/06 – 3/07). Jennifer gave me and Investigative Interview for something that was out of my control and other promoted station managers did not get an Investigative Interview for similar and worse things, like mail being left in the building and mail being hidden. I was given a low merit rating from Jennifer and Robert even though I had performed well. Robert Reynosa was sent to King Station by Yul Melonson and I out performed him with less people and he is the Manager, Customer Service Operations.

On 9/30/08 I filed an EEO on Corey Richards and Craig Colton for Discrimination and Retaliation. Corey and I were Craig's supervisors at North Las Vegas, I was at the main office and Corey was at the sister station Meadow Mesa. Corey and Craig made several decisions not to promote me on the 17 positions. Craig would not promote me because of Steven Phaup, and Corey would not promote me because of retaliation and unprofessional behavior along with discrimination.

On 10/31/08 I filed an EEO on the Nevada Sierra District for all the discrimination that had happened to me from the time that I got to Nevada. I was told by an attorney that I had been discriminated against all the time with all the issues.

The NEEOISO dismissed the 9/18/08 EEO and it happened again so on 1/15/09 I filed another EEO on Robert Reynosa, Jennifer VO, and Mark Martinez for the previous issues and Robert for the current issue of discrimination, retaliation. Robert and Yul had been calling me and Robert wanted to know "Why do you want to work in the field as bad as it is." I replied; it's no problem to do the work it's the other stuff, discrimination, disrespect, threats, lies, retaliation and stuff like that. Yul wanted to know when was I coming back to work, and I replied are you offering me the manager's position. I had a telephone interview for King Station and Robert gave it to someone else who went out on stress.

On 5/27/09 I filed an EEO on Yul Melonson for mental and physical discrimination along with gender and age discrimination. Yul also had me come to the City of Las Vegas under the pretense that I was going to be granted my request for a lateral until I was injured on 3/13/09 and filed a claim on 4/2/09. I have the records for proof if you need them.

I thank you in advance for your time and concern in this matter and I swear under penalty of perjury that the information in this letter is true and correct to the best of my knowledge.
I know it because it plays in my head everyday all day.

Sir, I can be reached by telephone at (562) 889-2662 or (562) 291-2691 if you need to call me. My mailing address is still 1236 W. 22nd St. #1 Los Angeles, California 90007-1770

Sincerely
Lola McGee

National EEO Compliance – Response from Postmaster General to Intervene October 28, 2010.

NATIONAL EEO COMPLIANCE & APPEALS PROGRAMS

UNITED STATES
POSTAL SERVICE

October 28, 2010

Ms. Lola McGee
1236 W. 22nd Street, Apartment 1
Los Angeles, CA 90007-1770

Dear Ms. McGee:

This is regarding your recent correspondence dated September 30, 2010, to Postmaster General John Potter.

In your letter you indicated that you had received a response to previous correspondence from Susan Johnson, Manager EEO Compliance and Appeals Region 1, and requested that Mr. Potter investigate and intervene.

Ms. Johnson reports that she recently returned a call you made to her regarding the status of your formal EEO complaint, Agency Case No. 4E-890-0120-08. During this conversation you indicated that you were waiting for the decision by the Office of Federal Operations, EEOC on your appeal.

You have addressed your issue concerning OWCP benefits with the District Manger Health Resource Management. If you have additional concerns regarding the processing of worker's compensation benefits, the appropriate forum to address those concerns is with the OWCP.

You have utilized or have access to appropriate appeal processes regarding these matters. It would be inappropriate for our office to comment on the merits of your case.

Sincerely,

Jeff Slye
Acting Manager, EEO Field Operations

cc: Manager, EEO Compliance & Appeals, Region 1

475 L'ENFANT PLAZA SW
WASHINGTON DC 20260-4135
202-268-3658
FAX: 202-268-6189
WWW.USPS.COM

October 5, 2010

To: US DEPARTMENT OF LABOR
OFFICE OF WORKERS' COMP PROGRAMS
PO BOX 8300 DISTRICT 13 SFC
LONDON, KY 40742- 8300

From: Lola McGee
1236 W. 22nd St. #1
Los Angeles, CA 90007

RE: Request for Reconsideration Appeal case # 132209923 additional medical (MRI)

This letter is being written as a follow up of my reconsideration request form dated July 6, 2010 that was accompanied by a letter dated July 7, 2010 explaining the lifting injury sustained on 3/13/09 at Spring Valley Station in Las Vegas, Nevada.

After one and a half (1 ½) years later I have finally gotten the MRI dated 9/10/2010 that should have been performed when Centennial Spine and Pain Center requested it from your agency back in April 2009.

In my CA-1 I stated that both knees had pain coming from them and they still due today. The lifting injury took me totally out; and I had to have in home health service to learn how to walk. I still walk on a claw cane to date.

I am sending a copy of the results of the MRI that was performed on 9/10/2010. I can be reached at (562) 889-2662 Cell or (562) 291-2691 Home

Sincerely
Lola McGee

* * * *

October 5, 2010

To: EEOC & Appeals Region 1
Pacific Area Field Office and United States Postal Services – Nevada Sierra District
P. O. Box 880546
San Francisco, CA 94188-0546

From: Lola McGee
1236 W. 22nd St. #1
Los Angeles, CA 90007-1770

RE: Intent to Sue case #4E-890-0120-08 and case #4E-890-0043-09, also there will be individual filings.

To all concern,

The purpose of this letter is to notify all agencies, offices, and departments involved, in the cases stated above along with certain individuals of my intent to file civil action against the United States Postal Service for the Discrimination, illnesses, and injuries I sustained while being on the job performing my duties as assigned.

In addition, I will be filing civil actions for those who retaliated against me for my prior EEO activity and physical injuries and mental illnesses.

Sincerely
Lola McGee

* * * * *

October 5, 2010

To: Employees' Compensation Appeals Board
200 Constitution Avenue NW, Room S-5220
Washington, DC 20210

From: Lola McGee
1236 W. 22nd St. Apt. #1
Los Angeles, CA 90007-1770

Re: Change of Address and Status of Claim #132198863

To All Concern,

I am writing this letter to notify the agency of my change of address listed above and I would like to know the status of my claim. If there has been any information mailed out to me regarding this claim number, I did not received it. I would like for the agency to notify me if there has been any information mailed out regarding this claim.

Sincerely
Lola McGee

* * * * *

October 11, 2010

To: US DEPARTMENT OF LABOR
OFFICE OF WORKERS' COMP PROGRAMS
PO BOX 8300 DISTRICT 13 SFC
LONDON, KY 40742- 8300

From: Lola McGee
1236 W. 22nd St. #1
Los Angeles, CA 90007

RE: Request for Reconsideration Appeal case # 132209923 additional medical, (MRI) of Both (Right and Left) Knees.

This letter is being written as a follow up of my reconsideration request form dated July 6, 2010 that was accompanied by a letter dated July 7, 2010 explaining the lifting injury sustained on 3/13/09 at Spring Valley Station in Las Vegas, Nevada.

After one and a half (1 ½) years later I have finally gotten the MRI Test completed dated 9/10/2010 that should have been performed when Centennial Spine and Pain Center requested it from your agency back in April 2009.

In my CA-1 I stated that both knees had pain coming from them and they still due today. The lifting injury took me totally out; and I had to have in home health service to learn how to walk. I still walk on a claw cane to date.

I am sending a copy of the results of the MRI dated 9/10/10 that was performed on both knees. I can be reached at (562) 889-2662 Cell or (562) 291-2691 Home

Sincerely
Lola McGee

December 19, 2010

To: DOL DFEC Central Mailroom
P. O. Box 8300
London, KY 40742

From: Lola McGee
1236 W. 22nd St. Apt. #1
Los Angeles, CA 90007

RE: Change of Address for Case #132209923 and #132210754 New Telephone number: (562) 889-2662 – Cell

To Whom It May Concern:

This letter is being written to notify the agency and all involved, regarding the above case numbers, of my new address and contact phone number. I want it to be known that every time that I have moved, which this will be the eight (8) move and seventh (7) within a year, I have notified the agency of the new address. I have mental and physical, on the job, illnesses and injuries that has made it very hard for me to stay in one place for an extended period of time. I'm not use to this and I know it must be difficult for you to keep up with, however, I have sent in written notice of my moves.

Thank you,
Lola McGee

* * * * *

December 19, 2010

To: EEOC/OFO
P. O. Box 77960
Washington, D.C. 20013-8960

From: Lola McGee
1236 W. 22nd St. #1
Los Angeles, CA 90007-1770

RE: Case #4E-890-0120-08 formal date 11/1/08 and Case #4E-890-0043-09 formal filed 5/27/09

The purpose of this letter is to request updated information regarding the above case numbers and to give my new mailing address to the agency. I would like to know what the statue is of the above cases in detail. Please forward the information to the above mailing address. I can be reached by telephone at (562) 889-2662.

Sincerely
Lola McGee

Race Discrimination Paper I wrote in March 2001 while in school.

Race Discrimination

Lola McGee
Univ. Of Phoenix
James W. Potts
MGT/434
Group 4GAR4433
Workshop Two
March 27, 2001

Race Discrimination

As an African American woman, it is no secret what my people have been through as it relates to race discrimination. Black people have been discriminated against since this country since before the Mayflower (Bennett-Alexander, 2001). In the middle 1600 Blacks were forced into slavery and since then they have not been treated as equal. This paper will discuss the racial discrimination that all minorities endure on a daily basis, and the degree in which it happens. In addition, the myth about discrimination will be addressed. If employers could look at an employee on his or her own merit, the workplace would be a better place to perform duties.

Racial Discrimination

Even though the Civil Rights Act of 1964 was passed, discrimination still exists in 2001. For over 200 years Blacks were in slavery (Bennett-Alexander, 2001). Because of such and ingrained behavior and mentality, Blacks are use to being treated as second-class citizens. Discriminatory behavior towards Black people by employers is nothing new and Black people tolerate it on a daily basis. According to Inc.,D/B/A/ Domino's Bradley v. Pizzaco of Nebraska, Domino's 939 f.2d 610 (8th Cir. 1991) Blacks men were being discriminated against because Domino's policy was for all men to be clean shaven. Because Black men have medically tested skin problems, it created a race discrimination issue. The policy implies that Black men cannot work for Domino's. The courts ruled that it was in fact discrimination. It is the law that employers ensure that every employee has an equal opportunity for employment and advancement in the workplace regardless of race (Bennett-Alexander, 2001). Laws like these are the only way that Black people will begin to be treated fairly in the workplace.

Degrees/Types

One would have to know that with racial discrimination being so prevalent among Blacks, there would have to be various types and degrees of discrimination with other minorities. Women are another group of people who are constantly discriminated against. A man can apply and get a computer position paying 60,000 a year, and a woman can apply and get the same job making 45,000 a year. The reasoning for this is that society believes that men are smarter, and more workforce productive than women. Men are also put in certain hierarchical positions that very few women may posses. In addition, men in the construction field believe that women should not make the same pay as they do. Women can be classified as a pipe fitter and receive $20.00 an hour, while a man can be classified at the same skill and receive $30.00 an hour. The problem here is that both are carrying the same material and weight. Women are looked upon as housewives and childbearing people. They are treated as second-class citizens just like Blacks are. Rather the discrimination is in the form of race, gender, are classification it is still discrimination.

Myths/Truths

Some of the most common myths are that Black people are paranoid, and that racism and discrimination is over. According to Bennett-Alexander, The single most common reason that discrimination continues to lye doormat in so many societies today is that those in the majority often simply refuse to believe that it exists (2001). Many people conveniently overlook discrimination in the workplace because it is easier to get along with others.

Discrimination 5

For most offices it's the culture of the office, and most people do not want to weather any storms. Unfortunately When discrimination is brought to the employer's attention he or she doesn't want to believe that it is happening.

Conclusion

If everybody were treated with dignity and respect the world would be a better place. Unfortunately we have race discrimination that is present in society. Also, there are several degrees and types of discrimination that takes place. On the other hand, there are myths about what was considered discrimination. With this element being apart of today's workplaces, minorities will always be treated as second-class citizens. Maybe one day we all will feel freedom.

Reference

Bennett-Alexander, D., Hartman, L.P., Employment Law for Business 3rd edition, 2001. New York, Irwin/McGraw-Hill Inc.

March 23, 2011

To: U. S Department of Labor
Employees' Compensation Appeals Board
200 Constitution Avenue, NW, Room S-5220
Washington, D.C. 20210

From: Lola McGee
1236 W. 22nd St. #1
Los Angeles, CA 90007-1770

RE: Request for submission of old and new medical information that was written in narrative form but actual test were not sent in regarding Case# 132198863 – Decision dated March 6, 2009

To Whom It May Concern:

I Lola McGee am writing this letter because I did not know that the MRI reports were suppose to be sent in if the doctor gave his findings and diagnosis in narrative form.

On 8/25/08 I Lola McGee, birth date 7/7/1962, was employed by the United States Postal Service as a Supervisor, Customer Services North Las Vegas Main Office 1414 E. Lake Mead Blvd. North Las Vegas, NV 89030. However, I was detailed to the Meadow Mesa Station where I sustained a traumatic injury to my Brain by having a panic attack when I was threatened by OIC North Las Vegas, Jerry Wilson. The claim was turned into an Occupational Disease, in which, I disagree.

In addition, I have MRI reports of my Brain and post operation Heart Monitoring Test which shows an increase in my Heart Palpitations since the operation on 2/25/10.

I would like for this information to be considered in the approval of my claim and I will be sending the DOL DFEC a copy of the information as well.

I can be reached at (562) 889-2662

Sincerely
Lola McGee

March 23, 2011

To: DOL DFEC Central Mailroom
PO BOX 8300
LONDON, KY 40742

From: Lola McGee
1236 W. 22nd St. #1
Los Angeles, CA 90007

RE: Request for Reconsideration Appeal case # 132209923 Addressing Background Information, and sending in Dr. Siamak Rouzroch Causal Narrative and referral

This letter is being written today in response to Cal Sagami, Senior Claims Examiner letter dated January 5, 2011 regarding my on the job injury dated 3/13/09 at Spring Valley Station in Las Vegas, Nevada where I was employed as a Supervisor, Customer Services for the United States Postal Service. I am now Medical Disability Retirement from injuries and illnesses sustained at the postal service.

In my statement that I filed on 4/2/09 I put that my back, left thigh, and knees were injured from lifting trays and tubs of mail into a hamper; however, on my CA-1 some how I left off the "S" on knees. I want it to be known that all my medical documentation states bi-lateral knees and I swear under penalty of perjury that I injured both of my knees; it was a mistake on my part to not put the "S" on the CA-1 form.

In addition, I want it to be known that I put the trays and tubs of mail into the hamper by myself; the limited duty carrier was not present. I apologize for the confusion with using words in my statement as if she was present with me. I was helping her because she had lifting restrictions.

I am sending a copy of Dr. Siamak Rouzroch narrative report which states on the job work injury on 3/13/09 to both-knee pain, back pain, and left thigh. I have a referral to see a pain management doctor.

I can be reached at (562) 889-2662

Sincerely
Lola McGee

March 23, 2011

To: EEOC/OFO
P. O. Box 77960
Washington, D.C. 20013-8960

From: Lola McGee
1236 W. 22nd St. #1
Los Angeles, CA 90007-1770

RE: Second request for information regarding Case #4E-890-0120-08 formal file date 11/1/08 and Case #4E-890-0043-09 formal filed date 5/27/09

The purpose of this letter is to request updated information regarding the above case numbers and to give my new mailing address to the agency. I would like to know what the statue is of the above cases in detail. Please forward the information to the above mailing address. I can be reached by telephone at (562) 889-2662.

Sincerely
Lola McGee

* * *

March 23, 2011

To: Employees' Compensation Appeals Board
200 Constitution Avenue NW, Room S-5220
Washington, DC 20210

From: Lola McGee
1236 W. 22nd St. Apt. #1
Los Angeles, CA 90007-1770

Re: Change of Address and Status of Claim #132198863

To All Concern,
I am writing this letter to notify the agency of my change of address listed above and I would like to know the status of my claim. If there has been any information mailed out to me regarding this claim number, I did not received it. I would like for the agency to notify me if there has been any information mailed out regarding this claim.

Sincerely
Lola McGee

Some of my medical reports from the beginning of Las Vegas Demise 2004 to current.

Human Behavior Institute
Clinical Services

August 26, 2009

Re: Lola McGee
DOB: 07/07/1962

To Whom It May Concern:

Ms. McGee was seen off and on at HBI for counseling and psychological services beginning in February, 2005. My first encounter with Ms. McGee was on May 2, 2005, and I met with her on 15 occasions between then and October 8, 2008.

The relevant diagnostic profile on 10/08/2008 was as follows:

* 309.81 – Post Traumatic Stress Disorder (w/ obsessive-compulsive features and panic attacks)
* 296.32 – Major Depressive Disorder, Recurrent, Moderate
"Cardiovascular abnormalities" reported
Psychosocial Stressors and Functioning--Moderate-Severe:
Occupational problems: conflict with supervisor(s); work stress
Economic problems: change in financial status

The focus of treatment was primarily on family issues and childhood trauma in relation to present-day experiences and stressors. Although it was not the direct focus of therapy, it was clear that there were interpersonal and organizational issues and conflicts related to her duties, responsibilities, and hierarchical relationships in her work with the USPS that were highly stressful to her. Ms. McGee had expressed considerable frustration as she reported having sent several communications regarding issues at work that seemed to her to generate little or no appropriate response. It was my impression that job and career-related stressors were significantly contributing to Ms. McGee's symptoms of anxiety and depression that were affecting her in personal as well as professional areas of her life.

Please contact me if I may be of further assistance in this matter.

Sincerely,

Michael S. Shepard, Psy.D.
Licensed Clinical Psychologist

*Diagnostic codes are per standard resources, DSM-IV-TR and ICD-9

2740 South Jones Boulevard • Las Vegas, Nevada 89146 • (702) 248-8866 • FAX: (702) 248-1339

Reed's Nursing &
Educational Services Inc.

September 11, 2009

To Whom It May Concern:

Lola Mc Gee (SS# xxx-xx-9539) reports that she was threatened by her boss on 8-25-08 and for the last two and one half years of being an acting manager for the post office she feels discriminated against because she states that she applied for 17 positions and was not promoted even once, two of the positions remained unfilled. In addition, she states that her bosses retaliated against her when she filed EEO's against them by not paying her on time, disrespecting her, and various other negative behaviors. Ms McGee has been under my care since 8-26-08, with a history of severe and prolonged psychiatric illness despite appropriate outpatient treatment, and is showing significant decompensation since returning to work on 3-9-09. She is exhibiting increase anxiety and panic attacks that resulted in her calling 911 on 4-13-09 due to severe chest pain and paralysis of her right arm. She was admitted to St. Rose Hospital for evaluation of sudden paralysis of her right arm.

She is incapable of performing the duties and responsibilities of her job description (Supv Customer Services, EAS -16). She exhibits severe anxiety, panic attacks, agoraphobia, low self-esteem/confidence, and ambivalence. She has difficulty concentrating and staying focused on task, and making rational decisions. She has experienced frequent episodes of panic attacks, mood swings with anger episodes and crying spells. Due to her severe depression, labile and rapid mood fluctuations it would be impossible for her to provide supervision to carriers and interact with the public. Regarding causality, in my opinion the above work related stressors contributed to the following diagnoses below:

DIAGNOSIS- DSM-IV TR:

Axis I 296.33 Major Depressive Disorder, Recurrent, Severe Without Psychotic Features
309.81 Posttraumatic Stress Disorder
300.21 Panic Disorder with Agoraphobia
Axis II V71.09 No Diagnosis on Axis II
Axis III 427.1 Paroxysmal Ventricular Tachycardia
785.1 Palpitations
785.2 Heart Murmur
786.50 Chest Pain
Axis IV Occupational Problems, Conflict with Manager/Supervisor
Axis V GAF: Current 41-50, Prior 81-90

Current Medications:

Pristiq 50mg po QAM
Klonopin 1mg po BID

Please contact me if you have questions or require additional information.

Sincerely,

Mary J. Reed PhD, APN, CS, BC

Kayenta Therapy Center · 9402 W. Lake Mead Blvd. · Las Vegas, NV 89134
Tel: (702)341-0010 · Fax: (702)254-7830
drreed@nursing-edu.biz · www.nursing-edu.biz

Santos H. Yu, M.D.
Clinical Neurophysiology
with emphasis on
neuromuscular disorders

Edgar B. Evangelista, M.D.
Clinical Neurophysiology
Sleep Medicine

Jimmy John Novero, M.D.
Board Certified

NEUROLOGY CENTER OF NEVADA

- General Adult Neurology
- Neuromuscular Consultation
- Electromyography & Nerve conduction studies
- Routine, Ambulatory, Extended EEG studies
- Sleep Disorder Consultation
- Botox Injection Therapy

"we can treat dizziness, stroke/TIA, memory problem, headache, muscle weakness, seizures, tremors, numbness/tingling, neck and back pain"

DATE: 12-Jan-10

To Whom It May Concern:

Lola McGee is a 46 year old female who numbness in her feet and weakness of her lower extremities. She was initially evaluated by me on December 16, 2008 while working for the US postal service, a job she has had for approximately 10 years. Her examination at the time revealed physical findings consistent with a peripheral neuropathy, with sensory loss in her distal lower extremities, decreased symmetrical reflexes, and mild to moderate weakness on the left lower extremity. She also presented with low back pain and had moderate lumbar tenderness and spasms.
To support her diagnosis, she has had neurophysiological studies / electrodiagnostic studies which showed findings consistent with a mainly axonal and more predominantly sensory neuropathy. The studies also showed abnormal bilateral superficial peroneal sensory responses and decreased recruitment of the peroneus longus and medial gastrocnemius muscles but no active denervation. The overall findings of the electrophysiological studies appear consistent with an early sensory peripheral neuropathy.
Additional work-up included MRI studies of lumbar spine and cervical and lumbar x-rays which revealed mild degenerative disease. Her laboratory studies essentially were unremarkable, including fasting glucose. She has no history of diabetes.
She has been treated with physical therapy and medications, including Lyrica and Lortab. She has had minimal significant improvement so far, with worsening numbness of her feet and pain during periods of prolonged sitting and standing. She has been continuing her work at the postal service which consists of loading trays of mail and heavy lifting. She has noted more pain especially since March 2009 while assisting a carrier when she felt what she described as a "pop" in her lower back and more severe pain in her left thigh.

Diagnosis and Prognosis: Lola McGee has symptoms, exam findings and electrodiagnostic evidence consistent with a peripheral neuropathy mainly affecting her lower extremities. This likely is a result of an idiopathic peripheral neuropathy. She also has low back pain which can be due to lumbar radiculitis and worsened by heavy lifting and bending. Still complaining of upper and lower extremity numbness, pareshtesias, and pain. She is also complaining of back pain and is having gait difficulties due to pain and weakness.

100 N Green Valley Parkway Suite 225 Henderson, NV 89074 (702) 247-9994 Fax (702) 651-9995
2501 W Charleston Blvd Las Vegas, NV 89102 (702) 382-7760
8285 W Arby Ave Suite 231 Las Vegas, NV 89113 (702) 270-3485
To schedule an appointment, please call (702) 247-9994
Page 1 of 2

1/12/2010 10:05:06 AM Neurology Center Of Nevada Fax: 7026519995 Page 3 of 3

McGee, Lola
DOB: 07/07/1962
5/4/2009

Page 2 of 2

Patient states that she had been "working in a hostile work environment, was threatened by her boss, felt discriminated and felt unfair tactics were used and felt disrespected." Patient states she had a panic attack on 8/25/08 and this was the the start of her symptoms and pain that she currently complains of. She was asymptomatic prior to 8/25/08. She states she had applied for different positions as acting manager in her job for 2.5 years but did not get any position.

Patient's neuropathic symptoms were likely aggravated or exacerbated by the work-related stressors she experienced back in August 2008 and which have been persistent since then. Her symptoms have been progressing since onset and treatment so far has been minimally effective. Full recovery is highly unlikely given the progressive nature of the illness; prognosis for partial recovery at this time cannot be determined and will depend on several factors, including follow-up evaluations as well as response to therapies and medications. Given her current medical status, she will be unable to perform her duties at her current job which may worsen and exacerbate her symptoms. And inspite of all the treatment and PT, she is Permanent stationary and will benefit with additional PT.

Sincerely,

Jimmy John Novero, M.D.

Board Certified Neurologist
100 N. Green Valley Pkwy.
Suite 215
Henderson, NV 89074

(702) 247-9994

100 N Green Valley Parkway Suite 225 Henderson, NV 89074 (702) 247-9994 Fax (702) 651-9995
2501 W Charleston Blvd Las Vegas, NV 89102 (702) 382-7760
8285 W Arby Ave Suite 231 Las Vegas, NV 89113 (702) 270-3485
To schedule an appointment, please call (702) 247-9994
Page 2 of 2

Oct 19 09 04:31p p.3

October 13, 2009

Patient: Lola Mcgee
DOB: 07/07/1962
Age: 47 Years

Lola Mcgee was seen in our office today, October 13, 2009. The following is a summary of today's visit.

Chief Complaint/Reason for visit:
This 47 year old female presents with peripheral neuropathy.

History of Present Illness

peripheral neuropathy

Patient reports that she has also developed neuropathy in her right arm. She reports that her right arm is numb, tingly,painful and burning. She also has lumbar radiculopathy and back pain due to sciatica and lumbar radiculopathy. According to the patient's account, her lumbar radiculopathy was aggravated by a lifting accident that occured on 03/13/09 becasue the patient went back to work against the doctor's advice. The collapse of her arm on 04/13/09 and that is when the neuropathy of her arm started. The neuropathy in her lower extremities per the patient, is unchanged but she claims all she knows is that she is in great deal of pain.

She has sciatic pain and low back strain in addition to her lumbar radiculopathy which got worse after her lifting accident on 3/13/09. She lifted tubs and trays of mail which weighed approximately at least 50 lbs.

She had seen the Centennial Spine and Pain Center on 4/28/09 and diagnosed with: cervical facet syndrome, lumbar facet syndrome, thoracic facet syndrome, lumbar radiculopathy, knee pain. She has right upper extremity burning pain and pain radiating to her right arm and hand, mostly 4th and 5th digits. This is related to her cervical radiculopathy.

Clinical Assessment
The patient is a 47-year old female with history of peripheral neuropathy and neck / low back pain related to cervical and lumbar radiculitis and radiculopathy.

Assessment/ Plan
Neuralgia / neuritis / radiculitis (729.2)
1. She will start topiramate 25 mg qhs x 1 week then 50 mg qhs for her neuropathic pain and symptoms.
2. Continue other medications as prescribed and phsyical therapy.
3. Follow-up as scheduled.

Peripheral neuropathy (356.9)
Pain-neck (723.1)
Pain-low back (724.2)
1. She will start topiramate 25 mg qhs x 1 week then 50 mg qhs for her neuropathic pain and symptoms.
2. Continue other medications as prescribed and phsyical therapy.
3. Follow-up as scheduled.

Orders
Follow-up:

Assessment	Follow-up	Reason	Timeframe	Comments
729.2	Office visit	Follow-up visit		6 Months
729.2	Office visit	Assess response to treatment		-today
729.2	Office Visit	Follow-up on medication		-today

Jimmy John Nobleza Novero, MD

Mcgee, Lola 07/07/1962 1/2

Oct 19 09 04:31p p.4

CC Providers:

Mcgee, Lola 07/07/1962 2/2

History and Physical

Patient Name:	Lola McGee	**Visit Date:**	November 20, 2008
Patient ID:	99176	**Provider:**	Frederick Goll, III MD
Sex:	Female	**Location:**	Greenvalley
Birthdate:	July 7, 1962		

Chief Complaint

- Hearing loss

History Of Present Illness

Lola B. McGee is a 46 year old female who is referred by Heather Harris NP for evaluation of mild loss of hearing involving both ears. The hearing loss began suddenly 3 months ago and may be related to threats from her boss on 8/25/08. There is no history of exposure to ototoxic medications, ear infections, an upper respiratory infection, severe emotional stress, head injury, stroke, recent swimming, recent cleaning of the ears, sinusitis, noise exposure, multiple ear infections, prior ear surgery, radiation therapy, surgery, and ear trauma. The patient reports additional complaints, including: tinnitus. The patient denies balance problems, otalgia, and otorrhea. There are no noted alleviating factors. The patient has not received any prior treatment for this condition. Her past medical history is noncontributory. The patient has no family history of hearing loss.

Lola B. McGee is a 46 year old female , who is referred by Heather Harris NP for evaluation of cough. The cough is nonproductive , has been present for 3 months , and occurs frequently. The symptoms began acutely and were related to threat from her boss on 8/25/08. The patient's symptoms remain constant throughout the day. The patient reports that she has also experienced nasal congestion, rhinorrhea, gagging, heartburn, and choking. The patient denies facial pain, throat discomfort, wheezing, and hemoptysis. The patient's past medical history is notable for gastroesophageal reflux disease (GERD). The patient's social and environmental history is unremarkable. She has not had any recent care for this condition. A chest x-ray has not been performed.

AUDIOMETRY FINDINGS:

Audiologic testing was performed today showing abnormal hearing Test results show a left greater than right sensorineural hearing loss. Sensorineural loss was noted to be mild to moderate and high frequency.

Tympanometry was performed today showing type "A" (normal) tympanogram on the right and type "A" (normal) tympanogram on the left.

Past Medical History

Reviewed None Changed

Past Surgical History

Reviewed None Changed

Medication List

Reviewed None Changed

Allergy List

Reviewed None Changed

Family Medical History

Reviewed None Changed

[Digital Signature Validated]

[History and Physical] [Lola McGee] [99176] [12/1/2008] Page 2 of 4

Social History
Reviewed None Changed

Review of Systems

Constitutional
- **Admits** : fatigue, fever, weight loss
- **Denies** : weight gain

Eyes
- **Denies** : eye discomfort, double vision, impaired vision, blurred vision, changes in vision

HENT
- **Admits** : SEE HPI

Cardiovascular
- **Admits** : chest pain, palpitations, shortness of breath with walking or lying flat, swelling or feet, ankles or hands

Respiratory
- **Admits** : shortness of breath, cough
- **Denies** : wheezing, spitting up blood

Gastrointestinal
- **Admits** : nausea, vomiting, diarrhea, constipation, loss of appetite
- **Denies** : abdominal pain, blood in stools, change in bowel movements

Genitourinary
- **Admits** : frequency, incontinence
- **Denies** : urgency, change in urine color, difficulty voiding, decreased libido, irregular menses, vaginal discharge

Integument
- **Denies** : rash, itching, skin dryness, change in skin color, change in hair or nails, varicose veins

Neurologic
- **Admits** : tingling or numbness, tremors, headaches
- **Denies** : seizures

Musculoskeletal
- **Admits** : joint pain, joint swelling, muscle pain, muscle cramps, back pain

Endocrine
- **Denies** : cold intolerance, heat intolerance, dry skin, excessive thirst or urination

Psychiatric
- **Admits** : depression, memory loss or confusion, insomnia, nervousness

Heme-Lymph
- **Denies** : lightheadedness, easy bleeding, easy bruising

Physical Examination

Constitutional
- **General Appearance** : well nourished, well-developed, alert, oriented, in no acute distress
- **Communication Ability / Voice Quality** : communication ability normal, voice quality normal

Head
- **Inspection** : normocephalic, no lesions present, atraumatic
- **Palpation** : no tenderness on palpation, no masses on palpation

Face
- **Inspection** : normal appearance, no lesions present, no evidence of trauma, jaw position normal
- **Palpation** : frontoethmoidal and maxillary sinuses nontender to palpation, no masses present
- **Facial Strength** : facial motion symmetric, normal eye closure strength bilaterally
- **Parotid Glands** : no tenderness on palpation, no swelling present, no masses present

Eyes
- **Ocular Motility/Alignment** : ocular alignment normal, ocular motility normal, no nystagmus present, visual acuity normal, no proptosis present
- **Eyelids/Adnexa** : eyelids within normal limits, lacrimal glands within normal limits, orbits within normal limits
- **Conjunctiva** : conjunctiva normal
- **Sclera** : sclera white

Ears
- **Hearing** : hearing to conversational voice
- **External Ears** : no auricle lesions or tenderness to palpation present, external auditory canals within normal limits without lesions or discharge
- **Otoscopic Exam** : tympanic membrane appearance normal, no lesions or perforations present. No fluid present behind

[Digital Signature Validated]

tympanic membranes
- o **Vestibular System** : physiologic nystagmus present on version testing

Nose / Nasopharynx
- o **External Nose** : appearance normal, no tenderness on palpation, normal size, no lesions, no evidence of trauma, nostrils patent
- o **Intranasal Exam** : nasal mucosa within normal limits, vestibule within normal limits, inferior meatus normal width and appearance, middle meatus normal, inferior turbinate appearance normal, middle turbinates within normal limits, nasal septum midline
- o **Nasopharynx** : nasopharynx within normal limits

Oral Cavity / Oropharynx
- o **Lips** : upper and lower lips pink and moist
- o **Teeth** : dentition within normal limits for age
- o **Gums** : gingivae healthy
- o **Oral Mucosa** : oral mucosa moist, no mucosal lesions present
- o **Floor of Mouth** : floor of mouth within normal limits, salivary ducts patent
- o **Tongue** : tongue moist and without lesions
- o **Palate** : soft and hard palates within normal limits
- o **Oropharynx** : appearance within normal limits, tonsils normal in appearance, peritonsillar regions within normal limits

Hypopharynx / Larynx
- o **Hypopharynx** : normal general appearance, no lesions present
- o **Larynx** : normal general appearance, epiglottis within normal limits, arytenoid cartilage within normal limits, vocal cord appearance normal
  Flexible Endoscopic Examination: normal general appearance, epiglottis within normal limits, *arytenoid cartilage erythema and edema present*, vestibular folds normal, vocal cord appearance normal, normal vocal cord position at rest

Neck
- o **Inspection and Palpation** : appearance normal, no masses or tenderness on palpation
- o **Thyroid** : size of gland normal, no tenderness, nodules or mass present on palpation, position midline
- o **Submandibular Glands** : normal size, nontender to palpation
- o **Lymph Nodes** : no lymphadenopathy present

Chest / Respiratory
- o **Respiratory Effort** : breathing unlabored

Cardiovascular
- o **Extremities** : no cyanosis or edema

Neurological/Psychiatric
- o **Orientation** : grossly oriented
- o **Cranial Nerves** : CN II-XII intact

Assessment

- Sensorineural Hearing Loss 389.10
- Tinnitus, Subjective 388.31
- Laryngopharyngeal Reflux 530.81

Plan

Orders
- o Impedance Testing (92567) - 11/20/2008
- o Comprehensive Audiometry Evaluation (92557) - 11/20/2008
- o Laryngoscopy, flexible fiberoptic, diagnostic (31575) - 11/20/2008

Medications
- o Tessalon Perles Oral Capsule 100 mg
  SIG: take 2 capsules by oral route 3 times a day for 30 days
  DISP: (180) capsules with 3 refills
  Prescribed on 11/20/2008

- o Prilosec Oral Capsule, Delayed Release(E.C.) 20 mg
  SIG: take 1 capsule (20 mg) by oral route once daily before a meal for 30 days
  DISP: (30) capsules with 6 refills

[Digital Signature Validated]

[History and Physical] [Lola McGee] [99176] [12/1/2008] Page 4 of 4

Prescribed on 11/20/2008

Instructions

- Discussed findings and options with patient
- Return to clinic as needed
- Handouts were given to patient

Disposition

- Call or RTC if symptoms worsen or persist.

Correspondence

- CC this document (Heather Harris NP) - 11/20/2008

Electronically Signed by: Frederick Goll, III MD on November 20, 2008 05:02:54 PM

[Digital Signature Validated]

Page No: 104

08/31/2009 14:15 7029908731 CCN PAGE 01/01

Cardiovascular Consultants of Nevada

Daejoon Anh, M.D
William W. Chu, M.D., Ph.D.
Michael A. Codina, M.D., F.A.C.C.
Herbert Cordero, M.D., F.A.C.C.
Robert P. Croke, M.D., F.A.C.C.
Paul V. Heeren, M.D., F.A.C.C.
Edward E. Holden, M.D., F.A.C.C.
Pamela A. Ivey, M.D., F.A.C.C.
Scott J. MacDonald, M.D., F.A.C.C.
Matthew J. McMahon, D.O., F.A.C.C.
Dhiraj Narula, M.D., F.A.C.C.
David L. Navratil, M.D., F.A.C.C.
Jeannette Nee, M.D., F.A.C.C.
Cuong T. Nguyen, M.D., F.A.C.C.
Jerry D. Routh, M.D., F.A.C.C.
Erik Sirulnick, M.D., F.A.C.C.
Harry M. Thomas, M.D., F.A.C.C.

MEDICAL RECORDS AUTHORAZATION

CCN # 391900 # of pages ______

☐ Sent to Medical Records for processing

☐ Completed in office by____________________ on ________

☐ Completed in Medical Records by Teresa Price on

To be completed by office CC: DR HARRIS/Reed/Navarro

I Authorize and request that Cardiovascular Consultants of Nevada release my medical records to

____*Please mail my records to me at my home address*
____*Send to a physician*
____*I would like to pick up my records at the clinical office.*

Please fill in blanks on the letter also included with the authorization
You may fax to 702-732-8948,
mail in the enclosed envelope
or bring both documents if picking up records at an office

Please sign, provide date of birth

Lola McGee
Please print your name

X [signature]
Signature

7/7/1962
Date of Birth

2300 Corporate Circle, Suite 100, Henderson, Nevada 89074 • 702.731.8224 • 888.559.9339 • www.ccnv.com

Sunrise Doctor's Pavilion / 933-9400 • St. Rose Siena Campus / 407-0110 • Summerlin Medical Center / 562-0344
Mountain View Campus / 360-7600 • Southern Hills Medical Center / 932-9820

CCN Cardiovascular Consultants of Nevada

Daejoon Anh, M.D.
Shaheen N. Chowdhry, M.D., F.A.C.C.
William W. Chu, M.D., Ph.D., F.A.C.C.
Herbert Cordero, M.D., F.A.C.C.
Robert P. Croke, M.D., F.A.C.C.
Paul V. Heeren, M.D., F.A.C.C.
Edward R. Holden, M.D., F.A.C.C.
Pamela A. Ivey, M.D., F.A.C.C.
Ninton S. Keide, M.D., F.A.C.C.
Scott J. MacDonald, M.D., F.A.C.C.
Dhiraj Narula, M.D., F.A.C.C.
David L. Navratil, M.D., F.A.C.C.
Jeannette Nee, M.D., F.A.C.C.
Cuong T. Nguyen, M.D., F.A.C.C.
Jerry D. Routh, M.D., F.A.C.C.
Frederick A. Schaller, D.O., F.A.C.O.I.
Erik Sirulnick, M.D., F.A.C.C.
Harry M. Thomas, M.D., F.A.C.C.
Branavan Umakanthan, D.O., F.A.C.C.
Nayab Zafar, M.D.

April 30, 2009

Heather Harris, FNP
500 E Windmill Lane Ste 125
Las Vegas, NV 89123

RE: Lola B. McGee
Patient Number: 391900
Patient DOB: 7/7/1962

Dear Ms Harris:

Ms. McGee is here to get test results to satisfy ourselves that structural cardiovascular disease is absent and that we are still dealing solely with a benign right ventricular arrhythmia.

We did a CT angio of the coronaries, CT of the remaining anterior structures of the chest, and CT of the carotid and intracranial vessels. All are normal. I have given the copies to the patient and her daughter.

CURRENT DIAGNOSES

1. Posttraumatic Stress Disorder, 309.814602
2. Paroxysmal Ventricular Tachycardia, 427.1
3. - Abnormal Test-Abnormal Exercise Stress Test, 794.30
4. - Palpitations, 785.1
5. Heart murmur, 785.2
6. Chest pain, 786.50

MEDICATIONS

1. Motrin 800 mg Tab, 1 p.o. daily prn pain
2. Baclofen 10 mg Tablet, 1 tab bid
3. Pristiq 50 mg Tablet Sustained Release 24 hr, 1 by mouth daily
4. Clonazepam 1 mg Tab, 1 p.o. b.i.d. prn
5. Lyrica 50 Mg Capsule, 1 by mouth twice daily
6. Ultram ER 300 mg Tablet Sustained Release 24 hr, 1 by mouth daily pt not sure of daily dosage
7. Verapamil 120 Mg Tab, 1 p.o. daily

PHYSICAL EXAMINATION

VITAL SIGNS:

Blood Pressure:	130/80 Sitting, Left arm, regular cuff
Pulse-	60/min.
Weight-	245.00 lbs.
Height-	69"
Temperature-	98.2
O2Sat-	96%
BMI-	36

2300 Corporate Circle, Suite 100, Henderson, Nevada 89074 • 702.731.8224 • 888.559.9339 • www.ccnv.com

Sunrise Doctor's Pavilion / 933-9400 • St. Rose Siena Campus / 407-0110 • Summerlin Medical Center / 562-0399
Mountain View Campus / [illegible]

RE: Lola B. McGee
Patient Number: 391900
Patient DOB: 7/7/1962

CONSTITUTIONAL
well developed, well nourished, in no acute distress

SKIN
warm and dry to touch, no apparent skin lesions or masses noted

PSYCHIATRIC
oriented to time, place, and person

NEUROLOGICAL
no gross motor or sensory deficits noted

MEDICATIONS UPDATED TODAY:
Verapamil 120 Mg Tab, 1 p.o. daily, #90

MEDICATION STOPPED TODAY:
Lyrica 50 mg Capsule

IMPRESSIONS/PLAN

This affirms my opinion stated two weeks ago that no structural cardiovascular disease is present. We need not undertake additional cardiac procedures. We will simply continue the verapamil. I assured a new prescription. We will see the patient in six months or the soonest we could be helpful. We hope that the administrative matters will have smoothed out at that time to reduce the patient's stress.

Sincerely,

Robert P. Croke, M.D., F.A.C.C.
RPC/jhs
cc: Mary Jane Reed, Ph.D., APN
Ms. Lola B. McGee

2

HeartCare
ASSOCIATES OF CONNECTICUT, LLC

Ricardo Cordido MD • Philip Fazzone MD • Samuel Hahn MD • Jack Hauser MD • Siegfried Kra MD • Marian Vulpe MD
Karin Augur PA • Alicia Burr APRN • Anna Rodonski PA • Douglas Stitz PA • Mark Whelan PA

February 1, 2010

Angelo Accomando, M.D.
Family Practice & Internal Medicine of
New Haven County
205 Main Street
East Haven, CT 06512

Re: **McGee, Lola**
DOB: 07/07/62

Dear Angelo:

I had the pleasure of seeing Lola McGee in the office today. As you know, she was initially seen on 1/19/10 for follow up cardiovascular care after returning from Nevada, where she was a patient of Dr. Robert of Cardiovascular Consultants of Nevada. She has a history of hypertension, hyperlipidemia, diabetes, obesity, and was diagnosed with RVOT VT by Dr. Robert, who reportedly explained to Ms. McGee that this diagnosis carries a benign prognosis, and would most likely not require more than pharmacologic therapy, which was started with verapamil-SR 120 mg qd. A nuclear stress test revealed an ischemic perfusion abnormality, however, a coronary CT angiogram revealed no obstructive CAD. A carotid ultrasound was reportedly normal. She has no history of diabetes or significant valvular disease. She also has a history of severe peripheral neuropathy and PTSD, on medical disability. She has been complaining of persistent and worsened exertional dyspnea, chest discomfort, palpitations, and lower extremity pain and edema. She was last seen by her former cardiologist in Nevada in 4/09.

Her current medications include verapamil-SR 120 mg qd, simvastatin 10 mg qd, HCTZ 12.5 mg qd, Lyrica, Pristiq, topiramiate prn, ibuprofen prn, Tramadol prn, and clonazepam prn. She has no known drug allergies.

On physical exam, her blood pressure is 118/68, with a heart rate of 80 and regular, and respirations of 16-18. Her weight is 258 pounds at 5'9". She has no neck vein distention. Her carotid upstroke is slightly decreased, without bruit. Her lungs are clear to auscultation. S1 and S2 are regular, without murmurs, gallops, rubs, or clicks. She has anterior chest wall tenderness. Bowel sounds are present, without organomegaly, guarding, or rebound. Her extremities reveal trace to 1+ bilateral lower extremity edema, without clubbing or cyanosis. There are no focal neurological deficits.

Her EKG showed normal sinus rhythm at 80, with frequent PVCs and episodes of ventricular bigeminy, which display a right inferior axis with a LBBB configuration; consistent with an RVOT origin.

A pharmacologic nuclear stress test from 1/26/10 revealed no evidence of infarct or ischemia, with an LVEF of 41% with mild fixed LV dilation (normal greater than 50%).

An echocardiogram in 1/10 revealed an EF in the low 40s, without regional variation, normal RV size and systolic function, and no significant valvular disease.

Based on these findings, I believe Lola has evidence of a non-ischemic cardiomyopathy, which appears to be mediated by a high ventricular ectopic burden of RVOT origin. Pharmacologic therapy with verapamil appears to have been ineffective. Although her symptoms appear to be multifactorial, they may be, at least in part, explained by a mild non-ischemic cardiomyopathy and considerable ventricular ectopic burden, which appears to have an RVOT origin and may be amenable to mapping and radiofrequency ablation. I have referred Lola to Dr. Blitzer to evaluate this therapeutic option, and have substituted

North Haven • East Haven • Hamden • Meriden • Wallingford • West Haven
Tel: 203 407 2500 • Fax: 203 407 2550 •

McGee, Lola
Page Two
2/1/10

Coreg-CR 20 mg qd for verapamil at this time. A 24 hour Holter monitor will be obtained shortly, with follow up in approximately four weeks.

Thank you for allowing me to participate in your patient's care. Please contact me with any questions regarding her care.

Sincerely,

Marian Volpe, M.D.

HeartCare
ASSOCIATES OF CONNECTICUT, LLC

Ricardo Cordido MD • Philip Fazzone MD • Samuel Hahn MD • Jack Hauser MD • Siegfried Kra MD • Marian Vulpe MD
Karin Augur PA • Alicia Burr APRN • Anna Rodonski PA • Douglas Stitz PA • Mark Whelan PA

24 Hour Holter Monitor Report

Name: McGee, Lola
Refer MD: Accomando/MV
Date: 2/3/10

Sex: F **DOB:** 7/7/62
Indication: Cardiomyopathy, dyspnea, PVCs, RVOT VT, palpitations
Meds:

Patient Diary

The patient did not submit a diary with this 24 hour full disclosure program.

Heart Rate and Rhythm

The underlying rhythm is sinus. The minimum, maximum and mean heart rates were 66, 117, and 86 bpm, respectively. There was appropriate diurnal heart rate variability. There were no significant pauses or episodes of marked bradycardia.

Ventricular Ectopy

There were frequent isolated premature ventricular complexes (more than 44,000), with episodes of sustained ventricular bigeminy. There were no episodes of ventricular tachycardia or other malignant ventricular arrhythmias.

Supraventricular Ectopy

There was no atrial ectopic activity.

ST Segments

There were no significant ST segment shifts during the monitoring interval.

Conclusion

1. Normal sinus rhythm, with frequent isolated PVCs and episodes of sustained ventricular bigeminy, without documented episodes of ventricular tachycardia.
2. No documented symptoms.
3. These findings were reviewed with the patient and Dr. Blitzer/EP referral.

MVulpe
Marian Vulpe, M.D.

North Haven • East Haven • Hamden • Meriden • Wallingford • West Haven
Tel: 203.407.2500 • Fax: 203.407.2559 • www.heartcareassoc.com

HeartCare
ASSOCIATES OF CONNECTICUT, LLC

Ricardo Cordido MD • Philip Fazzone MD • Samuel Hahn MD • Jack Hauser MD • Siegfried Kra MD • Marian Vulpe MD
Karin Augur PA • Alicia Burr APRN • Anna Rodonski PA • Douglas Stitz PA • Mark Whelan PA

Transthoracic Echocardiogram Report

Name:	McGee, Lola	**DOB:**	7/7/62
Ordering MD:	MV	**MRN:**	17191473
PCP:	Accomando	**Study Date:**	3/22/10
Indications:	Abn EKG, cardiomyopathy, dyspnea, RVOT VT	**Site/Tech:**	EH/SAW
Limitations:			
Ht/Wt/BSA/Sex:	5'9"/270/2.35/F		

M-Mode Measurements

LVEDD	4.5	(<5.6 cm)	AO	2.7	(<4.0 cm)
LVESD	3.6				
LV EF	53%	(>50%)	PWT	1.2	(<1.1 cm)
LA	2.8	(<4.0 cm)	IVS	1.0	(<1.1 cm)

2-D / Color Flow Doppler / Pulse Wave & Continuous Doppler Study

Left Ventricle, Interventricular Septum

Global size and LV systolic function are normal, without regional variation. There is mild LVH. LV diastolic function is normal.

Left Atrium, Interatrial Septum

There is mild extrinsic compression of the LA. The interatrial septum appears structurally normal, without color flow evidence of interatrial shunting.

Mitral Valve

Both mitral valve leaflets are mildly thickened. There is trace mitral regurgitation, without prolapse or stenosis.

Aortic Valve/Root

The aortic valve is trileaflet. There is no aortic insufficiency, stenosis, or aortic root dilatation.

Right Atrium, Right Ventricle, Tricuspid Valve, Pulmonic Valve

The right heart chambers are normal in size. RV systolic function is normal. The tricuspid and pulmonic valves are structurally normal. There is no tricuspid regurgitation, or pulmonic insufficiency or stenosis.

Pericardium, Extra-cardiac Structures

There is no pericardial effusion, intracardiac mass, thrombus, or vegetation.

Impression:

1. Normal LV and RV systolic function, without regional variation, and mild LVH.
2. Compared to the prior study from 1/25/10, LV systolic function is improved from 45%.

Marian Vulpe, M.D.

North Haven • East Haven • Hamden • Meriden • Wallingford • West Haven
Tel: 203.407.2500 • Fax: 203.407.2559 • www.heartcareassoc.com

HeartCare
ASSOCIATES OF CONNECTICUT, LLC

ICAEL

Ricardo Cordido MD • Philip Fazzone MD • Samuel Hahn MD • Jack Hauser MD • Siegfried Kra MD • Marian Vulpe MD
Karin Augur PA • Alicia Burr APRN • Anna Rodonski PA • Douglas Stitz PA • Mark Whelan PA

Transthoracic Echocardiogram Report

Name:	McGee, Lola	**DOB:**	7/7/62
Ordering MD:	MV	**MRN:**	17191473
PCP:	Accomando	**Study Date:**	1/25/10
Indications:	Abn EKG, CP, dyspnea, edema, hyperlipidemia	**Site/Tech:**	EH/SAW
Limitations:			
Ht/Wt/BSA/Sex:	5'9"/260/2.31/F		

M-Mode Measurements

LVEDD	4.4	(<5.6 cm)	AO	2.9	(<4.0 cm)
LVESD	3.4				
LV EF	45%	(>50%)	PWT	1.2	(<1.1 cm)
LA	2.7	(<4.0 cm)	IVS	1.1	(<1.1 cm)

2-D / Color Flow Doppler / Pulse Wave & Continuous Doppler Study

Left Ventricle, Interventricular Septum

The LV is normal in size. There is mild global LV systolic dysfunction, without regional variation. There is mild LVH and mild LV diastolic dysfunction due to impaired relaxation.

Left Atrium, Interatrial Septum

The LA is mildly dilated (2-D), with extrinsic compression of the LA, possibly by the descending thoracic aorta. The interatrial septum appears structurally normal, without color flow evidence of interatrial shunting.

Mitral Valve

Both mitral valve leaflets are mildly thickened. There is trace mitral regurgitation, without prolapse or stenosis.

Aortic Valve/Root

The aortic valve is trileaflet. There is no aortic insufficiency, stenosis, or aortic root dilatation.

Right Atrium, Right Ventricle, Tricuspid Valve, Pulmonic Valve

The right heart chambers are normal in size. RV systolic function is normal. The tricuspid and pulmonic valves are structurally normal. There is trace tricuspid regurgitation, without pulmonic insufficiency or stenosis.

Pericardium, Extra-cardiac Structures

There is no pericardial effusion, intracardiac mass, thrombus, or vegetation. The rhythm is sinus, with frequent PVCs.

Impression:

1. Normal LV size, mild LV systolic function, without regional variation, mild LVH, mild LV diastolic dysfunction, and mild LA dilation. Normal RV size and systolic function.
2. Extrinsic compression of the LA. Advanced imaging (chest CT) suggested if clinically indicated.
3. Sinus rhythm with frequent ventricular ectopic activity.

Marian Vulpe, M.D.

North Haven • East Haven • Hamden • Meriden • Wallingford • West Haven
Tel: 203.407.2500 • Fax: 203.407.2559 • www.heartcareassoc.com

HEARTCARE ASSOCIATES, LLC
CARDIOLOGY

PROGRESS NOTES

LAST NAME: McGee FIRST NAME: Lola

DOB: 7/7/62 DRUG ALLERGIES: NKDA.

DATE OF VISIT: 3/22/10 PCP: Accomando.

REASON FOR VISIT: 3 wk fu. / CCMO

AGE: 47 (MD/MA) MV/CM LOCATION: HAM CIRC CAM EH BV MER

BP: 130/90 (L) R Wt: 270 Ht: 5'9" Last INR: BMI:

Recent ER/Hospital Visits (Date and reason): (+) ablation HSP

MEDS:

Simvastatin 10 mg qd
HCTZ 12.5 mg qd
Lyrica
Topiramate 50 mg BID
Tramadol
Clonazepam

CARDIAC CONCERNS:

Review of Systems

Fever, chills, weakness, fatigue
Dizziness, Syncope, Pre-syncope
Blurred vision, double vision
Palpitations, Jaw pain, Throat Pain
Shortness of Breath, Chest pain
Abdominal Pain, Flank Pain
Swelling, Pain in extremities

MIBI 1/10 – NL perf EF 41%.

3/2 24° ... BP ... 57/160/90

Pt c/o CP due to ablation

( ) Diabetes
( ) Tobacco
(✓) Hyperlipidemia
( ) Hypertension
( ) Previous MI
( ) FHHD
( ) Rheumatic Heart Disease

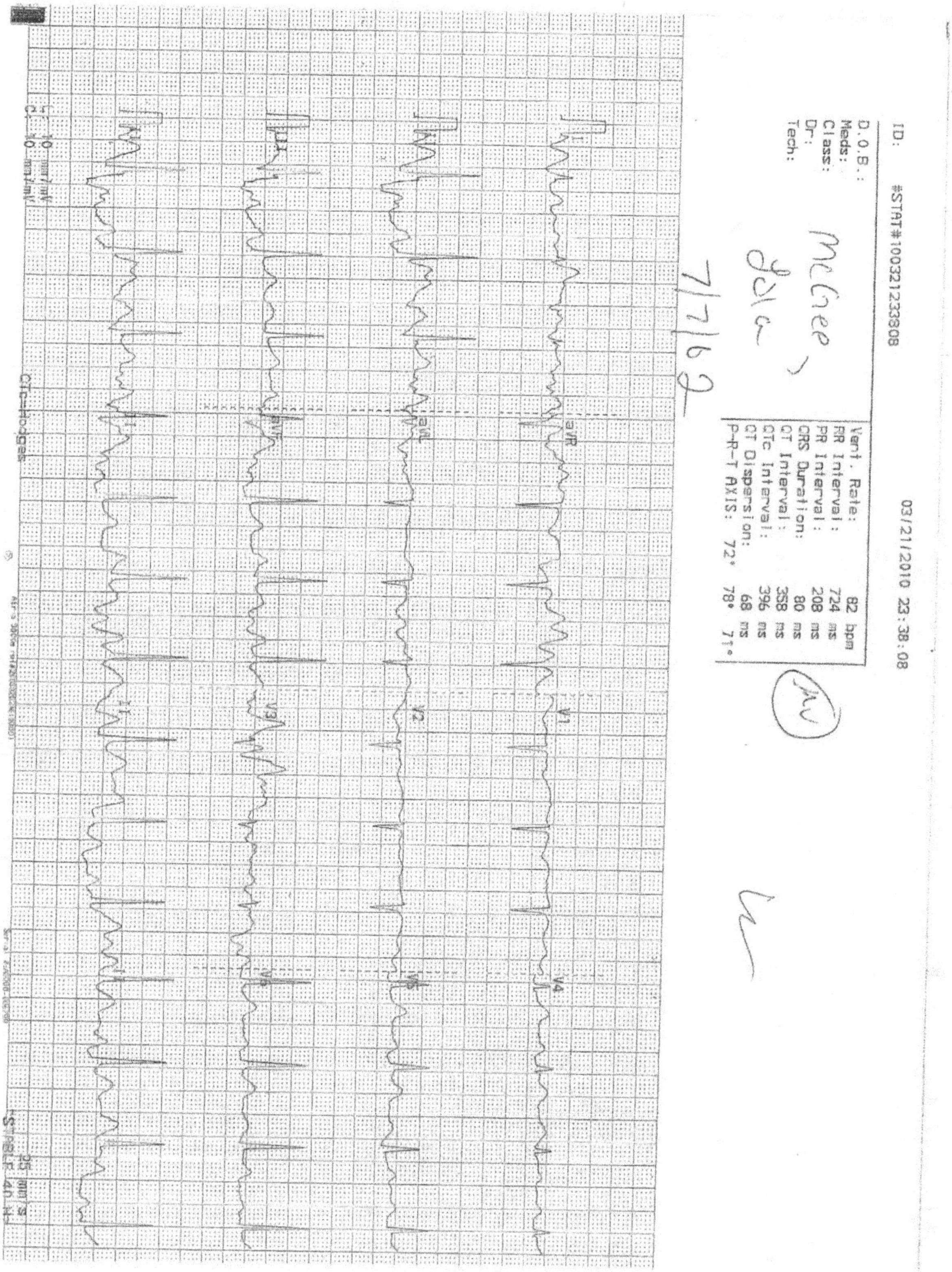
ID: #STAT#100321233808
03/21/2010 23:38:08
D.O.B.:
Meds:
Class:
Dr:
Tech:
Vent. Rate: 82 bpm
RR Interval: 724 ms
PR Interval: 208 ms
QRS Duration: 80 ms
QT Interval: 358 ms
QTc Interval: 396 ms
QT Dispersion: 68 ms
P-R-T AXIS: 72° 78° 71°
aVR
aVL
aVF
V1
V2
V3
V4
V5
V6
QTc-Hodges

Arrhythmia Center of Connecticut, P.C.
MARK H. SCHOENFELD, M.D., F.A.C.C. MARK L. BLITZER, M.D., F.A.C.C.
NIMROD LAVI, M.D.

Orchard Medical Center
330 Orchard Street • Suite 210
New Haven, CT 06511
Tel (203) 867-5400
Fax (203) 867-5401

March 25, 2010
(DOS February 25, 2010)

Marian Vulpe, M.D.
2200 Whitney Avenue
Hamden, CT 06518

Re: Lola MCGEE

Dear Marian:

I wanted to update you on Lola McGee who underwent an EP study and ablation today. As you know, she is a 47 year old with a 2½ year history of high-grade unifocal PVCs. These have failed suppression attempts with both beta and calcium channel blockers. She recently developed mild cardiomyopathy with an EF estimated between 41-45% by MIBI and echo. There is no evidence of any underlying coronary artery disease. She feels the palpitations multiple times each day and finds them distressing. She has had several episodes of near syncope, and they have been correlated with runs of nonsustained VT. Given her significant symptoms, as well as the larger concern that PVCs may be contributing to the cardiomyopathy, she was brought in for an EP study and RF ablation.

The PVCs mapped to an identical site that would be predicted by her surface EKG, i.e., high in the RV outflow tract approximately 1 cm under the pulmonary valve, along the free wall. She was in persistent bigeminy prior to the ablation. The first burn successfully obliterated all of the PVCs. I then placed six additional lesions surrounding the successful site. We observed her approximately 45 additional minutes and pulsed her several times with isuprel without return of any PVCs. I finished the case relatively late in the day and kept her overnight. She had no PVCs overnight either. We discharged her home the following day in good condition, off both beta and calcium channel blockers. With your permission, I would check a Holter monitor in several weeks, and then ask you to check an echo in a month or two to see if her LV function has improved. Certainly, I am hopeful that it will.

Thank you very much for allowing me to participate in her care.

Sincerely,

Mark L. Blitzer, M.D.

MLB/la

cc: Angelo Accomando, M.D.
Family Practice & Internal Medicine
205 Main Street
East Haven, CT 06512

Arrhythmia Center of Connecticut, P.C.
MARK H. SCHOENFELD, M.D., F.A.C.C. MARK L. BLITZER, M.D., F.A.C.C.
NIMROD LAVI, M.D.

Orchard Medical Center
330 Orchard Street • Suite 210
New Haven, CT 06511
Tel (203) 867-5400
Fax (203) 867-5401

March 10, 2010

Marian Vulpe, M.D.
Heart Care Associates
2200 Whitney Avenue
Suite 180
Hamden, CT 06518

Re: Lola MCGEE

Dear Marian:

I had the pleasure of meeting with Lola McGee 2 weeks after her RVOT VT ablation. As you know, Ms. McGee is a lovely 47-year-old. She has a 2 ½ year history of palpitations. This was managed by her Nevada cardiologists conservatively in light of her structurally normal heart. Nonetheless, she remained quite symptomatic including runs of VT. She had been refractory to attempts at suppression with verapamil and Coreg. Further, she has had a recent fall in her EF into the 40s. We thought this likely PVC mediated.

We brought her in for PVC mapping and RF ablation. It went beautifully. The PVCs mapped to the free wall of the outflow tract just under the pulmonary valve. The first ablation site completely rid her of all PVCs. She previously had been in a bigeminal pattern. I delivered additional lesions around the successful site.

She recuperated fine without PVCs overnight and has continued to thrive. She reports cessation of all palpitations. She feels her chest wall no longer "jumps funny". Her "wheezing" has gone away. As you know, she and her daughter are moving to Hollywood, California in 2 weeks. The weather in Connecticut did not agree with them.

Her medications include Motrin, Pristiq, Lyrica, Ultram, clonazepam, Zocor, Topamax and a "water pill".

On exam, she looked comfortable. Her blood pressure was 118/68. Her heart rate was 80. Her weight was up several pounds to 272 pounds. HEENT exam revealed no thyromegaly or lymphadenopathy. Her lungs were clear. Her cardiac exam revealed an irregular pulse, normal S1, S2 without S3 gallop. She had no significant murmur. She had no JVD. Her carotids were 2+ with brisk upstrokes and no bruits. Her abdomen was non-tender without organomegaly. Extremities showed no edema.

EKG demonstrated sinus at 80. She had a normal PR, narrow QRS and normal corrected QT interval. There were no PVCs.

She had a Holter monitor done in anticipation of today's visit. It looked beautifully improved with 100 PVCs throughout the day. The majority occurred between 9AM and 10AM, although she does not recall anything particular going on at that point. The PVCs have several different morphologies. This represents almost 500-fold improvement to her prior PVC density than when she was in bigeminy much of the day.

Overall, I congratulated her on her success. The next step would be to check an echo to see if her LV function has normalized now that the PVC

03/19/2010 FRI 16:07 FAX 203 8675401 001/001

ARRHYTHMIA CENTER OF CONNECTICUT, PC
330 ORCHARD STREET, SUITE 210
NEW HAVEN, CONNECTICUT 06511
203-867-5400

Patient Information

Name :MCGEE, LOLA
DOB :07/07/1962
Address :43 Victor Street
:East Haven, CT
Indications :s/p ablation, VEA
:
Medication :no cardiac meds.
:

ID :008510
Age :47 Sex :F
Height : Weight :
Physician :Mark L Blitzer MD

Holter Report Summary

Report Number : 008510
Order No. :
Report Date : 03/05/2010
Test Date : 03/02/2010

Starting Time : 11:56
Hours Analyzed : 24:16
Artifact : 0:03:02
Analysis Mode : CONFIRM

Total Beats : 132082
Unknown Beats : 0
Others : 0

Rate Dependent Events

Heart Rates: Min	57 BPM at 14:16-1	Bradycardia Runs :	0	Pauses :	0
Max	160 BPM at 23:01-1	Longest :		Longest :	
Avg	90 BPM	Min Rate :			

Ventricular Events

Total Beats	112	Couplets	1
Forms	7	Triplets	0
		Bigeminy Runs	0
AIVR / IVR Runs	0		
Longest			
Min Rate			
V Tach Runs	0		
Longest			
Max Rate			
Max VE/Minute	19 beats at 09:22-2		
Max VE / Hour	68 beats 09:00-2 - 10:00-2		
Mean VE / Hour	4.6		
VE / 1000	0.8		

Supraventricular Events

Total Beats	0
Couplets	0
SVTach Runs	0
Longest	
Max Rate	
Max SVE/Minute	0
Max SVE / Hour	0
Mean SVE / Hour	0.0
SVE / 1000	0.0

Impressions and Findings

Basic rhythm is sinus with sinus tachycardia 57- 160 BPM; average heart rate 90 BPM. 112 ventricular ectopics, including 1 ventricular couplet; some are interpolated.

Ectopy is asymptomatic. Patient reports a stinging in her back (123 BPM), pain (109 BPM), felt my heart (106 BPM).

Geraldine A Fallon
Holter Technologist
INTERPRETATION: Sinus rhythm with average heart rate 90 BPM. PVCs, mostly between 9 and 10 am, of 7 different morphologies. Ectopy is asymptomatic.

Mark L Blitzer MD

Signed ________ Date 3/18/10

Mon Mar 08 2010 10:56:01

DEL MAR 25268-401 A1 Page 1 / 2

M. Vulpe, M.D.
March 10, 2010
Page 2

Re: Lola MCGEE

density is near nil. I think she is scheduled next week just prior to her planned move to California.

Hopefully she will continue to thrive. Thank you for sending along this interesting case.

Sincerely yours,

Mark L. Blitzer, M.D.

MLB/dmp
cc: Angelo Accomando, M.D.
205 Main Street
East Haven, CT 06512

05/14/2010 16:28 562--531-4400 FEDEX OFFICE 0583 PAGE 99

JAN-29-2002 01:39P FROM: TO:17022600876 P:2/2

American Optometric Association

DR. SCHEFFEL'S EYE CARE CENTER

Craig Scheffel, O.D. & Associates

17 Lakewood Center Mall

Lakewood, CA 90712

Telephone: (562) 633-6443

Rx FOR Lola McGee DATE 9/14/07

ADDRESS

		SPHERICAL	CYLINDRICAL	AXIS	PRISM	BASE
DISTANCE	O.D.	-0.50	-3.25	178		
	O.S.	-0.50	-3.25	170		
ADD	O.D.		ADDITIONAL SPECIFICATIONS			
	O.S.					

EXPIRATION DATE [illegible]

This prescription expires on the date shown above, and is not to be duplicated after this date

Rx EXPIRED

______________________ O.D.

~~[illegible]~~ = 8/25/08

Before

05/14/2010 16:28 562--531-4400 FEDEX OFFICE 0583 PAGE 99

DR. CONRAD L. ...CHNER III, O.D.

DR. Vorapat Thu..yalaksal, O.D.

1450 Horizon Ridge Parkway, # B313

Name: Lola McGee P.D. 1 Exam Date: 25 Sept 08

RX		SPHERICAL	CYLINDRICAL	AXIS	PRISM	BASE
DISTANCE Rx	OD	-2.50	-3.00	130		
	OS	-0.75	-2.50	152		
NEAR Rx	OD	+1.50				
	OS					

~~Before~~ 8/25/08

After

Telephone: (562) 904-1969

DEA # AB2756142
Lic. # G52712

BRIAN M. BROWN, M.D.

Eye Physician & Surgeon

10933 Lakewood Blvd. Downey, California 90241

PATIENT'S NAME: Lola McGee DATE: 11/17/2010

ADDRESS:

℞

~~ZYMAR® 0.3%: 5ml~~ EXP 11/17/2011

~~1 drop QID X 1 week to~~

~~start 1 day prior to surgery.~~

-0.50 -3.25 X180

-0.50 -2.00 X145

ADD +1.75

Refill - 1 - 2 - 3 - 4 - PRN

☐ Do Not Substitute

☐ Spanish

B-035657-012309

M.D.

20ncr

LAST Check-up

Brian M. Brown, M.D.
Eye Physician & Surgeon
10933 Lakewood Blvd.
Downey, CA 90241
(562) 904-1989

William Hornstein, M.D.
1045 Atlantic Avenue, Suite 719
Long Beach, CA 90813
Fax #: (562) 437-1054

Re: Lola McGil
DOB: 07/07/1962

DOE: November 17, 2010

Dear Dr. Hornstein:

Thank you very much for referring the above patient for evaluation of possible amaurosis fugax. The patient reported that she woke up one morning and was not able to see from the right eye approximately two weeks ago. The patient reported she gets blurry and double vision at times monocular and at times binocular. She stated that she had a peripheral sensory neuropathy.

OBJECTIVE: Significant ocular examination findings were a best corrected visual acuity of 20/30 in both eyes. There was no afferent pupillary defect. At distance and near correction, the patient was orthophoric. Dilated fundus examination revealed normal disc, macula and blood vessels.

IMPRESSION AND PLAN: History of transient loss of vision. I found no abnormal ophthalmic findings on today's examination. I did request an OCT of the optic nerve and her visual field to rule out optic nerve disease. As you know, episodes of transient loss of vision may be caused by thrombus or emboli and carotid and cardiac noninvasives are recommended. I requested the patient follow up with me in two weeks.

Again, thank you very much for allowing me to participate in the care of your patients.

Sincerely,

Electronically signed and authenticated by Brian M. Brown, M.D. @ 11/20/2010 11:54:00 AM

Brian M. Brown, M.D.

BB/cgm

Faxed **McGil,Lola-1119x184328-Brown** @ 11/24/2010 6:47:51 PM

WILLIAM HORNSTEIN, M.D., INC.
BAUER PROFESSIONAL BUILDING
1045 ATLANTIC AVE., SUITE 719, LONG BEACH, CA 90813
PHONE: (562) 591-1324 • Fax: (562) 437-1054

NAME LOLA McGEE DATE 12/16/10

℞ ADDRESS 1236 W. 22nd St. LA, CA 90007 CALIF.

PAIN MANAGEMENT, - 1040 ELM ST #100
DEAR DR BERNADETT OR DOCHERTY
THIS PT. WITH POLYNEUROPATHY
& MULTIPLE PARESTHESIAS/
DYSESTHESIAS c̄ PERSISTENT PAIN.
PLEASE EVALUATE & TREAT
FOR PAIN SYMPTOMS.
THANKS— (562) 901-2453

REP _____ TIMES
NE REP. ☐
DEA: AH8143074
ST. LIC.: G036575 _____ M.D.

Social Security Disability Approval May 17, 2011.

SOCIAL SECURITY ADMINISTRATION

Refer To:

Office of Disability Adjudication and Review
SSA ODAR Hearing Ofc
Suite 1200
606 South Olive Street
Los Angeles, CA 90014-9818

Date: May 17, 2011

Lola B. Mc Gee
1236 W. 22nd Str.
Apt. 1
Los Angeles, CA 90007

Notice of Decision – Fully Favorable

I carefully reviewed the facts of your case and made the enclosed fully favorable decision. Please read this notice and my decision.

Another office will process my decision. That office may ask you for more information. If you do not hear anything within 60 days of the date of this notice, please contact your local office. The contact information for your local office is at the end of this notice.

If You Disagree With My Decision

If you disagree with my decision, you may file an appeal with the Appeals Council.

How To File An Appeal

To file an appeal you or your representative must ask in writing that the Appeals Council review my decision. You may use our Request for Review form (HA-520) or write a letter. The form is available at www.socialsecurity.gov. Please put the Social Security number shown above on any appeal you file. If you need help, you may file in person at any Social Security or hearing office.

Please send your request to:

Appeals Council
Office of Disability Adjudication and Review
5107 Leesburg Pike
Falls Church, VA 22041-3255

Time Limit To File An Appeal

You must file your written appeal **within 60 days** of the date you get this notice. The Appeals Council assumes you got this notice 5 days after the date of the notice unless you show you did not get it within the 5-day period.

The Appeals Council will dismiss a late request unless you show you had a good reason for not

Form HA-L76 (03-2010)

See Next Page

Lola B. Mc Gee

If you have any other questions, please call, write, or visit any Social Security office. Please have this notice and decision with you. The telephone number of the local office that serves your area is (866)964-7401. Its address is:

Social Security
1115 W Adams Blvd
University Village
Los Angeles, CA 90007-9821

David J Agatstein
Administrative Law Judge

Enclosures:
Form HA-L15 (Fee Agreement Approval)
Decision Rationale

cc: Charles E. Binder
Binder & Binder
4000 Metropolitan Dr.
Suite 350
Orange, CA 92868

Form HA-L76 (03-2010)

SOCIAL SECURITY ADMINISTRATION
Office of Disability Adjudication and Review

DECISION

IN THE CASE OF	**CLAIM FOR**
Lola B. Mc Gee (Claimant)	Period of Disability and Disability Insurance Benefits
(Wage Earner)	(Social Security Number)

JURISDICTION AND PROCEDURAL HISTORY

This case is before the undersigned on a request for hearing dated May 18, 2010 (20 CFR 404.929 *et seq.*). The claimant appeared and testified at a hearing held on May 17, 2011, in Los Angeles, CA. Also appearing and testifying were Harvey L Alpern, M.D. and David Peterson, Ph.D., impartial medical experts, and Sandra Schneider, an impartial vocational expert. The claimant is represented by Charles E. Binder, an attorney.

The claimant is alleging disability since August 25, 2008.

ISSUES

The issue is whether the claimant is disabled under sections 216(i) and 223(d) of the Social Security Act. Disability is defined as the inability to engage in any substantial gainful activity by reason of any medically determinable physical or mental impairment or combination of impairments that can be expected to result in death or that has lasted or can be expected to last for a continuous period of not less than 12 months.

There is an additional issue whether the insured status requirements of sections 216(i) and 223 of the Social Security Act are met. The claimant's earnings record shows that the claimant has acquired sufficient quarters of coverage to remain insured through December 31, 2014. Thus, the claimant must establish disability on or before that date in order to be entitled to a period of disability and disability insurance benefits.

After careful review of the entire record, the undersigned finds that the claimant has been disabled from August 25, 2008, through the date of this decision. The undersigned also finds that the insured status requirements of the Social Security Act were met as of the date disability is established.

APPLICABLE LAW

Under the authority of the Social Security Act, the Social Security Administration has established a five-step sequential evaluation process for determining whether an individual is

See Next Page

Social Security Administration is responsible for providing evidence that demonstrates that other work exists in significant numbers in the national economy that the claimant can do, given the residual functional capacity, age, education, and work experience (20 CFR 404.1512(g) and 404.1560(c)).

FINDINGS OF FACT AND CONCLUSIONS OF LAW

After careful consideration of the entire record, the undersigned makes the following findings:

1. **The claimant's date last insured is December 31, 2014.**

2. **The claimant has not engaged in substantial gainful activity since August 25, 2008, the alleged onset date (20 CFR 404.1520(b) and 404.1571 *et seq.*).**

3. **The claimant has the following severe impairments: peripheral neuropathy, anxiety and depression (20 CFR 404.1520(c)).**

4. **The severity of the claimant's impairments meets the criteria of section 12.04 of 20 CFR Part 404, Subpart P, Appendix 1 (20 CFR 404.1520(d) and 404.1525).**

In making this finding, the undersigned considered all symptoms and the extent to which these symptoms can reasonably be accepted as consistent with the objective medical evidence and other evidence, based on the requirements of 20 CFR 404.1529 and SSRs 96-4p and 96-7p. The undersigned has also considered opinion evidence in accordance with the requirements of 20 CFR 404.1527 and SSRs 96-2p, 96-6p and 06-3p.

The claimant's impairments meet the criteria of section 12.04. The "paragraph A" criteria are satisfied because the claimant has major depression and anxiety. The "paragraph B" criteria are satisfied because the claimant's impairments cause marked restriction in activities of daily living, marked difficulties in maintaining social functioning, marked difficulties in maintaining concentration, persistence or pace, and four or more episodes of decompensation, each of extended duration.

The medical experts so testified.

After considering the evidence of record, the undersigned finds that the claimant's medically determinable impairments could reasonably be expected to produce the alleged symptoms, and that the claimant's statements concerning the intensity, persistence and limiting effects of these symptoms are generally credible.

The State agency medical consultant's physical assessment and psychological consultant's mental assessment are given little weight because other medical opinions are more consistent with the record as a whole and evidence received at the hearing level shows that the claimant is more limited than determined by the State agency consultants.

See Next Page

SOCIAL SECURITY ADMINISTRATION
Office of Disability Adjudication and Review

ORDER OF ADMINISTRATIVE LAW JUDGE

IN THE CASE OF	**CLAIM FOR**
Lola B. Mc Gee (Claimant)	Period of Disability and Disability Insurance Benefits
(Wage Earner)	(Social Security Number)

I approve the fee agreement between the claimant and her representative subject to the condition that the claim results in past-due benefits. My determination is limited to whether the fee agreement meets the statutory conditions for approval and is not otherwise excepted. I neither approve nor disapprove any other aspect of the agreement.

YOU MAY REQUEST A REVIEW OF THIS ORDER AS INDICATED BELOW

Fee Agreement Approval: You may ask us to review the approval of the fee agreement. If so, write us within 15 days from the day you get this order. Tell us that you disagree with the approval of the agreement and give your reasons. Your representative also has 15 days to write us if he or she does not agree with the approval of the fee agreement. Send your request to this address:

William J. King, Jr.
Regional Chief Administrative Law Judge
SSA ODAR Regional Ofc
5th Floor
555 Battery St
San Francisco, CA 94111-2305

Fee Agreement Amount: You may also ask for a review of the amount of the fee due to the representative under this approved fee agreement. If so, please write directly to me as the deciding Administrative Law Judge within 15 days of the day you are notified of the amount of the fee due to the representative. Your representative also has 15 days to write me if he/she does not agree with the fee amount under the approved agreement.

You should include the social security number(s) shown on this order on any papers that you send us.

/s/ David J Agatstein
David J Agatstein
Administrative Law Judge

May 17, 2011
Date

Form HA-L15 (03-2007)

DESERT RADIOLOGISTS

2020 Palomino Lane #100, Las Vegas, NV 89106, (702) 759-8600
3920 S. Eastern Ave. #100, Las Vegas, NV 89119, (702) 794-2100
7200 Cathedral Rock Dr. #230, Las Vegas, NV 89128, (702) 759-4300
60 N. Pecos Rd., Henderson, NV 89074, (702) 759-4400
2811 W. Horizon Ridge Pkwy., Henderson, NV 89052, (702) 759-4500

MEDICAL IMAGING REPORT

Report Status: FINAL

Patient Name: **MCGEE, LOLA** DOB: **7/7/62** Age: 46Y Sex: F
MRN: **652459** Service Location:
Account Number: 000016002

Ordering Physician: SANTOS YU, MD
100 N GREEN VALLEY PKWY STE 215
HENDERSON, NV 89074

Accession Number: 0035632 Order Number: 000033782
Service Date/Time: 1/13/2009 3:49PM
Study Description: **000463 XR L SPINE 4 OR MORE VW**

ORIGINAL
ASHOK GUPTA, MD 1/14/09 7:07 am
LUMBAR SPINE: 1/13/2009 4:34 PM

CLINICAL HISTORY: Low back pain

TECHNIQUE: Five views of the lumbar spine were obtained.

COMPARISON: None.

FINDINGS: Five routine views of the lumbar spine demonstrate no fracture or vertebral body height loss. There is no destructive osseous process. Normal anatomic alignment is preserved. There is no spondylolisthesis. Mild endplate osteophyte formation is seen throughout the lumbar spine. There is mild disk height loss at the L5 -- S1 level.
Oblique projections demonstrate normal facet alignment and no spondylolysis. There is no gross evidence of bony neural foraminal alteration.

IMPRESSION:

1. No fracture or significant malalignment.
2. Mild multi-level degenerative change. If there are radicular or myelopathic symptoms, consider further evaluation with MRI.

CONFIDENTIALITY NOTICE

This message is intended for the use of the person or entity to which it is addressed and may contain information that is privileged and confidential, the disclosure or re-disclosure of which is governed by applicable law. If the reader of this message is not the intended recipient or the employee or agent responsible to deliver it to the intended recipient, you are hereby notified that any dissemination, distribution or copying of this information is STRICTLY PROHIBITED. If you have received this message by error, please notify us immediately by phone and return the original message to us by mail. Thank you.

Date Printed: 2/11/2009 Page 1 of 2 Recipient:

Patient Name:	**MCGEE, LOLA**	DOB: **7/7/62**	Age: 46Y	Sex: F
MRN:	**652459**	Service Location:		
		Account Number: 000016002		

Original By: ASHOK GUPTA, MD 1/14/09 7:07 am

CC Physicians:

Radiologist: ASHOK GUPTA, MD
Date Signed: 1/14/09 7:07

CONFIDENTIALITY NOTICE

This message is intended for the use of the person or entity to which it is addressed and may contain information that is privileged and confidential, the disclosure or re-disclosure of which is governed by applicable law. If the reader of this message is not the intended recipient or the employee or agent responsible to deliver it to the intended recipient, you are hereby notified that any dissemination, distribution or copying of this information is STRICTLY PROHIBITED. If you have received this message by error, please notify us immediately by phone and return the original message to us by mail. Thank you.

Date Printed: 2/11/2009 Page 2 of 2 Recipient:

DR
DESERT RADIOLOGISTS

2020 Palomino Lane #100, Las Vegas, NV 89106, (702) 759-8600
3920 S. Eastern Ave. #100, Las Vegas, NV 89119, (702) 794-2100
7200 Cathedral Rock Dr. #230, Las Vegas, NV 89128, (702) 759-4300
60 N. Pecos Rd., Henderson, NV 89074, (702) 759-4400
2811 W. Horizon Ridge Pkwy., Henderson, NV 89052, (702) 759-4500

MEDICAL IMAGING REPORT

Report Status: FINAL

Patient Name: **MCGEE, LOLA**
MRN: **652459**

DOB: **7/7/62** Age: 46Y Sex: F
Service Location: XR HORIZON
Account Number: 000016002

Ordering Physician: SANTOS YU, MD
100 N GREEN VALLEY PKWY STE 215
HENDERSON, NV 89074

Accession Number: 0035628
Order Number: 000033781
Service Date/Time: 1/13/2009 3:49PM
Study Description: **000429 XR C SPINE ROUTINE 5 VW**

ORIGINAL
ASHOK GUPTA, MD 1/14/09 7:06 am
CERVICAL SPINE: 1/13/2009 4:34 PM
CLINICAL HISTORY: Pain.
TECHNIQUE: AP, lateral, odontoid, and bilateral oblique projections of the cervical spine were obtained.
COMPARISON: None.
FINDINGS:
There is no fracture or vertebral body height loss. Normal anatomic alignment is maintained. The minimal endplate osteophyte formation is seen at the C4 through C6 levels. There is no evidence of bony injury. There is no evidence of spondylosis or significant congenital anomalies. The adjacent soft tissue structures are normal. No osseous neuroforaminal stenosis.

IMPRESSION:
Mild degenerative changes are seen.

Original By: ASHOK GUPTA, MD 1/14/09 7:06 am
CC Physicians:

Radiologist: ASHOK GUPTA, MD
Date Signed: 1/14/09 7:06

CONFIDENTIALITY NOTICE

This message is intended for the use of the person or entity to which it is addressed and may contain information that is privileged and confidential, the disclosure or re-disclosure of which is governed by applicable law. If the reader of this message is not the intended recipient or the employee or agent responsible to deliver it to the intended recipient, you are hereby notified that any dissemination, distribution or copying of this information is STRICTLY PROHIBITED. If you have received this message by error, please notify us immediately by phone and return the original message to us by mail. Thank you.

Date Printed: 2/11/2009 Page 1 of 1 Recipient:

DR
DESERT RADIOLOGISTS

2020 Palomino Lane #100, Las Vegas, NV 89106, (702) 759-8600
3920 S. Eastern Ave. #100, Las Vegas, NV 89119, (702) 794-2100
7200 Cathedral Rock Dr. #230, Las Vegas, NV 89128, (702) 759-4300
60 N. Pecos Rd., Henderson, NV 89074, (702) 759-4400
2811 W. Horizon Ridge Pkwy., Henderson, NV 89052, (702) 759-4500

MEDICAL IMAGING REPORT

Report Status: FINAL

Patient Name:	**MCGEE, LOLA**	DOB: **7/7/62** Age: 46Y Sex: F	
MRN:	**652459**	Service Location:	MR HORIZON
		Account Number:	000016002

Ordering Physician: JIMMY NOVERO, MD
100 N GREEN VALLEY PKWY STE 215
HENDERSON, NV 89074

Accession Number: 0041994 Order Number: 000040895
Service Date/Time: 1/26/2009 7:30AM
Study Description: **000213 MR LUMBAR WO CONTRAST**

ORIGINAL
KEIR HALES, MD 1/26/09 9:40 am
CLINICAL INDICATION: Low back pain. Patient presents with left leg pain and radiculopathy.

TECHNIQUE: Noncontrast MRI of the lumbar spine.

COMPARISON: Plain film x-rays of the lumbar spine dated January 13, 2009.

FINDINGS: Noncontrast MRI of the lumbar spine demonstrates appropriate termination of the spinal cord at T12. There is no abnormal signal within the cord. Vertebral bodies are in near anatomic alignment. There is disk hydration at L3 -- 4, L4 -- 5 and L5 -- S1. Marrow signal is within normal limits.

Evaluation of the axial images demonstrates a moderate disk bulge at L3 -- 4. This measures 4 mm and narrows the spinal canal to 10 mm. In addition, there is 4 mm of ligamentum flavum hypertrophy.

At L4 -- 5, there is a 4-mm disk bulge which narrows the spinal canal to 8 mm. In addition, there is 5 mm of ligamentum flavum hypertrophy.

At L5 -- S1, there is a 4-mm disk bulge which narrows the spinal canal to 13 mm.

The sacroiliac joints are intact.

IMPRESSION: Mild disk bulges are present at L3 -- 4, and 4 L4 -- 5 and L5 -- S1 as outlined above. These are most prominent at L3 -- 4. Critical stenosis is not felt to be present.

CONFIDENTIALITY NOTICE

This message is intended for the use of the person or entity to which it is addressed and may contain information that is privileged and confidential, the disclosure or re-disclosure of which is governed by applicable law. If the reader of this message is not the intended recipient or the employee or agent responsible to deliver it to the intended recipient, you are hereby notified that any dissemination, distribution or copying of this information is STRICTLY PROHIBITED. If you have received this message by error, please notify us immediately by phone and return the original message to us by mail. Thank you

Date Printed: 2/11/2009 Page 1 of 2 Recipient:

Patient Name:	**MCGEE, LOLA**	DOB: **7/7/62** Age: 46Y Sex: F	
MRN:	**652459**	Service Location:	MR HORIZON
		Account Number:	000016002

Original By: KEIR HALES, MD 1/26/09 9:40 am

CC Physicians:

Radiologist: KEIR HALES, MD

Date Signed: 1/26/09 9:40

CONFIDENTIALITY NOTICE

This message is intended for the use of the person or entity to which it is addressed and may contain information that is privileged and confidential, the disclosure or re-disclosure of which is governed by applicable law. If the reader of this message is not the intended recipient or the employee or agent responsible to deliver it to the intended recipient, you are hereby notified that any dissemination, distribution or copying of this information is STRICTLY PROHIBITED. If you have received this message by error, please notify us immediately by phone and return the original message to us by mail. Thank you.

23-JUN-2010 16:05 Gold-Fax Message Page 2/3

44A-062310
MRI BRAIN W/WO

23-Jun-2010
O/P
MAGNETIC RESONANCE IMA

ST. MARY MEDICAL CENTER
1050 Linden Avenue
Long Beach, CA 90813

*** FINAL COPY ***

MRI BRAIN WITHOUT/WITH CONTRAST: 6/23/10

History: Multiple motor sensory deficits in all extremities; rule out demyelinating disease, mass lesions or ischemic change.

Procedure:

MR images of the brain were obtained using sagittal and coronal T1 weighted sequences. Axial T2 weighted and FLAIR sequences were obtained. Diffusion weighted images were also obtained. Following intravenous injection of the standard amount of Omniscan, images were also repeated in the axial and coronal projections.

Findings:

Sagittal T1 weighted images show no acute hemorrhage. T2 and FLAIR images show mild cortical atrophy consitent with the patient's age. There is a focal area of increased signal in the deep white matter in the right frontal region best seen on FLAIR images measuring 3 mm in diameter. There is some increased signal adjacent to the occipitals horns bilaterally. There is also a focal area of increased signal seen on FLAIR images in the left pons measuring approximately 2.5 mm in diameter. Sagittal FLAIR images through the corpus callosum do not show perpendicular lesions. Post contrast images show no enhancing lesions. No vascular malformation or aneurysm is identified. The cerebellopontine angle appears normal. Diffusion weighted imaging shows no evidence of acute infarct.

IMPRESSION: There are focal areas of increased signal in the right frontal region and left pons consistent with deep white matter degenerative change, deep white matter inflammatory change or microinfarcts.

There is also some mildly increased signal adjacent to the occipital horns bilaterally. The findings appear less prominent on MRI than the reported clinical findings. In addition, sagittal images of the corpus callosum do not show lesions suspicious for MS.

Page 1

MCGEE,LOLA BONITTA
534872

WILLIAM HORNSTEIN MD
1045 ATLANTIC AVENUE #719
LONG BEACH CA 90813

FEMALE 47
07-Jul-1962
O/P

23-Jun-201015:25

JUN-2010 16:05 Gold-Fax Message Page 3/3

44A-062310
MRI BRAIN W/WO

ST. MARY MEDICAL CENTER
1050 Linden Avenue
Long Beach, CA 90813

23-Jun-2010
O/P
MAGNETIC RESONANCE IMA

*** FINAL COPY ***

signed: GREGORY T. VANLEY, M.D.

GV/sl

Page 2

MCGEE,LOLA BONITTA
534872

FEMALE 47
07-Jul-1962
O/P

23-Jun-201015:25

WILLIAM HORNSTEIN MD
1045 ATLANTIC AVENUE #719
LONG BEACH CA 90813

-2010 08:00 Gold-Fax Message Page 3/5

55B-121010
MRA NECK W/CONT

13-Dec-2010
O/P
MAGNETIC RESONANCE IMA

ST. MARY MEDICAL CENTER
1050 Linden Avenue
Long Beach, CA 90813

*** FINAL COPY ***

MRA NECK: 12/10/10

History: Visual changes, amaurosis fugax.

Procedure:

MR angiogram of the neck was obtained using axial 3-D inflow MIP technique following the intravenous injection of the standard amount of Omniscan.

Findings:

The origin of common carotid artery appears normal bilaterally as do the left subclavian artery and right subclavian artery and innominate artery. The carotid bifurcation appears normal bilaterally. The left internal carotid artery shows some kinking or artifact approximately 3.7 cm from its origin. The area of questionable focal narrowing seen on the MRA head in the left distal internal carotid artery at the level of the foramen lacerum appears normal on this exam which would confirm artifact as the cause of this abnormality on the MRA brain.

The right internal carotid artery appears normal.

The vertebral arteries are well visualized and appear normal. The basilar artery appears normal. The visualized intracranial circulation also appears normal.

IMPRESSION: The examination is within normal limits.

signed: GREGORY T. VANLEY, M.D.

GV/sl

MCGEE, LOLA BONITTA
5348772

FEMALE 48
07-Jul-1962
O/P

WILLIAM HORNSTEIN MD
1045 ATLANTIC AVENUE #719
LONG BEACH CA 90813

12-Dec-201010:43

ec-2010 08:00 **Gold-Fax Message** Page 4/5

55C-121010
US CAROTID DUPL

13-Dec-2010
O/P
ULTRASOUND

ST. MARY MEDICAL CENTER
1050 Linden Avenue
Long Beach, CA 90813

*** FINAL COPY ***

BILATERAL CAROTID DUPLEX ULTRASOUND WITH SPECTRAL ANALYSIS:
12/10/10

History: Visual changes, evaluate for carotid stenosis.

Procedure/Findings:

Bilateral carotid duplex imaging was performed. Examination included imaging of both common carotid and internal carotid arteries and external carotid arteries. Real-time high resolution images were performed in the sagittal and transverse planes. Duplex Doppler imaging was then obtained at all levels to measure peak velocities. Scanning was then attempted to image the vertebral arteries.

	PSV	EDV		PSV	EDV
RCCA PROX:	75.2	19.2	LCCA PROX:	93	32.0
RCCA DIS:	54.4	24.0	LCCA DIS:	62.4	27.2
RICA PROX:	44.8	24.0	LICA PROX:	45.8	26.0
RICA DIS:	72.0	46.4	LICA DIS:	62.6	33.6
RECA:	40.0	12.8	LECA:	61.1	21.4
RT VERTEBRAL:	35.2	17.6	LT VERTEBRAL:	38.2	18.3
Antegrade:	X		Antegrade:	X	

RIGHT ICA/CCA PSV RATIO: 0.96 LEFT ICA/CCA PSV RATIO: 0.67

Stenosis Grading

0-30% NORMAL-MILD stenosis
PS<110cm/sec
ED<40cm/sec
IC/CC ratio<1.8

40-50% MODERATE stenosis
PS<130cm/sec
ED<40cm/sec
IC/CC ratio<1.8

60-79% SEVERE stenosis

80-99% CRITICAL stenosis

(cont'd)
Page 1

MCGEE LOLA BONITTA
534872

FEMALE 48
07-Jul-1962
O/P

WILLIAM HORNSTEIN MD
1045 ATLANTIC AVENUE #719
LONG BEACH CA 90813

12-Dec-201010:15

-2010 08:00 Gold-Fax Message Page 5/5

55C-121010
US CAROTID DUPL

ST. MARY MEDICAL CENTER
1050 Linden Avenue
Long Beach, CA 90813

13-Dec-2010
O/P
ULTRASOUND
*** FINAL COPY ***

(continued - US CAROTID DUPL)

PS>130cm/sec PS>250cm/sec

IMPRESSION: No flow limiting stenosis seen.

Antegrade flow is seen in bilateral vertebral arteries.

signed: GREGORY T. VANLEY, M.D.

GV/sl

Page 2

MCGEE,LOLA BONITTA
534872

FEMALE 48
07-Jul-1962
O/P

12-Dec-201010:15

WILLIAM HORNSTEIN MD
1045 ATLANTIC AVENUE #719
LONG BEACH CA 90813

13-DEC-2010 08:00 *Gold-Fax Message* *Page 2/5*

55A-121010
MRA HEAD W/O CO

13-Dec-2010
O/P
MAGNETIC RESONANCE IMA

ST. MARY MEDICAL CENTER
1050 Linden Avenue
Long Beach, CA 90813

*** FINAL COPY ***

MRA CIRCLE OF WILLIS: 12/10/10

History: Visual changes, amaurosis fugax.

Procedure:

MR angiogram of the circle of Willis was obtained using axial 3-D inflow MIP technique.

Findings:

The vertebral arteries appear normal bilaterally as does the basilar artery. The posterior cerebral arteries appear normal. The left internal carotid artery shows questionable narrowing vs bony artifact as it passes through the base of the skull. No significant stenosis is noted on the right. The distal internal carotid arteries appear normal bilaterally as do their bifurcations into the A1 and M1 segments. The visualized anterior and middle cerebral arteries appear normal.

IMPRESSION: Possible focal stenosis vs bony artifact of the left internal carotid artery as it passes through the base of the skull at the foramen lacerum. √

No other abnormality is detected.

signed: GREGORY T. VANLEY, M.D.

GV/sl

MCGEE, LOLA BONITTA
534872

FEMALE 48
07-Jul-1962
O/P

12-Dec-201010:30

WILLIAM HORNSTEIN MD
1045 ATLANTIC AVENUE #719
LONG BEACH CA 90813

From: FAXmaker To: dr Page: 1/2 Date: 10/11/2010 11:12:55 AM

Liberty Pacific
MEDICAL IMAGING • LONG BEACH

LPMI of Long Beach
2708 E. Willow Street
Signal Hill, CA 90755

Phone: 562-216-5120
Fax: 562-733-5880

To: SIAMAK ROUZROCH, M.D.
1703 TEMINO AVENUE #107
LONG BEACH CA 90804

Patient: LOLA MCGEE
MRN 111488
DOB 07/07/1962
Gender Female

EXAM: MRI Left Knee W/O Contrast
DOS: 09/10/2010

History: Knee pain.

Technique: Using the 1.5 Tesla Siemens Symphony MR imager, sagittal and coronal proton density images and sagittal, axial, and coronal proton density fat-saturation images of the knee were obtained.

Interpretation:

The medial meniscus exhibits extensive intrasubstance signal without definite communicating articular surface tear evident.

The lateral meniscus exhibits intrasubstance signal without communicating articular surface tear evident.

The anterior and posterior cruciate ligaments as well as medial and lateral collateral ligaments, patellar and quadriceps tendons are intact.

A small joint effusion is present.

Mild chondromalacic change affects all three compartments of the knee.

Conclusion:

1. **The medial meniscus exhibits extensive intrasubstance signal without definite communicating articular surface tear evident.**
2. **The lateral meniscus exhibits intrasubstance signal without communicating articular surface tear evident.**
3. **A small joint effusion is present.**
4. **Mild chondromalacic change affects all three compartments of the knee.**

Thank you for referring your patient to our imaging center.

From: FAXmaker To: dr Page: 2/2 Date: 10/11/2010 11:12:56 AM

Patient: MCGEE, LOLA MRN: 111488

Interpreting Radiologist:

James Amster, M.D.
Electronically signed

It's been said, get in where you fit in, but now I realize that there would not have been anywhere for me to fit in because of my integrity, and I don't know the rules to playing the game with people's lives and welfare. Any page of this book is the reason why people go postal. Management is the ultimate reason why any adverse behavior or action happens in the postal service because they are supposed to be in control of the organization. I can't say it enough, yet they act like themselves.

Management sit around the table and create lies that they call communication on an issue. Creative thinking is normally of a positive nature. However, one can use it to be very malicious. These games are played with employees from the top to the bottom in hierarchy; it does not matter what position you hold (Craft to Postmaster General). Management passes the buck downward, and people throw rocks and hide their hands. This mentality is also passed downward. It's like a cult. If the top says to do it then it's done, regardless if it's wrong. You do it or you're on the list and probably will never get off. The pressure that comes from being defiant to management is insurmountable. While you're trying to do your job, the papers are already written on how to get it served.

By the way, did I tell you that employees' lives, welfare, health, and families are affected by the decisions that are very unethically made by senior management, and management has no dignity and respect for their subordinate employees?

There are more women in the world, yet men are running it as far as the workplace goes in hierarchy. Mary Magdalene is a high states woman in the Catholic Religion, yet men continue to discriminate and disrespect women, even the Catholic men.

There are senior managers in the postal service who proclaim to be of the Catholic religion, yet they are the same managers that threatened, lied, used, misused, discriminated, disrespected, and denied me treatment, after getting ill for their own self-gain, but I forgot I'm an African-American woman who was trying to be judged on her own merit not race, color, are gender.

Men used me to gain higher status. It's no different than women in stables, and they need to know that they have a false sense of statue and status.

After senior management has done their dirt to employees, they sit around the table and laugh, make fun, and crack jokes about what had been achieved, regardless of the harm caused to the employee. At the same token, they are leery because they don't know if any repercussions are going to come. Management starts collectively creating lies, plotting to cover up their decisions. The rules and regulations no longer apply to everyone.

I've just been trusting in the Spirit of the Lord, and hope I can discern the difference to have proper direction now that I'm mentally ill. I've been relying on the advice of my doctors and hope I'll get better soon. However, I have a dire need to protect the twenty-four years of sobriety that I acquired from Ms. Pearl Mobley, my counselor and tribe leader from the Hillsman Drug and alcohol center, also known as Bricks Kicks. I don't need any more adversity in my life, because being drug-free, as I know it, is what I want my life to be in civilization. I will not allow the psychotropic drugs that I am taking to become a dependency and take away my sobriety. I worked too hard to achieve it. In addition, I don't think Ms. Mobley would appreciate it at all. Her presence in my life gave me a brand-new lease on life. I was taught to live a very productive life by changing my attitude and behavior. That is who I was when I worked at the postal service. Daily, I struggle to keep as much of me as possible. Because of my mental and physical disabilities and my suffering, it's a daily struggle, the most I can do is make the best of my life and continue to help others, even though my friends, family, and I are very distraught.

On August 25, 2008, when the powerless, insecure, cowardly officer-in-charge decided to threaten me with his Caucasian, male superiority, the aimless, insurmountable damage that was done is totally unexplainable to me. It is unfortunate that a cowardly behavior can have such a devastating impact on anyone in the postal service or any other organization. No one should be able to have that much of an effect on any employee, and get away with it, without an investigation. However, I'm ill from head to toe, and I have to use painful and injured parts of my body to aid other parts. When one area hurts more than the other, like my back and legs, the arm or hand I'm using is in pain also.

My work ethic and performance that got the others promoted and in charge was the same work ethic that should have gotten me promoted and in charge. I know how to manage people and achieve the desired results without misusing them and treating them with dignity and respect. After it's all said and done, those are the employees that will help me achieve my desired bottom line. Why wouldn't I find a way to motivate them to be on my team?

Racism, hatred, and embedded discrimination, is only envy, jealousy, and ultimate fear. If I was a temperamental, violent, ragging, person, I have been through enough to have gone "Postal" three fold. Fortunate enough for me and them that no one is worth my freedom or life.

Equal Employment Opportunity (EEO)

The United States Postal Service investigates its own claims and EEOs, and in that case there is no fair ground for the claimant or any employee that feels discriminated against, this is a monopoly within the government agency and there needs to be something done about it.

There needs to be a check the checker as it relates to the investigation of the postal services' EEO complaints and claims of injury. Sorry to say, but the Department of Labor/ Office of Workers' Compensation Programs is not the answer. The DOL/OWCP is the same as the postal service investigating itself, they are a federal team that plays games with the employees, it's sad but it's true, I've been going through it for over two years now.

I want it to be noted that I did not need an attorney to perform my duties and I should not need an attorney if I get threatened or injured while working for any agency of the federal government. Simply put, there needs to be a committee formed to check the checker for EEO complaints, claims of injury/illness in the postal service. I know I've said it before but I truly have learned to endure pain in various ways, it's sad but it's true.

The Sand Box

Normally when you think of a sandbox you think of elementary school children. However, I want you to know that there are managers in the United States Postal Service that have the same mentality as the elementary school children that play in the sandbox.

The children have the mentality to gain ground by doing bad things to others until they are taught differently. Unfortunately, we have adult managers that play tit for tat and/or this is my territory not yours. Consequently, if you don't do this my way then I'm going to do this to you for being defiant against me. The game is played day in and day out with craft employees, management, and in addition, the employee unions. Depending on any given day who ever wins the round, then the other will strike back. I do not know how else to describe this mentality but to call it "The Sand Box."

The sandbox mentality is what fuels the temperamental person, employee, manager, etcetera to going postal. Something foul was done on either side by the craft employee or the management employee and that person felt defeated and their temperament caused them to lose their mind and go into a rage.

Sometimes when people "Go Postal" it's not because they have done any thing wrong to management; it's because they were treated wrong by management and they can't seem to find the way to win the battle and it has affected their entire lives, such as me.

I was treated very wrong by management and I thought by being in management and with my good record that I would be treated fairly, but that was not the case. I was treated badly, used, misused, lied on and lied to, threatened, discriminated against, and retaliated on, denied claims, and EEOs, had to work in a hostile work environment and after all that I was treated even worst. I was left to deal with my illnesses, injuries, and welfare on my own. The ultimate was that they questioned my integrity and now have me under surveillance. How could you not be angry and struggle to keep your sanity while knowing you worked for an agency that you gave your life to with the notion that you all were a team.

All I want is peace of mind and for justice to prevail; to God be the glory, honor, and praise.

Finding a life because mine was taken away

I am trying to find a life as I learn how to live the one that I have now. I have moved seven times within a year and a half, and I'm still not happy or comfortable. I have inner turmoil along with physical challenges, to say the least. I want to have some sort of relationship but that is not going well either. My mind is not the same, something happened to it when I had the panic attack. Sometimes I ask myself, "Why did I say that are what did I say?" My memory is terrible, but I play what happened to me in the postal service in my mind every day verses what my life used to be like. I hope this book helps me and others with similar situations or who are going through them right now. I desire a relationship, but it's going to take a very special person to be with me because I say things that do not make sense and expect them to interpret what I mean. I intend to say the correct words, but they just don't come out of my mouth correctly. Also, I can't seem to find the correct words to say as I converse with others or with someone of interest; so things come out of my mouth and it offends people. I don't mean any harm, but the damage is done and the perception has been formed by that time. I push myself as much as possible, but I'm still finding new challenges with my condition. I find new things with my mind, body, ability, and functionality on a daily basis.

Abnormal Behavior and Situations

On April 5, 2008, while at King Station in Las Vegas, I was demonstrating to my staff how I wanted the floor to be run and in the interim, I inadvertently touched a carrier who happened to be a union steward. The carrier had been disciplined two weeks prior and she was bitter about it. She committed a safety infraction by talking on her cell phone while driving. The steward and I had always been very respectful and I thought had a very good amicable relationship. She would come and talk to me about issues in the office and we would sit down and resolve them at the lowest level possible. She even shared some of her personal information with me. We shared a common bond with both of our children going to college and she would speak to me every day. However, on April 5, 2008, the employee decided to state that I touched her that morning at approximately 8:30 a.m., but she did not report a problem until 2:30 p.m.

On March 6, 2009, a former friend was visiting me in Las Vegas at my apartment after I moved out of my home with my significant other. Unfortunately, I left a tub of bath water running and it overflowed by the time it registered with me that night. The water was about four to six inches high in the bathroom and had flooded into my bedroom. Needless to say, I had a serious problem on my hands, especially with me living on the top floor of the building. Of course, the water soiled the carpet and seeped down into my neighbor's apartment. My friend did help with assisting me with the clean up, but of course maintenance had to be called. It took them from Saturday through Monday to clean, replace, and dry up the mess that I caused.

On Saturday, March 7, 2009, I went over to the former home I had moved out of on November 26, 2008 to retrieve a vehicle I had purchased with my former significant other as this person could no longer pay the note without my financial help. I made it clear that I was no longer going to help financially and I needed to get the vehicle and that there was another vehicle available. Additionally, I needed to pick up other things. However, I was not allowed to take the vehicle so a struggle over me starting the QX56 Infiniti SUV and that person trying to stop me created chaos. Two other people were over at the time, and the police was called. I went to jail for being at my own home trying to retrieve my own property. I had deep bleeding scratches on both my arms and nothing was wrong with the other person. I was the one bleeding, but I was also the one that went to jail because the two friends said that I had hit my significant other. We were in a relationship for eight years and I had never done anything remotely close to domestic abuse, and I would not have started on March 7, 2009. My significant other told the police that no assault had taken place, and a report would not be filed stating so, and an innocent woman was not going to be sent to jail for something she did not do. I was bailed out of jail by my daughter and went home to the flooding disaster.

While the police were talking to me, I got a phone call with terrible news that a very close family friend had passed away. So, I had all of this on my mind, even my return to work on March 9, 2009 after being out for over seven months. Because of the death, I returned to work on March 13, 2009 instead.

I can imagine how my ancestors felt with trying to do away with Slavery, Harriett Tubman and the others like her. I then can identify with the Jim Crowe Laws for African-American people trying to gain their rights to vote and be treated equal.

I feel somewhat ashamed of the fact that I thought I could actually work and be overqualified for some of the positions and not get one because of the color of my skin, age and gender. I was a normal, high achiever, with knowledge, skill, ability, will, determination, perseverance, education, training, accolades, great interviewer, professionalism, serious, private, focused, team player, motivating leader, great decision maker, and respectful person that saw only one thing: my responsibility to my career and duties. Unfortunately, it was all to my demise. I devoted my life to my career and eventually lost my private haven. I was disciplined and knew how to keep my life in order of importance. It was a job, but I did it.

I did not know that I was a challenge to a fault for upper management, nor did I know that my accomplishments and unknown life feared them so much to the point that they had several personal reasons why the powers that be did not promote me. This is not including the discrimination because that was number one. One thing I can say is that I earned the promotions and was qualified.

My mother told me a long time ago: "People are okay in their on way. It's just some people don't weigh enough."

Loyalty vs. Communism

I should have stayed in Reno, Nevada. I believe that things would have gone differently for me, even though I was already ill. I was truly loyal to Craig, Robert, Jennifer, Mark, Yul, and ultimately Grady Griffin. My loyalty should not have been bypassed by Shaun Mossman or Sylvester Black. They alone could have made better decisions had they chose to do so. I believe it's a shame that managers at their levels would allow such behavior from their subordinates. I demonstrated my adaptability by going to several stations with great diversity in culture and race. Even my detail to Reno, although they did not know, I had never stayed in a hotel room by myself. I have witnessed, what I perceived to be sexual harassment, by Craig and Yul, yet I did not say anything to either one of them. Craig and I had a mutual doctor and he told me that he was going to make an appointment just to see her because he liked the way she wore low-cut blouses and she was a little spunky thing. I endured to a fault the decisions that Craig made with keeping the harassing supervisor working at North Las Vegas Main Office even though I shared my concerns. Yul and I were discussing our daughters, who are now in college, and he said to me that today's young female believes that having oral sex still makes them a virgin and I replied, how could they think that and Yul said I don't know, but I was born in the wrong generation. I wanted to throw up at the fact that he would say something like that. I believe that it is a disgrace to women. I was not focused on their personal lives. I was there to do a job, and that's it. I trained supervisors, and worked long hours, and some Saturdays, but it wasn't enough.

Robert was the manager that denied most of the seventeen positions that I applied for. I did not get one of them, but, I made all my bosses look good and they were promoted several times. I was given low ratings on my merit rating in National Performance Assessment (NPA) database. I worked ten to twelvehour days and didn't say a word. I did not call to tell them that I was working long hours and I didn't call to tell them that I was working Saturday's. I just did what I had to do to improve my offices. If they called or came by they would know that I was there, and sometimes that was the case. I'm a private person that don't do too much small talk or gossip. However, Robert would say things to me and I never gave an opinion. He made a remark one day at King Station, saying "It's probably good Mark is leaving, that will save a lot of people their jobs." I replied, "Oh really, you think so?" He replied, "Yea." Robert wanted the supervisors to be switched at Paradise Valley Station, but that was just to make waves for me and to satisfy his sand box mentality issue. I did not get the job and the supervisors were still there when I left. I was never to succeed in any office after the meeting I called with Jennifer, Robert, and Mark, but I did. Every improvement that was made was down played. Mark decided that he did not like me and all of this was discrimination on all my bosses' parts. Jennifer transferred with a promotion and her husband needed his transfer and she asked me to process his paperwork for her and I did. One of my staff was suppose to do the paperwork because he was the craft employee.

Communism is in the postal service culture. Management decides the longevity of an employee's career by their likes and dislikes, not by their merit, or talent of the person. When Robert called and asked me to come from Reno to King Station, he stated: "It's evident that you can communicate. Will you come and work at King for me?" I now see that it was perceived that as an African-American woman, I was not able to communicate with all nationally of people, because there was only one African-American employee at Sun Valley Station, the majority were Caucasian. I want it to be noted that I have a sense of innocence about me and I see people, not their race or color. A person's race or ethnicity does not matter to me, I have a job to do and I'm going to do my job. I will not tolerate anyone being treated without dignity and respect, which starts with self.

The Big Set Up

I want it to be known that I now see the set up with Yul, Craig, Shaun, and Jerry; they did not know how to get rid of me so they sent Jerry Wilson to threaten me and lie on me. During the week of August 22, 2008, after Jerry told me the first time that I went over his head with Craig, Yul called me and stated over the phone that "Jerry said that I was going to file an EEO on Las Vegas for not getting Huntridge." I hesitated, sighed, and finally after I could not stop myself from saying it, I stated to Yul that he is telling a "Damn Lie." Then Yul called me on August 22, 2008 and authorized me to bring in the Transitional Employees and when asked by Jerry about it, Yul told Jerry that he only authorized three TEs to come in early. I was then, on August 25, 2008 addressed by Jerry over the phone about the TEs earlier that morning and I told him that Yul allowed me to bring them in and Jerry stated that Yul said he authorized three and you brought in all of them at 7:30am. I stated that I only brought in three at 7:00 a.m. and three at 9:00 a.m., so that isn't true. My staff did not make the best decisions even though we talked about it. Next, Jerry showed up at the office and later on is when he threatened and lied on me in his statement and on all of the paperwork concerning my claim for injury and EEO. My mother told me a long time ago, "Cast iron steel will wear out if you use it enough." I was a very solid rock. However, I was worn out and used to a fault, and I'm trying to stay sane in order to build a new life in which I know nothing about.

There is no agency, organization, department, or any workforce that should be allowed to get away with this kind of treatment to employees and go on with business as if it did not happen, because the employee (craft or management) is left trying to survive, to get well, to be financially stable, to keep their family together, their relationship/marriage, and ultimately their health. No workplace should have the power to intentionally destroy a person's life. God gives life and God takes life in His time.

I know of several stories and situations that happened in the United States Postal Service. Some that made the news. I'm going to reveal them to help you understand that it is not just me, I'm one of many.

Chapter 10

Tragic Stories

I first want to apologize to the families and friends of these tragedies for having to relive them through this book. I only hope that the government will see a need to change the procedures and policies to correct the problems that plague varies organizations and agencies. There needs to be a bill passed for this very reason. In the meantime, we need to hold management accountable because there are people going through this type of abuse right now, and I can't say it enough. May God Bless The United States Federal Government and the entire world.

Two years ago, in Los Angeles, as a carrier was delivering his route, he walked up on a fatal shooting. He was in shock and had to have someone from the station come and get him. All he asked was to be moved from the route/station and the United States Postal Service denied his request. His doctor reported that he could not work on the same route anymore. He was sent to therapy and is now training on computers, so eventually the postal service and the Department of Labor will put him in another job. However, it will not be federal, meaning he will not work for the postal service anymore. This gentleman has a wife and children and it has totally affected the whole unit.

Years ago there was the Goleta tragedy that left several dead and injured, and also the neighbor of an ex-postal employee. This is the type of mentality that some people have after working for the postal service. The games that senior management play are just too much for employees to handle. The sandbox mentality, of course, is elevated to ruthless, traitorous, and diminishing behavior. Some of the employees play games by not performing and management play games with them and then produce paperwork in a progressive manner to get rid of them. Ultimately, management feels that they have won the war at this time, it's a sick mentality. Those who play these games are just as sick as the other, but management always has the choice to correct the situation. However, some people in management have personal, immature behavior, and they should not be supervising or managing any employees because they do not have the ability to be effective. Then you have senior managers that tell subordinate supervisors, and managers what discipline that they want you to give a particular employee and that is against postal policy, but they do it anyway.

A few weeks ago, I was passing by a television, and I saw where there had been a killing spree at a Budweiser plant. Eight were killed, and the shooter stated that he wished he could have gotten more. Is this type of mentality and behavior acceptable? Of course not, however, what and who pushed that man to be so violent to want that many people dead?

I'm not a violent person, but I have the mental diagnosis that almost made me not know my own surroundings, and that's what I stayed prayed up for. I have 24 years of sobriety, and I'm now required to take narcotic medication to sustain my mental turmoil and physical pain; and it's not by choice.

Not long ago there was a situation in Washington, DC where the Postmaster General had to step in and terminate an employee (Plant Manager) on the spot for getting so angry at his girlfriend because he wanted her to retire or resign. The girlfriend was a Manager, Distribution Operations (MDO) and she was accused of not making her numbers, which made him look bad. The reason for the termination was violence on the workroom floor, which is a postal policy.

I would like to know why Jerry Wilson wasn't terminated for threatening me, while we were in my office. I guess "Unknown" is a good enough reason to question my integrity after it was not questioned why they had me working all around the district in different offices without being promoted. Before I worked with Jerry, they knew my abilities, and my professionalism. Jerry Wilson wasn't terminated because I am Black and Female, and Jerry is White and Male. The postal policy does not apply to me, because if it did, then there would have been an investigation by senior management, Jerry, and myself. There is a Zero-Tolerance Policy in the United States Postal Service, but it did not apply to me on August 25, 2008, after I had a Panic Attack and somehow drove myself home.

Years ago in Las Vegas the Manager of Labor Relations was shot and killed by a plant employee who actually came to kill the Plant Manager. Management was warned by the wife of the employee that he was under the influence and was coming to hurt someone at the postal service. However, they did not use any precautions. The Manager, Labor Relations saw the employee in the parking lot, went to his car, saw the gun, and they struggled with it and the employee shot and killed him. The built-up rages in most employees are against management for what they believe to be injustice, and sad to say but most times they are correct. I don't want it to seem like I condone the psychotic behavior, but you have to admit anyone who feels the need to behave to this magnitude needs the issues to be addressed as to why it's happening and what really causes a person to act out in this manner. Some even commit suicide after their act of violence. For the record, the employee in this case did go to prison.

In Las Vegas right now there are several Supervisors, Customer Services, and Managers, Customer Services that are out on Stress. I remember the time when management never called in sick; however, senior management is making decisions that are not conducive to its staff, and they are calling in and going out on Stress, and this is a very important time of the year for the postal service, the Holiday Season 2010.

Another violent act that happened in Las Vegas was in May 2009 when a male supervisor started yelling at a female supervisor. As he yelled derogatory language at her and told her that she did not do anything around the office, and all the manager does is sit in the office and act like he's manager, he slammed his hands down on the desk, then picked up a stapler and slammed it down on the desk. He stood up with his fists balled up and walked towards her as she was sitting at her computer. As he continued towards her, she got up, and he was yelling, "Fuck you, fuck you," continuously. The female supervisor asked him, "What are you going to do?" He was very hostile and in a rage. Two craft employees came to her rescue, one (male) got in between them and the other walked up with her fist balled up and stated, "Not today," and he turned and yelled, "Fuck all you motherfuckers," and walked out the door. The female supervisor called the station manager, and he asked if he had to come in. The manager finally came and interviewed the craft employees, and both supervisors. She called the A/Manager, Customer Service Operations and had to leave a message. She called the Postal Inspection Service, and he told her to write him a statement. The next business day (Monday), the female supervisor walked into the office and the male supervisor, and the station manager were at the Supervisors Desk talking. She sat down at her computer, did her work and asked the manager if she could speak with him. She told him that she was not feeling well, and that she was going to the doctor. The Executive Postmaster of the City of Las Vegas called and asked her if it was from being in Formal A, or is it because of what happen on Saturday. She stated it is what happened on Saturday, and she need to go to the doctor. She went to the doctor, and the doctor put her off work and stated that she could not work with the male supervisor anymore. The Executive Postmaster, at the time, moved her to another station and then had to change his decision because it was not the correct decision to make. He sent the A/Manager, Customer Services Operation to correct his bad decision. She was at the other station for one day, then they switched the supervisors, and the male supervisor went to the station where he had previously sent her. While the male supervisor was at the station, he fell out on the floor and had to be taken away by ambulance. He had a tumor in his brain and went through an operation and months of recovery. The female supervisor was out due to Stress and was to return in three weeks, which was December 2010.

A retired EAS manager from Los Angeles describes why people go postal as employees getting fed up with the bullshit coming from upper management. Upper management gives instructions that they know are wrong and not by the policies, procedures, or written instructions, but they make the employee do whatever it is anyway. Also, management is giving out discipline that they know is not warranted and there is no just cause. The employees just get tired of the games that upper management play with their subordinates and the employees know that there will not be any recourse against them. The instructions are followed out because of fear of reprisal from the subordinate. In addition, upper management is never to give instructions as to what level of discipline an employee is to receive by their supervisor because of an infraction, but upper management does it day in and day out. Thus, the same infraction could be done by another employee, but management will not follow the protocol and give that employee any discipline at all. Managers show favoritism and employees get tired of it.

Former carrier from California describes why people go postal as employees getting tired of the injustice that upper management does with their militant way of thinking. She says, "I have seen grown men cry because of the promises that have been made to them and unfairness of the way they have been treated. She states that favoritism, and discrimination is the epitome of going postal. There was a Black acting supervisor (204-b) that had been active in the position for five years and when the position became available to fill they gave it to the White acting supervisor (204-b) that did not do the job only on a fill-in basis. Also, she states that she has witnessed regularly a supervisor casing a female's route because he liked the woman even though she was married.

It is this types of decision-making that management makes that create hostility in the workplace and when an employee who has witnessed such behavior or decision making, it makes them lose respect and then management wants to hold them accountable, but the moral of the office and the integrity of the manager has been lost. As management progresses with the discipline, the anger builds in the employee, and they go postal.

In the late '60s and early '70s in Plainview, Texas, a carrier was bitten by a large dog on his neck. He had a successful surgery and went back and forth with the U. S. Department of Labor/Workers' Compensation Programs paperwork requests. However, the carrier was later mysteriously found dead in his bed after acquiring an attorney to fight the case for him; nothing ever became of this situation.

Another carrier out of Lubbock, Texas was a seasonal employee for about five years and one day a White carrier who normally used the postal jeep was not at work and the Black seasonal working carrier asked to use it and the Postmaster, after going back and forth with him, kicked the carrier and told him, "No, Nigger, you're going to walk like you always do." The carrier acquired an attorney to fight his case and won. However, when the seasonal carrier returned to work, the Postmaster told him that he no longer had any work for the season for him.

This is the perspective of an Acting Supervisor, Distribution Operations from Los Angeles, CA. She states that employees go postal because they get tired of being treated like shit; and fucked up. Management dog people out when they want to take off, and employees work hours are being compromised. Management committed Sexual Harassment on employees. Employees have FMLA cases approved, and management still harass them with being in their time frequency. She stated that management used profanity while yelling at employees and treating them less than what they are, a human being.

It is heart wrenching how after the effort, energy, perseverance, creativity, skill, will, knowledge, experience, education, ability to do the job very well, and achieve good, as I did with working with my staff and employees, for the United States Postal Service can be reversed to the mentality by management to achieve malice against their subordinate. It is unbelievable and mind-boggling to me. The more the challenge became the more vicious they became in their "Sandbox behavior" to achieve ill will against me, when I was on their team, no matter what degree of damage came to me and my family.

A psychiatrist with diplomat status responds to the question, "Why do people go postal?" he states that it depends on the person and how much they can take as it relates to the situation or behavior. Some people can take more than others, but the build- up of pressure in a person's mind will make them believe they have no other recourse and they respond with what they believe to be the answer to resolve their problems and feeling. They act out in various ways and most times its violence in the workplace.

What Do You Want From Me?

I was a model employee who did not have any conduct issues, and I was at work every day completing my responsibility. I had one unscheduled day absence in over eleven years of service. I did my job, trained others, helped where ever needed, revamped entire operations, terminated employees when warranted, facilitated effective communication, worked over and beyond the call of duty. I was professional, respectful, serious, adaptable, reduced high-dollar payout grievances, performed to budget, managed my staff to perform, improved and performed excellent in difficult challenging offices, delivered the mail timely and efficiently, protected resources, received accolades, was not temperamental, dependable, worked well with others of diverse nationalities, worked well with union organizations, followed rules, processes, and regulations, cut overtime, captured under time, treated everyone with dignity and respect, got my postmasters promoted with my performance, reduced accidents, served community issues and request, made and reduced percent to standard, made and reduced carriers out past 1700, got mail processed timely, worked with plant issues, trained new supervisors to be responsible rather I was in the office, or not; they could perform very well. This type of person is not the one that should be treated badly, without dignity and respect, nor discriminated against. She is to be commended and promoted. Yet, I'm under surveillance and the agency is wasting good federal resources and time. They make me afraid and it increases my anxiety with them following me, tapping my phones, and utilizing their spy technology just for me. It is sad that I'm that important at this point for ill reason regarding them. Not only do I feel like I'm going to die, but I feel they want me to die, and that way their poor ruthless decision-making and mentality will not be revealed. I have to rotate sleeping on my sides because of the pain and numbness in my arms, the right arm is worse because of the collapsing of it on April 13, 2009. My ears ring and I have hearing loss, which causes me to talk louder, and that is annoying. My vision has changed three times since August 25, 2008.

I cannot smell normal odors, and it makes me feel abnormal. My nerves are damaged to the point where my feet contort by itself and my nerves move by themselves throughout my body. I actually slap myself when my nerves move by themselves, because I think something is crawling on me.

United States Department of Labor/Office of Workers' Compensation Programs

I want it to be known that I know first-hand how the postal service destroys your life and family. I no longer have my relationship or my home. I was not cooking, cleaning, shopping for groceries, paying bills, having sex, doing laundry, watching movies, going out to eat or socializing. My entire life changed, and I did not have the strength or energy to do anything but go to work, and go to sleep. On the weekends, I would go and gamble, I totally lost my discipline. After I went back to work on March 13, 2009 and got injured from lifting, all I could do was learn how to walk again. I lost my mind and everyday I feel like I'm going to die. I was defecating and had continence issues throughout the day. I had home therapy, because physical therapy told my doctor that the emotional issues need to be handled before the physical issues can be treated. I am still in therapy to date, 2011. Regardless of the doctor reports, I am still not approved for worker's compensation. I have been medically retired from U.S. Office of Personnel Management and the Social Security Administration, but not receiving approval of worker's compensation.

Legal Assistance

After all efforts to allow the United States Postal Service to do the right thing and admit to all the wrongs done to me while working in a hostile work environment, being discriminated against, lied to and lied on, threatened with a zero-tolerance policy, my civil rights taken away from me and being treated without dignity and respect, I sought legal assistance. However, I found out that there are very few attorneys that represent those of us that have been wronged by the U.S. Government. This is injustice within itself.

Everyone deserves to be represented by legal counsel and not having to pay thousands of dollars ahead of the filings. Most of all, I found out that they do not want to take a case that they know that they have a great chance of losing or getting their status diminished. There needs to be a program or legal policy put in place by the government to help those that have been wronged, I'm talking about normal human beings.

Everyone is not bad or wrong because they challenge the U.S. Government on its decisions. All of us are created equal, and we all fall short of the Glory of the Lord; I don't care what position you hold in service. Those in hierarchy positions treat their subordinates unjust, causing the employees to have to endure their mistreatment without any recourse or support from a higher manager, such as the Postmaster General, in my case, John E. Potter. I received no help or intervention from John Potter even though I was done wrong by the postal investigation. My EEOs and the Department of Labor/Office of Workers' Compensation Programs processing my injury and illness claims from on the job with the U. S. Postal Service.

Under Severe Surveillance

People follow me and watch what I'm doing. I'm mostly in my home asleep daily. I have cameras in my apartment; if I get up and use the restroom at 2:00am they are looking at me, I hear them. I was on Las Vegas Blvd., and a guy took a picture of me from his car. Cameras are outside and there are people in the building working with whatever federal agency that feels a need to watch me. I feel insulted and appalled. Helicopters follow me when I lose the person that is following me in my car. I'm just trying to find life again, and it's very hard and mind boggling. I feel offended and frustrated along with paranoid by the surveillance, because I don't know to what degree they will go. My car recently got vandalized, behind the security gates in (11/2011) and no one knows what happened. They do something with the water and air hose. All kinds of sounds are mysteriously created, and I do hear them. My surveillance is every day all day. I wake up at 2:00 a.m. or 2:00 p.m. they are always there, and I hear them in the ceiling, and I live on the top floor.

Mental/Physical Affects and Feelings

I have mental breakdowns where it feels like an eighteen wheeler hit me while my back was turned. Sometimes I feel like I was in a 25-year marriage, and my husband died suddenly, and I was left to deal with the entire grieving process all alone. My heart is in turmoil along with my mind and brain. I truly feel crazy and do not know what to do about it, even though I have some mental health experience. My vagina gets numb as I sit on the toilet and pain shoots through my thighs and up and down my back. My arms ache, with numbness. I'm often confused and boggled, left with no answers. I have moved eight times in the last year trying to find some clarity and peace of mind. There is a thin line between sanity and insanity, so when I feel like I'm going too far to the insanity side, I just stay still and pray.

Emotionally, I have made some very poor choices and decisions based on my feelings. I attach myself to whatever feels good, but that may not be good for me, and it hasn't been. I'm very needy and it's hard to live life like I do, but I'm trying very hard to find my way in this new life. Pain is actually a part of my daily life, and I can't do anything about it. I'm so sick of complaining that I pretend that I'm not hurting around people, unless the pain has reached a high level. Furthermore, I try to act as if I'm upbeat and feeling good mentally because I don't want family and friends to see me so down all the time. After all, it has been three years, and I'm still trying to stay sane rather than not know my surroundings. I tried to be self-sufficient, but it just did not work for me. I live with family and friends as I need to move to keep trying to have peace of mind. My peace of mind has nothing to do with the people around me; it's me not feeling peaceful or not having any joy.

I aimlessly stare for long periods of time and all I think about is what has happened to me from my superiors at the postal service. My anxiety just comes in the spur of the moment, and I can't control my thoughts or mind anymore. I still have head shocks, and my eyeballs hurt. I've learned how to turn into the bed to decrease my pain in my back and spine. My knees pop and buckle and I'm so afraid of falling.

The stronger parts of my body have gotten weak from overuse in trying to get around. It still angers me and causes inner turmoil with not being able to phantom the treatment I received from my superiors after not having a conduct, performance, or attendance problem my whole career until I got sick. I still don't see how people can treat me so ruthless and without thought. I was used beyond measure, and it was allowed by their superiors.

Even after I retired, they would not even let me post a flyer or send an email, as others have been able to do, to notify my employees and staff members of my retirement party. People who think negatively always think others are the same. Everyone does not think maliciously; there are people that go by the rules and do not need to step on anyone in order to succeed. Craig told me when I changed North Las Vegas Main Post Office, and the grievances stopped along with the National Association of Letter Carriers Steward resigning that all we needed was a different approach; I smiled at Craig. This is one of the reasons that Human Resources came to North Las Vegas Main Post Office to personally meet me. Shelby Kruger-Duncan and Patti Hanson wanted to see who Lola McGee was.Shelby asked, "You can get your numbers and still treat people with dignity and respect?" I replied, "Yes." I told Shelby that it was the manager's mentality and how they treat their staff, and employees are the key. I also stated that employees want to be held accountable, just as they want management to be held accountable. Shelby told me that she had talked with some of the employees, and they said that you believed in them and you want to succeed, and they know it. Shelby stated, "Good for you Lola." There are too many management personnel that is, what I call "Postalize," they think you have to be big, bad, ruff and tough to get employees and staff to do their jobs, and it just isn't so.

In addition to that, we had the highest voice of the Employee Survey in 2005--81.1%. Even though I have an education, there are times that I can't even think of small words to convey my thoughts in a conversation. I have Memory Loss and it is confusing and sad to me, but I thank God for just waking up in the morning that is a blessing within itself. My thought process is awkward; I don't think rational nor do I make rational decisions. In my attempt to be independent I have had my family move me in and out of apartments and houses, and they are tired. I've gone from places to storages five times with a house full of furniture, and I have very heavy furniture; some are custom made. My higher learning is absent sometimes, and my vocabulary has sporadic presence. My mind and brain just go blank. Sometimes I speak so out of context to where I try and clean it up in conversation, but the damage is already done. I still cry often from what was done to me. I want to be active, and playing sports, going for walks, having my kind of sexual activity, cooking, and lifting what I want, and hosting social gatherings, but I'm too limited to do any of that. I am so out of character with this mentality that it is embarrassing yet reality. When I say the wrong words, this sometimes causes arguments and confusion along with questioning my love for some and character for others. The reason why this is so terrible is that I don't mean any harm to those that are around me and definitely not my love ones. What's so bad is that I often have to wonder what is it that I did to offend them.

Expertise vs. Lack of Knowledge

I was an expert in what I did for the United States Postal Service, and I had plenty of experience at doing my job duties. I could walk into an office with a new eye, and I could see the forest and the trees. I had the processes that the Nevada Sierra District enforced intact, and I knew how to follow the rules within the Employees Labor Unions and do my job efficiently. I was experienced in running business matters, personally and professionally long before I ever entered the grounds of the postal service. The only thing that I needed was the process rules and regulation down of the postal service to run my operations.

On February 21, 2011, I was told by a friend that Dr. Oz from the Oprah Winfrey Show confirmed and explained how Panic Attacks affect people and the symptoms. She told what was said, and I told her that I had the confirmation for the fourth time that something happened to my brain on the day that OIC North Las Vegas, Jerry Wilson threatened me. Dr. Oz described something like fight or flight, and I told her that I did the flight behavior because I'm not a person to fight, and I'm scary. In addition, I'm not going to jeopardize my life or freedom. I have people who love me and a child who depends on seeing me as her mother. My child loves me beyond life, and I'm her best friend.

In the interim, there were issues and things that happened on both sides. Yul came back to the office after a manager's meeting one day and stated to me, "You lied to me." I stated suddenly and with sincerity, "What are you talking about?" "Craig said that the employees hated you." "Well, I don't know, but they carried undertime for me, and we received an eighty-one point one percent (81.1) on voice of the employee survey (VOE)." Craig also told me that I was the reason that he came to North Las Vegas Post Office every day, so Craig lied to Yul not me because I was there I know.

Every post office that I managed, the employees would always tell me that they were happy that I was there. I addressed attendance, grievances, discipline and safety issues, which altogether improved the office's bottom line and moral. Yul said to me one day, you have no friends in the post office, and that includes me, remember that. I truly know I don't have any friends in the postal service. I feel like a tadpole sipped sucked my life, blood, and health from my body, until it's all gone, and management has just had the best cup of coffee of their lives.

I failed a mock OSHA Audit at Paradise Valley Station in 2007. The assistant in my office did not like me very much, and she showed it to me not knowing I knew how she had assisted others. It was my first time with being a manager and having certain requirements of the audit completed. I did not know the process, but I'm glad it was a mock and not real. I had my hands full with the other office tasks, and I needed a little more time with the assistant to be able to understand what I needed to put in place for passing. I found out that one thing was signing some binders, but if I had known, then I would have done that.

Once in a manager's meeting I was paying attention to the graphs, and I did not here Shaun Mossman say the postal service had a loss of $800,000 at the time, and he called on me to state the deficit of the $800,000 loss. I was embarrassed. When I would arrive at an office, I would have five staff members, and shortly after that the staff would be taking and put in other offices, which led me to have to help run my office sometimes to give my staff members a day off. I completed everything at NLV daily, including decision making for Yul, except for clerk $100 cash counts.

At forty-years old, I could play sports. I want to cook my large delicious meals and have my love ones over. I want to maintain my own home and have a choice as to where I am and what I live in. I love music and socializing, and I want to be energized enough to capture all the love that is shared when I'm in the presence of those who love me.

I love watching NBA games and picking my favorite team to win, but I have a problem with focusing on one thing at a time for any length of time; this condition makes me have anxiety and crazy thoughts running through my mind, sometimes I feel like I'm not going to have sanity or know my surroundings. This is the scariest feeling a human being can experience, in my opinion. Noise irritates me to no end, and I feel very disturb by it. Swelling in my feet, legs, ankles, and thighs is crippling, and it prevents me from doing the things I desire. I have pain that extends from the top of my neck to the bottom of my feet. I live with this pain every moment of the day, and some are more intense than others. I was once a very confident person, but now I just procrastinate daily. I think uncontrollably, and nothing gets done in a timely manner; this is really crazy and mind-boggling to me. I have racing thoughts and insomnia at times. I can only enjoy penetrating sex to have a climax, because my vagina has nerve damage and numbing, so oral sex does nothing for me anymore. I may not need to be thinking about a relationship, but I desire to have someone in my life that can accept my disabilities as I am today. I'm a person that is used to being in a relationship.

Going to a restaurant and on other outings really gets me fatigued and in contraction with severe pain, and emotional stress from all that I have to endure to enjoy a little pleasure. My buttocks and in between has numbing and pain that are beyond one's imagination, so I often have to sit to the side and pamper and juggle my body in an attempt to relieve my pain and numbing body. My eyes have gone from one prescription to three prescriptions as of September 25, 2008, and now they have gotten even worse to where I can't even see out of my current prescription. In addition, I now have another prescription as a result of my right eye going blind back in March of this year 2011. I cannot smell or hear very well, and this distorts my ability to discern what people are saying and how food taste. My feet and ankles swell to the point of distorted recognition, looking like Flintstone feet. My back is in so much pain to where I have a normal pain tolerance level which is high within itself. Walking, sitting, standing, and using the toilet is a very big challenge for me; it's really a shame. My personal caring for myself is very limited from the person I use to be. When you have taken care of yourself for all your adult life, it's hard to depend on others to take care of you. I am now forty-nine years old, and I can't even cook me a decent meal or even wash a load of clothes and process them to completion. My job, for me, at this time, in my life is to keep my sanity.

August 8, 2011 was a very profound day. It was reaffirmed for me by Dr. Condoleezza Rice, a Republican from Birmingham, Alabama; which is where my father was born. She stated that black people had to do things twice as good as whites in order to get ahead. I affirm that I did my very best over and beyond, which was providing great work and service for my country, the United States of America via the United States Postal Service. Ms. Rice stated that it was now known that racism is present and probably won't be rid of or gone in her lifetime. This is why I stated earlier that there needs to be a check the checker to have balance and truth in the postal service and all other federal agencies. Federal agencies, as they are today, are making people very ill and with injuries, and they do not care. I'm a prime example of how they care. They don't even care afterwards with known knowledge. Racism and discrimination, along with a hostile environment is the epitome of scum, and it happens in the United States Postal Service every day.

DEPARTMENT OF THE TREASURY
FINANCIAL MANAGEMENT SERVICE
019846 P. O. BOX 1686
BIRMINGHAM, AL 35201-1686

THIS IS NOT A BILL
PLEASE RETAIN FOR YOUR RECORDS

03/01/11

LOLA B MCGEE
APT# 1
S72438465 1236 WEST 22TH STREET
LOS ANGELES CA 90007

As authorized by Federal law, we applied all or part of your Federal payment to a debt you owe. The government agency (or agencies) collecting your debt is listed below.

Debt Management Servicing Center
Financial Management Service
DMSC - Birmingham Office
P. O. Box 830794
Birmingham AL 35283-0794
888-826-3127 (888) 826-3127
PURPOSE: Non-Tax Federal Debt

TIN Num:
TOP Trace Num: S72438465
Acct Num: 2010124893A
Amount This Creditor: $496.15
Creditor: 33 Site: H3

The Agency has previously sent notice to you at the last address known to the Agency. That notice explained the amount and type of debt you owe, the rights available to you, and that the Agency intended to collect the debt by intercepting any Federal payments made to you, including tax refunds. **If you believe your payment was reduced in error or if you have questions about this debt, you must contact the Agency at the address and telephone number shown above.** The U. S. Department of the Treasury's Financial Management Service cannot resolve issues regarding debts with other agencies.

We will forward the money taken from your Federal payment to the Agency to be applied to your debt balance; however, the Agency may not receive the funds for several weeks after the payment date. If you intend to contact the Agency, please have this notice available.

U. S. Department of the Treasury
Financial Management Service
(800) 304-3107
TELECOMMUNICATIONS DEVICE FOR THE DEAF (TDD) (866) 297-0517

PAYMENT SUMMARY
PAYEE NAME: LOLA B MCGEE
PAYMENT BEFORE REDUCTION: $1984.63
TOTAL AMOUNT OF THIS REDUCTION: $496.15
PAYING FEDERAL AGENCY: Office of Personnel Management

PAYMENT DATE: 03/01/11
PAYMENT TYPE: EFT

FOR OFFICIAL USE ONLY: 0000016235 S724384651435592592335281600 3ALTR-P01LOLA016235
RL0709

Chapter 11
Where Did The Love Go?

It is my hope that this letter brings about understanding of the mystery behind the love I lost for our relationship. We were truly in love with one another when we arrived in Las Vegas. You know who you are, and I hope that you read this with an open heart and mind for clear understanding. I miss what we had.

After purchasing our house, we made it a beautiful, loving, and spirit filled home. We were very happy and proud of the changes that we had made in our lives through the transition from California to Vegas. Even though we were both domestically inclined with the upkeep of our home you were more electronically inclined and I more business minded. This really made it easy to compliment each other. I still thank you for cleaning those bathrooms for me. We may have had a beautiful home, but we lived in it to the fullest. I still remember us preparing one of our favorite meals, colossal crab, rib-eye steak, fully loaded baked potato, and a fresh salad, as we watched a movie and shared our love with each other.

Even though we had our quirks, we still managed to love one another and enjoyed being together every day. We were friends as well as lovers. We enjoyed socializing together and with others, and we died laughing at each other's jokes. Fun was a part of our daily lives. We lived life to the fullest, and were even competitive in board games. We enjoyed going out and getting away, but we loved being at home together most of all. We had great conversations about life and the world around us. Most of all we talked about the GOD in which we serve. Consequently, I started having problems at work, and they would come home with me. You know I loved my job and had desires for upward mobility, and no one knew better than you my potential to rise above my circumstances and persevere. You pushed and supported me to no end, and it became overwhelming for you. I was under great pressure at North Las Vegas Post Office, as a supervisor; and when I started working as an A/Manager for the Nevada Sierra District. Unfortunately, my health began to decline; and I became a person that was different than the one you had known in all of our eight years together. I did not know what was wrong with me and you definitely did not know. As I continued to pour myself into my work yet go to the doctors, my lack of energy and attitude begin to create negativity in our home. I did not know nor could I see that I was the problem.

I was in denial about my depression diagnosis and that made things worse. I became a robot on auto-pilot and subconsciously forgot about my home, relationship and the quality of life we had created. I do not even remember when I stopped having sex, cooking, doing laundry and dishes, paying bills, and not being able to maintain my life. It was as if I woke up one day, and you started arguing with me and calling me lazy and stating how I don't do anything, and that is when I began to look back and see the big picture. All I knew was that I had to go to work and when I got home, I did not have any desire to do nothing but get prepared for the next days work and go to sleep. Our relationship as I look back was in turmoil because of me and my problems at work.

As you know, the more I gave the more they took, but I was never promoted and that made both of us upset. In the interim of North Las Vegas Post Office issues, working as an A/Manager, and being disrespected by upper management on telecons, I became very ill with Heart Palpitations, Chocking Cough, Depression, Post-Traumatic Stress Disorder, and Obsessive-Compulsive Disorder, all diagnosis by 2007.

I was gambling out of control and not even paying my bills correctly. The mortgage was kept up but not to your liking; I changed from the way I did it in the beginning. All of this brought about a change within our relationship and our household. Consequently, on August 25, 2008, I was threatened by Jerry Wilson, and the Emotional Trauma resulted in me having a Panic Attack. We did not know the effect of this tragedy, but we knew something else was wrong with me. This was the straw that took me out for over seven months from work.

During that period, I was emotionally out of control from the person you once knew. My brain, values, principles, morals, and character changed for the worse. I moved out of the bedroom and started talking to my friends oppose to talking to you. You'd asked me why was I not talking to you, but I can talk to my friends. My reply was, "I don't want to talk to you because all we do is argue, and I shut down." I told you that all I wanted was "Peace of mind, and I don't feel it in this house anymore." I stopped paying the mortgage, and I stated that if I had a $1,000,000,000, I would not pay another note. You did not understand that I did not want to be connected to Las Vegas anymore because it brought me so much hurt and pain. The house made me feel like I was trapped. I was a wounded woman in my life, not just in our relationship. I no longer had any feelings of true emotions for you or me. I was lost, and it was very scary. I want to say that I'm very sorry for getting sick and losing my strength, and way. I know it's hard to believe, but it's true. I totally lost my way, and I was going crazy. I left to get peace of mind and try to find some way to live and not die. It was about me not you. You were feeling hurt from loving me, and I was not feeling at all; I was trying not to die. I truly thought that I was going to die every day that I woke up, so the only thing for me to do was to get out of that space and place. My life depended on it, to me. The love I had for you just vanished from my heart, because I, not meaning to, associated you with the post office. I'm sorry I hurt you so badly, truly I am.

I Can't Believe What Has Happened

I'm a very sick, injured, ill woman, and I thought I was special. My bosses smiled in my face and stabbed me in my back. They used my skills and abilities to their advantage then they callously calculated a plot to get rid of me because I was a model employee with an excellent record and conduct. They did not know what to do with me to try to stop me from desiring to move up and advance to higher heights; so the plot took place.

Craig, Mark, Jennifer, Robert, Shaun, Sylvester Black, NALC, then Yul, Robert, Craig, Jerry, Cory, and Grady Griffin all had a plot; I see it so clearly know, and let's not forget the part that Pat Miner condoned. These managers are so spineless that they do not have enough "Ass" to keep their nuts off the sheets. They do not have any backbone to stand up for their behavior. They just throw rocks and hide their hands. They had the mitigated gall to make ill-will statements, yet not stand up as men and women, to back up their own words. I was determined to be the best and get promoted, but they had another agenda.

Now I'm very ill, family, friends, life, and spirits are affected and broken. Communication was my strong and weak points, now it's more of the latter in my life today. I was disrespected on telecoms by Robert Reynosa and Mark Martinez. One day we were having a telecom on percent to standard, and Mark told me that he was not easily impressed, and it wouldn't make a difference. I stated, "You will be proud and give me Kudos," and he stated, "Don't wait on it." I replied, "Okay."

When I arrived at Paradise Valley Station there were four supervisors and one acting supervisor. Shortly after my arrival one supervisor was sent to another station on loan and the 204-b acting supervisor was not allowed to work because we needed him on his route to carry mail so I only had three staff members to do the job. It was challenging but we performed great numbers. I was sent there because I was intended not to succeed in an office with so many challenges. I did it without the evil spirit, but they thought I could not, Mark, Jennifer, and Robert. This is because I called the meeting and they took it personal.

The morning I arrived at Paradise Valley Station with the mail being brought back in March 2007, miraculously I had an auditor arrive to check the process and mail in the building. I believe now it was a set up by Jennifer, everything that could go wrong did go wrong. My DCD – mail counter did not work, mail needed to be counted that was processed from the machines at the plant, so I only had one supervisor and myself to do the job. I knew the auditor, so I asked him to help me. He fixed the DCD, and he helped me count mail from one zone- zip code area. He left, and I had to input the mail into the computer program and get the carriers started and to make sure there was a carrier on every route even if it meant calling in someone. I set the floor, and I called Jennifer to let her know about the mail being brought back from prior day. My third supervisor was not going to be in until 9:30am so I had to deal with my work and the floor, and I did. At 9:30 I informed my staff member of the issue on the floor and asked her why didn't she tell me about the mail being brought back the prior day, and she stated the businesses were closed even though we had six carriers out on two routes for what they brought back they marked it closed and took it out of the system. I stated ok and went to my office to do my work. Jennifer did not give me a chance to give my staff members an investigative interview. Instead, she made a decision to give me an investigative interview. I was not disciplined with a letter, but I was sent back to North Las Vegas as a supervisor in my permanent position. I worked at P.V for seven months and did a great job.

The decision making, as it refers to mail being brought back by the carriers because the businesses were closed, was not handled properly, in my opinion. Of course, my staff member thought she was doing the right thing by marking the mail business closed. However, she did not inform me the prior day when I left early, but I had called her twice, and she told me everything was ok. She put the mail volume into the program where it reflected the decrease in mail delivered that day, but I was not informed of the non delivery until the next morning when I arrived at work. Because I had given a staff member the day off, I ran the unit for the morning operation in getting the mail out, then went on to do my own work and left my two staff members to run the operations. One was responsible for getting the mail to the street, and the other was responsible for processing the mail to the carriers so that it can make it to the street.

As you remember other managers did not even deliver their mail; and, some had mail that wasn't even sent to the plant. Some had outgoing mail that was left in the office, and those promoted managers did not even get an investigated interview; but I was just so terrible in my performance at Paradise Valley Station an investigated interview was warranted according to Jennifer, Mark, and Robert. This was discrimination and retaliation towards me.

August, 9, 2011 was one of the best days that I have had since 2007. I watched four television programs this week to my recollection. I watched Oprah Winfrey Master Class on OWN; how amazing. This is a show that I was truly devoted to everyday and watched. The shows were from July 26, 2011, but I did not watch them until August 9, 2011. It took quite sometime, because I have to get up even off the bed from sitting with my legs up, and I have a great mattress set with pillow top; however, I did it. I really enjoyed watching the Master Class show.

Pain is always profound in two of the areas that are injured in my body; mental, physical or emotional daily. Two are always set aside from all the rest, but there are days regularly when all three areas are profound and breathtaking. I'm still trying to figure it all out; however, one thing I know is that I will always have the heart that God gave me, and I will never stop being a helper even in my state of being.

I'm a Helper – I need so much to help myself, and I still try to help others.
My Confidence – I'm not very confident anymore.
My Keen Mentally – Reaching masses of people every chance I get.
Embarrassment: To a degree; I guess my dignity, and pride gets in the way of help sometimes. I don't want to rely on certain medical products for my physical and mental disabilities. I'm still young, and I'm trying to do without a raised toilet or a scooter, or stop driving my car. My mental state is maladaptive and not always productive. I have severe paranoia. I do not trust people anymore, I question all of them rather I say it verbally, or I just think it. I've experienced it, but I really don't understand how people can be so inhumane to others in any kind of way. How can the very people that cooked your food, took care of your children, worked your business, and kept your entire house be second class when they have done first class duties for you? I would not eat anything from someone I thought was less than. In actuality, no one is less than!!! Please hurry up and understand me.

We all work to achieve and want exactly what Oprah said in her final Oprah Winfrey show (Acceptance, Acknowledgment and Worthiness – do you hear me and does what I say and do mean something to you). I did all of that, and the U. S. Postal Service treated me like I was inhumane. What do you think the world would be like if we all we're just cooks, or construction workers? I think we would be in a pitiful place, and that's the reason why we are diverse, yet all human beings with different desires (I'll take my fraction and make it a whole number for God's glorification).

Integrity – is my first name.
Serious – is my second.
Fairness – is my third.
Respect – is my fourth.
Dignity – is my fifth.
Class – is my sixth.
Discipline – is my seventh.

As I grew and developed I changed the hand dealt to me, and I created my own hand; with the grace and mercy of God, it is a must to survive and improve your life.

Accountability

I originally asked for me to be made whole, even though there isn't any amount of money that could be exchanged for my health (mentally or physically). I never asked for anyone's job or for anyone to be terminated even in my Darkest Moments. However, now I want for jobs to be taken away and my original request for an official apology to be given. I still want my upgrade merits and 10% increase by two levels, consecutively, because I earned my accolades repeatedly. I want everyone, all upper management, to be terminated or retired at my rate of pay right now $42,000 per year. This includes my social security, and I don't want them to receive any more than that.

My mind is constantly thinking about what I used to do while multi tasking. I believe the glass is half full not half empty. Remember, I was a physically and mentally strong woman so my drive and will to live was far greater than the average person. Please don't judge me because I'm trying to see and find a better life than I have right now, because thinking about what I can't do is counter-productive to growth and development.

Activity

Sports—volleyball, softball, running; sex—my way, dancing—my way, which is provocative, cooking, social functions, television, dominoes, Bid Wiz, outside outings daily living, and plays. Now, someone else takes care of me; I can't. I'm trying not to go insane. I want the United States Postal Services to pay for this book, and any other expenses that it accumulates as it relates to my mental and physical well being. This (writing) undertaking is a prescription directly from my doctor in an effort to help restore my mental health. I do not want to be penalized for something that I did not bring upon myself. I do not want my pension or social security to be affected because of it.

My conscience consists of fairness, dignity, respect and integrity. My spirit will not allow me to hold on to this injustice, so I have to get this off of me. My heart believes in treating people fairly, and I demonstrate it with actions not just words. Truly, I'll tell on myself, so I can sleep at night. All fall short of the glory of the Lord, period!!!

As Oprah said so many times on her show "Now they can't say that they don't know." This book stands as notification since the powers that be covered up their wrong doing to me. If nothing is done, then no one cares about the peoples lives that the United States Postal Service effects in an adverse way, and often to their demise. Hostile work environments, discrimination, and threats of violence or ill-will to another human being are not what people give their service for to their respective organizations. Please know it; everyone is different no matter how hard you try to force your rigidity upon them. People will not respond in the manner of your desired, positive, results, which impede on the productivity of growth in the workplace. All people are not coming to work for bullshit and gossip; most people come to work to do a good job and give their best. Please start appreciating your subordinates, and get help with your short comings to be an effective leader.

I want a bill passed by the President of the United States of America to change the processes in which the postal service chooses promotions, handle injured employees, mental and physical claims, hostile work complaints, discrimination complaints, so that there will be a just approving or denying the body that governs these issues aside from the federal agencies themselves. There needs to be impartiality.

I want to thank the Office of Personnel Management for making a decision that was just based on the information that they received from me, medical etcetera. Management tells lies and controverts claims to save their face, in the meanwhile the employee is in pain and suffering mentally, physically, emotionally, and financially, in turn the welfare and lives of the employee are devastatingly damage. Their family is also distraught by the effects of their love one. Most often injured employees lose their jobs because they are not able to perform to the required standards and duties, and they put a feather in their cap because you are out of the way and off the rolls.

Why Didn't I Leave?

I was asked by someone, "Why didn't you leave?" I have a series of events that happened, and some did not surface until the demise of me in the postal service. Initially, it took one year for me to get my transfer/lateral from California to Nevada, and I had already started the process for purchasing a home. Escrow closed in March of 2004, and I was assigned to North Las Vegas in May of 2004. I loved Las Vegas before I worked there. I came into a hostile work environment, and I was correcting the deficiencies. I thought the disrespect of the other supervisor would stop; however, I began counseling for the effect it all had on me. I was in denial of my diagnosis of depression, because I did not think that I was acting to my interpretation of a depressed person. My focus was determination to achieve upward mobility. I truly was better than the next person, and I earned my place with going the extra mile and going over and beyond. I'm a person that stays the course, but not knowing that discrimination was playing a part.

I was a very confident person who stood and walked tall, but that characteristic was no longer as positive as it was in the beginning. I was told that I was the person for the job, and Craig stated to me that he felt good with making his decision to hire me as his supervisor. It is ironic that he later told me that I was too confident in myself as a manager, but I got the job done. I have always believed in myself along with my preparation of acquiring knowledge, skills, ability, education, and my measuring tools were my accolades, even though I deserved more than I was given. My accolades validated me. I facilitated and effectively communicated the right information to my staff as it went forth to my employees. I became focused on my health issues, loss of energy, fatigued, Choking Cough, Heart Palpitations – 44,000 extra beats per day, Depression, Anxiety, Panic Disorder, Memory Loss, Post-Traumatic Stress Disorder, Pain, loss of an eight-year relationship, two fifteen-year plus friendships, lumbar ridiculopathy, entire back pain, pain in buttocks, neck pain, chest pain, sciatica, sprain knees, thigh pain, neuropathy, vision impaired, hearing loss, facial shocks, numbness, swelling, tingling, burning, hurt, angry, mind confusion, immobility, crippled, bi-lateral knee pain with damage, mental turmoil, drug usage – medication vagina numbness, loss of love and libido, emotionally unavailable, uncontrollable sleeping, crazy uncontrollable thoughts, racing thoughts, nightmares, insomnia, poor decision making, talking out of my head, stuttering with words, right arm collapsed, blindness twice in my right eye, heart surgery, remembering my surroundings, and trying to live and not die.

I was oblivious to what my superiors actually thought of me, because they laugh in my face and made me believe that I was genuinely on their team by the offices they sent me to. Before I came back in March of 2009, before the lifting injury, I did put in for other offices in different states. However, I was in denial of that because I was already very ill. The going back on March 13, 2009 actually crippled me for life as I see it. I did not put in for until April 2009, and it was approved in September 2009.

I feel like the black lady who worked in the Department of Agriculture and was fired for being perceived prejudice by a white reporter, and then they offered her a job back after the whole story was told. "Why don't they know that we can all work together, she replied" It is my belief that they are so afraid that we will excel above their status that they fear us and don't know it, but some just have ingrained hatred with personal issues of dislikes, and that's when you become the Black Nigger in their eyes. Once this elementary mentality presents itself the sky is the limit on how far they will go to keep their foot on your neck. If by chance a Black person gets promoted, they are looked at with a fine-tooth comb, and they must follow protocol, or they will be out themselves. The cult is very deep and controlling to a fault. I can't say it enough; we can all work together and treat each other with dignity and respect, along with being fair about the situations, challenges, promotions, merits, and issues. Why envy or fear the other man or woman; learn from them and get like them. I believe if a leader has personal issues that they take to the workplace, and then counseling is where they need to be, not trying to vent their frustrations out on subordinate employees.

Chapter 12
If I Was...

If I had not been threatened by the Officer in Charge of North Las Vegas, and there was no investigation, then this book would not have been written.

If I was the type of person that gossiped and shared my business, then this book would not have been written.

If I was a White Male, then this book would not have been written.

If I was a White Female, then this book would not have been written.

If I was not a strong confident Black Woman, then this book would not have been written.

If I did not know how to communicate orally and in written form to my staff and employees then this book would not have been written.

If I was not a non-violent person then this book would not have been written.

If God had not made me who I am then this book would not have been written.

If I was not a hard working, focused team player to my superiors then this book would not have been written.

If I did not have self respect and for others then this book would not have been written.

If I had not been lied to and on, then this book would not have been written.

If I was a good follower in order to become a great leader, then this book would not have been written.

If I did not intimidate and be misunderstood by senior management, then this book would not have been written.

If I did not have a strong voice and spoke with conviction and confidence to senior management, then this book would not have been written.

If I was not respectful of senior management and spoke the truths as things arose, then this book would not have been written.

If management did not have a problem with my material things (new home, two new vehicles, beautiful jewelry, some things they had and didn't have, then this book would not have been written.

If management did not know that I have an accomplished daughter who graduated from Howard University, with Honors, and Yale University with Honors, then this book would not have been written.

If I was paid for the days that I worked training others for managers and doing postal arbitration testimonies, by right, then this book would not have been written.

If I had not been lied to by the A/Manager, Customer Service Operations, and called a meeting with the promoted Manager, Customer Service Operations, and the Executive Postmaster of the City of Las Vegas (because I had done so well in my first office as A/Manager, Customer Services at Huntridge Station), then this book would not have been written.

If I had not been the A/Manager, Customer Services at Paradise Valley Station for seven months and was performing extremely well for a split zone office, but they promoted the person that I replaced the prior seven months, then this book would not have been written.

If I had not been given an investigative interview for something that I did not even know about, but other promoted office managers had mail that never left the building, and some were hiding mail that was supposed to be delivered, and they did not get an investigative interview, then this book would not have been written.

If I had not worked in a hostile work environment and report the issues to the postmaster and Officer in Charge, then this book would not have been written.

If games had not been played with me regarding my merit input and lateral transfer because I could not work with the postmaster who had gotten the job, then this book would not have been written.

If I was not discriminated against (for being Black, Female, and forty-six years old) after working as an acting manager in the Nevada Sierra District for two and a half years (While my Non-Black Female and Male coworkers were promoted with less experience, education, and only worked one office with 13-15 routes AS-19, while I worked EAS-20, EAS-21, and EAS-22, offices that were more challenging with 29-95 routes then this book would not have been written.). I demonstrated my adaptability by flying back and forth to Reno, but they always found a way to not promote me.

If I had not filed EEOs on several senior managers that were all denied (the postal service investigates its own complaint), then this book would not have been written.

If I had not gotten ill and injured and the United States Postal Service, Nevada Sierra District controverted all my claims, and they were denied, then this book would not have been written.

If I was a methodically, callous, calculating, person, then this book would not have been written, I would be in jail or hell for doing something that is not my normal character.

If I did not respect everyone and treat people as people, then this book would not have been written!!!

I spent over a year wearing a beaning because my hair fell out and I did not have the strength or desire to come it consistently.

I made my bed and I was so proud of myself that I took a picture of it 9/2011!!!!!!!!!

In addition to the catastrophic mental, physical, and emotional injuries I suffered while working for the U. S. Postal Service, I was left to find a way to live a life that I was not familiar with. I actually lived outside of my body and mind, as if I was in a dream. I am proud to report that I'm doing much better today.

I had to live moment by moment, because day to day was not an option. I prayed even when I did not feel the power of my prayer. I literally would stop in my tracks and pray to not lose my awareness of my surroundings. I woke up every day thinking I was going to die. I received care around the clock, for a grueling four (4) years, with cooking, cleaning, and laundry. I was driven to and from my doctor's appointments. I slept around the clock and had very little interaction with others because I just wanted to sleep. My mental state was so debilitating, to I had trouble conveying my thoughts to others. I had racing thoughts and mind confusion to the point where I wasn't able to concentrate on the task at hand. I experienced the inability to respond normally to traumatic stimuli; I have a blunted affect. The trauma caused me to be emotionally unavailable. I was a walking zombie with slurred speech. I was bitter, hostile, angry, and in mental turmoil. I moved twelve (12) times in four (4) different states because I couldn't find a peace of mind or feel safe.

My only recourse was to stretch out on faith. It is my faith in God that got me to where I am today. Today, I live alone and I take care of myself. I have gotten my independence back. I may live a different life today, but at least, I'm living and we don't know what tomorrow will bring.

Thank God for faith and Courage

This Book Is God's Devine Order For My Life
Use Me Lord For Your Service,

To God

Be

All The

Glory

Honor

And Praise

THE END

www.ingramcontent.com/pod-product-compliance
Lightning Source LLC
Chambersburg PA
CBHW081911170426
43200CB00014B/2706